LORD MANSFIELD

Lord Mansfield

Justice in the Age of Reason

NORMAN S. POSER

McGill-Queen's University Press
Montreal & Kingston • London • Ithaca

ISBN 978-0-7735-4183-2 (cloth)
ISBN 978-0-7735-8979-7 (EPDF)
ISBN 978-0-7735-8980-3 (EPUB)

Legal deposit third quarter 2013
Bibliothèque nationale du Québec

Printed in Canada on acid-free paper that is 100% ancient forest free (100% post-consumer recycled), processed chlorine free

McGill-Queen's University Press acknowledges the support of the Canada Council for the Arts for our publishing program. We also acknowledge the financial support of the Government of Canada through the Canada Book Fund for our publishing activities.

Library and Archives Canada Cataloguing in Publication

Poser, Norman S., 1928–, author
Lord Mansfield : justice in the age of reason / Norman S. Poser.

Includes bibliographical references and index.
Issued in print and electronic formats.
ISBN 978-0-7735-4183-2 (bound). – ISBN 978-0-7735-8979-7 (EPDF)
ISBN 978-0-7735-8980-3 (EPUB)

1. Mansfield, William Murray, Earl of, 1705–1793. 2. Law – Great Britain – History – 18th century. 3. Great Britain – Politics and government – 1714–1820. 4. Judges – Great Britain – Biography. I. Title.

KD621.M3P68 2013 347.42'02734092 C2013-902698-3
C2013-902699-1

This book was typeset by True to Type in 11.5/14 Bembo

To Arthur T. Vanderbilt
Chief Justice of New Jersey (1948–57)

Contents

Preface

William Murray, 1st Earl of Mansfield, has been strangely ignored by biographers. He was the greatest lawyer of the eighteenth century, a leading politician of his age, and a judge of at least equal stature with such great American jurists as John Marshall, Joseph Story, Oliver Wendell Holmes, and William Brennan. His influence on the law of the English-speaking world, evidenced by the fact that the United States Supreme Court has cited his decisions over 330 times, has continued into the twenty-first century.

Despite Mansfield's influence and achievements, no full-length life story has been written in modern times. English lawyers C.H.S. Fifoot in 1936[1] and Edmund Heward in 1979[2] each wrote a short book about him, but both focus mostly on Mansfield's decisions as a judge and do not provide much information about his personal and political life. In 1992, Professor James Oldham of Georgetown University Law Center published a two-volume summary and analysis of Mansfield's decisions and trial notes, which includes an introductory biographical chapter.[3] An abridged version was published in 2004.[4] Other than that, there is nothing except John Holliday's 1797 biography, which contains some interesting, though not always reliable, information about Mansfield's early life;[5] and several chapters (comprising 282 pages) about Mansfield in John Campbell's *Lives of the Chief Justices of England*, published in 1849.[6]

Two highly qualified individuals planned to write biographies of Lord Mansfield. The first was John Buchan (1875–1940), a Scottish lawyer and politician who, as Lord Tweedsmuir, became governor general of Canada, but is best known today as the author of *The Thirty-Nine Steps* and other spy thrillers. Buchan greatly admired Mansfield and, in preparation for writing a biography, analyzed and classified every one of his decisions,[7] but unfortunately never got around to writing it.

The other was Arthur T. Vanderbilt (1888–1957), a champion of law reform who served as dean of New York University Law School and then as chief justice of New Jersey. He had been drawn to Mansfield ever since his days studying contract law in law school. Beginning in 1935, he and his researchers spent twenty-two years collecting and transcribing a vast amount of archival material on Mansfield in British and American libraries, including letters, reports of cases, diary excerpts, and newspaper articles. Judge Vanderbilt's research was extraordinarily thorough. When his principal researcher, William Hamilton, then a graduate student and later a history professor at Duke University, wrote to him from London in 1938 that he had unearthed a quantity of correspondence and manuscripts of unreported cases, or cases that had better reports than those in the printed reports, Vanderbilt's reply was brief and to the point: "Get everything."[8]

Judge Vanderbilt planned to write the biography upon his mandatory retirement from the bench at the age of seventy; however, he died suddenly a year earlier, leaving all his papers, including seventeen boxes of research material on Mansfield, to Wesleyan University, his undergraduate alma mater. It is impossible to overstate the debt I owe to Wesleyan and to the Vanderbilt family for giving me access to this treasure trove. It provides much of the primary source material that I used to write this book. Over a period of eighteen months, I examined it at the Olin Library at Wesleyan in Middletown, Connecticut.

Doing the research for this book has been a thrilling experience. It has taken me to Scone Palace in Perth, Scotland, still the residence of the earls of Mansfield; and to Mansfield's Palladian country house of Kenwood on Hampstead Heath, five miles from central London, where for nearly four decades Lord and Lady Mansfield entertained politicians, foreign diplomats, nobles, generals, bishops, judges, lawyers, artists, actors, friends, and relatives. Although most of the documents I read were photocopies, on microfilm, or transcriptions, I had the experience, in the J.P. Morgan Library in New York, of holding in my hands (most delicately, I assure the librarian) a long letter written by William Murray in 1744 to the mother of the mad Marquess of Annandale.

Writing the life of a judge raised two fundamental questions. The first was how much law I should include. If the book covered too many of the judge's decisions and too much of his legal thinking, the general reader (and even some lawyers) would find the book tedious. On the other hand, no biography can ignore the life work of its subject; for Mansfield, the law was at the centre of his life for over sixty years and cannot be separated from his life story. I have steered a middle course, exploring Mansfield's principal contributions to Anglo-American (including Canadian) law, as well as some of his most significant decisions. Where a point can be made by describing a case that is readily accessible or would be particularly interesting to a non-lawyer, I have chosen that one, rather than another more complex or legally technical case that deals with the same legal issue. I have largely ignored some areas of the law in which Mansfield decided important cases, such as real estate law, because those decisions had much greater significance in the eighteenth century than they have today.[9]

The second question, closely related to the first, was whether to treat Mansfield's life and work chronologically or thematically. Here, too, I have chosen a middle course. To make sense of his views in a particular area, such as religious freedom, slavery, or commercial law, it is necessary to describe those legal decisions in one place in the book, even though they may have occurred over several years. His personal and political life, however, can best be depicted chronologically. For this reason, some chapters take a thematic approach and others a chronological. Overall, I have tried to portray the trajectory of Mansfield's life as it actually occurred in all of its complexity as he simultaneously lived the life of lawyer, politician, judge, and statesman.

Completing this book is a source of pleasure, but it is mixed with a tinge of regret. It has been a joy to wake up every day knowing that I am going to spend the morning, and perhaps a good part of the afternoon, with Lord Mansfield. I will miss him.

New York
February 2013

Chronology

	Historical events	Events in the life of William Murray (Lord Mansfield)	Important legal decisions of Lord Mansfield
1688	Glorious Revolution: King James II abdicates the thrones of England and Scotland and sets up a Jacobite court in France		
1699	Scotland's Darien Venture in Central America fails, causing a financial collapse		
1705		William Murray, fourth son of David Murray, Viscount Stormont, born at the Palace of Scone, near Perth,Scotland	
1707	Union of Scotland and England		
1714	Queen Anne, the last Stuart monarch, dies; succeeded by George I, Elector of Hanover		
1715–16	Jacobite Rebellion defeated	William's brother, James Murray, participates in the rebellion, escapes to France; his brother, David Murray, and his father fined and imprisoned	
1718		Travels alone to London and enters Westminster School	
1721	Robert Walpole heads Whig ministry		
1723		Enters Christ Church, Oxford	
1725		While travelling in France, secretly pledges allegiance to the exiled Stuart Pretender to the throne	

	Historical events	Events in the life of William Murray (Lord Mansfield)	Important legal decisions of Lord Mansfield
1727	George I dies; succeeded by George II	Receives B.A. degree from Oxford University	
1727–30		Studies law at Lincoln's Inn	
1730		Receives M.A. degree from Oxford; travels in France and Italy; called to the bar	
1730s	Opposition to Walpole emerges under the leadership of William Pulteney	Becomes a friend of members of opposition to Walpole ministry, including William Pitt, George Grenville, and Viscount Bolingbroke	
1737		Counsel for provost of City of Edinburgh in House of Lords and House of Commons in the Porteous affair	
1738		Counsel for merchants petitioning House of Commons for action against Spanish outrages at sea	
		Marries Lady Elizabeth Finch, sister of Earl of Winchilsea and granddaughter of Earl of Nottingham, former lord chancellor	
1739		Trial counsel for defendant in *Cibber v. Sloper*, criminal conversation (adultery) case	
		Counsel for merchants of Antigua in House of Commons against usury law	
1740	Outbreak of War of Austrian Succession; Britain joins Austria, against France, Spain, and Prussia		
1741		Becomes adviser to the Duke of Newcastle	
1742	Fall of Robert Walpole as prime minister; succeeded by Lord Carteret	Appointed solicitor general and elected to Parliament	
1743	Henry Pelham becomes prime minister; he and his brother, the Duke of Newcastle, head the government	Becomes chief spokesman for the ministry in the House of Commons	
1745–46	Jacobite Rebellion defeated	Prosecutes the rebel lords for high treason	

	Historical events	*Events in the life of William Murray (Lord Mansfield)*	*Important legal decisions of Lord Mansfield*
1747	Peace of Aix-la-Chapelle ends War of Austrian Succession	Defends the peace treaty in the House of Commons	
1752	Introduction of Gregorian calendar; Britain loses eleven days		
1753		Accused of Jacobitism; clears himself before the Cabinet	
1754	Death of Henry Pelham	Appointed attorney general; buys Kenwood House in Hampstead from Lord Bute	
1754–57	Struggle among William Pitt, Henry Fox, and Newcastle to control the ministry	Lets it be known he is not interested in heading the ministry, but doubtful whether he would have been chosen	
1756	Outbreak of Seven Years' War; Britain joins Prussia against France and Austria	Appointed chief justice of Court of King's Bench, raised to the peerage as Baron Mansfield, and appointed a member of the Privy Council; declines the post of lord chancellor	
1757	Newcastle becomes prime minister; he and Pitt head the government	Appointed (temporarily) chancellor of the exchequer; is a member of the Cabinet; helps broker the Pitt-Newcastle alliance	
1758			*Miller v. Race* (commercial law) *Heylin v. Adamson* (commercial law)
1760	George II dies; succeeded by his grandson, George III		*Moses v. Macferlan* (unjust enrichment)
1761			*Pelly v. Royal-Exchange Assurance* (marine insurance)
1762	Newcastle replaced by Lord Bute as prime minister; Tories take control after forty years of Whig rule	Switches his allegiance to the Tories	*Rex v. Barker* (religious toleration)
1763	Bute resigns as prime minister; replaced by George Grenville Peace of Paris ends Seven Years' War; gives Britain rule over Canada and India John Wilkes arrested for libel for publishing *The North Briton,* no. 45, and *An Essay on Woman*	Ceases to be a member of the ministry but continues to advise the King	*Rex v. Delaval* (law and morals)

	Historical events	Events in the life of William Murray (Lord Mansfield)	Important legal decisions of Lord Mansfield
1764	Wilkes flees to France; convicted *in absentia*; expelled from the House of Commons and declared an outlaw		
1765	Newcastle and Marquess of Rockingham head Whig ministry; American Stamp Act enacted		*Pillans v. Van Mierop* (contract law) (overruled by House of Lords in 1778)
1766	Repeal of Stamp Act Pitt (now Earl of Chatham) becomes prime minister	Supports taxation of American colonists in the House of Lords	*Carter v. Boehm* (insurance fraud)
1767		Appointed (temporarily) chancellor of the exchequer Speaks in the House of Lords on behalf of Protestant dissenters	
1768	Wilkes returns to England		*Rex v. Wilkes* (outlawry) *Lowe* v. Peers (marriage contracts) *Rex v. Webb* (religious freedom)
1768–69	Wilkes elected to Parliament three times and each time expelled by the House of Commons		
1769			*Millar v. Taylor* (copyright) (overruled by House of Lords in 1774)
1770	Lord North heads ministry	Appointed Speaker of the House of Lords; continues as member of the Privy Council and adviser to Lord North and the King	*Perrin v. Blake* (property law) *Rex v. Woodfall* (seditious libel, freedom of the press)
1771		Again declines the post of lord chancellor	
1772			*Somerset v. Stewart* (slavery)
1773	Boston Tea Party		

	Historical events	*Events in the life of William Murray (Lord Mansfield)*	*Important legal decisions of Lord Mansfield*
1774			*Mostyn v. Fabrigas* (international law)
			Campbell v. Hall (taxation of colonies)
1775–81	American Revolution	Advises the King, ministry, and House of Lords to take tough measures against the American colonists	
1776		Appointed Earl of Mansfield	*Rex v. Tubbs* (impressment of seamen)
			Rex v. Minish (nuisance)
			Foone v. Blount (religious freedom)
1778			*DaCosta v. Jones* (illegal wager, right of privacy)
1779			*Hawkes v. Saunders* (unjust enrichment)
			Liardet v. Johnson (patent law)
1780		His house in Bloomsbury Square and his books and papers destroyed in the Gordon Riots	
1781			*Rhodes v. Peacock* (commercial law)
1782	Marquess of Rockingham becomes prime minister		*Folkes v. Chadd* (expert witnesses)
1783	William Pitt the Younger becomes prime minister at the age of 24		*Ringsted v. Lady Lanesborough* (status of married women)
			Rex v. Eccles (labour unions)
1784		Death of Lady Mansfield	*Rex v. Shipley* (seditious libel, freedom of the press)
1786		Ceases to sit in the court but continues to be chief justice	

	Historical events	*Events in the life of William Murray (Lord Mansfield)*	*Important legal decisions of Lord Mansfield*
1788		Resigns as chief justice; succeeded by Lord Kenyon	
1789	Beginning of French Revolution		
1793		Dies at Kenwood; buried in Westminster Abbey	

William Murray (Lord Mansfield) about the year 1737, when he was thirty-two, and already a leading member of the bar and a friend of many noblemen and political leaders. Portrait by Jean-Baptiste van Loo. © National Portrait Gallery, London.

Lady Elizabeth Finch (left) and her sister Lady Henrietta Finch around the year 1732, six years before Elizabeth married Lord Mansfield. The Finches were one of England's richest and most prominent families, the sisters' grandfather having served as lord chancellor in the seventeenth century. Portrait by Charles Jervas. © English Heritage.

Alexander Pope, the greatest poet of early eighteenth-century England and a close friend of Lord Mansfield. He thought Mansfield better suited for a literary rather than a legal or political career but, nevertheless, helped him improve his oratory. Portrait by William Hoare. © National Portrait Gallery, London.

Philip Yorke, Lord Chancellor Hardwicke. Mansfield developed his skills as a lawyer in Hardwicke's court, saying of him: "When his Lordship pronounced his decrees, wisdom himself might be supposed to speak." Portrait by Michael Dahl. © National Portrait Gallery, London.

Thomas Pelham-Holles, Duke of Newcastle, the leading politician of mid-eighteenth-century England. Through Newcastle's influence, Mansfield was appointed solicitor general and elected to Parliament. Mansfield became Newcastle's friend and one of his closest advisers. Portrait by William Hoare. © National Portrait Gallery, London.

William Pitt, Earl of Chatham, Britain's leader in the Seven Years' War. Pitt and Mansfield were political rivals and debating opponents in the House of Commons and later in the House of Lords. Portrait by Richard Brompton.

Kenwood House, Lord Mansfield's home in Hampstead, which he bought from Lord Bute in 1754. Mansfield engaged the Scottish architect Robert Adam to expand and redecorate it, making it one of England's great country houses. © English Heritage.

The library of Kenwood House, which has been called "one of the most important Neo-Classical rooms in Europe and one of Adam's finest achievements." Here, Lord and Lady Mansfield entertained many of the leading aristocrats, politicians, clergymen, artists, foreign dignitaries, and members of the bench and bar. © English Heritage.

Lord Mansfield in 1777. While chief justice of the Court of King's Bench, he also was a member of the House of Lords and an adviser to King George III and Prime Minister Lord North. His strong opposition to the demands of the American colonists influenced Britain's policy. Portrait by David Martin. Courtesy of the Scottish National Portrait Gallery.

Lady Mansfield in 1776. The Mansfields' harmonious marriage lasted forty-six years until her death in 1784, and was marked by mutual affection, trust, and respect. She took an active interest in political affairs and was her husband's confidante and adviser. Portrait by David Martin. From the Collection of The Rt Hon. The Earl of Mansfield and Mansfield, Scone Palace, Perth, Scotland.

LORD MANSFIELD

Introduction

William Murray, 1st Earl of Mansfield, dominated the world of law in eighteenth-century Britain. Mansfield's long life (1705–1793) covered almost the entire century, and for thirty-two of those years he served as chief justice of the Court of King's Bench. Through the power of his intellect and the clarity of his writing, he changed the laws of England and the Commonwealth nations forever. When the American colonies gained their independence, many of Mansfield's innovations became the law of the United States.

Mansfield's life and work need to be seen in the context of the age he lived in. Eighteenth-century England was spent in the shadow of the Glorious Revolution of 1688, which replaced a political system based on authority with one based on reason. The revolutionaries of 1688 rejected the absolute-monarchy model of Louis XIV of France, in favour of a new kind of state that reduced the power of the monarchy, fostered the growth of industry and commerce, and promoted a religiously tolerant society.[1] The guiding light of this momentous change was the seventeenth-century philosopher John Locke, who espoused political freedom, religious toleration, and economic individualism. Mansfield was a child of the Revolution, and Locke's teachings showed up repeatedly in his arguments as a lawyer and his rulings as a judge.

The political change brought about by the Revolution was accompanied by the birth of modern scientific method. In the early seventeenth century, Francis Bacon had emphasized that by careful examination of the natural world, patterns would emerge from which general principles could be drawn.[2] But it was the genius of Isaac Newton that laid the groundwork for the scientific and technological advances of eighteenth-century Britain. Newton brought to English science and philosophy an empiricism consisting of inquiry, observation, and experiment; and Newton's followers applied his scientific method to politics and law.[3] Mansfield, pragmatic and innovative, inherited these ideas. He favoured reason over tradition, experience over abstraction. In the world of law, he was the foremost representative of the Age of Reason.

Mansfield was the founder of modern commercial law. He enfolded into the ancient common law of England the customs and usages of the merchants and industrialists. But his influence affected almost every area of the law. Much of his thinking seems strikingly up-to-date today. For example, he saw that the influence of money on elections was a threat to democratic institutions, and he recognized that individuals had a right of privacy. To this day the courts of the United States,[4] Canada,[5] and the United Kingdom[6] apply legal rules that he established more than two hundred years ago. The United States Supreme Court alone has cited Mansfield's decisions more than 330 times, including cases in 2004 and 2008 ruling that a prisoner at Guantanamo Bay was protected by the writ of habeas corpus.[7]

Like United States Supreme Court Justice William Brennan in the twentieth century, Mansfield believed that the courts should be engines of social change. He saw morality as the basis of all law, and his court the guardian of public morals. He was willing to supplement the reforms enacted by the legislature and, where he deemed it necessary, to make new law in order to achieve justice and protect the weak.[8] But his attempts to temper the rigidity of the common law were not always popular with fellow judges, and some of his innovations were undone after he retired.

Born William Murray, a younger son of a Scottish nobleman, he travelled alone to London at the age of thirteen, never to return to Scotland. His parents and two of his brothers were supporters of the exiled Stuart kings, known as Jacobites, who staged two unsuccessful rebellions during his lifetime. Throughout his life, Mansfield's political enemies nurtured the suspicion that he had Jacobite sympathies. Nevertheless, by dint of his extraordinary ambition, hard work, legal talent, social skills, and an advantageous marriage, he overcame the handicap of a Scottish Jacobite family to become a friend, adviser, and political associate of many of the landed noblemen who, in effect, ruled Britain. Mansfield's life was an extraordinary journey, from a treasonous Scottish family to the very heart of the oligarchic establishment of eighteenth-century Britain.

Within a decade of being admitted to the bar at the age of twenty-five, Murray had become England's most highly esteemed lawyer. The Duke of Newcastle, the most powerful politician of the day, retained Murray to help with his private legal affairs, but soon saw that Murray could also be a political asset. Under Newcastle's patronage, Murray was elected to Parliament and appointed solicitor general of England. For fourteen years, he was chief spokesman for the Whig ministry in the House of Commons. The opposition was led by William Pitt, known as the Great Commoner. In an age of great orators, Murray and Pitt were the stars; when they debated, the House was packed and one could hear a pin drop.

In 1756, King George II appointed Murray chief justice and raised him to the peerage with the title of Lord Mansfield. While a judge, he remained an active politician, the notion of separation of powers not being part of the unwritten English constitution. He was a potent force in the House of Lords, which not only had a veto over all legislation but also was Britain's highest appellate court. For many years, Mansfield was a confidant of the King and an adviser to the ministry. Although many exaggerated his influence over government policy, there is no doubt that he remained an important political figure throughout the turbulent period of the American Revolution and until the end of Lord North's administration in 1782.

Either as a judge or as a politician, Mansfield was involved in almost every important issue that confronted Britain during his active life. His decision in the famous *Somerset* case to free a recaptured slave did not end slavery in Britain, but it set the nation on the path to abolition of the slave trade and eventually of slavery. Mansfield consistently supported religious toleration, both of Catholics and of Protestants who dissented from the established Anglican Church. As a result, he became a victim of the worst disturbance in London's history, the week-long anti-Catholic Gordon Riots of 1780. The rioters targeted Mansfield's home in Bloomsbury Square, burning down the house and destroying virtually all of his books and papers – an incalculable loss to history as well as to Mansfield and his family.

He fiercely opposed the demands of the American colonists and counselled the King to treat them as rebels and traitors, a misguided policy that led to the loss of the colonies, Britain's worst defeat of the century. His suppression of freedom of the press by imposing harsh penalties for violations of the seditious-libel laws was the most conspicuous departure from his otherwise nearly constant support of individual freedom.

Mansfield's character abounded in contradictions. He could be ambitious or timid, avaricious or generous, secretive or sociable, vain or humble, severe or kind. In an age when patronage and nepotism were rife, he was shameless in his efforts to find lucrative positions for his family members, including a nephew whose diplomatic career he successfully promoted and who was to become the heir to his title and wealth, and a corrupt army officer who was widely believed to be his illegitimate son. He was revered by many but hated by his political opponents and many members of the public. Although he was severe in his enforcement of the draconian laws of his day (about 160 crimes were punishable by death), particularly economic crimes such as forgery, he showed mercy and kindness to the weak and vulnerable.

Three themes ran like threads through Mansfield's long career. First, the Jacobitism of his family played an important part in shaping his character and, in particular, made him reluctant to challenge the authority of the government. His vulnerability to charges of Jacobitism was one of the reasons for his timidity as a politician, and for his decision to pursue a career as a judge rather than to aim for the highest rung on the political ladder. The second theme, closely related to the first, was the sharp contrast between Mansfield's conservatism and cautiousness as a politician and his boldness as a judge. In the words of a twentieth-century American judge: "As a judge [Mansfield] was brilliant, valiant, daring and resourceful. He possessed not only great intellectual courage, but real moral courage as well. He sounded a note vibrant and clear for ethical values in the law. He had a fine sense of justice, a keen insight into the future trend of the law ... In the political arena he was most unhappy. On the Bench he was completely at home; there he was sure of himself; there he was fearless."[9] The third theme was Mansfield's unwavering support for commerce. Most obviously, it drove his decisions that created modern commercial law, his greatest and most enduring contribution to Anglo-American law. But in other areas of the law, including slavery, status of women, religious toleration, labour relations, law of nuisance, and intellectual property, he always seemed to be considering whether his ruling would facilitate trade and enhance Britain's position as the world's leading commercial power.

Mansfield had an astonishingly wide circle of friends, including dukes and duchesses, bishops, politicians, poets, and actors, as well as judges and lawyers, but he revealed little of his private thoughts even to his closest friends. Friends and relatives came to him for personal advice, perhaps because he did not hold back when he believed that bluntness was appropriate. He was free of the usual vices of British noblemen: gambling, excessive drinking, and promiscuous sex. His main pleasures were reading (particularly the classics), horseback riding, and entertaining his friends. That said, it is necessary to add that his only passion was the law.

His marriage of forty-six years to an intelligent, sociable, and well-liked noblewoman was happy, though childless. Lady Mansfield died in 1784, and he retired from the bench four years later. He spent the remaining years of his life peacefully at his country home of Kenwood, cared for by loving nieces and great-nieces, one of whom was Dido Elizabeth Belle, the illegitimate daughter of a naval-officer nephew and an African slave. He emancipated Dido and left her a legacy, which enabled her to marry and have a family. During his life he amassed a sizable fortune through his legal practice, his salary and perquisites as a judge, and his canny investments in mortgages.

John Buchan wrote of Lord Mansfield: "In many ways he is the most imposing figure in the history of the English bench. He had a profound effect upon the development of law; he held one or the other of the great law offices for almost half a century; and he dominated his colleagues as no other Chief-Justice has ever done. But it is possible to disregard this technical side, and still find a wonderful figure of a man, a statesman, and a scholar ... The great Lord Chief-Justice may be profitably studied apart from his profession."[10] That is what I have attempted to do in this book.

PART ONE

Becoming Lord Mansfield

1

Scotland

Without study, nothing can be acquired.

William Murray, in a letter to his brother Charles

Nothing in William Murray's ancestry would have led anyone to predict the legal genius or extraordinary career of the future Lord Mansfield. The Murrays were not lawyers or scholars; they were landowners, politicians, and warriors who had owned large estates and served as sheriffs in the Scottish Lowlands for six hundred years. The family's most illustrious member was David Murray, who entered the household of King James VI as the king's cupbearer and in 1584 was appointed the king's "master stabler" and his consort Queen Anne's "first esquire."[1] The King knighted him in 1598 and appointed him a privy councillor shortly afterwards.[2]

Sir David's fortunes rose in 1600, when he helped defeat an attempt by a Scottish nobleman, the Earl of Gowrie, to kidnap – and probably kill – the King.[3] Later, he sat on the panel of officers that investigated the conspiracy. In gratitude for his services, the King gave Murray all of Gowrie's lands in southeastern Scotland, including the Palace of Scone and its ancient Augustinian Abbey, where the kings of Scotland had been crowned since the fourteenth century.[4] Scone is about a mile and a half from the city of Perth, forty miles north of Edinburgh in the Scottish Lowlands. In 1603, when King James VI succeeded to the English throne, Sir David was one of the ministers who accompanied him to England. He was appointed one of the Scottish commissioners to negotiate a closer union with England. In 1621, the King raised him to the Scottish nobility, with the title of Viscount Stormont.[5]

Sir David died childless, so the peerage descended to other members of the Murray family. William Murray's grandfather, a first cousin of Sir David, succeeded to the title in 1658 as the 4th Viscount Stormont, and ten years later William Murray's father, also named David, became the 5th Viscount.

The French envoy to Scotland later described him as "a man of great resolution, strict probity and uncommon presence of mind,"[6] an apt description, too, of his famous son.

In 1688, Stormont married Marjory Scott, the only daughter of David Scott and Nicola Grierson. She came from an old Scottish warrior family. Her most notorious kinsman was a cousin, Sir Robert Grierson of Lag, a leader of the Episcopalians in their savage religious war against the Presbyterians (who were known as Covenanters) during the late seventeenth century. He was the only member of William Murray's ancestry known to have been a judge, though hardly one of whom Lord Mansfield, who believed in religious toleration, would have been proud.[7] To be a Covenanter was punishable by death, unless the person was willing to take an oath giving up his Presbyterian faith. Having defeated the Covenanters, Sir Robert opened a military court of justice in Wigtown on the banks of the Solway River and, to avoid any chance of a condemned person being reprieved, ordered that sentences of death be executed within three hours of the verdict. In 1685, he sentenced two women Covenanters, one an aged widow and the other a girl of eighteen, to death by drowning, which was the ordinary way of executing women in seventeenth-century Scotland. The so-called Wigtown martyrs were tied to stakes planted in the river between low and high tide, and suffocated slowly as the tide came in. The two women refused to give up their faith and sang hymns until the rising water drowned them out.[8]

William Murray, David and Marjory's fourth son and eleventh child (they had fourteen children in all: six sons and eight daughters), was born at the Palace of Scone on 2 March 1705.[9] Although Scotland's religious wars were over, the country was in political and economic turmoil. Ten years earlier, many Scots had invested heavily in a trading company that attempted to establish a colony at Darien in the strategically located Isthmus of Panama, with the hope of creating an emporium for world commerce. Lacking provisions and succumbing to disease, most of the colonists died or were captured by the Spanish, and the Scots who had bought shares in the venture lost their entire investment.

The collapse of the Darien Venture left Scotland in economic ruin and made clear to Scottish merchants that Scotland had no alternative to a union with England, its much richer neighbour. The union, which created the United Kingdom, took effect two years after Murray's birth and has lasted until the present day. There were many in Scotland, including Lord Stormont, who bitterly resented the disappearance of Scotland as an independent nation.

For a century before the union, England and Scotland had been ruled jointly by the Stuart monarchs. On the death of Queen Elizabeth I in 1603, King James VI of Scotland inherited the English throne, becoming James I of England.[10] In 1688 his grandson, James II, an unpopular Catholic ruler of Protestant England, was forced to abdicate and go into exile in France, and was replaced by his Protestant daughter Mary. Mary's Dutch husband, William of Orange, became the leader of a European coalition in the wars against Louis XIV of France, England's traditional enemy. The exiled King James had the support of Louis, who himself was a relative of the Stuart kings.[11] Louis gave James a palace at St Germain, outside Paris, where he held court and plotted to recapture the throne of England and Scotland. When James died in 1701, his son, James Edward Stuart, took up his father's claim to the throne. The younger James, who was known as the Pretender,[12] and his followers were called Jacobites.[13] William Murray's father, Lord Stormont, and William's older brother, James, were ardent Jacobites.

Since Jacobitism played a crucial role in William Murray's life, it is important to understand why the Jacobite cause aroused fervent loyalty as well as violent hatred in the English and the Scots. The threat posed by the Jacobites to the government and people of Great Britain during the first half of the eighteenth century was not an idle one. They staged two invasions, in 1715 and 1745 – the latter one coming within 125 miles of London before the rebels retreated to Scotland, where a British army defeated them in battle.

The threat of Jacobitism to Britain was powerful because it touched on four elements that were of vital concern to Britons. First, many Scots opposed the union with England and hoped that a Jacobite victory would restore Scottish independence. Second, the Pretender was given asylum and support by France, Britain's traditional enemy. Fear of the Jacobites was linked to fear of a powerful foreign nation, just as during the Cold War many in the United States and western Europe felt threatened by communism, backed by the Soviet Union. Third, in an age of strong religious feeling, the Jacobites, if they had been successful, would have placed a Catholic king on the throne of overwhelmingly and passionately Protestant Britain. Finally, many Englishmen as well as Scots, and Protestants as well as Catholics, felt loyalty to the Stuart Pretender as the legitimate heir to the British throne. Unlike the communists, who never gained substantial support among the post-war American public, the Jacobites had a homegrown base of support within Britain.

Murray's rise to the highest level of influence and esteem in eighteenth-century England, despite being a member of a family that ardently supported the Jacobites, was an extraordinary personal achievement. It is also a tribute to the spirit of toleration that informed the English elite after the 1688 Revolution. His ascent to the British aristocracy and his appointment as chief justice was as unlikely in Murray's time as a person with a family that sympathized with communism being appointed chief justice of the United States Supreme Court in the 1950s.

Murray's vulnerability throughout his life to accusations of Jacobitism shaped his character in important ways. It made him cautious and unwilling to take a stand on political issues or to challenge the authority of the government; arguably, if it had not been for his Jacobite connection, his enormous talents might well have made him prime minister during the government crisis of the 1750s. Yet it is just as well that he did not reach the very top of the political hierarchy, for his contribution to Anglo-American law was far more important and long-lasting than anything he might have achieved as a politician.

Although the consequences of Murray's Jacobite associations lay in the future, their roots were present in the first two decades of the eighteenth century, when Murray was only beginning to become aware of political events. After the 1707 union of the two countries, his father, Lord Stormont, travelled throughout Scotland to raise support for a Jacobite Rebellion. He was the first Scottish nobleman to place his signature on a "memorial" addressed to Louis XIV, accepting his protection and assuring him that upon the Pretender's arrival in Scotland the country would arise "and the present government will be entirely abolished." The French king was unwilling to provide help and the insurrection died quietly, but the government in London took note of Stormont's disloyal activities. After a brief imprisonment in Scotland, he was summoned to London and required to give a bond to ensure his future good behaviour.[14] William's mother also seems to have been a Jacobite sympathizer; years later, when the Pretender's son, Charles Edward Stuart, invaded Scotland, she (by then a widow) made Charles and his followers welcome at Scone Palace.

While his father was flirting with treason in the early years of the century, William Murray was living at Scone Palace, set near the banks of the River Tay, Scotland's longest river, amid the beautiful rolling agricultural country of southeastern Scotland. Soon he began his studies at the Perth Grammar School. Founded in the twelfth century, it was considered one of Scotland's first-rate schools, celebrated for the scholars it produced.[15] The Scots took education seriously and were willing to spend money on their educational institutions, from the universities of the Scottish Enlightenment to parish schools such as the Perth Grammar School.[16] Primary education was compulsory, and every parish was required to have a school.[17] The school was associated with the church, its main purpose being to train its students for careers as clergymen. The students – all of whom were boys – came from all classes of society: the sons of the gentry sat side-by-side with the sons of tradesmen as well as of the poor, whose tuition was paid by the Perth Town Council.[18] Thus, from an early age Murray gained familiarity with those whose backgrounds were very different from his own.

Six days a week, young William would walk with a satchel on his back or ride a pony to school. The curriculum centred on the study of Latin. From the very beginning, Murray applied himself diligently to his studies, a habit that remained with him throughout his life. "Without study," he later wrote to his younger brother, "nothing can be acquired; a meer soldier or sailor is a very despicable thing, yet either profession join'd to learning may make you one of the greatest men in the three Kingdoms."[19]

Murray was usually at the head of his class. Soon he was able to translate into English the works of the Roman poet Horace and the historian Sallust, to talk with ease in Latin, and to compose Latin prose and verse. His father bought Caesar's *Commentaries* for him when he was ten and Livy's *History of Rome* two years later. Murray also received a thorough education in English grammar and composition, subjects not taught in English primary schools. On some occasions, the boys delivered orations from a stage erected for that purpose, and there were frequent performances of scenes from plays, attended by parents and others.[20] Murray's persuasiveness as an advocate in court, brilliance as an orator in Parliament, and clarity of expression as a judge can be traced to his education in the Latin classics and English grammar at the Perth Grammar School.

In 1713, when William Murray was eight, his parents, most likely for reasons of economy,[21] moved from their ancestral home of Scone to a small house they owned at Camlongan, a hundred miles away near the English border. They left William and his younger brother Charles in the charge of John Martin, the school's headmaster.[22] For providing room and board for the two boys, Martin received a quarterly payment of £60 Scots (less than five English pounds) and an allowance of oatmeal.[23] His accounts (in Scottish pounds) for other expenses related to the two boys, sent to Stormont's agent in Edinburgh, included seven pounds, four shillings for books for William; twelve shillings for cutting the two boys' hair; three pounds, twelve shillings for a pair of boots for William; as well as minor expenses for delivering the books to William and for posting letters to his mother and sister.[24] Although his parents kept in touch with him, William had no family life from the age of eight.

When William was ten, Perth became the headquarters of the first of the two Jacobite invasions of Britain. A year earlier, Queen Anne, the last of the Stuart monarchs, had died childless. The Act of Settlement, passed by the English Parliament in 1701, excluded any Catholic or spouse of a Catholic from the throne. Accordingly, the British crown passed to Anne's nearest Protestant relative, George, Elector of Hanover, one of the princely states of Germany, who became King George I of Britain.[25] Many Scots were strongly opposed to the Hanoverian succession and also hoped that by reinstating the Stuarts they could undo the union with England. Moreover, a large part of the population of both Scotland and England – Protestants as well as Catholics – regarded the exiled Pretender as the legitimate British king. Dudley Ryder, then a young lawyer in London and later to be attorney general and a close colleague of William Murray, wrote in his diary: "Monday, July 25 [1715] ... Went to John's Coffee House ... Had some talk about the public affairs. Mr Witnoom thinks we must call in foreign forces to assist us if the Pretender makes an invasion, that we cannot depend upon our English troops, the common people are so poisoned with Jacobitism and so much set against the present government."[26]

The leader of the 1715 rebellion was John Erskine, Earl of Mar, who had briefly been a member of George I's Privy Council. After falsely assuring the King of his loyalty, Mar travelled in disguise to Scotland in August 1715 and summoned a large number of noblemen and gentlemen to meet him for a supposed hunting party in Aboyne in northern Scotland. William Murray's father, Viscount Stormont, was one of those who attended. There, on 27 August, Mar told the assembled rebels "that he would do everything in his power to make his countrymen again a free people, and restore to them their ancient liberties which had been surrendered into the hands of the English by the accursed treaty of union." On 6 September, at Braemar, Mar issued a proclamation declaring James Stuart king of Scotland; and three weeks later he entered Perth with a force of 5,000 men.[27]

The government in London immediately took steps to suppress the rebellion. On 30 August, a number of Scottish noblemen, including Stormont, were summoned to Edinburgh, under pain of a year's imprisonment, to pledge allegiance to the government. He did not go; two others who obeyed the summons were immediately imprisoned. Once the 1715 rebellion began, Stormont prudently returned to Camlongan and declined to do any more to help the rebel cause.

For the next four months, Mar sat at Perth accumulating troops and supplies. An incompetent general, he led his forces in several excursions from the town with the goal of capturing Edinburgh, but each sortie ended in failure. On 22 October, after advancing to Dunblane, near Stirling Castle, the headquarters of the Duke of Argyll's government forces, Mar returned to Perth. Three weeks later the rebel army left Perth again, but was decisively defeated by a much smaller government force on 15 November at the Battle of Sheriffmuir. The Pretender arrived in Scotland on 22 December and spent three weeks at Scone Palace, hoping to be crowned in the Abbey of Scone as King James VIII of Scotland. But it was a lost cause. At the end of January, a council of war decided to retreat to Dundee on the North Sea coast. On 4 February, James Stuart, seeing that the rebellion had failed, re-embarked for France. For all practical purposes, the rebellion was over.

Stormont, accompanied by his oldest son, David, went to Stirling Castle, where they surrendered to Argyll. On 24 July 1716, the Judiciary Court sentenced each of them to a year's imprisonment and a £500 fine for contempt and willful disobedience for not appearing before the court when ordered to do so at the start of the rebellion.[28] Although some Scottish noblemen and gentry who joined the rebellion paid for their participation with their lives, most of the others were reprieved.[29] Mar, who had gone into exile in the Pretender's court, became a secret agent for the British government, returned to England, and in 1721 actually received an annual pension of £2,000 from King George I.[30]

Stormont's second son, James Murray, then twenty-five years of age, was deeply involved in the rebellion. A man of ability and graceful manners, he had been admitted to the Scots bar in 1710 but never practised law. During the last years of Queen Anne's reign, James was an influential member of the Tory-dominated Parliament.[31] In London he became a political disciple and ally of Henry St John, Viscount Bolingbroke, a prominent Tory minister under Queen Anne. Upon the accession of George I to the throne in 1714, Bolingbroke fell from power, and he and James Murray both became committed Jacobites.[32] In preparation for the uprising, James Murray had travelled to France, where the Pretender appointed him as his secretary of state for Scotland in his government in exile. On 28 September 1715, the same day that Mar's army entered Perth, James Murray arrived there from France, having travelled incognito from Dover with letters from the Pretender assuring Mar of help and a promise that he would shortly join him in Scotland, a promise that he soon fulfilled.[33]

The ten-year-old William Murray, attending school at Perth, must have seen, or at least been aware of, the comings and goings of the rebel army and been affected by the inevitable disruptions of daily life. His presence at the centre of the failed rebellion, led by an incompetent general, with potentially catastrophic results for members of his family, undoubtedly influenced his thoughts and character. His observation of these events may have contributed to his cautious nature and his lifelong reluctance to challenge governmental authority. Nevertheless, as we will learn, in his youth William Murray harboured sympathetic feelings to the Jacobite cause.[34]

Stormont's Jacobite activities did not end with the 1715 rebellion. There is a report that in 1719 or 1720 Stormont was visited at his home in Annandale by an envoy from the Jacobite court, which was plotting another uprising in the Scottish Highlands. In 1720, he participated in another attempt to place the Pretender on the Scottish throne, passing along information to other conspirators concerning the supposed approach to Scotland of a Spanish fleet.[35] The plot was aborted when the plotters were betrayed to the British government.[36]

James Murray, William's older brother, having followed the Pretender into exile, spent many years as prime minister of his court, with the Jacobite title of Earl of Dunbar. William's sister Marjory married Colonel John Hay, who had accompanied the Earl of Mar to Scotland in 1715 and had joined him in proclaiming James Stuart as king. Later, Hay, to whom the Pretender gave the title of Earl of Inverness, also became a courtier at St Germain, and his wife became the Pretender's close friend and adviser – some said his mistress.[37] These treasonable family connections were to haunt William Murray all his life. Over seventy years later, an English newspaper reminded its readers that a brother of the revered Lord Mansfield had participated in the failed rebellion of 1715.[38]

By the time William reached the age of thirteen, the question arose as to where he would continue his education. His father had intended him to go to the University of St Andrews, Scotland's most important educational institution, but instead it was decided that he would go to Westminster School in London.

As a schoolboy in Perth, William was already remarkable for the clearness of intellect, powers of application, and regularity of conduct that characterized his later career.[39] Lord Stormont consulted his older son, James, on the question of William's career. Although James Murray was now in exile at the Pretender's court in France, he and his father remained in touch.[40] James saw that William's talents might make him a useful ally in the Jacobite cause. James had formed a friendship with another avowed Jacobite, Francis Atterbury, Bishop of Rochester and Dean of Westminster, whose responsibilities included supervision of Westminster School. (Atterbury too was to be exiled, in 1723, for his involvement in yet another unsuccessful plot to install the Pretender on the British throne).[41] James Murray may have persuaded Atterbury to admit his precocious younger brother to Westminster School and then persuaded his father that William's unusual aptitude and diligence would get him an appointment as a King's Scholar, which ensured financial support for his education, and the virtual certainty of a scholarship at Christ Church, the college of Oxford University with which Westminster had a close relationship. Stormont agreed to the plan for his younger son, and William was duly admitted to Westminster School.[42]

To journey from Perth to London, travellers' choices were limited: the Edinburgh coach, which started once a month and claimed to take only ten days but often took considerably longer; and the trading ships that sailed from Edinburgh's port of Leith two or three times a month and sometimes took as long as six weeks to reach London.[43] Rejecting these alternatives, thirteen-year-old William Murray made the trip of over 360 miles overland by himself – evidence of not only his courage and maturity but also his parents' confidence in him. He rode a pony given to him by his father, with the idea that he would sell the animal to defray his expenses once he arrived in London.

Although in later life Murray was sometimes described as timid, there was nothing timid about his setting out alone at this young age on a lengthy journey in early eighteenth-century Britain. Most of the roads in England and Scotland were so poor that long-distance travel was uncommon and no one could cover more than ten miles a day.[44] Based on the road system built by the Romans in the first century AD, the highways either had been dismembered or had fallen into decay. The administration of roads had passed into the hands of local communities, whose responsibility for upkeep was limited by parish boundaries. There was no police force to suppress highway robberies; highwaymen, undaunted by the virtual certainty of being hanged if caught, were an ever-present danger.[45]

Despite these inconveniences and perils, Murray's journey appears to have been uneventful. He left Perth on 15 March 1718, going by way of Camlongan to say goodbye to his parents, and then proceeding through Gretna Green on the Scottish-English border to Carlisle, the nearest English town of any size. He arrived in London without mishap on 8 May.[46]

According to most accounts, Murray never returned to Scotland or saw his parents again. Throughout his career as a lawyer, politician, and judge, any visit to Scotland might have triggered suspicions that he, like his father and brother James, was a secret Jacobite. Nonetheless, there is an incongruity that is difficult to explain in his relationship to his family. On the one hand, he was able to distance himself from his parents for the rest of his life, although there is no sign that he ever felt any hostility toward or estrangement from them. On the other hand, he seems to have had a strong attachment to other members of his family, especially to several nieces and great-nieces, and to his nephew David Murray, who eventually succeeded to his title of Earl of Mansfield.

2

Westminster and Oxford

Mr Murray is reckoned one of the finest scholars there.

Westminster classmate of Murray,
in a letter to Murray's brother-in-law John Hay

The London that greeted William Murray when he arrived by pony in May 1718 was a rough, noisy, dangerous, but exciting city. London comprised two cities: the City of London (commonly called "the City"), the commercial capital – the square mile that centred on St Paul's Cathedral; and Westminster, a mile or so to the west, the seat of government – the King and his St James's Palace, Parliament, and the law courts. By the time of young Murray's arrival, however, London and Westminster, together with the borough of Southwark on the south bank of the Thames, were generally regarded as a single metropolis called "London."[1]

London was the largest city in the western world, with a population of about 600,000, ranging from the wealthiest, comprising about 1,500 families, to the abject poor.[2] The disparity between wealth and poverty was extreme, often remarked upon by visitors.[3] Great mansions of noblemen and rich merchants, opulent shop windows, splendid carriages, and elegantly dressed gentlemen and ladies were in close proximity to utmost squalor. Miserable shanties actually leaned against the walls of the magnificent Westminster Abbey.[4] One might be confronted at one moment by the dazzling spectacle of pompous wealth, and at the next by the fevered pleading of a ragged beggar for just a penny to relieve his starving family.[5]

The streets were paved with rough stones, which made travel by carriage a bone-jarring experience. Gutters ran down the centre of the streets, collecting rainwater, sewage, household garbage, and other detritus, and emptied into streams that joined the Thames. The law required that human waste be collected at night and taken to pits outside the city, but it was often honoured in the breach. It was easier and cheaper for the collectors of "night soil" to deposit it in the gutters.[6] London was noisy as well as smelly. The cries of street vendors hawking their wares – muffins, oysters, pies, candlesticks, stockings, crockery, flowers – could be heard everywhere. Grinders of knives, menders of chairs, and solderers of pots and pans added to the din. And overlaying this: the clatter of carriages over the cobblestones and the noise of street performers, from fiddlers and harpists to women who sang bawdy songs, gathering around them listeners that included "idlers, fools, and pickpockets."[7]

The city was crowded with traffic. There were "chairmen," carriers of sedan chairs who carried passengers for a fee or were employed by the wealthy to take them around town. There were porters, known as "carmen," who trundled goods from place to place or from the Thames-side docks to warehouses. Twenty thousand horses were used for riding or for hauling carriages and carts. Pedestrians had to take care not to be run over or pushed against the walls of the houses lining the narrow streets. Given the arduousness of street travel, the best highway for many journeys was the Thames, where nine hundred licensed "watermen" conveyed people and freight up and down the river between Westminster and the City[8] or across the river (London Bridge was the only bridge until 1750, when Westminster Bridge was built[9]).

Manners on the streets were rough. Historian Jerry White records: "In 1718 [the date of Murray's arrival in London] it was said there were so many thieves in the City that people were afraid to shop or visit the coffee houses after dark."[10] Mob violence was endemic. A well-dressed man was in danger of being pelted with mud by unruly citizens. If two pedestrians claimed the right of way on a narrow street, it was not unusual for a fight to ensue. The city marshal in 1718 reported: "Now it is the general complaint of the taverns, the coffee-houses, the shopkeepers and others, that their customers are afraid when it is dark to come to their houses and shops for fear that their hats and wigs should be snitched from their heads or their swords taken from their sides, or that they may be blinded, knocked down, cut or stabbed; nay, the coaches cannot secure them, but they are likewise cut and robbed in the public streets, &c. By which means the traffic of the City is much interrupted."[11]

Despite the noise, the smells, and the roughness, London was a city of considerable beauty. Much of it had been rebuilt since the Great Fire of 1666, most notably Sir Christopher Wren's masterpiece, St Paul's Cathedral, but there were also many new churches and public buildings. Older edifices, including the Tower of London and Westminster Abbey, added to the city's grandeur. The red brick used for many of the houses and shops added to the physical attractiveness of London in the early eighteenth century.[12]

For seventy years, Westminster was at the centre of William Murray's life. He received much of his education at Westminster School; earned his reputation as a lawyer in the courts that sat in Westminster Hall; presided in Westminster Hall as chief justice of the Court of King's Bench for thirty-two years; served as a member of Parliament in Westminster Palace, first in the House of Commons and, after his appointment to the peerage, in the House of Lords, where he from time to time sat as Speaker of the House; and finally, was buried in Westminster Abbey among the kings, statesmen, poets, and other notables of England.[13]

When Murray arrived in London, he immediately got in touch with John Wemyss, a Scottish apothecary who had lived on the Stormont estate at Scone. Wemyss got him settled in Westminster. He helped Murray sell his pony and found him lodgings with George Tollett, whose two sons had attended Westminster School a few years earlier. Tollett and his wife ran one of several boarding and lodging houses where Westminster boys lived, in Dean's Yard, a large square adjacent to Westminster Abbey and Westminster Palace. Wemyss sent Murray's mother, Lady Stormont, accounts of the money that he laid out on William's behalf after arrival: he outfitted William with a sword, two wigs, and pocket money, and paid his entrance fees for Westminster School as well as his tailor and his landlord.[14]

The total charges for board and tuition ranged from about £25 to £35 a year, which included charges for candles and schoolbooks (about 30 shillings, or one and one-half pounds), an entrance fee of a guinea (one pound and one shilling), a tuition fee of a guinea a quarter, and Christmas gifts to the masters. Although it is impossible to be precise in converting the purchasing power of money in the eighteenth century to its current purchasing power, £1 in 1751 would be roughly equivalent to £180 (or US/CA$290) in 2012. Thus, £35 would be around £6,300 (or US/CA$10,000) today.[15]

Westminster School, like many other English so-called "public schools," had been founded by clergymen in the Middle Ages, and it remained under the auspices of the Church of England. Although Eton would eclipse Westminster later in the century as the country's leading boys' school, when Murray arrived at Westminster School, it was the training ground of the elite: its graduates included politicians, bishops, peers, generals, admirals, lord chancellors, high-society doctors, and numerous artists and writers.[16] Among its alumni were poets John Dryden and William Cowper; architect Christopher Wren; historian Edward Gibbon; philosopher John Locke; and theologian Charles Wesley (brother of John Wesley, the founder of the Methodist movement).[17] Many of the political leaders with whom Murray was later to be closely associated were Westminster graduates, including four future prime ministers: John Carteret, William Pulteney, the Duke of Newcastle, and the Marquess of Rockingham.

The school's proximity to the seat of government was itself a source of privilege. The students could go in and out of the Houses of Parliament and listen to the debates whenever they liked. They had the privilege of sitting below the gallery of the House of Commons, on a level with the floor of the House, and on the very steps of the throne in the House of Lords.[18] A nineteenth-century Westminster student recollected: "Westminster School was to me a portal to the House of Commons, for I made good use of the ancient privileges Westminster scholars have of going in and out of the Houses of Parliament when they like. We could go under the gallery and on a level with the floor of the House of Commons, and could appear at the bar of the Lords."[19]

There was a strong *esprit de corps* among the five hundred Westminster boys, which sometimes turned into unruliness. In one case, a master allowed the actor father of a pupil to come drunk from the stage at Drury Lane and play his part again to an audience of delighted Westminsters.[20] On another occasion, a not-too-scrupulous bookseller and publisher named Edmund Curll (who had once been sentenced to stand in the pillory for publishing politically sensitive material,[21] and whom Daniel Defoe had called "a contemptible wretch")[22] had published, without the consent of its author, a student named Barber, a garbled version of a funeral eulogy given in honour of a clergyman who had been connected with the school. Shortly afterwards, Curll made the mistake of straying close to the school. The boys seized him, wrapped him in a blanket, tossed him in the air, and then took him, still imprisoned in the blanket, to Dean's Yard, where he was forced to kneel and ask Barber's pardon, after which he was summarily kicked off the premises.[23] The Westminster camaraderie continued long after graduation from the school. Although Newcastle and Carteret were political opponents, this did not prevent them, when well into their forties, from joining in drunken revels after a school feast.[24]

Despite the tomfoolery, Westminster School was a serious institute of learning, with highly qualified teachers. Oddly, this training ground of the elite was run by Jacobites, men who wished to overthrow the government and install the Stuart Pretender as king. In the aftermath of the Jacobite Rebellion of 1715, sympathizers to the cause who had not joined the rebellion were generally treated with toleration and allowed to keep their positions. The school was under the supervision of Francis Atterbury, Dean of Westminster and Bishop of Rochester, a man of brilliant attainments and forceful personality, and a professed Jacobite.[25] Atterbury was to be exiled and deprived of his clerical position in 1723 for his involvement in a plot to install the Pretender on the British throne.[26] The headmaster was Robert Freind, a celebrated Latin scholar, poet, and clergyman. He was a personal friend of Atterbury and of Dean Jonathan Swift, the Irish cleric and author of *Gulliver's Travels*. Both Atterbury and Freind were graduates of Westminster School and of Christ Church, Oxford, which was also a hotbed of Jacobitism. Although Freind too was a Jacobite and a Tory, he had the confidence of the Whig noblemen and gentry who sent their sons to Westminster.[27] The assistant headmaster was John Nicoll, another clergyman, who later succeeded Freind as headmaster. Nicoll was no disciplinarian, and his lenient attitude toward his charges may have influenced Murray, who as a judge later in life said that severity was not the way to rule over boys or men (although he was not averse to corporal punishment of schoolboys).[28]

When Murray arrived at Westminster in 1718, some of his classmates were amused by his thick Scottish accent (which he never entirely lost),[29] but many were soon won over by his agreeable manners and impressed by his abilities.[30] If a newspaper article, written much later, is to be believed, Murray already had acquired the cautiousness and financial acumen that he was to show throughout his life: "When at school he was not remarkable for personal courage or for mental bravery. Though one of the studious boys of his standing he has been beat by boys a year or two below him! And though acute and voluble his opinions were suppressed and restricted by [those] less powerful but more intrepid than his own. Of his money allowance he was always so good a manager that he could lend to him who was in need."[31]

Murray excelled at the Westminster course of study, which consisted chiefly of reading ancient Roman writers, including the poets Martial, Ovid, and Virgil. He also excelled in oratory, an ability that was to serve him well in later life.[32] Even at this early stage of his life, he was being compared to Cicero, the great Roman orator and politician, who had perfect mastery of all the weapons of an advocate and was especially famous for his ability to communicate pathos.[33]

On 21 May 1719, almost exactly a year after his arrival, Murray was elected to the "foundation," as his brother James had predicted, receiving the title of King's Scholar and, more important, a free education. The foundation was a royal scholarship, created by Queen Elizabeth I.[34] Murray's election was undoubtedly due principally to his merit as a scholar and orator, but the influence of James's friend Bishop Atterbury, who participated along with the teachers in examining the boys, may also have played a part.[35]

It was no easy feat to become a King's Scholar. If a student proposed himself as a candidate, he would challenge another boy to contend with him in Latin and Greek grammatical questions. The two boys would fire questions at each other for five hours at a time, with the headmaster sitting as umpire. At the end of eight weeks of constant challenges, the eight boys who did the best would be chosen as King's Scholars. The privileges of King's Scholars were not only financial. The boys lived together in the college dormitory and were set apart from other students by the cap, gown, and college waistcoat that they wore. Most important, King's Scholars were almost guaranteed admission to Christ Church, the college of Oxford University with which Westminster School had a traditional relationship, beginning in the sixteenth century, when Queen Elizabeth I assigned a number of scholarships at Christ Church to boys who had been educated at Westminster.[36] With the other King's Scholars, Murray, in a white surplice with a white taper in hand, attended the funeral of the great essayist, poet, and politician Joseph Addison in 1719.[37]

By the time he was sixteen, Murray was considered mature enough and had reached such proficiency in the classics that he was tutoring the two sons, aged ten and eleven, of George Henry Hay, Earl of Kinnoull. Murray was related to Hay by marriage: his sister Marjory was married to George Henry Hay's brother, Colonel John Hay. On 10 August 1721, a Westminster classmate of Murray wrote to John Hay: "Your brother Mr Murray is reckoned one of the finest scholars there, and is so manly a young lad and so very much esteemed [by his headmaster and by the two boys' father] that they have thought it needless to have any other tutor for your nephews and have left them entirely in his care."[38]

One of Murray's two pupils, Robert Hay-Drummond, who later became chaplain to the King and still later Archbishop of York, displayed the kind of coolness under fire as a Westminster student that upper-class eighteenth-century Englishmen aspired to. While Hay-Drummond was acting in Shakespeare's *Julius Caesar* before an audience that included the King and Queen, the plume of ostrich feathers on his cap caught fire. Perfectly unflappable, he pushed the cap off his head and went on with his speech as if nothing had happened.[39] (One cannot resist mentioning that one of Murray's Westminster classmates was actually named Julius Caesar. He later became a major general in the army and died during a campaign in Germany as a result of falling off his horse.[40])

On one of his vacations while at Westminster, Murray was invited to stay with Lord and Lady Kinnoull, the parents of his two young pupils. Observing him with a pen in hand and a thoughtful look on his face, Lady Kinnoull asked him if he was writing his theme for school and what, in plain English, the theme was. Murray's answer rather surprised his hostess: "What is that to you?" She replied: "How can you be so rude? I asked you a very civil and plain question and did not expect from a schoolboy such a pert answer." The boy said: "Indeed, my Lady, I can only answer once more: 'What is that to you?'" The subject of his Latin thesis was "Quid at te pertinet?" – in English: "What is that to you?"[41]

The story shows Murray's self-possession and perhaps a subtle sense of humour, even as a teenager. It also reveals that Murray had high-placed family connections in London who kept a friendly eye on him while he was at Westminster School.[42] The Kinnoulls were an influential Tory family. Lady Kinnoull was the daughter of the Earl of Oxford, who had been prime minister under Queen Anne; and Lord Kinnoull was one of the sixteen Scottish peers who were elected to sit in the House of Lords. He was later appointed British ambassador to the Ottoman Empire.[43]

One cannot overestimate the importance of Westminster School to Murray's later career. The bonds between old Westminsters were very strong. A graduate could always be sure of access to persons with political power if they also were Westminster graduates.[44] Many of the contacts with influential people that Mansfield made at Westminster School lasted the rest of his life. But for the connections he made there, it is questionable whether he would ever have become a lawyer, let alone been appointed chief justice or raised to the peerage as Lord Mansfield. England's ruling class was built on an intricate system of groups and families, many of whom sent their sons to Westminster.[45] Historian William Hamilton has described perceptively the milieu of upper-class England in which Murray came of age, and which helps explain his lifelong ambition to establish his own noble lineage:

> Men then as now desired power and prestige[46] ... The sense of family was strong, and through it men groped after ... the attainment of a sense of long and well established lineage, and its perpetuation or establishment through office, service to the state, and a solid foundation on blood and wealth ... The ruling class was made up of just such families, and those ... who were on the way up took care that connections were established or kept with those who had arrived ... Personal friendships pass [were not only of] mild and incidental interest. Political and professional influence and ability [were] of vital importance. All these things were stepping stones to advancement in church and state.[47]

All his life, Murray had an extraordinary ability to cultivate people who could further his career. As a teenager, he seems to have been the kind of precocious, respectful boy whose intelligence and amiable manners were sure to please his elders. While a student at Westminster, he was a frequent visitor to the home of Lionel Sackville, Duke of Dorset, the head of a family of great wealth and power.[48] It is unclear how that connection was established. Years later, when Murray, then solicitor general of England, had to defend himself before the Cabinet against accusations of having once been a Jacobite sympathizer, Dorset spoke up for him, assuring his colleagues of Murray's loyalty to the government in his youth.[49] Lord George Sackville, Lionel's youngest son, became Murray's lifelong friend. When George, by then an army general, was court-martialed for disobeying orders in battle, Murray offered him advice, thereby incurring the King's displeasure.[50]

Another friend that Murray made at Westminster was a boy named Vernon, who took him home to meet his father, a textile merchant on Ludgate Hill near St Paul's Cathedral, who was a Jacobite sympathizer. Although details are murky, it seems that after young Vernon died at an early age, his father treated Murray as if he were his own son. According to Murray's earliest biographer, when Murray married in 1738, Vernon stood forward in place of a parent, and he later willed to Murray an estate of 500 acres in the Midlands of England worth at least £10,000. Murray retained the gift, according to the biographer, "without imbibing, or adhering to the tainted [Jacobite] principles of the donor."[51] This may be so, but more than thirty years later, when Murray had reached the important post of solicitor general, he was accused of having drunk toasts to the Jacobite Pretender in Vernon's home.[52]

It was at Westminster that Murray met Andrew Stone, the son of a Lombard Street banker and goldsmith. The two were also fellow students at Oxford. Stone later became Newcastle's private secretary, and he most likely introduced Murray to Newcastle, which, as we will see, had significant consequences for Murray's career.[53]

Two other fellow students at Westminster School who became Murray's lifelong friends were Thomas Newton and James Johnson. Newton became a clergyman and eventually Bishop of Bristol. He was one of the many clerics among Murray's circle of friends. Johnson, who also was a fellow student of Murray at Oxford, also went into the church and taught for a while at Westminster School. In 1753 he was appointed Bishop of Gloucester.[54] He was later accused, along with Murray and Stone, of being a secret Jacobite. Johnson too became a protege of Newcastle.

Throughout his life, Murray retained an active interest in Westminster School. He was a trustee of the school from 1741 until his death, and he regularly attended its annual meetings and plays given at the school. In 1742, about twenty years after he left Westminster, Murray, then solicitor general of England, and William Pulteney, Earl of Bath, another leading politician, together visited their former headmaster, Dr Freind, then in retirement. Their purpose was to discuss with Freind the possible appointment of Dr Nicoll, the then headmaster of Westminster, as dean of Christ Church, Oxford. After the meeting, Pulteney suggested to Newcastle, who was then a secretary of state, that they get together to decide the matter.[55] Nicoll did not get the job, but it is significant that three prominent Westminster alumni took an interest in his career long after they had graduated from the school. Ten years later, Murray was one of the old Westminsters involved in choosing a new headmaster of the school.[56]

Thus, Westminster alumni in positions of power looked after the interests both of the school and of their former teachers. In 1758 Murray was one of the stewards for an anniversary dinner held in the Great Room, Dean Street, Soho, attended by more than 200 Westminsters. The other guests included the Duke of Newcastle, the Earl of Winchilsea (Murray's brother-in-law), the Lord Mayor of London, and numerous other dukes, earls, bishops, and at least one army general.[57] And when Murray died in 1793 the captain (i.e., head boy) of Westminster declaimed Latin verses honouring him.

On 18 June 1723, after a rigorous examination, Murray, then eighteen years of age, was first on a list of King's Scholars who were admitted to Christ Church, Oxford.[58] Christ Church was founded, as Cardinal College, in the sixteenth century by Cardinal Wolsey, a lord chancellor under Henry VIII. The college remained closely attached to the Church of England, and its faculty and students were proud of the fact that its college chapel was also the cathedral church of a diocese.[59] Christ Church was one of the most prestigious of the Oxford colleges, prompting Dr Samuel Johnson to say, "if a man had a mind to *prance*, he must study at Christ Church and All-Souls [another Oxford college]."[60] Christ Church's popularity meant that it was overcrowded; while some students had handsome and commodious apartments, others lived in dismal garrets accessible by a steep staircase.[61] Given Murray's noble connections, it is likely that he lived comfortably at Oxford. The diary of another well-off undergraduate noted that he was woken up at eight by his "scout" (i.e., servant) to announce that the bell had rung for prayers, but he stayed in bed till ten. Breakfast, eaten in his room but shared with friends, consisted of a round penny roll, tea with cream and sugar, with a "bit of butter on a pewter plate."[62]

Oxford University, and particularly Christ Church, was notorious for the Jacobitism of both students and teachers.[63] Many of the clerics who ran Oxford University were "non-jurors," i.e., they refused to swear allegiance to George I because they regarded the exiled Pretender as the rightful king. William Pitt once described the university as "a seminary of treason."[64] This was certainly an exaggeration, but many of the Whig gentry who had supported the Hanoverian succession would not send their sons there. Dudley Ryder wrote in his diary in 1715 that the students were so infected with Tory principles that a Whig was looked upon as a kind of monster.[65]

Another reason why many parents avoided sending their sons to Oxford was the riotous living that prevailed there. According to one contemporary, "swearing and drinking and railing is what completes an Oxford scholar at this time of day."[66] Murray seems to have avoided these temptations, and while his "contemporaries were fostering the gout, and insuring premature old age, he preserved his constitution unimpaired."[67] The most important social meeting of the year, beginning on the first Tuesday of August and attended by people from the town as well as undergraduates, were the horse races, held about a mile and a half from town. In view of the popularity of betting among the English, one has to believe there were plenty of bets laid. Booths were set up where beer was sold. On the third day of the races, there was a "smock-race," where "women in nothing but a shirt and petticoat without a blouse and the men shirtless and in short breeches run a race for the prize of a shirt."[68] At Christ Church, every now and then there was dancing and singing in the senior common room, which cost the students seven shillings.[69]

Given Murray's Jacobite family connections and his education at Westminster under the supervision of Bishop Atterbury, it is possible that he harboured sympathies for the "cause"; however, if he did, he kept them to himself. The known Jacobitism of his father, his brother James, and his brother-in-law John Hay made it all the more important for Murray, if he planned to pursue a legal or political career, to make clear to everyone who knew him that he supported the Hanoverian succession. Thirty years later, George Stone, the brother of Murray's friend Andrew Stone, wrote to George Sackville, another friend of Murray: "I well remember that the Jacobites of Oxford used to speak of [Murray] with resentment and abhorrence."[70] In view of Murray's close family relationship with Jacobitism, they must have regarded him as a traitor to their cause.

Murray's need to avoid any hint of Jacobitism increased in August 1724, when his sister Marjory arrived in England in an attempt to reach Scotland in order to straighten out her husband's financial affairs. She never got to Scotland. She was arrested in London and kept a prisoner there for several months on suspicion of being a spy for the Pretender. She eventually gained her freedom and rejoined her husband in Rome.[71] It is unclear whether she had any contact with William Murray during her time in England, but her presence there must have been an embarrassment for him.

In 1753, when Murray had to defend himself before the Cabinet against an accusation of Jacobitism, he insisted on his political loyalty during his time at Oxford. His statement was self-serving, but there is no reason to dismiss it entirely: "When I went to the University, as I was upon a foundation, I took all the oaths to the Government. When I took them, I well knew the force of those engagements; I was not ignorant of the nature of the question (if it can be called a question; for I never could see the doubt). That a Protestant should reason himself into a Jacobite is as incomprehensible in politics as it is in religion that a man should reason himself into an Atheist."[72]

The eighteenth century is customarily regarded as the low point of the Oxford and Cambridge universities as educational institutions; the traditional view is that "routine and lethargy reigned" there.[73] Some said that the public lectures were useless, and that many young men went to Oxford for the sake of being able to say they had been at the university, not for any knowledge they might acquire there.[74] Yet Christ Church offered a serious education, focusing on the classics. Undergraduates were taught a system of ethics and politics based on the Roman ideals of justice, temperance, prudence, and fortitude.

Each Christ Church undergraduate was under the direction of a tutor, with whom he met periodically and who was paid £20–30 a year. Most of the tutors were clergymen, who were well qualified to perform their educational duties.[75] Fortunately, we do have a record of Murray's studies. His tutor was a don named Henry Sherman, about whom little is known except that he had a reputation for dullness.[76] Murray's prescribed readings included Cicero's *Orations*, Homer's *Iliad*, and Virgil's *Aeneid*.[77] In addition, he read works of science and philosophy, as well as the Old Testament books of Genesis and Deuteronomy in Hebrew, a language that he had most likely already studied at Westminster School, where there was a strong tradition of Hebrew studies.[78]

In theory if not always in practice, the undergraduate course of study was rigorous, covering logic, mathematics, natural and moral philosophy, religion, and prescribed classical writers. Students were required to compose verses and themes in Latin and Greek and to engage in public debates.[79] Great stress was laid on the importance of expressing thoughts in Latin and on the ability to translate from colloquial English into Latin. While at Christ Church, Murray demonstrated his prowess by translating Cicero's *Orations* into English and then re-translating them back into Latin.[80] He also gave an oration, in Latin, in praise of Demosthenes, the Greek orator and statesman.[81]

In addition to a tutor, undergraduates were taught by graduate students, called "moderators." The moderators tended to be only a few years older than the undergraduates, and in many cases they had been fellow students at Westminster.[82] Four times a week, the moderators lectured on Aristotle and conducted disputations with the students, alternately in Greek and Latin. Also four times a week, undergraduates were required to attend a lecture in rhetoric; the lecturer examined them on the lectures of the previous week. Undergraduates were required to declaim in Latin or Greek on alternate Saturdays.[83]

Besides the classics, undergraduates at Christ Church were required to attend lectures in science. John Keill, the Savilian Professor of Astronomy, who had been a student of Isaac Newton, gave a course in "mechanical and experimental philosophy." The course included classes in mechanics, the laws of nature, the nature of fluids, and optics.[84] It is tempting to speculate that Murray acquired from Keill his appreciation of Newton's scientific method of inquiry, observation, and experiment, which he later applied to questions of law.

The Whig ministry proposed to improve the Oxford curriculum by introducing the study of modern history and languages, but this was chiefly for political rather than educational reasons.[85] In 1723, the year that Murray entered Christ Church, the government was trying to bring the clergymen who served as teachers at Oxford and Cambridge under its political control. It appointed Edmund Gibson, an influential Anglican clergyman, Bishop of London, with the power to appoint clerics who were loyal to the government. Gibson proposed to appoint a professor of modern history and languages in each of the two universities, along with at least two assistants and twenty scholars. The positions were to be filled by Whig loyalists, who would train the scholars to be public servants.[86]

The project never came to much. However, it is worth noting because Murray applied for one of the Oxford scholarships, not because he wanted or needed it, but because, as he later admitted with extraordinary candour, it was a way of announcing to the world that he supported the Hanoverian succession and was not a Jacobite:[87] "The first year that I came to the University, the late King ... founded a professorship in Modern History. I applied to be one of the scholars. I could propose no advantage from it; by its being known that I had made the application, I had all that I wanted; it showed the light in which I then wished to be considered."[88] In 1727, shortly before he left Oxford, Murray again demonstrated his loyalty to the Hanoverian regime by entering (and winning) a competition to compose a Latin poem lamenting King George I's death. This was his first victory over his fellow undergraduate and contender for the prize William Pitt, who was to become Murray's lifelong political opponent.[89]

There is evidence that Murray's rejection of Jacobitism was insincere and opportunistic. On 6 August 1725, as a twenty-year-old Oxford undergraduate travelling in France on his vacation, he wrote a highly unusual letter to his brother-in-law, John Hay. Hay was a trusted adviser of the Jacobite court, which had moved to Rome a decade earlier.[90] This, in its entirety, is Murray's letter:

> My Lord, – I beg leave to lay hold of the first opportunity I have had to offer your Lordship my most humble respects and to assure you of the warmest sentiments of a sincere friendship which I am sorry I have never been able to show by any kind of service and that this is the first time I have dared to give this small testimony of it. At the same time I flatter myself you'll excuse the ambition of a young man if I make use of the freedom I at present have [i.e., being away from England] to desire you to make a tender of my duty and loyalty to the King [i.e., the Pretender] – a very small present but all I have to offer. It will in some measure excuse my presumption for offering my service though in so private a station as not to be able to render any considerable – that I do it at a time when so many are wanting to their duty that 'tis some merit to protest against it and the intention will I hope be acceptable as presented by you. The chief end I would propose from my studies and education and the greatest glory I can aim at is to be able to serve his Majesty in any way that he pleases to command me. I ask pardon for taking up so much of your time and beg leave to assure your Lordship that I am with great respect, your most affectionate Brother and obedient servant, Will. Murray.[91]

Hay replied, but unfortunately we do not have his letter. A second letter to Hay, which Murray wrote on 30 October 1725, while again (or still) in France, indicates that Hay had commiserated with Murray about his accidental fall down a flight of stairs that caused a cut tendon on his finger. Murray assured Hay that the injury was not serious ("the cuts the surgeon gave me were much worse than those I received by the fall"). Murray's letter continued: "It is impossible to confer a greater obligation upon me than to let me know if I can be of any way serviceable to your Lordship here or in England when I return."[92]

Murray's offer of his loyalty and services to the Pretender strongly suggests that he was a secret Jacobite sympathizer in his youth – not an unlikely conclusion, given the known Jacobite sentiments of his family members. If this is the case, the two letters show that Murray's enemies were not far off the mark when they charged him, throughout his life, with being duplicitous about his Jacobite sympathies. His offer of services to Hay in England can be interpreted as a treasonous offer to support the Pretender if he attempted to seize the British throne.

Alternatively, it is possible that Murray wrote to Hay in a spirit of family loyalty, without seriously entertaining any Jacobite views, in which case he was not being candid with Hay. The truth is we do not know what Murray's real political opinions were at this time of his life. The two letters do, however, provide a clue to one aspect of Murray's character: his inclination to present a persona to the outside world that was not necessarily consistent with his real thoughts. His inability to express his views with moral persuasiveness was his most glaring weakness as a politician; this inability reflected the inner contradictions in his life.

Whatever Murray's real opinions about Jacobitism, by writing the two letters he departed from his habitual caution and his primary concern with furthering his own career and ambitions. All his life, he must have regretted writing them and shuddered at the possibility they would come to light or that he would be blackmailed, particularly when twenty-eight years later, as solicitor general of England, he was forced to deny an accusation that he had drunk toasts to the Pretender as a youth, a serious charge at the time. In eighteenth-century England, the label of Jacobite was sufficient to damn a person who wished to hold high public office.[93] Disclosure of the two letters would most likely have ended Murray's political career, prevented his ascent to the bench, and perhaps even have led to his prosecution as a traitor to his country.

Murray's fear of Jacobite charges doubtless had an important influence on his later life. His political rival William Pitt made Murray cringe on more than one occasion by obliquely (but unmistakably) accusing him of Jacobitism in parliamentary debates. The fear may also have played a part in Murray's desire to seek the security of the bench rather than high political office, and it very likely accounts for the timidity and moral cowardice that many accused him of. His fear of accusations that he was a Jacobite and therefore a traitor contributed to his conservative political views and his extreme reluctance, both as a politician and as a judge, to challenge authority. Throughout his life, the guilty knowledge of the two letters written in his youth to John Hay – virtual ticking bombs – gave real substance to his fear.

3

Lincoln's Inn

Few successful practitioners can have entered upon their careers with so wide a range of legal knowledge.

Arnold D. McNair, "Dr Johnson and the Law," *The Law Quarterly Review*

It is not clear exactly when William Murray decided to become a lawyer. Although this was one of the possibilities that he discussed with his father before leaving Scotland in 1718, nothing seems to have been decided at that time.[1] A likely consideration was that a legal education was expensive, and Viscount Stormont was not a rich man. However, William did need a profession. As a younger son, he could not expect to inherit much from his father: under the British system of primogeniture, Stormont's landholdings, which constituted the bulk of his wealth, would go to his eldest son. A career in the army or navy was not a practical option because a Scot whose family had supported the 1715 rebellion had little chance of rising to the top of the British military establishment.[2] Since a military or legal career was eliminated, this left the church, and it seems that, when he arrived at Westminster, Murray was resigned to becoming a clergyman.[3]

Nevertheless, the law attracted him. He loved scholarly pursuits and excelled in them and, given his ability as an orator and his facility with words, the law held a promise of success and financial reward if he could find the wherewithal for a legal education. While a student at Westminster School, Murray sometimes visited the courts at Westminster Hall, which was adjacent to the school, to listen to the arguments of the lawyers and the questions, comments, and opinions of the judges.[4] But it was his ease in forming friendships and acquiring sponsors who could assist him, combined with his intellectual gifts and great appetite for hard work, that, provided Murray with the opportunity to become a lawyer (just as twenty years later the patronage of the Duke of Newcastle would open up a political career for him). One such friendship, begun at Westminster School, was with Thomas Foley, the only child of Baron Foley, whose ancestors had acquired a fortune in iron mining and manufacturing in the seventeenth century.[5]

At some point, Murray mentioned to Thomas Foley his disappointment at being unable to afford a legal education. Young Foley, who later attended Christ Church with Murray, invited him to visit his father's country estate over the holidays (probably in 1723, when Murray was eighteen), where he impressed Baron Foley with his conversation and intelligence. The Baron offered to give him or lend him (it is not clear which) an annual sum of £200 to finance his legal education. The Foleys were closely connected by politics and marriage with the Harley family, whose members included Murray's relatives by marriage Lord and Lady Kinnoull. Furthermore, several members of the Foley family had gone to Westminster School.[6] So there were plausible reasons why the wealthy Baron Foley would have been willing to help Murray get started in his career.

Murray obtained the consent of his family to the proposed arrangement and became a member of Lincoln's Inn, one of the four "Inns of Court," on 23 April 1724, three years before he completed his studies as an undergraduate at Christ Church.[7] Thus, while residing at Oxford, he was also theoretically training for the law in London.

Murray did not forget his benefactor. In the early 1730s, when he was beginning to practise law in London, he would spend weekends visiting Baron Foley, who lived outside the city. When a barrister asked Murray why he visited Lord Foley, he replied: "It is enough ... if I contribute by my visits to the entertainment of my *fast friends*, or, if I fail in that, I am sure to contribute, by lassitude, to the repose of my *own faculties*."[8]

Baron Foley died in 1733, but forty-five years later, sitting in the House of Lords as Lord Mansfield, Murray was still grateful to the man who made his career possible. A cousin of Baron Foley, another Thomas Foley, had inherited the title. When he died in 1777, his two sons had run up debts in the enormous sum of £200,000. Thomas's will set up a trust, designed to ensure that the debts were paid, but the sons managed to introduce a bill in the House of Lords to set aside the will. Mansfield argued that the will should be upheld, because it clearly showed Thomas Foley's intention and the House of Lords lacked the authority to rewrite a will. But he made a point of adding that his long course of uninterrupted friendship with the Foley family made him sorry that he was compelled to oppose the wishes of Lord Foley's sons.[9]

In 1727, after obtaining his bachelor's degree from Oxford, Murray began his legal education at Lincoln's Inn, one of the Inns of Court that had been established in the Middle Ages to govern the legal profession and to train law students. The Inns of Court, private institutions run by lawyers, not by the courts or the government, had the authority to license students to practise law. Lincoln's Inn was physically located about halfway between the City, the centre of England's commerce, and Westminster, the site of government and the courts.

Although the Inns of Court were originally founded to provide legal education, by the eighteenth century, law students were pretty much left to their own devices. A few law students gained their education by being apprenticed as clerks to practising attorneys, with the aim of eventually buying the practice.[10] This was expensive; an active legal practice might cost as much as £1,000. A regular system of "reading in chambers" with a barrister, a kind of legal apprenticeship, was not established until half a century after Murray's days as a law student.[11]

The Inns had formal requirements that students participate in "moot" court exercises and attend lectures given by "benchers," as senior members of the Inn were called, but these requirements could be waived by paying a fee at the time that a student was called to the bar.[12] The main requirement for joining the legal profession was to be, at least in theory, in residence at one of the Inns for a period of seven years and to eat a certain number of dinners there. The most likely reason why Murray, like many other candidates for the law, had joined Lincoln's Inn soon after he arrived at Oxford was to start the seven-year residence period running as early as possible, even though he was not physically present at the Inn.[13] But even this fictitious residence requirement was not strictly enforced; Murray was called to the bar in November 1730, just six and a half years after his admission to Lincoln's Inn.

Contemporary writers criticized the system. In the law, which among the professions was the most difficult to study, students were left without an instructor. Comparing English legal education "in ancient times" with that of the eighteenth century, an advertisement for a "treatise" on this subject stated:

> Their exercises, in those days, were not mere matters of form, but real tests of the student's proficiency. They did not then, as now, eat their way to the bar; and other certificates were required besides those of

> having regularly and decorously swallowed their mutton. Readers laid down, in their lectures, the principles of particular parts of the law, explaining the difficulties, and reconciled seeming contradictions; removed the obstructions, and smoothed the ruggedness, which are so apt to discourage beginners, and which all beginners must meet, in this untrodden path, without a guide.[14]

Lincoln's Inn was not the largest of the Inns of Court; during the 1720s, the Inn called an average of only seven students to the bar each year, fewer than half as many as two of the others, the Middle Temple and Inner Temple.[15] But it was known as the Inn "for lawyers"; while many young men from wealthy families joined an Inn without any intention of practising law, most of the students at Lincoln's Inn, including several who were the sons of barristers, seriously intended to pursue a legal career. Its members included many of the greatest lawyers of the day, and it dominated the legal profession during most of the eighteenth century.[16]

Law students were not held in high regard at the time Murray began his studies at Lincoln's Inn at the age of twenty-two. Without any kind of parental or collegiate supervision, many of them paid little attention to the study of law. A description of the activities of a student at one of the other Inns of Court sums up what must have been fairly typical: "The *Law* was his Profession, but Poetry his Study. *Love* was the sphere he mov'd in, and *Fornication* the Center of all his Happiness. His *Books* were of no other use but to Adorn his Study; and he never thought of Pleading at any other *Bar* but a *Vintners*. The Morning he spent in *Dressing*, the Afternoon in *Courtship*, and the most part of the Night in *Debauchery*."[17] There was plenty of opportunity for debauchery. As a law student, Dudley Ryder, who later became Murray's colleague and preceded him as chief justice, wrote in his diary: "Went to the playhouse. The whores are always in the passage to it and continually lay hold of me."[18] Lincoln's Inn was near the theatres, where prostitutes openly plied their trade.[19]

There is very little first-hand information about Murray's daily life while he lived and ate his dinners at Lincoln's Inn, but there is no hint in his correspondence and that of his friends and associates in later years that he ever devoted any time to the common vices of eighteenth-century English gentlemen: drinking, gambling, and promiscuous sex.

It was during this period of his life that Murray began to acquire the encyclopedic knowledge and understanding of the law of England and other nations that helped make him a great judge. There being no system for a student to read the law under the supervision of an experienced lawyer, he mainly educated himself during his three years in residence as a student at Lincoln's Inn. An attorney named James Booth, whose father was a Catholic with Jacobite leanings, instructed him in real property law, but that was an exception. A few years later, when Murray had a legal practice, he tried to throw some business Booth's way.[20]

Long after he had become chief justice, Murray wrote down his prescription for a course of law studies in a "letter to young friends." Although one cannot be certain, it is very likely that he was describing his own self-education, or at least something similar to it. He began the letter by declaring that, because "general ethics ... are the foundation of all law," he recommended first reading the classical writers Xenophon, Cicero, and Aristotle, as well as William Wollaston's *The Religion of Nature* (1722), in which this early eighteenth-century English philosopher argued that religion and morality were identical and that religion is the pursuit of happiness, by following the dictates of truth and reason.

Next, Mansfield recommended studying "the law of nations, which is partly founded on the law of nature," particularly the works of Hugo Grotius and Samuel Pufendorf, two seventeenth-century legal philosophers who had a great influence on his thinking about the nature of law. In *On the Laws of War and Peace* (1625), Grotius, a citizen of the Netherlands, wrote that the laws of all countries derived from an unalterable law of nature, which in turn was based on the nature of man as a sociable being. Thus the particular laws of different countries were based on a natural law that was shared by all civilizations. Grotius believed that everyone had a natural right to protect his person and his property. He advanced two fundamental laws of nature: first, an individual was permitted to defend his own life; and, second, he was permitted to acquire and keep those things that are useful for life. It followed that individuals had a fundamental right to increase their wealth, so long as they did not impinge on the rightful property of others. Grotius's theory of natural law provided intellectual support to the expansion of Dutch commerce in the seventeenth century, just as Mansfield's judicial decisions supported British commerce in the following century.[21]

The German Samuel Pufendorf, writing fifty years later than Grotius, was likewise a believer in a natural law, which was promulgated by God and rested on natural reason. In *On the Duty of Man and Citizen* (1673), he wrote that people have vices, including greed, lust, avarice, desire for glory and unnecessary possessions, and a passion for insulting others. Thus, laws were required to keep them from coming into conflict with each other. In order to be safe, it was necessary for men to be sociable; and the laws of sociability, which teach people how to become useful members of society, are called natural laws. Writing twenty-five years after the Treaty of Westphalia (1648) had validated religious diversity in Europe, Pufendorf combined a strong belief in God with an ecumenical view of religion.[22] He saw that "a new morality able to gain the consent of all Europeans to the new political order ... would have to be independent of the confessional differences that divided them, yet also permit belief and practice of these rival religions within the moral framework."[23] Pufendorf's influence can be seen in the spirit of religious toleration that ran throughout Mansfield's long career.[24]

Mansfield's advice to law students continued: "When you have laid this foundation, it will be time to look into those systems of positive law that have prevailed in their turn. You will begin of course with Roman Law ... After this, it will be proper to acquire a general idea of Feudal Law, and the Feudal system, which is so interwoven with almost every constitution in Europe, that, without some knowledge of it, it is impossible to understand modern history." Only after learning "general notions, general leading principles," did Mansfield think it useful to begin the study of any "municipal" law, by which he meant the particular laws of England, Scotland, and France.[25]

Although in his own studies Murray may not have pursued a program as carefully organized as the one he later recommended to law students, there is no doubt that as a student he himself read many, if not most, of the authors on his list. What is equally interesting about his concise letter (when transcribed, it covers little more than one double-spaced page) is his emphasis on mastering general principles before taking up the specifics of learning the law. Throughout Murray's life, a cornerstone of his thinking, not just about the law but also about finance and politics, was to establish or find an overriding principle that would provide guidance for the future when dealing with the details of a problem. This is one of the reasons why many of the legal precedents he established have endured until the present day as part of Anglo-American legal systems.

The texts on English law available to a law student in the early eighteenth century were limited. *Coke upon Littleton*, published in 1628, remained the standard legal textbook until the nineteenth century.[26] Blackstone's *Commentaries*, which was to become a principal text for generations of law students, had not yet been written when Murray studied the law.[27] Dudley Ryder's diary as a law student a decade earlier shows that he spent many hours with *Coke*, and it is likely Murray did the same. Ryder also read works of the seventeenth-century philosopher John Locke, which he said "gives the best and clearest account of trade and its interest of anything I have met with."[28] Murray too included Locke in his studies; Locke's laissez-faire philosophy clearly influenced his thinking about many important issues, including economics and religious toleration. Later, when arguing in court, Murray on at least one occasion cited Locke's *Several Papers Relating to Money, Interest and Trade*.[29]

Yet these books barely scratch the surface of Murray's readings as a law student, which included works on ethics and history, Roman civil law, and the French commercial code.[30]

What led him to take on the additional work and extend his readings to the legal systems of other nations, international law, and Roman law cannot be readily explained. His ambition was to shine at the English bar, but the English common law was highly insular and bound by ancient procedural rules that did not require familiarity with other legal systems. In fact, English lawyers and judges discouraged the study of Roman law.[31] It was Murray himself, after he became chief justice nearly thirty years later, who introduced elements of Roman, foreign, and international law into the English common law.

One partial explanation for the extraordinary breadth of Murray's interests is that, as a Scot, he wanted to know more about Scottish law, which resembled the civil law of continental Europe and retained its separate identity even after the union of Scotland and England. Murray's classical education, beginning as a schoolboy in Perth and continuing at Westminster School and Christ Church, had introduced him to Roman law and had most likely made him want to learn more about other legal systems. According to one writer, "few successful practitioners can have entered upon their careers with so wide a range of legal knowledge. There is evidence that it included, in addition to English law, Roman law, Scots law, the French commercial code and [possibly] the law of nature and of nations."[32]

The breadth of Murray's legal education – which was largely self-education – played a significant part in making him one of the greatest and most influential judges in history. The legal historian Sir William Holdsworth wrote:

> It was because Mansfield was learned in other systems of law besides the common law that he was able by his decisions to develop and modernize many of the rules and principles of the common law. His knowledge of other systems of law helped him to come to right conclusions as to the correct legal principle to apply in the case before him; and his knowledge of English law helped him to give to that legal principle a technical form which was in accordance with authority … He was a learned Scots lawyer. This affected his mind in two ways. First, it made him familiar with sometimes more reasonable rules of Scots law. Second, it helped give him a Scots outlook on the law … He considered that attention should be paid not so much to the actual decision in any given case, but to the principle underlying that decision.[33]

Aside from his readings, Murray chiefly learned the law by attending the courts in Westminster Hall regularly and analyzing the decisions of the judges.[34] A few years earlier, Dudley Ryder, whose diligence in learning the law may have approached (but did not match) Murray's, wrote in his diary: "It is good to attend the courts constantly though one does not find one's self much the better for every particular time one goes, for it insensibly habituates one to think in their manner and accustoms one to their style and practice. I intend therefore to be very constant in my attendance upon them."[35]

Participating in something similar to the common practice in modern North American law schools of forming study groups, Murray would meet regularly with other students to discuss legal questions and debate points of law. They prepared their arguments with great care; he found many of these discussions and case analyses useful later, not only as a practising lawyer but also as a judge during his long career spanning nearly sixty years.[36] Although largely self-educated in the law, Murray was exceptionally well prepared for a legal career when he was admitted to the bar in 1730.

4

A Rising Lawyer

There is no tongue carries a better edge.

Edward Young, poet and Murray's legal client,
in a letter to the Duchess of Portland

By June 1730, when Murray obtained a Master of Arts degree from Oxford, he had laid the groundwork for his career. But it is unlikely that anyone could have predicted that within ten years he would be England's foremost lawyer and eventually the greatest judge of the eighteenth century. His diligence and dedication to the law matched his ambition. He had acquired an extraordinarily broad knowledge of the law of England and other nations, as well as of history and the classics. He had already demonstrated the eloquence and persuasive ability that he would soon use to good effect in the courtroom and in Parliament. His days at Westminster and Christ Church had given him contacts with the highest circles of English society; and his urbane manners enabled him to make the most of his knowledge, abilities, and contacts. To borrow the words of novelist Anthony Trollope, "he lived quite at ease with people of the highest rank."[1]

Finally, Murray's chosen profession gave him social mobility. In eighteenth-century English society, professionals occupied their own niche between the ruling class of landowners and the rising class of merchants, bankers, and tradesmen. Lawyers, particularly, with their easy access to the world of public affairs and political intrigue, were well placed to exploit the social and economic opportunities that their position offered.[2]

Nevertheless, Murray faced serious obstacles. First of all, he was a Scot. Dislike of the Scottish nation had become almost a mania among the English, including the elite as well as the general populace.[3] Dudley Ryder voiced a popular sentiment when he wrote that the Scots "seem to be men very fit for business, intriguing, cunning, tricking sort of men that have not much honour or conscience, but that are ready to comply with the court in anything."[4] Secondly, the well-known Jacobitism of his father and siblings created the suspicion, not entirely unfounded, that Murray secretly harboured Jacobite sympathies.

Moreover, Murray owned no land, in an age when the great property owners dominated both Parliament and polite society.[5] Ownership of land was valued, not only as an investment but also for the political and social cachet that it provided.[6] Murray's only source of wealth was his ability as a lawyer. And despite the advantages that lawyers naturally enjoyed, there was a social prejudice against them: a feeling that they were encroaching on a sphere reserved for their superiors in birth and fortune. Historian George Otto Trevelyan wrote of the "small esteem in which gentlemen of the long robe [i.e., the law] were generally held ... Everybody was greedy but the lawyer was selfish. Everybody was ready to change sides with the rest of the connection to which he belonged; but the lawyer rattled alone, and at a moment which suited his individual interest."[7]

Although Murray came from a noble family (albeit Scottish rather than English) and had good connections acquired at Westminster and Oxford, some regarded him as a "climber," a fortune hunter.[8] He would soon overcome his lack of money and status through his dazzling success at the bar, his marriage into a prominent family of the English nobility, and his ability to make friends with an ever-widening circle of influential people.

During the summer of 1730, Murray travelled in France and Italy.[9] It was usual for upper-class Englishmen to make what was known as the Grand Tour, often under the guidance of a well-educated tutor who could lead his disciples through France and particularly Italy (often including a trek through the Alps) and explain the antiquities to them. It is not known with whom Murray travelled, but if he made an extended trip of this kind,[10] his tutorial companion very possibly was his friend Rev Joseph Spence, a thirty-one-year-old professor of poetry at New College, Oxford. That summer, Spence led a tour that included Charles Sackville, Earl of Middlesex, one of Murray's classmates at Westminster and Christ Church.[11] The itinerary of the trip is not recorded, but another Grand Tour led by Spence included the major cities of Italy as well as Paris and Geneva.

A similar lack of evidence means we also do not know whether Murray used this travel opportunity on the Continent to make contact with his relatives at the exiled Pretender's court, as he had done five years earlier. Given his family's Jacobite connections, it is unlikely that he took such a risk at the threshold of his career.

On 23 November 1730, Murray was admitted to the bar and began the practice of law. Although he retained his residence at Lincoln's Inn for several years,[12] he moved into chambers at No. 5 King's Bench Walk, near the Thames at the Inner Temple, one of the four Inns of Court. The building was partly designed by Christopher Wren after the Great Fire of 1666. This section of London, wedged between the mainly commercial area that constituted the City of London and the rapidly growing West End where the nobility and the wealthy lived, was the domain of lawyers. In the coffee houses around the Temple, the talk was generally not of politics, poetry, or theatre, but of "causes, costs, demurrers, rejoinders, and exceptions."[13]

At first, business came to Murray slowly. It appears that he had no business at all during his first two years as a lawyer.[14] From his third year, he had a growing practice, although it took seven years at the bar before he made £2,000 a year. He used his first professional earnings to buy a china and silver-plate tea set. His sister-in-law, Lady Stormont (his oldest brother, David Murray, had inherited the Stormont title when their father died in 1731), who may have helped him financially while he was a law student, sent him food packages, including Scottish marmalade, when he was a young lawyer.[15]

Murray's Scottish birth and his knowledge of Scottish law turned out to be an important professional advantage. Appeals from Scotland's Court of Session were heard by the House of Lords, which was both Great Britain's upper legislative chamber, comparable in some ways to the Senates of Canada and the United States, and its highest court of appeals. A favourable word from his friends to Scottish attorneys, as well as his family connections, may have brought him this business.[16]

Murray's first case of any importance was a securities dispute involving the South Sea Bubble, the speculative craze that had seized investors in England and Scotland in 1720. Murray represented a Scottish investor who had purchased South Sea stock and then sued his broker when the price of the stock plummeted and he lost his entire investment. A Scottish court awarded the investor damages; unsurprisingly, there were appeals, and the case finally came to the House of Lords in March 1733, an astonishing delay of thirteen years after the South Sea Bubble burst. (When Murray became chief justice, one of his first court reforms was to speed up the judicial process and prevent the kind of delays that occurred in this early case.) Murray lost the case – which must be one of the earliest securities lawsuits on record – on the ground that his client had only his own credulity and greed to blame for his misfortune.[17]

Nevertheless, there was great admiration for the force of Murray's argument, in which he vividly described the fraud concocted by the defendant in the case.[18] The following year he was successful in another appeal to the House of Lords from the decision of the Scottish Court of Session. In *Hoggan v. Wardlaw*, the twenty-two electors of a borough had agreed in writing to act in concert in the election of magistrates, under penalty of 500 marks "and of being esteemed infamous and unfit for society."[19] The Scottish court upheld the agreement, but Murray was one of the two lawyers who obtained a reversal of its decision. The House of Lords found the agreement illegal because it prevented the electors from acting as free agents according to their consciences. This was the first of several election disputes that Murray was to argue.

He soon began to build up a considerable practice arguing Scottish appeals in the House of Lords.[20] His skill as an advocate brought him to the attention of the lord chancellor, Philip Yorke, Earl of Hardwicke, whose advice the other peers usually relied on when deciding appeals. Next to Mansfield, Hardwicke has been described as the greatest lawyer of the eighteenth century, a period that was singularly rich in great lawyers.[21] Although Hardwicke, like so many of his countrymen, was prejudiced against Scots, that did not prevent a mutual respect from developing between the two men.

Murray called Hardwicke "a truly great man ... who from very humble means, and without family support and connections, became Lord High Chancellor of England on account of his virtue, his talents, and his diligence."[22] By virtue of his office, he "was a member of the legislature – he acted as speaker of the House of Lords – a member of the executive who sat in Cabinet, and, in what was left of his time, sat as a judge" in the Court of Chancery.[23] According to one of Hardwicke's biographers, "No man, by the scope of his own activities, ever more utterly confounded and laid low the doctrine of the separation of powers."[24] It was said that no important government measure was executed without his previous consent.[25] However, he was principally a man of the law; Lord Chesterfield wrote: "Men are apt to mistake, or at least seem to mistake, their own talents ... Thus Lord Hardwicke valued himself more on being a great minister of state, which he certainly was not, than on being a great magistrate, which he certainly was."[26]

Hardwicke had risen to the successive positions of solicitor general (in 1720), attorney general (in 1724), and chief justice of the Court of King's Bench (in 1733), the exact career path that Murray was later to follow. However, after only four years as chief justice, Hardwicke was appointed lord chancellor. Murray and Hardwicke espoused a similar mixture of political conservatism and legal progressiveness. Both were familiar with Roman law, which Hardwicke had learned in order to decide appeals from Scottish cases.[27] Murray, Hardwicke's greatest disciple, said of him: "When his Lordship pronounced his decrees, wisdom himself might be supposed to speak."[28]

Hardwicke was known for the fairness of his rulings and also for his courtesy; he never interrupted a legal pleading or indulged in sarcastic humour at the expense of a lawyer or his client.[29] People would flock to Hardwicke's court to hear him pronounce judgment, much as they would go to the theatre to hear the great actor David Garrick. But Hardwicke commanded admiration rather than affection. There was no lighter side to his character, nor any record of any recreation that he enjoyed, and he seems to have had few friends.[30] It is not surprising, therefore, that the professional respect that developed between Hardwicke and Murray never grew into a personal friendship.

The Chancery Court, where Hardwicke sat as presiding judge, dealt largely in disputes involving real estate transactions; wills, trusts, and estates; and marriage settlements. Since land ownership was the principal source of wealth in pre-industrial England, much of the everyday work of lawyers involved disputes relating to real estate. In this court, Murray developed his skill in mastering complex factual situations and wringing from them simple issues of law that could readily be understood. It was here that he gained the respect of judges and fellow barristers.

England and its colonies were unique in having two sets of courts: the common law courts, where a plaintiff could recover damages from the defendant for a wrong done to him; and the Chancery Court, a court of "equity," which could order a defendant to do or refrain from doing a specific action. A litigant could bring a suit of equity in the Chancery Court if an adequate remedy in damages was unavailable. Equity provided relief from the rigidity and formalism of the common law.[31] Scottish historian and law professor John Millar explained the special benefit of the court of equity: "it is necessary ... to forego in many cases the benefit of that uniformity and certainty derived from the strict observance of a general rule, and by introducing an exception from the consideration of what is equitable in particular circumstances, to avoid the hardship which would otherwise fall upon individuals."[32] For example, a borrower who through no fault of his own was unable to pay off a mortgage on the required date could not obtain any relief from the common law courts, but might be able to obtain an "equity of redemption" from the Chancery Court prohibiting the lender from foreclosing on the property.

The flexibility exercised by the Chancery Court often gave a plaintiff the justice that the rigid requirements of the common law courts were unable to provide. Under the common law, a claim could not be pursued unless it fit into one of the traditional categories for lawsuits, known as "forms of action," which required pleaders in court to use particular language mandated by the respective category. A lawyer departed from the required words at his peril: his client's claim would be denied. The disadvantage of the Chancery Court was that its procedures were notoriously complex and slow. Noting the circumstances of a man who had pursued an estate case in Chancery for thirty-three years, until he was over eighty years of age, Mansfield suggested facetiously that the case had kept the man alive.[33] When the owner of a horse complained to Lord Chesterfield that the animal was restive and unruly, leaping over every fence within which it was placed, Chesterfield replied: "Put him in the Court of Chancery, and I'll warrant you he'll never get out of it."[34]

Later, sitting on the bench as the highest-ranking common law judge, and aiming for justice, Murray introduced into the common law some of the principles of equity that he had learned from Lord Hardwicke.[35] Conservative judges and lawyers would accuse Murray of subverting the English legal system by blurring the distinctions between the two systems of law.

Murray represented clients in a wide variety of disputes, some of them trivial or ridiculous. In one 1736 appeal before Lord Hardwicke, he represented a defendant who had been convicted of having ten partridges in his house, in violation of a 1694 law prohibiting unauthorized persons from having game in their homes. Murray implausibly argued to the court that the defendant might have acquired the partridges before the law was enacted. Hardwicke rejected Murray's argument and affirmed the conviction, perhaps on the ground that the stench of forty-year-old dead birds would have made the home uninhabitable.[36]

Murray gained a reputation for brilliant advocacy in a few high-profile cases. He first attracted public attention in 1737 in the Porteous case, a highly political matter, where he represented the city of Edinburgh, arguing before the bar of both Houses of Parliament against a proposed bill. (Lawyers were permitted to argue in Parliament for or against legislation.) Smuggling was rife along Scotland's east coast, and Andrew Wilson, a smuggler who had robbed a customs officer, was sentenced to death. After Wilson had been publicly hanged in Edinburgh, a riot ensued. The rioters hurled stones at members of the guard, at which point John Porteous, the captain of the guard, ordered his men to fire into the crowd. They killed eight people and wounded twice as many. Porteous was arrested, tried, and condemned to death by a Scottish court for having given the order to fire without first ordering the rioters to disperse, as required by the Riot Act.[37] However, Queen Caroline, who headed a regency council while the King was away in Hanover,[38] ordered Porteous's execution postponed in order to allow for an appeal.

Fearing that Porteous would be reprieved, many in Edinburgh were enraged at the delay. A mob forced its way into the prison, seized Porteous while he was trying to hide in a chimney, and hanged him.[39] A bill was brought before the House of Lords to discipline the city of Edinburgh and imprison Alexander Wilson,[40] its provost, for his failure to prevent the lynching. Appearing in the House of Lords on behalf of Provost Wilson, Murray argued forcefully that the bill would be a grave insult to the Scottish capital, that nothing Wilson did proceeded from malice, and that it would be unjust to punish the many for an offense by a few people who could not be identified. Nevertheless, the House of Lords passed the bill on the advice of Lord Hardwicke, who strongly supported it despite his admiration for Murray's legal ability.

The bill was then sent to the House of Commons, where Murray again represented the provost. He argued that the very example of Porteous made Wilson cautious in quelling riots and, furthermore, that Wilson had taken reasonable steps to prevent the riot. Influenced also by Prime Minister Robert Walpole, who thought moderation preferable to severity in preventing future crimes, the Commons reduced the harshness of the bill, which it then passed.[41] As a result, neither Wilson nor any other individual was punished, and the only penalty imposed on Edinburgh was a fine of £2,000 to provide for Porteous's widow.[42]

The Porteous case made Murray a hero In Edinburgh, which a few years later presented him with the key to the city in a gold box.[43] More important, it established his reputation in England as a gifted advocate. From then on, he began getting a flow of lucrative cases in the Chancery Court. So sudden was Murray's rise to prominence at the bar that he was reported to have said that he never knew the difference between a total want of employment and the fairly substantial income of £3,000 a year.[44]

Another 1737 case gave Murray an opportunity to help his alma mater, Christ Church, Oxford. The college had dismissed Thomas Lamprey, a chaplain, for marrying, and Lamprey petitioned Lord Hardwicke's court for reinstatement. Murray defeated the petition on the ground that Lamprey was not only a chaplain but also a fellow (or member) of the college, and English universities traditionally prohibited their members from marrying. Therefore, Lamprey's marriage was a lawful cause for his dismissal.[45] The dean of Christ Church was so delighted with Murray's success that he gave him the right to nominate a student to Christ Church, along with a scholarship. Murray nominated the son of Lord Milton, a judge of the Court of Session, Scotland's highest court, who had been kind to him as a boy.[46] His decision showed keen political judgment, for Lord Milton was the confidential agent of the Duke of Argyll. The duke, a loyal supporter of the Hanoverian succession to the throne, was the most powerful Scottish nobleman,[47] who was sometimes called the uncrowned king of Scotland.[48]

One sensational case, which came before the Court of King's Bench in 1738, demonstrates Murray's skill in framing a dispute in a way that best served his client. Theophilus Cibber, the black-sheep son of Colley Cibber, who was both poet laureate and a prominent actor, sued William Sloper for "criminal conversation" (the term used for adultery in the eighteenth century) with the younger Cibber's wife, Susannah Cibber, an actress and a celebrated beauty.[49] In a criminal-conversation suit, a husband could potentially recover enormous damages from a man who had sexual relations with his wife, on the ground that the adulterer had deprived the husband of his wife's "services." The husband had only to prove that he was married to the woman and that she had committed adultery with the defendant.

In arguing for the defendant in *Cibber v. Sloper*, Murray did not attempt to dispute the evidence that the adultery had taken place, and he emphasized that he did not support immorality. But, he said, this was not a prosecution for immorality; the only question for the jury to decide was whether the defendant had injured the plaintiff. The evidence, given by a servant, showed that Cibber had consented to his wife's adultery with Sloper, even to the extent of coming into the room where they lay in bed together and putting a pillow under their heads.

In addressing the jury, Murray suggested that Cibber and his wife were engaged in a racket whereby they "lay a snare for an unwary young gentleman, take a sum of money from him, and when he would part with no more, then come for a second sum to a court of justice." The jury found for the plaintiff but awarded him the derisory sum of £10, the smallest banknote then in circulation.[50] Forty-four years later, Murray, then the famous lord chief justice, may have been thinking of his successful advocacy in the *Cibber* case when he instructed the jury in a similar criminal-conversation case: "If upon the evidence you think the husband was privy to, consenting, and encouraging this debauchery, he ought not to have a verdict." In that case the jury awarded the plaintiff damages of only one shilling.[51]

Murray worked very hard, but he made it look easy. The poet William Cowper later recalled that Murray was "wonderfully handsome, and would expound the most mysterious intricacies of the law, or recapitulate both matter and evidence of a cause ... with an intelligent smile on his features, that bespoke plainly the perfect ease with which he did it. The most abstruse studies (I believe) never cost him any labour."[52] A portrait painted around 1742 by French artist Jean Baptiste van Loo shows him as he must have appeared in the courtroom, dressed soberly in black with a white collar and two short strips of linen hanging below his neck.[53] He wears a light grey wig and is clean-shaven, both of which were the custom for upper-class men of his day. He has a long patrician nose, a cleft chin, and thin lips and eyebrows. The success he had achieved in his profession is reflected in a slightly supercilious smile, and one gets the impression of a man who cares a great deal about his appearance. The portrait does not show him full length, but according to one biographer, "the only natural advantage which he did not possess was height; as he was on the small side."[54]

In an age that loved eloquent oratory and legal argument, Murray was a great attraction. One observer wrote: "Often when the audience part of the court of King's Bench would begin to thin from the expectation of no material business coming on, no sooner was the cry given of 'Murray being up,' than the crowds would run back so as not only to fill the court, but all the avenues leading to it."[55]

One indication of the success of Murray's law practice is the high social standing of many of his clients. He represented Lord Sidney Beauclerk, the son of a duke and an illegitimate grandson of King Charles II, in a disputed parliamentary election for Windsor.[56] Another client was the Earl of Pembroke (known as the "architect earl" because he was largely responsible for building Westminster Bridge), in a dispute with the Duchess of Portland. On land granted to her, she had planted a terrace with trees that obstructed Pembroke's view of the Thames. Murray was able to prove that Lady Portland did not own the land on which she had planted the trees. Despite his effective advocacy against her, Murray was to become a lifelong friend of Lady Portland, the granddaughter of a former prime minister and the mother of a future prime minister.[57]

Murray's most distinguished client was the imperious, quarrelsome, and very rich Sarah Churchill. She was the widow of John Churchill, Duke of Marlborough, the great army general of the wars against Louis XIV, and an ancestor of Winston Churchill. A woman with a "passion for government," Duchess Sarah had exercised power in her own right as a confidante of Queen Anne during the early years of the century.[58] After hearing Murray's eloquent courtroom defence of a client, Sarah decided to use Murray as her lawyer. She sent him the enormous retainer of a thousand guineas, which he returned to her, less five guineas, which he said was his usual retainer.[59]

One evening, Murray returned to his home at King's Bench Walk to find the duchess's carriage, accompanied by numerous footmen and other servants, waiting for him. Sarah met him when he entered the house and exclaimed haughtily, "Young man, if you want to rise in the world you must not sup out."[60] Evidently Murray ignored her advice, for the duchess called on him another evening and again found him gone. She waited in her carriage until after midnight, and finally left in a rage. When Murray returned from a supper party, his clerk told him that there had been a caller and added, "I could not make out, sir, who she was, for she would not tell me her name, but she swore so dreadfully that I am sure she must be a lady of quality."[61]

The most famous of Murray's friends during his years in law practice was not a lawyer or politician but the greatest poet of his day, Alexander Pope. They may have met through Joseph Spence, a mutual friend. The earliest contemporary evidence that they knew each other dates from 1735, when Murray and Pope together visited Spence.[62] Their friendship lasted until Pope's death in 1744. Although crippled by tuberculosis since childhood and humpbacked, he had a pleasant disposition and vivacity that attracted many people to him.[63] By 1737 Murray and Pope had became close friends, despite the difference in their ages and backgrounds: Pope was seventeen years older than Murray; he was the son of a wealthy London linen merchant. Pope often stayed with Murray at his house in Lincoln's Inn Fields (where Murray lived after his marriage in 1738), sometimes writing and receiving his letters there, and more or less treating Murray's home as his own. Murray in turn was a frequent weekend visitor to Pope's idyllic villa at Twickenham, on the banks of the Thames outside London.[64] Murray spent Christmas of 1742 at Twickenham with Pope and other friends.[65] It was said that they also wandered together over the hills of Hampstead Heath, near Kenwood House, which Murray was later to buy for a summer home and which eventually became his chief residence.[66] The suave, well-dressed Murray and the infirm Pope, no taller than a twelve-year-old boy, must have made an unusual-looking pair.

Pope had risen to literary prominence despite considerable obstacles. As a Roman Catholic, he was under numerous severe restrictions that had been imposed by Parliament in the late seventeenth century. He was not allowed to hold any public employment; to inherit, purchase, or own land; or to practise his religion publicly. His home was subject to forcible entry at any time upon the authorization of a justice of the peace.[67] In addition to these legally imposed handicaps, Pope suffered from illness throughout his life.[68] They may have been drawn to each other because both were outsiders, members of two groups against which most Englishmen were prejudiced: Catholics and Scots. One can speculate that the religious tolerance that Murray later displayed as a judge owed something to his friendship with Pope when he was a young lawyer. They also shared a love – and deep knowledge – of the writings of the ancient Greeks and Romans.

Pope greatly admired the young barrister. In 1736, he wrote to William Fortescue (who held the judicial post of master of the rolls) that Murray was "one of the few people whom no man that knows, can forget, or not esteem."[69] Two years later, he wrote to Fortescue: "Pray remember me to Mr Murray. You need not tell him I admire and esteem him, but pray assure him I love him."[70] And in 1739 he wrote to Jonathan Swift that he particularly cultivated the friendship of young people, because they are likely to be honest, whereas the old often are not; he mentioned Murray as one of very few persons "whom I would never fear to hold out against all the corruption in the world."[71]

Knowing Murray's abilities, Pope thought it a pity that he had chosen a legal career; he believed Murray's talents better suited to a literary life and would have liked Murray to lead a life as happy as his own.[72] Comparing

Murray and William Pulteney, a leading politician who, like Murray, was known for his eloquence, to two great Classical Roman poets, he wrote, in the first book of the *Dunciad*: "How sweet an Ovid, Murray was our boast! / How many Martials were Pulteney Lost!"[73]

Pope had "a capacity to react warmly and intelligently to excellence in areas quite foreign to his own skills and experience."[74] Although he was disappointed that Murray was not inclined to become a poet, he admired Murray's oratory and was captured by the beauty of his voice.[75] Pope made great efforts to help his friend develop his skills as an advocate. During visits to Murray's law chambers, he would spend hours instructing him in the art of oratory, not so much in the substance of what he said but rather in the intonations he used. According to one story, an unannounced visitor once found Murray practising oratory in front of a mirror, while Pope sat by, coaching him.[76]

In return, Murray acted, very effectively, as Pope's lawyer, as he did for other friends.[77] In November 1737 he brought a lawsuit under the Copyright Act in Chancellor Hardwicke's court on behalf of Robert Dodsley, a well-known publisher and bookseller in Pall Mall, against James Watson, a printer. Pope had set up Dodsley in business[78] and had sold him the right to publish his works. Watson had pirated copies of an edition of Pope's letters. Watson quickly settled the case, paying £100 to Pope, delivering to Dodsley the whole impression of the pirated books, and giving his bond not to print any more copies.[79] Twenty years later, soon after Murray had been elevated to the bench, Dodsley showed his appreciation of his former lawyer by publishing *An Ode on the Powers of Eloquence to the Right Hon. Lord Mansfield*.[80]

As a close friend, Pope was privy to Murray's romantic attachments. Campbell, Murray's biographer, states that around 1738 Murray proposed marriage to a young lady of beauty, accomplishments, and birth, and she listened favourably to his suit. Her family, however, refused to allow the marriage because he was only a lawyer, not a landowner of wealth, and they married her off instead to a country squire. In his despondency Murray retired to a small cottage on the banks of the Thames, near Pope's villa at Twickenham.[81] In view of Murray's increasingly busy practice, his self-imposed withdrawal could not have lasted long.

Pope consoled him in verse. In an English imitation of the Roman poet Horace's "Ode to Venus," published in March 1737, he compared Murray to Horace's friend, the lawyer Paulus Maximus. The poem included flattering lines that obliquely referred to Murray's disappointment in love:

Again? new tumults in my breast?
Ah, spare me Venus! let me, let me rest!
. . . .
To *number five* direct your doves,
There spread round Murray all your blooming loves,
Noble and young, who strikes the heart
With every sprightly, every decent part;
Equal the injur'd to defend,
To charm the mistress, or to fix the friend,
He, with a hundred arts refin'd,
Shall stretch thy conquests over half the kind …[82]

"Number five" referred to the address of Murray's chambers at King's Bench Walk. Colley Cibber, a mediocre poet who had often been the butt of Pope's wit – and who may still have been smarting from Murray's recent destruction of his son's criminal-conversation suit – mocked Murray in a parody of Pope: "Persuasion tips his tongue, whene'er he talks / And he has chambers in the King's Bench Walks."[83]

A good indication that Murray recovered quickly from his romantic setback is that only a few months later a friend wrote that Pope "dined with Mr Murray and Lady Betty, and was very drunk last Saturday night."[84] Lady Betty was Elizabeth Finch, whom Murray married the following year. It is possible that Lady Betty's brother, John Finch, a lawyer at the Inner Temple between 1736 and 1739, introduced the two to each other.[85]

Another of Murray's friends was William Warburton, whom he met through Pope in the 1730s.[86] Born in 1698, Warburton began his career as a lawyer but soon changed his mind and took holy orders. Warburton became Pope's literary executor when the poet died in 1744. Murray acted as his lawyer in connection with the publication of Pope's works as well as on other matters, including a consultation on a point of law regarding the fortune of the mistress of one of Warburton's friends, for which Warburton paid Murray a fee of two guineas.[87] A decade later, Murray and Warburton vacationed together at Bath when Murray visited the spa for his rheumatism,[88] and Murray was instrumental in getting Warburton an appointment as preacher at Lincoln's Inn. In 1760 Warburton became Bishop of Gloucester, very possibly through Murray's intervention on his behalf with the Duke of Newcastle, who controlled patronage, including ecclesiastical appointments.[89]

Warburton was a prolific, intemperate, and controversial writer, a strenuous advocate of the literal truth of the Old and New Testaments, vigorously attacking anyone who disagreed with him, including deists, atheists, and Methodists.[90] Although he made many public enemies, he was a warm and constant personal friend. In 1767 he dedicated a volume of his sermons to Lady Mansfield, reminding his readers that she was the granddaughter of "that great Magistrate" the Earl of Nottingham; and a year later Warburton gave the very large sum of £500 to Mansfield to endow a course of sermons at Lincoln's Inn to prove the truth of revealed religion.[91]

Another prominent friend of Murray during his years as a practicing lawyer was Henry St John, 1st Viscount Bolingbroke. Born in 1678, Bolingbroke was a Tory secretary of state under Queen Anne and a confirmed Jacobite. After the Hanoverian succession in 1714, he fled to France and entered the service of the Stuart Pretender. He was impeached *in absentia* for high treason, but a year later he broke with the Pretender. He received a pardon from the King in 1723 and was allowed to return from exile but not to resume his place in the House of Lords.[92]

Bolingbroke's writings on politics, government, religion, and philosophy were widely read at the time and had an important influence on Murray's thinking. His *Letters on the Study and Use of History* stated the "exemplary theory" of history, which derived from the thinking of Roman historians. The main message of the *Letters* was that the study of history was mandatory for a career in politics because it furnished examples of human conduct that could be distilled into principles and rules to guide the action of politicians. In 1736 Bolingbroke gave the manuscript of the *Letters* to his friend Pope, who printed the work privately and sent copies to Murray and others.[93]

In Bolingbroke's most influential book, *The Idea of a Patriot King*, published in 1739, he advocated greater royal power and replacement of the party system by less corrupt, albeit more authoritarian, methods of government.[94] Bolingbroke's economic philosophy followed the laissez-faire economics of John Locke, whom Bolingbroke acknowledged as his teacher. Murray, who likewise was influenced by Locke's writings, and the much older Bolingbroke became friends;[95] Murray revered Bolingbroke and was attracted to his authoritarian political philosophy. Bolingbroke, for his part, respected Murray's legal ability; he retained Murray to act as his attorney during an absence from England in 1740.[96] *Patriot King* would have an important impact on the thinking and policies of King George III, who chafed under the restrictions imposed by a constitutional monarchy, upon his accession to the throne in 1760.

Bolingbroke was skeptical by nature, a child of the Enlightenment, exemplified by the philosophers Rousseau, Voltaire, and Locke. He was a deist, rejecting formal religion and believing that the existence of God was demonstrated through nature. This brought Bolingbroke into conflict with the choleric, religiously orthodox Warburton. Pope hoped that his two friends, both men of high intelligence, could settle their differences. In the spring of 1744, not long before Pope's death, Murray, Pope, and Warburton had dinner together, probably at Pope's home in Twickenham.[97] Warburton shocked Pope by telling him that Bolingbroke did not believe in the moral attributes of God. Pope told Warburton that he must have been mistaken, and later asked Bolingbroke about it. Bolingbroke denied the accusation and Pope, who tended to believe the best about everyone, was overjoyed to hear this and happily told Warburton, "I told you you must be mistaken."[98] It is not known what part Murray played in this conversation, but it is likely that, ever the cautious lawyer, he kept his thoughts on the controversial topic of religion to himself. Though Murray was a member of the Church of England all his life, there is no evidence that he had strong religious beliefs.

Pope died not long afterwards, and by his will made Murray one of his executors. Among his bequests, he left Murray a marble head of Homer by the great Italian sculptor Bernini, which was to grace Murray's home at Kenwood, and another of Sir Isaac Newton by Guelfi.[99] Twelve years later, after Bolingbroke and Pope were both dead, Warburton, who was never given to restraint in expressing his views, published a violent criticism of their "life, morals, politics, and conversation."[100] In a long unsigned letter, Murray chastised his friend Warburton for his attack on his other two friends.[101] Murray must have been very angry, for this was one of the very few times that he departed from his habitual restraint: "You have let many strange similes, allusions, and expressions fall from your pen, and most astonishingly conclude the whole in a piss pot ... Poor Pope did not deserve to the treated by you with so much cruelty, contempt, and injustice; and in my conscience I believe you do not mean it, and I have wrote with so much haste, as to have weighed the force of your own words and manner."[102]

Murray had other literary friends. During the late 1730s he helped the career of a young poet, Christopher Smart, born in 1722. Smart's father worked at Raby, a grand medieval castle in northern England, the home of William and Henrietta Fitzroy, Duke and Duchess of Cleveland. Henrietta was a sister of Lady Elizabeth Finch, who was to become Murray's wife. Smart's father died when the boy was eleven, and he and his two sisters were sent to live at Raby.[103] At the age of thirteen, Smart seems to have developed a puppy love for Henrietta, who was thirty-three, describing her as a "beautiful young lady" in a poem he wrote to her. Henrietta must have been flattered, and also impressed with his literary talents: she gave him an allowance of £40 a year to pay for his education at Cambridge.[104]

Around the time of his marriage to Henrietta's sister at Raby Castle in 1738, Murray was introduced to Smart.[105] He was impressed by Smart's talents as a classical scholar, and it was very likely at his suggestion that Smart translated Pope's "Ode on Saint Cecilia's Day" into Latin.[106] The translation won Smart a £20 scholarship at Cambridge and launched his career as a poet. It was his first publication. Encouraged by his success, Smart wrote to Pope in 1743 asking for permission to translate another of his poems: "Mr Murray told me that it would, he thought, be agreeable to you to see a good Latin version of your *Essay on Man*, and advised me to undertake it … I should not have presumed to have given you this trouble had not Mr Murray assured me that I might safely venture."[107] Pope was not interested, perhaps because his health was failing.

Murray continued to encourage Smart, who followed Pope's example of writing a poem for Murray. Titled "After Dining with Mr Murray," it imitated the Latin poet Catullus and went:

> O Thou, of British orators the chief,
> That *were*, or *are in being*, or belief;
> All eminence and goodness as thou art,
> Accept the gratitude of Poet Smart.[108]

Although Smart became well known as a poet, his life was unhappy. His behaviour became increasingly erratic, including his writing of magazine articles under the pseudonym of "Mrs Mary Midwife," and Murray distanced himself from the young man. In 1757, Smart's father-in-law, who was also his publisher, had him committed to a lunatic asylum, where he remained for six years. Murray met him at least once more, though not under the best of circumstances. In 1771, as Chief Justice Mansfield, he committed Smart to debtor's prison, where he died later that year.[109]

Murray's circle of literary friends also included Edward Young, the author of *Night Thoughts*, a poem whose publication in 1742 made him famous, but today is almost completely forgotten. Like Pope and Warburton, Young availed himself of Murray's legal talents. The Duke of Wharton, Young's patron, had broken a promise to give Young two annuities. Murray represented Young when he sued the duke in the court of Chancellor Hardwicke, who ordered the duke to pay one of the two annuities and reserved judgment on the other. In a letter to their mutual friend the Duchess of Portland, Young paid tribute to Murray's exceptional skills as an advocate:

> This day by your friend Murray's assistance I carried just one half my point, the other is referred to Prince Posterity. Mr Murray ... helped me to the wing without cutting off the leg. For the matter stood *thus*: I had two annuities of different dates, that of the second date he sliced off for me with infinite address and dexterity, and left that of the first date still sticking to the Duke's estate. Though I must do him this justice, that if any man alive could have cut off the leg he had certainly done it; for there is no tongue carries a better edge.[110]

Although Murray never visited America, as a practicing lawyer he was constantly involved in American affairs. As solicitor general and attorney general, he gave many legal opinions to the government involving the North American colonies. Later, as an unofficial adviser to King George III, he helped shape British policy in its dealings with the American colonists. Beginning in 1734 and lasting into the 1740s, he represented several of the American colonies before the Commissioners for Trade and Plantations, commonly called the Board of Trade, as well as committees of the King's Privy Council, in boundary disputes with adjacent colonies. He was the attorney for New Hampshire in a long-standing dispute over its border with the Massachusetts Bay colony; for Rhode Island in a dispute with Massachusetts; for the three sons of William Penn, John, Thomas, and Richard, the proprietors of Pennsylvania, in a long-drawn-out dispute with Lord Baltimore over the boundaries of Maryland; and for the Trustees of Georgia in a dispute with South Carolina. He also was counsel for Samuel Mason, the agent for the Mohegan Indians, in a suit against Connecticut.[111]

Some of these disputes raised issues relating to the rights of the colonies vis-à-vis the King and Parliament, issues that were to become of critical importance in the years leading up to the American Revolution. For example, in the Pennsylvania–Maryland dispute, Murray argued before the Board of Trade that the King did not have the right to nominate a deputy-governor of three disputed counties (which later became the state of Delaware); and that, as proprietors of the counties under a seventeenth-century grant from the Crown, the Penn brothers had that right, subject to a veto by the King.[112]

The Georgia Trustees, who were controlled by James Oglethorpe, the founder of the Georgia colony, first retained Murray as their counsel in late 1736. He represented the trustees for several years, first in a dispute with the adjacent colony of South Carolina and its opposition to laws enacted by Georgia prohibiting the rum trade and regulating trade with the Indians in Georgia. The colony of South Carolina claimed that these laws cut her off from this lucrative business, and enacted a law indemnifying its traders for any penalties imposed on them under the Georgia statute. At a meeting of the Board of Trade on 9 June 1737, Murray made a long speech on behalf of the Georgia Trustees, arguing that the South Carolina indemnification law had the effect of repealing the Georgia statute, and that Georgia law was paramount within the boundaries of the colony.[113]

The case continued into 1738, when Murray appeared before a committee of the Privy Council on behalf of the Georgia Trustees. This dispute happened to be a rare occasion when a client was unhappy with Murray's legal representation: Charles Wesley, who was present, noted in his journal that his argument was "so little to Mr Oglethorpe's satisfaction that he started up, and ran out."[114] Nevertheless, the Privy Council settled the case to the satisfaction of the Georgia Trustees, by giving South Carolinians certain trading rights, which the Georgia counsel said they already had.

One of Murray's American cases marked an early occasion showing his support for freedom of commerce and finance, which would become a central tenet of his judicial philosophy. In 1739, he acted as counsel for merchants in the Caribbean colony of Antigua, who protested against a statute of that island that restricted the rate of interest that lenders could charge. Murray argued before the Board of Trade that no benefit could arise from the statute, because "money will always find its own price, in proportion to the plenty or scarcity of it." To support his argument, he read the Board several paragraphs of the work of John Locke, the great seventeenth-century philosopher.[115] Here Murray was being canny, for the members of the Board of Trade were likely to be impressed with anything Locke had written; Locke's philosophy of limited monarchy laid the theoretical foundation for the Glorious Revolution of 1688 and was the creed of the ruling Whig party.[116]

On the subject of usury, Locke had written that, since a person cannot be prevented from giving away his money, he also should not be prevented from lending it at any rate he pleases. The consequences of a usury law, Locke argued, would be disastrous. It would make it difficult to lend and borrow money, and so obstruct trade; it would hurt those who most need help, such as widows and orphans and other unsophisticated people; it would benefit bankers and scriveners, who will always find ways to get round the law; and it would cause people to perjure themselves.[117] Murray's adherence to Locke's laissez-faire theory of money was to play an important part in several of his judicial decisions.

Murray's American law practice was varied. A divorce at that time could be obtained only by legislative permission. Murray represented Edward Manning, a resident of Jamaica who had obtained a divorce in 1739 through passing of a statute by the Jamaican assembly. This was the first colonial divorce statute. Murray argued on behalf of Manning before the Board of Trade, but lost the case when the Board disapproved the Jamaican statute and the Privy Council agreed with the Board's report.[118] Three years later, the Georgia Trustees again retained Murray (despite Oglethorpe's previous unhappiness with him) in a very different kind of case. He argued successfully in the House of Commons against a petition by one Thomas Stephens for the establishment of Georgia as a royal colony. The petition, which set forth the advantages of the slave trade and accused the trustees of embezzlement, was denied and Stephens was reprimanded, on his knees, in the House of Commons.[119]

By 1738 Murray, only thirty-three, had risen to the top of his profession. He had a substantial income from his practice and a promising future. And he was ready to make an advantageous marriage. On 20 September, he and Lady Elizabeth Finch (whom contemporaries often called Lady Betty) were married at Raby Castle in Durham in northern England, the home of Elizabeth's sister Henrietta, Duchess of Cleveland. As a marriage settlement, she and her ducal husband promised to pay the wedding couple an annuity of £500, making provision that it continue to be paid from the duke's estate after his death.[120]

The marriage lasted forty-six years, until Lady Betty's death in 1784. They had no children. The bride was a member of one of the richest and most powerful families in England. The Finches were a family of lawyers going back several generations; one of her ancestors defended Sir Francis Bacon in his trial for corruption in 1621. Lady Elizabeth's paternal grandfather, Heneage Finch, as solicitor general of England, conducted the trials of the regicides who had tried and executed King Charles I in 1649. After the Restoration, Charles II raised Finch to the peerage as Earl of Nottingham.

Finch served as lord chancellor from 1675 until his death in 1682.[121] Heneage Finch was one of the great judges of his day; he has been called the father of modern equity.[122] He was believed to be the author of the Statute of Frauds, the 1677 law that requires many kinds of contracts to be in writing in order to be enforceable.[123] Legislation that derives from the original Statute of Frauds is still part of Anglo-American law.[124]

Lady Elizabeth's father, Daniel Finch, was born in 1647 and succeeded to the titles of Earl of Nottingham and Earl of Winchilsea (the latter title upon the death of a cousin). He was known as "Dismal Finch" for his stubbornness, self-centredness, and dour temperament.[125] He supported the Toleration Act of 1689, which removed some of the restrictions on Protestant dissenters (i.e., Methodists, Quakers, and other Protestant sects that refused to subscribe to the sacrament of the Anglican Church) but not the restrictions on Catholics. On two occasions he served as one of the two secretaries of state who managed the business of the government. Despite his support of religious toleration, he became the active head of the High Church party during the reign of Queen Anne; but, unlike many other Tories, he steered clear of any connection with the Jacobites. Nevertheless, he was dismissed from his post of president of the Privy Council because he advocated leniency to the Jacobite peers under sentence of death for their participation in the 1715 rebellion.

Daniel Finch had one daughter by his first wife, who died young. His second wife, Lady Elizabeth's mother, was Anne, the daughter of Christopher, Viscount Hatton, a member of another ancient noble family. She gave birth to the incredible number of thirty children, of whom seven were stillborn and ten died young.[126] Daniel Finch died in 1730, eight years before his daughter married William Murray.

Lady Betty Finch was thirty-four, a year older than Murray, at the time of their marriage. A full-length portrait of her with her sister Henrietta, painted around 1732 by Charles Jervas, shows an attractive young woman with auburn hair, dressed elegantly in black. Her left hand delicately touches that of her sister, while in her right hand she holds a circlet of myrtle as if to crown a suitor.[127] Six years later, Murray accepted that crown and, according to John Holliday, his earliest biographer, "the couple lived together in great harmony and domestic happiness almost half a century."[128] The same could be said of Murray as was said of his near-contemporary Edmund Burke: "What was rare in fashionable London, after [his] marriage [his] name never was associated with that of any other woman."[129]

At a time when the average age of marriage of English noblewomen was under twenty-five,[130] the lateness of Betty Finch's marriage despite her good looks, wealth, and social prominence is puzzling. But aristocratic unmarried young women could enjoy a good life in London in the 1730s. Theatre, opera, masquerade balls, pleasure gardens, and the latest books and periodicals were all available to them.[131] By all accounts, Betty Finch was intelligent and sociable, so this life may have appealed to her. She had had previous opportunities to marry: newspapers published rumours that she was expected to marry Sir Thomas Newton in 1726[132] and the Earl of Westmoreland six years later.[133] But Newton seems to have had few interests aside from breeding horses, and Westmoreland was more than twenty years her senior. One could speculate that Betty Finch was willing to wait for an exceptional man who was free of the common vices of eighteenth-century English noblemen: drunkenness, sexual promiscuity, and gambling. According to a social historian of eighteenth-century England: "Elite women sought prudent affectionate matches, that they might share in the prestige and the pleasures of genteel family life."[134]

Many years after his own wedding, in a letter congratulating a young friend who had just wed, Lord Mansfield described the qualities that he valued in a wife: "I think you have made a wise choice – a lady well born, well educated, a good person, good connections, a healthy family, all her brothers remarkably clever ... I think fortune, where a man has [one] or is in a rising way, no object."[135] It is hard to believe that Mansfield was not thinking of his own wife when he wrote this, and his letter tends to negate any suggestion that the wealth of Lady Betty's family played an important part in his choice of a wife.

Lady Betty's friends were of two minds about the marriage, the doubts stemming from Murray being a mere Scottish lawyer, without a title or land to his name – but the overall verdict was favourable. Lady Mary Wortley Montagu wrote to a friend: "I suppose it is no news to you that Lady Betty Finch is married to Mr Murray. People are divided in their opinions, as they commonly are, on the prudence of her choice. I am among those who think ... she has happily disposed of her person."[136] Another aristocratic lady wrote: "The Mr Murray Lady Betty Finch has married is the same Pope celebrates, and I believe he is by everybody that know him well spoken of."[137] Interestingly, the writer identified Murray not by his success as a lawyer or his ancient noble family but as the dedicatee of one of Alexander Pope's poems.

Nonetheless, Murray's political enemies sometimes attacked him as a social climber who had opportunistically married into one of England's greatest families. An anonymous pamphlet, which some believed was written by

Murray himself, refuted this charge by pointing to his own noble background:

> If Mr M----y, or Strix, as you injudiciously call the most poignant and harmonious orator of the age, be ally'd by marriage to an English family of distinction, he has brought into it the highest personal merit, and the noble blood of all the ancient nobility of Scotland: A nobility known all over Europe, and distinguished for hospitality, valour and patriotism, long before the name of Englishman was heard of.
>
> Therefore, though Mr M----y has married into a family as distinguished and ancient, as most English families are or can be, yet persuade not yourself that he has acquired any new honours by the alliance.[138]

So, to what extent did Murray's marriage, and the connections acquired through it, contribute to his acceptance within the highest circles of English society and his rise through the government ranks to chief justice of England? Eighteenth-century England was effectively ruled by a small number of noble families, interlocked by marriage. Without Murray's connection to the Finches, it is unlikely that dukes, marquesses, and earls would have accepted a "mere lawyer" as a close associate and near-equal.[139]

Murray's marriage also increased his acceptability as a candidate for high office. Although the Finches were not in the first rank of politicians, they were part of the inner circle of the nobility that ruled Britain. Lady Betty's oldest brother, Daniel Finch, Earl of Winchilsea, served in many positions, including member of the Privy Council and first lord of the admiralty. As a member of the ministry of William Carteret, the prime minister in 1742, Daniel may have been influential in persuading the King to approve Murray's appointment as solicitor general.[140] Lady Betty's younger brothers, Edward and William, had positions in George II's household; Edward would play cards with the King in the evening and, after Carteret fell from power, was the conduit by which Carteret's views reached the King.[141] Edward and William Finch also served in diplomatic positions: Edward as minister to Sweden and Russia, and William as envoy to Sweden and the Netherlands. Another brother, John Finch, was a member of Parliament and surveyor of general works.

Lady Betty's sister Cecilia Isabella, known as Lady Bell, also was in a position to help Murray's career. Lady Bell, who never married, was for many years first lady of the bedchamber and private secretary to Princess Amelia, the King's daughter. An important figure at George II's Court, Lady Bell was "at the centre of the political world in her own right and had her own networks of political influence."[142] She frequently entertained leading politicians in her home, including Sir Robert Walpole and the Duke of Newcastle, with whom she had been friends for thirty years.[143] Newcastle sometimes asked her to use her influence at Court for him, and she in turn asked him for patronage on behalf of others.[144] Newcastle may have sought help from Lady Bell in 1756 when he was trying to overcome the King's resistance to raising Murray to the peerage.[145] Another of Lady Betty's sisters, Mary, was the mother of the Marquess of Rockingham, who twice served as prime minister during the reign of George III. In addition, Lady Betty was related through her mother's family to George Grenville, who was a friend of Murray and a brother-in-law of William Pitt. Grenville and Pitt both were to serve as prime minister.

As a result of his marriage, Murray did receive a small but perhaps significant advantage to his law practice: access to the private papers of his wife's grandfather, the 1st Earl of Nottingham. In a case that he argued as solicitor general in 1750, he referred to a decision by the famous lord chancellor of the previous century and added, "according to his own manuscript from whence I cite it."[146]

Nevertheless, the influence on Murray's career of his connection with the Finch family should not be overstated. The principal factor that launched Murray on his political career and eventually led to his appointment as chief justice was his close relationship with the Duke of Newcastle. As the leading politician of the mid-eighteenth century, Newcastle saw that Murray's impressive abilities could be useful to him on both a personal and political level.[147]

After a decade of legal practice, Murray had risen to the top of his profession. Despite his relative youth, he was one of the most sought-after lawyers in the country. A contemporary who heard him argue a contested election case in 1741 wrote: "Never was a case better opened, nor a reply made in a stronger manner, than was done by Murray in this case. The man is a miracle. No argument was missed; none urged but with the greatest precision: no circumstance omitted which could create an impression; none thrown in, but with the greatest propriety that judgment could suggest, or fancy improve."[148]

It was a mark of Murray's social, professional, and financial success that soon after his marriage he moved from his chambers near the Temple to a handsome house that he bought in Lincoln's Inn Fields.[149] This was a large square at the eastern edge of the rapidly growing West End of London, which at the time was a suburb of stately houses, the homes of the rich, the aristocratic, and the noble.[150] The Fields itself, despite its proximity to Lincoln's Inn, was not the exclusive preserve of lawyers; it was lined with the residences of noblemen, including the Duke of Newcastle, the Earl of Sandwich, and the Countess of Middlesex.[151] Government ministers, lawyers, judges, and foreign ambassadors occupied the houses on three sides of the square.

Earlier in the century, part of Lincoln's Inn Fields had lain waste, "a receptacle for rubbish, dirt, and nastiness of all sorts."[152] It was also a dangerous place where robberies and assaults were frequent and several persons had been killed. In 1735, responding to a petition from its residents, Parliament imposed a tax to "enclose, clean, and adorn" the Fields. By the time the Murrays moved there, Lincoln's Inn Fields was surrounded by wooden palings and criss-crossed by paths.[153] Considered one of the principal sights of London, it was primarily a residential square; but it was also the site of some commercial activities, including a theatre (where John Gay's *The Beggar's Opera*, London's favourite play, was shown),[154] a printing shop (where Benjamin Franklin once worked), and a library with a "handsome" collection.[155] Here the Murrays lived for the next fifteen years, and here, regularly at parties on Sunday evenings, they entertained leading politicians, judges, lawyers, noblemen, and members of Parliament.[156]

Murray's rise to the top of the legal profession in about ten years from the time he was admitted to the bar is astonishing. Hard work, ambition, intellectual ability, social skills, and an advantageous marriage all contributed to his success. He acted effectively in several capacities: as a trial lawyer, an appellate advocate, and a legal and financial adviser. It was only a short step from legal practice to the political arena.

5

Entering Politics

The only objection that can be made to him is what he can't help, which is that he is a Scotchman.

Duke of Richmond, in a letter to the Duke of Newcastle

Murray's emergence as a political figure must be seen against the background of British politics of the 1720s and 1730s. For nearly half a century after the failed rebellion of 1715, the Tories, many of whom had supported or at least sympathized with the rebels, could not shake off the taint of Jacobitism. In the public mind, Toryism became associated with disloyalty and even treason; meanwhile the Whigs, who had engineered the Hanoverian succession, enjoyed uninterrupted control of the government until the early 1760s. For twenty-one of those years (1721–42), British politics was dominated by Sir Robert Walpole, who was both the leader of the House of Commons and first lord of the treasury.[1] In fact, if not in name, Walpole was Britain's first prime minister.[2] In an age when the King still had considerable real power, including the right to choose his ministers, Walpole performed a delicate balancing act. He had to satisfy both the King, because to incur his displeasure risked dismissal, and Parliament, because it could (and eventually did) drive him from office.

Walpole's ministry was on the whole a successful one. He was hardworking and had a large fund of practical knowledge and common sense. He increased the power and prestige of the House of Commons, maintained a policy of peace with France and other foreign nations, and handled the country's finances with great success.[3] But Walpole had major faults. He engaged in wholesale bribery of voters, spent huge sums of money to subsidize newspapers that supported him and his policies,[4] and surrounded himself with mediocrities in order to keep all potential rivals for power at a distance.[5]

Denied an active role in the government, some of the ablest men of the time formed an informal and unofficial opposition to Walpole's ministry.[6] Although they were Whigs who were devoted to the principles of the Glorious Revolution of 1688, they differed from Walpole and his followers in their interpretation of the Revolution. Walpole believed that the Revolution was "necessary and brief" and that it placed sovereignty in the hands of parliament, not in the hands of the people. The Whigs who went into opposition maintained that the Revolution was "transformative and chronologically open-ended" and that it established popular, not parliamentary, sovereignty.[7] The differences in principle between Walpole and the opposition should not, however, be overstated. To some large extent, the opposition was motivated by personal ambitions and grievances.

The opposition included a number of men who belonged to the nobility and were related to each other by birth or marriage. Several of them entered Parliament during the 1730s and were to become the next generation's political leaders. Murray made lasting friendships with several of these men; however, unlike them, he was not a landowner, a nobleman, or a possessor of inherited wealth. Although he came from an old and distinguished Scottish family, he was a self-made man whose main assets were his extraordinary legal talent and his ability to make friends.

The opposition to the Walpole ministry originally formed around Richard Temple, Lord Cobham, who had distinguished himself as a general in the early eighteenth-century wars against France. Cobham went into opposition after King George II deprived him of his regiment in 1733 because he supported a parliamentary proposal for an inquiry into the South Sea Bubble financial scandal.[8] The King had been a secret participant in the venture and had made a substantial profit.[9] Cobham's followers became known as "Cobham's Cubs,"[10] or sometimes as the "Boy Patriots" because most were still in their thirties. Several became Murray's friends, including Cobham's nephew, George Grenville, and Grenville's brother-in-law, William Pitt. Other of Murray's friends who were members of this coterie included Pitt's cousin George Lyttelton, who had been at Christ Church, Oxford with Murray, and the celebrated wit and conversationalist Henry Hyde, Viscount Cornbury, a Tory member of Parliament with Jacobite leanings, whose family had close ties to the Stuart monarchs.[11] The aging, imperious Duchess of Marlborough, a legal client of Murray, became the opposition's "matriarch, gadfly, and immortal, undecaying Toast."[12]

The intellectual leader of the opposition was Murray's friend and legal client, Henry St John, Viscount Bolingbroke. Soon after his return from exile, Bolingbroke began taking part in the intrigues that eventually undermined Walpole's ministry. In 1726 Bolingbroke and William Pulteney founded *The Craftsman*, a weekly newspaper that constantly attacked the Walpole ministry.

The political leader of the opposition was the vastly wealthy Pulteney, who, like Murray, was educated at Westminster and Christ Church. A scholar, wit, and potent pamphleteer, Pulteney was also considered one of the greatest orators ever to sit in the House of Commons.[13] He had hopes of becoming prime minister after Walpole fell from power in 1742 (he did serve in that post for two days – probably the shortest tenure of any British prime minister), but his leadership of the opposition ended that year when he accepted the offer of a peerage and moved from the Commons to the Lords as the 1st Earl of Bath.[14]

Pulteney had a nasty temper and as a youth was given to picking quarrels, which sometimes led to fistfights or even duels. He married a very beautiful woman, who, like him, had a sharp tongue. Horace Walpole, the son of Sir Robert Walpole and London's busiest gossipmonger, referred to the two of them as "my Lord and Lady Bath who live in a vinegar bottle."[15] Others, including Murray's wife, Lady Betty, disliked him. Lord Marchmont, another of Cobham's Cubs, wrote in 1744: "Lord Bolingbroke told me, that there was no danger of any connexion formed ... between Lord Bath and Mr Murray's family, for Lady Betty Murray had avoided any intercourse with them, and told him that Lord and Lady Bath were the ridicule of the place for their avarice, which was grown up to the greatest excess."[16]

Murray often visited the country estates of Cobham's Cubs. Letters they wrote to each other give us some idea of how this group of friends spent their leisure time.[17] In the autumn of 1742, Cornbury wrote to Grenville, who was travelling on the Continent, apparently for his health: "Mr Murray has given me, this recess, a great deal of his time, and consequently made mine, as you will easily believe, very delightful. He gave me above a fortnight here, and most of the rest of his time we rambled together. Mr Pitt has not yet been here, but I expect him in a few days. Mr Murray was not gone from hence when I received your letter. I need not tell you how much he is your friend."[18]

Three weeks later Murray, then staying at Lyttelton's country estate of Hagley in Worcestershire, wrote a chatty, gossipy letter to the still-travelling (and still single) Grenville, offering to introduce him to an eligible young lady:

> Dear George, – I have long had a strong impulse to write to you; you are much in my heart, and often in my thoughts. I am very impatient for your recovery, and rejoice in the favourable accounts I hear. I rambled about as usual during the leisure time I had, and amongst other places I was at, I spent three days most agreeably at Hagley, with our friends Lyttelton and Pitt, where you may believe you were not forgot ... Pope is at Bath, perched upon his hill, making epigrams, and stifling them in their birth, and Lord H[ervey] (would you believe it?) is writing libels upon the King and his Ministers. It does not become him to be so employed ...
>
> I have a friend and near relation at A____on, a lady whose acquaintance you would be pleased with, and who would show a great regard to any one I have so great a friendship for as I have for you. Let me know if your route is like to lie that way, and I will send you a letter to her. No man more ardently wishes to see you return soon to us in strength and health than your most affectionate, etc., W. Murray."[19]

As Murray's letter to George Grenville suggests, their mutual friend Alexander Pope was close to Cobham's Cubs; according to Pope's biographer, he became their "moral inspiration."[20] Pope supported Bolingbroke's ideal of political non-partisanship, writing: "In moderation placing all my glory, / While Tories call me Whig, and Whigs a Tory."[21] In 1738, Pope wrote a poem attacking the corruption of the ministry and almost begging Murray to join the opposition. Dedicated to Murray, the poem was an appeal that he take the side of political morality and avoid any temptation to become part of the ministry.[22]

Although Pope's poem did not achieve its purpose, it brought Murray to the attention of the reading public.[23] Murray carefully avoided identifying himself too closely with Cobham's Cubs. Cautious by nature and very ambitious, he would have been unwise to commit himself politically to any party or faction, especially in view of his vulnerable position as a member of a Jacobite family. His social skills enabled him to remain on good terms with an astounding mixture of people.[24] If he was to build a celebrated professional, and perhaps political, career, he could not afford to jeopardize the goodwill of the Walpole ministry.

Professionally as well as socially, Murray was edging into the political arena. As counsel for various clients, he argued not only in court but also before the bar of the House of Commons on proposed legislation and on election disputes. The first legislative matter in which Murray attracted public notice was the Quaker Tithes Bill. In 1735, the Walpole ministry sponsored legislation intended to benefit the Quakers, who had given him political support.[25] Although Quakers and other dissenting Protestant sects were no longer actively persecuted as they had been in the previous century, they were constantly being imprisoned for failure to pay tithes to the Church of England.[26] The proposed legislation would make it possible for Quakers to defend suits for tithes before local justices of the peace rather than in the higher ecclesiastical or secular courts, thus saving them litigation expense and very likely giving them a fairer hearing.

The clergy of the Church of England opposed the bill and petitioned to be heard in the House of Commons. Murray, who later as a judge would be a consistent supporter of the rights of dissenters and Catholics, this time appeared as counsel for the established church, arguing against the bill.[27] Nevertheless, the bill passed the House of Commons, although it was defeated in the Lords.

Murray's opposition to the bill won him a reputation as a defender of the existing order. A year later, when there was a vacancy for a seat in Parliament for Oxford (a very conservative district), it was proposed that Murray fill it. Nothing came of the idea, for he was intent at the time on furthering his legal career. Later, he recalled that the large legal fees he was earning for arguing on behalf of clients before the bar of the House of Commons made it "imprudent" for him to think of becoming a member of Parliament at that time.[28]

In 1738, Murray argued before the bar of the House of Commons on a critical issue of British foreign policy. The Spanish, who had colonized much of South and Central America, were involved in constant disputes and skirmishes with British merchants who chose to ignore a treaty with Spain that limited their trading with the Spanish possessions. Merchants and sea captains flooded Parliament with petitions against actual or supposed Spanish atrocities, which included the boarding of British ships and bringing them into Spanish ports, where the ships were confiscated and the cargoes seized on the ground that the British were engaged in smuggling.[29] In some instances, the Spanish were accused of abusing or mutilating the ships' captains and crews.

The government resisted the pressure to take action against Spain, believing (with some justification) that the popular outcry was largely manufactured by the mercantile interests, some of whom were engaged in smuggling. Walpole, who throughout his long tenure in office pursued a policy of avoiding war at all cost, thought a war against Spain would not only be expensive but would also give France an opportunity for mischief. He feared that while Britain was occupied in fighting Spain, the French might encourage (and even assist) the Stuart Pretender to invade Britain and pull down the entire British political structure, which was based on the Hanoverian succession to the throne.[30] Nevertheless, the stories of Spanish atrocities aroused anger throughout the country and provided a unique opportunity for politicians who opposed the ministry. The opposition claimed that Walpole's pacifism was a betrayal of the principles of the Glorious Revolution, among which was a policy of bellicosity toward France and, by implication, any European power that threatened British naval dominance.[31]

After appealing to the King without success, the merchants took their grievances to the House of Commons by means of a petition of "divers merchants, planters, and others, trading to, and interested in, the British Plantations in America," which was presented to the House on 14 March 1738.[32] They complained that the Spanish searches and abuses threatened Britain's commercial and naval interests, and they prayed for the Commons to hear Murray, whom they had retained as their counsel. Walpole opposed allowing lawyers to be heard, on the ground that they would use their skills as advocates to inflame passions. Nevertheless, the House decided to hear Murray's argument.[33]

On 28 March, Murray appeared before a packed House of Commons, with 438 members present (said to be the largest attendance since the debate on the Act of Union with Scotland thirty years earlier), and in a gripping speech described the alleged outrages by the Spaniards. He called as witnesses several seamen, including a captain named Robert Jenkins, who testified that seven years earlier a Spanish commander had boarded and pillaged his ship, tied him to the mast and torn off one of his ears, telling him to take it to King George with the message that if he were present he would be treated in the same way. Jenkins's testimony stirred up great outrage and patriotic feeling in the House.[34]

After Murray had finished, opposition leaders Pitt and Pulteney also argued in favour of war. The ministry refused to budge, but Murray had been so persuasive that a year later, when the merchants again petitioned to be heard through him, the ministry denied the petition.[35] Walpole eventually succumbed to the clamour, and the government declared war against Spain on 19 October 1739. Known to history as the War of Jenkins's Ear, it was subsumed a year later into a general European war, the War of the Austrian Succession.[36] Murray, although still a practicing lawyer and not yet a member of Parliament or a holder of political office, had helped move the country toward war.

Despite Lady Betty's dislike of Pulteney, Murray maintained a highly useful professional and political connection with him. Pulteney retained Murray as counsel in several election contests, the most important of which was the Westminster election of 1741. The government and the opposition each put up two candidates. The election went on for several days, and as was often the case in contested elections, there was rioting and tumult at the polling places. The government overreacted: they closed the polls, called out troops who surrounded the hustings, and declared the government candidates the winners. Pulteney petitioned the House of Commons to reverse the result and retained Murray as counsel. In his appearance before the bar of the House, Murray played on the fear – widespread in England at the time – of military intrusion into civil affairs. He argued that a civil magistrate had no power to call in the army to suppress a riot, even if he found that the civil authorities were unable to do so. The House of Commons, fearing that a standing army threatened English liberties, agreed and awarded the election to the opposition candidates.[37]

Horace Walpole was present at the argument and wrote to a friend that Murray spoke "divinely ... On summing up the evidence on both sides ... Murray was, in short, beyond what was ever heard at the bar." Despite the admiration for his advocacy, Murray could not shake off the stigma of his Scottish background and Jacobite connections. In Horace Walpole's otherwise complimentary account of Murray's argument for limiting the power of the civil authorities to call out the troops, Walpole added: "Is this not the work of Jacobites? Have they any other view than to render the Riot Act useless? And then they may rise for the Pretender whenever they please."[38] The Westminster election not only won accolades for Murray but also marked the end of Walpole's quarter-century domination of English politics. Beset by enemies and disconsolate at the loss of much of his political influence, he stepped down as prime minister in February 1742.

Another important politician who was both Murray's friend and client was John Carteret, Earl Granville (not to be confused with the Grenvilles). Like Murray (and so many of his political associates), he had gone to Westminster School and Christ Church, Oxford. A member of Parliament at the age of twenty-one, he supported the Hanoverian succession in 1714 and then served as a highly successful foreign minister and, later, in several diplomatic posts. In 1724 he broke with Walpole and joined Pulteney in opposition. Although some considered Carteret the greatest statesman of his day, politics was more of a game than a vocation to him, and he had little interest in the political infighting of the House of Commons.[39]

Carteret was known for his good looks, his congenial manners, and his powerful oratory in Parliament. He was a scholar, a lover of the classics, and a close personal friend of Jonathan Swift, who wrote that at the university Carteret learned "more Greek, Latin and Philosophy than properly became a person of his rank."[40] He was deeply in love with his first wife. When she died in 1743, he married a twenty-two-year-old beauty who was younger than his daughters by his first wife and was known as the "reigning toast" of London society. Horace Walpole wrote that he saw them "all fondness, walk together, and stop every five steps to kiss."[41] But two years later she too died. Carteret's only fault, perhaps, was an excessive fondness for alcohol; his brief 1742–44 tenure in power was sometimes called "the drunken administration." It was during Carteret's ministry that Murray entered politics as a member of Parliament and solicitor general of England.

Walpole's resignation did not lead to any significant change in policy: "what occurred amounted to no more than a reshuffle of offices among ambitious politicians."[42] George II asked Pulteney, Carteret, and the Duke of Newcastle to get together and form a new ministry. The next two years saw a struggle for power among these three politicians, resolved eventually in Newcastle's favour. Acknowledged as one of the most extraordinary politicians of the eighteenth (or any) century, Newcastle draws our attention because he was to become Murray's patron and friend, and was to have an unparalleled influence on his career.

Born in 1693, Thomas Pelham-Holles was, like so many other eighteenth-century politicians, educated at Westminster School. At the age of eighteen he inherited immense wealth from his uncle, including estates in eleven counties, from Sussex in the south to Dorset in the west and Yorkshire in the north;[43] and in 1715 he inherited the title of Duke of Newcastle. He supported the Hanoverian succession and in 1716, when only twenty-three, the King appointed him lord chamberlain, a job that was largely ceremonial but included wide patronage powers.

In 1724, Newcastle was made one of the two secretaries of state, a post he retained for the next thirty years;[44] in the same year his brother, Henry Pelham, became secretary of war. The administration of every government function not immediately concerned with finance was under the control of two secretaries of state, one for the northern department and one for the southern,[45] who were responsible for conducting foreign affairs and maintaining order at home.[46] The two secretaries of state formally had the same responsibilities, a situation that could lead to some confusion over who should be dealing with a particular issue;[47] but as a practical matter, they usually divided up the duties on an ad hoc basis. For two decades Newcastle served as Walpole's political lieutenant, and from 1730 until the 1760s he was the leader of the government in the House of Lords.[48]

Despite his great power, Newcastle had a child-like insecurity, with a constant need for recognition, and even love.[49] He was perpetually anxious that he might be deprived of his power, and he was perpetually excited and bustling, qualities that often made him the butt of ridicule.[50] He was totally unable to handle his own finances and, despite the great wealth that he inherited, he did not experience a single debt-free moment during his adult life. He spent huge amounts – which even he could not afford – on building and maintaining five great houses, notably Claremont in Surrey near London, where for half a century he entertained the elite of the British establishment and important foreign visitors.[51] At one memorable feast that Newcastle hosted, ninety-six tables were set, and provisions included five oxen, thirty-nine sheep, fourteen calves, six hogs, three hundred fowl, forty bushels of wheat, four hundred and eighty pounds of butter, and large quantities of port, brandy, claret, Burgundy, toddy, and beer.[52] Great expense also went into entertaining and feeding voters in parliamentary elections. Newcastle's prodigality was not just politically motivated: he simply loved good food. Included among his personal expenses was £500 to build houses and equipment to grow pineapples, a rare luxury in eighteenth-century England.[53]

According to a modern historian, "Newcastle's remarkable longevity in office (1724–56, 1757–61) owed not a little to the fact that he was a dutiful and competent servant of his country and the Hanoverian regime."[54] Unlike many politicians of the time, he was not financially corrupt; in addition, he was hard-working and possessed judgment and common sense.[55] His great strength was his recognition of his own deficiencies, and he made up for them by choosing men of superior talents as his confidential advisers.[56] In 1718, Newcastle met Philip Yorke, a lawyer from Kent, who later was appointed lord chancellor and raised to the peerage as Earl of Hardwicke – and to whom Murray would express indebtedness as his principal legal mentor. Hardwicke provided Newcastle with the calm judgment that he himself lacked. By 1735, Hardwicke had become Newcastle's chief confidant and adviser, and throughout the rest of his political career, Newcastle consulted him on every important decision.[57] Newcastle called Hardwicke "My Lord Chancellor, with whom I do everything, and without whom I do nothing."[58] The long association between Newcastle and Hardwicke was to become the most powerful friendship of eighteenth-century politics.[59]

To complete the network of friendships that supported Murray's career, we must also mention his Westminster School friend Andrew Stone, two years older than Murray. In August 1732, at an entertainment given by Newcastle at Claremont, Stone's brother-in-law, William Barnard, then chaplain at the estate, introduced Stone to Newcastle, who was instantly captivated by him. "I have had the charmingest man with me at Claremont I ever saw," Newcastle wrote to his wife. "He has more learning, more parts, and as agreeable as any man I ever saw in my life."[60] Three weeks later, he appointed Stone as his private secretary at the generous salary of £200 a year.

Although he received the title and salary of under secretary of state in 1734, Stone was in reality Newcastle's aide and companion, writing his speeches, giving advice, negotiating on his behalf, and carrying out political and diplomatic errands.[61] He made himself so invaluable that Newcastle came to regard him as a necessity of life.[62] Stone was a member of Parliament for several years – Newcastle having secured him a seat for the town of Hastings – but he does not seem to have had any higher political ambitions of his own. He was content to exercise power from behind the scenes as Newcastle's right-hand man, upon whom Newcastle could rely to handle the day-to-day details of his political life.[63]

Although Horace Walpole described Stone as a cold, mysterious man,[64] Stone may have preferred real power to public acclaim because he knew that he was not tough enough for the hurly-burly of public life. On one occasion, he reacted with unusual sensitivity to a slighting remark from Newcastle. Later that day, Murray wrote to Newcastle:

> I am so grieved at what happened this morning I don't know what to do. You saw my embarrassment and in a moment recovered yourself with your natural good humour. But when I turned ... I saw [Stone] crying bitterly, which I never saw before. When we left you I saw him too deeply mortified to talk upon that subject. I have upon another pretense wrote to him to desire he would come and breakfast with me tomorrow; I will say everything in my power to heal his wound; but my eyes tell me the blow had struck very deep.[65]

Newcastle replied that he was sorry he had hurt Stone, but dismissed the whole affair by saying that Stone resented hearing another's opinion.[66]

It was most likely Stone, around 1739 or 1740, who introduced Murray to Newcastle, an encounter that soon led Murray into public office and eventually to eminence as a judge.[67] It is also possible that Hardwicke made the introduction. Although he did not have much personal affection for Murray, he admired Murray's legal talent, which he had seen demonstrated in his court. For the next twenty years Murray, Stone, and Hardwicke formed a close-knit team of personal and political advisers to Newcastle, which endured even after Murray was appointed chief justice in 1756. Newcastle wrote to Murray two years after he became chief justice: "It is the greatest comfort to me to be within your advice. I know I am always sure of it; I am sure, I always desire it ... I am not above owning, I often want help."[68]

At first, Newcastle found Murray's legal skills useful in his personal affairs. By 1738, Newcastle's debts had reached the huge sum of £158,193.[69] Newcastle was childless, and the death of the two sons of his younger brother Henry Pelham a year later created the possibility that two cousins, Lord William Vane and his brother Henry Vane, would inherit his estates.[70] Newcastle came to an understanding with the Vanes under which they would relinquish their claims in return for a payment of £60,000. In order to raise the money, Newcastle was forced to sell or mortgage some of his lands.[71] He brought in a battalion of highly placed lawyers, including Hardwicke and Attorney General Sir Dudley Ryder, to help work out the complex legal arrangements, but he enlisted Murray as his principal negotiator and drafter of the documents.[72]

Murray's conscientiousness as a lawyer, enhanced perhaps by his awareness of the exalted position of his client, is apparent from the anxiety he expressed about the possible consequences of a minor drafting error in the description of a legal title. The error had inadvertently occurred in a preliminary memo that Newcastle and the Vanes had signed before the execution of the final settlement. In view of the highly technical nature of England land law, Murray feared there was a remote possibility that the error might later lead to a dispute. In August 1741, he wrote about the problem to Hardwicke's secretary, and three days later he and Hardwicke discussed it for a few minutes when they happened to meet on the road while on horseback. He wrote to Stone: "I am still of the opinion that the slip in the description of the copyhold though it has given me great anxiety is of no consequence, and may easily be rectified almost in any way."[73]

As Murray predicted, the minor fault in the preliminary memo did not cause any trouble, and a final family settlement was signed on 17 November 1741. Soon afterwards, Newcastle wrote to Hardwicke: "I cannot but think myself greatly indebted to Mr Murray, who from the great pains he has taken in the way of his profession, has singly procured the consent of all parties, without which I should not have been thoroughly easy."[74] Murray received the very substantial fee of 300 guineas for his professional services.[75] Newcastle was so grateful that he asked Hardwicke, as a favour, to make Murray a King's Counsel (K.C.), a status awarded to outstanding barristers who had been in practice for at least ten years. Being a K.C. had a practical advantage; lawyers who had the title were given precedence when arguing in court. Hardwicke at first refused, perhaps because he had a prejudice against Scots but perhaps also because he feared that Newcastle's increasing reliance on Murray might eclipse his own favoured position with the country's leading politician. On being appointed solicitor general in 1742, Murray received this honour, known as "taking silk" (from the fact that a K.C. was entitled to wear a silk gown).[76]

So impressed was Newcastle with Murray's ability in handling his private affairs, and with his reputation as an advocate, that he saw the young lawyer as a potentially useful political associate to act as the ministry's spokesman in the House of Commons. As discussed in the next chapter, after Walpole's resignation in early 1742, there was no firm political leadership. Newcastle and other members of the Walpole ministry remained in office; Carteret, who had experience in foreign affairs and who had the ear of the King, abandoned the opposition to become a secretary of state; and Pitt continued to lead the opposition.

A critical issue in Parliament was the role that Britain should play in the War of the Austrian Succession, which had broken out in Europe in 1740 and which pitted France and Prussia against Britain's ally, Austria. Pitt continually criticized the conduct of the war.[77] He preferred fighting the French in North America and India in order to enlarge the British Empire, to committing British forces to a war in continental Europe. Newcastle needed a forceful advocate who had the ability to beat back Pitt's attacks on the ministry in the House of Commons, and Murray was his choice.

Fortuitously for Newcastle and Murray, James Tyrell, a member of Parliament who represented the borough of Boroughbridge in Yorkshire, suddenly died. Boroughbridge was known as a "burgage" borough, where the right to vote was confined to a limited number of tenants who were beholden to the owner of the burgage.[78] In effect, the owner of the burgage could nominate members of Parliament; the Boroughbridge voters, of whom there were only seventy-four, risked losing their rights as tenants if they did not vote in accordance with the owner's wishes. Burgages, or part interests in them, could be bought and sold, and Newcastle had made it his business to buy up as many as possible, including a majority interest in Boroughbridge. Newcastle diplomatically consulted first with Andrew Wilkinson, the minority owner of the burgage, who replied: "Your Grace's Recommendation of Mr Murray to the Borough can't but be very agreeable to us; everybody are sensible of Mr Murray's great abilities."[79]

It was shrewd of Newcastle to bring Murray into Parliament to be a spokesman for the ministry. Murray was not only a superb orator but was also on friendly terms with many of the principal members of the opposition. Newcastle saw that he could defeat the opposition by taking advantage of Murray's connections with Cobham's Cubs. In September 1742, Newcastle described his plan to Hardwicke: "The best way to defeat all this is to get the better of them in their own way, if it can be done without disobliging our own friends ... and I think I have now in my hands a sure way of doing it. I know ... that I can absolutely depend on Mr Murray. He will beat them all with their own friends. I mean Pitt, Lyttelton, etc. The death of poor Tyrell gives me an opportunity of bringing him immediately into parliament, which I am disposed to do and indeed at present fully intend."[80] Hardwicke agreed.[81] Newcastle's letter at the very least suggests that he thought he could count on the ambitious Murray to be disloyal toward his friends.

In November, Newcastle formally recommended Murray to the voters of Boroughbridge, and he was duly elected to Parliament. (He was to be re-elected in the general elections of 1747 and 1754.[82]) But even becoming a prominent politician did not satisfy Murray's ambition. His first love and his greatest aptitude were for the law, and he was unwilling to take on political duties in the House of Commons unless he had a legal position in the ministry. He wanted to be solicitor general, one of the two law officers of the Crown (the other being the attorney general).

In order to get the appointment, Murray had to surmount three obstacles. First, he was a Scot, and it was unprecedented for a Scot to achieve high office in England. Murray overcame that objection by his recognized legal ability and the excellent connections he had made with the leaders of English politics and society since his days at Westminster.[83] The Duke of Richmond wrote to Newcastle that he approved of Murray's appointment as solicitor general, but added: "The only objection that can be made to him is what he can't help, which is that he is a Scotchman, which (as I have a great regard for him) I am extremely sorry for."[84] Murray's education at Westminster School and Oxford also reduced the handicap of his Scottish birth: referring specifically to Murray, Dr Johnson famously said, "much may be made of a Scotsman, if taken young."[85]

The second objection was that there already was a solicitor general in place, Sir John Strange. But Newcastle was able to persuade Strange to resign, with the promise of later being appointed master of the rolls, the third highest judicial post in England, after the lord chancellor and chief justice. Strange did indeed become master of the rolls, but not until eight years had gone by.[86] Murray later explained Strange's resignation very simply, if disingenuously: "In the year 1742, the present Master of the Rolls, from a warmth of friendship peculiar to him, resigned the office which he then held, that I might succeed him in it."[87]

The third difficulty that Newcastle had to overcome was the objection of the King. George II, thinking of James Murray, counsellor to James Edward Stuart at his court-in-exile in Rome, said he'd be damned if he and the Pretender had brothers for advisers.[88] But the King was persuaded to go along with Murray's appointment, perhaps at the insistence of Carteret. One of the few supporters of the shaky ministry was Lady Betty Murray's brother, the Earl of Winchilsea, who held the office of first lord of the admirality. Winchilsea may have asked Carteret to intervene with the King on Murray's behalf. And it cannot have hurt at this critical point in Murray's career that two other brothers-in-law, William and Edward Finch, and a sister-in-law, Isabella Finch, were members of the King's official household.[89]

Thus, expedience, influence, and Murray's unquestioned abilities all combined to smooth the way to high political office. Nevertheless, it was Newcastle who was chiefly responsible for Murray's election to Parliament and appointment as solicitor general. Years later, when Murray had become one of the great figures on the bench, Newcastle wrote to Andrew Stone: "Only the most determined resolution and support from me" made his political career possible.[90]

Strange's sudden retirement and Murray's appointment surprised the public, for Strange was a supporter of the Carteret–Newcastle administration, while some suspected Murray of secretly harbouring Jacobite sympathies. A long anonymous satirical poem, published in 1743 and awkwardly titled "The Causidicade. A Panegyric-Satiri-Serio-Comic-Dramatical Poem. On the Strange Resignation, and Stranger-Promotion. By Porcupinus Pelagius," described Murray's appointment as a cynical deal cooked up by the ministry and the King.[91] Of course, it was unquestionably a political transaction: Newcastle had sound practical reasons for installing Murray in office, and there does not appear to have been anything unethical in the promise of a judgeship to Strange in return for his resignation as solicitor general.

It is understandable that Murray's willingness to join the ministry might have been regarded as disloyalty by some of his friends who remained in opposition. As a lawyer, he had publicly supported the opposition on a critical matter of foreign policy and in a key election dispute. But Newcastle offered the ambitious Murray an appointment that promised to – and did – lead to political prominence and eventually to the chief justiceship of England. Eighteenth-century English politics was much more a matter of persons than of principles. In the same year that Murray joined the government (1742), both Carteret and Pulteney abandoned the opposition when opportunity knocked. Carteret, in fact, had already done so and had become prime minister by the time Murray joined the government; and Pulteney was bought off by the offer of an earldom.

After becoming solicitor general, Murray maintained his friendships with many of Cobham's Cubs, as well as with Alexander Pope. Bolingbroke enthusiastically supported Murray's appointment, writing from abroad to a mutual friend: "I love the man, and ... I rejoice ... that personal merit is a recommendation, and that men are raised in the state for the sake of the public, and not merely for the encouragement and service of any party."[92] The one important exception was Pitt. While recognizing Murray's abilities, Pitt not only opposed his views on several important issues but also nursed a lifelong hostility to him that he never fully explained. It may simply have been that he regarded Murray as a turncoat when he joined Newcastle's ministry.[93]

The King appointed Murray solicitor general on 27 November 1742, and he took his seat in the House of Commons in early December.[94] From the time that he became a member of Parliament, he invariably defended the policies of the government. Although technically the voters of Boroughbridge had elected him to office, in fact he represented Newcastle. It is not too much to say that he became Newcastle's creature. In the years that followed, Murray was not only the chief spokesman for the Newcastle ministry in the House of Commons but he also constantly advised Newcastle on personal as well as political matters, on one occasion even acting as an intermediary when a dispute arose between Newcastle and one of his relatives.[95]

Murray's main weakness as a politician was that he had no policies or following of his own. He was always the lawyer, with the government his client. Murray's political foe, William Pitt, was his intellectual inferior, but whether right or wrong on a particular issue, Pitt always spoke with moral conviction, and the opinions he expressed were his own. Listeners felt the force of Pitt's forthright character in a way that they did not with Murray, however much they may have admired his intellect and eloquence.

6

Law Officer of the Crown

Mr Pitt and Mr Murray ... are beyond comparison the best speakers ... You might hear a pin fall while either of them is speaking.

Lord Chesterfield, in a letter to his son

When William Murray, newly appointed solicitor general of England, kissed the hand of King George II on 26 November 1742, he was thirty-seven years old. His elevated social standing meant he was now on friendly terms with many of the Whig magnates, most of them peers of the realm and holders of enormous wealth, who dominated Parliament and in effect ruled the country. In the eighteenth century, "politics was a matter of the triangular relations of Court, ministry and Commons; and the ministry was the virtual preserve of the peerage."[1] Although Henry Pelham headed the ministry from the House of Commons, his brother, the Duke of Newcastle, exercised great power not as an elected member of the Commons but as a hereditary member of the House of Lords. William Pitt, known as the Great Commoner, cried out, when he was the leading voice of the opposition, that the ministry had become a cabal of nobles.[2]

Much later, when an aspiring biographer asked him to describe his life, Murray pointed to the advantages with which he had been born:

> My success in life is not very remarkable. My father was a man of rank and fashion. Early in life I was introduced into the best company and my circumstances enabled me to support the character of a man of fortune. To these advantages I owe chiefly my success and, therefore, my life cannot be very interesting. But if you wish to employ your abilities in writing the life of a truly great and wonderful man in our profession, take the life of Lord Hardwicke for your object: he was, indeed, a wonderful character; he became Lord Chief Justice of England and

> Chancellor of Great Britain, purely from his own abilities, for he was the son of a peasant.[3]

Murray's self-assessment was accurate up to a point, but he was being too modest (assuming that his modesty was genuine). It is true that he was a member of an old noble family, and that he did have valuable connections with the British nobility. But he owed his success much less to these advantages than to his legal genius, his dedication to hard work, and his ability to make friends.

With his appointment as solicitor general, Murray became a member of the ministry but not of the Cabinet, which was composed of about sixteen high officials.[4] Many eminent men had preceded him in the position, including Sir Edward Coke, the great legal scholar, prosecutor (of Sir Walter Raleigh, among others), and judge, in the late sixteenth century; Murray's wife's grandfather Heneage Finch, Earl of Nottingham, in the seventeenth century; and Philip Yorke, later Lord Hardwicke, in the eighteenth century. Loyal government service was a desirable qualification for any lawyer whose ambition was to be a judge,[5] and the office of solicitor general was the first stop on a well-worn path to becoming chief justice of the Court of King's Bench or lord chancellor. Coke became chief justice; Finch, lord chancellor; and Yorke, chief justice and then lord chancellor. And Sir Dudley Ryder, at that time attorney general, had earlier been solicitor general and later became chief justice. Thus, Murray's appointment augured a rise to high judicial office.

Ryder was attorney general during Murray's twelve years as solicitor general. The son of a London linen draper, Ryder had established a reputation as a highly competent lawyer and a man of integrity. Largely through having good connections, he was elected to Parliament in 1733 to fill a vacancy in a government-controlled borough, appointed attorney general in 1737, and knighted in 1740. Despite his unquestioned abilities, he lacked self-confidence and was dominated by his wife, who tended to avarice. While attorney general he desperately wanted to be created a peer, but his wife didn't want him to accept this great honour and rise in status unless he also received a salary increase.[6] In 1754, when Chief Justice Sir William Lee of the Court of King's Bench died, Ryder was appointed to succeed him, and Murray in turn succeeded to Ryder's office.

Ryder's main duties as attorney general were to prosecute major crimes and to advise the government on legal questions. He delegated many of his responsibilities to Murray, and although Murray was formally subordinate to Ryder, in fact they occupied an almost equal position.[7] Ryder and Murray usually worked together as a harmonious team. Most of the legal opinions given to the government were signed by both of them, whereas during the two years that Murray was attorney general, many opinions were signed only by him. Generally, Murray drafted the opinion, and Ryder then added his notes and comments.[8] As solicitor general, Murray performed Ryder's duties in his absence or incapacity.

Unlike Ryder, Murray was an important politician from the time he became solicitor general.[9] The scope of his activities, both legal and political, is astonishing. He acted as the principal spokesman for the ministry in the House of Commons, taking the lead in debates, often crossing swords with the equally eloquent and sometimes overpowering William Pitt. Murray was an unofficial but invaluable adviser to the Duke of Newcastle. Together with Ryder, Murray acted as the official legal adviser to the government, providing opinions of law to the ministry, the King, the Privy Council, the Board of Trade, the Treasury, and the Admiralty. In addition, he drafted legislation, prosecuted treason and other major crimes, and represented the government in civil lawsuits. Finally, he continued to conduct his own private practice of law: this was permitted at the time, and one of the benefits of the position of law officer of the Crown was that it attracted lucrative private business.

In addition to these official and professional duties, Murray took on the office of treasurer of the Society of Lincoln's Inn, to which he was elected in 1743. We have the extremely detailed accounts he kept during 1744, which included payments of nearly £3,000 "including 8s [eight shillings] for the stamps on the admittances of several [members'] sons." There also were substantial payments for port and Madeira wine. In addition, Murray managed the Society's investments; one payment that year was £800 for 3 per cent government annuities.[10]

It is hard to understand how Murray found the time to attend to these multifarious duties and activities. But attend to them he did, thanks to the habit, first acquired as a schoolboy at Perth Grammar School, of applying painstaking thoroughness to each task before him. On a typical working day he would spend the morning arguing cases in the Court of Chancery. Around noon, he might attend a meeting of the Cabinet (although not a member, he was frequently called upon to provide information or an opinion) or argue an appeal at the bar of the House of Lords. In the afternoon, he might be at the House of Commons to defend the policies and actions of the ministry.[11]

This brief summary of his activities does not include the hours he must have spent studying documents, writing and reading letters, and talking to his colleagues and clients. The absence of modern means of communication and transportation was to a large extent mitigated by the fact that he could accomplish most of his activities within the conveniently narrow confines of Westminster, the home of Parliament and the courts. And many of Murray's associates in Parliament and the courts were the same people with whom he dined and exchanged information and views in letters and conversation.

When Murray became solicitor general, the political leadership of the country was in flux. A few months before Murray's appointment, Sir Robert Walpole had resigned as first lord of the treasury after two decades in the office, but nobody had yet taken his place as the recognized head of the government. A figurehead, the Earl of Wilmington, succeeded Walpole as prime minister, but the real power was in the hands of the two rival secretaries of state: Carteret, secretary for the north, and Newcastle, secretary for the south. During the next few months, these two struggled for ascendancy, Newcastle being assisted by his younger brother, Henry Pelham, a colourless but effective politician and administrator, who held the office of paymaster of the armed forces.

At first Carteret was in the ascendant, but by mid-1743 Pelham had gained control of the House of Commons. The King, who would have preferred the genteel and courteous Carteret, reluctantly appointed Pelham first lord of the treasury, with the newly recruited Murray as his chief political aide. Meanwhile, Pelham's brother, Newcastle, controlled the House of Lords. Carteret was forced to resign as secretary of state in 1744, and for the next ten years Newcastle and Pelham together ran the government.

As chief spokesman for the policies of the Pelham ministry in the House of Commons, Murray had as his chief opponent William Pitt. In an age of great oratory, Murray and Pitt were the foremost orators of the day. Lord Chesterfield wrote to his son: "Mr Pitt and Mr Murray ... are beyond comparison the best speakers ... They alone can inflame or quiet the House; they alone are so attended to in that numerous and noisy assembly that you might hear a pin fall while either of them is speaking."[12]

They were very different, however, both in style and character, and it showed in their oratory. "Murray excelled in lucidity of statement and force of argument, but was incapable of those bursts of fiery eloquence with which his great rival awed or charmed the House of Commons."[13] Lord Macauley's comparison of them tells us something about Murray's strengths and weaknesses as well as the direction of his ambitions:

> [Murray] far surpassed Pitt in correctness of taste, in power of reasoning, in depth and variety of knowledge ... Intellectually, he was ... fully equal to Pitt; but he was deficient in the moral qualities to which Pitt owed most of his success. Murray wanted the energy, the courage, the all-grasping and all-risking ambition, which make men great in stirring times. His heart was a little cold; his temper cautious even to timidity; his manner decorous even to formality. He never exposed his fortunes or his fame to any risk which he could avoid. At one point he might, in all probability, have been Prime Minister. But the object of all his life was the judicial bench. The situation of Chief Justice might not be as splendid as that of [Prime Minister]; but it was dignified; it was quiet; it was secure; and therefore it was the favourite situation of Murray.[14]

In the eyes of most observers, Pitt usually had the better of Murray in parliamentary debates. Although an accomplished orator, Murray "sank beneath the thunder of [Pitt's] more vigorous powers."[15] The scorn that Pitt and some others in Parliament felt for Murray is illustrated by an anecdote wherein Pitt's sarcasm reduced Murray almost to tears. On one such occasion, when the actor-playwrights Samuel Foote and Arthur Murphy were listening to the debate in the gallery of the House of Commons, Murphy asked Foote: "Shall we go home now?" Foote replied: "No, let us wait till he has made the little man vanish entirely."[16] Others had a more positive opinion: "Murray was all grace, ease, suavity, and mellifluence; his bare narrative was said to be worth any other man's argument; but this arose from the perfection of his logic, the excellence of his arrangement, and his thorough mastery of the subject in hand."[17]

Beyond the fact that Pitt and Murray were political foes, there was a personal animosity between them that lasted until Pitt's death in 1778. Pitt was even unwilling to sit next to Murray in the House of Commons.[18] It is likely that he disdained Murray for abandoning the ranks of the opposition, with its ardent patriotism and its hatred of corruption, to become a mere mouthpiece for the ministry. Pitt took every opportunity to insinuate that Murray was a secret Jacobite. He may have honestly believed this or, more likely, he simply used the suspicion of Murray's Jacobitism as a convenient weapon against him.

Murray's first chance to state the government's case in the House of Commons came on 7 December 1742, only a few days after he was sworn in as solicitor general.[19] The question being debated was whether the British government should pay for 16,000 Hanoverian troops fighting on her side on the European continent in the War of the Austrian Succession, but it also involved important issues concerning the balance of power between king and Parliament. King George II was not only King of England but also elector (i.e., ruler) of the German state of Hanover, to which he made frequent extended visits.[20] He much preferred his small electorate, where he was an absolute ruler, over England, where he was subject to the limits imposed by a constitutional monarchy and by the wealth and arrogance of the great Whig noblemen.[21] Pitt and others accused Secretary of State Carteret of ministering to the King by putting the interests of Hanover above those of his own country. The dispute came to a head when Carteret, without the approval of Parliament, agreed to put the Hanoverian troops in the pay of the British government.[22] A motion was made in the House of Commons to dismiss the Hanoverian troops, and Murray spoke in opposition to the motion.

His argument on behalf of the ministry was fluent and thorough, the advocacy of an experienced lawyer who not only persuasively stated the government's case but anticipated and refuted the arguments that could be made against it. First, he characterized the motion as an attack on the prerogative of the Crown to declare war and to decide how the war should be prosecuted. Under the unwritten English constitution, he said, this was not within the province of Parliament.

He then analyzed the current military situation in Europe, showing a full understanding of the relative positions and the policies of Austria, France, Holland, and the other nations involved in the war. He argued that the King's direction of the war had been successful, but that England could not continue to prosecute it without the help of foreign troops, and it had not been shown that any troops other than the Hanoverians were available. He dismissed the allegations that the Hanoverian soldiers were cowardly and that they disobeyed the orders of British generals, saying that in wartime, instances of cowardice and lack of discipline always arise but can be controlled through prudent conduct by the commanding officer. Returning to the question of the powers of Parliament, Murray said that the lawmakers should not even advise the King on military matters unless they had full information, which they did not, and that, given the King's success in prosecuting the war, there was no reason to give him advice.

Murray then turned to the central issue: whether the war was being prosecuted not in Britain's interest but rather in order to gain more territory for Hanover. As an experienced lawyer, he did not try to avoid the issue but faced it squarely. If Hanover reaped an advantage from the war, he said, Parliament should not begrudge it: it did not hurt Britain. Furthermore, to suggest that the war was being fought for Hanover's benefit was dangerous, because it would tend to alienate the British people from the Hanoverian succession and could only come from a republican or Jacobite spirit. Thus, he gratuitously dragged in the issue of Jacobitism, perhaps to anticipate and negate in advance any attack on himself as a Jacobite sympathizer.

Finally, Murray stated, somewhat disingenuously in view of his detailed discussion of the situation, that not being a member of the Cabinet he was not privy to its secrets, but he believed that the war was being fought for no other purpose than to bring France and Austria to the peace table and secure the tranquility of Europe.[23] Despite Murray's protest to the contrary, it must have been obvious to close observers that his friend Andrew Stone, Newcastle's private secretary and confidant, had been keeping Murray informed of what went on at Cabinet meetings.[24] Although his tone was one of great modesty, his bearing was that of a man who knew his authority and the value of his position.[25]

It was a masterful speech, but Pitt rose immediately to support the motion to dismiss the Hanoverian troops. His approach was much broader than Murray's, and he made a strong appeal to patriotism. Pitt had "a keen sense of opportunism"; one of his "foremost characteristics was the ability increasingly to convince himself that his own interest and the national interest were one and the same."[26] Pitt attacked Britain's policy of becoming engaged in a continental war with no concrete result other than a benefit for Hanover: "why should the Elector of Hanover exert his liberality at the expense of Great Britain? It is now too apparent that this great, this powerful, this formidable kingdom is considered only as a province to a despicable electorate."[27]

The House rejected the motion to dismiss the Hanoverian troops because the ministry had the votes, but the general opinion was that the debate was a triumph for Pitt. According to Pitt's biographer, Murray was so cowed that he "never opened his lips on the same subject for the rest of the year."[28] One benefit for Murray was that his defense of the King's prerogative earned him the goodwill of George II.[29] But, while Pitt persuasively expressed his own views with patriotic fervour and deep moral passion, Murray was always the advocate, expressing (albeit with great force) the views of his client, the government. A fellow member of Parliament wrote about the debate:

> The one spoke like a pleader, and could not divest himself of a certain appearance of having been employed by others. The other spoke like a gentleman, like a statesman, who felt what he said, and possessed the strongest desire of conveying that feeling to others, for their own interest and that of their country. Murray *gains* your attention by the perspicuity of his arguments and the elegance of his diction. Pitt *commands* your attention and respect by the nobleness, the greatness of his sentiments, the strength and energy of his expression, and the certainty you are in of his always rising to a greater elevation both of thought and style.[30]

On another occasion, when Pitt denounced the members of the House of Commons for their levity when discussing bribery and corruption, Horace Walpole, who never had a liking for Murray, wrote that Pitt's thunderbolt "confounded the audience. Murray crouched, silent and terrified."[31] But Pitt did not always get the better of Murray. Murray was particularly effective in several debates in the House of Commons in late 1755. In a debate on appropriations for the navy, Pitt implied having been offered a post in the government. Murray then rose and said he had never heard of the offer, and Pitt was forced to admit that no such offer had been made. Two weeks later, Murray again spoke on naval matters, arguing against a bill that was designed to encourage recruiting for the navy by giving all prizes (i.e., captured enemy ships and their cargoes) to the officers and crews of the captors. Although the bill failed to pass, it was later reintroduced and was eventually enacted into law.

In a December 1755 debate on European treaties, "Murray spoke admirably, keeping closely to the point, and unanswerably."[32] Pitt spoke in opposition, but now he treated Murray with more caution. Turning to Murray, he said: "Then I would come to another learned gentleman, but it is difficult to know where to pull the first thread from a piece so finely spun."[33]

There was a great deal of camaraderie, joking, and learned allusions among the mostly well-educated members of the House of Commons, and Murray got on along well with his colleagues. He sat next to Henry Fox, a leading politician. On one occasion, Fox held up a copy of a bill, which after two readings had been altered throughout in red ink. Glancing at the document, Murray commented: "How bloody it looks." "Yes, but you cannot say I did it," Fox replied, pointing to Attorney General Ryder, who had altered the bill, adding then, in parody of Marc Antony's lament over Julius Caesar's toga: "Look what a rent the learned Casca made; through this, the well-beloved Brutus stabbed."[34]

Many of Murray's actions and utterances during his fourteen years as a law officer of the Crown foreshadowed the public policy to promote the growth of commerce that he later encouraged as a judge and anticipated the free-trade philosophy that his fellow-Scot, Adam Smith, expounded in his monumental work *The Wealth of Nations*, published in 1776. Murray spoke in the House of Commons in 1747 opposing a bill that would prohibit British insurers from insuring enemy ships in time of war. At the time, England was engaged in a naval war with France and Spain. Murray's speech demonstrated his strong support of freedom of commerce (even when it meant trading with the enemy), his firm grasp of the details of the matter, and his emphasis on the consequences if the bill were to be enacted into law.

He began his speech by citing examples of how previous trade restrictions had had an adverse impact on English merchants and manufacturers. For example, a prohibition on the import of Irish agricultural products in the seventeenth century had the unintended consequence of harming English farmers and merchants. Before the prohibition, Murray said, the Irish had sold their cattle and pigs to English farmers, who had fattened them up and sold them in the market. The prohibition forced Irish farmers to do the fattening up and the selling – to the French – themselves, thus helping the Irish and French economies at the expense of the English.

Murray warned his fellow members of the House to be cautious when imposing regulations on trade and pointed out that even in wartime the French and Spanish did most of their insurance business in London. The French were the most enterprising people in Europe, he said, and the consequence of the proposed regulation would be to strip English insurers of this profitable branch of business and transfer it to the French. Soon, the French would not only be insuring their own ships but also those of Spain and Portugal.

Murray then addressed the argument that English insurers of French ships might give intelligence of the location of English warships to the French. He turned the argument around: he had never heard of this; on the contrary, he had heard that some of the richest prizes taken by the English in the war "fell into our hands by intelligence communicated by those employed to get insurances upon them." In other words, English insurers were more likely to betray their French clients than their own countrymen.[35] Despite Murray's eloquence, patriotism won the day over commerce, and the bill passed. His prediction that it would shift the maritime insurance business to the French proved correct: within five years insurance offices had opened in Paris, Bordeaux, and Calais.[36]

Murray showed his interest in commerce and industry in other ways. He supported patent protection of inventors. A man with the unusual name of Onesypherous Paul invented a process for preparing cloth for scarlet dye that greatly improved the finished product. His patent petition was referred to Solicitor General Murray, who recommended it be granted.[37] On another occasion the problem of skilled artisans being induced to leave the country, thus depriving Britain of their skills, was referred to Murray. He reported that nothing could be done after the artisans had left, but recommended that diligent efforts be made to discover in advance their intentions of leaving, and especially the foreign agents who enticed them to leave.[38]

The Privy Council relied almost exclusively on Murray in deciding matters involving trade and the ownership of prizes taken at sea. According to one observer: "The precision, the impartiality, the consummate knowledge, the clear discernment and dispatch with which these causes have been determined, are the admiration of the world."[39]

During his time as solicitor general, Murray became deeply involved in Britain's foreign policy, both as a parliamentary defender of the ministry and as a private adviser to Newcastle, who as secretary of state had primary responsibility in foreign affairs. The war that the British had fought against France and Spain in Europe, the West Indies, and North America for nearly a decade had been expensive and inconclusive. It ended in 1748 with the Treaty of Aix-la-Chapelle, which essentially returned the belligerent nations to the status quo. Britain agreed to return to France the important fortress of Louisbourg at the mouth of the St Lawrence River, which it had captured during the war (and even agreed to send two noblemen to France as hostages for its surrender). On its part, France returned Madras in India to Britain and agreed to remove its troops from fortresses in the Low Countries that had been overrun during the war.[40] The Spanish attacks on British ships, which had precipitated war in 1739, were not even mentioned in the treaty. Many in Britain, particularly Pitt and his followers, denounced the treaty as humiliating and unnecessarily submissive.[41]

Murray was called upon to defend the treaty in the House of Commons, at a time when not only the treaty but also "disturbing social dislocations caused by military demobilization after the war" had placed Pelham's ministry on the defensive.[42] Again, he demonstrated his skill as an advocate and his command of every important detail. As in the debate about the Hanoverian troops, he professed to know nothing beyond what he read in the newspapers, a statement that nobody listening could have believed, especially after he began knowledgeably discussing and defending each provision of the treaty. He began by focusing on the treaty's most favourable terms: notably that the French had given up their conquests in Flanders to the Dutch. From the enemy's concessions, one would think Britain had been everywhere victorious in the war. But no, Britain had suffered defeat after defeat, not for any lack of bravery by its troops but because of the enemy's superior numbers. The peace was necessary to save Britain's ally, Holland, from destruction at the hands of the French. And there were financial reasons for making peace: Britain's public credit was in danger of "being entirely blown up." Then, speaking as an experienced attorney who had settled many lawsuits, Murray claimed that the treaty, though not perfect, was the best possible result: "All treaties of peace are founded upon the parties at war being respectively convinced that they can do no better."

But he was not through. Having argued that the terms of the treaty were favourable in view of Britain's lack of success in the war, he then turned the argument around and boasted of her victories. The navy had destroyed the enemy's commerce and had protected Britain's own commerce by destroying enemy privateers. He was convinced that Britain's numerous naval victories "forced [the French] to agree to reasonable terms of peace, notwithstanding their signal success upon the continent of Europe."[43] All in all, it was a masterpiece of advocacy, which goes far in explaining why Newcastle and other members of the ministry relied upon Murray to be the government's chief spokesman in the House of Commons.

Murray acted as an intimate adviser to Newcastle on political and foreign affairs. In May 1750 he reported to Newcastle, who was in Hanover with the King, on discussions that he had on separate occasions with Carteret (who now had the title of Lord Granville) and Pelham, first lord of the treasury.[44]

On 31 May 1752, Newcastle, who was again in Hanover with the King, sent Murray a long letter, marked "very private," in which he described Britain's current relations with France, Prussia, and Austria.[45] Murray replied the same day, giving Newcastle his advice on these matters.[46] On 17 July, Andrew Stone reported to Newcastle that he had dined the previous Wednesday with Pelham, Murray, and Lord Holdernesse (the other secretary of state, along with Newcastle), and that they discussed foreign affairs.[47] A week later, Murray wrote to Newcastle, giving advice on foreign affairs and warning of the danger of a rupture in the relations with Austria, which had been Britain's ally in the previous war but would later become its enemy in the Seven Years' War.[48] In August 1755, Murray, Stone, and Earl Waldegreve together went over a packet of dispatches that Newcastle had sent to Stone for their review.[49] Although not a Cabinet member and holding only a legal office in the government, Murray was engaged in policy discussions on the highest level and his advice was valued by government leaders.

Murray also continued to give personal advice to the leading politician in the land. In November 1950, upon Newcastle's return to England after one of his visits to Hanover with the King, Murray wrote to him, with extraordinary candour:

> I have just learned that you all landed at Dover yesterday morning in perfect health which I heartily rejoice at, and that you propose staying even there till you hear the King is landed or upon the Coast ...
>
> I am sure I would be wanting in the friendship with which I am attached to you if ... I did not ... earnestly press you to immediately [come] to town or at least to Claremont [Newcastle's home near London]. Your loitering at Dover without a reason will, I fear, be liable to many serious comments and what in great affairs and stations is even worse, much ridicule.[50]

Newcastle's finances were the subject of most of Murray's personal advice. Despite the family settlement of 1741, drafted and negotiated by Murray, which was supposed to end Newcastle's personal financial troubles, the duke was unable or unwilling to control his extravagances. In the summer of 1749, King George II dined at Newcastle's Claremont estate at enormous cost; the ceremonies included music, bell-ringers, and gunners for royal salutes.[51] Murray continued to assist and advise Newcastle, arranging mortgages on his estates in order to stave off bankruptcy.[52] In 1752 Newcastle asked Murray to make a detailed study of his affairs and suggest a remedy. According to one of Newcastle's biographers, "Murray's study of Newcastle's tangled financial situation was the most thorough and business-like ever made, and the duke actually made an effort to live by his recommendations."[53] On 18 October, Murray wrote to Newcastle: "I have ... boldly ventured to execute a scheme, without the privity of any mortal or communicating with any agent, by which I hope to reduce the great debt upon your estate at the rate of 3-1/2 per cent. I have already succeeded in part, but till my scheme is completed, I beg your Grace not to say a word of it to anybody whatsoever. If you do, it will fail. When we meet I will explain it more at large."[54]

Murray followed up his proposal with a memo, dated 16 January 1753, giving Newcastle some detailed practical advice. The paper gives us a picture of Murray's sometimes-brutal candour, common sense, ethical values, command of detail, psychological acuity, and business experience. Any person in financial difficulties would be fortunate to have such an adviser. He began by reporting that Newcastle's enemies had spread malicious rumours about his financial troubles in order to bring his creditors down upon him, but that they were unsuccessful because Newcastle had recently paid a large sum of his debts. But "it may be useful from this example of what malice can do, in order to guard against it for the future." Murray continued:

> Where a large sum is owing, to different people, in order to keep up credit, such a proportion of money is always wanted, as is necessary to answer what is called the circulation. People die, their representatives must be paid. People fail, their creditors must be paid. People have a present occasion – as marrying a child, etc. They grow surly and impatient if not paid.
>
> Whenever a demand of that sort shall be made, and not satisfied, the less the sum is (if the demand cannot immediately be answered) the worse it will be.

Murray then moved on to his most important point: Newcastle and his duchess must themselves make an overall financial plan and stick to it:

> What I would therefore earnestly recommend is that his Grace would make an entire plan of the expenses of this year, of every sort. And

> when any particular case comes under consideration, to consider it as relative to the whole. As to this or that particular item or expense, it is immaterial. But let the whole be such, as his Grace under the present circumstances approves of. And if it is necessary to spend in any one place, let there be a proportionable saving in another.
>
> Is there any plan settled as to his number of servants, or persons to live in the family? Is any resolution taken and executed as to his pensions and charities? Or as to the expenses with a view to elections?

After discussing more details of Newcastle's revenues and expenses, always raising the question as to how they would affect the overall plan, Murray, recognizing that the economies he was suggesting would be distasteful to Newcastle, sweetened the pill by astutely reminding him how he would benefit from his increased creditworthiness:

> Another thing – His Grace will not wonder, if there should be in some persons some little diffidence at first setting out, whether he will obstinately pursue a plan of this kind. Whereas, if there was the experience but of a year, that he is absolutely determined to do it, and after that, any sudden emergency or distress should happen, persons might be induced to lend any moderate sum, for which there may be immediate occasion, in confidence of his perseverance of it.[55]

Despite Murray's counselling, Newcastle's inability to control his expenses continued, and he continued to seek Murray's advice long after Murray became chief justice.

In the eighteenth century, the two law officers of the Crown were allowed to engage in the private practice of law. The enhanced reputation they enjoyed as a result of their official positions brought them clients, thus making these offices extremely lucrative. Lord Chesterfield wrote to his son in 1754: "The present Solicitor General, Murray, has less law than many lawyers, but has more practice than any; merely upon account of his eloquence, of which he has a never failing stream."[56] We do not know exactly what Murray's income was during his years as a law officer, but it was considerable. Besides his salary, which was £7,000 as attorney general,[57] he earned perhaps another £10,000 in fees from private clients and from legal opinions rendered to the Admiralty and other government departments.[58] In today's currency, he had an annual income of at least £3 million (or US/CA$4.5 million).

In some instances, the attorney general and solicitor general acted as co-counsel on behalf of a private client,[59] while in others they were on opposing sides.[60] The artist and society woman, Mary Delany, wrote to her sister, Ann Dewes, in 1752 that she had tried to retain both Dudley Ryder and William Murray to represent her in a lawsuit, "but Mr Murray (it is said), has been long retained on the other side, and Sir Dudley Rider [*sic*] too, who will be a great loss to us."[61]

The only limitation on private practice was that the law officers could not appear against the government without a special dispensation.[62] Murray seems to have been able to obtain such dispensation, for in 1754 he appeared in the Surrey assizes on behalf of a man who had been indicted for a minor crime. Murray sought a writ to move the case to the Court of King's Bench; Ryder, now chief justice of King's Bench, who only a few months earlier had been Murray's colleague as attorney general, decided the case in his favour.[63]

During his years as a government law officer, Murray represented private clients in a wide variety of lawsuits. Among other things, they included disputes over wills and trusts, real estate, the appointment of Church of England clergy, collection of debts, and patents and copyright. Although Murray was acting as an advocate on behalf of his clients, many of the views he expressed – support for freedom of commerce, religious toleration, impatience with obsolete laws – show a continuity between the attorney and the judge-to-be. Moreover, the qualities that Murray later displayed as a judge – pragmatism, fairness, and clarity – were already manifest.

A lawsuit in which Murray represented a private party demonstrates his reverence for the English common law (i.e., judge-made law, as opposed to legislation by Parliament), his preference for common sense over legal niceties, and the spirit of religious toleration that later informed his decisions as a judge. His argument contained the essence of his thinking about the function of law in society. *Omychund v. Barker*[64] was a dispute over the sale of goods in India, but the question before the court was whether the testimony of a witness who refused to swear a Christian oath could be admitted in evidence in a British trial. Commissioners had been sent to India to take written evidence; and several witnesses who were called by the plaintiff to testify swore an oath in the manner of their "Gentoo" (i.e., Hindu) religion, which was to touch the foot of a Brahmin priest with their hand.

Representing the plaintiff, Murray argued that since there was no binding legal authority on whether this kind of oath was sufficient, "the only question is whether upon principles of reason, justice, and convenience, this witness ought to be admitted." Then he explained the key role of the courts in making law, because the legislature cannot predict all the eventualities that may occur after it enacts a statute: "All occasions do not arise at once; now a particular species of *Indians* appears; hereafter another species of *Indians* may arise; a statute very seldom can take in all cases, therefore the common law, *that works itself pure* by rules drawn from the fountain of justice, is for this reason superior to an act of parliament."[65]

Finally, Murray offered a practical reason for allowing witnesses to be sworn in the manner of their own religion. A solemn oath is a security for a person's speaking the truth, he said; it is an appeal to God for the truth. It would therefore be self-defeating to compel a man to swear by a God in whom he does not believe. Chancellor Hardwicke agreed and admitted the testimony of witnesses who had been sworn according to the Gentoo religion.

Murray's varied experience during his twelve years as solicitor general and attorney general completed his development as a lawyer and politician. By 1756, when he was appointed chief justice, his views were fully formed and his legal skills well-honed. He was without peers in the legal profession.

7

Murray and the Jacobites

No Murray can be faithful to his King.

Casca's Epistle to Lord Mansfield

The threat of a second Jacobite invasion (the first having occurred in 1715) became a concern in the early 1740s. Sir Dudley Ryder wrote in his diary in 1741 of strong Jacobite sentiment in Leicestershire and other parts of the country. Many people, he learned, frequently drank toasts to the Pretender and wore white and blue ribbons (white signifying the exiled Pretender and blue, loyalty to the Stuart cause).[1] The possibility of a Jacobite invasion also jeopardized the position and reputation of Solicitor General Murray, given his family members' involvement in the cause.

During the whole eighteenth century, the most serious threat to the Hanoverian government was the 1745 Jacobite Rebellion.[2] That summer, with Britain at war and a large part of its army on the Continent, Charles Edward Stuart (known to history as Bonnie Prince Charlie), the twenty-five-year-old son of the Pretender, landed with a tiny band of men in the western isles of Scotland. On 19 August, at Glenfinnan in the western Highlands, in the presence of about 1,300 supporters, he proclaimed the Pretender king of England and Scotland.[3] Soon many of the Highland clans, which had never become reconciled to the union between Scotland and England or to the rule of the Hanoverian kings, rallied to support him. Charles's forces entered Perth on 4 September,[4] where he was conducted in triumph to nearby Scone Palace, the home of Viscount Stormont, Murray's eldest brother. Stormont, though friendly to the Jacobite cause, was unwilling to risk his life and property for the sake of the Stuarts. He absented himself, while his mother, who shared the Jacobite sympathies of her late husband and apparently had no such compunctions or fears, received Bonnie Prince Charlie and provided him and his followers with room and board at the palace during their short stay at Perth.[5]

The rebellion was at first successful. Charles's forces entered Edinburgh and defeated a British army at the Battle of Prestonpans in southern Scotland in late September. His Highlanders crossed into England with a force of only 5,000 men and besieged Carlisle, the city nearest the border. Six days later, Carlisle surrendered. Leaving a garrison to hold the city, the rebel forces made their way south, reaching Derby, only 125 miles from London, in early December.[6] There they halted. An even greater danger to Britain was that France was mobilizing an invasion force to support the rebels.[7] A French invasion, however, never materialized.

It is possible that the rebels could have reached London and toppled the government, but they were plagued by internal squabbles and also disappointed by the small number of Englishmen who joined the rebellion.[8] Although many of the English disliked the German-speaking Hanoverian monarchs and were willing to drink toasts to the exiled Stuart king, few were willing to fight their fellow countrymen in a civil war or to risk their own property and lives.[9] On 6 December, the rebels began a retreat to Scotland. They were decisively defeated by royal forces under the Duke of Cumberland, one of the King's sons, at the Battle of Culloden Moor, near Inverness, on 16 April 1746, thus ending the rebellion.[10]

Cumberland set out to extirpate Jacobitism from the Highlands, and did it with such brutality and sadism that he earned the sobriquet "Butcher Cumberland." Many Highlanders were summarily executed without a trial and their homes levelled. Soldiers under one of Cumberland's generals burned down 7,000 houses and fired cannon into heaps of wounded Jacobites for sport.[11] In one incident, country girls were made to strip naked and ride on horseback at Cumberland's camp for the enjoyment of the soldiers.[12] Charles Stuart escaped to France after many perilous adventures, but a number of those who joined the rebellion were caught and prosecuted. Murray played a large role in advising the government as to who deserved prosecution and, later, in prosecuting treason charges against several of the rebels. In both of these capacities, the fairness that he displayed, in the face of public outrage at the rebellion, was admirable. He neither shirked his prosecutorial task nor bent over backwards to be harsh to avoid any suspicion that he harboured Jacobite sympathies.

Whatever Murray's sympathies might have been twenty years earlier, he was now an important government officer and had nothing to gain and everything to lose from a Jacobite victory. Moreover, the English trading and manufacturing community strongly supported the government, and Murray, who had represented many merchants in his private practice, had political and economic views that were closely aligned with theirs. The Pretender was, in effect, a client of France, and a Jacobite success would inevitably have subordinated English commercial interests to those of the French.[13] Murray's rising career depended on the failure of the rebellion.

Once the rebels were defeated, Murray did not succumb to witch-hunting those believed to have helped the Jacobites. Two suspects were Joseph Backhouse and John Pearson, mayor and town clerk respectively of Carlisle, who had surrendered the city in November 1745 and afterwards proclaimed the Pretender as king. The Duke of Newcastle asked Ryder and Murray to examine affidavits and other accusatory documents, and to give an opinion as to whether the two men should be put on trial. On 28 March 1746, three weeks before the rebels' final defeat at Culloden, the law officers opined in a report to the King that there was not sufficient ground for a criminal prosecution. Ryder and Murray reported that Backhouse and Pearson had not supported the Pretender voluntarily, but were forced to do so by the rebels, and there was unexceptionable evidence of their good character and affection for the King.[14] Given the anti-Jacobite hysteria that pervaded the country at a time when the rebel army was still undefeated, this opinion shows considerable courage on the part of both law officers.

Murray also gave opinions to Newcastle that a long list of people involved in the rebellion, including the legendary Flora MacDonald, who helped Bonnie Prince Charlie escape to France, were triable in England for high treason.[15] About 120 of the rebels were executed, a third of them deserters from the British army. Murray acted as prosecutor in several of these treason trials, one of which was against a man named Townley, who had been a member of the Jacobite garrison of Carlisle that surrendered to the King's forces in the waning days of the rebellion. A jury found him guilty and, along with eight others, he was executed on Kennington Common in London on 2 August 1746. Townley's head was displayed upon Temple Bar, near Lincoln's Inn.[16]

Public attention focused on four Scottish noblemen, lords Kilmarnock, Cromarty, Balmerino, and Lovat, who had supported the rebellion and were tried in the House of Lords for high treason.[17] Murray questioned only one witness in the joint trial of Kilmarnock, Cromarty, and Balmerino in July 1746, with most of the prosecution being conducted by Attorney General Ryder. However, the Jacobite associations of Murray's family came up near the end of the trial in a way that must have unsettled him. After the peers had withdrawn to deliberate, Murray approached Balmerino and insolently asked him why he had given the House of Lords the trouble of hearing his case, when his own lawyer had told him that he could not possibly avoid being convicted.

Balmerino, who had not previously met Murray, asked bystanders who this person was and, on being told, he exclaimed: "Oh, Mr Murray! I am extremely glad to see you. I have been with several of your relations. The good lady, your mother, was of great use to us at Perth."[18] The three Scottish lords were convicted on 1 August 1746. Only Cromarty, who had a large family and whose wife was pregnant, was reprieved, while the other two were beheaded.[19]

The separate treason trial of the fourth rebel lord, Simon Fraser, Lord Lovat, in Westminster Hall in March 1747 was a major public attraction, provoking an "unseemly scramble for tickets."[20] Lovat was a fervent, though devious, Scottish nationalist, who had plotted a Jacobite rebellion as early as 1703 and had been involved in Jacobite as well as anti-Jacobite intrigues during the years since then.[21] When Charles Stuart landed in Scotland, Lovat waited to see which side was likely to win; but after the Jacobite victory at Prestonpans in September 1745, he declared his support for the rebels. Even then, he remained cautious; he did not join Charles Stuart but sent his son, while remaining at home and giving encouragement and sending supplies to the rebels. Even after the defeat of the rebellion at Culloden, he urged Charles to fight on. He himself tried to escape to France but was captured and brought to London to be tried by the House of Lords for treason.[22] Because Lovat had not actually taken up arms in the rebellion but had only given assistance, he was not indicted as a criminal, but instead was impeached by the House of Commons and then tried in the House of Lords.

Although Ryder was the principal manager in Lovat's impeachment trial, Murray questioned witnesses and made the concluding statement, summing up the prosecution's case. His play on the emotions as well as the intellects of his audience brings to mind Marc Antony's oration over Caesar's dead body. Aware that the Lords might be reluctant to condemn to death one of their own, especially one believed to be nearly eighty years old, he refrained from attacking Lovat personally.[23] Pointing out that Lovat had called no witnesses, he said that it was his duty not to "press down the Load heavier" on him, but rather "to satisfy your Lordships now, and the World hereafter, from the Nature of the Evidence by which this Accusation has been supported, why no Part is attempted to be answered."

Murray then brought up the fact that Lovat had not been allowed representation by a lawyer (counsel was allowed to defendants in court trials for treason, but not in trials in the House of Lords). He turned Lovat's disadvantage around to make it appear a benefit to him, and at the same time he flattered the Lords by appealing to their better natures. The central part of his address to the Lords is worth quoting:

> The Law requires you, as his Judges, to be his Counsel … I am persuaded, Compassion, inseparable from noble Minds, has been ingenious to suggest to your Thoughts Doubts and Objections, in favour of one standing in that Place, who certainly labours under some Infirmities, and is allowed to defend himself by no other Tongue than his own.
>
> If Scruples have arisen in the Minds of your Lordships, they will gain Strength from that Consideration; and the honest Prejudice you must feel from his Want of Assistance may be of more Advantage to him than the ablest Assistance he could have.

Having almost certainly captured the attention of his audience, Murray advised them on the applicable law. He made it seem simple. There were only two things, he said, that the Lords had to decide: whether the evidence was convincing proof of the treason, and whether there was any reason for them to believe the evidence. He then cited an ancient definition of treason as either of two things: imagining the death of the King, or levying war against the King in his realm. As to the first, he conceded that the defendant could not be guilty of treason unless he performed some overt act that showed his secret intention. The evidence produced in the trial, he said, showed several overt acts; one was that Lovat had written a letter to Charles Stuart declaring that he was Charles's "most zealous and active partisan in the North of Scotland." It may well have crossed Murray's mind that he himself had written a similar letter twenty years earlier, pledging his allegiance to Charles Stuart's father, the Jacobite Pretender. Turning then to the second type of treason – levying war against the King – Murray argued that, even though Lovat never himself joined the rebel forces, the letters of encouragement that he wrote to Charles and his followers, and his provision of supplies, constituted levying war.

Murray summarized the evidence in plain language that his audience could easily understand. To Lovat's argument that the witnesses who had testified against him ought not to be believed because many of them were accomplices who were trying to save their own lives, Murray replied that, while hope of life or fear of death may have induced some witnesses to give evidence, they had every incentive to tell the truth: if they were caught lying they would be in a far worse situation. Finally, he dismissed Lovat's last-ditch plea for a delay so that he could call witnesses for the defence: "These are Pretexts, but he [i.e., Lovat] let fall the true Reason why he has no Witnesses – there is no making Brick without Straw; – there is no calling Witnesses without Facts; – there is no making a Defence without Innocence; – there is no answering Evidence which is true. He has not so much as suggested what these Witnesses could prove, if they were here."[24] The only purpose of Lovat's request to call witnesses, said Murray, was to delay the completion of the trial. The request was denied.

After Murray concluded, the Lords withdrew to deliberate and returned shortly afterwards with a unanimous verdict of guilty. The next day, they reconvened for the sentencing, but first they gave Lovat an opportunity to speak. This crafty man used the opportunity to make a speech that on the surface showed unusual generosity to his prosecutor but nevertheless revealed some of the anger he must have been feeling. While he praised Murray, he subtly reminded his audience of Murray's Jacobite connections:

> Mr Murray ... I must say with Pleasure, is an Honour to his Country ... whose Eloquence and Learning is beyond what is to be expressed by an ignorant Man like me. I heard him with Pleasure, though it was against me. I have the Honour to be his Relation,[25] though perhaps he neither knows it, nor values it. I wish that his being born in the North may not hinder him from the Preferment that his Merit and Learning deserves. Till that Gentleman spoke, your Lordships were inclined to grant my earnest Request, and allow me further Time to bring up Witnesses to prove my Innocence; but, it seems, that has been over-ruled.

Lovat was sentenced to be beheaded. The condemned Jacobite was taken to the Tower, while his prosecutor, still suspected by many to be a Jacobite at heart, returned to his home in Lincoln's Inn Fields. Lovat was beheaded on Tower Hill on 9 April 1747, going to his death with courage and apparent equanimity.[26]

The defeat of the rebellion of 1745 ended the immediate Jacobite threat, but it fueled anti-Scottish feeling in England.[27] It showed that the Highland clans, if they had France's support, might have the ability to overthrow the Hanoverian government.[28] Jacobitism remained a hot political issue that would continue to require Murray's attention as solicitor general and also plague him personally in the following years. In February 1748, rowdy pro-Jacobite demonstrations at Oxford University led the ministry to put pressure on Ryder and Murray to take action against the vice chancellor of the university for not taking adequate steps to punish the rioters. Murray advised Ryder that it would be best to do nothing, because heavy-handed action would only inflame the nation, which was still divided between intransigent Jacobites and fierce supporters of the government. The matter was quietly dropped.[29]

A much more serious episode occurred in 1753, when Murray was forced to defend himself against a public accusation of having been a Jacobite in his youth. Its origin can be traced to 1751, when Prince Frederick, George II's eldest son, died, and the King's grandson, Prince George, then thirteen years of age, became heir to the throne (he would reign as George III from 1760 to 1820). The question of who would be the "governor" in charge of the young prince's education was a matter of great political importance, "because the integrity of the Hanoverian and Protestant succession [to the throne] continued to be such a touchstone of Whiggism" and "the system of balanced government brought into being by the Glorious Revolution of 1688."[30]

The Duke of Newcastle and his brother Henry Pelham, who together headed the government, chose two men to be Prince George's governors, Lord Harcourt and Thomas Hayter, Bishop of Norwich, neither of whom had any real qualifications as educators. Harcourt, according to Horace Walpole, knew nothing that he could teach the prince except hunting and drinking; whereas Hayter, though a sensible man and a clergyman, was a former buccaneer who "retained nothing of his first profession, except his seraglio."[31] In addition, Hayter disgusted the young prince with his dry and pedantic manners.[32]

Word got around that the prince's education was really in the hands of two of Newcastle's closest advisers, Andrew Stone and William Murray. There was some truth to this. Murray closely followed the progress of the prince's education and kept Newcastle continually informed about it, while Stone, who had been appointed sub-governor under Harcourt and Hayter, ingratiated himself with the prince's mother, the dowager Princess of Wales.[33] Murray even complained to Hayter that he was not paying enough attention to Stone's advice about the prince's education. When Hayter replied that Stone was subordinate to Harcourt, Murray interrupted him, saying that Harcourt "is a mere cipher, must be a cipher, and was intended to be only a cipher."[34]

In June 1752, Murray pointed out to Newcastle the shortcomings of Harcourt and Hayter as teachers,[35] and a month later he wrote that the prince showed every mark of confidence in Stone and listened to his instruction eagerly. In August 1752, he reported to Newcastle: "I was last Sunday at Court; everybody is delighted with the two princes [the other one being

Prince George's younger brother] ... Their behaviour is extremely polite and their conversation very manly and well understood ... Stone assures me their improvement in private is even beyond what it appears in public."[36]

In the autumn of 1752, Lord Chancellor Hardwicke and Prime Minister Pelham became alarmed at reports that Stone and Murray were teaching Prince George doctrines favouring the exiled Jacobites. Hayter found in the prince's possession a book, apparently *The Idea of a Patriot King*, by the former Jacobite, Viscount Bolingbroke, which advocated that the king assume a much more important role in Britain's constitutional monarchy.[37] A committee of three was appointed to look into the matter. The committee reported that the prince's younger brother had lent the book to the prince, and that their mother, the dowager Princess of Wales, or possibly their sister Augusta, had lent it to the younger prince.[38] Harcourt and Hayter were not mollified by this innocent explanation and, unable to get Stone dismissed as sub-governor of the prince, they both resigned,[39] to be replaced by Lord Waldegrave, a courtier of the King.

Despite the committee clearing Stone and Murray of the accusation, suspicion persisted that they were implanting Jacobite doctrines into the young prince's mind. Both men were unpopular with many persons in the government, Stone because of his great influence over Newcastle, which seemed out of proportion to his humble origins (he was the son of a London goldsmith), and Murray because he was a Scot with a Jacobite family.[40] An anonymous "memorial" (which Horace Walpole later admitted he had written[41]) was sent to several persons, complaining that "a Scotchman of a most disaffected family and allied in the nearest manner to the Pretender's First Minister" [i.e., William Murray's brother James] had been "consulted on the education of the Prince of Wales and entrusted with the most important secrets of government."[42] Some even believed that Murray and Stone, through their influence over Newcastle, were the men who actually governed the country.

It was at this juncture that Murray was specifically accused of Jacobitism. A lawyer named Fawcett from the city of Newcastle, who had attended Westminster School with Stone and Murray, was drinking coffee one evening in November 1752 with the Dean of Durham, when he saw in a newspaper that a Dr James Johnson was to be appointed Bishop of Gloucester.[43] Fawcett exclaimed: "That man has good luck." When asked what he meant by the remark, Fawcett replied: "That man is very lucky, for I remember, some years ago, that he was a Jacobite. I often met him at the home of my cousin, Mr Vernon, a mercer [textile merchant] on Ludgate Hill, a notorious Jacobite, where the Pretender's health was frequently drunk."[44] It may be recalled that Vernon, who was no longer alive, was the father of a classmate of Murray at Westminster School. Moreover, Vernon had befriended Murray and bequeathed a valuable estate to him.[45]

Fawcett's remark became the subject of gossip that spread to London and soon reached Pelham's ears. Pelham was concerned about the report, since he and Newcastle had recommended Dr Johnson for the bishopric, ecclesiastical appointments being within the patronage powers of the ministry. Although the mere drinking of a toast was hardly a treasonable act, Jacobitism and active treason were virtually synonymous in some people's minds – only eight years earlier a Jacobite army had invaded the country and come perilously close to taking the capital.

Disturbed by the reports about Johnson, Pelham asked a friend and relative named Vane, who had been a law client of Fawcett, to write and ask Fawcett whether he had made the remark about Dr Johnson's toast-drinking and, if he had, whether it was true. Fawcett replied evasively to Vane's letter, and Pelham then summoned him to London. Before leaving for London, Fawcett had several conversations about the matter with a certain Lord Ravensworth (who, incidentally, had been one of the recipients of Walpole's "memorial" attacking Murray and Stone). Fawcett told Ravensworth that he was not sure about Dr Johnson, but now, for the first time, said he remembered that Murray and Stone had on several occasions drunk toasts to the Pretender at Vernon's home.[46] Murray, Stone, Johnson, and Vernon's son were all old friends who had attended Westminster School together.

Questioned by Pelham in London, Fawcett – no doubt thoroughly frightened by the hornet's nest he had stirred up – said he wasn't sure about Johnson, and he didn't even mention Murray or Stone. This was how things stood when Ravensworth, a consummate busybody, arrived in London a few days later. Although Fawcett had earnestly asked him not to disclose what he had told him, Ravensworth repeated the accusation against Murray and Stone to anyone who would listen, including several noblemen and members of the ministry. He also made it known that he thought Stone should be dismissed as the Prince of Wales's tutor. In a second interview with Pelham, this time with Newcastle present, Fawcett said he could not substantiate the charge against Johnson, but now he insisted that he had seen Murray and Stone drink the Pretender's health.

An accusation of this kind against the solicitor general and the Prince of Wales's tutor could not be ignored. Pelham felt duty-bound to take it to the King. King George, who had a narrow but nevertheless shrewd intellect,[47] was not disturbed by the accusation; he said that, whatever Murray and Stone may have done when they were little more than boys, he was confident of their loyalty now.[48] If Newcastle had shown a firmer loyalty to Murray and Stone, he could perhaps have dismissed the accusation immediately, and the matter might have ended there.[49] But, given the widely held suspicion that his two closest advisers were Jacobites, Newcastle may have thought it more prudent to see them exonerated publicly.

The ministry convened the Cabinet council, which included Newcastle, Pelham, Hardwicke, the Archbishop of Canterbury, and several other noblemen, for a formal investigation into whether Stone and Murray had drunk toasts to the Pretender more than twenty years earlier. Ravensworth told the council what Fawcett had told him; but Fawcett, when sworn, lost his nerve and said that he couldn't remember having ever been present at Vernon's house with Murray or Stone when disloyal toasts were drunk.[50] At a second hearing, Fawcett testified that he thought he had heard treasonable healths drunk at Vernon's home when Stone and Murray were present, but that he could not swear to it. When asked about the time of the meetings, he said he couldn't be sure but believed they occurred in 1731 or 1732.

Several others, including Stone, flatly denied the toast-drinking. Murray, who at first had written to the King that he would sooner resign as solicitor general than suffer the indignity of having to defend himself against such an outrageous accusation, now asked to speak to the council. He made a long, detailed defence, denying that Vernon, or anyone else in his hearing, had ever proposed the health of the Pretender. He denied every part of Fawcett's accusation and pointed out falsehoods and inconsistencies in his story.[51] The council was persuaded and unanimously reported to the King that Fawcett had "shamefully prevaricated and contradicted himself" and that there was no ground for his "scandalous and malicious" allegations.[52]

Newcastle reported separately to the King that Murray "made the strongest and most able declaration of his firm attachment to your Majesty's government ... This speech made the greatest impression upon the Lords of the Council."[53] Despite the council's findings, the Duke of Bedford brought the issue to the House of Lords, proposing that the investigation of Stone and Murray be continued. In seeking to cast doubt on Murray's denial, Bedford strung together a series of incriminating allegations: that Vernon had been a notorious Jacobite: that Murray was Vernon's sole heir; and that Murray had advised Fawcett to let the matter drop.[54]

But once the ministry had exculpated Murray and Stone, it had little desire to pursue the matter further. Many of its members, including Newcastle and Hardwicke, spoke up in support of the two men. The latter "spoke in warm terms of the meritorious and irreproachable behaviour of Mr Murray, since his first appearance in the court of Chancery in 1742."[55] Lord Waldegrave, the Prince's new tutor, gave a speech affirming his confidence in Stone but not mentioning Murray, perhaps because he thought it expedient in view of Murray's Jacobite family connections.[56] William Pitt, although a political opponent of Murray who many times had insinuated that Murray was a secret Jacobite, asked his brother-in-law, Lord Temple, not to support Bedford in pushing the Jacobite charge.[57] So the matter was dropped, with only three other peers supporting Bedford.[58]

In a sense, the Fawcett affair was a tempest in a teapot. In the early eighteenth century, there were many people who regularly drank toasts to "the king over the water." The Pretender's health was frequently drunk at Oxford, where Murray was a student from 1723 to 1727.[59] In fact, the government had to contend with a continuing undercurrent of Jacobitism throughout much of the country, which manifested itself not only in quarrels in taverns but most noticeably in disturbances on public occasions such as royal anniversaries.[60] Some of the Jacobite demonstrations, no doubt, stemmed less from loyalty to the Pretender than simply from a desire to provoke the Hanoverian court and the Whig ministry.[61] In Kent, one "might have witnessed a band of Jacks on a drunken spree, drinking the Pretender's health on their knees and proclaiming his regality in the marketplace."[62] A historian of the Jacobite movement wrote, "If the drinking of toasts could have transformed the political situation, James or his son would have been carried back to the throne on a wave of enthusiasm and claret."[63] Henry Fox, the secretary of war, told King George that he himself had drunk the Pretender's health while a student at Oxford. According to Newcastle, Fox's declaration earned him Murray's "blind attachment."[64]

Although the affair created a furor in political circles, it did not create much public excitement. The days when an accusation of Jacobitism could arouse the populace were past.[65] The best proof of this, as well as the spirit of tolerance that informed the British elite, was that, only three years after Murray was forced to clear himself from the charge of Jacobitism, there was no public outcry when he was raised to the peerage as Lord Mansfield and to the exalted position of chief justice of England.

Nonetheless, there were those who believed that Murray and Stone had been whitewashed and that the investigation had been stopped by "dexterity and influence."[66] Lord Chesterfield wrote a few weeks later, with his usual wit, that he could not believe Murray and Stone's testimony that they had never been Jacobites: "This seems extraordinary, considering that they were of Jacobite families, bred up at Westminster School, and sent from thence to Oxford, the seat of Jacobitism. All I can say to this last particular is what Ariosto says of Angelica, who, after having travelled all over the world 'tête-à-tête' with her lover, professed herself an untouched virgin."[67]

The Fawcett affair had a lasting effect on Murray: it left him more cautious than ever, and indelibly loyal to King George II and later to King George III.[68] All the rest of his life, he would never challenge the authority of the Crown. His close brush with being tarred as a Jacobite may have subconsciously influenced his judgments after he ascended to the bench; for example, he vigorously enforced the seditious-libel laws that were used to prosecute critics of the government.

Murray's enemies never believed his denial that he had been a Jacobite, and they did not forget. In a November 1754 debate in the House of Commons on the army estimates, after a supporter of the ministry stated there were no Jacobites in England, Pitt brought up the subject of Jacobitism. Glaring at Murray, he declared that Jacobitism, far from being dead, was even suspected in high places. Continuing to look meaningfully in Murray's direction, he said that Oxford was paved with Jacobites and anyone bred there in Tory principles could not be trusted. One observer wrote: "Every word was Murray, yet so managed that no public notice could be taken of it ... and Fox declares that Murray, who was sitting next to him, suffered for an hour."[69] According to Horace Walpole: "Colours, much less words, could not paint the confusion and agitation that worked in Murray's face ... His countenance spoke everything that Fawcett had been too terrified to prevaricate away."[70] Twenty-one years later, the Fawcett accusation still was not forgotten; a pamphlet in verse addressed to Lord Mansfield even accused him of deceit when he prosecuted the lords who had assisted the Jacobite rebellion of 1745:

In youth, before dissembling was your trade,
To James libations on your knees you made;
Not loyalty, but fear has sheathed your sting;
No Murray can be faithful to his King.
. . . .
Once against rebels, 'twas your place to plead,
Your mouth condemn'd, your soul approv'd the deed.
Whilst round your heart sad disappointment hung,
Dissimulation oil'd your treach'rous tongue.[71]

8

Attaining the Bench and the Peerage

So greatly superior to the rest of his Profession, he stood without a Rival.

Lord Waldegrave, in his memoirs

As early as 1746, Murray's reputation as the foremost lawyer and legal scholar of his day led to rumours that he would be appointed chief justice of the Court of King's Bench, the highest permanent judgeship in England.[1] Although he was also a leading politician – the virtual leader of the House of Commons – and was respected by the nation and liked by the King, he had made it known that his main ambition lay in the law, not politics.[2] But for many years the job he wanted was not available. Chief Justice Sir William Lee remained in office until his death in 1754. In accordance with the usual practice, the attorney general, Sir Dudley Ryder, succeeded him, and Murray moved into Ryder's position. It was generally accepted that Murray would eventually be a judge. When Sir John Strange, the master of the rolls (and Murray's predecessor as solicitor general), died in 1754, Newcastle suggested to Chancellor Hardwicke that this senior judicial post be offered to Murray.[3] Hardwicke replied that, although he thought Murray fittest for the job and that it was due him, he also had little doubt that Murray would decline it.[4] Hardwicke knew that Murray's ambition was higher – to be chief justice. If Murray was indeed offered the master of the rolls, he rejected the offer.

When Ryder was appointed chief justice in 1754, his request for a peerage was turned down. The King had insisted that Ryder wait before being created a nobleman; Hardwicke, on whom the King relied heavily for advice, discouraged the peerage appointment, most likely because he was not happy having another prestigious "law lord" with him in the House of Lords. Finally, on 21 May 1756, the King relented and raised Ryder to the peerage in a ceremony held at Kensington Palace.[5] But Ryder was never able to enjoy his long-awaited title; three days later he died suddenly of a fever at his house on Chancery Lane.[6] There were immediate newspaper reports that Murray would be appointed chief justice.[7]

Murray did not hesitate in asserting his claim to the office. He had no competitors. According to Waldegrave, he was "so greatly superior to the rest of his Profession, that he stood without a Rival."[8] Newcastle had made a long-standing promise to Murray that he would be named Ryder's successor[9] – a repayment for the fifteen years that Murray had acted as trusted personal, financial, legal, and political adviser. Murray lost no time in asking Newcastle to fulfill his promise: only six days after Ryder's death, Newcastle wrote to Murray: "If you (as I know you will) persist in your resolution I will, as I said, as far as depends on me, assist you with cheerfulness, sincerity, and without grudge or complaint."[10] Newcastle's use of the word "persist" suggests that Murray had been pressing him to secure the appointment almost from the moment of Ryder's unexpected death.

Ryder's death and Murray's insistence on filling the vacancy could not have come at a worse time for Newcastle. The government was foundering, and Newcastle needed Murray's persuasive voice in the House of Commons as never before. The ministry, which for a decade had been led by the partnership of Newcastle and his brother, Henry Pelham, had come to an end two years earlier with Pelham's death. At that time Murray had been considered as a possible candidate to succeed Pelham as prime minister, but he was disqualified by his Scottish background and the accusation of Jacobitism made against him only a year earlier.[11] Newcastle took his brother's place as prime minister, but his ministry was unstable, owing largely to the rival ambitions of Henry Fox, the secretary of war, and William Pitt, the paymaster-general. The political lines were not between Whig and Tory – for all of the principal players were (or professed to be) Whigs – but rather between cliques, each led by a powerful politician.

For the time being, Fox supported Newcastle's ministry, but Newcastle did not think that Fox alone could stand up to the fiery and eloquent Pitt in debate in the House of Commons.[12] Pitt not only dominated parliamentary debates but also had a large following in the House of Commons and in the country at large. If Newcastle lost the services of Murray, he would be faced with the unpleasant necessity of inviting Pitt into the government, a prospect he wished to avoid. The King detested Pitt for constantly accusing him of putting the interests of his electorate of Hanover ahead of those of his British kingdom.[13] Furthermore, Pitt had not endeared himself to the King in allying himself with "Leicester House," the term used to identify the faction represented by Prince George, the heir to the throne, and his mother, the dowager Princess of Wales.[14] Referring to Newcastle's predicament and Hardwicke's jealousy of rivals, the politician Charles Townshend told Murray, "You will ruin the Duke of Newcastle by quitting the House of Commons, and the Chancellor by going into the House of Lords."[15]

A series of defeats and blunders had placed the government under attack from its parliamentary opponents. In 1756, the intermittent enmity between England and France had flared up into a war that would continue for the next seven years, and now French troops threatened to invade England from across the English Channel. England's former ally, Austria, had concluded an alliance with France; and England was ill-prepared for a continental war. Things were going badly in North America too, where French forces under the Marquis of Montcalm were attacking British outposts on the border with French Canada in what is now upstate New York.

But the most shameful defeat occurred almost simultaneously with Chief Justice Ryder's death. In May 1756, Admiral John Byng, commanding a British fleet in the Mediterranean, failed to engage the French fleet in battle off the coast of the British-held island of Minorca and instead retreated to Gibraltar, leaving Minorca to be captured by the French. News of Byng's withdrawal and the loss of Minorca was greeted with outrage throughout the country. It was aimed not only at Byng, who was immediately recalled and court-martialled for cowardice and negligence in the face of the enemy, but also at Newcastle and his government.[16]

Murray was in a hurry to be appointed chief justice because he expected the government to fall, in which case Newcastle, his chief sponsor, might no longer be in office.[17] He put pressure on Newcastle to use his political power and his influence with the King to get him the appointment as chief justice and also raise him to the peerage. Having seen the difficulty that Ryder had faced in being created a peer, Murray made it clear that he wanted a peerage at the same time as his appointment as chief justice. Newcastle, while reassuring Murray that he would not renege on his promise, equivocated. He tried to delay the appointment in order to keep Murray in the Commons as long as possible by appealing to Murray's loyalty to himself and the King. On 30 May, he wrote to Murray:

> Every Man who pretends to be a Minister in this Country, *is a Fool* if he acts a Day without the House of Commons; and a *Greater Fool* if he depends upon any of whom he cannot be sure ... Nobody but yourself

> will or can support me ... I must own, it would be most cruel to insist upon your remaining in the House of Commons, if you yourself don't see the Force and Reason of it. You have a right to the Chief Justice; it would be hard in the King to refuse the Peerage. I should blame you for taking the Chief Justice without it.[18]

While seeming to support Murray's ambition, Newcastle went on to tell him that the King needed a deputy in the House of Commons to do his business (Newcastle, being a peer, could not sit in the House of Commons) and that "the King can have no other deputy than yourself."[19] But Murray would not be deterred from his aim. Not only was a high judicial career his great ambition but he also did not relish staying in the House of Commons, where he would have to face the blasts of Pitt and his supporters over the Minorca defeat and other wartime failures. As Horace Walpole wrote, "he knew it was safer to expound laws than to be exposed to them."[20] Furthermore, although having sometimes been mentioned as a possible prime minister or secretary of state, Murray knew that the suspicion of Jacobitism that still clung to him would always bar him from the highest political office.[21] As chief justice, on the other hand, he would have security of life tenure in the event of a change in the ministry, and so would be less vulnerable to any accusations of disloyalty. And when he was chief justice and a British nobleman, his enemies could try all they wanted to tar him with his Jacobite family and alleged Jacobite past. From his lofty position on the bench and in the House of Lords, it wouldn't matter to him.

It does not appear that Murray answered Newcastle's ambivalent letter, but he must have made it clear to Newcastle in private conversation that he was unwilling to budge from his position.[22] For a couple of weeks, Newcastle postponed taking Murray's request to the King or doing anything else about it, and Murray accused him of not supporting his promotion to the bench. Newcastle, for his part, complained to Andrew Stone that Murray was ungrateful for the many favours he (Newcastle) had done for him.[23] Murray engaged in some hard bargaining: he made it plain to Newcastle that if he was not appointed chief justice he would return to private practice; he would quit the House of Commons and the attorney-generalship and cease supporting the ministry.[24] There was even speculation that he would instead remain in the House of Commons as a leader of the opposition.[25]

Realizing that Murray could not be dissuaded, Newcastle asked Hardwicke to take up Murray's request with the King.[26] Before doing so, Hardwicke met with Murray and ascertained for himself that Murray was unwilling to accept the chief justice position unless a peerage went with it.[27] Murray, like the careful lawyer he was, wrote to Hardwicke immediately after the meeting to make sure that Hardwicke understood this.[28] On 28 June, Hardwicke met with the King, and told him that both he and Newcastle backed Murray's claim. Although the King usually deferred to his ministers, he could be stubborn at times. He replied to Hardwicke: "As this is the opinion of you both, I am ready to make Mr Murray Chief Justice this term without further delay, [but] I will not make a precedent that when I advance [him] from the bar to that office, he should think that he has an immediate claim to a peerage." The King then reminded Hardwicke that Ryder had had to wait two years before being made a peer, and that Murray should get some experience as a judge before being raised to the nobility. Hardwicke replied that the two cases were different: Murray was a member of an ancient noble family, had made a great figure in Parliament, and would naturally wish to continue to be active there, though in the House of Lords instead of the Commons, rather than being excluded from all public business in the prime of his career.[29]

The peerage was an exclusive club, consisting of about 220 noblemen. Only eldest sons could inherit titles, and almost all peers were wealthy landowners.[30] The King, of whom it was said, "peerages were proverbially as difficult to extract … as banknotes,"[31] remained firm: he was willing to make Murray chief justice, but not a peer. He had already created four new peers that year,[32] and he did not want to further deflate the value of the peerage. It was difficult to get King George to do anything on which he had set his mind to resist.[33]

Two days later, Hardwicke again met with the King, and Newcastle then followed up with his own meeting. But all to no effect.[34] By this time Newcastle was thoroughly miserable with having to deal with an obstinate attorney general and an equally obstinate King. He also feared that the loss of Murray's support in the House of Commons would result in the fall of the ministry and his own removal from office. He reported to Murray on his interview with the King: "The King asked whether I had seen Murray. I said yes. Well what says he? Extremely sensible … of your Majesty's great goodness to him, but wishes not to accept the one without the other. [The king:] 'Why must I be forced? I will not make him a peer 'till the next session …'" Newcastle continued in his account to Murray: "I hope I have done right; I am sure I intended it, but it is my misfortune to be distrusted by those from whom I never did deserve it."[35] Murray replied graciously, thanking Newcastle for his intervention and reassuring him that he never suspected him of lack of friendship or affection, and suggesting that people with ill will toward Newcastle and Murray might have prejudiced the King against him.[36]

Persuasion having failed, Newcastle turned to bribery. If Murray agreed to stay in the House of Commons, he would be given the sinecure of the Duchy of Lancaster for life with a pension of £2,000 a year (he raised the offer to £6,000 in early October), with permission to remain attorney general at a salary of £7,000 a year. In addition, a valuable sinecure would be granted to Murray's nephew and presumptive heir, Viscount Stormont.[37] Wisely, Murray refused the bribes, knowing that acceptance of them would damage his reputation and make him new enemies.[38] All he was willing to do was delay his promotion until the autumn, in the hope that the King would by then be willing to grant him the peerage.

The whole episode showed several facets of Murray's character: his high ambition; his single-minded pursuit of any goal he set for himself; his devotion to the law; and his dislike of the turbulence of parliamentary politics, particularly in view of his vulnerability to accusations of Jacobitism.

The stalemate ended in mid-October, when the King backed down and agreed to give Murray the title of nobility that he insisted on. Why the King changed his mind is not clear, but it may be that he was simply tired of fighting his ministers and was preoccupied with foreign affairs, which were far more important to him than Murray's demand for a peerage. In late August, Frederick the Great's Prussian troops had invaded the German kingdom of Saxony, giving George reason to worry about the security of his electorate of Hanover.[39] Moreover, Murray had earned the King's trust and esteem by his loyal service as an officer of the Crown for fourteen years and his consistent support of the King's authority and prerogatives. It is also quite possible that Lady Mansfield's sister, Lady Bell, who handled financial and business affairs for Princess Amelia, the King's sister, exerted her influence on Murray's behalf, either through the princess or through her own social relationships with others at the court.[40]

On 20 October, Newcastle, thinking chiefly of the imminent dissolution of his ministry, gloomily told Murray: "My heart bleeds for the King, for my country, and for you. All my endeavours in my new situation shall be to serve the King, which includes the public too. As I have lived, I hope to die marked as your friend. But I dread universal ruin."[41] Newcastle, for all his expressions of self-pity, had acted honourably; he had kept his promise to Murray. Newcastle and Hardwicke had both put their own interests and preferences aside and had made a strong effort to overcome the King's reluctance to make Murray a peer. Murray wrote to Hardwicke: "It is impossible to say how much I feel your Lordship's great goodness and attention to me throughout this whole affair. The business of my life at all times, and on all occasions, shall be to show [my] gratitude."[42]

Both Newcastle and Murray had been correct in believing that the ministry would soon fall. It is doubtful whether Murray's departure made much difference; the military and naval defeats in Europe and North America had doomed the ministry in any event. In November 1756 Newcastle resigned, only to return to power the following year in a political alliance with his former opponent William Pitt.

On 25 October 1756, the King elevated Murray to the nobility as Lord Mansfield, Baron of Mansfield, and also appointed him chief justice of the Court of King's Bench.[43] (From here on in this book, Murray will be referred to as Mansfield.) The name Mansfield came from a small town in Nottinghamshire where Newcastle owned a manor, thus underscoring the fact that Lord Mansfield owed his peerage to his political sponsor.[44] A baron was a nobleman, but he stood on the lowest rung of the ladder of the nobility; on 7 December Lady Mansfield, who was the daughter of an earl, a much higher rank, wrote self-deprecatingly to Mansfield's nephew (her excitement and delight may have caused her to abandon any attempt at punctuation): "I am now at the fagg end of the nobility ... No one can rejoice more than I do that your Uncle amidst all the Confusions etc. is now got safely into Port or rather you please the Haven where I have long earnestly wish'd him to be ... The Motto bien choisis and the Promotion Universally applauded. What more is wish: but that he may long very long live and enjoy a Post which he already fills with much Dignity."[45] In the next thirty-two years, her wish would be granted.

Mansfield had not yet been appointed a serjeant-at-law, the highest rank of barrister. According to tradition, a chief justice had first to be a serjeant-at-law, so on Monday morning, 8 November, he received this additional honour at Westminster. At eight o'clock the same evening Mansfield was sworn in as chief justice by Lord Hardwicke at Hardwicke's house on Great Ormond Street, in the presence of the other three justices of the Court of King's Bench and most of the offices of the court.[46] This was followed by a "grand entertainment" at Lincoln's Inn, attended by the lord chancellor and numerous judges, lawyers, politicians, and members of the nobility.[47] This party not only marked Mansfield's appointment as chief justice but also his farewell to Lincoln's Inn, where he had received his legal education and had been a member for thirty years. He took the occasion to offer gracious praise to his legal mentor, Chancellor Hardwicke,[48] in whose court he had practised for over twenty-five years and who had helped persuade the King to bestow on him his new title of Baron Mansfield:

> If I have had, in any measure, success in my profession, it is owing to the great man who has presided in our highest courts of judicature the whole time I attended the bar. It was impossible to attend him, to sit under him every day, without catching some beams from his light. The disciples of Socrates, whom I will take the liberty to call the great lawyer of antiquity, since the first principles of law are derived from his philosophy, owe their reputation to their having been the reporters of the sayings of their master. If we can arrogate nothing to ourselves, we can boast the school we were brought up in; the scholar may glory in his master, and we may challenge past ages to show us his equal.[49]

The appointment of a new chief justice involved elaborate arrangements, at considerable expense to the appointee. He was expected to give commemorative rings to members of the royal family and the invitees to the "feast" at Lincoln's Inn. Wine – claret burgundy, champagne, port, and "sack" (Spanish dry wine) – had to be bought for the feast and was required, by tradition, to be sent to the other judges and serjeants. Then there was the appointment of clerks and other court officers, whose compensation consisted not only of salaries but also a cut of the court fees. These included a "tipstaff," whose chief duty was to accompany the chief justice whenever he went out in public. The chief justice was expected to have his own coach made; the coach of one of Mansfield's predecessors cost upwards of £500 and was so heavy that it needed two strong and active horses.[50]

Lord Mansfield presided for the first time as chief justice of the Court of King's Bench on 11 November 1756.[51] Eight days later, he was sworn in as a member of the King's Privy Council; this was a largely ceremonial appointment because by the eighteenth century the Privy Council, consisting of over eighty members, had mainly formal functions.[52] On 1 December, Mansfield took his seat in the House of Lords.[53] At the age of fifty-one, he had achieved his great ambition and was ready to begin a judicial career. But far from thinking he had won the prize of his life, Mansfield believed that he was only beginning the race.[54] He was right: he would go on to serve thirty-two years as a judge and irrevocably change the English common law. A fuller understanding of that accomplishment certainly invites a closer look at Mansfield's extraordinary judicial career, but equally consequential is his political and personal life.

9

The Judge as Politician

Lord Mansfield acts so shuffling a part that he has no credit with any party.

Earl of Sandwich, in a letter to Henry Fox

Although Mansfield preferred the more cloistered environment of the court to the tumult of the political arena, he never lost his taste for power and influence. The notion of separation of powers was virtually unknown in eighteenth-century England. It was not considered abnormal or unethical for a sitting judge to involve himself in politics as a supporter, and even member, of the ministry.[1] In fact, during his first twenty years on the bench, Mansfield played an even more significant role in foreign and domestic politics than he had as solicitor general or attorney general. As a member of the House of Lords, and at times of the Cabinet, Mansfield was constantly involved in the legislative and executive functions of the government. His influence was felt not only in debate in the House of Lords but also as a friend and confidant of several of the Whig magnates who ruled the country and as an unofficial adviser to King George II and, from 1760 on, to his grandson and successor, George III.

Although Mansfield had no qualms about himself as a judge being involved in politics, he did not believe that juries could be trusted in political cases. James Boswell asked him in 1773 whether a jury should have decided a certain case. Mansfield answered, "Yes, a jury if directed." Boswell asked, "Do juries always take direction, My Lord?" Mansfield replied, "Yes. Except in political causes where they do not at all keep themselves to right and wrong."[2] Mansfield may have been thinking of the seditious libel cases in which he had strictly limited the jury's role.[3] And in his old age, referring to the impeachment of his friend Warren Hastings, Mansfield expressed the view that there could be no justice in a political trial.[4]

Usually, Mansfield was able to combine his judicial and political activities without difficulty. One reason was that most trials were short, typically completed in a matter of hours or even less. For example, in July 1767, when he had a matter to discuss with the Bishop of Durham and the Duke of Newcastle, he wrote to Newcastle: "I have three special jury causes for Wednesday, but I will do everything possible to be able to finish them so as to be with the Bp. of D before 2 & come with him to Claremont [Newcastle's residence], & stay all night."[5] On some occasions, however, political obligations required him to forgo his judicial duties. In May 1773, a newspaper reported that Judge Ashurst sat in King's Bench for Mansfield, who was obliged to attend a council at the King's St James's Palace.[6]

Beyond that, he found time to draft statutes. In 1767, after George Grenville had been dismissed as prime minister and was actively opposing the government's policies, Mansfield gave him detailed advice regarding the language of a resolution that Grenville was proposing to introduce in Parliament. The subject of the resolution is not clear, but it appears to have pertained to the ministry's American policy.[7] When the Duke of Norfolk needed a parliamentary Act for the endowment, regulation, and enlargement of Sheffield Hospital, Mansfield drafted it for him in less than half an hour, while walking up and down the room.[8]

Mansfield's maiden speech in the House of Lords was occasioned not by a high affair of state but by an incident that, though trivial, shows his steadfast devotion to the monarchy. It was (and still is) traditional for the monarch to address the opening of Parliament, giving a speech on government policy that was actually written for him (or her in the case of a reigning queen) by the ministry. A spurious version of the King's Speech had been printed and sold in the streets, and there was talk in Parliament of starting a legal proceeding against the anonymous author. The King found the whole affair funny, saying: "I hope the man's punishment will be of the mildest sort, for I have read both speeches, and, as far as I understand them, the spurious speech is better than the one I delivered." But Mansfield was not amused. The author and publisher of the satire, he said, should be sent to prison and the speech burned in the Palace Yard by the common hangman: "Such an insult to the Crown and the two Houses [of Parliament], if taken notice of, could not be passed over or dealt with more leniently."[9] It is not known whether anyone was punished for writing or publishing the spurious speech, or whether its author was ever identified.

Less than a year after he was appointed chief justice, Mansfield performed what has been called his greatest service to the state.[10] He helped create the successful Newcastle–Pitt wartime ministry that led Britain during the Seven Years' War, during which Britain added India and Canada to its empire. In late 1756, with Britain at war with France, the Duke of Newcastle resigned as prime minister and was replaced by a caretaker ministry nominally under the Duke of Devonshire as prime minister but actually run by Pitt as secretary of state. Newcastle wished to return to power but was the target of public outrage for the loss of Minorca. Many thought that the real blame should be placed on Newcastle for not providing Byng with adequate naval forces and supplies.[11] Newcastle's position also was undercut by British military defeats at the hands of the French in North America and by diplomatic setbacks in Europe, particularly the loss of Austria as an ally.[12] He was also the victim of bad luck: a poor harvest and rising food prices fueled anger against the government.[13]

A court martial had convicted Byng of negligence but acquitted him of cowardice. Nevertheless, he was sentenced to death. His fate hung in the balance while the House of Lords debated whether to recommend that the King exercise mercy. By throwing all the blame on Byng and refusing to take any steps to prevent his execution, Newcastle hoped to divert public anger away from himself,[14] and Mansfield did all he could to help Newcastle. In December 1756, Mansfield told Pitt's sister that the King should not intervene to save Byng's life;[15] and on 14 February 1757, Mansfield told Lord Holdernesse, one of the two secretaries of state (the other being Pitt), that none of Byng's judges had any doubt about imposing the sentence of death.[16] This was untrue: three members of the court martial had already asked the King to commute Byng's sentence.[17]

When the House of Lords met on 1 March to consider whether to recommend mercy, Mansfield opposed the measure. He said that it was the duty of the Lords to step between the Crown and the people to block the King's intervention.[18] He denounced Byng's conduct, declaring that some naval captains would rather blow up their ships than retreat or be captured. He then proposed that the members of the court martial be called to the House and asked just two questions: first, whether, before they sentenced

Byng, they knew of any matter that would show that the sentence was unjust or procured by unlawful means; and, second, whether they thought themselves restrained by their oath from disclosing any such matter. In other words, Mansfield was cleverly trying to restrict the questions that the peers asked Byng's judges, giving them the difficult choice of either confirming the death sentence or admitting that they had imposed it illegally.

When the members of the court martial were called one by one before the House, each answered "no" to the first question (that they did not believe their conviction of Byng was unlawful) but, in response to questions by other members of the House, they made clear that they favoured mercy. They had sentenced Byng to death thinking that the sentence would never be carried out.[19] In an era when dozens of crimes carried the death penalty, it was not uncommon for judges to couple a guilty verdict with a recommendation for mercy.[20]

Horace Walpole, who hated Mansfield and accused him of "envy, jealousy, avarice, revenge, and treachery,"[21] commented acidly on his ferocity toward Byng: "One should not suppose that Lord Mansfield acted on personal motives, or from a desire of screening Newcastle ... As it is observed that timorous natures, like those of women, are generally cruel, Lord Mansfield might easily slide into rigour on this as he did on other occasions, when he was not personally afraid."[22] While Byng's conduct had not been beyond reproach, in reality he had become Newcastle's scapegoat. The King refused to grant mercy, and on 14 March 1757, Byng was executed by a firing squad on the quarterdeck of his ship, the *Monarque*, at the Portsmouth naval base.[23] Voltaire commented on Byng's execution: "In this country [England] it is useful to kill an admiral from time to time to encourage the others."[24]

The first few months of 1757 were occupied with a complex jockeying for power among the Duke of Newcastle, who controlled the House of Lords; Henry Fox, the leader of the House of Commons; Lord Waldegrave, a courtier and a favourite of the King; and William Pitt, the most dynamic and popular statesman of the day. The Devonshire–Pitt ministry was simply a stopgap, awaiting the formation of a permanent government. But there were difficulties.

Newcastle, though out of office, was the most powerful political figure in the country, with enough clout to topple any government he disliked.[25] Fox was a powerful and capable politician with tact, good temper, and broadness of mind. Although he despised lawyers and never lost an opportunity to show his aversion, he was an able advocate and could do battle with them on their own ground.[26] But he had little experience in foreign affairs, and a reputation for corruption.[27] Waldegrave, though close to the King, had little support in Parliament. Finally, as mentioned earlier, the King, who in the eighteenth century still had the power to choose his ministers, disliked Pitt for his attacks on the King as a foreigner who used the monarchy to promote the interests of his beloved electorate of Hanover.[28]

Mansfield acted as an intermediary among the players in the evolving political drama.[29] Newcastle at first suggested forming a ministry with Fox, with himself leading the Whigs in the House of Lords and Fox in the House of Commons, while Mansfield would be member of the Cabinet.[30] Because the contentious debate over Byng's fate continued to make Newcastle vulnerable to attack, Mansfield dissuaded him from trying to form such a ministry. On 5 March, he warned Newcastle that if he formed an administration without any certainty of real support from his new colleagues he would be "laying [his] head upon a table to be struck at."[31] Newcastle, recognizing Mansfield's "great good sense and great affection upon the subject," asked that Mansfield's advice be forwarded to the King.[32] Waldegrave accordingly told the King that it would be impossible to form a Newcastle–Fox ministry. Newcastle asked Mansfield to see Fox and convince him that "it would be madness for him, or us, to engage in anything till the inquiry [over Byng] is over."[33]

The jostling for position continued even after Byng's execution, with Mansfield and Hardwicke both guiding Newcastle through the crisis. On 26 March, Newcastle asked Mansfield to look over a draft of a letter he was about to send to the King.[34] Although we do not know the letter's subject matter, it most likely concerned his reluctance and/or inability to form a ministry. When the King received the letter he asked Waldegrave to ascertain Mansfield's opinion.[35] As it turned out, the King soon learned Mansfield's opinion directly from him.

On 8 April 1757, Henry Legge, a veteran politician and supporter of Pitt, resigned as chancellor of the exchequer (the equivalent of the Canadian minister of finance or the United States secretary of the treasury). The King summoned Mansfield to his "closet" (the room at Kensington Palace where he conducted his private business) and appointed him as a temporary replacement for Legge. So, while continuing to serve as chief justice, Mansfield added an important ministerial post to his responsibilities.

When appointed to the bench a year earlier, Mansfield became a member of the King's Privy Council, composed of about sixty notables, but not a member of the Cabinet. Given its size, the Privy Council was ill adapted for advising the King or for making and executing policy. In the late seventeenth century, the King had begun to summon five or six of his privy councillors for secret deliberations. This group became known as the Cabinet, or Cabinet Council. Originally just a subcommittee of the Privy Council, by the middle of the eighteenth century, the Cabinet had emerged as an independent part of the executive, executing most of the tasks previously performed by the Privy Council.[36]

During the eighteenth century, the size of the Cabinet fluctuated from about thirteen to twenty-one members.[37] After the first quarter of the century, the Cabinet met as frequently as the leading ministers wished, usually without the King's presence. According to historian Turner: "[A] small group of principal members predominated, and after a time tended to form an inner group apart ... [A] vast variety of business, all the important matters concerning the government of the realm, was transacted."[38] At Cabinet meetings, everyone had a chance to speak, and then they would consider and debate the issue and finally put it to a vote.[39]

The King, who had the sole power to appoint and remove members of the Cabinet, named Mansfield as a member in December 1757.[40] He remained a member for the next two decades, during the Seven Years' War and the turbulent years leading up to and during the American Revolution. He was appointed to the Cabinet in his individual capacity "as Lord Mansfield, not as chief justice."[41] Holding a specific ministerial post did not automatically entitle the official to membership in the Cabinet and, conversely, a person could be a member of the Cabinet without holding a specific government office. Mansfield's appointment to the Cabinet came several months *after* he had resigned as interim chancellor of the exchequer.[42] In a proposal for a new ministry in 1767, Mansfield and two others were described as "Cabinet Councillors Extraordinary."[43]

A few days after his hour-long meeting with the King on 8 April, Mansfield replayed the meeting for Newcastle over dinner. After paying Mansfield several compliments, the King took the opportunity to complain about Newcastle. Newcastle had refused not only to form a ministry, said the King, but had even refused to support those who were willing to do so. According to Mansfield's account, he loyally defended Newcastle, saying that Newcastle had been unwilling to come back into the government because he feared he would not be able to do the King any real service by it.[44] The King was not persuaded and asked Mansfield whether, if Newcastle were to go into opposition, the Whigs in the House of Commons would follow him. Mansfield, refusing to shy away from telling unpleasant truths, told the King that the Whigs would indeed follow Newcastle into opposition. This clearly was not the answer the King wanted to hear, and he made no reply.[45]

Newcastle, who believed that his enemies had been telling the King lies about him, was grateful to Mansfield for defending him. "It is a good comfort to me," he wrote to Mansfield, "to find that [the King] does justice to your zeal and abilities for his service; and that he will hear one, so able to give him good advice, and so ready upon all occasions ... to do justice to his friends, and particularly to myself."[46]

Even out of office, Newcastle, who had been a secretary of state for thirty-five years and still held the strings of patronage in his hands, was the most powerful political figure in the land. No ministry could be formed without him, but Mansfield shrewdly saw that Newcastle had to use his political power with extreme caution. A few days after meeting with the King, he advised Newcastle not to try to form a ministry unless he had the King's support. His letter to Newcastle goes far to explain why Newcastle and so many others relied on his judgment and followed his advice. The letter illuminates Mansfield's common sense, ethical standards, and political wisdom. His instinctive understanding of a political situation and its likely result was close to being perfect. His letter also illustrates the emphasis he always placed, in law as well as in politics, on establishing a principle for guidance in one's conduct, rather than being blown one way or the other by different circumstances or different persons' advice.

After referring to "the present nice difficult and dangerous situation you are in," Mansfield wrote to Newcastle:

> Unless you can fix a principle of action in your own breast and resolutely pursue it, you will be torn and distracted by variety of councils.
>
> All advice takes a tincture from the temper and motives of the giver, tho' well meant. The best intentioned friends are ingenious to support their wishes by refinements. Different opinions, tho' sincere, cast false colours upon the subject. It is impossible to be easy or act wisely without a determined ruling object.
>
> If ever your Grace returns to power unless it be with the King's favorable opinion, and by his inclination for his own sake; unless it be at

> least by the acquiescence of Leicester House [a shorthand reference to the separate court and centre of political power of the nineteen-year-old Prince of Wales, and his mother, the dowager Princess of Wales]; and as much with the good will of the best part of the people ... you had better end your days in an honourable retreat, for under any other circumstances you could have no comfort in place ...
>
> It has always been a favourite maxim of yours that honesty was the best policy. It is emphatically so upon the present occasion. The wisest man could not devise for you so cunning, so political a plea, as ... following the bent of your own inclination and character, by acting a clear and honest part.

Mansfield went on to say that Newcastle would be miserable if he forced himself upon the King. "But I will go further. To mix in factious opposition, after so many years of honourable service, would blast your fame and reputation forever."[47]

A month later Mansfield outlined for Newcastle a plan for a new ministry. Since neither Pitt nor Fox had the necessary support to form a government on their own, Mansfield told Newcastle that a Newcastle–Pitt government, with Newcastle as prime minister and Pitt as secretary of state, might just work. Even if it did not work, Newcastle would enhance his reputation by proposing it. According to historian J.C.D. Clark: "In either case, Newcastle held the balance. Pitt could destroy a ministry; only Newcastle could create one."[48]

Meanwhile, the King had concluded that the only solution to the Cabinet crisis was to allow Fox to form a new ministry. On 11 June 1757, Mansfield went to Kensington Palace simply to tender his resignation as temporary chancellor of the exchequer, but the meeting changed British history. Fox, who expected to be named prime minister that day, was waiting in the King's anteroom to receive Mansfield's seals of office, but first the King wanted to see Mansfield in private. The King lamented about the "melancholy" political situation and asked Mansfield what he thought. According to Mansfield's account of the meeting, "I did so very sincerely and made a good impression."[49] He laid out the whole situation before the King and told him that there would be general apprehension and even violence if Pitt were forced to resign and Fox were to form a government on his own.[50] Although the King despised Newcastle as a bumbler and hated Pitt, he realized he had no alternative but to follow Mansfield's advice. He told Mansfield to remain as chancellor of the exchequer for the time being and gave him full power to negotiate with Pitt and Newcastle to form a ministry – the very plan that Mansfield had proposed to Newcastle.[51]

Thus, Mansfield was the architect of the highly successful Newcastle–Pitt war ministry. Writing to Mansfield ten years later, Newcastle still recalled with gratitude the crucial role that Mansfield had played that day:

> I remember the great part which your Lordship took upon the same occasion, in the late reign, and the great success which immediately attended it.
>
> I remember when your Lordship went into the King's closet, to give back the Chancellor of the Exchequer's Seal, and when Mr Fox waited without, to receive it, that your Lordship, urged by a true zeal for his Majesty's interest and service, said that to the King, which made his Majesty refuse to take the Seal from your Lordship. His Majesty then employed your Lordship to go to us from him, and reinstated his former Ministers.[52]

Mansfield left the King's closet still holding his seals of office as chancellor of the exchequer, quickly whispering the outcome of the meeting to the astonished and increasingly angry Fox.[53] By chance, Mansfield met Newcastle as he passed Hyde Park Corner (whether on horseback – Mansfield's favourite mode of transportation – on foot, or in a carriage we do not know) and told him what had occurred. He then stopped by the homes of several Cabinet officers and told them not to hand in their resignations.[54] Although three days later, Mansfield's role of chief mediator in forming a Cabinet was handed over to Hardwicke, whose political and personal relationship with Newcastle was longer and closer than his own, Mansfield continued to be involved in handling the complex arrangements of creating a new ministry. On 14 June, Devonshire, the outgoing prime minister, used Mansfield as an intermediary with the King to lay before him a plan for a ministry that would be satisfactory to Hardwicke.[55]

The plan was presented to the King the next day: the new ministry included Pitt as secretary of state and Newcastle as prime minister.[56] Mansfield was to be a member of the Cabinet; and the Earl of Winchilsea, Mansfield's brother-in-law, first lord of the admiralty, though Pitt replaced him later that year. For the next four years. Pitt was in general charge of the conduct of the Seven Years' War, a global war with France, which included military and naval operations in Europe, North America, India, and the Caribbean. Like Churchill two centuries later, Pitt was a dynamic wartime leader, but one who was not universally admired. His character was flawed by political opportunism and "the ability increasingly to convince himself that his own interest and the national interest were one and the same."[57] But Pitt's power was not supreme. It was circumscribed by the development of a system under which ministers managed particular departments, such as the admiralty, ordnance, and treasury, and reported directly to the King, who remained head of the executive branch of the government.[58]

Newcastle, though prime minister in name, contented himself with handling patronage and election matters. Fox was palmed off with the highly lucrative consolation prize of paymaster of the forces, thereby ending his ambition for higher office. He held the office throughout the Seven Years' War, taking full advantage of its perquisites by using public funds to make speculative investments. By the end of the war, he had amassed a personal fortune of nearly £400,000, while leaving the office with a debt of £500,000.[59]

Mansfield resigned as chancellor of the exchequer on 2 July, and Legge resumed his old post. Nonetheless, Newcastle wanted Mansfield to remain in the Cabinet, in part to reinforce his own influence as a counterweight to Pitt's.[60] Pitt, despite being Mansfield's old enemy, respected his ability and supported his membership in the Cabinet.[61] In September, although Mansfield had not yet been appointed to the Cabinet, Holdernesse informed him that the King, recognizing his "zeal and superior talents," had commanded him to summon Mansfield to future Cabinet meetings. Holdernesse added that Mansfield's presence would "give me more frequent opportunities of learning your Lordship's thoughts upon the various intricate and nice points of business that must frequently occur."[62] Mansfield replied with fulsome humility: "I shall always be ready to contribute my mite, to the utmost of my poor ability, for the King's service, and to assist every one of his ministers cordially and frankly."[63]

Newcastle continued to rely on Mansfield for detailed advice on many issues, although Mansfield rarely spoke up at Cabinet meetings.[64] In June 1759 Newcastle wrote to Mansfield: "I must insist that you dine with me on Monday next at Newcastle House with [Andrew] Stone only – I have too many things to say."[65] Newcastle frequently sent Mansfield state papers by messenger to review in the evening and then discuss with him the next day.[66] For example, on one day in September 1760 Newcastle sent Mansfield more than thirty documents on a variety of matters, including the war in Europe, and asked Mansfield to dine "alone" (he underlined the word) with him to discuss them.[67] A week later, he sent Mansfield another package of papers on foreign and domestic affairs to review and asked him to spend the next weekend with him at Claremont, Newcastle's palatial residence outside London, so that they could discuss the cost of the war and the dim prospects for peace.[68]

Mansfield also visited the King at Kensington Palace from time to time to discuss politics and the progress of the war with France.[69] He was included in many discussions with Newcastle and other high-ranking ministers on affairs of state, whether they were on questions of foreign policy, taxation, elections, patronage, or simply political intrigue.[70] Although he was kept busy most of the day hearing cases in court, he nevertheless found the time for these political activities. And while riding circuit as a judge far from London, Mansfield kept Newcastle informed about economic conditions in the country. In July 1758, for example, he wrote from the town of Newcastle in northeastern England: "The talk universally is of a most plentiful crop of everything except hay, and that is so scarce here."[71]

Pitt's rapprochement with Mansfield did not last long. The old animosity between the two soon reasserted itself. According to gossip passed on to Newcastle by Count Viry, the Sardinian minister to England, who seemed to know everyone in London and had "a genius for intrigue,"[72] Pitt believed that Mansfield and Hardwicke were trying to turn Newcastle against him. Newcastle learned from Viry that Pitt said he got along fine with Newcastle but sometimes two little lawyers ["deux petits avocats," i.e., Mansfield and Hardwicke] put things into Newcastle's head; but that when Pitt reasoned with Newcastle he immediately saw the light and came to agree with Pitt.[73] Newcastle told Hardwicke that he had heard through Viry of Pitt's "implacable hatred" for Mansfield "and not a great deal less" for Hardwicke, though "they" were not so open in declaring their hatred against the latter because "they may think him more out of their reach."[74] It is not clear who "they" refers to, but Newcastle most likely meant Pitt and his Grenville relatives. Mansfield, for his part, was convinced that Pitt and Secretary of State Holdernesse were using Viry to transmit to Newcastle what they wished him to hear.[75] By 1759, there was so much acrimony at Cabinet meetings that Mansfield said he would no longer attend.[76]

There were several reasons for the hostility between Pitt and Mansfield, who had once been friends and political allies. The long history goes back to 1742 when Mansfield abandoned the opposition, of which Pitt was a prominent member, to join the Whig government as solicitor general. Pitt despised Mansfield as a timid lackey of Newcastle without independent principles or policies. But Pitt did not look kindly on *any* opposition. Although he was not formally prime minister, he and Newcastle had an understanding that he would be the de facto leader of the government, and he would not tolerate any interference with or questioning of his policies, particularly those that pertained to the conduct of the war. Moreover, Pitt seems to have had an aristocratic prejudice against lawyers, as evidenced by his contemptuous reference to Mansfield and Hardwicke as "two little lawyers." The suspicion of Jacobitism still clung to Mansfield, although by the late 1750s it was probably more a political weapon to be used against him than an actual belief in his disloyalty. Many regarded Mansfield and Hardwicke as dangerous influences on policy because, without having any official responsibilities as government ministers, they had the ear of both Newcastle and the King.

Eighteenth-century British politics was based on an elaborate system of patronage.[77] The Whig oligarchs who ruled the ministry had at their disposal a large number of government positions, including jobs in the dockyards and as collectors of excise taxes, which could be used to secure votes for candidates for Parliament who were friendly to the ministry.[78] Furthermore, many members of Parliament were themselves recipients of patronage. At mid-century about 220 members of the House of Commons, or 40 per cent of the membership, were office-holders.[79] According to historian Roy Porter: "patronage was power, and patronage scarcely bothered to wear a fig leaf."[80] One entered the civil service only through the recommendation of a person of influence, through patronage, or through nepotism.[81] There were many sinecures, positions that provided a salary but required little or no work.

Newcastle, the most notorious distributor of patronage in British history, sat at the centre of this web of influence and power. Advancement in the government, the military forces, the universities, or the church was difficult if not impossible without his approval.[82] He became a master of managing elections and has been called "the most hardened of political jobbers."[83] In a period when the successful conduct of public affairs depended upon personal contacts, he knew practically everyone.[84]

Clerical appointments were a significant part of Newcastle's patronage system, earning him the sobriquet "ecclesiastical minister."[85] Archbishops and bishops of the Church of England sat (and voted) as members of the House of Lords, which had a veto over all legislation, and Newcastle made sure that only clergymen who would cast their votes loyally with the ministry would be appointed.[86] However, he "did not exercise his patronage irresponsibly or without genuine regard for the interests of the Church."[87] Those seeking an appointment had no compunction about making a direct solicitation to Newcastle, even when the existing holder of the office was still alive. Thomas Newton, a cleric and a friend of Mansfield, wrote to Newcastle: "I think it my duty to acquaint your grace that the Archbishop of York lies a-dying and ... cannot possibly live beyond tomorrow morning if so long ... I beg, I hope, I trust your Grace's kindness and goodness will be shown to one who has long solicited your favour."[88] Newton did not get the appointment but he eventually became Bishop of Bristol.

Mansfield acted as a kind of junior partner of Newcastle in distributing patronage. As time went by, he was able to exercise his patronage power independently, through his position of chief justice and his own network of political and social relationships. Many who shared in ruling the country, from the King and Newcastle on down, relied on Mansfield for personal, political, and legal advice, which was usually candid as well as astute, and this created a sense of obligation toward him. Moreover, throughout his life Mansfield was persistent in getting what he wanted, either for himself or someone he favoured. His efforts to obtain high government posts for his nephew Lord Stormont[89] are the most extreme example of his relentless use of patronage.

Mansfield's correspondence with Newcastle is full of discussion about applications for clerical appointments, not just of archbishops and bishops but also of lower-ranking clergy. The latter included, for example, the chaplain of the church at Highgate, the village near Mansfield's home of Kenwood, where Mansfield worshipped.[90] Through Mansfield, William Warburton was appointed preacher at Lincoln's Inn in 1746. His long and close friendship with Mansfield probably played a part in Warburton's advancement to a bishopric. The experience of Edward Young, a cleric and poet who tried over many years to be appointed a bishop, offers a glimpse of the interlocking relationships used to exercise influence (which in this case failed). Young enlisted Margaret Cavendish, Duchess of Portland, who was both Newcastle's cousin and Mansfield's friend, in his pursuit of an appointment. When Newcastle failed or refused to act, the duchess went to

Mansfield, who was then solicitor general. Mansfield too was unwilling or unable to persuade Newcastle to make Young a bishop, but Young kept trying for ten more years, without ever achieving his ambition.[91]

Many of those seeking clerical appointments would try to reach Newcastle through Mansfield rather than going directly to Newcastle. In November 1752 Mansfield alerted Newcastle that he would soon get a request from Henry Vane, another cousin of Newcastle and friend of Mansfield, to appoint a relative of Vane as chaplain at Cambridge University. Mansfield wrote: "He is, I think, a Fellow of Trinity College. I don't know him, but the Bishop of Chester and other heads will give him a good character. I only speak to put in before other applications. If he is otherwise fit his connections in the county make him extremely so."[92] Mansfield's influence can be seen in many other clerical appointments. In 1752, Newcastle wrote to Mansfield that he knew it would please him to hear that Richard Trevor had been made Bishop of Durham and "our friend Johnson" Bishop of Gloucester.[93]

Mansfield could also rebuff solicitations, even from old friends. When George Lyttelton, a member of his circle of friends from his days as a private lawyer, asked Mansfield to make his brother a bishop, Mansfield turned him down gently but firmly:

> I am extremely flattered by the justice you do to my sentiments in believing that would contribute my utmost endeavours to bring about what you earnestly desire. Nothing could give me greater pleasure, but indeed you overrate my interest, upon such an occasion it would not weigh at all ... I am afraid the conjunction is not propitious to your making a bishop ... I have never been wanting, from the sincere love I bear you, to try to give your brother a life where I have seen a possible opportunity. I am afraid it is looked upon as a thing that wou'd not do at present, and improper to attempt.[94]

When David Garrick asked Mansfield to appoint his brother marshal of a prison, probably the one attached to the Court of King's Bench, Mansfield turned him down with a combination of extreme candour and flattery:

> I very well know that your brother, from his universal character, is worthy of the relation he bears to you. The office of Marshal I believe to be lucrative, but the conditions are irksome to a liberal mind, and dangerous. He must live in the prison ... He must execute it by him-

self, and he is liable for all escapes, so that he must live in the worst company, and often risk his fortune upon the trust he is obliged to put in bad men. I found your brother's course of business had not led him to any connection with, or experience in, the work of that office.[95]

On 25 October 1760, King George II died at the age of seventy-seven and was succeeded by his twenty-two-year-old grandson.[96] While the old king had ceded much of his influence to his ministers and Parliament, George III attempted to reclaim power for the Crown. He diligently learned the practice of politics, believing that the king should be as knowledgeable about government affairs as his ministers.[97] George's high notions of the sovereign's prerogatives were derived in large part from the writings of Viscount Bolingbroke, the former Tory prime minister under Queen Anne in the early years of the century. Bolingbroke had expounded the notion of a "Patriot King," who would rule the country with a Parliament reduced in power, in which political parties had been abolished.[98] Bolingbroke, who had been a friend and legal client of Mansfield, influenced Mansfield's political thinking by reinforcing his inclination to support monarchical authority.

The new king was deeply devout and (unusually, for a British king) faithful to his wife. He liked to eat plain meals with his family and to go to bed early.[99] He was a patron of the arts, amassing an enormous library (which eventually was acquired by the British Museum), and he was the founder of the Royal Academy. Known popularly as "Farmer George" (both by his supporters and by satirists of his restrained and frugal manner), he collected plants and farm animals, cultivated gardens, sponsored botanic missionaries, and promoted scientific agriculture.[100]

George III's accession to the throne ended the half-century supremacy of the Whig party. In making appointments, the new king used Bolingbroke's emphasis on personal merit as a means of replacing Whigs with favoured Tories in positions of power.[101] The accession brought to power the Earl of Bute, a Scot who for the previous decade had been the confidant and constant companion of the young prince and his mother, the dowager Princess of Wales. As the minister of a young king who wanted to exert personal power, Bute was inevitably unpopular with the Whig politicians who had ruled the country for nearly half a century and who, furthermore, were not happy to see a Scot for the first time become Britain's prime minister. Bute was not helped by a coldness of manner: "In ordinary intercourse, he was proud, sullen, and unconciliatory. He never looked at those to whom he spoke, or who spoke to him." A contemporary said that he "affected a theatrical air of great importance."[102] Yet he was a conscientious, hard-working statesman, who unfortunately came to office at a time of political instability. He also was a man of taste and science, who published a nine-volume treatise on botany, and a patron of writers, artists, and architects.[103]

Although Bute did not officially become prime minister until 1762 and had little support in Parliament, the young king's almost total reliance on him gave Bute unique power from the beginning of the new reign. It was clear from the outset that the days of the Newcastle–Pitt ministry were numbered. Within six weeks of the old king's death, Newcastle recorded his belief that Bute, although not yet a Cabinet member, intended to exclude Mansfield from the Cabinet.[104] This did not happen, and in fact Mansfield's continued importance in the ministry is suggested by Lady Mary Wortley Montagu, who wrote in 1761 that she thought Mansfield was "the real director of home affairs."[105] Although that was an overstatement, it indicated that Mansfield remained close to the centre of power.

Mansfield, characteristically, approached the new political situation with circumspection. Although he remained a member, along with Lord Hardwicke and Andrew Stone, of Newcastle's inner circle of advisers, he refused to commit himself to any policy. At a Cabinet meeting in November, three weeks after the change in the monarchy, Pitt proposed to the Cabinet a wartime "expedition" and went around the room asking for the vote of each member; Mansfield was the only one who declined to state an opinion.[106]

It was in this period of change and tension that Mansfield earned a reputation for duplicitous behaviour, switching sides whenever it seemed propitious in order to maintain his own influence within the government. His lack of political conviction had been commented on much earlier. In 1754, when Mansfield was solicitor general in Newcastle's government and his leading spokesman in the House of Commons, Henry Legge, the chancellor of the exchequer, had questioned Mansfield's political loyalty, calling him "the Tory head of a Whig body."[107] But Mansfield's friend Bishop Hurd had a much more positive assessment of him: "Too good to be the leader, and too able to be the dupe, of any party, he was believed to speak his own sense of public measures; and the authority of his judgment was so high, that, in regular times, the house was usually decided by it."[108]

Within two months after George III came to the throne, Newcastle was bemoaning his lack of influence over the King, who, showing "implacable hostility" to him, had refused to grant his patronage requests.[109] Mansfield advised him not to precipitate a struggle for power with Bute but rather to form an alliance with him. He suggested that perhaps Bute wished to work as closely as he could with Newcastle without giving offence to Pitt.[110] Newcastle seems to have taken this advice, for in March 1761, without consulting Mansfield, he supported the appointment of Bute as a Cabinet member, confiding later to Mansfield that, since Bute had the real power because of his close relationship with the King, it made sense to make him "responsible with the other ministers, and therefore more dependent upon them."[111]

This uneasy situation of Newcastle and Pitt being marginalized by Bute could not last long. By the summer of 1761, Newcastle was threatening to resign as prime minister. Again, Mansfield gave him savvy – if self-serving – political advice. It will be difficult to resign and escape public reproach, wrote Mansfield. If Newcastle decided to resign he should do it carefully to avoid any suspicion that he was resigning because he was no longer getting patronage. If, on the other hand, Newcastle agreed to stay in office, he should not make any conditions, because the King would not keep any promises he might make; and further, "the mention of terms destroys every public ground upon which you can stay in or go out with dignity."[112]

While the wary Newcastle took Mansfield's advice and temporized, the imperious Pitt had had enough. After learning of a secret treaty between France and Spain, Pitt proposed to the Cabinet in October 1761 that Britain make a pre-emptive strike against the Spanish fleet and colonies. When Bute and others opposed him, Pitt resigned, saying, "I will be *responsible* for nothing that I do not *direct*," thus bringing to an end a four-year ministry that had brought England unparalleled military and naval successes.[113] Newcastle stayed on for several more months, while Mansfield considered whether it might not be wiser to join Bute rather than oppose him.

Meanwhile, Bute, being sure of the King's support, waited for the right moment to strike at the Whigs. A preliminary peace treaty with France had been drawn up and approved by the King and Bute. Even though it enabled Britain to keep most of the huge gains it had acquired through military victories, including Canada, India, and several islands in the West Indies, Newcastle and Pitt (who remained powerful figures in Parliament) both opposed the treaty, wanting to take an even tougher line. The City bankers who had financed the war wanted peace, as did Mansfield.[114]

Another contentious issue was Britain's continued financial support of Prussia in its war with France and Austria on the European continent. In early 1762, Mansfield urged Newcastle not to continue subsidizing the Prussian army. Newcastle and Hardwicke, however, believed that Britain should not renege on a promise of support made to King Frederick the Great. Mansfield eventually agreed to the payments; Newcastle held fast but was overruled by Bute.[115] Seeing that he no longer had the support of other members of the Cabinet, Newcastle, again following Mansfield's advice, decided it was time to resign as prime minister.[116] When he told King George of his decision, the King answered coldly, without a word of thanks for Newcastle's services to the country for four decades: "Then my Lord, I must fill up your place as well as I can."[117] Newcastle resigned on 26 May 1762, to be succeeded by Bute.

Newcastle asked his followers to resign with him. Some did, but Mansfield stayed on, raising bitter feelings in Newcastle, who had brought Mansfield into politics and had been the principal promoter of his career from the time he became solicitor general and a member of Parliament twenty years earlier. It is difficult to disagree with a historian's comment that Mansfield "pursued a Machiavellian policy, clinging to Newcastle and Pelham as long as they had any power left, and abandoning them as readily to pay court to every new favourite, cultivating Whig connections with Tory principles."[118] Cracks in his relationship with Newcastle had begun to appear even before Newcastle's resignation. On 3 May 1762, Mansfield had to deny to Newcastle that he had been meeting with politicians behind Newcastle's back on the issue of Britain's participation in the European war.[119] Newcastle seems to have been satisfied with Mansfield's denial, for on the following day he acknowledged that Mansfield was acting as an intermediary between various groups in order to keep the ministry together.

The role Mansfield played was typically ambivalent. Having advised Newcastle to resign, Mansfield now told Bute that letting Newcastle go was a mistake. If Bute had allowed Newcastle to continue playing at being prime minister, he said, Bute could have secretly enjoyed the substance of power. The gradual introduction of Tories into all the government departments, Mansfield said, could have been accomplished more easily if Newcastle, the Whig leader, remained the ostensible leader of the government.[120]

Mansfield's decision to remain in the Cabinet after Newcastle resigned caused a temporary breach in their long-standing friendship. Newcastle was dismayed by Mansfield's conduct, which he regarded as disloyal as well as "mysterious, lamenting, but always concluding for, in support, of *this*, or perhaps any Administration."[121] A few months after he resigned, Newcastle wrote to Attorney General Charles Yorke, naming his "very few" best friends but not including Mansfield as one of them.[122] When the preliminary peace treaty was debated in the House of Lords on 9 December, the two former friends and political associates found themselves on opposite sides of the debate, Mansfield supporting the Bute ministry, making "a fine defence of the treaty," while Newcastle and Hardwicke opposed it. The Lords approved the treaty.[123]

Meanwhile, the Whig hegemony over English politics, which dated from the accession of George I in 1714, was rapidly being dismantled. On 31 October 1762, the King and Bute suddenly dismissed from court and government positions anyone who had been allied with Newcastle or his deceased brother, Henry Pelham. This coup d'état, which historians call "the slaughter of the Pelhamite innocents," has been described as one of the most momentous decisions of George III's reign.[124]

Although Mansfield had been Newcastle's protege and intimate adviser for twenty years, he escaped the carnage and remained in the Cabinet as its legal adviser. Just as he had abandoned Pitt and the "Boy Patriots" in 1742 in order to join the government, so twenty years later he abandoned Newcastle and the Whigs in order to ally himself with George III and Bute. A satire on Bute's ministry, written in late 1762, called Mansfield (along with Lord Chancellor Hardwicke) a "trimmer [who] marched with great dexterity in a kind of zig zag, but could never go the straight road."[125]

In 1763, Bute's ministry, lacking support from the Whig magnates, came to an end, although the King continued to seek Bute's private advice for a few more years.[126] Mansfield again switched sides. Declining to speak up for Bute in the House of Lords and seeing Bute's situation as perilous, Mansfield was unwilling to endanger his own political position for Bute's sake.[127]

Mansfield's relationship with the new king had not begun auspiciously. George III's attitude toward him was at first cold and suspicious. In June 1762, a few weeks after Newcastle's resignation, the King expressed belief that Mansfield had entered into a "league" against Bute that had been formed by Newcastle, Hardwicke, Pitt, and the Duke of Cumberland (the King's uncle).[128] When Mansfield failed to attend a Cabinet meeting, the King charged him with disrespect to his royal person. Mansfield explained, rather unpersuasively, that he did not attend because he was not sufficiently acquainted with the dispatches (on foreign affairs) that had been sent to him while on circuit as a judge.[129] After an audience with Mansfield in November 1762, the King wrote scathingly to Bute: "I was glad when I got rid of him. He is but half a man; timidity and refinement make him unfit for the present turbulent scene. He, I am certain, feels that, and therefore cries out against everything but *moderation*."[130] And two months later, the King, agreeing with Pitt that vanity was one of Mansfield's faults, wrote of Mansfield's "own opinion of his superiority of abilities over the rest of the world."[131]

By March 1763, however, the King had begun to warm up to Mansfield: he noted approvingly that Mansfield had supported Bute's advice concerning the peace treaty negotiations; and in April the King asked that Mansfield be given an advance copy of his speech to Parliament, so that he would not first learn of it when it was delivered; the King also declared himself to be "much hurt" by a request from Bute that he not speak to Mansfield on "the subject I have most at heart."[132] It is not clear what that subject was, but it may have involved Cabinet appointments after Bute's resignation as prime minister a few days earlier. Within the space of a few months, the value of Mansfield's pragmatic and astute advice and the pleasure of his company turned George III's initial contempt into respect. In August 1763, it was observed as a matter of interest that the King spent over an hour in private with Mansfield before holding his royal levee.[133]

During the first few years of his reign, George III had a succession of short-term prime ministers. His inability to establish a stable government was due, at least in part, to a difference of opinion between the King and his ministers as to the limits on the King's power.[134] When Bute resigned in April 1763, he was succeeded by George Grenville, Pitt's brother-in-law and Mansfield's old friend from the days when all three were out of sympathy with the Walpole ministry. History has been unkind to Grenville, whose ministry saw the enactment of the American Stamp Tax, one of the key events leading to the American Revolution.[135] Grenville was a competent, indefatigable politician, but he lacked imagination and political sensitivity. It was perhaps his misfortune to be "the wrong man in the wrong place at the wrong time."[136] Grenville was jealous of Bute's continued influence even while no longer in office; he complained to the King that he had only the appearance but not the reality of power, since the King continued to rely on Bute for advice.[137]

Although Grenville's ministry was at first considered temporary, he remained prime minister for two years. During the summer of 1763, George III was trying to bring Pitt, who had enormous popular support, back into the government. This was the time when Pitt and Mansfield were at odds over the seditious-libel prosecution of John Wilkes for publishing criticism of the government.[138] Pitt told Newcastle that he would not sit in a Cabinet meeting with Mansfield; he said that freedom of the press was an essential part of the English constitution and liberty of the subject, and on this issue he had an irreconcilable disagreement with Mansfield.[139] According to Horace Walpole (who disliked Mansfield and whose statements were not always reliable), Pitt also told the King that Mansfield was a Jacobite who planned to ruin the King's family.[140]

Not surprisingly, Newcastle refused to lift a finger on behalf of his former protege, writing to Hardwicke that "Mansfield's behaviour to the public, in the support he had given to ... Bute and his ministry, and his particular conduct towards me, had been such that I should not think myself concerned to keep ... Mansfield in the Cabinet Council."[141] The King continued to seek Mansfield's advice, in August sending him to study, while he was on circuit, a proposed marriage contract between his sister Princess Augusta and the Prince of Brunswick.[142]

A month later, however, Mansfield asked the King for permission to withdraw from the Cabinet, and the King consented.[143] It appears that Mansfield did not resign his Cabinet position, but asked only to be excused from participating in Cabinet deliberations. Meanwhile, negotiations regarding the makeup of the new ministry went on while Pitt attempted – as it turned out unsuccessfully – to form a new government. Opinion was divided as to whether Mansfield should be a member of any new ministry, some expressing anger that a man of Mansfield's abilities should be excluded,[144] others deploring his timidity and apparent lack of principle. "Lord Mansfield acts so shuffling a part," wrote Lord Sandwich, "that he has no credit with any party."[145] At one meeting, Newcastle reported, "they all agreed that ... Mansfield wanted courage so much, that he could go thro' with nothing."[146] Despite his growing prestige as a judge, he was regarded with disdain by many of the leading politicians for his lack of loyalty to any person or party.[147]

In 1766, George III raised Pitt to the nobility as Earl of Chatham and appointed him prime minister. A succession of bad harvests led Pitt to use the royal prerogative to ban the export of grain from England.[148] This arbitrary act, not backed by an Act of Parliament, was challenged in the House of Lords, where Mansfield reinforced his reputation for equivocation. According to Lord March, who was present at the debate, "Mansfield trimmed in his usual manner and avoided declaring his opinion, though he argued for illegality. Lord Camden attacked him very close upon not speaking out his opinion."[149] Even the young Duke of Portland, whose mother was a lifelong friend of Mansfield, was scathing in his criticism. In a letter to Newcastle, Portland wrote of his "dislike" and "abhorrence" of Mansfield. Dismissing Mansfield's opposition to the royal prerogative, which he had heretofore always supported, Portland wrote: "Half an hour's constitutional language or indeed lawyers' talk cannot efface or obliterate the few years' public conduct that I have been a witness of, much less remove those prejudices and I must say those just apprehensions and detestation of the principles and doctrines with which he artfully endeavoured to corrupt my system of Whiggism in my tenderest years."[150]

Nevertheless, Mansfield's adeptness in political manoeuvring and the respect that the King and many others had for his acumen and judgment assured his continued influence within the government. Newcastle, his close associate for more than twenty years, thought that "his advice is preferable to any others";[151] and during the turbulent 1760s, with the swift succession of six prime ministers,[152] many other leading politicians sought Mansfield's advice on legal and political issues. During the rapid turnover of ministries and shifting of alliances among the leading political figures, Mansfield was often deeply involved in the discussions and negotiations. A minute written by Newcastle in April 1767 during the Chatham ministry gives us an idea of the extent and nature of his participation in what apparently were negotiations for the formation of a new ministry:

> Mansfield was with me last night, and told me that ... Rockingham [the previous prime minister] had been with him the night before, and when his Lordship was there, Mr Grenville [the prime minister before Rockingham] came to the door ... Mansfield would have called him in, but ... Grenville was gone and returned to ... Mansfield after ... Rockingham had left him ... Mr Grenville told ... Mansfield that he would insist upon no condition for himself (but as his friends do for him) ...

> Mansfield expressed great concern that the negotiation had not succeeded, as he always feared it would not, knowing the difficulties that must attend it ... Mansfield most strongly recommended a continuance of civility and good humour. He was of opinion that, at present, things should remain as they are; and hoped, that time, temper, and events might bring that about which, if now pushed, might not be attended with success.[153]

In September 1767, Chancellor of the Exchequer Charles Townshend died, and Lord North having refused the post, Mansfield again took it on a temporary basis. A week later North changed his mind and replaced him.[154] The King often sought Mansfield's advice, particularly on questions related to forming a ministry and the personalities involved. After two meetings with the King in November 1767, Mansfield had a long conference with George Lyttelton, an old friend and a former chancellor of the exchequer, lasting until one in the morning. Lyttelton reported on it to Lord Temple, the brother of former Prime Minister George Grenville and brother-in-law of Prime Minister Chatham. The letter tells us something not only about what Mansfield was thinking but also what his political friends thought of him:

> He seemed very desirous that the present [Chatham] ministry should not continue, but equally unwilling that the King should be forced to remove them; full of contempt for Lord Rockingham and the Duke of Richmond, of hatred to Lord Chatham and all his friends ... I tried to draw from him what had passed in his two conversations with the King; he said the King's talk to him was gracious, but loose and inconclusive. He assured your brother [George Grenville], upon his honour, that nothing important had passed. I understand he has much credit with the Dukes of Bedford and Newcastle, yet perhaps less than he thinks. His great use to our party is in the House of Lords; for in his intrigues he is warped by many different views, by managements for various connections, by a great attention to the closet [i.e., the King], and by the uncertainty, the timidity, and over-refining turn of his mind.[155]

In January 1770 the revolving door of ministries ended with Lord North taking office as prime minister, a post he held for twelve years. Modern historians have refuted the long-standing belief that North was a mere puppet of George III. While the King had the power to choose his ministers, once he had chosen them he left it to them to govern the country.[156] North was a witty, popular minister, an able debater in the House of Commons, who remained on good terms with his political opponents.[157] Nevertheless, he was one of the architects of the disastrous policy that ended with the loss of the American colonies.[158]

Mansfield was to play an important, though unofficial, role during North's ministry. He declined the post of lord chancellor in 1771,[159] as he had when it was offered to him fifteen years earlier, but he gave the King detailed advice on who should fill the post.[160] Historian Paul Langford concludes that, widely considered the "*éminence grise* of the Cabinet, [Mansfield] played a large but unofficial part in ministerial deliberations."[161] He remained a member of the Cabinet until North's ministry came to an end in 1782.

Mansfield was the prime minister's chief legal adviser, a role usually filled by the lord chancellor; and North also leaned on him for political advice. For example, in September 1781, North sent Mansfield a packet of papers with detailed information on foreign affairs, writing that he was communicating only with Mansfield, the King, and perhaps Sir Joseph Yorke (a diplomat).[162] At the age of seventy, Mansfield still had the energy to participate in political discussions and decisions, without curtailing his role as chief justice. For example, in August 1775, he returned to Kenwood from assizes at Chelmsford in Essex on a Saturday evening, and on Sunday evening travelled to London to attend a Cabinet meeting at the lord chancellor's home.[163]

As evidence of Mansfield's continued interest in the nitty-gritty of politics, his papers at Scone Palace include a list, drawn up by him in 1779, of forty-one members of the House of Lords who, though holding no government office, generally voted with the government.[164] Mansfield also had direct access to the King, who no doubt valued his intellectual power, knowledge of the political situation, and practical common sense. An unfriendly newspaper reported in 1776 that Mansfield was often with the King and described him as "a truly adulating minister; he fawns."[165]

Mansfield was so closely involved in the government that he was accused of running the country. Lord Shelburne, a future prime minister, said that Mansfield, not North, was the real prime minister;[166] and Edmund Burke charged that George III was overthrowing the constitution by resorting to a "double cabinet," ignoring his formal ministry and ruling through private advisers.[167] There can be no doubt that Mansfield was one of those to whom he was referring. Mansfield's dual role as judge and politician also came under fire from the press. The *Public Advertiser* commented in December 1777 that "a man clothed with the robe of magistracy ought not to be a politician; a political judge was an improper and dangerous engine."[168]

Mansfield's influence on British foreign policy was recognized, even exaggerated, abroad. In 1777, when war between Britain and France seemed likely, the French foreign minister, Comte de Vergennes, informed his ambassador in London that Lord North had approached another French diplomat, suggesting that means be found to calm things down. Vergennes emphasized to his ambassador how important it was to find out to what extent Prime Minister North had the confidence of Mansfield and his nephew Stormont, who was then British ambassador in Paris.[169] Evidently, the French minister believed that Prime Minister North needed Mansfield's confidence in order to be able to speak for the British government.

In 1777, the king of Poland turned to Mansfield when he beseeched the British government to save his country from its enemies. Mansfield's connection with Poland went back two decades. Stanislaw August Poniatowski, whose mother belonged to the Czartoryski family, the most powerful and eminent in Poland (known as "The Familia"), had visited England in 1754, when he was twenty-two. He became a good friend of Lord Chancellor Hardwicke's son, Charles Yorke, who took him on a tour of the English countryside and introduced him to several friends of Mansfield, including Bishop William Warburton and Lord Temple and his brother, George Grenville. Although there is no definite proof that he also met Mansfield, it seems likely that he did. Stanislaw returned to Poland a confirmed Anglophile, and he kept up his contacts with his English friends and acquaintances.[170]

In 1756, when Mansfield's nephew Lord Stormont was British ambassador in Warsaw, he met and became friends with Adam Czartoryski, Stanislaw's cousin. Adam visited England the following year, and Stormont provided him with an introduction to Mansfield, who met and had discussions with him. In Poland, Stormont also became friends with Stanislaw, who wrote to Charles Yorke that he should tell Mansfield that he loved Stormont almost as much as his own brother.[171] Thus, from the 1750s Mansfield had contacts with members of Poland's leading family and was conversant with Polish political affairs.

In 1764 Stanislaw was elected king of Poland. A sophisticated aristocrat who as a young man living in St Petersburg had been Catherine the Great's lover, he turned out to be a zealous Polish patriot and a serious reformer.[172] By 1770, Polish affairs were on the verge of disaster, as Russia, Prussia, and Austria combined to carve up Poland. Mansfield's nephew Stormont, then ambassador to Vienna, "became involved in some shadowy private diplomacy" in a futile attempt to prevent the partition.[173] Nevertheless, in 1771 each of the three countries helped themselves to a slice of Polish territory, and threatened Poland with further incursions. During this time, Mansfield continued to involve himself in Polish affairs.[174] In February 1777, King Stanislaw wrote eloquently, not to Prime Minister North or one of the secretaries of state, but to Mansfield, imploring help from the country he most admired: "Such is my unfeigned opinion of your Lordship's greatness and sensibility of mind, that tho' the decision of justice to the subjects of Great Britain is your particular province, yet I think the circumstances of a faithful ally to your country, appearing in this manner before you to complain of his violated rights will move you to exert yourself even beyond your particular duty in my favour. I ask no justice but such as is honourable for your King, and useful for your nation to grant me. What can I say more." He added in a postscript: "I have sent ... a small phial of otter of roses for Lady Mansfield. I hope there is nothing improper in this mark of esteem."[175]

Unfortunately for the Polish nation, there was nothing Mansfield could do. By the 1770s, Britain had other priorities, particularly in its colonial empire and its relations with France, and had little interest in the affairs of eastern Europe.[176] After two additional partitions in the 1790s, Poland disappeared as an independent nation until it was re-established in 1919 after the First World War. Although Mansfield had not been of any help to the Poles, they, like the French, clearly regarded him as a key political figure with decisive influence over British foreign policy.

10

Family Affairs

He has friends, relations, and dependents amply provided for.

Earl of Shelburne, speaking about Lord Mansfield in the House of Lords

The few details that are known about the forty-six years of Lord and Lady Mansfield's life together suggest that theirs was a happy and companionable marriage.[1] The affection, trust, and respect that Lord Mansfield felt for his wife are made plain in the will he executed in 1782, two years before her death. Aside from certain specific bequests, he left all his personal property to Lady Mansfield for her life, and to his nephew and heir, Lord Stormont, after her death. This was not an unusual arrangement for a rich man to make for his wife, but he took special pains to make clear in his will that she should be under no "restraint in the Enjoyment of Chattels which are consumed by using, such as Carriages, Liquor, Horses, Cows, Hay, Implements. I give her the absolute Property of all such, with power also to convert to her own use while she lives, any part of the household Goods Furniture or Plate." He also appointed her as his executrix, along with Stormont as executor.[2]

Lady Mansfield moved in a circle of educated, talented women known as bluestockings, named after the Blue Stocking Society, a literary group (comprising men as well as women). Her close friends included Mary Delany, an artist and botanist who had ties with the royal family; Margaret Cavendish-Bentinck, Duchess of Portland; and Henrietta Howard, Countess of Suffolk, the former mistress of King George II.[3]

Despite her noble ancestry as the daughter of an earl, Lady Mansfield was a home-loving, unpretentious person. At their country home of Kenwood, she arose before six every morning, spending the time until breakfast managing her dairy farm.[4] Like some other aristocratic ladies of her era, she enjoyed managing a dairy: she and her neighbour Lady Southampton used to compete as to who made the best butter.[5]

Some notion of Lady Mansfield's friendliness and warmth may be glimpsed from a letter the Duke of Newcastle wrote to a friend in 1768, saying that he hoped that during the Easter holidays he would be able to visit the Mansfield country home of Kenwood and "drink his coffee there: not in the Hall, but in my Lady Mansfield's warm Dressing room."[6] She had gone to some trouble and expense to make sure that the room was an agreeable place to have a cup of coffee: an invoice of 1757 – three years after Lord Mansfield bought the property – shows that she, not her husband, paid £22 for "taking down the old green paper and cloth shipping and putting the cloth up again; new linen ... Printed Chinese Rail Border 18 inches wide put around the blue room."[7] This evidently was *her* project for *her* room, conforming to *her* taste in home decoration.

Lady Mansfield had a friendly affection for her husband's nephew, Lord Stormont. When Stormont, then British ambassador in Warsaw, wrote to Lady Mansfield that he had bought a set of Dresden china for her, she good-naturedly chided him: "Money certainly burns in your pocket ... Were you within reach of hearing (which by the way I am very sorry you are not) you would not fail having a good scold, but as that unfortunately is not now the case, I return you many thanks for which you must allow me to call an unnecessary token of remembrance and which I never shall or can want to put me in mind of l'amiable Mi Lord."[8] And when the china dishes arrived safely five months later, she wrote that they were "inimitably pretty and plainly show you to have un Goût Exquis [exquisite taste] even in crockery ware."[9]

Lady Mansfield was not one of the very few elite women who engaged in electoral politics; nevertheless, evidence suggests that she was one of those who took an active interest in her husband's activities and acted as his confidante and perhaps also adviser, providing him with "a discreet ... combination of support, criticism, direction, and strategy."[10] Her letters to Stormont were by no means confined to household affairs; they also were full of political news and gossip. A letter written in 1757 is typical: "The present administration seems in a tottering condition. Shou'd it continue as it now is three months longer, I shall think the time I have employ'd in studying Politicks was all thrown away ... Pitt [then heading the ministry in a duumvirate with Newcastle] has been lay'd up with the Gout almost ever since he came in, consults with no Man except his brother Temple." She then goes on to comment on the ongoing court martial of Admiral Byng and to describe the manoeuvrings at the latest session of Parliament, concluding: "I'm now at the end of my paper as well as at the end of my Politicks."[11] In another letter she gives Stormont detailed tidings of an imminent change of government, including who would fill each Cabinet post;[12] and in a third letter she predicts, accurately: "Tis now confidently said an arrangement must soon be made and our old Neighbour [i.e., Mansfield's ally, the Duke of Newcastle] comes in Sharing Power with orator Pitt [i.e., Mansfield's political enemy] and his Party, which if true verifys the old saying half a loaf is better than no Bread."[13]

Her letters suggest that dinner-table conversation between Lord and Lady Mansfield included serious discussions of politics, and that she processed with intelligence and interest the information that she learned from him and others. There were those who tried to use Lady Mansfield as a way of approaching Mansfield for a favour for a friend, but she was able to rebuff them politely when she wanted to; when Lady Hervey asked her to talk to her husband on behalf of an office seeker, "she said she certainly would though she did not believe he would want to be put in mind of it."[14]

When Mansfield was a young man, his sister asked him why he would not marry a certain lady who had a fortune. He replied: "Fortune! I'll make a fortune that you have no idea of."[15] And so he did. Beginning with few assets, he accumulated enormous wealth. It came from three principal sources: fees from his legal practice; investments in mortgages; and the salary and other emoluments from his position of chief justice. He also received fees for acting as Speaker of the House of Lords when the lord chancellor was absent.[16] Even before he was appointed chief justice in 1756, his financial success as a lawyer enabled him to buy Kenwood and to live in comfort and luxury there and at his London home in Lincoln's Inn Fields (and later in Bloomsbury Square). He banked with the eminent private banking firm of C. Hoare & Co., founded in 1672 (and continuing in business in the twenty-first century).[17]

An important figure in Mansfield's life was John Way, who for more than thirty-five years kept his accounts and managed his property and investments.[18] A letter that Way wrote shortly after Mansfield's death to Stormont (who had succeeded to the title as 2nd Earl of Mansfield) provided detailed information and advice on Mansfield's investments, indicating that Way was a knowledgeable and sophisticated steward of his business affairs.[19] In addition to serving Mansfield in his personal capacity, Way received an appointment for life as chief clerk of the Court of King's Bench, the profits of which he shared with his employer, an arrangement that was not considered illegal or even unethical at the time.[20] Mansfield continued to receive these profits even after he retired from the bench; in 1791 he received £4,431 from Way, in addition to his £12,815 income from investments.[21] Through his long service for Mansfield, Way accumulated enough wealth to become a member of the gentry; in 1787 he took his wife to the fashionable resort of Bath, from where he wrote to Mansfield about social as well as business affairs.[22] In his will, Mansfield left Way a substantial bequest and an annuity.[23]

In 1786, Mansfield's total assets amounted to about £400,000 (equivalent in 2012 to around £72 million or US/CA$115 million), not counting the value of his Kenwood estate and land he owned in the county of Cheshire.[24] Most of his wealth was in mortgages. When a country gentleman asked Mansfield for investment advice, he replied: "If you are satisfied with *principal* without *interest*, buy land; if you wish *interest* with your *principal*, purchase in the stocks; but if it is your desire to have *principal* and *interest* amply secured, lay out your money in mortgages."[25]

Mortgages were both an attractive investment for lenders such as Mansfield and an important service for noble property owners. According to Langford: "the mortgage was essential to the landed family's comfort, perhaps to its survival. Upon it depended the life-style of many families who found temporary exigencies too pressing to be met from ordinary revenue ... Even a great estate might depend on mortgagees who drew their interest from the land without contributing to its political management, or accepting any responsibility for its well-being."[26] Mansfield lent money, secured by mortgages, to several of the great British noblemen who, though endowed with huge landed estates, were often short of ready cash. When Lady Mansfield's nephew the Marquess of Rockingham, who twice served as prime minister, died in 1782, his estate was said to be encumbered with £180,000 of debt, of which at least £80,000 was owed to Mansfield.[27] In 1791, Mansfield's mortgage debtors included the young Duke of Rutland, whose recently deceased father, the lord lieutenant of Ireland, had a passion for gambling; Viscount Melbourne, whose son became Queen Victoria's first prime minister; Earl Fitzwilliam, a nephew of Rockingham; and the Duke of Portland, who, like Rockingham, also served twice as prime minister.[28]

Mansfield was sometimes accused of avarice, particularly during his last two years as chief justice, when he seldom sat in court but continued to draw his annual salary of £5,000. Aside from his salary, Mansfield received substantial emoluments from his office. Upon his appointment, Mansfield had about fifty offices to fill. To assist him in court, there were several clerks, cryers, ushers, tipstaffs, and jailers, a bag-bearer, a marshal, and a train bearer; for transportation, the chief justice had a footman, a coachman, and a postillion; and for entertaining, particularly when on assizes, he had cooks and a butler.[29]

The chief justice was permitted to enrich himself through the sale of these positions, a practice that was not illegal and was sanctioned by custom.[30] In 1784, at a time when Mansfield may have been thinking of Stormont's inheritance, he assured Stormont that he (Mansfield) and the other judges on the court had no doubt that the office of clerk of the rules of the Court of King's Bench, which had been left vacant by the death of its incumbent, was saleable.[31] When Sir Dudley Ryder had been appointed chief justice in 1754, he noted in his diary that the previous tipstaff had bought his position from the chief justice for £600 or £700.[32]

Court officers were willing to buy their positions because they were able to make money from court fees. The cooks compensated themselves by padding the bills for items that they purchased. The jailer at the King's Bench prison, which was under Mansfield's supervision, was able to earn £220 a year through the sale of such things as food and drink to prisoners.[33]

Mansfield took a portion of the court fees paid by litigants. In 1780 a newspaper charged that he had amassed the enormous sum of £220,000 by "going snacks" with court officers.[34] This figure was almost certainly an exaggeration, but the basic accusation was correct. We have already seen that he shared court fees with his chief clerk. It appears from John Way's accounts that Mansfield collected between £3,000 and £5,300 annually from court fees.[35] A newspaper reported that if a man was suing to recover a debt of as little as £5, he would have to pay a fee of 11 shillings and 8 pence (a little more than half a pound) just for writing the name of the case on the marshal's list before the trial; and more than half of this amount reportedly went into Mansfield's pocket, while the remainder was shared by the marshal and the cryer.[36]

There were rumours that Mansfield invested in the ambitious Adelphi Terrace venture of the Adam brothers to build residences and warehouses along the Thames near Charing Cross.[37] Influence was brought to bear on Parliament to appropriate public funds to straighten the riverbank. The project turned out to be a financial disaster, but antipathy to the Scots fed gossip that both Mansfield and the Earl of Bute profited from the venture. The Adam brothers, Mansfield, and Bute were all Scots, and Robert Adam was not only Mansfield's friend but also the architect who had made improvements to his country home of Kenwood. But no proof has been found that Mansfield was financially interested in the Adelphi development.[38] And it would have been uncharacteristic of the prudent Mansfield to get himself involved in a real estate speculation.

Perhaps because he had no children of his own, Mansfield was always ready to help the children and grandchildren of his brothers and sisters. He was never shy about using his highly placed contacts to advance the careers of his relatives. This was not unusual in eighteenth-century England, where nepotism was rife. For example, Edward Thurlow, who served as lord chancellor while Mansfield was chief justice, managed to get his brother a bishopric, and his son and nephews also gained valuable sinecures.[39] But the peppery earl of Shelburne was actually understating the case when he said of Mansfield in the House of Lords, "he has friends, relations, and dependents amply provided for; I will not say beyond their deserts, but this I may say, much beyond their expectations."[40]

During Britain's mid-century wars, many officers owed their commissions to political influence,[41] sometimes with unfortunate results for the armed forces. On several occasions, Mansfield attempted – usually successfully – to obtain military or naval commissions for family members. At Mansfield's behest, the Duke of Newcastle used his control over patronage to help advance the careers of Mansfield's relatives. In 1745, when suppression of the Jacobite Rebellion increased the need for military officers, Newcastle asked the Duke of Cumberland, who led the army that defeated the rebellion, to appoint Mr Lindsay, a relative of Mansfield, as a lieutenant and as the commander of a regimental company.[42] Lindsay was probably a son or nephew of Sir Alexander Lindsay of Evelick, who had married Mansfield's sister Amelia. A few years later, Lindsay having risen to the rank of captain, Newcastle thanked the Duke of Devonshire for recommending to the King that he be promoted to colonel, adding: "I forgot to acquaint the Att. General [i.e., Mansfield] with it, till very lately, he will return his thanks to you, in the strongest manner."[43] In 1758, Mansfield asked Newcastle to use his influence to obtain the command of a regiment for Mansfield's nephew, a Major Lindsay, whom he described as "a very pretty man."[44]

In 1747, when Mansfield was solicitor general and a party leader in the House of Commons, he managed to obtain two appointments for a Mr Murray (a member of the numerous Murray clan who was either one of Mansfield's brothers or, more likely, a cousin) as *both* an army lieutenant and a naval officer. The commander of the lucky relative's regiment complained about the solicitor general's use of influence, telling a Cabinet member that the military/naval Mr Murray was not performing his duties in either of his two capacities, and even threatened to take the matter to the King.[45]

By far the greatest beneficiary of Mansfield's influence and family feeling was his nephew, David Murray, Viscount Stormont, who inherited the title in 1748 from his father, Mansfield's eldest brother. Although Stormont became a conscientious professional diplomat, he rose to high office almost entirely because of his uncle's powerful sponsorship. He tended to be pompous and not particularly imaginative; a newspaper article described him as "rather mulish."[46] Like many people who rose to eminence not through their own abilities, he took himself very seriously. General Paoli, the Corsican patriot who was visiting England in 1783, observed irreverently: "Lord Stormont is so stately and walks so erect because he is full of wind, and were he to stoop, would f—t."[47] A caricature, now in London's National Portrait Gallery, shows Stormont as essentially clueless, wearing an inane smile. But Stormont's limitations did not stop Mansfield from championing him at every opportunity and defending him fiercely from attacks.

Although the Stormonts were members of the Scottish nobility, that gave them little standing among the British peerage. The 1707 Act of Union between England and Scotland allowed the Scottish peers to elect sixteen representatives of their number to sit in the British House of Lords. In 1754 Stormont was elected to be one of these representative peers, but he could not pass this right to his heirs. Mansfield, having no children of his own, was determined that Stormont should inherit his British earldom and thus establish a noble family line.

Through Mansfield's influence, Stormont was successively appointed envoy to Saxony and Poland (then under the same ruler), Vienna, and Paris. In 1759, while serving as ambassador in Warsaw, Stormont married a Polish woman, Henrietta Frederica Bunau. They had one child, Lady Elizabeth Murray, born in Warsaw in 1760. Soon after Henrietta's death in 1766, Lady Elizabeth was sent to live at Kenwood. She lived there until her marriage in 1785, and Mansfield developed a special fondness for her. In 1776, at the age of forty-nine, Stormont married again, this time to Louisa Cathcart, who was only fifteen at the time. She was the daughter of Lord Cathcart, a celebrated soldier and diplomat who had been shot in the face during one of Britain's European battles against the French and was known as "Patch Cathcart" because of the black silk patch he wore to cover the scar. Stormont and Louisa had five children, including a son who eventually inherited the Mansfield title and passed it on to his heirs.

In April 1761, when the British government was choosing envoys to be sent to the Congress at Augsburg to negotiate a peace treaty to end the Seven Years' War, Mansfield complained to Newcastle that ignoring his nephew's desire for the post was a personal insult to himself: "In the disposition for the Congress ... Lord Stormont (that is I) is not only not considered, but is never so much as put upon the Lists even in discourse. I cannot in justice and honour let him throw away his time and fortune longer where he is [in Poland]; and as I find my friendship can be of no use to him, he must come to try to make his own way."[48] Newcastle replied that he was doing all he could for Stormont, but that he had met with a cold reception from William Pitt, the country's wartime leader.[49]

Mansfield persevered, writing to Newcastle a month later: "Lord Stormont's situation points him out so strong to be one of this Congress: that if he is passed by, it is impossible either at home or abroad not to consider him as slighted & disgraced ... I do not believe that Mr Pitt will make any objection to him."[50] Mansfield's persistence paid off, and in April 1761 he was able to inform Stormont that he had seen the King, "who was pleased in the most gracious manner to comply with my Request." He then carefully instructed his nephew on the etiquette regarding acceptance of the post: "It is a considerable point you [are] much obliged to Ld Bute. In your answer to the notification you will take care to write properly acknowledging the mark of the King's Grace, etc."[51] Two years later Mansfield persuaded George III to appoint Stormont ambassador to Vienna.[52] But Mansfield's attempts in the early 1760s to obtain a British peerage for him were unsuccessful.[53]

Again through Mansfield's intervention, Stormont received his most important diplomatic position, as ambassador to Paris from 1772 until March 1778, when France entered the Revolutionary War on the side of the American colonists and he was recalled. In 1774, Mansfield visited Paris to attend the festivities celebrating the accession of Louis XVI to the throne. So far as is known, it was his only foreign trip after his visit to France and Italy in 1730, shortly before he was admitted to the bar. In Paris, he was presented to King Louis XVI and Queen Marie Antoinette, who treated him with marked courtesy. By this time, his reputation as a great magistrate had spread to the Continent. On his return to England he had his portrait painted in the clothes he wore for the Paris ceremonies.[54] The admiration that the French elite felt for Mansfield was expressed a few years later, even while France was at war with Britain, by Mme Necker, the wife of the French finance minister and the hostess of a famous literary salon. In a letter to Stormont, she described Mansfield as "ce grand homme admiré de toutes les nations cheri de tous les coeurs sensibles [this great man admired by all nations and dear to all sensitive hearts]."[55]

Stormont's obligation to Mansfield was so well known that Mansfield was described in the press as Stormont's "patron."[56] In fact, as ambassador to Paris, Stormont sometimes bypassed the ministry, communicating directly with Mansfield, and Mansfield took Stormont's diplomatic letters directly to the King.[57] In 1776, when Mansfield was elevated to the title of earl, he successfully achieved his goal of assuring that his title would eventually pass on to his nephew.[58]

While serving as ambassador to France, the most coveted of all British diplomatic posts, Stormont created an effective network of intelligence agents.[59] Nevertheless, he was accused of incompetence. It was commonly believed that the French government had deceived him as to its intention to enter the American war[60] on the side of the colonists and, after the French entered the war, that Stormont had not provided his government with information about the enemy fleet. Mansfield took the criticism as a personal insult and angrily defended his nephew at a Cabinet meeting.[61] A few years later, a newspaper alleged that, while Stormont was in France, a "gentleman spy" that he had hired had sold British secrets to the French government.[62] In the course of his diplomatic career, Stormont built up an extensive knowledge of European affairs, but his ideas about British foreign policy were, according to his biographer, "always orthodox, often outdated, and at times dangerously rigid."[63]

Throughout, Mansfield did everything that he could to advance his nephew's career. On the day after the death of Lord Cathcart in 1776, whose daughter Stormont had recently married, Mansfield wrote to an unidentified friend asking her to put in a word for Stormont in order to obtain a "sinecure" that Cathcart had held.[64] It is not clear what the sinecure was or whether Stormont got it, but Mansfield's ceaseless efforts on his nephew's behalf continued. A few months after Stormont's return from France, when the Duke of Queensberry, who held the sinecure of justice general of Scotland, lay dying, Stormont asked one of the secretaries of state to recommend him to the King for this office, which required no work.[65] This time he was successful, and he held the post until his death in 1796. Although Stormont had himself solicited the sinecure, it is doubtful whether he would have received it but for the efforts of his uncle, who personally thanked the King for making the appointment.[66]

Stormont's most controversial appointment was as secretary of state for the northern department in October 1779.[67] He was one of very few career diplomats of the eighteenth century to be thus appointed.[68] This was a Cabinet position with responsibility, among other things, for foreign relations with the Protestant states of northern Europe. A year later, *The London Courant* printed a diatribe against Mansfield for promoting his nephew to this important position. The newspaper stated that Mansfield had spent twenty-five years "doing so much mischief in the different situations he filled" and reminded its readers that the new secretary of state was also a nephew of James Murray, secretary to the Jacobite Pretender.[69] Although Jacobitism was no longer a threat to Britain or its government, it was still a handy tool for Mansfield's enemies to use against him and Stormont.

At the time of Stormont's appointment, *The Morning Post* took aim on a personal level and accused him of stinginess: "A noble Scotch peer lately made an English Secretary of State has refused, it is said, to give the customary fees to the attendants at St James's, always paid by those who attain to posts of profit and consequence. This comes with rather ill grace from his Lordship, who receives upwards of £20,000 per year of this nation's money."[70] A few days later, the same newspaper expressed disbelief at Mansfield's transparent pretense that he knew nothing about Stormont's appointment.[71] Thus, supported by Mansfield, Stormont held one high office after another. The childless Mansfield looked upon him as a son, to whom he would pass on his earldom and thereby integrate the Scottish Jacobite Murray family into the emerging British state.[72]

Even while recommending Stormont for high office, Mansfield was well aware of his nephew's shortcomings; in private, he gave him detailed instructions on how he should behave and occasionally chided him. Knowing that Stormont tended to be lazy, Mansfield told him that his dispatches from Dresden, where Stormont was ambassador, should contain more detail about what King Frederick the Great of Prussia "had done or was supposed to intend; what the [king] of Poland intended [and] what advice was given by the Austrian & French ministers."[73] Another time, he wrote to Stormont: "Write fully, be Diligent and active."[74] Ever cognizant of the importance of personal relationships, he also advised his nephew to "write sometimes a private letter" to the Duke of Newcastle.[75] In 1756, when Stormont, then ambassador to Saxony but under pressure from George II to move to Warsaw, wanted an appointment to a different post, Mansfield advised him on how to approach the King: "Lay in your Pretensions [i.e., his claim] modestly, but firmly. Note the great Expence this year at Dresden, the extraordinary charge of Warsaw – desirous to serve the King at any rate."[76]

When King Frederick invaded Saxony in August 1756, King Stanislaw fled to Poland, where he was also king, and the diplomatic corps followed him there. Stormont was reluctant to leave the beautiful city of Dresden for Warsaw, and it required an instruction from King George to get him to make the move.[77] It was while Stormont was in Poland that Mansfield became thoroughly exasperated by his behaviour. Nineteen-year-old Lord Titchfield was the son of Mansfield's friend the Duchess of Portland, and the heir to one of the greatest estates in England. He had gone to Westminster School and Christ Church, Oxford, but had left Oxford without a degree because of some unspecified problem. Mansfield believed that London would be the ruin of a rich but immature young man, but that he needed to see something of the world. Since France was at war with England, he saw Poland as an alternative. Mansfield's idea, which Titchfield's parents shared, was for him to study in Warsaw under a French tutor and to live with Stormont, who would supervise him and take care of all his needs.[78]

To Mansfield's annoyance and frustration, Stormont objected when asked to have Titchfield as his house guest.[79] At this point, Lady Mansfield wrote Stormont to support her husband's wishes: "You have always so readily comply'd with every Request made to you by your Uncle that I'm persuaded Ld Titchfield will on his arrival at Warsaw find a logement chez vous [lodging in your home]. One elsewhere will by no means answer either your Uncles or his Parents purpose." At the bottom of the letter, in a different handwriting, almost certainly Mansfield's, was the following canny postscript: "Lord Mansfield desires as soon as you receive this that you will write him an ostensible letter with regard to Lord Titchfield much as your last was, which he did not care to shew upon your objection of having him in the House with you. Let it be such a one as may shew; & to avoid the appearance of its being so; mention some other indifferent things in the letter."[80] Presumably, Stormont's letter was to be shown to the Duchess of Portland.

Ten days later, Mansfield wrote another letter to his nephew and gave it to Titchfield to carry with him to Warsaw. In it he gave Stormont peremptory and detailed instructions, which tell us something not only about his views regarding the proper education and upbringing of a young man but also about his manner toward his thirty-year-old nephew, whom he treats like an errant schoolboy:

> It is impossible to express how warmly I interest myself in every thing which nearly regards the Dss Of Portland. I love Ld Titchfield for his own sake. I make it therefore my earnest request that you will return to

him the Friendship which I have shown to you … I am sure your own inclination wou'd prompt you to do every thing I wish to Ld Titchfield, independent of my request.

He is to live in yr House with you, as one of the Family. It is left to you to order what Equipage or Servants he shou'd have, and upon what Footing.

You will likewise order what masters for exercise, languages or other accomplishments he ought to have, so far as they can be got.

I must beg of you to try to prevail upon Mr Langlois to direct, overlook and assist him in the courses of study proper for him to pursue at home, such as ancient History, Modern History, and General Law. You can give him the plans I chalked out for you and may very easily improve them. I mean these as severer studys, the Belles Lettres and Liveres du Temps are amusements and absolutely necessary to conversation …

Ld Titchfield has every good quality of the Heart. He has a great desire to do well … His only fault is that he don't think so well of Himself as I & every body else think of him …

He has resolved on two things. Never to play, or drink in the sense in which I use the words … Nobody will press a young man to either, after he is known to decline it. Let me recommend to you to see that he keeps both resolutions. Tho' I suspect you have no objection to lying in a bed in the morning [an obvious dig at Stormont's laziness], I wish he may be accustomed to rise early and not give too much into supping, because he has a tendency not to be lean.

The expence is not an object nor at all regarded in his case, so far as it is useful or proper. Yet he shou'd use himself betimes to that economy which teaches to keep regular accounts …

I shall be very anxious to hear how he goes on, and beg you wou'd send frequent accounts.

He has an unlimited credit, but he is to acquaint & consult you every time he uses it. Yours, etc. Mansfield[81]

Apparently not satisfied that he had adequately conveyed his message, Mansfield wrote again to Stormont four days later:

You must lodge him … I hope the letters have reached you, because I think you will be convinced & if you are not, you won't hesitate to give way to my positive opinion and earnest desire … If [Titchfield]

> turns out well he may be very considerable for he will have one of the greatest estates in the Kingdom ... I do most earnestly entreat you to do all in yr power to make a man of him. As to any expense of equipage or take a House for his Servants or Masters & in short every thing you think proper. Vous en êtes le maître [you will be his master] & be assured his living with you will not in the end put you to any expense.[82]

It appears that Stormont obeyed his uncle's detailed instructions, for two months later Mansfield thanked him for his attention to Titchfield, taking care to remind him again that Titchfield was by birth and fortune one of the first subjects in the kingdom.[83]

Another beneficiary of Mansfield's influence over the course of many years was Sir Thomas Mills, whose unexplained closeness to Mansfield gave rise to much speculation. Mills was widely rumoured to be Mansfield's illegitimate son; others believed he was an illegitimate son of Mansfield's sister Marjory and James Edward Stuart, the exiled Pretender to the throne.[84] Marjory was married to John Hay, a courtier at the Pretender's court, and was reputed to be the Pretender's mistress.[85] If this story of Mills's parentage is true, he was a grandson – albeit illegitimate – of King James II and thus had the distinction of royal blood.

One strange thing about Mills is that, despite his relative prominence (he was known to a wide circle of people in England and Canada), there appears to be no record of the date or place of his birth. He probably was born in the mid-1730s, not long before Mansfield's marriage.

Whether or not Mills was Mansfield's son or possibly his nephew, Mansfield ceaselessly promoted his career. Newspapers sometimes obliquely referred to Mills as a "relative" or "friend" of Mansfield, or called Mansfield Mills's "patron."[86] Sylvester Douglas, a prominent Scottish lawyer, politician, and diplomat, wrote many years later in his diary that he used to dine often with Mills, "whose connection with Lord Mansfield and great intimacy with him and influence over him were the subject of much conjecture and considered as very unaccountable or mysterious." Douglas goes on to say that Mills was illiterate but was "frank, friendly, dashing" and had served with "distinguished bravery" at the end of the "American war" (presumably the Seven Years' War, which ended in 1763).[87]

Douglas wrote in his diary that he did not believe that Mills was Mansfield's son because Mills was born in Scotland "of a mother always resident there at a time so distant from Lord Mansfield's only visit to Scotland since he first left it, that this was proved to be impossible." (Incidentally, Douglas's diary is the only known reference to Mansfield *ever* having returned to Scotland after leaving Perth at the age of thirteen.) Douglas said that Mills was born in Perth, the son of the wife of a slater named Milles [*sic*]. He also wrote that the actor and playwright Samuel Foote gave a different reason for believing that Mills could not have been Mansfield's son: Foote managed to insult both Mansfield and Mills in one sentence by pointing out that, unlike Mansfield, Mills "was as remarkable for want of understanding as [for] excess of courage."[88]

Nothing is known for sure about Mills until 1759, when he joined the British army as an ensign and served in Quebec soon after its capture from the French. Mills rose to the rank of major and shortly after returned to London, where he seemed to have had frequent social contacts with Mansfield. On one occasion he dined with Mansfield and several other eminent persons, including the actor David Garrick and Baron Smythe, one of Mansfield's fellow judges.[89] On another, Mills played host at dinner to Mansfield, Prime Minister Lord North, and Garrick.[90] He somehow achieved a knighthood (making him Sir Thomas Mills) and an appointment as receiver general of Quebec, a lucrative sinecure that placed him in charge of collecting and expending the revenues of the province. His questionable financial dealings made him known in Canada as "Corrupt Boy Mills."[91]

Mills held the office of receiver general for over twenty years, but spent little of that time in Canada. The office was administered by low-paid appointees or deputies, while Mills collected his salary and lived in London at the Adam brothers' high-end development of Adelphi Terrace. On at least one occasion Mills was presented to the King and Queen, almost certainly owing to Mansfield's sponsorship.[92] Mills spent lavishly and was always in debt. He gathered around him a group of men of literary and artistic talent who were happy to enjoy his hospitality.[93] His dining and drinking friends included the artist Sir Joshua Reynolds, who painted his portrait six times; the playwright and poet Oliver Goldsmith; and the actors Garrick and Foote.[94] These and many others may have been drawn to Mills by his widely believed family relationship to Lord Mansfield.

With all his faults, Mills appears to have been a man of courage. Returning to his London home one evening in 1772 in a sedan chair, he was accosted by four robbers. Although one of them held a pistol, he bounded from the chair and attacked them, causing them to flee, but not before he was slightly wounded.[95] Along with his courage, Mills had a violent side. He became involved in a dispute with his Adelphi Terrace neighbour Henry Hoare (known as Fat Harry), who had lent him nearly £2,000; he broke into Hoare's coach house and smashed the side panels of his coach with a pickaxe or hatchet.[96]

Mills had numerous connections with Mansfield, all of which tend to support the widespread speculation that they were relatives. In 1776, Lady Mansfield was one of three "sponsors" at the baptism of Mills's newborn daughter. A year later Mansfield's wife and niece socialized with Mills and his wife at Brighton.[97] And when a mob destroyed Mansfield's home in Bloomsbury Square in the 1780 Gordon Riots, Mills was at the house and, according to an account given to a newspaper (and to his own testimony in a trial of one of the rioters), escorted Lady Mansfield to safety.[98] Among Mansfield's possessions that rioters carried out of the house and destroyed was a portrait of Mills. Two years later, deeply in debt despite having held a lucrative office in India, Mills was forced to sell his house at Adelphi Terrace and its contents, which included a portrait of Mansfield by Sir Joshua Reynolds. Mansfield purchased these possessions, thus avoiding having them sold at auction to satisfy Mills's creditors.[99] It seems that Mills was in a position to pass on to Garrick gossip about law-court appointments – Serjeant Glynn (a leading barrister) had been appointed Recorder of the City; Bearcroft (another barrister) had failed to get the job – suggesting at least the possibility that Mansfield was the source of the information.[100]

Following the sale of his house and in order to stay out of debtors' prison, Mills left England secretly for India, leaving his wife and child behind.[101] Mansfield wrote a letter of introduction to his friend, Warren Hastings, governor general of Bengal, asking him to find employment for his protege.[102] Mills, wrote Mansfield, has been "the unjustifiable cause of his own distress. He has many friends and has kept the best company, but unfortunately he has been as careless and extravagant as any ... He is very active, behaved well as an officer in the last war, is very capable and conversant in business."[103] Hastings came through handsomely for his friend, finding Mills an appointment with a reported salary of £10,000 a year.[104] According to one newspaper, "he bids fair to return with one of the largest fortunes of late brought out of India."[105]

By 1787, Mills was back in London.[106] When a legislative council in Quebec examined the accounts of his office as receiver general, it discovered that he had used more than £3,000 of public money to pay his debts, and he was forced to resign. He died in 1793, three weeks before Mansfield's death. A government audit revealed that his office had a shortfall of more than £18,500.[107]

There is no definite proof that Mills was Mansfield's son or nephew, or that he obtained his knighthood or his sinecure as receiver general of Quebec through Mansfield's influence. Yet it is difficult to explain the longstanding and intimate friendship between the cautious, highly educated, sophisticated chief justice and the unruly, corrupt army officer, who was about thirty years his junior, unless some kind of undisclosed tie existed between them. It is unlikely that Mansfield would have recommended him to Warren Hastings or would have had his portrait hanging on the wall of his home if there had not been a family relationship. Horace Walpole called Mills "a noisy Fellow, who lived at a vast Expense without any visible means; but was supposed to be a natural Son of Lord Mansfield, & to be supported by him in that profusion." Another diarist wrote that Mills was certainly Scottish, but that "all beyond that was matter of conjecture, save only that it was universally understood that Mr Thomas Mills was under the protection of the great Lord Mansfield."[108] William Smith, chief justice of Quebec, who knew both Mansfield and Mills, referred to Mills in his diary simply as "a bastard of Lord Mansfield."[109] Whether this was true is still an open question.

Despite the numerous connections between Mills and Mansfield, there is no record of Mansfield ever having referred to their relationship. Interestingly, the archival material at Scone Palace, the seat of the earls of Mansfield, contains correspondence of Mills during the American Revolutionary War. One of these letters, written in 1777 to Mills by Sir William Grant, a Scottish-born army officer and lawyer, gives detailed information about the progress of the war.[110] We do not know how correspondence between two ostensibly non-family members came to be part of the Scone archives, which are otherwise limited to papers of the Murray/Mansfield family.[111]

Although there is no persuasive evidence that Mansfield ever returned to his native Scotland or saw his parents after leaving at the age of thirteen, he nonetheless maintained close ties to the members of his family all his life. For many years, he looked after his nieces and grandnieces at Kenwood, and he used his political influence to advance the careers of several of his nephews. Although his main motive for furthering Stormont's career was most likely to ensure that the precious earldom he had earned be passed down to future generations, Mansfield's devotion to his family cannot be doubted.

11

The Social Scene

His cold reserve and sharpness too were still too much for me. It was like being cut with a very, very cold instrument ... He chills the most generous blood.

James Boswell, journal entry about Lord Mansfield

Mansfield did not care for hunting, fishing, or shooting, the sports most favoured by the nobility, and although he was a Scotsman, he did not play golf. He particularly enjoyed riding (he suffered at least two injurious falls from his horse, once when he was seventy-six years old), walking, playing cards (though he had little interest in gambling), and visiting and entertaining his friends.[1]

Reading was also one of his great pleasures. His favourite toast was: "Old books and young friends."[2] Anyone who loved the classics – even the rabble-rousing John Wilkes – had a claim to his friendship. Although many, if not most, of his books were destroyed in the 1780 Gordon Riots, an inventory of his library at his London home in Lincoln's Inn Fields at the time of his death shows the extraordinary breadth of his literary interests. The library included, among others, volumes on English law (Blackstone, Bracton, Coke, admiralty law); foreign law (Scottish and Russian law, the law of the sea, Justinian's *Institutions*); jurisprudence (Grotius, Pufendorf); philosophy (the *Bhagavad Gita*, Paley's *Philosophy*, Beattie's *Essay on the Nature and Immutability of Truth*); politics (Francis Bacon, Bolingbroke, civil liberty and slavery); religion (Hebrew and Dutch Bibles); travel (Hakluyt's *Voyages*, Burnet's *Travels*, Lery's *Voyage en Amérique*); history (Thucydides; histories of Greenland, the East India Company, and Westminster elections); literature (*Robinson Crusoe*, Fitzgerald's poems, Lander's *Essay on Milton*, Pope's translation of *The Iliad*); science and medicine (Squire on longitude, Smith on Health, Hippocrates); art (*Pitture di Bologna*, Walter's *Paintings*); and a generous helping of classical writers in addition to those listed above (Tacitus, Euripides, Aristophanes, Cicero, Aristotle, Demosthenes).[3]

As Mansfield's wealth and importance grew, he needed a country house that could be easily reached from London and could be used for entertaining. In 1754, two years before he was raised to the peerage and the bench, he bought Kenwood, a modest brick villa, built in the late seventeenth century on a picturesque site at the northern edge of Hampstead Heath, about four miles northwest of London.[4] A contemporary described Kenwood as "a delightful place, and well suited to him, both as a man of business and a man of taste."[5] The property, which was sometimes referred to by its original name of Caen Wood, had been owned by a monastic order during the Middle Ages and was one of the religious houses confiscated by King Henry VIII in the 1530s. King Henry soon gave it to private owners, and by the eighteenth century it came into the hands of the Duke of Argyle, a powerful Scottish nobleman. Argyle bequeathed Kenwood to his nephew, the Earl of Bute, who was to become prime minister under King George III; and Bute sold it to Mansfield when he was solicitor general.[6]

Kenwood was situated on high ground, with a spectacular view overlooking London. A Hampstead chronicler described it: "To the north, where the grounds of Caen Wood come sweeping down to the brimming ponds, on which the swans 'float double, swan and shadow,' the landscape widens into one of rare beauty. Park-like beyond the park, in its alternations of lawny slope and little dells and groups of trees, it looks like a portion of the demesne, and not the least picturesque and lovely part of it."[7] Long before he bought the property, Murray was said to have been a frequent visitor to Hampstead. It is possible that strolls on Hampstead Heath with his friend the poet Alexander Pope caused him to fall in love with the surroundings and covet the house. According to an anonymous poet:

The Muses, since the birth of Time,
Have ever dwelt on heights sublime;
On Pindus now they gathered flowers,
Now sported in Parnassian bowers;
And late, when Murray deigned to rove
Beneath Ken Wood's sequestered grove,
They wander'd oft, when all was still,
With him and Pope on Hampstead Hill.[8]

Hampstead was a somewhat dangerous place in the mid-eighteenth century, and travelling between Kenwood and London was not without difficulty or peril. Highwaymen favoured the area since they could escape pursuit down one of the numerous lanes leading from the town and Hampstead Heath. Reciting that inhabitants and travellers "are exposed to robberies and other outrages," a statute was enacted in 1775 for lighting the streets of Hampstead and for establishing a nightly watch and an armed horse and foot patrol between Hampstead and London.[9] The highways between London and Hampstead were so narrow that on one occasion a lady traveller's coach was brought to a standstill until the road could be widened. It was not unusual for the wheels of a coach to be so embedded in the mud that extra horses had to be brought from the nearest farmhouse or village to drag it out.[10]

The house itself, with its rich furnishings, was a target for criminals. Twice in 1786, burglars broke in, the first time leaving behind a ladder that they had taken from Jack Straw's Castle, a nearby inn on Hampstead Heath[11] (the inn still exists). A few months later, thieves broke in again, plundered several of the rooms, and managed to escape, despite the presence of two watchmen who had been hired to guard the house after the Gordon Riots of 1780.[12] On two other occasions, the thieves were caught. Three men robbed a servant of Mansfield of a silver watch and some other personal belongings one evening while he was returning to Kenwood from the village of Highgate; in the other case, a horse belonging to Mansfield was stolen from a nearby field. The defendants in both cases were tried and sentenced to death.[13]

Despite the risk of crime and the difficulties of travel, Lord and Lady Mansfield spent a good part of the summer and autumn of every year at Kenwood, and they entertained many people there, including members of the nobility, the government, and the legal community. In May 1757, Lady Mansfield wrote to her nephew: "Kenwood is now in great beauty your uncle is passionately fond of it we go thither every Saturday and return on Mondays but I live in hopes we shall now soon go thither to fix for the summer."[14]

After 1780, when their Bloomsbury Square residence in London was destroyed in the Gordon Riots, Kenwood became their principal residence and remained so until Mansfield's death, although he continued to keep a place in town. The Mansfields' hospitality was not limited to the elite. In 1773, they hosted a dinner at Kenwood for about 400 poor people of the neighbourhood. After dinner, each guest received half a crown (two and a half shillings, or one-eighth of a pound) and a loaf of bread.[15] Three years later, the *Morning Chronicle* reported that Mansfield had subscribed very liberally to a subscription for the relief of the poor in Kentish Town and its vicinity, near his home in Bloomsbury Square.[16]

Soon after Mansfield purchased Kenwood, he enlarged the estate by acquiring additional land,[17] some of which he rented out.[18] After ten years of living there, Mansfield hired the fashionable and celebrated Scottish architect Robert Adam to make extensive alterations that turned Kenwood into an impressive residence, fit for a lord chief justice.[19] The Mansfields must have had many overnight guests, for the first work asked of Adam was the addition of an attic floor for extra bedrooms. Adam, who designed "the smartest interiors in England" for some of its greatest noblemen,[20] became Mansfield's personal friend.

The owners of country houses used their wealth to create exquisite interiors in keeping with neo-classical eighteenth-century taste.[21] In turning Kenwood into an elegant mansion, Mansfield was acting in accordance with his class and his times. Adam's most notable creation at Kenwood was the library, which he designed in 1767; there is general agreement today that it is "one of the most important Neo-Classical rooms in Europe and one of Adam's finest achievements."[22] It was intended as both a library and a room for receiving company. One end, semi-circular, was fitted with bookcases and screened by columns so that the main part of the room could be used for social gatherings.[23] In 1768, the Duke of Newcastle wrote Mansfield that he wanted to see "your improvements and particularly your great room, which, I hear, is a very fine and agreeable one."[24] Adam created a new mode of wall-decoration using mirrors made with French glass supplied by the furniture maker and interior designer Thomas Chippendale (although Chippendale did not supply the furniture).[25] On the walls were paintings, some with classical themes by the Venetian artist Antonio Zucchi, such as "Bacchus and Ceres" and "Diana and her Muses." The main attraction in the hall was Gian Lorenzo Bernini's bust of Homer, which Alexander Pope had bequeathed to Mansfield.[26]

An American visitor described Kenwood in 1776:

> The house elegant, not large – the centre is a noble portico; the walls of the hall, saloon, chambers, etc. covered with paper of Indian or Chinese figures, the library a beautiful room (having a fine prospect of St Paul's distant about seven miles, through a wood, over a lawn, and ending in a fine piece of water) contains the largest mirrors I ever saw, being seven-and-a-half feet high and three-and-a-half in breadth. In the hall are two tables of jet black marble, the walls hung with portraits of Lord Mansfield and Lady [who] was a daughter of Finch, Earl of Nottingham.[27]

Another visitor wrote: "It is a large and convenient house. There is one fine room, an oval form of 60 feet long, I believe by 30. I imagine ye whole front is 300 feet: this includes a greenhouse of 60 [feet] ... We conversed, looked at prints, walked on the terrace, which notwithstanding the rain that has fallen, was dry, the view from what I could distinguish was charming. We dined ... in the saloon: we had a dinner with attendance suitable to the house and the owner of it."[28]

After Mansfield's death, Stormont, who inherited both Kenwood and his uncle's earldom, planned to make extensive alterations and additions. A newspaper expressed sorrow over this possibility: "Whether the additions will be improvements or the contrary time will show. The library which is in a conical form and so divided by pillars that the centre forms a drawing room is so to be totally altered which those who wish to unite the utile [i.e., useful] with the dulce [i.e., attractive] will lament because there is no library in England built upon similar principles or thought upon so judicious a plan."[29] Fortunately for posterity, the 2nd earl died three years after his uncle, before he had time to destroy the library or other features of Adam's work.

Kenwood remained the Mansfield family's home until 1906, when it was leased to tenants, including at various times Grand Duke Michael Michaelovich, a grandson of Czar Nicholas II of Russia, and Nancy Leeds, an American millionairess. In 1925 the house was sold to the family trust of Lord Iveagh, the heir of the Guinness brewing company. Following Iveagh's death in 1927, Kenwood was opened to the public.[30] Nevertheless, it was allowed to decay; in 1938 a London newspaper reported that a family of two full-grown foxes and a cub had made their home in the house. The foxes were believed to be responsible for the loss of ducks and pheasants from the nearby woods and ponds.[31] Today the house is managed by English Heritage and is visited by 150,000 people annually.

In the mid-1770s, Lord and Lady Mansfield moved their London residence from Lincoln's Inn Fields, where they had lived for about fifteen years, to a leased house at the northeast corner of Bloomsbury Square, at the northern edge of London, close to the newly founded British Museum.[32] From here, Mansfield could look northward to see, crowned against the sky some four miles distant, the upland villages of Highgate and Hampstead, the site of his country home of Kenwood.[33] Immediately to the south, but hidden from view by masses of leafy foliage, lay the congested, bustling city of

London.[34] Bloomsbury Square, which the Earl of Southampton had developed in the late seventeenth century, conveyed a delightful atmosphere of leisure and repose, where often the only sounds came from the twittering and chirping of birds. The entire north side of the square was occupied by Southampton House (later renamed Bedford House), an elegant mansion with a spacious court in front for the reception of carriages.[35] Residents of Bloomsbury Square also included the Earl of Chesterfield, the poet Thomas Gray, and several other judges.[36] The square was considered such an enchanting place that visiting foreign princes were taken to see it as one of the wonders of England.[37]

Lord and Lady Mansfield usually spent November to May at Bloomsbury Square and the remainder of the year at Kenwood. Their time in London coincided with the height of the social season, which was also the political season.[38] When in London, Mansfield would hold a levee every Sunday evening.[39] These informal receptions were attended by a great variety of guests, including noblemen, politicians, generals, ambassadors, lawyers, and bishops. A newspaper account describes a levee held one October afternoon after Mansfield returned from Kenwood: "As soon as his Lordship's doors were opened they flocked in shoals to pay their disrespects [*sic*] to his Lordship's station, although his Lordship was so complaisant and obliging as not to permit some of them to depart without being escorted to their lodgings by one of his Lordship's attendants."[40]

James Boswell paints a pleasant picture of Mansfield at ease at one of his levees in 1772, "talking neatly and with vivacity," wearing his wig, his coat buttoned, his legs pushed in front of him, and his heels knocking frequently but not hard against each other.[41] At another levee that Boswell attended, Mansfield graciously mentioned Boswell's book about his tour of the Hebrides with Samuel Johnson. Mansfield: "We have all been reading your travels, Mr Boswell" and Boswell modestly replied: "I was a humble attendant on Mr Johnson." Mansfield then, referring to a dispute in Switzerland on whether Hell was eternal, laughed and said: "In this country they don't trouble themselves about Hell, whether it is eternal or not." A nobleman who was a guest at the levee entered into the humorous spirit of the exchange, saying: "They take it as they find it." Boswell commented primly in his diary: "This was upon the whole rather an improper exchange of pleasantry at the Lord Chief Justice's on a Sunday."[42]

Mansfield frequently attended the King's weekly levees held from November to May at St James's Palace, near Piccadilly in the heart of London. He used the opportunity of one royal levee to thank the King for an office that the King had bestowed on Mansfield's nephew, Lord Stormont.[43] On some occasions, the King would meet privately with Mansfield before the levee to ask his advice on some matter.[44] Mansfield also attended the public festivities to mark the King's birthday and the anniversaries of his accession to the throne and his coronation. Attending these events cannot have always been a very pleasant experience for the invited notables. A guest at the birthday celebration in June 1785 noted that Mansfield, then eighty years of age, was wedged closely together with Stormont and numerous other noblemen for hours while they waited for the King and Queen to arrive.[45]

Much of Mansfield's social life was spent with legal or political associates. In the 1760s Mansfield attended regular gatherings of lawyers and judges at the villa of John Dunning, a prominent barrister with whom Mansfield got along well, in the London suburb of Ealing,[46] where shoptalk undoubtedly dominated the conversation. On the first Sunday of the court term, Mansfield, several other judges, lawyers, aldermen, and sheriffs would hear a sermon at St Paul's Cathedral, which was followed by a dinner at Grocer's Hall, then, as now, an important banqueting venue in the City of London.[47]

Dinners tended to be lavish; vast quantities of fish and red and white meat of excellent quality were consumed.[48] Those who could afford it would indulge in what was then exotic food. In 1762, Sir Thomas Wroughton, then British envoy in St Petersburg, sent "some very fine curious rhubarb" by messenger to the King, Lord Bute, Mansfield, and one other person.[49] The Duke of Newcastle, a celebrated gourmand, would often invite Mansfield to feast with him while they discussed foreign and domestic politics, patronage, and other matters. On one occasion in June 1767, he asked Mansfield to join him and three or four other peers at Newcastle's palatial home of Claremont to share "a most prodigious fine turtle." Newcastle concluded his letter: "To be serious, the weather is very fine, the turtle very good, and, I believe I can promise you some good fruit. So pray come. You know there is always a bed for you there."[50] The fruit that Newcastle promised came from his own hothouses at Claremont, where he grew apricots, cherries, pineapples, peaches, and other varieties of fruit.[51]

Noblemen's dinners were almost always accompanied by heavy drinking,[52] although there is no known account of Mansfield ever being inebriated. Dr Johnson had told his biographer Boswell that Mansfield "drank champagne with the wits," but his favourite drink was not champagne but claret (Bordeaux red wine).[53] When his nephew Lord Stormont was ambassador in Warsaw, Mansfield asked him to ship him some Tokay, a Hungarian sweet wine.[54] The wine arrived almost a year later, but more than one-third of it had leaked out (presumably it had been sent in barrels) and the remainder had to be bottled.[55] Newcastle too liked good wine. When he accompanied the King on a visit to Hanover in 1748, he had some Rhenish wine sent to him in England.[56]

In describing a dinner with Mansfield and the Archbishop of York, the second highest-ranking clergyman in England, Newcastle wrote: "The archbishop, is all heart and zeal. My Lord Mansfield very friendly, very discreet, and prudent."[57] Mansfield's discreet nature, combined with his high office, made him an ideal person for entertaining visiting dignitaries from abroad. On at least one occasion he gave an elegant dinner at Kenwood for the entire foreign diplomatic corps.[58] In 1768, he attended a state dinner with the nineteen-year-old King Christian VII of Denmark, who had married one of King George III's sisters but a few years later was to engage in such bizarre and disreputable conduct that he was adjudged insane. He had already shown disturbing signs for a monarch, including "a liking for lowlife exploits in the brothels of Copenhagen";[59] Mansfield, after having had a conversation with him at dinner, reassured Newcastle: "He is very well behaved & says nothing improper & really has a very agreeable countenance."[60]

On another occasion, Mansfield helped Newcastle play host to Princess Ludwika Poniatowska, sister of Poland's King Stanislaw Augustus II, who visited England in the summer of 1767, accompanied by a few ladies. Mansfield took the princess on a tour of several of the great houses of the nobility, culminating in a visit to Claremont, Newcastle's sumptuous home.[61] The princess even joined Mansfield on circuit, most likely for only a short time, in order to give her a glimpse of the English justice system; she was present at the assizes at Croydon near London; after several criminals had been convicted, she interceded to "give respite" to one of them.[62]

It may be asked what part Lady Mansfield played in these social occasions, for her name seldom comes up in Mansfield's correspondence with Newcastle or his other friends and political associates. In his account of his dinner with King Christian of Denmark, Mansfield mentions the presence of another aristocratic lady, so it is reasonable to suppose that Lady Mansfield also was part of the company. On the other hand, Newcastle's invitation to Mansfield to enjoy a turtle and some fruit with him and a few other noblemen seems to have contemplated an all-male dinner. The fact that the principal purpose of many of Mansfield's dinners with Newcastle and other politicians was to discuss foreign and domestic politics also suggests that wives were not invited.

During the second half of the century, it was increasingly becoming the custom for dinners and other social occasions to include both sexes, and social events were coming to be regarded as women's domain.[63] Dinner-table conversation might include political affairs, as well as polite conversation and society gossip.[64] On other occasions, political discussion would be deferred until after dinner, when port and brandy were brought in for the men for a period of heavy drinking and toasting, and the lady of the house and her guests would withdraw. Polite women abhorred extreme drunkenness and complained about tobacco smoke."[65] It is likely that the intelligent and gracious Lady Mansfield fit into this mould: at mixed-sex dinners she acted her part as hostess or guest and then left the room with the other ladies, perhaps to chat over a cup of tea in the lady of the house's handsome drawing room (originally called the withdrawing room, because the ladies withdrew to it).[66]

Mansfield was an affable dinner companion. Richard Cumberland, a writer and civil servant, described him in a social setting:

> I cannot recollect the time when, sitting at the table with Lord Mansfield, I ever failed to remark that happy and engaging art which he possessed of putting the company present in good humour with themselves; I am convinced they naturally liked him the more for his seeming to like them so well …
>
> He would lend his ear most condescendingly to his company, and cheer the least attempt at humour with the prompt payment of a laugh, which cost his muscles no exertion, but was merely a subscription that he readily threw in towards the general hilarity of the table …
>
> He would not start new topics but easily led into anecdotes of past times; these he detailed with pleasure, but he told them correctly rather than amusingly. He would resort to society for relaxation and rest of mind rather than for anything that would cost him fresh exertions.[67]

In private conversations, particularly with others in the legal profession, Mansfield seemed a very different man from the one Cumberland described. James Boswell, who liked to visit Mansfield just to be in the company of a great judge,[68] wrote about a visit in his journal: "I ran home, drest, and went to Lord Mansfield's. Jenkinson was with him; but went away just as I came. My Lord and I were then left tête à tête. His cold reserve and sharpness too were still too much for me. It was like being cut with a very, very cold instrument. I have not for a long time experienced that weakness of mind which I had formerly in a woeful degree in the company of the Great or the Clever. But Lord Mansfield has uncommon power. He chills the most generous blood."[69]

Mansfield's humour could have a cruel side. On one occasion, Boswell was present when Mansfield was told that some boys had picked up handfuls of dust from the street and thrown them in the wind in front of coaches going by, in order to disturb the horses, and that the coachmen had cut one of the boys severely with his whip. "He deserved it," Mansfield replied, "and yet after all what are half the age doing but throwing dust in other people's eyes?"[70] Another time, Boswell told Mansfield that he had met a Scottish schoolmaster, who told him that the boys were beginning to be rebellious. "I told him, 'Don't spare them, Lord Mansfield allows you to whip them with a rod or [leather strap] as much as you please; but don't take improper modes of correction.' Mansfield: 'Nor correct in passion. You said right.' (laughing)."[71]

The number and variety of Mansfield's friends was extraordinary. The poet Alexander Pope, the clergyman William Warburton, the legal scholar William Blackstone, and the architect Robert Adam have already been alluded to. A full listing of his friendships would make for tedious reading, but a few others are worth noting.

Margaret Cavendish-Bentinck, Duchess of Portland (whose son was to become prime minister in 1783), became a lifelong friend after Newcastle introduced her to Mansfield in the 1740s. Immensely wealthy, she was famous for her zoo and botanical gardens and for the enormous collection of natural history and decorative arts that she created on her palatial estate of Welbeck Abbey. Mansfield corresponded with her on political as well as personal matters; a long letter that he wrote in 1757 concerning Polish affairs, when his nephew Lord Stormont was the British ambassador in Warsaw, indicates that she was knowledgeable about international politics and was even involved in diplomacy herself.[72] After her husband's death in 1769, the duchess and her son got into a dispute over the family estates, and she implored Mansfield to act as mediator. Mansfield at first refused but later agreed to meet with the parties and tell them how he thought the matter might be resolved.[73] As late as 1776 Mansfield was still trying to settle the dispute.[74] Despite her wealth, intellectual gifts, and interest in high affairs of state, the duchess was not too august to treat Mansfield for a sore throat, perhaps while he was a guest at Welbeck Abbey.[75] He was greatly distressed by her death in 1785.[76]

Lord George Sackville, eleven years younger than Mansfield, was a fellow Westminster School alumnus and a lifelong friend. As a young lawyer, Mansfield had been a frequent visitor to the home of Sackville's father, the Duke of Dorset.[77] Sackville joined the army; as a regimental commander he fought against the French with heroism and was shot in the breast and seriously wounded at the Battle of Fontenoy in 1745. But fourteen years later at the Battle of Minden, as commander of the British army fighting as allies of the Hanoverians, he ignored an order of the allied commander, Duke Ferdinand of Brunswick, to attack the French with his cavalry. The British and their allies won the battle but Sackville's failure to attack deprived them of a decisive victory. Disgraced, Sackville turned to Mansfield for advice about whether to ask for a court martial or a parliamentary inquiry into his conduct. Mansfield advised a court martial, because it could exonerate him while a parliamentary inquiry could not. He was court-martialed, found guilty of disobedience, and judged unfit to serve in the military. After that, Sackville had some bitter feelings toward Mansfield, although they renewed their friendship in the 1770s, when they both counselled the government to take a hard line against the American colonists.[78]

Mansfield had many friends among the higher clergy. His Westminster School classmates Thomas Newton, Bishop of Bristol, and James Johnson, Bishop of Gloucester, sometimes were visitors to Kenwood.[79] While on circuit in western and northwestern England, Mansfield used the opportunity to spend a few days each with Richard Hurd, Bishop of Worcester, and Bishop Halifax.[80] Hurd was a scholar, known for precision and pedantry; a friend of Dr Johnson called him "an old maid in breeches."[81] Nevertheless, Mansfield liked him. Hurd owed his advancement in the church to Mansfield and to Charles Yorke, Chancellor Hardwicke's son, who served as attorney general in the 1760s;[82] Mansfield left Hurd a bequest of £100 in his will as a token of his affection.[83]

Mansfield also had friends on the stage. Samuel Foote and David Garrick, two of the leading actor-playwrights of the day, as well as friendly rivals, were frequent guests at Mansfield's table, invited because they were brilliant additions to a dinner party.[84] On one occasion, everyone listened deferentially as Garrick began sermonizing about the importance of thrift and economy, citing the example of the playwright Charles Churchill, a mutual friend who had recently died after a life of waste and extravagance. Foote's biographer finishes the story:

> No one would have supposed it possible to dislodge [Garrick] from such vantage-ground as this, surrounded by all the decorums of life, and with a Lord Chief Justice at the head of the table. But Foote unexpectedly struck in. He said that every question had two sides, and he had long made up his mind on the advantages implied in the fact of *not* paying one's debts ... In the first place, it presupposed some time or other the possession of fortune, to have been able to *get* credit. Then, living on credit was the art of living without the most troublesome thing in the whole world, which was money. It saved the expense and annoyance of keeping accounts, and made over all the responsibility to other people. It was the panacea for the cares and embarrassments of wealth. It checked and discountenanced avarice; while, people being always more liberal of others' goods than their own, it extended every sort of encouragement to generosity ... And would anyone venture to say, meanwhile, that paying one's debts could possibly draw to us such anxious attention from our own part of the world while we live, or such sincere regrets when we die, as *not* paying them? All which, Foote put with such whimsical gravity, and supported with such a surprising abundance of sarcastic illustration, that in the general laughter against Garrick no laugh was heartier than Lord Mansfield's.[85]

Foote was famous for his licentious lifestyle and his witty repartee. In a famous exchange, the Earl of Sandwich, himself a notorious rake, said: "Foote, I have often wondered what catastrophe would bring you to your end; but I think you must either die of the pox [i.e., syphilis], or the halter [i.e., the gallows]." Without missing a beat, Foote replied: "That will depend on whether I embrace your lordship's mistress, or your lordship's principles."[86]

Perhaps the most important and interesting of Mansfield's friends was Warren Hastings, whose efforts, more than those of any other person, made India the jewel in the crown of the British Empire. Mansfield had known Hastings as a boy, perhaps through his nephew Stormont, who had been a student at Westminster School at around the same time as Hastings.[87] Many years later, when Hastings faced political difficulties, Mansfield recalled that as a boy "he took into his Head that he could fly & made a very ingenious pair of wings. It is true he broke his nose but that is nothing to the Purpose. I will answer for him that he overcomes all his Difficulties."[88] When Mansfield heard from Hastings in 1774, he called Hastings "an old friend."[89]

As governor general, Hastings believed that Bengal should be governed according to Indian customs and laws, a view that Mansfield fully agreed with.[90] Hastings was an unusual colonial governor for his time, leaving much of the administration in Indian hands, although under British direction. He was a patron of Indian arts and learning; became reasonably fluent in Hindi and Urdu, the principal languages of the subcontinent; and he sponsored translations of commentaries on Muslim and Hindu law. But he also had a strong authoritarian streak, which manifested itself both with Indian rulers who opposed him and with the five-member British supreme council of which he was the head. From 1774 on, he was engaged in bureaucratic warfare with a majority of the council, who accused him of corruption and of acting in a high-handed manner.[91]

In December 1781, Hastings sent his agent, Major John Scott, to London to represent his interests with the British government. Scott immediately went to see Mansfield, who received him warmly.[92] Scott's detailed letters to Hastings describe in detail how Mansfield acted as an informal adviser to Hastings, telling Scott that he should feel free to visit him "without Ceremony."[93] Over the next two years, Mansfield frequently dined with Scott, advised him on how best to deal with the ministry and Parliament, secured Scott more than one audience with the King[94] and himself put in a good word for Hastings with the King,[95] passed on to Scott political information that might be of interest and use to Hastings,[96] encouraged Hastings not to give in to his enemies on the council, and generally gave Hastings his unqualified support.

In return, Mansfield asked Hastings to find posts in India for relatives and friends. His successful application on behalf of the deeply indebted Sir Thomas Mills has already been mentioned, but there were others.[97] In July 1782, Scott wrote to Hastings that Mansfield "desired me to tell you ... that ... Judge Willis [an associate justice on King's Bench] has pressed him to recommend his Son in Bengal to your notice & that he shall be much obliged by any Favor you may show him. Lord Mansfield added that knowing your Situation, he was very averse to trouble you with Recommendations but this was an application he could not avoid complying with."[98]

When Hastings considered resigning from his office in 1783, Mansfield, with hyperbolic praise, begged him not to:

> [The position] requires many uncommon qualities and talents. He should be a statesman, a general, a merchant. He should have temper to bear contradiction, folly, and impertinence. He should be intrepid and resolute, and possess a mind full of resources … We lost the West Indies for want of such a man and, had it not been for you, we should have lost the East. If I live to see you return, I shall be happy to enjoy as much as you can allow me of your retreat, to talk over with you the wonderful events of your wonderful days, to contemplate the superior brightness of your setting sun. A Governor of India come back without avarice without rapine without corruption, without wealth, is a phenomenon which has not risen before. I am with the greatest affection etc. Mansfield.[99]

Mansfield praised Hastings in terms that he used for no other friend or acquaintance. Again and again, he told Scott that he regarded Hastings as "the greatest and most wonderful character of the Age"[100] and "the greatest man of the present age by far."[101] Scott reported to Hastings: "This great man's eyes glisten whenever he speaks of you."[102] In light of Mansfield's expression of his admiration to Hastings directly, it is unlikely that Scott was exaggerating. Mansfield was drawn to Hastings by a shared curiosity and love of learning and by a similar outlook on both politics and law. They both were authoritarian in their political outlook, but Hastings was a genuine empire-builder while Mansfield ruled only over a court of law. Few individuals, however successful, are entirely content with their lot, and perhaps Mansfield envied Hastings for achieving a kind of greatness that he wished for himself.

One of the accusations that Hastings's enemies made against him was that he had accepted huge gifts from Indian native rulers. This was true: he had sent more than £120,000 back to Britain during the first four years that he was governor.[103] Many British officials accepted gifts from Indian rulers, but Hastings took it a step further than most, and so earned criticism – and envy – from his critics in England. Mansfield encouraged him to accept a gift of one million rupees from a vizier, saying that "he must now think of himself."[104] Scott reported to Hastings that Mansfield was looking for an English estate for Hastings to buy and had found for him "one of the neatest Villas in England, which, with the Estate around it, he can get for £50,000, but he says you cannot afford to purchase it without this addition to your fortune."[105]

In early 1784, when Prime Minister William Pitt, the son of Mansfield's old political opponent, introduced a bill in Parliament that increased governmental supervision of the East India Company and in effect repudiated Hastings's administration,[106] Mansfield failed to support Hastings in the House of Lords, and the bill passed. In writing to his employer, Scott excused Mansfield: "I venerate Lord Mansfield so sincerely & am so certain that he has done all in his Power for you consistent with the Caution & Timidity attendant on old Age."[107] Yet the friendship seemed to survive. While Mansfield was staying at the fashionable spa-resort of Tunbridge Wells in October, soon after his wife died, he gallantly escorted Mrs Hastings to the assembly rooms and accompanied her on her walks every day.[108] The following year, Hastings resigned as governor and returned to England, but there is no record that the intimate talks about Hastings's life that Mansfield had looked forward to ever took place.

In 1787, led by Edmund Burke, the House of Commons impeached Hastings on charges of corruption and oppression. The real basis for the charges, however, was political: his parliamentary critics believed he had given preferential treatment to Scottish officers in India and that he had governed in an overbearing manner.[109] After a trial in the House of Lords that lasted seven years, he was acquitted, two years after Mansfield's death.

Mansfield also found the time from his legal and political activities to give personal advice and help to family members as well as friends. He investigated a possible fraud committed on Lady Mansfield's sister Isabella, and on his nephew the Marquess of Rockingham (the son of Lady Mansfield's sister Mary). He advised Rockingham that it was essential for him to keep precise accounts and to keep them up to date.[110] Among others, he helped the Duke of Portland, the son of his lifelong friend the dowager duchess, to put his financial affairs in order.[111]

Mansfield could be brutally honest in the advice he gave friends. He did not shrink from telling people what they did not want to hear. Perhaps they came to him because they could count on hearing the unvarnished truth from this urbane and wise judge. Charles Manners, 4th Duke of Rutland, who in 1784 was appointed lord lieutenant of Ireland, complained to Mansfield that he was being libelled because of his dissolute habits. Mansfield's reply was a model of prudent but straightforward advice:

> You are much in the right to despise being libelled for doing what is right ... but I have always listened to calumny so far as to examine whether it hits upon a sore place, and, if it does, to correct the thing immediately. The complaint the most general, and which hurts you the most, is drinking hard, and the irregularity of the hours of [Dublin] Castle. Many are ready and able to advise you in great matters, but in such points as these two, which I think of the utmost importance to your conduct and fame, I am the only man who will venture to give you a hint.[112]

Three years later, Rutland was dead at the age of thirty-three, very likely as the result of excessive consumption of claret. In his will, he appointed Mansfield as one of his executors and guardians of his children.[113]

The Annandales were Scottish noblemen related to Mansfield by marriage.[114] We know that Mansfield kept in touch with them, for in the early 1740s he was corresponding with Charlotta Van Lore, the dowager Marchioness of Annandale, about the mental and physical condition of her son, the Marquess of Annandale. The problem was that the marquess was insane. Mansfield wrote two letters to the marchioness that show a side of him that does not appear in his legal arguments or parliamentary debates: candid and pragmatic as always, he was also highly observant and sensitive to others' feelings and concerns. In October 1743 he wrote to dissuade her from going to see her son: "If he is not bad enough to be confined, which at present he is not, he will resent your coming, refuse to see you, and probably go the next morning abroad. If he is confined, the doctors won't allow you to see him ... You will forgive me giving you my advice so freely but my judgement is so clear upon this matter that if you receive this letter upon the road I would advise you to turn back."[115]

In 1744, the year the marquess was officially declared a lunatic by the Court of Chancery,[116] Mansfield wrote another letter to the marchioness from his chambers in Lincoln's Inn, in which he recounted a two-hour meeting with the mad marquess. His main object in writing seems to have been to persuade the marchioness not to interfere with her son's treatment but to leave it to the doctors, and even to avoid any contact with him:

> He [told me] that he had consulted physicians in France – Germany – Holland and they said it was La Maladie d'Esprit – by which he understood the having too high spirits ... He opened his bosom and showed

> me some bruises and hurts he had received – that his falls from post horses were innumerable ...
>
> These are a few sketches of a long conversation which affected me greatly. I could perceive he was much upon his guard, much in that sort of awe which respect and affection give, for he showed me a great deal of both ... He desired I would speak to the doctors that he should not be watched any more, as to everything else he was easy – he could not be in better lodgings, and would do what the physicians ordered – I undertook immediately to do it, that he was now well there was no occasion for them, but he must be much upon his guard and live regular and take what was prescribed ...
>
> In this unhappy affair I have had is all along much at heart to save you. For this reason I stopped your journey last year and advised you to refer everything to the opinion of the best physicians ... This last fit of illness is less known than his former, because he has gone by a feigned name. What I know I have communicated to nobody but you ...
>
> I think you should burn my letters and I desire you would. You will take great care, if you come up, to conceal the reason of your coming.[117]

It is not clear what further involvement Mansfield had with the marquess or his mother. In 1745, David Hume, the Scottish philosopher, was chosen to be the marquess's companion, while his mother and two other relations handled his affairs. According to Hume, Mansfield was called on for advice "now and then, but he did extremely little," while Mansfield for his part objected to Hume receiving an annuity of £100 for his services.[118] Be that as it may, Mansfield's letters to the marchioness show a caring side of him that belies, or at least qualifies, the generally held belief that Mansfield was an emotionally cold person. Hume also relied on Mansfield for legal assistance in connection with his services to the marquess.[119]

As a result of Mansfield's position as chief justice and his well-earned reputation for diligence and good judgment, he was a member of the governing bodies of several philanthropic organizations. He was a trustee of the Busby Trust, a charitable trust established in the will of Richard Busby, a seventeenth-century headmaster of Westminster School; the trustees, including the Duke of Newcastle, the Earl of Winchilsea (Mansfield's brother-in-law), and several other noble Westminster alumni, held their annual meeting and dinner in the cloisters of Westminster Abbey.[120] He was also a trustee of the British Museum, which was founded in 1753.[121]

In 1758, Mansfield was elected as one of the governors of Charterhouse, a position that was to involve him in controversy.[122] Charterhouse, founded in 1611 on the site of an old Carthusian monastery in the Smithfield section of London, was a hospital and a school (which moved to rural Surrey in 1872 and is today one of the nine elite English public schools). In the eighteenth century, governorships of Charterhouse were eagerly sought after, for they carried a great deal of prestige. Among the governors were several dukes and earls, as well as the Archbishop of Canterbury, England's highest-ranking prelate. Mansfield's election was bitterly opposed by his political enemies, William Pitt and Pitt's brother-in-law, Lord Temple.[123] A few years later, Mansfield's vote to admit his nephew (by marriage) the Marquess of Rockingham instead of George Grenville, another brother-in-law of Pitt's, to fill a vacancy on the Charterhouse board of governors, again angered Pitt.[124] Lord Chancellor Hardwicke commented: "I was amazed to read the account ... of the offence Mr Pitt has taken at my Lord Mansfield's concurrence in the election at the Charter House ... Is it the rule that because people differ from one another in politics, therefore all civil intercourse must be cut off?"[125] Apparently the answer was yes. According to one report, the animus ran so high that members of the Grenville ministry refused to speak to Mansfield.[126]

As a Charterhouse governor, Mansfield exercised his usual prudence and caution. When Lady Suffolk, the former mistress of King George II, called in some of her connections, including Mansfield and Newcastle, for the election of Dr Morton, librarian of the British Museum, to the influential post of headmaster of the school, Mansfield refused to commit himself.[127] Although "extremely flattered" by her request, he told her gently that because he considered his position as one of trust he would never commit his vote beforehand, in order to be left free to make the best choice. He agreed to speak to the Duke of Newcastle about it but suggested that her best course would be to go to him directly.[128]

In 1766, two boys attending the school were caught in some kind of sexual behaviour, and a meeting of the governors was called to decide how to deal with the situation. Mansfield, however, advised against having a meeting or taking any other action until the two boys had been taken away by their parents. The Archbishop of Canterbury wrote enigmatically to Newcastle: "I have yielded; and in part for a Reason, which I will acquaint your Grace, when I have the Honour of seeing you."[129] What action the governors eventually took is not clear. It seems astonishing that a leading politician, the highest-ranking clergyman in the land, and the chief justice all became involved in a matter of this kind. It is likely that one or both of the boys were members of an important family, and the governors' overriding concern was to avoid scandal.

As an individual, Mansfield presents an enigmatic study in contrasts. He was a very private person, in the sense that he almost always kept his thoughts to himself. Few, if any, people felt they really knew him. On the other hand, in an age that placed a premium on sociability, when "good breeding, conversation and discreet charm were the lubricants which would overcome social friction,"[130] he was the most sociable of human beings. As an important member of elite society, he performed the philanthropic and community duties that were expected of him but, beyond that, he clearly loved his busy social life. He had innumerable contacts in the world of the nobility, politics, religion, and the arts, and he often used his contacts to obtain favours for family members and others; but he gave at least as much as he received. Those who knew him best revered him not only for his greatness as a judge but also, on a personal level, for his willingness to give friendship and sage, candid advice.

Dido Elizabeth Belle (left) and Lady Elizabeth Murray, two of Mansfield's great-nieces. Dido, the daughter of John Lindsay, Mansfield's sea-captain nephew, and a West Indies slave, lived at Kenwood and cared for Mansfield in his old age. Lady Elizabeth, the daughter of Lord Stormont, Mansfield's nephew, also lived at Kenwood after her mother's death. Portrait by Johan Zoffany. From the Collection of The Rt Hon. The Earl of Mansfield and Mansfield, Scone Palace, Perth, Scotland.

David Murray, Viscount Stormont, Mansfield's nephew and heir to his title and estate. Although his abilities were limited, through Mansfield's influence he was appointed British ambassador in Dresden, Warsaw, Vienna, and Paris, and later one of the two secretaries of state. Etching by James Bretherton. © National Portrait Gallery, London.

Sir Thomas Mills, a British army officer who many thought was Lord Mansfield's illegitimate son. Mills lavishly entertained artists, actors, and playwrights in London; when he fell into debt, Mansfield helped him procure a lucrative post in India. Portrait of Sir Thomas Mills, oil on canvas by Sir Joshua Reynolds. McCord Museum, Montreal, M969.21.1.

John Wilkes, a champion of liberty and a popular hero. Mansfield's court found him guilty of seditious libel for a pamphlet criticizing the government. Wilkes later became lord mayor of London and a friend of Mansfield, with whom he shared a love of the classics. Etching by William Hogarth. © National Portrait Gallery, London.

An iconic portrait of Chief Justice Lord Mansfield by John Singleton Copley, an American artist who lived for many years in England. The portrait was first exhibited in 1783, but was probably painted a few years earlier.

Warren Hastings, colonial governor general of the Indian state of Bengal, whom Mansfield called "the greatest and most wonderful character of the Age." Mansfield advised Hastings on establishing a legal system for India, as well as on how to deal with his political enemies. Portrait by Sir Joshua Reynolds. © National Portrait Gallery, London.

London in the midst of the week-long Gordon Riots in June 1780. Moved by anti-Catholic feeling, the rioters burned Mansfield's Bloomsbury Square house to the ground and destroyed many of his possessions and papers. Etching by Francis Wheatley. © The Trustees of the British Museum.

Lord Mansfield at the age of eighty. Sir Joshua Reynolds wished he had painted the portrait eight or ten years earlier, before Mansfield lost his teeth. He wrote: "I have made him exactly what he is now, as if I was upon my oath to give the truth, the whole truth, and nothing but the truth." From the Collection of The Rt Hon. The Earl of Mansfield and Mansfield, Scone Palace, Perth, Scotland.

Sir Francis Buller, an associate justice of the Court of King's Bench, whom Mansfield tried unsuccessfully to get appointed as his successor. Buller was best known for his alleged ruling that a husband could punish his wife with impunity if he used a "stick no thicker than his thumb." Etching by James Gillray.

The monument to Lord Mansfield in Westminster Abbey, designed by John Flaxman. The chief justice is flanked by allegorical figures representing Justice and Learning. © Dean and Chapter of Westminster.

PART TWO

Justice in the Age of Reason

12

Chief Justice of the Court of King's Bench

The cause was like a great piece of veal ... Lord Mansfield found the joint at once and cut with greatest ease, cleanly and cleverly.

James Boswell, a journal entry

No sooner had Mansfield taken his seat as chief justice in November 1756 than he was offered the position of lord chancellor. Lord Hardwicke, along with Newcastle and the rest of the Cabinet, had resigned the same month. The lord chancellor had a special role in the English government;[1] besides being the chief judge of the Court of Chancery, he was also a Cabinet member and the presiding officer of the House of Lords. This was only the first of several times that the King asked Mansfield to take the post, but each time he turned it down, although it would have meant a higher rank and twice the salary.[2]

The question of job security may have played a part in Mansfield's unwillingness to accept the post. The chancellor was normally expected to resign whenever the ministry changed, while the chief justice had what amounted to life tenure. According to one observer: Mansfield "preferred a permanent £5,000 a year as Chief Justice to £10,000 as Chancellor when his party was in office – and a retiring pension of £5,000 when it was out. He was too wide awake for that."[3] In order to ensure the independence of the judiciary from the monarchy, the Act of Settlement of 1701 provided that a common law judge had life tenure unless found guilty of misconduct or removed by both Houses of Parliament.[4] The idea was that the will of the rulers should be subordinate to the rule of law, and that judges should no longer be "jackals of government" but independent referees between the Crown and the citizen.[5] The only exception to these safeguards was that a judge's tenure automatically expired upon the accession of a new monarch. However, even that possible source of judicial insecurity ended in 1761, when King George III, on Mansfield's advice, recommended to Parliament that, to ensure the "independency and uprightness" of judges, they should have life tenure during good behaviour, and Parliament agreed.[6] The poet David Mallet commented on the King's proposal:

The law must independent be;
Her ministers as in my sight
And mine alone, despensing right,
With temper firm, with spirit sage,
The MANSFIELDS of each future age.[7]

This reference to Mansfield suggests that after only five years as a judge he had already achieved a reputation for fairness, wisdom, and independence.

A second reason for Mansfield's refusing the post of chancellor was that the Court of King's Bench presented an irresistible challenge to him as a lawyer. While the principles of equity administered by the Chancery Court were more or less settled law, the ancient common law of England administered by King's Bench was badly in need of reform. In a legally minded age, a serious drawback of the law was that many practitioners regarded it as a fixed set of rules and procedures, rather than a system that could be adapted to the changing needs and circumstances of society.[8] As chief justice, the ambitious Mansfield would have a unique opportunity to make those changes.[9] It was a position that he had coveted for many years, and one for which he was well prepared.

The Court of King's Bench, with a history going back to the thirteenth century,[10] was one of the three central courts that tried cases under the English common law, the other two being the courts of Common Pleas and Exchequer. The common law was the customary law of England that had developed over the years, not so much by acts of Parliament (although the judges interpreted these acts) but by the judges' decisions, which served as precedents for later decisions. Although there were a number of inferior local courts, the three central courts supervised all common law litigation.[11] In addition to the three common law courts, the Court of Chancery, which had only two judges – the lord chancellor and the master of the rolls – administered a separate legal system, called equity, that existed side-by-side with the common law.

Originally, each of the three central common law courts had jurisdiction over different kinds of disputes,[12] but by the early eighteenth century each of the courts had managed to enlarge its own jurisdiction, encroaching on each other's turf to such an extent that they all competed for the same cases.[13] Attracting business was important to the judges because a good part of their compensation consisted of fees paid by the parties.[14] During Mansfield's tenure as chief justice, the fairness and clarity of his decisions, the speed with which he resolved disputes, and the public confidence in his integrity brought so many suitors to his court that the other two courts became veritable backwaters.[15] In each of the four three-week trial terms at Westminster Hall, the Court of King's Bench tried, on average, the amazing number of between 250 and 300 cases.[16] Mansfield attracted so much legal business to King's Bench that, as chief justice, he had "a princely income," greater than that of any of the other judges.[17]

Each of the three common law courts had a chief justice and three "puisne" (i.e., associate) justices, for a total of twelve judges. Although there were 4,000 attorneys in London,[18] only about 300 barristers were admitted to the bar, i.e., to argue cases in these courts.[19] Of these, a close-knit group of only 20 to 30 had a remunerative practice in the Court of King's Bench. The members of this small group were well known to each other, and there was an informal atmosphere among them and between them and the judges.[20]

The three common law courts, as well as the Court of Chancery, were all crowded together in Westminster Hall, built for King William Rufus in 1099 and enlarged under Richard II around 1395. This impressive structure still stands, though it no longer houses the law courts. A twenty-one-year-old nephew of Sir Joshua Reynolds, visiting London from Devonshire in 1775, described the ceremonial procession at the Hall on the first day of term in a chatty letter to his sister:

> Westminster Hall is an exceeding large building, and contains the chief Courts of Justice of England; the first entrance is into one of the largest rooms in the Kingdom; on the right hand a flight of steps leads to another room in which is held the Court of Exchequer; a little farther on the same side is a little nook, as it appears, in the wall, which forms another court; this is the Court of Common Pleas; at the further end are two other rooms; these are the Court of Chancery and the Court of King's Bench.
>
> The Ceremony is this: the approach of the Judges is signified by Beadles and Constables, who make a Lane; then 5 or 6 men in Great

> Wigs and Gowns (I don't know their titles) place themselves in a line about halfway up the Hall. The Lord Chancellor preceded by the Great Seal etc. which are always carried before Him wherever He goes) then walks up, salutes those who are plac'd to receive Him, shakes them by the Hand and passes on to his own Court, the Court of Chancery; I forgot to say that He is preceded by a prodigious large gold Mace, and 7 or 8 Pursebearers or Clerks (I believe) with green Bags, and one walks behind Him to bear his train, for they are all in their Robes ... When He is seated, the Lord Chief Justice (Lord Mansfield) makes His appearance, and goes through the same Ceremony; He has no Mace. Then all the other Judges according to their priority and preceded in the same manner, and with their Bearers, walk up and salute those officers, and retire to their respective Courts, where they proceed to do Business.[21]

Westminster Hall was a bustling place when the courts were in session. Besides the courts, it housed a range of counters and stalls for the sale of books, prints, and mathematical instruments. Seamstresses and others displayed their wares, giving the hall the appearance of a market or fair.[22] The different courts were not separated by partitions until about 1760, but even after that Westminster Hall was extremely noisy. Aside from the booksellers and other retailers and their customers, a large number of judges, lawyers, law students, jurors, witnesses, and spectators were often present, especially when an important or sensational case was to be heard.[23]

Here, for over thirty years, Lord Mansfield listened to testimony and legal arguments and handed down the decisions of the court. The part of Westminster Hall occupied by the Court of King's Bench was only about twenty-five feet square. The judges sat on a raised dais. Behind them was an embroidered tapestry showing the royal arms, and in front of them sat the clerks at a table covered with a green cloth. The jurors sat on one side, with a gallery for the spectators on the other side.[24] Once, when someone complained to Mansfield that the court was not large enough to hold even the barristers, he replied acidly that it was "much more than large enough for those who had business there."[25]

Given the absence of any well-organized legal education in England, attending the courts at Westminster Hall was a vital part of a law student's education. There they could learn not just the law but also the procedures of the court, the language of the law, and how lawyers were expected to conduct themselves.[26] Mansfield, who had gained much of his own legal education by attending trials at Westminster Hall, paid particular attention to the students, reserving a special section of the courtroom for them. He would require counsel to make a statement of his case for their benefit, and he would often stop the proceedings to explain, comment upon, or even refute, a point that a lawyer or a witness had made, solely for the enlightenment of the students.[27]

The courts sat in Westminster Hall during four trial terms, each lasting about three weeks: Michaelmas (October–November), Hilary (January–February), Easter (April–May), and Trinity (May–June).[28] Between trial terms, the twelve common law judges would hear cases in Guildhall in the City of London, as well as criminal cases at Old Bailey. In July and August, the judges, accompanied by members of the bar, also travelled on circuit, conducting trials, called "assizes," on six circuits throughout England. With very few exceptions, Mansfield travelled on circuit every summer from the time he became a judge until the age of eighty.[29] Most of the felonies tried at the assizes involved theft. Horse stealing, for example, was a capital crime, and Mansfield believed that imposing harsh penalties would serve as a deterrent.[30]

Two judges, each from a different court, usually travelled together on circuit.[31] For example, in the summer of 1758, Mansfield and Baron Sidney Smythe of the Court of Exchequer travelled on the Northern Circuit, visiting at least eight towns over a period of nearly two months.[32] The judges usually travelled from town to town by coach, accompanied by liveried outriders, while the lawyers rode on horseback.[33] Mansfield sometimes chose to ride, with his coach following him. On the one occasion when he travelled on the Midland Circuit, he did not even join the cavalcade of judges, lawyers, and court officials entering the town of Leicester, but stole into town late at night on a saddle horse.[34]

The number of cases to be tried in each town varied considerably. In the town of Newcastle, Mansfield reported to his friend and patron the Duke of Newcastle in 1758, there was so little business that it was all completed before dinner,[35] whereas in Lancaster, "there was more business than ever known" and the court continued to sit on Saturday night until it was completed.[36] During his first eight years on the bench Mansfield went on all six circuits, but after 1764 he confined himself to the Home Circuit, the closest to London.[37] He would often invite the judge accompanying him to his home at Kenwood on the Sunday before the circuit was to begin, and they would then set out together on Monday morning.[38]

The assizes in any given town usually lasted a limited number of days, during which all the cases had to be tried. As a result, justice was speedy, though not always fair. The judges entered the town in a ceremonial procession, escorted by sheriffs, and opened court that evening. The next day, after attending church and hearing a sermon, one of the two judges would instruct the grand jury, which would return indictments the same afternoon. Meanwhile, the trial jury was sworn, and it would sometimes hear several trials that day. Trials continued after dinner – when the jurors might have had a good deal to drink – and it was not unusual for jurors to doze off during a trial, even when a prisoner's life was at stake. Witnesses, too, sometimes testified under the influence of alcohol.[39]

The presence of the judges on circuit gave the local notables an opportunity to show their hospitality. When Mansfield was promoted to the bench, he paid a compliment to Oxford University by choosing the Oxford Circuit as the first circuit on which he travelled. The faculty and students of Christ Church were so appreciative of the honour he paid to his alma mater that they entertained him magnificently at a dinner in Christ Church Hall, and a student delivered a Latin oration congratulating him on his advancement.[40] On the Northern Circuit in 1758, Mansfield reported: "The Sheriff yesterday entertained 250 gentlemen. I am kept today for an extraordinary dinner the Mayor gives to the ladies in town; and in the evening Sir Walter Blacket carries me to his house, where I shall stay all day tomorrow."[41] In contrast to this hospitality, judges on circuit were sometimes victims of mobs who disagreed with their decisions. One such case occurred in Coventry in 1761, when a judge on circuit was obliged to take refuge in a private house to escape the fury of those who believed he had made an unfair ruling.[42]

The assizes also provided entertainment for the local populace, an exciting occasion for horse racing, balls, and private parties. But the trials were the main event. Men, women, and children crowded into the courtroom, eager to witness the drama of a capital case and to watch the lawyers in action.[43] On one occasion when Mansfield was on the Northern Circuit, his crier, a bold young man, took the opportunity to grope a country belle just before the judge entered the room. Responding to her shrieks, a group of male spectators were about to inflict physical harm on the miscreant. Seeing Mansfield approaching, he saved himself from a beating by shouting: "My lords, the king's justices do strictly charge and command all manner of persons to keep silence on pain of imprisonment." When told about the incident, Mansfield was more impressed by his crier's presence of mind than shocked by his behaviour.[44]

In Westminster Hall, Mansfield and his fellow judges handled both trials and appeals. A single judge conducted most trials, but if a trial was particularly complex or if an important question of law had to be settled, it would be heard by all four King's Bench judges sitting together as a court.[45] Trials ranged from matters of momentous importance, such as slavery[46] and freedom of the press,[47] to minor disputes, such as an assault claim occasioned by a quarrel over a sixpenny penknife.[48] A large percentage of the trials involved the interpretation of wills, deeds, leases, and marriage settlements, with a substantial number of marine-insurance and other commercial cases.[49]

It is a remarkable fact that during Mansfield's first twenty years as chief justice only twice was there disagreement among the four judges of King's Bench, with Justice Sir Joseph Yates being the sole dissenting judge on both occasions. Appointed to the court in 1764, Yates was known for his independent views and his competence as a judge; he was also an elegant man who enjoyed dancing, was something of a dandy, but had earned a reputation for integrity and kindness.[50] Although Yates and Mansfield treated each other with mutual respect, there was no personal warmth between them. Yates first dissented in 1769 in the important copyright case of *Millar v. Taylor*.[51] The second dissent occurred a year later in *Perrin v. Blake*,[52] a case involving the interpretation of a will, where Mansfield declined to follow settled law where the law was at odds with the clear intention of the testator.

During the entire thirty-two years of Mansfield's tenure, there were dissents in only twenty cases, and only six decisions of his court were reversed on appeal.[53] Mansfield was proud of this record of near unanimity, in part because the solidarity of the judges gave litigants confidence in the certainty of the legal principles that he had laid down, particularly in cases affecting commerce.[54] He also undoubtedly savoured the almost uninterrupted unanimity as an indication of his dominance of the court. One barrister who practised before Mansfield believed that the unanimity was due less to his uncommon abilities, integrity, and temper, than to sheer fear of him, which accounted for "four judges agreeing perfectly in every rule, order and judgment for fourteen years."[55]

Mansfield's relations with his fellow judges were usually harmonious.[56] At the time he was appointed chief justice, two of them, Michael Foster and Thomas Denison, had already been on the court for over ten years. They were both experts in the common law, and Mansfield was happy to learn from them. He asked Foster to write some of the court's opinions on intricate points of law. In order to get the benefit of their experience and knowledge, he would take one of them in his coach with him on his daily journey to Westminster Hall.[57]

On occasion, Mansfield's supremacy produced tensions. Sometimes Mansfield failed to show respect for a particular judge, either because he disliked him or perhaps because he wanted to impress on the minds of the spectators his domination of the court. In one instance he rudely turned away from Justice Willes just when Willes expected Mansfield to ask his opinion on a case; the indignant judge shrieked out in court: "I have not been consulted and I will be heard." Forty years later, the philosopher and social reformer Jeremy Bentham, who was present at the court that day, wrote: "At this distance of time ... the feminine scream issuing out of his manly frame still lingers in my ears."[58]

But, in general, when the associate justices disagreed with Mansfield they did not challenge him. On one occasion Mansfield refused to require a nobleman, who was in a legal dispute with his wife, to appear in court, saying that the court had no power over a peer until the House of Lords had been consulted. The other judges grumbled that Mansfield's ruling diminished the court's standing, but they were unwilling to oppose him directly.[59]

The best known of Mansfield's associate justices was William Blackstone, the author of *Commentaries on the Laws of England*, probably the most influential legal text ever written; but Mansfield and Blackstone sat together on King's Bench for less than four months. Although Blackstone, born in 1723, was nearly twenty years younger than Mansfield, they became friends. Their personalities were very different, Blackstone tending to be introverted and shy, while Mansfield had a pleasing personality and many friends. It may have been their similar literary tastes, centring on the classics, that drew them together. According to one of Blackstone's biographers, Mansfield introduced Blackstone to the first young woman who interested him,[60] and Mansfield was the best man at Blackstone's wedding.[61]

Blackstone had learned the law in large part by attending Mansfield's court. Although Blackstone never became a leading member of the bar,[62] Mansfield recognized his legal genius and, when the Oxford University Chair of Civil Law became vacant, recommended him for the post to the Duke of Newcastle, who controlled all such appointments. Interviewing Blackstone for the job, Newcastle asked him if "whenever anything in the political hemisphere is agitated at that University, you will, sir, exert yourself on our behalf?" When Blackstone declined to become Newcastle's political toady, merely saying he would fulfill his lecturing duties as well as he could, Newcastle turned him down.[63]

Nevertheless, Mansfield continued his efforts on Blackstone's behalf, advising him to settle at Oxford and persuading Charles Viner, a wealthy lawyer, to establish a professorship of common law. In 1758 Blackstone became the first occupant of the post.[64] His Vinerian lectures were not only the first occasion where English law was taught in a university but they also formed the basis for *Commentaries*, in which Blackstone for the first time presented English law as a rational and coherent system. It became a standard text for law students.[65] Mansfield and his fellow justice Sir John Wilmot read drafts of *Commentaries* and provided Blackstone with comments and corrections.[66] Thus, to Mansfield must go some of the credit for the famous *Commentaries*.

In February 1770, Blackstone was appointed as a justice of the Court of Common Pleas to replace a judge who had retired, but a week later he was appointed to the Court of King's Bench. The reason for this unusual series of events was that Joseph Yates, who had been an associate justice of the Court of King's Bench since 1764, wanted to leave the court, either because his poor health made the heavy workload difficult for him or because he disagreed with some of Mansfield's legal innovations and no longer wished to work under his powerful sway.[67] As a result, Blackstone and Yates agreed to switch courts.

But Blackstone too chafed under Mansfield's domination of the Court of King's Bench, and when Yates died in June 1770 at the age of forty-eight, creating a vacancy on Common Pleas, Blackstone took the opportunity to return there, where he remained for ten years.[68] There seems to have been a growing distance between Blackstone and Mansfield, perhaps due to Mansfield's resentment of his younger colleague's prominence as a result of the huge success of *Commentaries*.[69]

The three central courts not only tried cases but also heard appeals. This they did in an interlocking manner. Appeals from King's Bench went to the Exchequer Chamber, composed of the judges of Common Pleas and Exchequer, or directly to the House of Lords; appeals from Common Pleas went to King's Bench; and appeals from Exchequer went to Exchequer Chamber, which in such cases was composed of the judges of King's Bench and Common Pleas.

The court of last resort was the House of Lords,[70] whose presiding officer – and the highest-ranking judge in the land – was the lord chancellor.[71] In deciding appeals in the House of Lords, the lord chancellor sometimes sat alone or, more often, with one or two of the other "law lords," the judges who were members of the peerage, usually including Lord Mansfield. In practice, when the House of Lords was called upon to decide an appeal, it usually deferred to the law lords. Thus, sitting as a member of the House of Lords, Mansfield might play a role in deciding an appeal of a case on which he had sat as the trial judge. The Earl of Shelburne, who was usually critical of Mansfield, said that he had "the most indecent habit of attending the appeals against his own decrees in the House of Lords."[72]

Because noblemen and noblewomen were not required to appear in the common law courts, the House of Lords also conducted trials in which a peer was a defendant, such as the notorious bigamy trial of the Duchess of Kingston.[73]

Well before the time he was appointed, Mansfield must have given a great deal of thought to how he would conduct himself as chief justice. Seldom has any new judge been better prepared for his job. He handed down some of his most important and carefully thought-out decisions, particularly those involving commercial law and insurance law, during his first few years in office, and he continued to make significant contributions to the English common law for the next thirty years.

As soon as he took his seat on the bench, he began to impose his views and character on the court. His first important action, in the belief that "justice delayed is justice denied,"[74] was to speed up the court's procedures. It was a practice up to that time to allow counsel to argue a case two or even three times before the court pronounced judgment. On 12 November 1756, one day after he first sat as a judge, King's Bench heard argument in *Raynard v. Chase*,[75] an appeal in a bankruptcy case. After counsel had completed his argument, the court reporter stated: "As this was the first argument, it was expected, as of course, that it would be argued again." Mansfield quickly threw cold water on any such expectation, at the same time emphasizing that he meant not only to dispose of the case before him without any delay but also to educate future litigants as to the state of the law: "Where we have no doubt, we ought not to put the parties to the delay and expense of a farther argument; nor leave other persons who may be interested in the determination ... under the anxiety of suspense." Then, instead of postponing the decision, as was the custom in the past, he immediately rendered it from the bench and the other judges quickly made it unanimous.

Previously, the lawyers for the two sides in a lawsuit would often agree between themselves to postpone a trial or argument. Mansfield, thinking again of the interests of the clients in having their cases heard expeditiously, did not allow this. If a lawyer wanted a delay, he would have to apply to the court and show a good reason for the postponement.[76]

Mansfield was relentless in moving the work of the court along with dispatch. In England, there were (and still are) two distinct classes of lawyers: solicitors (sometimes called attorneys), who advised clients and drew up legal papers but normally did not try cases or argue appeals in court; and barristers, who had the exclusive privilege of appearing in court. On one occasion, when John Dunning, one of the foremost barristers of his day,[77] did not show up on time to try a case, Mansfield refused to delay the trial. He called on the client's solicitor to open the case. The other barristers present in court burst into laughter at this defiance of tradition and the discomfort of the solicitor, but Mansfield persevered, and the solicitor was forced to get up and state the case.[78] On another occasion, Mansfield told William Davy, another prominent barrister, that he wanted a case heard the next Friday. When Davy reminded him that that day was Good Friday, Mansfield said: "I do not care for that. I shall sit for all that." Davy replied: "Well, my Lord, to be sure you may do as you please, but if you do, my Lord, you will be the first judge to do business on a Good Friday since Pontius Pilate's time."[79]

In his determination to speed up the work of the court, Mansfield did not spare himself. In one trial, for example, the defence did not finish its case until nine in the evening; then the plaintiff's lawyer spoke in reply for an hour; and Mansfield, who was then in his seventies, did not begin his instructions to the jury until ten o'clock. A newspaper reported: "And notwithstanding he sat above thirteen hours on the bench his spirits did not appear in the least exhausted. He spoke for above an hour."[80] The length of this particular court session was unusual, but it was not unusual for the court to sit six days a week, from nine in the morning until three or four in the afternoon,[81] and if Mansfield deemed it necessary, a trial might go on until five, or even seven, in the evening.[82] By 1781, Mansfield had attended one hundred consecutive sessions of the court.[83]

His tireless devotion to the business of the court was not solely due to lifelong habit and the press of court business; he revelled in his judicial work. It was said that Mansfield enjoyed trying cases as much as others liked to engage in sports or fishing.[84] If there was anything for him to learn about a case, he sought it out with pleasure.[85] Soon after his appointment, when he sent a draft of an argument to a fellow judge from his home at Kenwood, he wrote: "While the company is at cards, I play my rubbers at this work, not the pleasantest in the world; but what must be done I love to do, and have it over."[86]

His insistence on handling the business of the court with dispatch was never at the expense of thoroughness. To be painstaking in his work was certainly an enduring personal practice, but he also felt it to be his duty as a judge. In one criminal case, he said: "I never give a judicial opinion upon any point, until I think I am master of every material argument and authority relative to it. It is not only a justice due to the Crown and the party, in every criminal case where doubts arise, to weigh well the grounds and reasons of the judgment; but it is of great consequence, to explain them with accuracy and precision, in open Court."[87] Yet his insistence on understanding the details of a case did not diminish his grasp of its overall significance. He had the same marvellous ability possessed by Florence Nightingale, who, it was said, had "both the smallest details at her fingers' end and the great general views of the whole."[88]

Mansfield insisted on fair treatment of the lawyers who practised before him. Until his appointment, the members of the bar argued their motions before the court in order of seniority. Each day, the court called upon the most senior counsel to make his motions, then the next senior, and so on. If time ran out, the same procedure was repeated the next day, so that junior barristers might have to sit in court day after day without getting a chance to argue their motions. Mansfield altered this procedure by allowing each lawyer to make only one motion in rotation and if all the motions had not been heard by the time the court adjourned, he would start next morning where the court had left off, until all the members of the bar with motions had been heard.[89] The new procedure encouraged and protected the junior lawyers, but even more important, it helped their clients by reducing the delay in having their cases heard.[90]

Mansfield, in robes of black velvet, bordered with gold, was a charismatic and commanding figure on the bench.[91] Boswell, who seems to have attended King's Bench to hear Mansfield pronounce judgment whenever he had a chance, wrote in his diary that he was "charmed with the precision of his ideas, the clearness of his arrangement, the eloquent choice and fluency of his language and the distinct forcible and melodious expression of his voice."[92] In all that he said, there was a happy mixture of good nature, good humour, elegance, ease, and dignity.[93] When he pronounced judgment, he spoke slowly, sounding distinctly every letter of every word. He never completely lost his Scottish accent (pronouncing "authority," "awtawrity" and "attachment," "attaichment") and he did not always observe the rules of grammar, but he was always understood.[94] He had a near-perfect memory; he seldom took notes during a trial or appeal, and when he did, he rarely consulted them.[95]

It was nearly impossible to fool Lord Mansfield. He "seemed to have a particular pleasure in discriminating between ingenious, clear, and convincing argument, and subtle metaphysical distinctions, tending to bewilder and mislead the tyros or students in the law."[96] John Campbell, Mansfield's nineteenth-century biographer, wrote: "No man has ever in an equal degree possessed that wonderful sagacity in discovering chicanery and artifice, and separating fallacy from truth, and sophistry from argument."[97] He laid it down as a rule that a person who, even legally, uses the court's procedures for illegal or wicked purposes may be punished for contempt of court. For example, a creditor who gets his debtor arrested for recovery of a just debt would be acting illegally if his purpose is to harass, injure, or defame the person, to prevent him from attending an election, or for some other illegal or improper purpose.[98]

An instance of Mansfield's impatience with deception occurred when a Frenchman appeared in court to justify his putting up bail of £1,000 for a defendant. The question was whether the Frenchman had sufficient assets to make bail of that amount. When he was cross-examined, he claimed not to understand English, and the lawyer questioning him seemed at a loss as to what to do. At that, Mansfield swung into action. He asked the man in the most elegant French whether he was a homeowner, where he lived, his occupation, how much he was worth, and how long he had lived in England. Upon Mansfield's questioning, the man confessed that he was not worth more than £400 and, despite his "no English," he had lived in England for seven years.[99]

Boswell used an unforgettable image to describe Mansfield's ability to get right to the heart of a dispute. Going to the court with a friend, Boswell predicted that Mansfield would reverse a decision of the fifteen-member Scottish Court of Session. "How will he do it?" asked his friend. Boswell replied: "By sleight of hand ... He won't tell you how he does it. But he'll let you see him do it." After Mansfield gave his opinion from the bench reversing the court's decision, Boswell said: "He has not only done it. But he has shown how he did it. The cause was like a great piece of veal or other meat. The Court of Session could not find the joint. It was handed about through the fifteen, and they tried at it but it would not do. Lord Mansfield found the joint at once and cut with greatest ease, cleanly and cleverly."[100]

The praise for Mansfield was not unqualified. During his lifetime he was criticized for his unswerving support of the authority of the government. One otherwise admiring observer wrote of this trait: "This conduct will leave a stain upon his character which time cannot obliterate. The great man's errors universally admitted to be such ought to serve as a beacon to minor judges."[101] The coldness and arrogance that he sometimes displayed to his fellow judges as well as to others left him open to accusations of vanity; and his attempts, not always successful, to change the law led to accusations of unconstitutional principles.[102] William Pitt, Mansfield's political opponent for more than three decades, was blunt in his criticism of Mansfield's willingness to depart from established legal precedents. Pitt accused Mansfield of inventing law "and no fond parent could be more attached to his offspring than he was to such inventions."[103] Pitt charged that Mansfield was "a very bad judge, proud, haughty to the Bar, [and] hasty in his determinations."[104] He also was critical of Mansfield's habit of attending appeals of his own decisions in the House of Lords.

Nevertheless, the vast majority of Mansfield's contemporaries as well as later writers recognized him as a great judge, in part because of his basic humanity and instinct for justice. Campbell wrote that while on the bench he encouraged the timid and awed the bold.[105] His demeanour to the lawyers who practised before him was usually dignified and courteous. He paid patient attention to their arguments and often would ask questions that assisted them.[106] But he could occasionally be cruel. When Serjeant George Hill, a particularly wordy and pedantic lawyer who had acquired the nickname of Serjeant Labyrinth,[107] was droning on and on, Mansfield interrupted him with, "The court hopes your cold is better," in a tone meant to ridicule the lawyer.[108]

If Mansfield thought a lawyer was wasting the court's time, he would read a newspaper or write letters during the argument.[109] On one such occasion, John Dunning, who was not intimidated by Mansfield, stopped in mid-argument. Mansfield said: "Pray go on, Mr Dunning." The lawyer paused and then answered: "I fear, my Lord, I am interrupting your Lordship's more important occupations. I will gladly wait until your Lordship finds leisure to attend to my client and his humble counsel."[110] Responding to Dunning's argument in another case, Mansfield exclaimed: "If that be the law, I may burn my law books." Dunning replied: "Better read them my Lord."[111]

And Mansfield loved the rare occasions when Dunning got taken down a peg. Once, when Dunning, an ungainly figure who was perpetually ill with bronchial troubles,[112] was cross-examining an attractive young woman, he asked her whether her master went to bed with her. She replied: "That trial does not come up today, Mr Slabberchops." Mansfield thrust his hand into the waistband of his breeches – his habit when he was amused – and asked Dunning whether he had any more questions to put to the witness. Dunning replied: "No, my Lord, I have done" and sat down.[113]

Despite – or perhaps because of – Dunning's refusal to be overawed by Mansfield, they got along well together. Dunning served as solicitor general in the late 1760s, and after he resigned in 1770 and resumed his legal practice as a private lawyer, Mansfield gave him the privilege of making motions in court directly after the serjeants, who were the highest-ranking members of the bar.[114] A few years later, Dunning represented a plaintiff who brought an action for reinstatement against Dr Warren, the rector of the parish of Hampstead, who had fired him as his clerk. The clerk had stood father for a bride and gave her in marriage. Warren fired him because, as soon as the ceremony was over, the clerk kissed the bride, without any objection from her. Dunning argued before Mansfield that Dr Warren probably fired the clerk because he was angry that he didn't get a kiss. Mansfield supported Dunning (though not his reasoning), ruling that the clerk was a servant of the parish, who could not be discharged at the pleasure of the rector because the clerkship was a civil, not an ecclesiastical, position.[115]

Mansfield occasionally liked to spice his remarks in court with humour, which sometimes had a sharp edge. Sir Fletcher Norton was an eloquent and aggressive lawyer whom Mansfield particularly liked.[116] He served as attorney general and later as speaker of the House of Commons. But Norton was known for his lack of culture. When arguing before Mansfield on a case involving real estate, Norton unfortunately said: "My Lord, I can illustrate the point ... in my own person: I have two little manors." Giving him a bland smile, Mansfield said: "We all know that, Sir Fletcher."[117]

In another case, involving the theft of a ladle, the prosecutor stressed that the offence was particularly serious because the prisoner was believed to be an attorney. Mansfield half-whispered to the prosecutor: "Come, come, don't exaggerate matters; if the fellow had been an attorney you may depend upon it, he would have stolen the *bowl* as well as the *ladle*!"[118] When a lawyer from Somersetshire asked Mansfield to remove a case from King's Bench to be heard in his home county, Mansfield replied: "I think Somersetshire the only place you can beat them in, consider[ing] 'tis your own dunghill."[119]

In a case involving the collision of two ships at sea, the witness was a sailor who arrived in court somewhat the worse for liquor. He testified that at the time of the accident he was standing abaft the binnacle. Mansfield asked where that was. The sailor said loudly: "A pretty fellow to be a judge, who does not know where abaft the binnacle is!" Instead of threatening to commit him for contempt, Mansfield replied sweetly: "Well, my friend, fit me for my office by telling me where *abaft the binnacle* is; you have already shown me the meaning of *half seas over*."[120] (Today, this might be translated as "three sheets to the wind."[121])

A witness named Elm, who was over eighty, gave remarkably clear testimony in a trial in which Dunning was counsel for one of the parties. Mansfield questioned Elm about his living habits and was told that he had all his life been an early riser and a temperate man. Mansfield (perhaps thinking about his own moderate habits) remarked: "I have always found that without temperance and early habits longevity is never attained." The next witness was Elm's older brother, who almost surpassed his brother as an intelligent and clear-headed witness. "I suppose that you are also an early riser," said Mansfield. "No, my Lord," he answered, "I like my bed at all hours and specially I like it in the morning." "Ah, but like your brother you are a very temperate man?" asked the judge, anxiously hoping to preserve the more important part of his theory. "My Lord, I am a very old man and my memory is as clear as a bell, but I can't remember the night when I haven't gone to bed more or less drunk." "Ah my Lord," Dunning exclaimed, "this old man's case supports a theory upheld by many that habitual intemperance is favourable to longevity." "No, no," replied Mansfield with a smile: "This old man and his brother teach us what every carpenter knows – that elm be it wet or dry is a very tough wood."[122]

Mansfield was truly shocked by injustice and used every power he had to correct it. There are many accounts of his assisting the defenceless. Anne Catley, a girl of fifteen who was a talented singer,[123] had been apprenticed by her father, a gentleman's coachman, to William Bates, a music teacher. After two years of her apprenticeship, and without the knowledge of Anne's father, Bates turned her over to the socially prominent Sir Francis Delaval,[124] ostensibly to continue her music lessons with him but in reality to live with him as his kept mistress. A lawyer named John Fraine drew up an agreement between Bates and Delaval providing that Bates would receive the profits derived from Anne's singing. Delaval then paid Bates £200 in payment for the girl.[125]

When the case came before Mansfield's court, he made short work of the attempt by Bates, Fraine, and Delaval to disguise the unsavoury transaction: "the girl goes and lives and still does live with Sir Francis, notoriously, as a kept mistress. Thus she has been played over, by Bates, into his hands, for this purpose. No man can avoid seeing all this; let him wink ever so much." Mansfield then moved to the key question of whether the Court of King's Bench had jurisdiction over an immoral transaction, even in the absence of a specific statute prohibiting it. The court, Mansfield declared in a crucial pronouncement, was the custodian of the morals of the people and had jurisdiction of offences against good morals. The sale of the girl was "notoriously and grossly against public decency and good manners." Thus, morality was an essential part of the English common law.[126] Moreover, Bates, Fraine, and Delaval had entered into a conspiracy, which was clearly within the court's jurisdiction.

Mansfield ordered Anne released from Delaval's clutches and also refused to turn her over to her father. Rejecting the traditional argument that a father should have absolute authority over his children, he pointed out that the girl had sworn that she received "ill usage" from him before he put her out as an apprentice, and that while she was apprenticed to Bates her father "seldom or ever came to see her, or ever gave her either advice or reprimand." Furthermore, he said, "it is even suspicious whether the father and mother were not parties to the conspiracy" and whether the father was carrying on the prosecution in hopes of extorting money from the defendant.

"Let the girl therefore be discharged from all restraint, and be at liberty to go where she will."

Mansfield then turned to whether criminal charges should be brought against the three conspirators. As to Delaval, who had "debauched" the girl, there could be no doubt. Bates too should stand trial because he knew that the girl had become Delaval's mistress but he never notified her father. Mansfield, who all his life loved and revered the legal profession, saved his special condemnation for Fraine, the attorney: "he has certainly acted inconsistently with the duty of his profession, and that chastity of character which it is incumbent upon an attorney always to support ... It was impossible for him to be ignorant of the real intention of this transaction: he could not imagine that she really bound herself to Sir Francis to be taught music by him; but must undoubtedly have been conscious of the true purpose for which these deeds and writings were calculated."[127]

In a somewhat similar case that was reported in a newspaper, a poor clergyman's fourteen-year-old daughter had been walking down the central London street of Holborn with a female friend when a coach drove up with three men in it, one of whom was the girl's brother. Two of them jumped out and tried to seize her, whereupon she ran into a shop for shelter. Nevertheless, the three men pulled her out of the shop and took her by force to a magistrate in order to have her committed to her brother's custody. The girl told the magistrate that she believed that her brother meant to carry her to a bawdy house. At that, the magistrate released the girl and committed two of the men who had seized her. They were brought before Lord Mansfield to be tried before a jury.

Since the girl had no attorney or friend to help her, Mansfield questioned her himself and learned what had happened. When he asked the girl why she thought her brother intended to take her to a bawdy house, she answered because he kept a bawdy house himself and she was informed that his associates made a practice of kidnapping young girls for noblemen and gentlemen who wanted them. The jury found the defendants guilty. The newspaper commented: "Thus from the candour and condescension of the noble judge to be counsel, attorney and sole friend of a helpless orphan girl ... stern justice overtakes the whole confederacy, whereof the unnatural brother is the chief ringleader."[128]

In yet another instance of Mansfield's protection of the weak, the counsel for a landlord who was trying to eject a woman of limited means read a long affidavit to support a motion that she had been properly served with process. Mansfield agreed that she had been properly served but "thought it cruel to load with such unnecessary and extravagant expenses a woman already so much distressed." He therefore ordered the plaintiff to pay her costs.[129] A newspaper correspondent observed: "The justice and humanity of the Court ... may serve as a proper hint to the wealthy that they may not hope to carry any oppressive point ... by running an indigent adversary to expenses which the party cannot probably support."[130]

Yet another example of Mansfield's basic humanity came where the overseers of a parish had caused a man to be indicted for converting his house into a hospital for unmarried women to give birth. The overseers claimed that the women then deserted their babies, leaving them to be supported by the parish. Mansfield expressed surprise that such an indictment could ever be found: "By what law is it criminal," he asked, "to deliver a woman when she is with child?" The indictment was dismissed.[131]

On one occasion, Mansfield offered the parties to a dispute his own services as an arbitrator, and he resolved the dispute with Solomonic wisdom. The case had been outstanding for eleven years. Charles Macklin, one of the greatest actors of his day, had been hired to perform at Covent Garden for three seasons at a salary of £400 a season. Macklin was a quarrelsome Irishman; he had once killed a fellow actor in a backstage brawl and was acquitted of murder but convicted of manslaughter.[132] For either political or personal reasons, theatre audiences were known to drive performers off the stage by hissing, catcalls, and physical violence, and the combination of a bellicose actor and an unruly audience could be explosive.[133] Early in the first season of the contract, as a result of a dispute between Macklin and some members of the audience, a riot broke out in the theatre during a performance of *Macbeth*.[134] He was unable to complete the performance, and the manager, not daring to let him appear again, considered the contract terminated. Macklin, however, offered to continue to play his part and demanded his salary. When the manager refused, Macklin brought suit. After lengthy proceedings in other courts, the parties appeared before Lord Mansfield, who decided that the time had come to bring the case to a close. He offered to settle the matter himself if both parties agreed, which they did. The rioting in the theatre was a common calamity, he said, in which the manager and the performer were equal sufferers. He therefore awarded Macklin half of his agreed-upon compensation and ordered each party to pay his own costs. As Macklin left the courtroom, he stopped to tell Mansfield that until this case he had never before known what justice was.[135]

The riot at Covent Garden that drove Macklin off the stage was the basis for a separate lawsuit that he brought for riot and conspiracy against several of the fomenters. Mansfield made a fine distinction between freedom of speech and conspiracy, based on the intention of the audience members who caused the riot. He observed that, while members of an audience had the right to hiss or applaud a performer in order to show their opinion of his performance, they had no right to "execut[e] a pre-concerted design ... to drive him from the theatre and to promote his utter ruin."[136] This was just one example of the important point he made that an action that is perfectly legal if done for an innocuous purpose may be illegal if done for an improper purpose.[137] Macklin, however, told Mansfield that he was not looking for revenge, but only for compensation for his monetary losses from the riot. Mansfield, who always supported a just settlement of any dispute, replied: "Then I think you have done yourself great credit and honour by what you have now said; and I think your conduct was wise too ... You have met with great applause to-day. You never acted better."[138]

Mansfield's contemporaries differed in their views of how impartial he was in his treatment of lawyers and their clients who appeared in his court. Almost certainly he acted impartially most of the time. In a case tried before Mansfield at Guildhall, a Paris wine merchant sued an important London magistrate over his bill. A newspaper reported: "The Court in general expected the judge would have taken some particular notice of such an action but his Lordship ... took no more cognizance of it than if it had been against the most unimportant individual."[139] On another occasion, Mansfield went out of his way to put in his place someone who assumed he would be treated with special deference. Dr Brockelsby was a well-known physician and a friend of such luminaries as Samuel Johnson, Edmund Burke, and John Wilkes. It was said that he was "obsessed with politics, so harassed by the claims of his avocation that he has no time for the practice of medicine."[140] Brockelsby had met Mansfield the previous evening at supper and happened to be a witness in a case that came before him the next day. On taking the stand, the doctor nodded familiarly at the judge. Mansfield took no special notice of him and, when he summed up the case for the jury, he took pains to show his disdain as well as to distance himself from the witness, saying:

"The next witness is one Rockelsby or Brockelsby, Brockelsby or Rockelsby – I am not sure which – and … he swears he is a physician."[141]

Mansfield himself said: "It is a rule with me – an inviolable rule, never to hear a syllable out of Court about any case that either is or is in the smallest degree likely to come before me as a judge." Lord Camden, chief justice of the Court of Common Pleas, who disagreed with Mansfield on most matters, was not so fastidious. "Now I, for my part," he said, "could hear as many people as chose to talk to me about their cases, it would never make the slightest impression on me."[142] Mansfield's prophylactic approach seems preferable to Camden's self-confidence that he was immune from improper influence.

On the other hand, Mansfield did not always act impartially. He was accused of favouring young lawyers who had been educated at Westminster. John Scott, the future Lord Chancellor Eldon, moved his law practice from the Court of King's Bench to the Chancery Court because "I soon perceived, or thought I perceived, a preference in Lord Mansfield … for young lawyers who had been bred at Westminster School and Christ Church [Oxford] … Lord Mansfield, I do believe, was not conscious of the bias; he was a good man."[143] When important people were involved in a case, Mansfield sometimes displayed a deference that was inappropriate for a judge. An example was the Duchess of Kingston, the defendant in a notorious bigamy case.[144] When she appeared in Mansfield's court, escorted by the Duke of Newcastle and two other notables, she was allowed to wait in an antechamber, separate from all the other litigants and witnesses, until Mansfield and his fellow judges were ready to receive her.[145] James Boswell, though an admirer of Mansfield, noted in his diary "Lord Mansfield's strange behaviour in the case of the Duchess of Kingston. I said it was shocking to see a Lord Chief Justice so partial."[146]

Mansfield's greatest strength as a judge rested on his ability to dispense justice in the particular disputes that came before him and at the same time advance the interests of society generally. Mansfield's belief that a wise judge, even if not educated in the law, could rely on his instinct for justice is illustrated by the advice he once gave a high military officer in Jamaica whose responsibilities also included acting as a judge: "General, you have a sound head, and a good heart; take courage and you will do very well, in your new occupation, in a Court of Equity. My advice is, to make your decrees as your head and your heart dictate, to hear both sides patiently, to decide with firmness in the best manner you can; *but be careful not to assign your reasons*, since your determinations may be substantially right, although your reasons may be very bad, or essentially wrong."[147] However, Mansfield did not believe that this advice, while appropriate for a layman, should be followed by a professional judge. He himself gave reasons for his decisions, because he believed that a judge's job included setting down rules, based on general principles, which would provide guidance for future litigants. But, above all, his job was to dispense justice.

Mansfield wrote no books or articles describing his views on the role of the law and the courts in society. It is possible that a speech or article of this kind was among his papers that were destroyed in the Gordon Riots of 1780; if so, it is irretrievably lost. What we know of his legal philosophy must therefore be gleaned from his judicial decisions and from letters. A letter he wrote in 1775 to his long-time friend Warren Hastings, the governor general of Bengal, gives us a valuable window into his thinking. At the time, Hastings faced the task of creating a legal system for Britain's newly acquired colony of India. Instead of imposing British laws on the Indians, he decided to leave existing Indian laws in place (subject, of course, to British supervision). He sent a translation of these laws to Mansfield for his comment.

Mansfield began his reply by praising Hastings for not trying to change the laws of a foreign country with a culture radically different from that of England: "No measure could be more barbarous, in every sense of the epithet, than to change the laws of any people, except by slow degrees, and in consequence of long experience." The worst laws that are familiar to a society, he said, are preferable to the best laws to which it is a stranger.[148] But, while the laws of each society reflect its particular culture, customs, and traditions, all legal systems have a common root in reason and morality.

Mansfield's letter continued, going to the heart of his judicial philosophy:

> As to right and wrong, human reason is much the same at all times and in all places. Greeks, Romans, Arabians, Gentoos [i.e., Hindus], and Christians draw the same conclusions from principles of natural justice and equity, but every people and age have to have them vouched by the authority of their own doctors.
>
> You have done like the great lawgivers of Greece and Rome in calling together their pundits to make a collection of their laws. I am delighted with the specimen you have sent me. It is very curious: the

> peculiarities, and the resemblance to European modes of thinking afford matter of great and equal entertainment. By this time you know that we have not been so absurd as to attempt changing the Hindoo laws. They are left by us as entire and untouched as they were by the Mahomatan Government.[149]

Mansfield believed in "natural law": namely, that the particular laws of a country, however different in their particulars, are based on "an eternal and immutable moral code."[150] His belief was based on his education in the classics, his study of the legal systems of other nations, and his experience as a lawyer and judge.

Natural law has a long history. According to the legal philosopher and educator Roscoe Pound, the ancient Greeks "had the notion of an ideal form of the social *status quo* – a form that expresses its nature, a perfect form of the social organization of a given civilization – as that which the legal order is to further and maintain. They are to measure all situations by an idealized form of the social order of the time and place and are so to shape the law as to make it maintain and further this ideal of the social status quo."[151] The idea that there was a "determinable law of nature" can be traced from the ancient Greeks to the Romans. The Roman statesman, orator, and philosopher Cicero believed that all law was based on general principles that were grounded in the universality of human reason.[152] Natural-law doctrine was passed on from the classical writers to medieval scholars.[153] St Thomas Aquinas wrote in the thirteenth century that "every law framed by man bears the character of a law exactly to the extent to which it is derived from the law of nature. But if on any point it is in conflict with the law of nature, it at once ceases to be a law; it is a mere perversion of the law."[154] As indicated earlier, the seventeenth-century legal philosophers Hugo Grotius and Samuel Pufendorf also were proponents of natural law.[155]

Mansfield was familiar with all these writers, but none influenced his thinking as much as the seventeenth-century English philosopher John Locke. Locke explained his theory of law and politics in *Two Treatises Of Government*, published in 1690. Locke rejected the theory that kings ruled by divine right and replaced it with a theory of government based on a social contract. He hypothesized that before the existence of any government, men were free to do what they liked with their own selves and their possessions. They were governed only by natural law, laid down by God, which dictated that no one ought to harm another in his life, health, liberty, or property. Because there were transgressors who might deprive people of their God-given rights, members of the community agreed by a social compact to give up to the government their individual right to punish transgressors, in exchange for protection against them. But the positive laws established by the government should, to the extent possible, be guided and inspired by natural law, which is based on morality and reason.[156]

Mansfield's approach to the law was essentially humanist; his focus was more likely to be on the minds and actions of individuals rather than on the operation of abstract rules. Thus, in interpreting the meaning of a contract or a will, he attempted to fulfill the intention of the party to the contract or the maker of the will, even if this interpretation contravened a well-established legal rule.[157] In the context of the criminal law, Mansfield set forth the principle that a person who attempts to commit a crime is guilty of a criminal act, even if he is unsuccessful in accomplishing the crime.[158]

Mansfield's judicial decisions reflect his belief that all legal rules serve as illustrations of fundamental principles of reason and morality. This can be seen in how he dealt with the question of precedent. The English common law was an elaborate and ancient structure, based largely on the precedents established by centuries of judicial decisions and, to a much lesser extent, on statutes enacted by Parliament. Much like a coral reef, case grafted on case created a comprehensive body of law. Instead of trying to persuade Parliament to codify the nation's laws, as the French had done under Louis XIV in the seventeenth century,[159] Mansfield believed that it was more effective – and more in accord with English tradition – to improve the law gradually through judicially decided cases that would provide precedents for future disputes.[160] "General rules," he once argued as a lawyer, "are ... varied by change of circumstances. Cases arise within the letter, yet, not within the reason, of the rule; and exceptions are introduced, which, grafted upon the rule, form a system of law."[161] The common law, he said, "*works itself pure* by rules drawn from the fountain of justice."[162]

Mansfield respected precedent, but only if the reason for the precedent continued to exist. He ignored or construed narrowly precedents that he believed no longer had relevance to modern society. He followed this practice even when interpreting statutes enacted by Parliament. Thus, he refused to enforce – or interpreted very narrowly – the harsh anti-Catholic laws adopted a century earlier, since the political reasons for their adoption had ceased to exist. He told his friend David Garrick: "A judge on the bench is now and then in your whimsical situation between Tragedy and Comedy; inclination drawing one way and a long string of precedents the other."[163] Mansfield realized that it was sometimes necessary to sacrifice the advantage of a fixed rule in order to prevent a miscarriage of justice. His legal colleagues recognized, even if they did not always approve of, the very contingent nature of his quest for certainty in the law. Shortly after Mansfield had overruled several long-established decisions, one of the participants at a dinner of judges and lawyers rose to toast ironically "the glorious uncertainty of the law."[164]

He believed that the principle underlying a particular decision was more important than the decision itself:[165] "The law of England would be a strange science indeed if it were decided upon precedents only. Precedents serve to illustrate principles, and to give them a fixed principles run through all the cases according as the particular circumstances of each have been found to fall within the one or other of them."[166] Where there was no exact precedent to guide the court, Mansfield would make a new precedent based on "reason, justice, and convenience," or by analogy to other cases.[167] Sometimes he bowed to an established precedent against his inclination, but more often he was able to find a way around it by distinguishing its facts from that of the case before him, or he would simply overrule a precedent.[168] If the English common law did not provide him with an answer, he would sometimes seek it in foreign law. It was here that his readings in Roman law and European civil law helped him reach a just result based on principles of natural law.[169]

Mansfield believed that the law was not some arcane system of knowledge understood only by monkish professionals, but that it existed to serve society: "As the usages of society alter," he said, "the law must adapt itself to the various situations of mankind."[170] Mansfield's view of the role of the courts in society was very similar to that of twentieth-century United States Supreme Court Justice William Brennan, who also believed that the courts should be agents for social change. Brennan once said: "Courts have a creative job to do when they find that a rule has lost its touch with reality and should be abandoned or reformulated to meet new conditions and new moral values." In the absence of a precedent, Brennan argued, "the courts must hammer out new rules that will respect whatever values of the past have survived the tests of reason and experience and anticipate what contemporary values will best meet those tests."[171]

As one legal historian has pointed out, Mansfield "wished to decide cases upon ideally right principles, but he recognized that established rules ought not to be overturned."[172] Mansfield said: "In mercantile contracts especially, for the sake of certainty, it is better to adhere to decisions, even if they were at first erroneous. All new contracts are made in the sense of the judicial determinations; and supposing an interpretation at first wrong, it becomes afterwards highly unjust and highly inconvenient to vary from it."[173] Mansfield emphasized the need for fixed rules also in matters involving real estate, to the extent that even "if an erroneous or hasty determination has got into practice, there is more benefit derived from adhering to it, than if it were to be overturned."[174]

Whether regarded as inconsistency or flexibility, Mansfield exercised wide discretion in how he decided cases. This was a time when only a relatively small segment of English life was governed by statutes enacted by Parliament. He achieved his most important contribution to English law – the creation of a comprehensive system of commercial law – without any action being taken by Parliament. Some judges and lawyers criticized Mansfield for his legal "innovations," and particularly for importing some of the principles of equity into the more rigid common law. Mansfield believed that it would make the life of litigants easier if law and equity were fused into a single system,[175] and he himself reportedly said that he "never liked the law so much as when it was most like equity."[176] It may be said that he had empathy with the litigants who appeared before him, which a modern writer has described as "the ability to stand in the shoes of another, to understand that others have concerns and feelings and values different from our own."[177] Mansfield has been criticized for usurping the function of the legislature by changing the law,[178] and some of the changes he made in the law were later undone. Yet it is doubtful whether Parliament had the institutional ability to make the legal changes necessary to facilitate Britain's commercial and industrial expansion.

Mansfield's greatness as a judge rests on two principal bases: first, the long-term influence of his decisions, which was a result of his insistence on adapting the law to changing conditions and on basing his decisions on fundamental principles; second, the morality he brought into the law. In the words of a biographer, "No judge ever impressed so forcibly upon the jurisprudence of this country the peculiar qualities of his own mind."[179] More than two centuries after his lifetime, many of the rules he set forth are still followed by the Anglo-Saxon courts. Whether we turn to substantive law, such as commercial law or patent law, or to procedural issues, such as the admissibility of the testimony of expert witnesses or the attorney-client or doctor-client privilege,[180] we find that Mansfield neatly defined the issue before him and had something definitive to say about it. His rulings were clear, pragmatic, and adaptable to changing times and mores. As one of his contemporaries wrote: "The simplicity and at the same time energy of the language are certainly well calculated to be an antidote against ... ostentatious pomp of diction."[181] In formulating a rule, whether in affairs touching commerce or daily life, Mansfield was always thinking ahead: what would be the practical consequences of the rule?

There was also a strong moral component to Mansfield's jurisprudence. He subscribed to John Locke's view that law was based on reason, common sense, and morality.[182] He regarded his court as the guardian of public morals and declared that there was no injury or wrong for which the law does not provide a remedy.[183] His conviction that morality was a foundation of the law was a source of his greatness as a judge. Mansfield was a true child of the eighteenth-century Enlightenment, which consisted of "openness to new ideas, inquisitiveness, interest in knowledge, the tendency to question established opinions, emancipation from superstitious fears."[184] His rulings supported fairness, religious freedom, and protection of the weak.

It is true that some of Mansfield's decisions do not accord with twenty-first-century values, such as his enforcement of capital punishment and other harsh penalties for many crimes, his hostility to workers' efforts to improve their conditions, and his suppression of freedom of the press by strenuously enforcing seditious-libel laws. To say that he was a man of his times is true, but it is not a fully adequate response, for many of his contemporaries criticized him for these decisions. Yet Mansfield's admirable qualities and his contributions to the law and to society outweighed his flaws.

13

Commerce and Industry

The great object in every branch of the law, but especially in mercantile law, is certainty.

Lord Mansfield, *Milles v. Fletcher*

When Mansfield became chief justice in 1756, he already had a quarter century's experience in mercantile matters. As a practicing lawyer he had argued on behalf of merchants both in court and before the bar of the House of Commons. As the principal spokesman for the ministry in the Commons he had advised the government against imposing restrictions on foreign trade. As solicitor general and then attorney general he had advised the Board of Trade on numerous issues involving commerce.

Mansfield thus came to the bench not only knowledgeable about commercial matters but also deeply sympathetic to the interests of merchants and industrialists. Throughout his career, he adhered to the economic philosophy of John Locke and the principles of the Glorious Revolution of 1688, which sought to develop England's manufacturing capacity and to transform its economy into one based on the value of labour rather than of land.[1] As a judge, he was steadfast in promoting commercial interests. In 1759, only three years into his tenure as chief justice, the East India Company expressed its gratitude by naming a newly launched ship the *Lord Mansfield*.[2]

Mansfield's appointment as chief justice came at an opportune time in the development of British commerce and industry. Britain was already the most important manufacturing and commercial country in the world.[3] The per capita wealth of its population was the highest in the world.[4] It was not yet the great industrial nation that it was to become in the nineteenth century, but it was no longer the collection of peaceful rural communities that poets such as Thomas Gray in the "Elegy Written in a Country

Churchyard" and Oliver Goldsmith in "The Deserted Village" wrote about with nostalgia and regret. Dr Samuel Johnson commented in 1756 that "there never was from the earliest ages a time in which trade so much engaged the attention of mankind, or commercial gain was sought with such general emulation."[5] To cite just one indicator among many, the tonnage of ships entering the port of London quadrupled during the eighteenth century.[6] Mansfield's shaping of English law enabled it to serve – and to further – the great changes that, during his thirty-two-year tenure on the bench, led directly to the Industrial Revolution and Britain's greatest days as a world power.

At mid-century, British industry, commerce, and society were in the midst of a profound transformation. Industry was expanding, particularly in the manufacture of textiles and metal products. The expansion was accompanied by changes in industrial organization: cottage industries were moving into factories, and populations were moving from country to city. These changes were made possible by, and in turn stimulated, technological advances, improvements in transportation and communication, expansion of domestic and foreign trade, and the development of a unified national economy. The use of new financial instruments and developments in the law, the latter spearheaded by Mansfield, provided an infrastructure for the newly semi-industrial country.

The metalworking industries were growing rapidly in the Midlands around Birmingham. The Lancashire cotton mills and Yorkshire woollen mills were producing inexpensive cloth, much of which was exported. Pottery, hosiery, and brewing industries, among others, were expanding. Although landownership was still the source of most of the wealth of the country, several of the great noblemen who owned enormous estates were investing their capital in industrial and commercial development. Historian Langford has well summed up the complex interrelationship between industry and agriculture and its impact on society:

> Individual landowners needed little reminding of their dependence on the market for agricultural produce created by a commercially diverse and growing nation. Many, too, derived profits, either directly or indirectly, from mining, manufacturing, or government securities. The concern of men who made their money in something other than land to sink the proceeds of their enterprise in a landed estate is an enduring feature of English history. It showed no sign of letting up with industrial growth. One of the main functions of the manufacturing cities, as

contemporaries were well aware, was to manufacture propertied gentlemen for export to rural neighbourhoods and metropolitan life-styles.[7]

In popular imagination, the eighteenth-century English aristocracy had disdain for commercial activity, but this was far from the truth. In fact, it showed great common sense, energy, and commercial entrepreneurship.[8] Many of the great landowners invested their excess capital in industry and infrastructure. To take one famous example, in 1761 the Duke of Bridgewater invested the enormous sum of £350,000 to build a canal that greatly reduced the cost of shipping coal from the mines on his property to the industrial centre of Manchester.[9] Conversely, capital created by industry and commerce was invested in improvement of the land and methods of cultivation, which greatly increased agricultural productivity.[10]

The changes in industrial organization improved the productivity of manufacturers. The diary of Sir Dudley Ryder, Mansfield's predecessor as chief justice, includes an illuminating entry as early as 1715. Ryder, then a law student, wrote that he met a man at dinner who, foreshadowing at least the concept of the assembly-line innovations of Henry Ford nearly two centuries later, told him that "our manufactures ... are capable of very great improvement and he thinks it would tend very much to it if in our manufactures that consist in several parts, as most of them do, and require different sorts of work to bring them to an end, every distinct part be put into different hands and one person be not used upon different part of it."[11] Later in the century, a diarist wrote, with apparent approval, that the growth of manufacturing in Birmingham was due in part to specialization of functions in factories, so that the repetitive work "becomes so simple that ... children of six or eight years old do it as well as men."[12] Factories, where employees worked for set hours at a fixed rate of pay, were beginning to replace cottage industries, where the workers were paid for work done in their own homes. In the 1760s, for example, the manufacturer Matthew Boulton built a factory on the outskirts of Birmingham for a variety of metal and tortoise-shell goods; housing 600 workers, it became the largest factory of its kind in the world.[13]

Advances in technology were beginning to change English society as well as its landscape. The theoretical foundation for these advances had been laid in the seventeenth and early eighteenth centuries. The rational empirical method of thought and the emphasis on inquiry, observation, and experiment that characterized the work of such scientists as Robert Boyle and

Isaac Newton had immense practical consequences, leading directly to a stream of inventions that transformed British industry and society in the mid-eighteenth century.[14] Newton's working out of the theory of gravity "created the mechanics that laid the groundwork for steam engines and the Industrial Revolution."[15] James Watt's invention of the steam engine, used initially to pump water out of deep coal mines, was soon harnessed to a variety of manufacturing processes, particularly smelting iron. Technological inventions in spinning and weaving that transformed the textile industry included James Hargreaves's "spinning jenny" (1767), Richard Arkwright's "water-frame" (1769), and Samuel Crompton's "mule" (1775).[16] New techniques for iron- and steel-making and for fusing silver, copper, and brass made a variety of metal products available at a reasonable cost.[17]

Commerce required an infrastructure that only the national government could provide. Entrepreneurs ceaselessly petitioned Parliament for appropriations to make rivers more navigable, to build canals, and to develop a system of turnpikes to replace decayed roads, like those young William Murray had taken on his journey from Perth to London in 1718. In fact, Parliament's main activity was to pass private Acts for turnpike roads and other economic measures.[18] These improvements in transportation helped create an integrated national economy, in which regions could specialize in manufacturing the goods that they could produce most efficiently.[19] The engineering genius of James Brindley led to the creation of a network of canals that criss-crossed the country. In mid-century, Josiah Wedgwood, who introduced industrial methods into the manufacture of pottery, lobbied in Parliament for the building of a canal that would bring the excellent clay of Cornwall to his factory in Staffordshire without the great expense of overland transport.[20] Manufactured products could now be carried inexpensively by water to London, Liverpool, and other ports for shipment to overseas markets.[21]

Owing to a lower death rate, a better food supply, and improved medical services, the population of England increased from six to seven million during the reign of George II (1727–60). A larger population combined with industrial growth led to increasing urbanization: the manufacturing centres of Birmingham, Sheffield, Leeds, Nottingham, Leicester, and Manchester changed from small towns into important cities within the space of a few years.[22] The numerous coffee houses in London and the provinces became important centres for business meetings and exchange of information as well as social discourse.[23] The advent of daily and weekly newspapers had an important political impact but also helped foster a national economy by bringing people of all ranks into contact with each other. Merchants demanded free flow of information to conduct their trade.[24] *The Daily Advertiser*, a commercial paper founded in 1730, circulated in business houses, coffee houses, and taverns. It regularly published stock prices, rates of exchange, and lists of exports and imports. By 1757, London had three morning papers and several evening papers, in addition to several weekly and semi-weekly journals, which contained advertisements as well as political and commercial news.[25]

Industrial growth was fed by the needs of an increasingly prosperous society, which demanded sophisticated products and amenities. The Wedgwood potteries partly owed their success to the newly formed English habit of drinking tea.[26] Tea had been introduced into England in 1662 by King Charles II's Portuguese wife, Catherine of Braganza, whose dowry included a chest of China tea. For many years only aristocrats sipped this exotic beverage. In 1689, the East India Company began importing tea from India and China. In 1721, the Company received a monopoly on the tea trade. It exported textiles to India and China, and tea became a profitable cargo on ships returning to England. By the end of the century, the tea trade was its chief source of profit.[27] Popularized in the coffee houses that proliferated in the late seventeenth and early eighteenth centuries, tea became the national drink of the English. And the public began sweetening their tea (as well as coffee and chocolate) with sugar, "transform[ing] them into heavenly brews."[28] Sugar was the principal product of West Indies plantations, worked by African slave labour under appalling conditions; and the increased demand for sugar stimulated the growth of the British-dominated transatlantic slave trade.[29]

Industrial growth stimulated shipping and foreign trade. Overseas trade in commodities increased fourfold during the eighteenth century, the most expansive years being between 1745 and 1764, a period when the bulk of British trade was turning from markets in Europe to those in the West Indies and the North American colonies.[30] Britain's exports to North America of manufactured goods, particularly agricultural implements, also were growing apace.[31] A significant part of British commerce, however, was in slaves. British ships carried captive Africans to the West Indies and North America, where they were exchanged for sugar or tobacco, which was then carried to Liverpool or Bristol. As a practicing lawyer, Mansfield represented West Indian interests, including those involved in the slave trade either as merchants, planters, financiers, or ship captains. As we will see, in 1772 he was forced to address the tension between the development of commerce and the infamy of slavery.[32]

The needs of the government also stimulated financial innovation and institution building. In order to finance the wars of the mid-eighteenth century, the government borrowed huge sums, on the security of the country's tax revenues.[33] The Bank of England, founded in 1694, was the primary lender to the government, but consortiums of merchants in the City of London also helped fund the national debt.[34] The government's issuance of credit instruments, and the trading of these instruments on the Stock Exchange, founded in 1773, made London the world's most important financial centre.[35]

Consistent with his support of British commerce, Mansfield opposed legislation that restricted trading, even with the enemy.[36] As described earlier, when he was solicitor general he argued, unsuccessfully, in Parliament against a law that would prohibit British companies from insuring enemy ships in time of war.[37] He believed that the laws restricting trade should be construed narrowly. In 1773, English lace-makers tried to enforce a statute that fined any person who imported foreign-made lace into the country and also required that the imported lace be burned. A lawsuit was brought against a nobleman who had brought waistcoats and breeches into England that he had bought in France for his own use. When the offending clothes were produced in court, Mansfield became caustic. He said he could not conceive that Parliament intended that a gentleman returning from abroad be stripped stark naked and also be subject to a penalty. Obviously, the statute only prohibited importing foreign lace *for resale* in England. As to the burning of the offending lace, Mansfield pointed out that the statute required that only the lace embroidery be burned but said nothing about the clothes on which the lace was sewn.[38] Following Mansfield's instructions, the jury brought in a verdict for the defendant.[39]

Mansfield also narrowly interpreted traditional monopolies that had been granted to certain trades. There were watermen, who carried goods and passengers up, down, and across the Thames; carters, who carried goods through the streets; and chairmen, who carried passengers. These guild members were licensed and claimed the exclusive right to perform their callings.[40] In one case, a merchant with his own cart, who had a shipment of cheese on board a ship docked at a Thames quay, brought a suit against one of the carters for obstructing pickup of the shipment by putting his cart between the merchant's cart and the quay. Mansfield noted that the rules expressly applied only to licensed carts, and that unlicensed carts were not covered by the rules. He said it was a strange proposition that a man could not use his own cart to transport his own goods. Therefore, he construed the carter's monopoly as applying only to carrying goods for hire.[41]

In another case, an auctioneer had taken rooms in the town of Guilford to sell a variety of goods by auction. The local tradesmen, who wanted no competition, encouraged their servants to go to the auction room and disrupt the sales. The defendant's attorney introduced evidence in court that some other disturbance may have interfered with the auction. Mansfield would have none of it. He "explained the danger that would attend admitting such an extenuation of a very grave offence which virtually meant prohibiting all auctions where a few thought proper to associate and assemble under the pretense of innocently amusing themselves and thereby obstruct the trade."[42] The auctioneer – and freedom of trade – prevailed.

In a very different kind of lawsuit in which Mansfield supported freedom of trade, a man sued the master of Jonathan's coffee house in Exchange Alley for an assault by pushing him out of the house. According to a newspaper report, after it was proved at the trial that the coffee house had been a market for buying and selling government securities, the jury brought in a verdict for the plaintiff. The report concluded that Jonathan's coffee house was a free and open market, open to all, Although we do not have a record of Mansfield's charge to the jury, it seems likely that the jury was following Mansfield's instructions.

By the mid-eighteenth century, about one in five English families was directly involved in commerce, in addition to the farmers and industrialists whose profits depended on foreign and domestic trading.[43] For all of these people, clear and predictable legal rules governing commercial and credit transactions were essential. Although most mercantile disputes had been resolved through private arbitration,[44] the English common law courts had decided mercantile disputes since the sixteenth century, but neither Parliament nor the courts had created a coherent body of mercantile law.

The chief shortcoming that prevented the development of commercial law during the first half of the eighteenth century was the absence of any underlying principle to guide the outcome of isolated decisions.[45] Typically, when a dispute involving the sale of goods, maritime insurance, or a credit instrument was brought to the court, the judge directed the jury to decide the case according to its individual circumstances.[46] All the evidence was thrown together and left to the jury, with no legal principle to provide guidance for future litigants. As a result, there was no general consensus as to how to deal with these disputes. The courts' decisions were often inconsistent with the established usages of merchants.[47]

Mansfield's great achievement was to construct a settled system of principles and rules upon which merchants, lawyers, and judges could rely.[48] "Nothing is more mischievous," he said, "than uncertainty in mercantile law. It would be terrible to paper negotiation [i.e., the use of notes and bills in commerce] to put every case on its own bottom and to have no certain rule but to depend on what juries might think."[49]

The "law merchant," which reflected the customs and usages of merchants, was first developed in the great commercial centres of Venice, Florence, and Milan. It arose from the practical requirements of merchants, and its two guiding principles were, first, participation by the merchants in formulating and applying the rules and, second, speedy resolution of disputes.[50] The law merchant was international: the ability of mercantile courts to decide disputes on the basis of generally accepted custom and usage, rather than on local law, greatly facilitated international commerce.[51] During the seventeenth century, the law merchant had gradually begun to be absorbed into the English common law and become part of established precedent.[52] But it was Mansfield, deeply steeped in Roman law and the civil law of continental Europe, who completed this process.[53]

Where English common law was unsettled or unclear, Mansfield looked to the law merchant for guidance.[54] Thus, the rules that had been developed informally by merchants became the law of the land.[55] Mansfield emphasized that these rules, based on reason and justice, were the same all over the world; that they should be easy to understand by non-lawyers; and that they should be certain so that traders could depend on them.[56]

When a commercial case came before him, Mansfield made use of special juries, often composed of merchants, who would be likely to understand the business context of a dispute. Special juries existed before Mansfield's time, but he saw how they could be used to ascertain mercantile practices that could be brought into the common law.[57] For example, in an insurance case where the question was how to estimate the damages, he said: "The special jury (amongst whom there were many knowing and considerable merchants) found the defendant's rule of estimation to be right, and gave their verdict for him. They understood the question very well, and knew more of the subject of it than any body else present; and formed their judgment from their own notions and experience, without much assistance from any thing that passed."[58] Mansfield would converse freely with the jurors in court and sometimes talked to them privately – occasionally even entertaining them at dinner, a practice that would seem distinctly odd to modern lawyers and judges.[59]

Mansfield looked to custom and usage in disputes related to property rights too. In a case involving the right of a tenant of farmland to crops after the expiration of his lease, he declared: "The custom of a particular place may rectify what otherwise would be imprudence or folly ... The custom does not alter or contradict the agreement in the lease; it only superadds a right which is consequential to the taking ... although not mentioned in the ... lease."[60]

Where the English common law did not address a problem, Mansfield sometimes looked to foreign law: modern juridical writers from France, German, Holland, or Italy; the "law of nations" as expounded by theorists of international law, particularly the Dutch Hugo Grotius and the German Samuel Pufendorf; or Roman civil law.[61] Mansfield's early self-education in civil and international law and his familiarity with modes of thinking outside the common law enabled him make landmark innovations in commercial law, many of which have survived to the present day.

"The maritime law," he wrote, "is not the law of a particular country, but the general law of nations."[62] In one maritime case, he stated: "I wish this case to be spoken to by civilians [i.e., experts in the civil law of continental Europe]. We can have no light from our own law. I have been looking into a French Commentary."[63] In another maritime case, he cited the ancient law of the island of Rhodes, the Ordinances of Louis XIV, and half a dozen other ancient and modern continental European sources.[64]

To understand fully the facts and issues involved in a case, Mansfield would sometimes go outside the court for information.[65] In one marine insurance case, he said: "I have taken the trouble to inform myself of the practice of the Court of Admiralty in England ... and I have talked to Sir George Lee, who has examined the books of the Court of Admiralty."[66] In another insurance case, he said: "I ... endeavoured to get what assistance I could by conversing with some gentlemen of experience in adjustments."[67]

In yet another case, which turned on the fairness of the practice of owners (or their agents) buying their own goods at auction, Mansfield looked to popular opinion as to whether it was ethical. Mansfield said that he had questioned many non-lawyers "upon the morality and rectitude of the transaction." If the practice was unfair, "it is no argument to say it is a frequent custom: gaming, stock-jobbing and swindling, are frequent. But the law forbids them all." Mansfield concluded that the practice was unfair and a fraud, because buyers of the goods were led to believe "that the articles set up to sale will be disposed of to the highest real bidder."[68]

Mansfield's willingness to bring mercantile practices into the common law was not unlimited. Even though he might on occasion stretch, or even abandon, a legal precedent if he thought the reason for it had ceased to exist, he would not depart from a precedent that was clear and certain. Mansfield emphasized certainty in the law because he thought it was important for merchants and others to be able to predict the consequences of their actions and the actions of those they dealt with. Furthermore, while the customs of merchants might be persuasive to him, they were not conclusive; they had to square with standards of honest dealing and good faith.[69]

Mansfield's decisions in commercial cases, as in other areas of the law, were intensely practical. Where he thought it necessary or appropriate, he abandoned the formality of traditional common law pleading rules in order to provide legal protection to a broad range of commercial assets, transactions, and practices.[70] His aim was to get as quickly as possible to the essential issue or issues involved in a dispute and to resolve the dispute in accordance with principles of justice and fair dealing. He stated in one opinion: "I never like to entangle justice in matters of form, and to turn parties round on frivolous objections where I can avoid it. It only tends to the ruin and destruction of both ... The question therefore ... is ... whether the facts support the merits of the defendant's plea."[71]

Commerce is based largely on contract. Merchants, manufacturers, and carriers of goods make agreements to buy and sell goods and services, to be delivered or provided in the future. Trade depended on merchants being able to rely on the word of others, and Mansfield's decisions in contract cases showed a strong bias in favour of enforcing promises.[72]

An important issue in contract law was the idea of "consideration." The common law had long required that, in order for a promise to be legally binding, there had to be a consideration for it; i.e., a promise of something in return. A bare promise (such as the promise of a gift), or in the legal Latin that lawyers used, a *nudum pactum*, without any consideration for it, could not be enforced. In *Pillans v. Van Mierop*,[73] Mansfield rejected this ancient doctrine because it was contrary to the usage and law of merchants. His knowledge of Scots law and the civil law of continental Europe informed his decision.[74] After pointing out that it was the custom of merchants to honour a written promise in the absence of any consideration, he boldly declared that "the ancient notion about the want of consideration was for the sake of evidence only." If a promise was in writing, no consideration would be necessary because the writing provided evidence that the promise had actually been made. But here Mansfield's rejection of precedent was unsuccessful. Thirteen years later, the House of Lords overruled *Pillans*, restoring the consideration requirement even where a promise was in writing.[75]

Mansfield, ever resourceful, got around the House of Lords, at least to some extent, by broadening the definition of consideration. In *Hawkes v. Saunders*,[76] the executrix of an estate had promised to pay all of the decedent's debts but failed to do so, even though there were sufficient assets in the estate. Mansfield held that the executrix's *moral* obligation to pay the debts was an adequate consideration for her promise. Then, in order to give guidance to future litigants, he mentioned three other situations where a moral obligation would be adequate consideration. First, if a debtor was discharged from his debt in bankruptcy but then made a new promise to pay the debt, his moral obligation to pay was sufficient consideration to support the new promise. Second, the debt of a minor, which was not enforceable, could be re-established by a new promise to pay the debt after the minor comes of age. Third, a debt that was barred by the statute of limitations was enforceable if the debtor made a new promise after the statute had run.

Despite his bias in favour of enforcing promises, Mansfield would not enforce promises that were illegal, immoral, or contrary to public policy. Mansfield was severe when a person took advantage of those who could not defend themselves, such as minors. In one case, a banker had given a minor £650, and the minor promised to pay the banker £100 a year for the rest of his life. In declaring the transaction void, Mansfield excoriated "bankers and other monied men [who] from motives of avarice and selfishness ... draw young men or even boys at school or college to make foolish bargains by advancing them sums of money ... merely to supply their vices, their follies and pernicious pursuits or their utter ruin; it was therefore necessary to take every advantage the law could give to strike at the root of this great and growing evil."[77]

Mansfield fixed his sights on fraudsters. The governors of Greenwich Hospital sued a person who had contracted to sell meat to the hospital. The defendant had contracted to supply good ox beef but instead substituted beef of an inferior quality. The defendant's lawyer argued that the bills for the objectionable beef had been paid and that wiped away any inference of fraud. Mansfield in his charge to the jury rejected this "frivolous and evasive plea with equal humanity and justice. He remarked upon the iniquity of practising a fraud in the very article of life upon so extensive a charity."[78] Without leaving the courtroom, the jury gave a verdict for £100 damages and full costs of the suit. In another case, Mansfield fulminated against a chemist who was sued for selling fake medicine for coughs and sore throats. The jury awarded the plaintiff considerable damages and costs. A newspaper editorialized that the verdict would have a deterrent effect.[79]

He was equally hard on medical quacks, who were pervasive in eighteenth-century London.[80] A labourer asked a "rupture surgeon" to cure him of a rupture that he had had for twenty years. Being indigent, he gave the surgeon four promissory notes in payment of the fee of 20 guineas. In a lawsuit over the fee, expert witnesses testified that the labourer had a common puncture, the repair of which should not have cost more than 1 guinea. In charging the jury, Mansfield denounced medical quacks who, he said, "were the most dangerous and pernicious of all imposters." In a few minutes, the jury awarded the labourer damages of 100 guineas.[81] In another medical case, a patient sued to recover 25 guineas he had paid in advance to a famous oculist who had assured him that he could cure a bad disorder of the eyes. The oculist gave the plaintiff six bottles of a liquid and six small jars of ointment to be used in the doctor's absence, since the doctor had to go away for a while. Nine months later, the plaintiff's eyes were worse. After summing up the evidence for the jury, Mansfield observed that the doctor had given his patient a positive assurance that he had not fulfilled. Mansfield instructed the jury to find a directed verdict for the plaintiff, which they did without hesitation.[82]

As noted earlier, legal procedures under the common law were based on forms of action, pleading forms that lawyers were required to adhere to when bringing a claim in court.[83] One form of action was for "money had and received," under which a lawyer might state that his client had lent money to a person, who had promised to repay it but had not done so.

Mansfield expanded the action of money had and received in order to reach a just result in cases brought before him.[84] He developed the principle of unjust enrichment, which has become an important part of modern Anglo-American law. He ruled that a person should not be allowed to keep money or other assets that were not rightfully his, even though he had made no promise to pay them to the rightful owner.[85] For example, someone who has collected life insurance proceeds on the life of a person who later turns out to be alive should not be allowed to keep the proceeds, even though he made no promise to repay the insurance company. The idea of unjust enrichment may seem simple and obvious today, but until Mansfield's time it was by no means clear that someone who was unjustly in possession of money could be compelled to give it up unless he had made a promise to repay it.[86]

An example of unjust enrichment was the case of *Longchamp v. Kenny*.[87] Teresa Cornelys, who was well known for the fashionable "Venetian" masked balls that she sponsored at Carlisle House in Soho Square,[88] had consigned a number of tickets to one of her balls to Longchamp, a waiter at a club on St James's Street, to be sold to members of the club. Longchamp was supposed to hand over to Mrs Cornelys the proceeds of the sales as well as any unsold tickets. One of the tickets got into the hands of Kenny, the manager of the club. When Mrs Cornelys asked Longchamp to account for the tickets, he said that Kenny had one of them. Kenny, however, told Mrs Cornelys to get the money from Longchamp, to whom she had given the ticket. When Longchamp was threatened with arrest, he paid 5 guineas (the value of the ticket) to Mrs Cornelys and sued Kenny, using the traditional legal form of action for recovering money that had been paid out or loaned. Kenny argued that he had made no promise to return the ticket or return it to Lonchamp, but Mansfield cut through the legal niceties. If Kenny had sold the ticket, the proceeds did not belong to him. Kenny had not produced the ticket in court, so it was a fair presumption that he had sold it. Mansfield would not allow Kenny to be unjustly enriched.

As Mansfield said in another case: "Where a man is under a legal or equitable obligation to pay, the law implies a promise though none was ever actually made."[89] To achieve fairness, Mansfield used the legal fiction that a contract was implied; a legal claim for unjust enrichment is still known among lawyers as a "quasi-contract." Morality required that any unjust enrichment be returned.[90]

Domestic and foreign trade depended on the use of credit. Business was largely done on a credit basis; merchants, shopkeepers, and large industrialists were increasingly acting as bankers.[91] Mansfield's most important contribution to commercial law was in the area of negotiable instruments, the written documents on which the country's credit system was based. The clarity and dependability of Mansfield's decisions in cases on negotiable instruments attracted a great volume of business to his court from the mercantile community in the City of London.[92]

The use of credit created a need for sophisticated financial instruments. A borrower might give the lender a promissory note: a direct commitment in writing to pay a sum at a given time. As foreign and domestic trade expanded, more complex credit arrangements came into use. The most commonly used instrument was the bill of exchange, which had found its way into England from continental Europe in the seventeenth century.[93] A bill of exchange, like a modern bank cheque, was an order by one person (the drawer) directing a second person (the drawee) to pay a sum of money to a third person (the payee).[94] Blackstone in his *Commentaries* pointed out that the bill of exchange enabled "a man at the most distant part of the world [to] have money remitted to him from any trading country."[95]

The use of promissory notes and bills of exchange called for clear and consistent legal rules that all the parties involved could depend on, particularly with respect to their negotiability (i.e., whether the instruments, like money, could be freely transferred). These instruments had been used in commerce for years, but the rights and duties of parties were still unclear at the beginning of Mansfield's tenure as a judge.[96] Although merchants had developed the concept of negotiability in the seventeenth century, it was left to Mansfield a hundred years later to incorporate mercantile custom regarding negotiable instruments into the common law.[97]

Two years after he became chief justice, Mansfield decided the landmark case of *Miller v. Race*.[98] A promissory note issued by a bank for the relatively small amount of £21, 10 shillings, made out to "William Finney or bearer," had been stolen from the mails. The thief or one of his cohorts sold the note to an innkeeper in the ordinary course of his business. The innkeeper had paid "a full and valuable consideration" for the note, without any knowledge that the note was stolen. By the time the innkeeper applied to the bank for payment on the note, the bank had found out that the note was stolen, and it refused to pay, on the ground that the innkeeper could not have acquired title to the note from the thief. The innkeeper sued the clerk of the bank, and a jury found in the innkeeper's favour.

On appeal, the question before Mansfield's court was whether the innkeeper had acquired good title to the note, even though the person who sold it to him (the thief) did not have good title. Characteristically, Mansfield emphasized the practical implications of the dispute. Trade and commerce "would be much incommoded" if the innkeeper could not collect on the note. He emphasized the unique characteristics of negotiable instruments and pointed out that they were generally treated in commerce as the equivalent of money: "They are not goods, not securities, nor documents for debts ... but are treated as money, as cash, in the ordinary course and transaction of business, by the general consent of mankind, which give them the credit and currency of money, to all intents and purposes. [They] are never considered as securities for money, but as money itself ... So, in case of money stolen, the true owner can not recover it, after it has been paid away fairly and honestly upon a valuable and bona fide consideration."[99]

In the case at hand, Mansfield said, the innkeeper had taken the note from a person who looked like a gentleman. It was reasonable for the innkeeper to do so; if the note had been for £1,000, it might have been suspicious, but this note was for a small amount. So a person who paid good money for a stolen note and had no reason to believe that it was stolen, gained good title to the note. He became a "holder in due course," a term that has continued to be used to the present day.

Finally, Mansfield returned to the importance of negotiability to commerce: "A bank-note is constantly and universally, both at home and abroad, treated as money, as cash; and paid, and received, as cash; and it is necessary, for the purpose of commerce, that their currency should be established and secured."[100] Mansfield's decision was revolutionary. Nearly a century later the great American senator, lawyer, and orator Daniel Webster still had to persuade his fellow Americans that the definition of "currency" should include instruments such as banknotes and bills of exchange.[101]

Although Mansfield usually looked for guidance to the customs and usages of merchants in commercial cases, he would not do so if the law on a particular point was already settled.[102] In one case, the payee of a bill of exchange had endorsed it to another person, but the endorsement had omitted the customary words "or order."[103] In the trial of the case, Mansfield had allowed the testimony of merchants to be admitted that the usage of merchants required the words "or order" to be in the endorsement. On appeal, Mansfield admitted that he had been wrong in admitting the testimony: "Since the trial, I have looked into the cases, and have considered the thing with a great deal of care and attention, and thought much about it: and I am very clearly of opinion that I ought not to have admitted any evidence of the particular usage of merchants in such a case. Of this, I say, I am now satisfied: for the law is already settled."[104]

Mansfield then held that, in accord with previous cases, it was not necessary to insert the words "or order" in the endorsement, for a bill of exchange is negotiable in its original creation, and a defect in an endorsement could not change that. Common sense and the requirements of trade dictated that a bill of exchange be fully negotiable in order to serve its purpose, and Mansfield's view was that details of wording were secondary to that purpose.[105] It was the intent of the parties that mattered. Also, he was not afraid to admit that he had been wrong. On another occasion, when asked why he had changed his mind on a particular point of law, he answered that it only showed that he was wiser today than he had been the day before.[106]

In his decisions on negotiable instruments, Mansfield's aim was always to expedite commerce. Toward the end of his tenure as chief justice, Mansfield again described the nature of a negotiable instrument "because it is important that general commercial points should be publicly decided." In *Peacock v. Rhodes*,[107] a case involving a holder in due course of a stolen bill that had been endorsed in blank, he stated that the situation of the holder of a bill of exchange or promissory note was different from that of an assignee of a contract. An assignee took the thing assigned, subject to any defences against the original owner. "If this rule applied to bills and promissory notes," Mansfield continued, "it would stop their currency. The law is settled that a holder, coming fairly by a bill or note, has nothing to do with the transaction between the original parties, unless, perhaps ... a note for money won at play [i.e., gambling] ... I see no difference between a note indorsed in blank, and one payable to bearer. They both go by delivery, and possession proves property in both cases."[108]

An example of Mansfield's pragmatic approach to complex legal questions was *Whitfield v. Le Despencer*,[109] where a banknote given to the postal service in London to be mailed to a person outside the city was stolen by a letter sorter in the post office.[110] The owner of the note sued the postmaster general for negligence. Mansfield cited legal authority that the postmaster was not liable for the fault of an employee, but he continued by pointing out that the owner could very easily have avoided his loss: "What have merchants done ... as a caution and security against a loss? They cut their bills and notes into two or three parts, and send them at different times: one, by this day's post, the other, by the next. This shows the sense of mankind as to their remedy."[111]

Mansfield's strong bias in favour of freedom of commerce showed itself in cases involving the legal wrong of "nuisance." A nuisance typically occurs when a business creates unpleasant smells, noises, or sights that annoy or harm local residents. In an era of burgeoning commerce and industrialization, it is not surprising that nuisance cases came up with some frequency in Mansfield's court.[112] They included such activities as keeping a dog kennel near a public highway, polluting the air because of manufacturing, or obstructing shipping by depositing large pieces of timber in the Thames.[113]

In nuisance cases, Mansfield balanced the benefits to commerce from the offensive activities against the discomfort caused to neighbours. He thought three factors were critical: the location of the business (an activity that might be objectionable in a residential district might be tolerated in a commercial setting), the degree of discomfort to residents or neighbours, and whether the defendant had taken reasonable steps to limit the disagreeable activity.[114] In keeping with his steadfast support of commerce, Mansfield usually leaned toward allowing the activity to continue. In some cases, he was able to get the parties to compromise or to submit the dispute to arbitration.[115]

In one nuisance case, a candle-maker in Soho was indicted for melting grease, animal guts, and other substances to the detriment of the neighbours. Witnesses testified that the smell was so offensive that it made people sick or caused them to quit their houses. Mansfield was unconvinced. He said that some useful trades, though disagreeable, must be tolerated in London. The defendant had been carrying on his business for six years and had done everything he could to make it inoffensive to the neighbours. He had bought and melted the best materials. Moreover, if the jury found him guilty he would either be forced to discontinue his business and lose all the expenses of his equipment, or to pay such a heavy fine that he could no longer continue his trade. It took the jury only a few minutes to find the defendant not guilty. The newspaper report of the case commented: "Whereby it would seem that tallow melters as well as chandlers [i.e., candle-makers] are authorized to carry on their trade in all places."[116]

In another dispute, a London chemist was indicted for setting up a laboratory, where he burned quantities of bones in order to extract ammonia from them, in the neighbourhood of a hospital. Witnesses for the prosecution, including physicians, agreed that the smell was disagreeable, with some neighbours testifying that the stench was almost unbearable. Witnesses for the defendant pointed out, however, that ammonia previously had to be imported; it was one of the ingredients used for the manufacture of sulfuric acid. The defendant's production of ammonia had lowered its price and, as a result, England was likely to become an exporter instead of an importer of sulfuric acid.[117] In view of the defendant's contribution to commerce, Mansfield was not persuaded that his laboratory was a nuisance:

> It has been proved that his manufactory is of great utility to commerce and physic as it prevents the importation of the same medicine which was not so good from other countries and it is a very ingenious and surprising invention ... The being disagreeable to a neighbourhood does not decide it to be a nuisance. Tallow chandlers, brewers, butchers are all disagreeable but they are no nuisance. Waterworks are a nuisance to some on account of the smoke but they are found necessary and there is no or more convenient place.[118]

After deliberating for two and half hours, the jury handed down a verdict in the defendant's favour.

Mansfield did not always decide in favour of the offending businesses. In a case decided early in his tenure on the bench, he and his fellow judges affirmed a jury verdict against the owners of a factory consisting of twenty buildings that made nitric acid and sulfuric acid in the pastoral London suburb of Twickenham on the banks of the Thames. According to the neighbours, "the air was impregnated with noisome and offensive stinks and smells; to the common nuisance of all the King's ... subjects inhabiting ... and travelling and passing the King's common highway." Mansfield said that for such an activity to be a nuisance, "it is not necessary that the smell should be unwholesome: it is enough, if it renders the enjoyment of life and property uncomfortable." As a result of the decision, the factory owners demolished the factory and, by the consent of the parties, were fined only the nominal sum of 6 shillings, 8 pence each.[119] The bucolic location of the factory no doubt influenced the court; if it had been in central London it is unlikely that Mansfield would have found it to be a nuisance.

The development of the law of insurance was essential to the growth of international trade. As British commerce grew during the eighteenth century, ship owners and merchants needed to lay off the risk that their vessels and cargoes might be lost or damaged.[120] Maritime insurers became indispensable participants in international trade, and London was the centre of a worldwide insurance industry. One of Mansfield's great achievements was to establish clear rules governing maritime insurance. The parties to these transactions were experienced businessmen who were familiar with international customs and usages, which Mansfield in his decisions enfolded into the English common law. The merchants and insurers who frequently signed insurance contracts valued predictability in the law that governed these contracts. Mansfield always emphasized the importance of certainty in insurance decisions and took pains to explain his decisions. In *Milles v. Fletcher*,[121] an insurance case, he said: "The great object in every branch of the law, but especially in mercantile law, is certainty, and that the grounds of decision should be precisely known."[122]

Mansfield made an essential contribution to commerce by developing fundamental principles of insurance law. The first was that an insurance policy was an agreement of indemnity, meaning that the person who wished to insure a vessel, goods, or other assets had to have an "insurable interest" in the thing or person insured.[123] In the absence of an insurable interest, the supposed insurance contract was nothing but a wager.

Two of Mansfield's decisions illustrate this point. In the first, a petty officer of a ship sailing for China paid a £20 premium to an insurer, in return for which the insurer agreed that if the ship arrived in China later than a certain time, he would pay the officer £1,000. Mansfield ruled that the agreement violated a statute that prohibited all gaming or wagers about shipping, and he added: "This is a general caution to all persons concerned with shipping to keep to the original intent of the insurance – a contract of indemnity between the parties against inevitable loss."[124]

In the second case, Mansfield upheld an agreement where a supplier of beer to the army insured against losing his expected profit of £1,000 if the beer was lost in transit from England to Quebec. The agreement, Mansfield said, was not an illegal wager because the shipper of the beer had an insurable interest; he would have received a certain profit from his contract with the government if the beer had not been lost.[125]

Mansfield emphasized, however, that, since an insurance contract was a contract of indemnity, the insured was not entitled to recover any more than the loss he suffered. Where a shipload of sugar was damaged in transit and had to be sold immediately to avoid further spoilage, the owner of the sugar could recover the difference between the value of the spoiled sugar and its value if the damage had not occurred, rather than the difference between the price the sugar was sold for and the value assigned to it in the insurance policy. The latter rule, Mansfield said, "would involve the underwriter in the rise or fall of the market: it would subject him, in some cases, to pay vastly more than the loss; in others, it would deprive the insured of any satisfaction."[126]

Another fundamental principle he established was that insurance is protection against risk: if the insurer does not run the risk, he is not entitled to the premium and must return it to the insured. In *Stevenson v. Snow*, a ship was insured to sail under convoy from London to Nova Scotia, apparently during wartime. The convoy sailed before the ship could join it. The owner demanded that the insurer return the premium, but the insurer refused. Mansfield agreed with the owner: "Equity implies a condition 'that the insurer shall not receive the price of running a risque, if he runs none.'"[127]

In *Carter v. Boehm*,[128] Mansfield established the fundamental principle of good faith in all insurance contracts. Neither the insurer nor the insured may conceal facts that he knows. George Carter, the governor of Fort Marlborough on the Island of Sumatra in the East Indies, bought a one-year insurance policy against the loss of the fort to a foreign enemy. After the French captured the fort, Carter demanded payment from the insurer. The insurer refused, claiming that Carter had committed a fraud by concealing the weakness of the fort and the likelihood of its being attacked by the French. Carter sued and a special jury of merchants brought in a verdict in his favour. When the case was appealed to the Court of King's Bench, Mansfield and the other judges agreed with the jury verdict.

Mansfield then carefully laid out the law of concealment in insurance cases. If an insured knows any special facts that the insurer doesn't know, it is a fraud for him to conceal them, because in that case the risk actually run by the insurer would be different from the risk that the insurer understands he is running. On the other hand, the insured need not mention what the insurer already knows or ought to know. For example, if a ship or its cargo is being insured, the insurer is bound to know the natural perils of the voyage, such as lightning, hurricanes, earthquakes, etc. The ultimate question is whether, under all the circumstances at the time the policy was written, there was a fair representation or a concealment. If the concealment was intentional, the insured has committed a fraud. Even if the concealment was not intentional, it was not a fair representation if it materially changed the risk that the insurer understood he was running.

In this case, Carter was not guilty of concealment of the risk. At the time the policy was written, the insurer, sitting in London, was actually in a better position than Carter to judge the likelihood that the fort might be attacked, a contingency that depended on such matters as the success of the war in Europe and the naval forces that the British and the French had sent to the East Indies.

In *Pelly v. Royal Exchange Assurance*,[129] an interesting case that Mansfield decided only a few months after he became chief justice, he established the important principle that an insurer is assumed to know the usual risks that accompany a venture. In that case, the defendants insured against the loss of the tackle and other equipment of a sailing ship on a voyage to China. When the ship arrived at its destination on the Canton River, the equipment was stored in a warehouse while the ship was being cleaned and refitted. While in storage it was destroyed by a fire. The question the court had to decide was whether the insurers were liable for this loss, which occurred on land, not while the ship was at sea.

Mansfield decided the case against the insurers. He first pointed out that the defendants had insured the ship's equipment against fire during the whole time of the voyage, without any restrictions. Since what happened was within the words of the policy, it was up to the defendants to show that they had not insured against the loss that occurred. He then listed the rules of marine insurance, which he said were the same all over the world: If a voyage is altered by the fault of the captain or owner of the ship, the insurer is no longer liable; but the insurer is liable for everything done "in the usual course and manner of doing it. Everything done in the usual course must have been foreseen and in contemplation, at the time [the insurer] engaged. He took the risk upon a supposition that what was usual or necessary would be done ... For the means must be taken to be insured, as well as the end." Since it was necessary to store the ship's equipment on land while the ship was being cleaned and refitted, the loss was within the terms of the insurance policy.

Mansfield treated life insurance cases with the same clarity and pragmatism as he did marine insurance cases. In these, the plaintiff (usually the estate of the insured) had the initial burden of proving that the insured was in reasonably good health when the insurance policy was written. Once this proof was made, the insurer could rebut it by showing that the insured was guilty of fraud or concealment as to his or her condition.[130]

These principles were not always simple to apply to particular cases. In *Ross v. Bradshaw*,[131] a one-year term insurance policy had been written on the life of Sir James Ross, who had warranted that he was in good health. In fact, he had received a wound in battle twelve years earlier, which gave him palsy and rendered him incontinent, a fact not known to the insurer. A month before the policy expired, Ross died of a "malignant fever," and the insurer contested the policy on the ground that he had concealed his condition. Mansfield told the jury: "The only question is whether he was in a reasonably good state of health." Although Ross was troubled with spasms and cramps, he was in as good a state of health when the policy was written as he had enjoyed for a long time. A warranty of good health "could never mean that a man has not in him the seeds of some disorder. We are all born with the seeds of mortality in us." The jury found the insurer liable.

Mansfield decided a similar case involving insurance on the life of Sir Simon Stuart. When he took out the insurance, Sir Simon had not told the insurer that he had been troubled by gout for several years, and the insurer sought to escape liability on the ground of concealment. Mansfield disagreed. He told the jury that nobody is entirely free from complaints; it was enough that Stuart was not afflicted with any disease that was likely to hasten his death. His "disorder did not preclude him from being an insurable life."[132] The jury followed Mansfield's instruction that the plaintiff was entitled to recover on the policy.

Mansfield's views on employment and labour were conventional for his time. His decisions and his statements from the bench showed that he shared the opinion of the ruling class that Britain's commercial prosperity required keeping labour costs down.[133] In the 1760s and 1770s, the change from cottage industry to factories, and from human power to water-powered (and eventually steam-powered) mills, meant that men, women, and even children began to work for a fixed number of hours a day, sometimes as many as twelve.[134] Longer hours, lower wages, and the introduction of machinery led to strikes and sometimes riots by miners, weavers, construction labourers, merchant seamen, and other workers.[135] Parliament's reacted by enacting statutes in 1721 and 1726 prohibiting workers from combining to demand higher pay or shorter hours.[136]

These laws were hardly necessary, for Mansfield consistently ruled that trade unions were illegal conspiracies under the common law. In *The King v. Eccles*,[137] seven employees of a Lancaster tailor who demanded higher wages were convicted of conspiring to prevent the tailor from carrying on his trade. When they appealed, Mansfield did not even bother to hear the prosecutor's arguments but immediately delivered his opinion: "Every man may work at what price he pleases, but a combination not to work under certain prices is an indictable offense." The seven men were each sentenced to six months in prison.

In another case, an employer had fired two men, apparently for sexually harassing a maidservant. Several of their co-workers agreed to refuse to work until the two men were rehired. They were indicted for conspiracy. In instructing the jury, Mansfield said:

> It is of great consequence in every country, especially a free country, that individuals should not be oppressed by conspiracies. All conspiracies are crimes, even if they are to do lawful acts ... Here several workmen joined in an act by means of which they deprived the master of the advantage of choice. The master has a right and may choose to employ some particular man; and they conspired to prevent him from so doing. What condition would masters be in if half the workmen in town were to conspire not to work for a particular master, there would be an end to all regularity or certainty.

The jury found the defendants guilty. The newspaper report of the case states that the sentencing was postponed until the next term of the court.[138] We do not know whether the two men were rehired.

Despite the conspiracy laws, labour organizers found ways of intimidating those who were willing to work for lower wages. A newspaper reported in 1762 that the clerk of a "weaver's club" was indicted for tying two weavers back to back on a horse and leading them through the streets because they were willing to work for low wages. Although a large number of weavers came to court to support the defendant, he was sentenced to three months in prison.[139] A newspaper reported a few years later that a large group of journeymen carpenters had assembled to have their wages raised and to punish all who worked at a low price. They bound one journeyman with cords on a donkey with his face to the tail, tied a saw on his back and a label with the words "Working under price," and led him that way through the streets of Wapping, a section of London. The local constable and peace officers rescued the man, arrested four of the rioters, and took them to Newgate prison in handcuffs.[140] We do not know whether Mansfield tried the case against them, but there can be little doubt that if he had, he would have dealt with them severely.

Although Mansfield had no doubt that labour combinations were criminal conspiracies, unless a workman who participated in a concerted action was a labour organizer or agitator, or participated in a riot, Mansfield and other judges were seldom willing to impose harsh penalties. Employers often shied away from pressing charges, either for fear of retaliation or of losing valuable employees. The penalties that were imposed had little deterrent effect, and employee combinations increased during Mansfield's long term in office.[141]

Mansfield recognized the duties of employers as well as employees. In one case, a woman gave a doctor's prescription to an apothecary, but the shop boy sent over powder instead of the prescribed pills, in six times the quantity prescribed. The woman became very ill from the overdose and sued the apothecary. In his charge to the jury, Mansfield articulated a rule of what is now called agency law. Every person who keeps a shop, he said, was responsible for everything that was done in it, either by himself or by any other person to whom he had entrusted the management of the business. This rule applied in all the professions but had particular application to that of an apothecary or chemist, by whose errors the lives of people were at stake. Even if the apothecary had been absent, he would have been answerable for the mischief. The jury awarded damages of £20 to the plaintiff.[142]

Mansfield's most important and lasting contribution to the law came in his decisions affecting commerce. His fellow justice Francis Buller was fully justified in his opinion that Mansfield "may be truly said to be the founder of the commercial law of this country."[143] In this area we see most clearly his salient qualities as a judge: his ability through his decisions to create a coherent body of law based on principles to guide future litigants; his pragmatic outlook; his clarity of thought; his willingness to look to foreign law or general principles of fairness and reason where the English common law did not supply answers; and his adaptation of the law to fit Britain's new situation as the world's leading commercial and industrial power. Moreover, Mansfield's consistent support of commerce can also be seen in other branches of the law, including his criminal law decisions.

14

Freedom of the Press

Fiat justicia, ruat coelum [let justice be done, though the heavens fall].

Lord Mansfield, at John Wilkes's outlawry trial

In eighteenth-century England, the government controlled the press largely through the libel laws. Any criticism of the government could be the basis for a criminal charge of seditious libel. As a prosecutor and then as a judge, Mansfield believed that vigorous enforcement of the seditious libel laws was a way of supporting the government and arresting what he saw as a decline in the moral condition of the country.[1] This earned him the enmity of much of the general public as well as of many members of the ruling elite, who accused him of denying their fundamental rights of liberty and freedom of the press. One pamphleteer wrote: "Lord Mansfield has succeeded so far in his vile, his infamous design of destroying the liberty of the press, that there is not one bookseller [that] has now resolution enough to publish the most trifling essay wrote with any kind of spirit in defence of the common rights of mankind."[2]

Mansfield's suppression of any criticism of the government can plausibly be ascribed, at least in part, to his fear of being labelled a Jacobite and a traitor. Three events in Mansfield's life seem to have influenced his character and policies in this direction. First, at the age of ten, living in Perth, he witnessed the debacle of the Jacobite Rebellion of 1715, which his father as well as two of his brothers had supported. Second, he cannot have forgotten that at the age of twenty he wrote two letters to his brother-in-law, Colonel John Hay, pledging his loyalty to the exiled Pretender. Finally, in 1753 he had to defend himself before the Cabinet against charges that as a young man he had drunk toasts to the Pretender. His decisions in seditious libel cases contrast sharply with his emphasis on individual freedom in other areas, particularly religious toleration.

Truth was no defence to a criminal charge of seditious libel; on the contrary, Mansfield was quoted as saying that the truth of a libel is an aggravation of the defendant's guilt: "the greater the truth the greater the libel."[3] Reinforcing the government's tight control of the press, he insisted that the judge, not the jury, decided whether a particular statement was libelous; the jury was asked only to decide whether the defendant was the author, publisher, or printer of the offending statement. The penalties for seditious libel could be harsh, including fines, imprisonment, and standing publicly in the pillory; the latter punishment could be painful or even fatal, because the prisoner was at the mercy of a sometimes-hostile mob. One newspaper commented that, by means of the pillory, "murder is sometimes committed in a civilized nation."[4]

Mansfield was much less severe in civil libel suits. In one case he ruled that calling a person a thief was not libelous because the defendant did not mean to accuse the plaintiff of a felony. The expression was just a vulgar phrase from which no special damage could arise.[5]

Mansfield's enforcement of the seditious libel laws followed existing precedent. As a young barrister in 1731, he attended a trial where Attorney General Philip Yorke (later to become Lord Chancellor Hardwicke) prosecuted Francklin, the printer of a prominent anti-government newspaper, *The Craftsman*, for attacking the Robert Walpole ministry. A large crowd of spectators attended the trial, including persons of high rank who themselves were critical of the government and came to support the defendant. Yorke argued that it was immaterial whether the statements made by Francklin were true or not. Liberty, he said, does not mean "a licentious and an unbound liberty to libel and scandalize his Majesty or his principal officers and ministers of state, or his magistrates, or even any of the meanest of his subjects, whenever they think fit; for that would be a dangerous liberty indeed, and be of a very pernicious consequence." The jury found Francklin guilty and sentenced him to a fine of £100 and a year's imprisonment.[6]

As an officer of the Crown, Mansfield prosecuted several libel cases and gave legal opinions to government departments regarding libel. The views he expressed as a prosecutor suggested that as a judge he would be no friend of freedom of the press. In prosecuting a libel case in 1752, he told the jury that the only question for them to decide was whether the defendant published the offending pamphlet; whether or not its contents were libelous was for the judge to decide.[7] In 1755 the commissioners of excise asked Mansfield as attorney general for an opinion concerning an entry in Samuel

Johnson's famous *Dictionary of the English Language*. Johnson had defined the word "excise" as: "A hateful tax levied upon commodities, and adjudged not by the common judges of property, but wretches hired by those to whom excise is paid." The commissioners asked Mansfield whether this definition could be considered a libel and, if so, whether it was proper to proceed against the author. Mansfield opined that it was a libel, although he added: "But under all the circumstances, I should think it better to give him an opportunity of altering his definition; and, in case, he do not, to threaten him with [prosecution]."[8] Johnson never changed the definition, but the commissioners decided that it would be more prudent not to prosecute him, either because of his standing as a literary figure or because a prosecution would only publicize the unpopular excise taxes.[9]

Mansfield believed that obscene or blasphemous works were libelous. In 1749, he approved the government's seizure of a supposedly obscene book entitled *Memoirs of a Woman of Pleasure* (popularly known as *Fanny Hill*).[10] He also inveighed against writings that questioned or criticized organized religion. Although he believed in freedom of worship, this did not include attacks on Christianity. In December 1755, Chancellor Hardwicke asked Mansfield's opinion on whether the author of such a pamphlet should be prosecuted. Mansfield replied:

> Though I have dipped but little into writings of this kind, I think I may venture to say it is the most impudent libel upon Christianity that ever was printed, because it consists only of bold, blasphemous assertions, without attempting proof or argument ... I really think there cannot be a properer case [to set an] example ... If the author or printer should be persons of any note or consequence or obnoxious characters this is an additional reason for Government to interpose a public prosecution.[11]

A few months later, a man named Jacob Ilive was convicted of printing and publishing a libel in which he questioned the truth of all revealed religion. It is not clear whether this was the pamphlet Mansfield was referring to in his letter to Hardwicke. Ilive was sentenced to stand in the pillory three times: at Charing Cross, the Royal Exchange, and Chancery Lane; to be imprisoned at hard labour for three years; and at the end of that time to give security of £200 for his good behaviour for life.[12]

After becoming chief justice, Mansfield privately warned David Hume, the Scottish philosopher, that if he published two treatises that attacked organized religion and attempted to prove that there was no such thing as an immortal soul, he would be prosecuted. Although Hume had already had the treatises printed, he took Mansfield's advice and refrained from publishing them. On his death, he left the treatises to his nephew, asking him to publish them himself if no bookseller or publisher would. A letter writer commented: "I think Lord Mansfield will again interpose: for with all desirable freedom left to the press there is still I conclude some legal restraint upon the publication of certain atrocious attacks upon the establishment with which Christianity, thank God! as yet makes a part."[13]

By far the most famous seditious libel defendant of the eighteenth century was John Wilkes. Wilkes was feared and hated by the government as a demagogue, but the London mob, as well as many merchants and tradesmen, idolized him as a heroic supporter of their civil liberties.[14] He based his criticism of the government on history, insisting he was a supporter of the Glorious Revolution of 1688, and that liberty was its fundamental principle.[15]

Wilkes was born in London in 1726, the son of a distiller. He was well educated in the classics, both in England and for a time in Holland. He was an ugly but charming man, with a long protruding chin. He was fearless in attacking authority but unprincipled in his political and private life. His marriage to Mary Mead, a woman of considerable wealth, gave him the wherewithal to run for a seat in Parliament. After one defeat, he was elected in 1757 by giving a guinea apiece to each of the 250 voters in the district.[16]

That same year, Wilkes's marriage broke up. Upon his separation, John agreed to pay Mary £200 a year for the rest of his life. Soon, however, he was in debt and he asked her to give up her alimony. When she refused, he sued her in the Court of King's Bench. It was the first of several encounters between Chief Justice Mansfield and Wilkes. Mansfield refused to upset the separation agreement and dismissed the case.[17] Wilkes never saw his wife again, never remarried, and soon gained a reputation in London's West End as a libertine, gratifying his sexual desires with a series of female servants and courtesans, and fathering at least one illegitimate child.[18]

In Parliament, Wilkes at first supported the Newcastle–Pitt ministry but was unable to persuade Pitt to give him a post on the Board of Trade. He attributed his failure to the influence of Lord Bute, who had become prime minister in 1762. The fact that Bute was a Scot may have contributed to Wilkes's anti-Scottish prejudice. Soon afterwards, Wilkes took over *The*

North Briton, a weekly political journal with a circulation of 2,000 that published a series of attacks on the government as well as on the Scots.[19] The most violent of these attacks was No. 45 of *The North Briton*, published on 23 April 1763, a week after Bute had been replaced as prime minister by George Grenville, Pitt's brother-in-law.

In No. 45, Wilkes went far beyond reviling the Scots. He attacked the proposed peace treaty with France as being too lenient; he suggested that Bute, the King's favourite, though no longer holding office, still exercised an influence in the government; and he concluded with an attack on the government in language that could be regarded as a call for revolution:

> A despotic minister will always endeavour to dazzle his prince with high-flown ideas of the *prerogative* and *honour* of the *crown*, which the minister will make a parade of *firmly maintaining*. I wish as much as any man in the kingdom to see *the honour of the crown* maintained in a manner truly becoming *Royalty*. I lament to see it sunk even to prostitution ...
>
> The *prerogative* of the crown is to exert the constitutional powers entrusted to him in a way not of blind favour and partiality, but of wisdom and judgment. This is the spirit of our constitution. The people too have their *prerogative*, and I hope the fine words of Dryden will be engraved on our hearts: Freedom is the English Subject's Prerogative.[20]

No. 45 aroused the fury of the ministry and the King, who called for legal action against Wilkes. Although the Cabinet was divided on whether to prosecute Wilkes for seditious libel,[21] Grenville, sensitive to criticism of his newly installed ministry, acted immediately and forcefully. He authorized Earl Halifax, one of the secretaries of state, to issue a "general warrant" for the arrest of the authors, printers, and publishers of No. 45 and for the seizure of their papers. The general warrant, without naming any particular persons, authorized government "messengers" to arrest anyone whom they had probable cause to believe had participated in the seditious libel. On an inaccurate tip, the messengers broke into the house of a printer named Dryden Leach, who was *not* the printer of No. 45, arrested twenty of his employees, and seized bundles of papers. Other messengers broke into the bookshop of George Kearsly, who *was* the publisher of No. 45, arrested him and his employees, and seized his papers. In all, forty-nine people were arrested,[22] among them Wilkes, who claimed parliamentary privilege on the ground that as a member of Parliament he was immune from arrest for any crime except a felony, breach of the peace, or treason, and that publishing a supposed libel was none of these. Nevertheless, he was imprisoned in the Tower of London.

The government's fierce overreaction to No. 45 made Wilkes a popular hero. Troops of his friends and supporters, including some members of the nobility, visited him in prison.[23] His friends obtained a writ of habeas corpus from Chief Justice Charles Pratt of the Court of Common Pleas. Pratt had a distinguished legal background; his father had served as chief justice of King's Bench and he himself had been attorney general before being appointed to the bench. A short vigorous man, he combined a love of the law with a love of the pleasures of life, including good food and wine, as well as opera and theatre.[24] As a defence lawyer and later as attorney general, he had gained a reputation as a champion of civil liberties by asserting the right of the jury to decide the ultimate issue of whether a publication was libelous.[25] He had a reputation as a "sound, penetrating, and lucid judge."[26]

A close friend and political ally of William Pitt, Pratt shared Pitt's dislike of Mansfield for his rigid enforcement of the seditious libel laws and his consistent refusal to question the policies of the government. Wilkes was represented by John Glynn, a member of Parliament and one of the most highly regarded barristers of his day, rated "the first man in Westminster Hall for legal knowledge."[27] Pitt called Glynn "a most ingenious, solid, pleasing man, and the spirit of the constitution itself."[28] Although Glynn acted as Wilkes's counsel throughout his long legal struggles, they were not close personally. When at a later date the King asked Wilkes about Glynn, Wilkes replied, displaying his own fundamentally conservative nature: "Sir ... he was my counsel – one must have a counsel; but he was no friend, he loves sedition and licentiousness, which I never delighted in. In fact, Sir, he was a Wilkite, which I never was."[29]

Appearing before Pratt in the Court of Common Pleas, Glynn argued that the general warrant was an illegal use of government power and also that Wilkes was immune from arrest on the ground of parliamentary privilege. To nobody's surprise, Pratt agreed. On 6 May, he ordered Wilkes released from prison, to the outspoken joy of a pro-Wilkes mob attending the hearing.[30] Mansfield, who could hear the clamour from his adjacent court in Westminster Hall, was furious at Wilkes's release. Newcastle, who knew Mansfield as well as anybody, ascribed Mansfield's rage to his rivalry with Pratt, believing that Mansfield thought the motion for habeas corpus should have been made in his own court.[31]

Besides writing No. 45 of *The North Briton*, Wilkes had engaged in literary activity of a very different kind. During the 1750s, a friend of Wilkes named Thomas Potter had written *An Essay on Woman*, a salacious parody of Alexander Pope's long poem *An Essay on Man* and also of the rather pompous notes on Pope's poem by Bishop William Warburton, his literary executor. Pope, who died in 1744, had been a close friend of Mansfield, and Warburton also was Mansfield's friend. After revising *An Essay on Woman* and adding some of his own bawdy poems, Wilkes had ordered printers to run off twelve copies for the edification of his fellow members of the Hell-fire Club, a group whose main activities were drinking, mockery of religion, and sex with high-class prostitutes, as well as a thirteenth copy for the club's library. Wilkes cautioned the printers to observe the utmost secrecy. *An Essay on Woman* has been described as "the dirtiest poem in the English language."[32] To give some idea of its nature, the title page pictured an erect penis next to a ten-inch scale, and one of the shorter poems from Wilkes was entitled "The Dying Lover to His Prick."[33] Government agents seized the manuscript of the *Essay* when they searched Wilkes's house.[34]

For the time being, Wilkes was a free man, but the establishment, urged on by the King, decided to move against him on two fronts: the legislature and the courts. A secret plan, not even known to most of the members of the Cabinet, was hatched to prosecute him for libelling Warburton in *An Essay on Woman*. As a bishop, Warburton was entitled to bring suit in the House of Lords. When the House met on 17 November 1763, the Earl of Sandwich, one of the two secretaries of state, read out some portions of the *Essay* that he claimed were not too shocking, saying it was necessary to do so in order to support the charge against Wilkes. Even so, one lord was so outraged that he asked Sandwich to stop reading, but other members eagerly urged him to go on. Witnesses were examined to prove that Wilkes was the author of the *Essay*. Lord Temple, Pitt's brother-in-law and a supporter of Wilkes, asked for an inquiry into whether copies of the *Essay* had been obtained legally. Mansfield then brought his formidable legal authority into the debate, calling Temple's objection absurd. Coming by evidence illegally, he said, did not make that evidence illegal in the trial of a criminal. He ridiculed the objection (which, incidentally, would have considerable force under the modern constitutional law of the United States or Canada[35]) so effectively that members called out for a vote. Mansfield rose again and made the rather obvious point, reminiscent of the trial of the Knave of Hearts in Lewis Carroll's *Alice in Wonderland*, that it might be irregular to convict Wilkes without first allowing him to be heard. Sandwich said he would defer the vote.[36]

Meanwhile, the King, determined to see Wilkes sent to prison, asked the House of Commons to review Judge Pratt's decision releasing him on the ground of parliamentary privilege.[37] Grenville, acting on Mansfield's advice that the courts would never be able to satisfy the King's desire to punish Wilkes,[38] agreed to this unusual procedure, in which the House of Commons was to act as a court of appeals. A vigorous debate in the House followed, in which a member of Parliament and former secretary to the Treasury named Samuel Martin, whom Wilkes in one issue of *The North Briton* had called a "treacherous, base, selfish, mean, abject, low-lived and dirty fellow," had his opportunity to use similar invective on Wilkes, calling him a "cowardly rascal, a villain and a scoundrel." Wilkes challenged Martin to a duel. They exchanged pistol shots in Hyde Park; Wilkes's pistol misfired, but Martin shot Wilkes in the abdomen. Wilkes recovered from his wound. Some thought that the duel was a setup, and that Martin had been paid by the government to assassinate Wilkes.[39]

Prevented for the moment by Wilkes's parliamentary privilege from imprisoning him, the government took the easier course of punishing his product, No. 45 of *The North Briton*. On 3 December, the publication was to be burned by the common hangman at the Royal Exchange. But when the magistrates assembled to witness the ceremony, a riot broke out. The mob seized the condemned paper from the hangman, and pelted and beat up the constables, crying "Wilkes and Liberty!" Three days later, when the House of Lords met to decide whether the magistrates were to blame for the fiasco, Mansfield spoke up in their defence.[40] Wilkes, believing that Mansfield's court would convict him of blasphemy for writing *An Essay on Woman*, fled to France in January 1764.[41]

Until this time, Mansfield's involvement with Wilkes had been peripheral, but it was to become much greater in the years ahead. On 10 July 1764, the Court of King's Bench found the printers of the *North Briton* guilty of seditious libel. Glynn, counsel for the defendants, told the jury that they were the judges of both the legal question (whether the publication was libelous) and the factual question (whether the defendants published the offending work). Mansfield angrily insisted that the jury had no competence to decide the legal question.[42]

When Dryden Leach, the printer, brought suit in the Court of Common Pleas against the government agents who had mistakenly broken into his house and arrested him pursuant to a general warrant, the jury awarded him damages of £400. On appeal to the Court of King's Bench, Mansfield affirmed the verdict, on the ground that the warrant did not authorize the arrest of Leach, who was neither an author, printer, nor publisher of No. 45 of *The North Briton*. Mansfield and the other three judges agreed that general warrants were illegal and void. They could not be justified by usage, because usage "will not hold against clear and solid principles of law"; in any case, the usage would have to be general, but "this has been the usage of only one office and officer against the practice of all other conservators of the peace."[43]

In January 1764, after Wilkes had fled to France, the House of Commons expelled him and the attorney general charged him with seditious libel. The following month, he was tried *in absentia* before Mansfield and found guilty of libelling Warburton in *An Essay on Woman* and the government in No. 45 of *The North Briton*. In August 1764 he was ordered to appear before the Court of King's Bench to be sentenced. When he failed to show up, he was declared an outlaw.

Wilkes spent the next four years in exile in France and Italy. In 1768, having been told that Mansfield had changed sides and was no longer the bitter enemy he had been,[44] Wilkes returned to England and ran for Parliament in an election to represent the County of Middlesex. He was elected in March 1768, but in order to take his seat it was necessary for him to get his outlawry reversed.

Mansfield issued a writ calling for Wilkes's arrest as an outlaw, but Wilkes appeared voluntarily in Mansfield's court on 20 April 1768, accompanied by three or four friends.[45] A large crowd had gathered in Westminster Hall to see him.[46] Wilkes first made a speech in his own defence, stating that *The North Briton* was not aimed at the King but at the ministry; and that *An Essay on Woman* had never been published, since only thirteen copies had been printed, and these were for his friends.[47] The attorney general asked the court to commit Wilkes to prison, while Wilkes's lawyer asked that he be freed on bail. Mansfield refused to grant either motion, ruling that nothing could be decided until the question of Wilkes's outlawry was resolved.

At around this time, Mansfield had injured himself, apparently in a fall from his horse; on 24 April a friend wrote that Mansfield had almost recovered "but the bruises are still very black in his face."[48] The injury must have been fairly serious, for three weeks later he was still convalescing; the Duke of Newcastle wrote to Mansfield that he was "extremely glad to hear that [Mansfield] was getting well apace."[49]

After surrendering himself to the sheriff, Wilkes was back in court again on 27 April asking to be released on bail. After a long debate, Mansfield denied the motion and ordered him to be committed to the King's Bench prison to await a hearing on the question of his outlawry. The marshal of the prison put Wilkes in a coach that set off to the prison in the custody of several tipstaffs (i.e., court officers), but before they could get halfway over Westminster Bridge an angry mob stopped the coach, painted the words "No. 45" on its side panels ("45" had become a slogan for support of Wilkes), and unhitched the horses. Wilkes tried to dissuade them and warned the tipstaffs to flee, which they did. The mob turned the coach around and pulled it down the Strand and Fleet Street, and finally to a tavern in the City of London.[50] Wilkes managed to slip away through a back door and go quietly to the prison where he gave himself up.[51]

It is important to understand the state of agitation and fear that existed in London during the weeks before Mansfield finally ruled on Wilkes's outlawry. During May, supporters of Wilkes, mostly middle- and working-class people,[52] gathered at the door of the House of Lords, crying "Wilkes and Liberty."[53] Mansfield may have put off the hearing only because of the injury he had suffered in April, but the delay increased the tension. The ranks of Wilkes's supporters increased every day, and members of the government debated whether the only alternative to being governed by a lawless mob was for a standing military force to maintain order, a solution unknown to the British constitution.[54] Wilkes's counsel again requested that he be released on bail; Mansfield again denied it.[55] Meanwhile, even Mansfield's closest political associates had no idea how he would rule on the question of Wilkes's outlawry.[56]

Finally, on 8 June, Mansfield delivered his opinion to a crowded court packed with Wilkes's supporters. Although the opinion is memorable for its stirring language proclaiming the independence of the judiciary, there is a strange disconnect between Mansfield's sanctimonious words and his actual decision. Mansfield began by pointing out that Wilkes brought the consequences of outlawry on himself "by fleeing from the justice of his country." Courts do not *make* the law, he said, their job is to *interpret* it. The court "can't prevent the judgment of the law ... It does not belong to us to interfere with punishment, we have only to declare the law." He continued:

> We are bound upon our oath upon our conscience to give such a judgment as the law will warrant and as our reason can approve such a judgment as we must stand or fall by in the opinion of the times and of posterity ...
>
> But consequences of a public nature, reasons of state, political ones have been strongly urged, private anonymous letters sent to me I shall pass over and avowed publications ... have endeavoured to influence or intimidate the Court and so prevail upon us to trifle and prevaricate

with God, our conscience and the public. It has been mentioned that consequences of a frightful nature will flow from the establishment of this outlawry ... These are arguments which will not weigh a feather with me. If insurrection or rebellion are to follow our determination we have not to answer for the consequences though we should be the innocent cause. We can only say *fiat justicia, ruat coelum* [let justice be done, though the heavens fall] ...

I wish earnestly for popularity. I will seek and will have popularity which follows, and not that which is run after ... But the threats have been carried further, personal violence has been denounced unless public humour be complied with. I do not fear such threats. I do not believe there is any reason to fear them.[57]

Having said all of this – and more – Mansfield must have astonished the large crowd in Westminster Hall when he reversed Wilkes's outlawry on the merest of technicalities. The sheriff's writ declaring Wilkes's outlawry had stated that it was executed at "my County Court," omitting to state that it was at the County of Middlesex. Although Mansfield conceded that there was no uncertainty as to which county was being referred to, he declared that legal precedents required him "to say that, for want of these technical words, the outlawry ought to be reversed."[58] Thus, Mansfield's long, eloquent opinion reproaching Wilkes consisted only of empty words. Despite Mansfield's self-righteous claim of immunity to the lure of popularity and threats of violence, it seems he succumbed to them. Horace Walpole thought that he acted out of cowardice.[59] A nineteenth-century historian commented more mildly: "It would on this occasion have been more dignified to make less parade of independence,"[60] while a twentieth-century biographer has argued charitably that Mansfield opposed the prosecution of Wilkes, believing that the matter would die away if Wilkes were left alone, and that he simply found a reason to support a decision he had already reached.[61]

Mansfield's decision was greeted with joy by the mob and instantly, if only temporarily, made him a popular figure. They cheered the decision and wanted to draw Mansfield home in his coach, just as six weeks earlier they had pulled Wilkes's coach through London, but Mansfield declined this unwanted honour.[62]

The reversal of Wilkes's outlawry saved him from a lifetime in prison,[63] but it did not absolve him of the libel convictions obtained against him *in absentia* four years earlier. He was remanded to prison to await his sentence. On 18 June 1768, Wilkes was brought back to the court, where Justice Yates, the senior judge after Mansfield, sentenced him to a fine of £500 and ten months in prison for No. 45 of *The North Briton* and a fine of £500 and twelve months in prison for *An Essay on Woman*.[64] It is not clear why Mansfield, who was on the bench with Yates, did not impose the sentence on Wilkes – perhaps he wanted a more severe sentence and the other three judges disagreed, and Mansfield did not want to suffer what he might have regarded as the indignity of being in the minority in his own court. Although Wilkes's supporters thought the sentence unjustifiably severe, Grenville said it was very lenient, comparing it to the sentence that Mansfield had imposed ten years earlier on Dr Shebbeare, who, like Wilkes, was convicted of libel for criticizing the government. Shebbeare was sentenced to be fined, to stand in the pillory three times, and to be imprisoned for three years.[65] Walpole, who frequently commented on Mansfield's supposed timidity, thought that he did not require that Wilkes suffer the humiliating and potentially dangerous punishment of the pillory, the usual punishment in seditious libel cases, because he was afraid of Wilkite rioters. Another possible reason Wilkes escaped the pillory, perhaps the most likely, was that the attorney general did not ask the court to impose this punishment.[66]

While in prison, Wilkes ran three times for election as a member of Parliament for Middlesex. Each time he won, and each time the House of Commons refused to seat him. In the third of these elections, held on 13 April 1769, he received 1,143 votes, while his opponent, Henry Luttrell (who, like Wilkes, was a notorious rake[67]), received 296. Nevertheless, the House declared Luttrell the winner.[68] In 1770, Pitt, who had been raised to the peerage as Earl Chatham, introduced a bill in the House of Lords reversing the decision of the House of Commons to seat Luttrell. Mansfield opposed the bill, arguing that the House of Commons had the ultimate power to decide the qualification of its members.[69] The bill was defeated. Wilkes finally took his seat in Parliament in December 1774, and eight years later the House of Commons voted to expunge from the record its previous resolutions expelling him and declaring him ineligible to be elected.[70]

In later years, Wilkes, the erstwhile rabble-rouser, became a member of the establishment. In 1774 he was elected lord mayor of London, and a few years later King George III, who had hated Wilkes bitterly, was reconciled with him.[71] Perhaps even more surprising, he and Mansfield became quite friendly. A mutual friend told Wilkes that he heard Mansfield say at a dinner party in March 1783, that "Mr Wilkes was the pleasantest companion, the politest gentleman, and the best scholar he knew."[72] Not long before Mansfield retired from the bench, when they were both at the resort of Tunbridge Wells, a newspaper reported on an example of Wilkes's dark humour at Mansfield's expense:

> All the country around Tunbridge Wells means to assemble on purpose to uphold the regenerating work of Mr Wilkes going to church next Sunday with his new prayer book.
>
> Lord Mansfield says it will be one of the noblest sights in the universe. Mr Wilkes replies that there might be one still more noble – the sight of his Lordship with a prayer book and a nosegay.[73] [It was often the custom for criminals about to be executed to carry a prayer book in one hand and a nosegay in the other.]

Mansfield and Wilkes shared a love of the classics, and on more than one occasion Wilkes made gifts of books to Mansfield. In 1788, Mansfield wrote to Wilkes from Kenwood: "Lord Mansfield returns Mr Wilkes many thanks for his elegant edition of Catullus, and congratulates him upon those enjoyments, which an early taste for the classics has put in his power."[74] Unlike Mansfield, however, Wilkes was a supporter of the American colonists in the Revolutionary War, who demonstrated their gratitude to him and to another British supporter of the colonists' cause, Colonel Isaac Barré, by bestowing their two names on the city of Wilkes-Barre, Pennsylvania.[75]

Next to Wilkes, the most prominent seditious libel cases involved the anonymous letters written by "Junius." The identity of Junius remains a secret to this day.[76] Many of the Junius letters were published between 1769 and 1772 in *The Public Advertiser*, edited by Henry Sampson Woodfall, which has been described as "one of the great papers of the century."[77] Before it began publishing the letters, the paper had a circulation of about 3,000; during their publication it rose to 4,800.[78] The letters attacked the Duke of Grafton, who was prime minister at the time, as well as the King.

Woodfall was charged with seditious libel and tried in June 1770 before Lord Mansfield at the Guildhall in the City of London. Mansfield told the jury that the only question for it to decide was whether Woodfall was the publisher of the letter. This, he said, was a question of fact, but whether the letter was a libel was a question of law for the judge to decide. After deliberating several hours, the jurors took coaches from Guildhall to Mansfield's home in Bloomsbury Square. Mansfield stood at the door of his parlour and made the jury give their verdict in the hall where the footmen were.[79] The verdict was "guilty of printing and publishing only,"[80] a verdict that stopped short of finding Woodfall guilty of seditious libel. When Mansfield heard it, he turned and withdrew without a word. He refused to accept the verdict and ordered a new trial.

Before Woodfall could be retried, Mansfield tried another seditious libel case, this one against John Miller, who was accused of reprinting Junius's letter to the King in the *London Evening Post*. A large crowd waited impatiently for several hours outside Guildhall to hear the verdict. Again Mansfield returned to his home while the jury deliberated, and again the jurors took hackney coaches to Bloomsbury Square to tell Mansfield their verdict, this time with a crowd of several thousand following in procession on foot. This time, the jury brought in a simple verdict of "not guilty." It was said that the roar of the crowd could be heard throughout London.[81] It was now apparent that no jury in London would bring a guilty verdict against a publisher of the Junius letters.

On 14 November 1770, *The Public Advertiser* published Junius's letter No. XLI, a personal attack on Mansfield, referring to his Scottish background, his Jacobite brother, and his supposed sympathies with the Pretender as a youth: "Like a honest man, you took part in politics which might have been expected from your birth, education, country [i.e., Scotland], and connections ... Why did you not follow the example of your worthy brother? With him you might have shared in the honour of the Pretender's confidence; with him you might have preserved the integrity of your character; and England, I think, might have spared you without regret."

Junius continued his attack on Mansfield by referring to his rulings in seditious libel cases, including the prosecution of Woodfall earlier the same year: "I see, through your whole life, one uniform plan to enlarge the power of the Crown at the expense of the liberty of the subject ... When you invade the province of the jury in matter of libel, you in effect attack the liberty of the press." The letter also attacked Mansfield for introducing foreign law and principles of equity into the English common law. Finally, Junius, like Horace Walpole thirteen years earlier in the debate over the fate of Admiral Byng,[82] denigrated Mansfield's character as having feminine traits:

"Yet I own, my Lord, that yours is not an uncommon character. Women, and men like women, are timid, vindictive, and irresolute. Their passions counteract each other; and make the same creature, at one moment hateful, at another contemptible."[83]

Attorney General William de Grey wanted to prosecute *The Daily Advertiser* for libelling Mansfield. Mansfield demurred, perhaps not wanting to promote more public discussion on the sensitive subject of his Jacobite family and of the old accusation that he himself had been a Jacobite sympathizer in the past.[84] Nevertheless, he maintained his tough stance against publishers of attacks on the government. Four years later, Woodfall was again prosecuted, this time for publishing a disparagement of the Glorious Revolution of 1688 and of King William and Queen Mary, who reigned at that time and had been dead for over seventy years. Although Woodfall's counsel argued that a statement could not be libelous unless it was calculated to excite sedition, Mansfield instructed the jury that criticism of a dead king could be libelous and that "whenever a man publishes he publishes at his peril, for there is no entering into the secret thoughts of a man's heart." After deliberating for several hours, the jury found Woodfall guilty of publishing the paper but not of it being a libel. Mansfield replied that they must bring in a general verdict: guilty or not guilty. They repeated that they found him guilty of publishing the paper. Mansfield said: "That is, you find the defendant guilty" and handed down a judgment of guilty. Woodfall was fined 300 marks and sentenced to imprisonment until the fine was paid.[85]

Mansfield decided numerous other libel cases during his career as a judge. One was against John Almon, who was convicted of publishing one of Junius's letters. When the case was appealed to Mansfield's court, Almon's lawyer argued that although several copies of the offending letter were printed in Almon's shop, it was done without his knowledge or consent, and that as soon as he learned of it he stopped the sale of the letters. Mansfield and his fellow judges made short work of this defence, ruling that where a pamphlet is sold in the shop of a bookseller and publisher of pamphlets, the owner of the shop is responsible for the sale, unless there is some exculpatory evidence. The court affirmed Almon's conviction.[86]

Regrettably, in seditious libel cases, Mansfield did not display the forward-looking attitude that he did in his rulings on religious toleration and commercial law. This can be attributed to his unwillingness to allow any criticism of the government. It is unfortunate that in these cases Mansfield subordinated the spirit of rationality and individualism that informed his decisions in other areas of the law, including commerce and religious freedom, to his almost unquestioning respect for royal authority. To Mansfield, any author or publisher who challenged or criticized the government was guilty of seditious libel.[87]

Many of Mansfield's contemporaries agreed with Junius that in depriving jurors of the right to decide whether a writing was libelous, Mansfield's decisions were intolerable restrictions on civil liberty.[88] The young poet Thomas Chatterton attacked Mansfield in a poem entitled "The Whore of Babylon":

And who shall doubts and false conclusions draw
Against the inquisitions of the law;
With gaolers, chains and pillories must plead
And Mansfield's conscience settle right his creed.
Is Mansfield's conscience then, will Reason cry,
A standard block to dress our notions by?
Why what a blunder has the fool let fall,
That Mansfield has no conscience, none at all.[89]

15

Crime and Punishment

Considering your crime, and its consequences ... I think myself bound in duty and conscience to acquaint his Majesty you are no object of his mercy.

Lord Mansfield, addressing a convicted forger of a stock certificate

The criminal courts were busy places in the eighteenth century, for London was a crime-ridden and disorderly city. Many cases arising from episodes of assault, robbery, false imprisonment, prostitution, drunkenness, and fraud came before the Court of King's Bench, which was the only one of the three central courts with jurisdiction to try criminal cases. Lord Mansfield heard these cases in Westminster Hall, at the Guildhall in the City of London, at the principal criminal court of Old Bailey, and on circuit outside London during the summer.[1] He also sat at Old Bailey with an Admiralty judge and a jury at sessions of the High Court of Admiralty, in cases involving mutiny and privateering.[2] Mansfield saw the large amount of street crime that he had to deal with as evidence of a general degeneration of society.[3]

Mansfield was aggressive in his administration of criminal justice and took a broad view of his court's jurisdiction. The absence of a statute proscribing a particular activity did not deter him from trying a case if the activity was contrary to good morals. When counsel argued that the Court of King's Bench lacked jurisdiction to punish election bribery, Mansfield replied that "wherever a practice, which is wrongful or unreasonable, has happened to have been introduced for want of sufficient advertence to the consequence of it, the best way is to set it right immediately, as soon as the inconvenience is observed, if former cases be not affected by the retrospect."[4] In a case that involved a conspiracy to corrupt the innocence of a young woman, Mansfield stated that his court had the power under the common law to punish those guilty of immoral acts, even though there had not been any previous prosecution for the same offence.[5]

Another important way in which Mansfield enlarged the jurisdiction of the criminal courts concerned attempted crimes. As late as 1769, English common law did not regard an attempt to commit a crime as a criminal act. Mansfield began to erode this doctrine in *Rex v. Vaughan*,[6] where he ruled that it was a crime to offer a bribe to a government official, even if the offer was not accepted. However, *Vaughan* did not make all attempts criminal, since the offer of a bribe was itself a substantive offence. In *Rex v. Scofield*,[7] decided in 1784, Mansfield, who customarily focused on the *intent* of an individual in determining the legal consequences of his actions, created the modern doctrine of attempt. He ruled that a person, indicted for arson, who attempted to burn down a house was guilty of a crime, even though the attempt failed.[8] It is today accepted that attempted crimes are themselves crimes.

Street riots were a constant threat to law and order, the worst being the riots for "Wilkes and Liberty" in the 1760s and the anti-Catholic Gordon Riots in 1780, when the rioters burned down Mansfield's home in Bloomsbury Square.[9] But there were numerous other serious disturbances in mid-century, which required troops to be called in, including riots in the Strand in 1759 that left all the windows of the office of a coach company without a pane of glass;[10] and a riot of London silk weavers in 1763 protesting the opening of the English markets to French silks after the war with France ended.[11]

Fights were common in the streets; it was not unusual for men to carry thick cudgels to protect themselves.[12] In 1758, a gang of about twenty young men invaded the area around Fleet Street every night, where they knocked people down "in order to see the claret [i.e., blood] run." When a constable tried to disperse them, eight or ten threw him down and broke his leg.[13] Most Londoners were victims of crime at one time or another, whether it was pickpocketing, burglary, or street or highway robbery.[14] The pickpockets in the area around the Drury Lane playhouse were so numerous that it was said to be difficult to go to the theatre without having one's pockets rifled.[15]

Prostitution was widespread in London, both on the streets and in brothels.[16] A visitor from the Continent observed that there were more prostitutes in London than in Paris and that they had more effrontery than those in Rome: "About nightfall they range themselves in a file in the footpaths of all the great streets, in companies of five or six, most of them dressed very genteelly ... They accost passengers in broad daylight and above all foreigners."[17] In 1760, a newspaper reported: "The common prostitutes of Ludgate Hill, the Old Bailey, etc. are become ... a public nuisance ... One of them ... took up a young man who refusing to go with her she took a pair of scissors and cut off the lower part of one of his ears."[18] Another London newspaper reported that an army sergeant had bequeathed in his will a glass of gin to every whore on Exeter Street (near the Strand in central London). According to the paper, his "fortune" was about £40, but it only left a thimbleful for each claimant.[19] Even allowing for a certain amount of exaggeration – £40 would have bought about eighty *gallons* of gin – the report suggests that there was a large population of prostitutes on a single London street.[20]

Drunkenness was a major problem. Testimony given in the House of Commons in 1750 showed that 16,000 London houses, or one house in fifteen, sold liquor.[21] Benjamin Franklin said that when he was a printer in London in the early years of the century, his companion at the press drank six pints of beer a day, beginning before breakfast.[22] But gin was replacing beer as the drink of choice, and its consumption was so extensive and excessive that it threatened to destroy the working classes of London. In 1736, when the government tried to put a stop to it by imposing a prohibitive tax on the sale of gin, there was widespread rioting in London.[23] Members of the upper classes also drank to excess – chiefly rum punch or wine in their clubs.[24] Drinking led to crime. A newspaper reported in 1787:

> The gin shops about St Paul's have very greatly added to the nightly riots and disturbances of that neighbourhood. When abandoned women have drunk themselves to intoxication, they lie before the doors and the watchmen, constables, etc. are the bait of their profligate abuse which they return with great vociferation to convince their employers that they are on duty. A correspondent had the misfortune to miss his way and to wander into this district. He was immediately surrounded by these fiends who wanted to strip him of his clothes. On applying to the officer he was told nothing could be done with them as the parish had no place for their confinement.[25]

There was no national police force to enforce the law. When there were riots, magistrates had to ask the home secretary to call in troops. The idea of a professional police force met strong opposition, for fear of corruption and tyranny.[26] Mansfield believed that enforcing the law should be left to local magistrates, who could be punished for failing to do so, and that the use of troops to suppress riots would only enrage the people and magnify the riots.[27] To the extent that there was law enforcement, it was in the hands of justices of the peace appointed by the lord lieutenants of the counties, who were usually noblemen of great wealth and prestige. The Duke of Newcastle, for example, was lord lieutenant for the counties of Sussex, Nottingham, and Middlesex. The justice of the peace investigated cases of serious crime, examined felony suspects, and wrote a report for the trial court. He also tried minor crimes, such as drunkenness, vagrancy, and profanity.[28] Local constables were often unable to keep the peace because they were intimidated or attacked by mobs they could not control.[29] Law officers received some protection from the law: Mansfield ruled that a constable could not be sued for arresting a man who turned out to be innocent if the constable acted in a way that was "bona fide, honest and regular in every degree."[30]

After an arrest in London, the accused would be examined at the Bow Street Magistrate's Court, presided over by the government-appointed principal magistrate. In 1748, this office was filled by Henry Fielding, the novelist. He was succeeded upon his death in 1754 by John Fielding, his half-brother, who had been blind from birth. John Fielding earned a reputation for fighting corruption in law enforcement and has been described as "the most innovative magistrate of the eighteenth century."[31] In 1755, he established a small group of constables, known later as the Bow Street runners, who were the forerunners of London's first metropolitan police force.[32] At the Bow Street Magistrate's Court, Fielding and his magistrates, who served on a rotating basis, conducted pretrial examinations in a courtlike setting. Persons suspected of serious crimes were vigorously questioned, in the hope that they would reveal their guilt. Lawyers for the accused were allowed to cross-examine witnesses for the prosecution but not to conduct other aspects of the defence. Victims and members of the public were allowed to attend the pretrial examinations, which were held in a large noisy room. Where probable cause was found, the case was sent to the Old Bailey or King's Bench for trial.[33]

In a pretrial hearing in 1780, a lawyer named Thomas Ayrton, representing a man accused of robbery, interrupted the questioning by Magistrate William Addington, who was trying to cross-examine the prosecutor. Addington objected to Ayrton's conduct, and the two traded insults, with the result that Addington ordered Ayrton's arrest. Ayrton sued Addington for assault and false imprisonment before Lord Mansfield in the Court of King's Bench The jury found in Ayrton's favour and also awarded him costs. At the hearing, Attorney General James Wallace condemned Bow Street examinations for their prejudicial nature. According to a newspaper, Wallace said that:

> The *public* examination[s] at Bow Street were productive of most mischievous consequences to Society. The injury done to individuals who might be innocent was such for which no possible compensation could be made ... the prisoner came for his trial without the possibility of fair inquiry, the minds of the people were influenced, the jury prejudiced and, where, any possible guilt lodged, the prisoner hardly stood the chance of a fair acquittal. [In newspaper accounts,] the evidence was given at large, crimes magnified, prisoners calumniated, prejudiced and, in the minds of men, adjudged before hearing.[34]

Mansfield agreed, calling the public examinations "subversive of every principle of justice."[35]

Perhaps as a result of Mansfield's criticism, some of the more unfair aspects of pretrial examinations, such as forcing the accused to incriminate himself or herself, were eliminated. In general, Fielding's reforms were beneficial. According to a modern scholar, Fielding's "most important legacy was the opening of the pretrial process to the public through the establishment of a rotation system [of the magistrates] at Bow Street that kept the office open for eight hours every day and the establishment of [a] purpose-built courtroom opened in 1772."[36]

The system of public justice was not restrained by any compunction about "cruel or unusual punishment."[37] A man or woman charged with a capital felony (other than treason) who refused to plead guilty or not guilty suffered the savage punishment of *peine forte et dure* (severe and hard punishment).[38] This procedure, which had been used since the early fifteenth century, was described by a judge in 1721: "The Prisoner ... shall be laid upon the bare Ground without any Litter, Straw or other Covering, and ... upon his Body shall be laid so much Iron and Stone as he can bear, and more."[39] When a judge threatened a prisoner with pressing, or soon after the pressing had begun, he usually decided to plead. But some prisoners, either in the hope of making a plea bargain with the court or for some other reason, persisted in remaining mute and were slowly crushed to death.[40]

There is at least one occasion when Mansfield showed himself willing to impose *peine forte et dure*. In 1757, when a man who was accused of mail robbery refused to plead guilty or not guilty to the indictment, Mansfield ordered the jailer to take him away, to be "pressed gradually with weights till he agreed to plead, otherwise in that manner to press him to death (which is the punishment the law appoints for those that will not plead)." The threat was effective, for the man immediately changed his mind and pleaded not guilty. He was then tried, found guilty, and sentenced to death. After the execution, he was hung in chains in the place where he had committed the robbery.[41] *Peine forte et dure* continued to be used until 1772, when refusal to plead to a felony was henceforth accepted as the equivalent of a guilty verdict. A statute of 1827 provided that "standing mute" would be taken as a *not guilty* plea.[42]

In the absence of an efficient method of law enforcement, reliance was placed on the deterrent effect of draconian punishment for a broad range of crimes. By the eighteenth century, Parliament had enacted "one of the bloodiest criminal codes in Europe."[43] In theory, all felonies were punishable by death, but the harshness was partly ameliorated by the institution of "benefit of clergy." Originating in the Middle Ages as an ecclesiastical system of mercy, benefit of clergy had become part of the secular criminal-justice system. It meant that a person convicted of a felony for the first time would escape the death penalty but would be branded on the thumb and would most likely be sentenced to transportation to the American colonies for indentured service for seven years.

As trade and wealth increased and attacks on property became more common,[44] Parliament reacted by making more felonies "non-clergyable" by statute.[45] During Mansfield's tenure as chief justice, about 160 offenses were punishable by death, including forgery, stealing assets worth more than 40 shillings from a residence, shoplifting of anything worth more than 5 shillings, and stealing from anybody's physical person.[46] One reason why violent crime was common in the streets and highways was that, with so many non-violent crimes punishable by death, a highwayman or other thief or robber had every reason to believe that he incurred no additional risk of execution if he killed or injured his victim.[47]

By mid-century, benefit of clergy had been largely replaced by a system of pardons for those convicted of a capital crime. In most cases, the trial judge would give the prisoner a temporary reprieve to allow him to apply to the King for a pardon. The King, sitting with his Privy Council, could pardon a convicted criminal or commute his sentence.[48] Knowing this, juries would often return a guilty verdict, coupled with a request that the court ask the King to exercise mercy.[49] If the pardon was absolute, the prisoner would go free, just as if he had been acquitted. If the pardon was conditional, the death sentence would be commuted to transportation to America for a period of fourteen years.[50]

Historians differ as to the percentage of death sentences that were actually carried out during Mansfield's tenure on the bench,[51] but public executions were not infrequent. On a single day in 1757 nine "malefactors" were hanged at Tyburn (the present site of Marble Arch, at the corner of Hyde Park), and six weeks later another twelve were hanged there, for crimes that included theft, forgery, burglary, highway robbery, and clipping gold coins.[52] The number of executions generally fluctuated with changes in the level of public concern over the prevalence of serious crime, reaching a peak of about ninety executions annually in the mid-1780s.[53]

In cases of theft, the harshness of the law was sometimes relieved by undervaluing the stolen goods, at least if the culprit was not a gang member or professional criminal. In one case, Mansfield suggested to the jury that, to avoid imposing the death penalty, they find a gold trinket that a prisoner had stolen to be worth less than 40 shillings. The prosecutor objected, saying "Under forty shillings, my Lord? Why the fashion alone cost me more than double the sum." "That may be, my friend," Mansfield replied, "yet God forbid that we should hang a man for fashion's sake."[54] On the other hand, Mansfield showed no mercy to professional criminals. When the confessed leader of a gang of housebreakers was convicted, Mansfield ordered his immediate execution (after his wife was briefly released from prison to see him before he died) "to strike the greater terror into" other members of the gang.[55]

Execution days were unofficial public holidays; permanent wooden grandstands were erected at Tyburn, on the city's western edge, for public enjoyment of the spectacle, and people paid for good seats.[56] Mansfield presided at the treason trial of Dr Hensey, a physician who was accused of selling state secrets, such as the sailing of the fleet and the launching of a man-of-war, to the French. After a trial lasting ten hours, the jury needed only half an hour to find him guilty. Hensey was sentenced to be hanged, drawn, and quartered at Tyburn.[57] This was the traditional punishment in England for treason. The prisoner would be hanged, but taken down from the gallows while still alive, revived if he had fainted, then castrated and disembowelled, after which he would be decapitated and his body would be cut into quarters.[58] Shortly before the time set for his execution, Hensey was pardoned, probably because a post-sentencing hearing by the Cabinet had revealed that he was a double agent who had acted as a spy for both sides.[59] When his reprieve was announced, quarrels broke out at Tyburn. Several persons who had paid 2 shillings and sixpence for seats at the grisly spectacle insisted on getting their money back.[60]

Public executions were so popular that they threatened to impede economic activity. They were preceded by a well-attended procession from Newgate Prison near the Old Bailey, through the streets of London, to Tyburn.[61] The dense, excited crowds along the way furnished a rich opportunity for pickpockets.[62] In 1783, the place of execution was changed from Tyburn to outside Newgate prison in the heart of London, eliminating the long procession and the disruptions to business and traffic that it caused. Another possible reason for the change of venue was that the area around Tyburn had become a centre of genteel urban development, whose residents found gruesome executions incompatible with their sensibilities.[63]

Lesser crimes were punished by whipping, the pillory, imprisonment, and branding on the hand. The last of these punishments was abolished in 1779.[64] In some cases, a convict could escape sentencing by agreeing to serve in the army, often in a regiment stationed overseas, or in the navy.[65] Whipping was a common penalty for minor theft or for the production of shoddy goods. For example, in 1757 four journeymen hatters were drawn through the streets and whipped for using dog's hair instead of beaver in making hats;[66] and a young woman, naked to the waist, was whipped through the public streets for stealing four pounds of silk from her employer.[67] Army deserters, if not executed, were severely whipped, one being sentenced to 500 lashes, which was probably the equivalent of a death sentence.[68]

The pillory, which as late as 1814 was called "a pillar of our legislative system,"[69] was a common form of punishment for a variety of crimes, including seditious libel,[70] sodomy,[71] assaulting a minor,[72] fortune-telling,[73] keeping a brothel,[74] and perjury.[75] The pillory consisted of a platform on which was fastened a post and a frame; the prisoner was made to stand behind the frame for an hour or so, with his head and arms thrust through holes in the frame. The severity of a sentence to the pillory depended largely on the attitude of the crowd toward the prisoner and on the nature of his (or her) crime. With a hostile crowd, the prisoner could easily be killed by the objects thrown at him, including dead cats and dogs and even stones, and by being otherwise manhandled.[76] When two men were put in the pillory for conspiracy to accuse two other innocent men of a highway robbery that they themselves had committed, one was killed by the mob and the other's head was so bruised and swollen that it was thought he would not recover.[77] Another example was a sixty-year-old tailor who had been convicted of attempted sodomy on a young man: he was severely pelted; then a woman climbed onto the pillory, cut off his breeches, and battered and whipped him until the blood came.[78]

On the other hand, persons whose crimes the public did not disapprove of, or who were popular with the crowd (including the author Daniel Defoe[79]), were treated gently in the pillory and even applauded.[80] A pilloried man who had been convicted of keeping a "disorderly house" was able to talk and shake hands with his friends, and share a drink with the spectators. When it was over, he walked around the pillory bowing to the onlookers and thanking them for their good company and kind treatment.[81]

Pillorying was a common punishment for violating the unpopular seditious-libel laws, which made criticism of the government a crime; although John Wilkes, the most famous eighteenth-century figure accused of that crime, escaped the pillory, perhaps owing to Mansfield's unwillingness to face the fury of the mob.[82] Another notorious seditious-libel case was that of Dr Shebbeare, who was tried before Mansfield in 1758. Shebbeare had written several *Letters to the People of England*, attacking the policy of the government and satirizing the dead kings William III and George I.[83] In his charge to the jury, Mansfield said that Shebbeare's conduct approached high treason.

Shebbeare was convicted and sentenced to stand in the pillory at three London locations and then to be imprisoned for three years. Arthur Beardmore, a lawyer who was acting as under-sheriff, mitigated the punishment by not requiring Shebbeare to bend his head uncomfortably forward through the hole in the pillory. (One woman who was pilloried for fortune-telling was almost strangled to death because of the narrow confinement of her neck.[84]) Instead, Beardmore raised the upper board of the pillory as high as possible and fastened it there, so that Shebbeare was able to stand upright and look through the wide opening between the upper and lower boards. It is not noted that any spectator objected to Shebbeare's lenient treatment. Attorney General Charles Pratt, however, was incensed at the indulgence shown the prisoner and brought an action for contempt of court against

Beardmore, Shebbeare's protector. At his trial Beardmore defended himself by saying, correctly though disingenuously, that he could see Shebbeare's head through the pillory. Mansfield, unmoved, fined Beardmore £50 for contempt, remarking that this was the most ingenious evasion of perjury he had ever heard.[85]

Imprisonment for debt was one of the great abuses in eighteenth-century England. London had seventeen prisons, nine of which held debtors.[86] The writer of a letter to a newspaper in 1761 mentioned the "multitudes" of debtors who "are entombed alive in the gaols of this kingdom where they are a burden upon their relatives and friends or upon the charitable part of mankind instead of doing anything to subsist themselves."[87] In the 1770s, almost half the prison population consisted of debtors, many of them owing very small amounts.[88] In 1793 a newspaper reported: "There is now a man confined for debt in Newgate who has been a prisoner there over fifteen years for a debt, the sum of which does not exceed forty-five shillings."[89]

Mansfield had little sympathy for debtors, despite receiving many letters complaining of the injustice of imprisonment for debt and appealing to his humanity and to the Magna Carta and the English unwritten constitution. In 1781 an Insolvent Debtors Bill was introduced in Parliament to release from prison those with debts of less than £500, on condition that the debtor allow a justice of the peace to examine his personal estate, publish a notice in a London newspaper that he is seeking release from prison, and provide a detailed schedule of his assets for his creditors to review. The bill passed the House of Commons unanimously. In the House of Lords, Mansfield made a long speech reluctantly supporting the bill, but fulminating against "a mistaken compassion which in [recent] years had got such possession of the minds of men that the edge of the law was frequently turned against the honest and deserving creditor in order to protect the advantage of the fraudulent debtor." He argued that life in prison was so pleasant for some debtors that they preferred staying there to paying their debts; if the prisons were made uncomfortable for debtors, such as by rigidly enforcing the rule against allowing alcohol in the prisons, they would be more likely to pay their debts in order to gain their liberty. Mansfield concluded his speech by saying that he had frequently met a cruel debtor who had abused his creditor but he had rarely known of a cruel creditor unless upon great provocation.[90] The Insolvent Debtors Bill passed the House of Lords and became law.[91]

Some persons convicted of seditious libel, like Dr Shebbeare, were sentenced to lengthy prison terms, which became more common after the beginning of the American Revolution, when transportation to the American colonies was no longer feasible. When it became apparent that the war would not be over quickly, Parliament enacted the Hard Labour Act of 1776 (more commonly called the Hulks Act), under which convicts could be sentenced to hard labour dredging the River Thames.[92] The law specified that the prisoners should be "fed with bread and any coarse and inferior food and water or small beer."[93] During a period of nine months, forty of the convicts died and many others sickened from the work, but some believed that the nature and novelty of the punishment improved the prisoners' manners and helped rehabilitate them. Mansfield, who supervised the program, thought that the convicts should have minimum contact with their friends and no access to liquor, and that those who gave proof that they had reformed should be recommended for a pardon.[94] A newspaper reported that one of the convicts was a man who had posed as a clergyman and was sentenced to work five years on the Thames, "where he may officiate as chaplain to the convicts."[95]

Management of the prisons was farmed out to wardens who paid large sums for the position and then extorted what they could from the prisoners.[96] There was a fee to be paid upon entry into the prison, and additional fees for bed and board.[97] The prisons were crowded and filthy, and their evil and dissipation were said to be worse than any on the Continent.[98] At times, Mansfield was unable to sentence a prisoner because there was no room in the prisons.[99] A man who had been convicted of vagrancy and sentenced to Bridewell, the prison used to punish minor offenders, was found dead of hunger and cold after seven weeks of incarceration.[100]

Louse-borne typhus, then called gaol fever, was endemic. When prisoners were brought from the filthy conditions of Newgate into the courtroom at Old Bailey, they brought with them a "putrid effluvia"; not surprisingly, the fever spread to the lawyers and judges. During the so-called "Black Sessions" of 1750 at the Old Bailey, a total of forty or fifty persons, including four of the six criminal-court judges, as well as lawyers, clerks, jurymen, witnesses, and spectators, died of gaol fever.[101] The following year, Mansfield wrote to his friend Andrew Stone: "Death is very busy among us ... It is extraordinary that many who were [at Old Bailey] have died and others have been ill of fevers. Sir Daniel Lambert is dead; my Lord Mayor is dying;

the under-sheriff is dead; Lord Chancellor's trainbearer is dead; my attorney is dead."[102]

As a judge, Mansfield showed some concern about prison conditions. In 1780 he severely reprimanded and threatened with punishment a jailer for extorting money from the prisoners for such amenities as a bed.[103] The following year, after the King's Bench Prison, where political prisoners and better-off debtors were incarcerated,[104] had been severely damaged in the Gordon Riots, Mansfield and his fellow justice Francis Buller visited the prison to see if it was in a condition to receive prisoners.[105]

While the poor suffered in prison, a wealthy or influential prisoner might have his own apartment where he could receive visitors.[106] In 1776, a newspaper correspondent asked Mansfield to inquire into the practices of the officers of debtors' prison renting out apartments to prisoners for 1,000 guineas.[107] On one occasion, Mansfield ordered the marshal of the King's Bench Prison not to permit the wives and children of prisoners to lodge there, nor to permit visitors to stay for hours drinking with the prisoners.[108]

In view of the opposition to a national police force and the use of troops, the cheapest and least oppressive method of law enforcement was to pay rewards to private persons who brought criminal prosecutions.[109] A private person had the same right to institute a criminal action as the attorney general, regardless of whether or not he was a victim of the supposed crime.[110] This system of law enforcement was often efficient but it could lead to extortion, perjury, and wrongful convictions. The testimony of informers was admitted in evidence in capital-punishment cases, even if the witness was entitled to a reward if the defendant was convicted.[111] Typically, the private prosecutor was the victim of the alleged crime or a member of the victim's family, but his sole incentive might be to gain a reward authorized by statute. A notorious example of this was the carpenter Payne, who for a time obtained substantial rewards by accusing persons of violating the severe anti-Catholic laws.[112] If the prosecution resulted in the defendant being sentenced to stand in the pillory, it was the custom, said Mansfield, for the prosecutor to pay the expenses of the court officer who executed the sentence.[113]

The victim of an economic crime might himself offer a reward to anyone who helped him recover stolen property. In a case tried before Mansfield and a special jury in 1782, a group of London merchants had made an offer in the newspapers of a reward of 10 per cent of the value of £2,000 in banknotes that their clerk had stolen. An Oxford Street perfumer followed the clerk to France and somehow recovered the notes. The perfumer sued the merchants for the promised reward, and the jury awarded him not just the reward but also his expenses to and from France.[114]

Another method of law enforcement used frequently at Old Bailey was the Crown witness system. As a practical matter, it was the only way of dealing with professional criminals and gangs. A person indicted for a felony could plead guilty and agree to testify against his accomplices. If his testimony helped gain a conviction, the Crown witness would be eligible to be considered for mercy; if not, he would be sentenced to death on his guilty plea.[115] It does not take much imagination to see that the Crown witness system was an invitation to perjury. Nevertheless, Mansfield approved of it: "If [the Crown witness] act fairly and openly, and discover the whole truth, though he is not entitled of right to a pardon, yet the usage, the lenity, and the practice of the Court is, to stop the prosecution against him; and he having an equitable title to a recommendation for the King's mercy."[116]

The victim of a crime could choose either a criminal or a civil action, the theory being that a person who brings a criminal action does so on behalf of the state, while one who brings a civil action does so only on his own behalf. In a case that came before Mansfield, a man had been robbed of all his household furnishings and his books by his wife and her attorney while he was confined in a debtor's prison. Although the man's lawyer advised a criminal prosecution, the grand jury suggested that he bring a civil action; this would allow him to recover some of his property, which he could not have done in a criminal action. Mansfield expressed his abhorrence of the defendants' "glaring injustice and pitiful chicanery" and gave a verdict for the plaintiff after only one witness was called.[117] In a case of false imprisonment, where a man had been detained in custody in India for over a year, Mansfield told the plaintiff that he could proceed with either a criminal or a civil action but not both; if he dropped the criminal action, he would be able to obtain restitution of his damages.[118]

Criminal justice was speedy. Juries in felony cases seldom took more than an hour to reach a verdict.[119] Most criminal cases were disposed of in minutes rather than hours, and it was rare for a trial to last more than a day. At a typical three- or four-day session at Old Bailey, the principal court for trying felonies committed in London and Middlesex County, fifty felony cases might be tried. This extraordinary speed was possible because an accused was not entitled to a lawyer, except in cases of petty crimes. A felony defendant, whose life might well be in jeopardy, had to handle his own defence. Only in the 1730s were defence lawyers permitted to examine and cross-examine witnesses, but the accused was on his own when it came to making opening and closing statements to the jury.[120] Mansfield and other judges were able to dispatch so many cases in a three- or four-day court session because juries were picked quickly, without any attempt to probe the jurors' backgrounds and attitudes, and because the judges' instructions to the jury tended to be perfunctory, sometimes simply consisting of an instruction to find the defendant guilty, which they often did.[121]

There was no effective system of appeals from conviction for those without money or influence. One man accused of robbery of some silver plate on a Monday was arrested on Tuesday, examined at Bow Street police court and committed to prison on Wednesday, tried and convicted on Thursday, and hanged on Saturday.[122] In another case, a man was convicted of murder on a Friday and sentenced to be hanged the following Monday.[123] But if the defendant was fortunate enough to have family or friends to intervene for him, he might have the time to appeal directly to the King for mercy.[124]

Undoubtedly, the speed of investigation, conviction, and punishment caused many innocent persons to be executed or to suffer other penalties. At best, the criminal-justice system was slipshod; at worst, it was disastrous. A newspaper reported in 1780 that a secretary of state had been handed a pardon from the King for a criminal who had been sentenced to be executed the next day: "The noble secretary, as he was wont, forgot the favour of his sovereign, drank his five bottles after dinner and the man was hanged in the morning."[125]

Sitting as a criminal judge, Lord Mansfield conducted himself with calmness, courtesy, and dignity, but he was merciless in punishing the guilty, particularly for crimes affecting commerce.[126] His decisions on the bench reflected the interests of the trading classes, whether they were wealthy merchants, industrialists, shopkeepers, or itinerant peddlers, all of whose livelihoods depended on the preservation of law and order.[127] Whether sitting as a trial judge or hearing an appeal, Mansfield was implacable in imposing the death penalty in forgery cases, because he saw forgery as a threat to the free flow of commerce.[128] He believed that, in order to protect commercial credit, persons should be able to rely on the authenticity of the signature on a note or other credit instrument.[129] When the convicted forger of a stock certificate begged Mansfield to ask the King for a pardon, Mansfield told him "not to flatter himself with vain hopes of that mercy which was not to expected," for, "considering your crime, and its consequences, in a nation where there is so much paper credit, I must tell you ... I think myself bound in duty and conscience to acquaint his Majesty you are no object of his mercy."[130]

Although Mansfield was not the judge who tried the most famous forgery case of his day, his influence with the King ensured that the forger would be executed. Dr William Dodd was a well-known and fashionable preacher, who served as chaplain to the young Earl of Chesterfield, whose tutor he had been. Dodd lived extravagantly and got himself deeply in debt. When pressed by his creditors, he forged Chesterfield's name on a bond for £4,200 and took the bond to a broker, telling him that the earl needed a loan but wanted to keep it secret. The broker signed the bond as a witness to the signature although, of course, he had not seen Chesterfield sign it. He found two bankers who accepted the bond and turned over £4,200 to Dodd. Afterwards, the bankers showed the bond to their lawyer, who became suspicious and took the bond to Lord Chesterfield, who repudiated the signature.

It was not difficult to trace the bond to Dodd. He was immediately arrested and charged with forgery, a capital offence. Chesterfield's lawyer told him that the only way to save himself was to make restitution, which he was able to do with the help of friends.[131] Nevertheless, the lord mayor of London insisted on pressing charges. Dodd admitted the forgery but said he did not intend to defraud Chesterfield because he planned to return the money.

Dodd was tried at Old Bailey on 22 February 1777. After deliberating for half an hour, the jury found him guilty but recommended mercy.[132] Dodd remained in jail while the trial judge discussed with the other Old Bailey judges whether the trial testimony given by the broker, who had falsely stated that he had witnessed Chesterfield's signature, was admissible, since the broker was a co-defendant with Dodd. Three months later, the judges concluded that the conviction was lawful, and sentenced Dodd to death. There was widespread sympathy for him and 23,000 people signed a petition for his reprieve on a parchment thirty-seven yards long.

Dodd was an excellent candidate for mercy. It was his first offence, and he had made restitution and had been assured that if he did he would escape the death penalty. A meeting of the King and the Privy Council to consider Dodd's case was set for 13 June 1777. As chief justice, Mansfield had the most influential voice in appeals of this kind. Dodd persuaded Dr Samuel Johnson, the great literary figure, to draft a letter to Mansfield, admitting the crime and imploring Mansfield to persuade the King to commute the sentence of execution to imprisonment and banishment.[133] Dodd sent the letter, which was signed "Your Lordship's most humble suppliant, William Dodd," to Mansfield two days before the meeting of the Privy Council. The King may have initially been inclined to pardon him, but when Mansfield advised against it he accepted the advice.[134]

Mansfield believed that severity would have a strong deterrent effect on future forgers, and that making an exception in Dodd's case would make it difficult to impose the death sentence on less prominent culprits. There had been several recent cases of forgery; at the time of Dodd's trial over twenty persons were in prison for forgery.[135] A year earlier, Daniel and Robert Perreau, two brothers who were respectable apothecaries, had been executed for forging bonds, and Mansfield was reported to have said: "If Dr Dodd does not suffer the full sentence of the law, the Perreaus may be said to have been murdered."[136] Moreover, the long petition that had been sent to the King on Dodd's behalf actually worked against Dodd, because some of those in authority regarded the petition as an attempt by the populace to interfere with justice.[137] In any contest between the people and the royal authority, Mansfield was on the side of authority. Dodd was hanged at Tyburn on 27 June 1777.[138]

Another crime that particularly irked Mansfield was perjury, since it directly affected the dispensing of justice. A newspaper reported that, "To the great honour of Lord Mansfield there is no crime whatsoever which seems to rouse his resentment so much as that of perjury."[139] Professional witnesses plied their trade in Westminster Hall, offering litigants "testimony for hire."[140] There was much public condemnation of so-called "Jew bail," where accusations of perjury intersected with widespread anti-Semitism.[141] Jew bail was the term used for impecunious Jewish bail bondsmen swearing falsely as to the amount of their assets.[142]

But concerns about perjury went far beyond professional witnesses and bail bondsmen. In 1786, a meeting of judges held in Mansfield's chambers agreed that nothing but capital punishment would be sufficient to deter persons from committing perjury and that a bill should be prepared to make this crime punishable by death.[143] Although nothing came of the proposal, severe penalties were sometimes imposed on convicted perjurers. In one 1784 case, which involved fraud in the public purchasing accounts and therefore claimed the attention of the mercantile part of the city, Mansfield's court sentenced a perjurer to a year's imprisonment, an hour in the pillory, and a fine of £2,000.[144]

Mansfield's severity was sometimes tempered by mercy. In one case, he pardoned a convicted highwayman who became blind without any possibility that his sight would be restored.[145] In another, the judges of a county in Wales had recommended mercy for a woman they had convicted of murdering her illegitimate child. The judges gave no reasons for their recommendation except that the act was committed without cruelty and that it was the first such instance ever known in the county. Lord Halifax, a secretary of state, asked Mansfield for his opinion. Mansfield said that, while the judges should have given more reasons, he thought their recommendation was sufficient to support clemency.[146]

Mansfield could also be lenient when the defendants in a criminal case were important persons. In 1779, four members of the Council of the East India Company were tried before Mansfield and two other judges of the Court of King's Bench for the arrest and false imprisonment of Lord Pigot, the governor of Madras, with whom they had had a serious dispute that had led to civil warfare and Pigot's death.[147] After deliberating for fifteen minutes, the jury found all four defendants guilty, and Mansfield sentenced each of them to pay a fine of £1,000 and to be imprisoned until the fine was paid. They instantly paid the fine and left with smiles on their faces.[148] A newspaper commented: "The affluence of the criminals enables them to laugh at the sentence; and the part of the sentence which condemns them to imprisonment until the fine shall be paid is so ridiculous as only to excite laughter."[149] A letter sent to another paper pointedly contrasted the leniency shown to the four defendants with the heavy fines and prison terms imposed on printers for publishing criticism of the government.[150]

16

Betting and Lending

It is astonishing how prejudice should have kept common sense so long out of the world!

Lord Mansfield, *Chesterfield v. Janssen*

Several cases involving wagers or usurious loans that Mansfield argued as a lawyer and decided as a judge provide illuminating examples of the forcefulness and clarity of his mind and the modernity of his thinking.

If gin drinking was the vice of the lower classes in eighteenth-century England, gambling was the mania of the elite.[1] At the private clubs on St James's Street, losses on hazard, a dice game, often reached £4,000 in a single night, a huge sum at the time.[2] Noblemen and sons of rich merchants would lay bets for colossal sums of money on just about any uncertainty.[3] For example, at Brooks's Club on St James's Street, two members made a bet on whether William Beckford, the lord mayor of London and richest commoner in the country (who had made his fortune from slave plantations in Jamaica and happened to be a friend of Mansfield) would be raised to the peerage.[4] He was not awarded that honour, although he was elected to the House of Commons. On the occasion of the Prince of Wales's coming of age in 1783, spectators at the Court of King's Bench wagered on whether or not the King would use the occasion to pardon several prisoners.[5] It was not uncommon for a wager to consist of taking out an insurance policy on another person's life; this amounted to a bet that the insured person would die sooner rather than later.[6]

Some of the bets were bizarre. A newspaper reported that a lady bet 200 guineas (£210) that she could go backwards in her carriage, with two servants on horseback also going backwards, from Coventry to London, a distance of ninety-three miles, in fourteen days. She told a newspaper what day she proposed to set out and entreated travellers not to crash into her.[7]

Gambling was popular in the fashionable resorts where the upper classes gathered. In the resort town of Bath, when the subscription books were opened for prayers at the Abbey and gaming at the rooms, there were twelve for prayer and sixty-seven for play. A newspaper commented in verse:

The Church and Rooms the other day,
Open'd their books for Prayer and Play.
The Priest for twelve, Hoyle sixty-seven,
How great the odds for Hell 'gainst Heaven![8]

There is no known record of Mansfield having engaged in gambling. Given his careful nature and shrewd financial sense, it is unlikely that he ever made any substantial wagers. But if he didn't play, he was sometimes present at the clubs where noblemen played for high stakes. In 1750, he wrote to the Duke of Newcastle about a night of gambling at White's Club. He reported that gambling would keep Newcastle's cousin Vane in town a little longer, and also that Andrew Stone, who was Mansfield's close friend and Newcastle's secretary and adviser, "would not dare to play for so much money in a year as Dick [Leveson] lost that night."[9] Leveson was the twenty-four-year-old younger son of the Earl of Gower and a member of Parliament. Perhaps as a result of a dissolute life, he died only three years later.

Gambling was not confined to the upper classes. In a bizarre case that came before Mansfield in 1775, a London tailor had won a bundle of asparagus (a great delicacy at the time) from a surgeon in a card game. An evening was set when the tailor and the surgeon, each with a friend, would eat the asparagus (apparently bought by the surgeon) at an inn on Tottenham Court Road. The surgeon arrived late and found that the tailor and his friend had eaten all the asparagus. A fight ensued, and the tailor was thrown out of the inn. Although he was not injured, he sued the surgeon for assault, and the jury awarded him damages of £5. The tailor then sued another person who had participated in the fight, but, according to a newspaper report of the case, "the second jury, not being composed of so many tailors as the first," awarded him damages of only 1 shilling.[10]

A statute of 1711[11] prohibited wagers of over £10 on horse races, cockfights, and other games (other than the popular sport of cricket);[12] and in 1745 the prohibition was extended to the game of roulette (known then as "roly poly").[13] George II loved to gamble, which was probably why the 1745 statute exempted gaming in the King's residences.[14] On Twelfth Night of 1760, the seventy-six-year-old King played the dice game hazard "with several persons of quality according to annual custom" until midnight; his son, the Duke of Cumberland, was the big winner.[15] Later the same year, Mansfield enforced the 1711 law by allowing a person to recover £20 that he had paid when he lost a bet on a horse race.[16]

Wagers that did not involve games were regarded as legal contracts unless they violated some principle of morality or public policy, and many lawsuits were brought to recover on such bets.[17] Mansfield's decisions in this area provide insight to his thinking on what morality and public policy demanded, and some seem distinctly relevant today. In *Jones v. Randall*,[18] a lawsuit was brought to collect on a wager over whether the House of Lords would reverse a decision of the Court of Chancery. Mansfield saw no objection to the wager on the ground of public policy but pointed out that if the wager had been made with the judge who had tried the case or with a member of the House of Lords it would have been illegal as a bribe.

In *Allen v. Hearne*, a case reported in a newspaper, Mansfield ruled that a wager of £100 between two voters on the outcome of an election was unenforceable because it violated public policy:

> The constitution of this kingdom depends upon this principle that *all elections should be free* and that every voter should be free from influence. This is a wager between two voters and the event laid on is the success of their respective candidates; from the moment the wager is laid each party is in *fetters*; he is not free; his conduct is influenced by the advantage he is to get if his candidate succeeds; it therefore in its nature biases his opinion; it may induce him to spend money to gain the election ... A gaming contract is never to be encouraged or suffered if it has a dangerous tendency and affords a bad example; it may be used as a bribe without a possibility of detection ... This wager ought to be void from the contraction of sound policy.[19]

Mansfield's concern over the influence of money on elections resonates in the twenty-first century, when it may pose an even greater threat to democracy than it did in the eighteenth. In the 2010 United States Supreme Court case of *Citizens United v. Federal Election Committee*,[20] Justice John Paul Stevens seemed to echo Mansfield's concern when he wrote in his dissenting opinion: "On numerous occasions we have recognized Congress' legitimate interest in preventing the money spent on elections from exerting an 'undue influence on an officeholder's judgment' and from creating 'the appearance of such influence,' beyond the sphere of quid pro quo relationships."[21]

The most notorious wager cases of the century involved the Chevalier d'Eon de Beaumont, a diplomat who had come to England in the 1760s as secretary to the French ambassador, but after the ambassador's departure had remained in England as minister plenipotentiary in charge of French affairs.[22] He may also have been acting as a spy for Louis XV. At some point in the 1760s, d'Eon had begun to wear women's clothes, and bets totalling more than £300,000 were made as to whether he was a man or a woman.[23] Several lawsuits were brought to enforce these wagers, two of which came before Lord Mansfield. The uncertainty about d'Eon's sex was increased in 1776 by an order of King Louis XVI declaring that he was a woman, and requiring him to return to Paris and to wear women's clothes as a condition of receiving a promised royal pension.[24]

In *Hayes v. Jacques*,[25] Hayes, a surgeon, had paid 100 guineas to Jacques, a broker and underwriter, and Jacques had signed a policy of "insurance" to pay Hayes 700 guineas if Hayes could prove that d'Eon was a woman. The case was tried in the Court of King's Bench in an atmosphere of great interest as well as merriment. Hayes claimed that he had indisputable proof that d'Eon was a woman. He called as witnesses another surgeon, who testified that he had made a physical examination of d'Eon and found him to be a woman; and de Morande, the editor of a French newspaper in London, who testified that d'Eon had told him that he was a woman, let him put his hand on his breasts, and displayed his wardrobe, which contained petticoats and other feminine clothes.[26] By this time, the spectators, especially those with whom Jacques had made similar wagers, were enjoying themselves thoroughly. Jacques's lawyer did not attempt to refute this evidence but argued that the contract was unenforceable on the ground of immorality.[27]

Mansfield did not appreciate the humour or the salaciousness in his court. A newspaper reported: "Mansfield with his usual delicacy and precision expressed his abhorrence of the whole transaction and the more so their bringing it into a Court of Justice."[28] He said that he wished the dispute had been settled privately or, failing that, that the jury could make both parties lose. But then he indulged in a little judicial humour of his own. He mentioned a bet of £100 concerning the dimensions of the Medici Venus (a Greek sculpture now in the Uffizi Gallery in Florence). One of the bettors said he had measured the dimensions himself. The other replied: "Do you think I would be such a fool to lay [i.e., bet] if I had not measured it? I will lay it for all that." According to the press, the court erupted in laughter.

Then Mansfield got serious. He said that since d'Eon had appeared as a man and was employed by the French court as a man, there was a presumption that he was a man. Hayes therefore had the burden of proving that he was a woman. This Mansfield left to the jury, who found that Hayes had met the burden and awarded him damages of £700. Although Mansfield was clearly disgusted with the case, he ignored the argument raised by the defence that the wager (or "insurance policy," as the parties had designated it) was unenforceable because it was against good morals and public policy.

The decision in the *Hayes* case was unpopular with the professional brokers who had bet huge sums on d'Eon being a man, and who suspected Hayes's witnesses of perjuring themselves. Several of the brokers refused to honour their bets, which led to new lawsuits being brought to enforce the agreements.[29] A few months after the *Hayes* decision, another d'Eon lawsuit, *Da Costa v. Jones,* came before Mansfield's court.[30] In 1771, Da Costa had paid Jones 75 guineas (about £79), and Jones promised to pay Da Costa £300 if d'Eon turned out to be female. After the *Hayes* decision, Da Costa sued Jones for the money, and the case was tried before Lord Mansfield in December 1777. A jury found the wager to be valid and awarded Da Costa damages of £300 and costs of 40 shillings.

By this time, Mansfield had had time to think about the implications of these wagers. When Jones's lawyer, Edward Bearcroft, moved to reverse the jury verdict on the ground that the wager tended to introduce indecent evidence, Mansfield helped him by suggesting an additional ground for reversal: that the wager materially affected the interest of a third person (d'Eon). Mansfield then reversed the verdict, reasoning that enforcement of the wager by the court would invade d'Eon's privacy: "That two men by laying a wager concerning a third person, might compel his physicians, relations, and servants, to disclose what they knew relative to the subject matter of the wager, would have been an alarming proposition." He compared the wager about d'Eon's sex to other types of wagers that would invade a person's privacy:

> Suppose a wager that affects the interest or the feelings of a third person ... that ... a woman has committed adultery. Would a Court of Justice try the adultery in an action upon such a wager? Or, a wager that an unmarried woman has had a bastard. Would you try that? Would it be endured? Most unquestionably it would not. Because it is not only an injury to a third person, but it disturbs the peace of society; and in either of these two cases, the party to be affected by it would have a

> right to say, how dare you bring my name in question? If a husband complains of adultery, he shall be allowed to try it; because he is a party injured ... But third persons, merely for the purpose of laying a wager, shall not thus wantonly expose others to ridicule.[31]

Mansfield then turned to the wager about d'Eon's sex:

> Shall two indifferent people, by a wager between themselves, injure him so, as to try an action upon that wager, whether ... he is a cheat and an imposter? or, show that he is a woman, and be allowed to subpoena all his intimate friends, and confidential attendants, to give evidence that will expose him all over Europe? It is monstrous to state ...
>
> The question is upon the sex of a person, to the appearance of all the world, a man; and who, for reasons of his own, thinks proper to keep his sex a secret. The medium of proof upon such a question must arise from the circumstances that distinguish the sexes. This necessarily tends to introduce all the indecent evidence such an enquiry can involve. Suppose two persons were to lay a wager upon a mark or defect in a woman's body. Will the Court say they would suffer her chambermaid to be called, to give evidence upon such a question ... A wager whether the next child shall be a boy or a girl hurts no one. But the present case is indecent in itself, and manifestly a gross injury to a third person; therefore ought not to be endured.[32]

In the *Da Costa* case, Mansfield, without using the term "right of privacy," established that the English common law recognized such a right. The concept resonates today, particularly in the United States, where the right of privacy has become a focal point for constitutional debate. (The right also is recognized in Canada.[33]) Although the U.S. Constitution does not explicitly mention a right of privacy, Mansfield's statement that such a right existed echoes in several decisions of the U.S. Supreme Court. Most notably, in *Griswold v. Connecticut*,[34] Justice William O. Douglas ruled that a state law forbidding the use of contraceptives was an unconstitutional invasion of a couple's right of marital privacy, and in *Roe v. Wade*,[35] Justice Harry Blackmun ruled that, within certain limits, the right of privacy prohibits the government from denying a woman's right to decide whether or not to terminate her pregnancy.[36]

As a result of Mansfield's decision in *Da Costa*, many people who had received premiums when they bet on d'Eon's sex had to give back the money.[37] D'Eon himself claimed to be a woman.[38] After living in France for several years, he returned to England in 1785. Although he continued to dress in women's clothes, he conducted himself in a decidedly unfeminine way, for example by giving exhibitions of fencing, a sport in which he excelled and which was not normally open to women.[39] In 1786, a fashionable lady wrote to a friend that one evening she had been in the company of "Madam d'Eon, or Monsieur (whichever you please), for certainly there is more of a grenadier than a lady in her appearance. She was very easy in her conversation, and I was much entertain'd"[40] On d'Eon's death in 1810, a doctor examined his body and found him to be a man.

Sometimes it was not easy to decide whether a particular transaction was a wager, an insurance policy, or a loan. In eighteenth-century England, the usury law prohibited any agreement to charge more than 5 per cent per annum on a loan or mortgage, and the lender was liable to forfeit three times what he had lent.[41] A lender might be able to get around the law, however, by the expedient of buying an annuity on the borrower's life. For example, the lender might pay the borrower £1,000, in return for which the borrower promised to pay £150 per annum for the rest of his or her life. The lender could then avoid the risk that the borrower would die before paying off the £1,000 by buying an insurance policy on the borrower's life.[42]

From the beginning of his career, Mansfield was opposed to all usury laws. Following the teachings of John Locke, he believed that ways would always be found to evade these laws and that money, like any other commodity, would inevitably find its own price in the market.[43] The purchase of an annuity to disguise a usurious loan was an example of such an evasion. But as a practicing lawyer, Mansfield had sometimes argued on behalf of a client that a loan was usurious and therefore unenforceable. In 1741 he represented Sir William Stanhope, a young man who, having run into debt, had sold an annuity to one Spinks. Spinks had paid him £800, in return for which Stanhope promised to pay Spinks an annuity of £108 for the rest of his life. Later, Stanhope sued in the Court of Chancery to be relieved of the bargain. Mansfield argued before Lord Hardwicke that the agreement was a usurious loan and also an oppressive and fraudulent bargain. Although Chancellor Hardwicke disliked contracts where loan sharks preyed upon heirs of great fortunes, he recommended that the parties settle the case, which they did. Stanhope returned the money he had received, as well as the arrears of the annuity, plus interest. Mansfield cannot have been very happy with the settlement, but in this case Hardwicke did not believe that Stanhope was a victim: he had not been able to prove that he was in financial distress when he made the bargain with Spinks.[44]

It was not uncommon for a young nobleman who was short of funds and pressured by tradesmen and other creditors to make a contract to sell his expected inheritance in advance, usually at a steep discount. The best known of these cases was *Chesterfield v. Janssen*,[45] decided in 1750, while Mansfield was solicitor general but also represented private clients. Abraham Janssen, a member of Parliament, had paid £5,000 to Spencer, the thirty-year-old favourite grandson of the Duchess of Marlborough, in return for which Spencer promised Janssen that he would pay Janssen £10,000 if he outlived the duchess, who was seventy-eight. Although the agreement was clear enough, it was not easy to categorize. Was it a bet on whether Spencer or the duchess would die first (she was older by almost fifty years), a usurious loan by Janssen to Spencer, or an insurance policy on the duchess's life? The reality was that Spencer had sold his expected inheritance to Janssen at a 50 per cent discount.

After the duchess died (at the age of eighty-four), Spencer repeated his promise to Janssen to pay him the £10,000. However, Spencer died two years later, after paying Janssen only £2,000, and Janssen demanded the remaining £8,000 from Spencer's executor. The executor brought suit before Lord Chancellor Hardwicke to be relieved of Janssen's demand on the ground that the contract was an unconscionable (i.e., grossly unfair) agreement and also a usurious loan.

Mansfield was one of the lawyers who represented Janssen, and his arguments give a wonderful picture of his skill as an advocate. Appealing to Hardwicke's common sense, he argued that the deal was a fair one for Spencer, who seems to have been a wastrel on a grand scale. Spencer had to have the money, and have it quietly, and he chose the most expedient method available to raise it. Mansfield argued: "From all the evidence ... he was addicted to women and wine. He had contracted £20,000 debts, and ... he was pressed by tradesmen." The contract, he said, was a kind of life insurance policy. If an insurer writes a policy without taking stock of the lives involved, he would be a candidate for a lunatic asylum. In this case, his grandmother had a good chance of outliving him. Debauchery, venereal disease, carelessness of health, "intemperance so inveterate as to get into his bones made Spencer's an uncertain life, although he was but thirty." On the other hand, the duchess, though nearing eighty, took good care of herself.[46]

Having argued that the contract was a fair bargain, Mansfield said that the only possible way of invalidating it was through the usury statute. But this contract was not a loan but a wager on the life expectancy of the two parties to the contract. Having argued that the usury statute did not apply to the case, Mansfield then frontally attacked the statute, which derived from the medieval religious concept that it was illegal to lend money on interest: "It is astonishing how prejudice should have kept common sense so long out of the world! Why is not money a commodity, as well as anything else? He cited John Locke, who, opposing all usury laws, had written that "the rate of interest should not be fixed at all, but left to find its own rate of interest in the market."[47]

Hardwicke was persuaded by Mansfield that the contract was not unfair and that it was not a usurious loan but rather an enforceable wager. Janssen was entitled to recover what he had been promised in his agreement with Spencer.

Despite his personal dislike of the usury law as a restraint on freedom of commerce, Chief Justice Mansfield did not shy away from enforcing it when it clearly had been violated.[48] In one case, where a lender took advantage of a borrower in financial distress to charge an illegally high rate of interest, a newspaper reported: "after a full and impartial hearing it was clearly proved to the satisfaction of the Court and jury that the defendant had taken a most exorbitant premium for a loan of £100. The jury without hesitation found a verdict for the plaintiff by which defendant loses his whole principal money advanced and pays all costs." The report continued: "This decision ought to be a lesson to men of an avaricious usurious disposition not to take too great an advantage of men unhappily involved in distresses and misfortunes."[49]

In another usury case tried before Mansfield, the lender argued that the transaction was not a usurious loan but a legal sale of an annuity. After the jury had been deliberating for some time, Mansfield left the court and went home. The jurors still had some questions to ask Mansfield, so they went by coach to his house in Bloomsbury Square. After a conversation with him they returned a verdict of £1,260 for the borrower.[50] When the lender moved for a new trial, Mansfield went right to the heart of the matter: What was the substance of the transaction? What was the intention of the parties? "The substance here," he said, "was plainly a borrowing and lending. [The borrower] had no idea of selling an annuity; but his declared object was to borrow money." The motion for a new trial was denied.[51]

17

Slavery and the Somerset *Case*

The black must be discharged.

Lord Mansfield, stating the conclusion in the *Somerset* case

The kidnapping or purchase of West African natives by Portuguese explorers to work as slaves on sugar plantations on the island of Madeira off the African coast began in the fifteenth century.[1] Between 1650 and 1700 sugar production, which depended on African slave labour, shifted to the Caribbean islands.[2] By the mid-eighteenth century, Britain, now the world's leading commercial nation, dominated the slave trade. The growing European demand for sugar and tobacco fueled a highly profitable commerce in African slaves to work on sugar plantations in the West Indies and, to a lesser extent, on tobacco plantations in Virginia and other British colonies in North America.[3]

The slave trade was a complex commercial enterprise, requiring the participation of African sellers of slaves, merchants, financiers, transatlantic carriers, plantation owners, and consumers of the product of slave labour, as well as support and subsidy by the British government.[4] It was a triangular trade: English merchants financed slave ships that sailed from English ports, mainly Bristol and Liverpool, to West Africa, where they bought slaves, most of whom had already been enslaved by other Africans,[5] in return for gold or English goods; the slaves were transported under unimaginably brutal conditions to the West Indies, where those who survived the so-called Middle Passage were sold to plantation owners in return for West Indian sugar and rum; those products were then shipped to England, North America, or the European continent.[6]

During the eighteenth century, the slave trade expanded greatly; by the second half of the eighteenth century, an average of 75,000 slaves a year were transported across the Atlantic.[7] The total number, from the sixteenth to the nineteenth centuries, was an astounding 12 million.[8] Liverpool, with a population of only 10,000 in 1700, had grown to become England's second city a century later, largely as a result of its merchants' trading in slaves and slave-produced commodities, particularly sugar and tobacco.[9] Bristol was not far behind, although it lost ground to Liverpool because of Liverpool's superior port facilities, and because Bristol's location near the English Channel made its shipping vulnerable to French privateers.[10]

The slave trade contributed immensely to the prosperity of English plantation owners, merchants, and shipping interests. The British owners of West Indian slave plantations were among the richest people in England.[11] Many highly respected citizens, including London aldermen, were involved in the slave trade as merchants or financiers.[12] William Beckford, mayor of London during the 1760s (and a lifelong friend of Lord Mansfield), owned eleven sugar plantations in Jamaica with 1,737 slaves.[13] Slaves were not regarded as human beings; in both commerce and law they were chattel property that could be bought and sold and used as collateral for loans.[14] To treat a slave as anything but property raised complex issues of contract and property law.

Slavery also existed within Britain, although the British economy, unlike those of the West Indies and the southern colonies of North America, was not slave-based, and no attempt was ever made to import boatloads of slaves into England.[15] In the 1770s, there were probably between 10,000 and 15,000 blacks in Britain, many of them free blacks or domestic slaves whom North American planters had brought with them when they returned to England.[16] Advertisements to buy and sell slaves, and to return escaped slaves, were published in the newspapers, and there was an active trade in ornamental collars and padlocks for slaves.[17]

One justification made for slavery was that blacks were not Christians; logically, therefore, if a slave were baptized in the Anglican Church, he or she would automatically become free. In 1760, the Archbishop of Canterbury, the head of the Anglican Church, questioned Lord Chancellor Hardwicke as to whether a slave could legally be prevented from going to church to be baptized.[18] We do not have Hardwicke's reply, but it was probably affirmative, since the lord chancellor was no opponent of slavery: as attorney general he had given an opinion that the baptism of a slave did not confer freedom,[19] and as a judge he had twice ruled that a slave does not automatically gain his freedom when he first treads on English soil.[20]

Despite these rulings, the notion that a slave would be free by becoming a Christian was believed so widely that slave owners went to great lengths to prevent their slaves from being baptized.[21] In 1760, a nine-year-old black girl in London who had escaped from her mistress because of mistreatment fled to a church to be baptized. The mistress followed her there and, while the minister was conducting the service, "violently forced her down the church and dragged her along the streets like a dog without pity or remorse regardless of her cries and tears, telling the people about her that the girl was her slave and she would use her as she pleased."[22]

As in the United States in the next century, slavery divided English society.[23] John Locke, whose writings on philosophy and economics exercised a great influence on Mansfield's thought, wrote in 1690: "Slavery is so vile and miserable an estate of man, and so directly opposite to the generous temper and courage of our nation, that it is hardly to be conceived that an 'Englishman,' much less a 'gentleman,' should plead for it."[24] Many agreed with him, but the West Indian planters and merchants had a powerful lobby in Parliament and, not surprisingly, many people in Liverpool and Bristol whose livelihood and wealth depended on the slave trade supported the institution.[25] By the 1770s a growing fear that emancipation would create a large number of unemployed blacks dampened abolitionist sentiment.[26]

Nevertheless, there was growing revulsion to slavery and the slave trade in England. Quakers and Methodists, in particular, mobilized abolitionist opinion.[27] (On the other hand, some rich Quakers were slave owners or slave traders.[28]) There were several active abolitionists, the most prominent and persistent being Granville Sharp. The grandson of an Anglican archbishop, he had begun his career as an apprentice to a linen draper. He learned Hebrew only so that he could argue the Talmud with a Jewish fellow apprentice. After failing in a business venture, he obtained an appointment as a junior clerk in the government's Ordnance Department.[29] He was sufficiently wealthy to keep a barge on the Thames, where he hosted musical concerts.[30]

Sharp spent much of his time in indefatigable efforts to end slavery and the slave trade, as well as to rescue individual slaves in England who had escaped and been recaptured. He petitioned the Archbishop of Canterbury and the prime minister to use their high positions to help abolish slavery, but most of all he employed the law courts to that end. In 1769 Sharp protested to the lord chancellor that a public advertisement for the sale of a black girl was a breach not only of the laws of nature but also of English law. His main argument was that nobody could claim a black as private property unless he could prove that blacks were not human beings and subjects of the King, who were entitled to protection from arbitrary imprisonment and from being arbitrarily shipped out of the country.[31]

The legal status of slavery in England was confused and contradictory. In 1677, an English judge had ruled "that *negroes*, being usually bought and sold among merchants, as merchandise, and also being infidels," could be the subject of a suit of "trover," which was the legal writ used to recover personal property that was illegally in the hands of another person.[32] Twenty years later, Chief Justice Sir John Holt took the opposite position, asserting that a black was not a chattel (i.e., personal property) but rather a "slavish servant," a human being whose freedom was restricted but not eliminated.[33] In 1705, Holt went further, saying that "the common law takes no notice of negroes being different from other men. By the common law no man can have a property in another ... there is no such thing as a slave by the law of England."[34]

Despite Holt's opinion, the question of slavery was far from settled. In 1729, the two law officers of the Crown, Attorney General Philip Yorke (later to become Lord Chancellor Hardwicke) and Solicitor General Charles Talbot (later to become chief justice), gave a legal opinion that a slave did not automatically become free when he was brought to Britain from the West Indies, that baptism did not make him free, and that his master could legally compel him to return to the plantations.[35] Although the Yorke-Talbot opinion did not have the same force of law as a judge's decision, slave owners heavily relied on it, just as abolitionists relied on Chief Justice Holt's opinions.[36]

William Blackstone, in the first edition of his famous *Commentaries on the Laws of England*, published in 1765, disagreed with the Yorke-Talbot opinion. Blackstone stated that "a slave or a negro, the moment he lands in England, falls under the protection of the laws, and with regard to all natural rights becomes [in that instant] a freeman."[37] In the second edition of the *Commentaries*, published a year later, Blackstone qualified his opinion and further confused the issue by adding the following words to the passage: "though the master's right to his service may still continue."[38] The change may have been due to Mansfield's influence.[39] Blackstone himself later explained the change by saying that the slave may have made a contract with his or her master to continue serving the master, ignoring the obvious fact that a contract made by a slave cannot be an expression of his free will.[40] The Archbishop of Canterbury aptly summed up the actual situation in England at the time: "Some have said that as soon as [slaves] set their foot on English ground they are free. But I believe the practice hath been otherwise."[41]

The existence of slavery in England and British participation in the African slave trade created a dilemma for Mansfield. There was a tension between his rational and humane beliefs and his unwavering support of British commerce and the sanctity of property. He understood the importance of the slave trade to British merchants, yet he knew that slavery could not be justified on any rational or humanitarian ground.[42] Less concerned about liberty than about social and economic damage control, Mansfield hoped to avoid having to reach a decision whether slavery was legal in England.[43]

Slavery and the slave trade were increasingly coming under attack in intellectual and establishment circles. In Adam Smith's *The Theory of Moral Sentiments*, first published in 1759, the great Scottish social philosopher and political economist described slave owners as "wretches who possess the virtues neither of the countries which they come from, nor those of which they go to, and whose levity, brutality, and baseness, so justly expose them to the contempt of the vanquished."[44] Mansfield's old friend Bishop William Warburton, a staunch conservative, denounced the slave trade in a 1766 sermon.[45]

Human bondage contradicted the ideals of liberty and natural rights that were becoming current in the 1770s.[46] A prominent exponent of this view, who very likely influenced Mansfield's thinking, was James Beattie, professor of moral philosophy at Marischal College in Aberdeen, Scotland. In 1770, Beattie published *An Essay on the Nature and Immutability of Truth*, which rationally and eloquently refuted arguments made by the philosopher David Hume that blacks were inherently inferior to whites. In his essay, Beattie pointed out that the apparent inferiority of Africans to Europeans was due to the absence of any civilizing influence. Britons and Frenchmen were as savage 2,000 years ago, he wrote, as Africans were now. "One may as well say of an infant, that he can never become a man, as of a nation, who barbarous, that it never can be civilized." [47] After refuting Hume's arguments one by one, Beattie called on the pride and patriotism of his countrymen to end slavery: "Let it never be said, that slavery is countenanced by the bravest and most generous people on earth; by a people who are animated with that heroic passion, the love of liberty, beyond all nations ancient or modern."[48]

The Essay on Truth was an enormous success and made a celebrity of Beattie. Soon after it was published, he visited London and for the first time met many of its leading intellectuals, including the literary giant Samuel Johnson, the actor David Garrick, the painter Sir Joshua Reynolds, and Lord Mansfield. In August 1771, only a few months before he was to decide the *Somerset* case, Mansfield heard that Beattie was in town and invited Beattie to dine alone with him. (According to Beattie, the invitation may have come to him because Mansfield had a grudge against Hume, who had publicly criticized one of his judicial decisions.[49]) Their conversation lasted nearly six hours and covered a variety of topics, of which slavery must have been one. Beattie wrote of Mansfield to a friend: "I have never seen a person of more easy and more agreeable manner ... He praises my Essay in the strongest terms. I write, he says, like a man in earnest, who feels what he writes, and he approves me for it."[50]

Although there is an absence of proof, it seems likely that Beattie helped persuade Mansfield that slavery could no longer be sanctioned by English society. Mansfield later prevailed on the King to grant Beattie a pension; when Beattie called on Mansfield to thank him, Mansfield "received him with his usual kindness" and told Beattie that he had learned from the King, "with whom he had had frequent conversations about Beattie," that the King planned, without being asked, to give him some kind of sinecure office.[51]

Although Mansfield may have been gradually moving toward revulsion at slavery, he was reluctant to make any decision that would call into question the legality of the slave trade or slavery. The slavery cases he decided before the famous *Somerset* case in 1772 did not require that of him. In 1758, he presided over a trial of two West Indian planters and the master of a slave ship for kidnapping a lady's black coachman and trying to take him out of the country "under pretence that he was their slave." Having offered no defence, presumably because they had seized the wrong man, the defendants were found guilty.[52]

In 1771, Mansfield heard another slavery case in which he again was able to avoid deciding whether or not slavery was legal in England. Thomas Lewis, a black, had once been the slave of one Robert Stapylton. After Spanish privateers captured a ship on which Stapylton and Lewis were passengers, Lewis was released from slavery and worked for wages in the American colonies as a free man before moving to England.[53] He was living in Chelsea, then a suburb of London, when Stapylton had him kidnapped by two watermen. Lewis was forcibly put on board a ship anchored in the Thames, to be sold as a slave in Jamaica. Granville Sharp, the abolitionist, learned of Lewis's capture and obtained his release by a writ of habeas corpus.

The writ of habeas corpus required that any person who had detained another bring the prisoner before a judge along with an explanation (called a "return") for the detention. If the return did not satisfy the judge that the detention was legal, the prisoner would be released.[54] That is what happened in the Stapylton case. English common law judges had developed habeas corpus over the previous centuries. It was not based on any statute, but rather on custom and the King's prerogative to ensure that no subject of his was imprisoned illegally. It has been called "the Great Writ of Liberty."[55] Originally, habeas corpus applied only to the imprisonment of persons accused of a crime, but by the mid-eighteenth century it was used to obtain the release of persons who were not accused of any wrongdoing, such as a purported slave or a seaman who had been seized by a press gang.[56]

After Lewis's release, Sharp brought a criminal action in the Court of King's Bench against Stapylton and the two watermen for their attempt to take Lewis out of England without his consent. In summing up the case for the jury, Mansfield stressed the fact that Lewis had been captured by the Spaniards, thus breaking the chain of Stapylton's title to his slave, and told the jury to consider whether Lewis still remained Stapylton's property after he had gained his liberty in America.[57] Thus Mansfield assumed, without deciding, that a person *could* legally be a slave in England. The jury found no evidence that Stapylton owned Lewis, a verdict that let Mansfield off the hook and infuriated Sharp, who was pressing for a clear decision that slavery was illegal in England.[58] Not hiding his relief that he did not have to decide the issue, Mansfield said: "I hope it never will be finally discussed. For I would have all masters think they were free and all negroes think they were not because then they would both behave better."[59]

The *Somerset* case was similar in some ways to Stapylton's but, unlike the earlier case, it gave Mansfield much less room to avoid deciding whether slavery was legal in England. Charles Stewart[60] was a Scottish merchant who had held the position of cashier and paymaster of customs in the port of Boston, Massachusetts. In 1769 he brought his slave, James Somerset, to

England. Notwithstanding his captivity, Somerset was baptized in August 1771, with three abolitionists acting as godparents.[61] Two months later, he escaped but was seized by slave-capturers hired by Stewart. When Somerset refused to return to Stewart's service, he was forcibly taken to the *Ann and Mary*, a ship anchored in the Thames, and held there in chains until he could be taken to Jamaica to be sold in the slave market. Somerset's abolitionist godparents learned of his captivity and obtained a writ of habeas corpus from Mansfield, requiring John Knowles, the captain of the *Ann and Mary*, to bring Somerset into court and to explain why he should be held as a captive in England and forced to leave the country against his will.[62]

After Mansfield ordered Somerset released pending a hearing on the merits, Somerset was introduced to Granville Sharp, who from then on took an active part in the case.[63] In contrast to the *Stapylton* case, there was no break in the chain of Stewart's ownership of Somerset. Since Somerset was unquestionably Stewart's slave at the time he escaped, Mansfield could not easily avoid deciding whether slavery was legal in England, as he had been able to do in the *Stapylton* case.

Mansfield went to great lengths to prevent the case coming to trial. In his opinion in the case, he stated that "in five or six cases of this nature, I have known it to be [settled by] the parties; on it's first coming before me, I strongly recommended it here." He suggested to Somerset's abolitionist protectors that they buy him from Stewart, but they refused.[64] At least twice he suggested to Stewart that he free Somerset, but he too refused;[65] the West Indian planters and merchants, who had taken over Stewart's legal expenses, had extracted a promise from him not to settle the case.[66] Both the abolitionists and the West Indians wanted a clear decision whether slavery was legal under English law. Although the question of the legality of Britons engaging in the slave trade (as opposed to the legality of slavery in England) was not directly at issue, the planters and merchants saw the case as a possible threat to their interests.

Mansfield, who as a lawyer in private practice had represented West Indian merchants and who throughout his career had been a strong supporter of commercial interests, was concerned about the implications of the case for the mercantile community.[67] One sign of his uneasiness was that, although he usually decided cases immediately from the bench or within a short time after hearing the lawyers' arguments, in this case he did not press for a speedy resolution. When counsel for Somerset asked for an adjournment to give him more time to prepare, Mansfield granted the delay, apparently hoping that the case would be settled. Somerset had escaped on 1 October 1771, and was recaptured on 26 November. Captain Knowles produced him in court on 9 December, but it was not until 22 June 1772, after several hearings, that Mansfield rendered his opinion.

The case quickly became a *cause célèbre*. A historian of slavery has noted: "In terms of popular mobilization the difference between the *Somerset* case and all previous ones lay in its notoriety ... Mansfield, by recessing the case from one session to another, actually enhanced its impact. Newspapers published extensive excerpts and summaries of the legal arguments."[68] There was extensive speculation in America as well as in England on the effect of the decision.[69] A large number of free blacks attended the hearings, believing that the day might be coming when English slavery would be abolished.[70]

Eminent counsel made arguments on both sides. Somerset was represented by a team of barristers led by John Glynn, none of whom would accept any compensation.[71] Glynn was highly regarded for his legal knowledge and his upright character; he was a liberal in politics who, when representing John Wilkes and others, had opposed Mansfield's position on the rights of juries in libel cases.[72]

Stewart's lead counsel, John Dunning, was regarded as the leading advocate of his day and was also a member of Parliament. Although he frequently sparred with Mansfield in court, their relationship was one of mutual respect. Dunning had been an avid supporter of civil liberties and had represented the slave Thomas Lewis in the Stapylton case. He was criticized for agreeing to represent Stewart.[73]

The first day of the trial was 7 February 1772. William Davy, one of Somerset's lawyers, argued that no man could be a slave in England, and that the laws of Virginia were not binding in England. Glynn continued the argument, asserting that other countries' laws could not be imported into England; for example, if galley slaves were brought into the country, would their master be allowed to keep them in captivity? At this point, Mansfield adjourned the case until the court's next term.

Lengthy arguments continued on 9 May, 14 May, and 21 May. Dunning and his colleagues, arguing on behalf of Stewart, said that it would be unjust to deprive Stewart of his rightful property in the slave and also pointed out the likely economic consequences of setting free 16,000 slaves in England, with a value of £800,000. Davy replied that it was high time to end the practice of buying and selling slaves, for an immoral contract was not enforceable (a position that Mansfield subscribed to in other cases). Referring to the Bible, Davy made the interesting (though irrelevant) observation that the first slave was Joseph. Mansfield, matching Davy's Biblical erudition, disagreed: it was Hagar, a bondswoman, he said.[74]

Mansfield adjourned the case for another month, but not before making several comments that indicated the direction of his thinking and laying the groundwork for the opinion he planned to give if the case was not settled before the court reconvened. His comments were, as usual, clear and concise. He had strongly recommended that the case be settled, "but if the parties will have it decided, we must give our opinion." His decision would be ruled by the law, not by compassion for Somerset nor by inconvenience for the slave owners. In an apparent attempt to mollify the slave owners, he made the gratuitous observation that a contract for the sale of a slave was good in England. But this case, he said was different: since it was brought under a writ of habeas corpus, the "person of the slave himself" was the object of inquiry. The only question before the court was whether Captain Knowles's return, which stated that Somerset was Stewart's slave, was sufficient justification for his detention.

Then Mansfield, the consummate legal craftsman, framed the precise question to be decided as narrowly as he could and in a way that attempted to reconcile his humane principles with his reluctance to interfere with the slave trade. The question, he said, was "whether any dominion, authority or coercion can be exercised in this country, on a slave according to the American laws?" In his desire not to interfere with the commercial interests of the West Indian slave owners, Mansfield was inconsistent with a position he had taken in the past: as solicitor general he had advised the Privy Council that the English common law, such as the law governing the rights of married women, superseded any contrary colonial law.[75] But on the subject of slavery he was unwilling to disturb the law of the colonies, although he conceded that Parliament had the latent power to overrule colonial law.

The way Mansfield framed the question was whether colonial slavery laws could be enforced in England in the same way, for example, that a marriage contracted in a foreign country would be recognized in England. To legalize slavery, he noted, would have many consequences "absolutely contrary to the municipal law of England."[76] On the other hand, he asserted that setting free 14,000 or 15,000 men (Mansfield's guess as to the number in England) would have "disagreeable" consequences. But, he said, his job was to enforce the law, regardless of the consequences. Then Mansfield, using the same words that he had used four years earlier in the *Wilkes* case – words that have been quoted countless times since that day – pronounced: "*fiat justitia, ruat coelum*" (let justice be done, though the heavens fall).[77] Finally, he suggested that, if the merchants thought the matter of great commercial concern, they should ask Parliament to legitimize slavery in England. Still hoping that the case would be settled, he adjourned the hearing.

No settlement having been reached, the court met again on 22 June 1772 for Mansfield to give the court's unanimous opinion. The courtroom in Westminster Hall was crowded with lawyers, West Indian planters, abolitionists, blacks, as well as the merely curious. Some people could not get into the courtroom.[78] To placate the concerns of the West Indian and North American planters and merchants, Mansfield again made clear that the case did not involve the legality of the slave trade; it was authorized by the laws of Virginia and Jamaica, and slaves "are goods and chattels; and, as such, saleable and sold."[79] However, the only question for the court to decide was whether the return to the writ of habeas corpus when the case was first brought before him (i.e., that Somerset was the property of Stewart) was sufficient to allow Stewart to keep him in captivity and to take him out of the country against his will. On this narrow question, Mansfield then stated his conclusion and that of the Court of King's Bench:

> So high an act of dominion must be recognized by the law of the country where it is used. The power of a master over his slave has been extremely different in different countries. The state of slavery is of such a nature, that it is incapable of being introduced on any reasons, moral or political; but only positive law ... It is so odious, that nothing can be suffered to support it, but positive law. Whatever inconveniences, therefore, may follow from a decision, I cannot say this case is allowed or approved by the law of England; and therefore the black must be discharged.[80]

Many people, particularly the blacks who were attending the hearing, believed that Mansfield had put an end to slavery in England.[81] Once Mansfield had given his decision, they bowed to him and the other judges, joyfully shook each others' hands, and congratulated themselves that blacks had recovered their rights as human beings.[82] Although Mansfield was careful to leave the transatlantic slave trade intact, his decision raised concern among the West Indian planters and merchants.[83] Even before he handed it down, they had attempted to get a bill through the House of Commons legalizing the slave trade, but it was rejected. After the decision, they brought in a bill to overrule it, but this too was unsuccessful.[84]

The *Somerset* decision did not end slavery in England. The recapture and deportation of escaped slaves continued until the 1790s. Slaves continued to be bought and sold in England.[85] Advertisements for the sale of slaves at auction continued to appear in the newspapers.[86] In May 1772, in the midst of the drawn-out *Somerset* case, an advertisement appeared in two London newspapers offering a reward for the recovery of a runaway black, last seen in Highgate (which, ironically, happened to be in the neighbourhood of Mansfield's home of Kenwood).[87]

The decision may have deterred some West Indian slave owners from bringing their slaves to England, but it did not invalidate colonial slave law.[88] Mansfield insisted on several later occasions that his decision was a narrow one, only preventing Somerset from being taken by force out of the country.[89] In a suit brought in 1782 for breach of a contract to purchase a slave, there was no suggestion that Mansfield considered such a contract to be void on the ground of illegality or immorality.[90] Thirteen years after the *Somerset* decision, he commented that previous court decisions "go no further than that the master cannot compel [the slave] to go out of the kingdom."[91]

One has to question the accuracy of Mansfield's narrow characterization of his *Somerset* decision. The ruling was not as narrow as Mansfield later claimed; if it had been, he might possibly have refused to release Somerset and simply ordered Stewart to refrain from deporting him; although it is arguable that the procedural posture of the case – it being brought on a writ of habeas corpus – gave him no alternative but to either order Somerset's release or deny it. As a historian of habeas corpus has written, habeas corpus could set one slave free, but it "could not enable a judge to declare illegal an entire system of bondage created by colonial legislatures."[92] Mansfield had made the fine distinction that, while slavery was not illegal in England, the court would not recognize a slave owner's dominion over a slave. It was therefore hardly surprising that many people gave the decision a broader interpretation. The decision also made the important point that habeas corpus protected blacks as well as whites.[93]

Long after deciding the *Somerset* case, Mansfield continued to regard black slaves not as human beings having inalienable rights but as chattels – personal property that their owners could dispose of as they wished. He exhibited this view most chillingly in the infamous case of the slave ship *Zong,* decided in May 1783, eleven years after his *Somerset* ruling.[94] The captain of the *Zong*, en route from West Africa to Jamaica with a cargo of several hundred slaves, lost his way in the Caribbean and was delayed at sea for several days. With water running out, 60 slaves died of thirst, 40 desperately threw themselves into the sea and drowned, and another 150 were thrown overboard.[95] The ship owner brought a lawsuit against the insurer of the ship and its cargo of slaves for recovery of the value of the slaves who had been thrown overboard.

A jury gave a verdict against the insurer, on the ground that the loss of the slaves was a result of the normal perils of the sea.[96] On appeal, Mansfield ruled that there had to be a new trial, because the ship owner had not shown that it was necessary to throw the slaves overboard. Apparently it had rained before the ship arrived in Jamaica; it was therefore possible that some water was available for the slaves. It was implicit in Mansfield's decision that if the ship owner could prove that sufficient water was lacking it would have been legal – and within the terms of the insurance policy as one of the normal perils of the sea – to throw the slaves overboard. Nowhere in his short opinion was there any suggestion that the captain and crew of the *Zong* were murderers.

Light was also shed on Mansfield's views after the *Somerset* case from another, albeit not disinterested, source. In 1790, the Earl of Sheffield, who was opposing abolition of the slave trade in Parliament, wrote to Mansfield's nephew Lord Stormont that Mansfield had told him a year earlier that, in his view, abolishing the slave trade would not help the slaves, who would be transported across the Atlantic on less well-regulated foreign ships; not to mention the fact that merchants in Bristol and Liverpool would lose revenues.[97]

Although the *Somerset* decision did not end slavery or the slave trade, it was far from meaningless. Although the case had little immediate effect in England, it provided support for the growing abolitionist sentiment. In Scotland, however, it had an almost immediate effect. Less than two weeks after the decision, an African slave in Scotland named Joseph Knight read in a Scottish newspaper that Somerset had been freed, and he decided that he too was entitled to be free. Knight brought suit in the magistrate's court in Perthshire in November 1773; after more than four years of litigation, the highest court of Scotland took the decisive step that Mansfield had been unwilling to take. The court freed Knight, declaring "that the state of slavery is not recognized by the laws of this kingdom, and is inconsistent with the principles thereof."[98]

In England, emancipation came much more slowly. By the early 1790s, deportations from England of escaped slaves had ceased, and Mansfield's narrow interpretation of the case gave way to a broader interpretation "that British slavery within Britain had been repudiated *in toto*."[99] In 1793, Mansfield himself acknowledged to Granville Sharp that the *Somerset* decision had undermined British slavery.[100] Despite Mansfield's efforts to minimize the importance of the decision, it has been aptly called "the opening act of the antislavery drama,"[101] which set England on its course of abolition of both the slave trade and domestic slavery. According to a historian: "without [Mansfield] to apply the light of reason to the centuries-old institution of slavery and expose it in precise legal terms, the Abolitionists would have found it infinitely harder to persuade Parliament to declare it illegal."[102] Yet the British slave trade actually expanded during the years after *Somerset*, reaching its peak in 1799.[103] Britain did not abolish the slave trade until 1807 and slavery until 1834, sixty-two years after the historic decision.

A distinction should be made between Mansfield's decisions as a judge who consistently furthered the interests of merchants and property owners even at the expense of fundamental human rights, and his humane conduct of his personal life. Dido Elizabeth Belle, born about 1763, was the illegitimate daughter of Mansfield's nephew, Sir John Lindsay, a captain in the British navy and a veteran of many sea battles, and a black slave whom he had encountered in the West Indies. Lindsay was the son of Sir Alexander Lindsay of Evelix, the head of an ancient Scottish family, and Amelia Murray, Mansfield's youngest sister. Thus, on her father's side Dido was related to two important clans, the Murrays and the Lindsays. It is not known what happened to Dido's mother. Her father being at sea most of the time, Dido was sent at an early age to live at Mansfield's home of Kenwood. There she became a member of Mansfield's household, acting as a companion to his great-niece, Lady Elizabeth Murray, who had lived there since her own mother's death in 1766.

At Kenwood, Dido had an intermediate status: she was neither a full member of the family nor a servant. For example, she did not take her meals with the family, but she would join the ladies for after-dinner coffee. She worked at the house, which under Lady Mansfield's supervision was not only a home but also a kind of genteel farm, managing the dairy and poultry yards. A painting by Johann Zoffany from about 1780, now at Scone Palace, shows Dido to be quite beautiful. In 1785, when Lady Elizabeth Murray married and left Kenwood, Dido stayed on to help look after Mansfield, who was now eighty and whose wife had died the previous year. When Dido's father died in 1788, he left her a legacy of £1,000, not an inconsequential sum at the time.[104]

Mansfield became very fond of Dido and was grateful for her care of him in his old age. In his will, executed in 1782, he confirmed her freedom, which he apparently had bestowed earlier, and bequeathed her £100 a year for life. In two separate codicils executed in May 1786 he bequeathed her an additional £500, explaining: "I think it right, considering how she has been bred & how she has behaved, to make a better Provision for Dido."[105] In 1793, soon after Mansfield's death, Dido married; she had three sons: twins born in 1795 and a third son born in 1800. She died in 1804, at the age of about forty-one.[106]

The *Somerset* case had important repercussions in Britain's North American colonies. The case was widely noted in colonial newspapers and its perceived threat to the institution of slavery may have provided a stimulus to the desire of Virginia and the other southern colonies to seek independence.[107] Within a year after the decision, slaves in Massachusetts began agitating against the institution. The stark contradiction that many of the "Sons of Liberty" were slave owners gave rise to Samuel Johnson's famous remark: "How is it that we hear the loudest yelps for liberty among the drivers of negroes?"[108]

But while discussion of the *Somerset* case "quickly fed into the developing conflict" between Britain and the American colonists,[109] it is too much to say that it "sparked" the American Revolution, as two historians have asserted.[110] The issues between the colonies and the British government that led to the American Revolution, particularly those relating to taxation of the colonies, had been coming to a boil for a decade before Mansfield's historic decision.[111]

In fact, the tinderbox of the revolution was Massachusetts, the colony where slavery was least important and abolitionist sentiment strongest. The principal events directly leading up to the American Revolution – the Boston Massacre of 1770, the Boston Tea Party of 1773, and the Battle of Lexington and Concord in 1775 – all occurred in Massachusetts and did not involve the issue of slavery. And it should not be forgotten that in deciding the *Somerset* case, Mansfield went out of his way to reassure the West Indian planters that the legality of the slave trade or of colonial slavery was not an issue before the court. So, while *Somerset* was a source of concern to American slave owners and a source of hope to their slaves, the decision's role in the American Revolution should not be overstated.

18

The American Revolution

If you do not kill them, they will kill you.

Lord Mansfield, speaking of the American colonists in the House of Lords

Although Lord Mansfield never visited the western hemisphere, he was closely involved with America throughout his career, beginning with the years when he was practicing law. His knowledge and experience of American affairs gave added weight to his advice to the King and ministry before and during the American Revolution. As a lawyer, Mansfield had represented many American clients, including several of the colonies in border disputes with other colonies, before English courts and the Board of Trade.[1] As solicitor general and then as attorney general, he gave legal opinions to the ministry, the Board of Trade, and other government departments on a variety of American issues, some of which anticipated the complex constitutional questions that perplexed the British government in the 1760s and came to a boil in the American Revolution.[2] Most momentous was the question of the respective roles that the King, the Cabinet, Parliament, the English courts, the royally appointed colonial governors, and the elected colonial assemblies should play in governing – and particularly in taxing – the North American colonies.

On American matters, as on others, Murray consistently supported the authority of the King and Parliament to keep tight control over the colonies. In 1746, for example, Mansfield as solicitor general and Dudley Ryder as attorney general jointly advised the Privy Council to disallow a Virginia statute that enabled a married woman to dispose of her own property, regardless of whether or not her husband was living. It would be a dangerous precedent, the two law officers wrote, to permit a colony to alter so settled a point of law as giving a married woman this power (which she did not have in England).[3] Twenty-six years later, however, Chief Justice

Mansfield took a different view of the supremacy of English law. In the *Somerset* slavery case, while declining to support the institution of slavery in England, he nevertheless insisted that the English common law did not override colonial law on the legality of slavery in the American colonies.[4]

In a far-reaching opinion in 1744, Mansfield and Ryder said that Parliament held the ultimate power to tax a colony;[5] and eleven years later Mansfield, then attorney general, opined that a tax enacted by a colony was invalid. In the latter case, he stated that a Maryland statute taxing convicts should be repealed or nullified because it was "of public concern and derogatory to the Crown and legislature of Great Britain. By the same reason," he argued, a colony "might levy a duty upon, or even prohibit, British goods."[6] A few months later, he again supported the supremacy of English laws over those of the colonies, opining that the King in council had authority to hear an appeal from the decision of a Massachusetts court over a dispute over title to a large tract of land.[7]

Aside from performing his official duties as a law officer of the Crown, Mansfield acted as an unofficial adviser to the Duke of Newcastle on many political issues, including some that concerned America. In 1754, while British forces were engaged in warfare with French Canadians and Amerindians along the Ohio River, Mansfield wrote to Newcastle about a discussion he had with a legal client, an American planter, whom he found intelligent and well informed: "Upon a general Question or two put to him, he opened his general Notions of the State of the British Empire in America, and the proper Method to put the Government in a constant posture of Defence ... I have desired him to throw his thoughts upon paper, which He very readily said he would last night. I will communicate them to your Grace." Mansfield added that his informant's thoughts might be of use to Charles Townshend, a lord of the admiralty who had drawn up a concerted plan for the defence of the colonies (and who was to play a key role in American affairs when he was chancellor of the exchequer in the 1760s).[8]

Both before and after Mansfield became chief justice, Newcastle made a habit of sending him packages of state papers, many of them dealing with American affairs, and asking him look them over and respond the next day with his comments.[9] The two also had detailed conversations in which Mansfield would give the duke political advice. For example, in 1767 Mansfield told Newcastle that he disapproved of the House of Commons reducing the authority of the British-appointed governor of New York over the elected New York assembly, and that he favoured a suggestion made by a member of the Commons for the billeting of British troops in New Yorkers' homes.[10]

Mansfield had little sympathy for the desire of the colonists to govern themselves. Nevertheless, he believed that it was unproductive and futile to impose the laws of one country on the citizens of another country with different traditions and a different culture.[11] He supported the right of the French Catholic inhabitants of Canada to practise their religion after Canada became a British colony, and he believed that a legal system for newly British India should take Indian traditional laws and customs into account.

But the nationality of the American colonists was not clear, either to the politicians in London or to the colonists themselves. Had they acquired an American nationality of their own, which was entitled to respect from the British government, or were they British subjects who happened to live across the Atlantic? The colonists believed – and most British politicians, including Mansfield, agreed – that they continued to be subject to British sovereignty when they migrated to the new world.[12] As historian Gordon Wood stated: "Almost to the moment of independence the colonists had continued to define themselves as British and only reluctantly came to see themselves as a separate people called Americans.[13]

Nevertheless, from the early years of the English colonization of North America in the early seventeenth century, the settlers had attempted to assert their autonomy from Britain.[14] Unlike Spain, which had established strong institutions of imperial control in its Latin American colonies, Britain had allowed its colonies to develop on their own through the enterprise of the colonists. No Act of Parliament authorized the establishment of the colonies; instead, they operated under charters from the King, which gave them a degree of self-rule.[15] Mansfield himself believed that chance, not political wisdom, played the decisive role in the settlement of English America: in a letter written in 1777 to the author of a history of America, he noted that "government left private adventurers to do as they pleased."[16]

Although the British government tried to control the colonies, it had to contend with a growing desire by the settlers for independence in fact, if not in name. Largely through their own efforts, the colonies had become an important adjunct to the British nation, and the colonists had a growing sense of their own importance. During the twenty-five years before the American Revolution, the population of the colonies doubled from one million to two and one-half million (one-fifth of whom were African slaves).[17] Philadelphia, with a population of 34,000, was the second-largest city in the British Empire, second only to London.[18] By the early 1770s, North America had become Britain's leading trading partner, accounting for 26 per cent of its exports and 15 per cent of its imports.[19] As Britain's interest in the colonies increased, the colonists began to see themselves, though remaining British, as an independent nation with its own separate interests.

The Peace of Paris in 1763 confirmed Britain's removal of a French military presence from Canada and the Ohio valley. With the end of the French threat, the American colonists no longer felt a need for the protection of the British army. The British government, under a ministry headed by George Grenville, disagreed. The events that followed led, a decade later, to the American Revolution, Britain's worst defeat of the eighteenth century. Grenville, who had been Mansfield's friend for more than thirty years, has received considerable bad press from history. Although George III disliked him and called him a man "with the mind of a counting-house clerk,"[20] Grenville was a conscientious, hard-working politician, with a thorough understanding of commerce and public finance.[21] His faults were a tendency to take large risks when he thought the odds favoured him, and "a lack of broad vision and sensitivity in politics."[22] Grenville's policy to tax the American colonies was based largely on his dismay at the size of Britain's debt and his obsession with enforcing the law. It is likely that any prime minister would have followed the same course, though perhaps not quite so aggressively.[23]

Grenville insisted that, since British troops were in North America primarily to protect the colonists, it was reasonable to tax the Americans to cover the costs and to reduce the national debt that Britain had incurred during the war. As the colonists pushed westward across the Appalachians to occupy the land captured from the French, they came into increasing conflict with the native Indian population. The British authorities decided to maintain a standing army in America to keep the peace in the West, and insisted that the Americans should bear a portion of its high cost.[24]

The first important step that led to the American Revolution came in March 1765, with the enactment of the American Stamp Tax. Before proposing the Stamp Act to Parliament, Grenville consulted with Mansfield on whether Britain had the constitutional power to impose the tax on the Americans. Mansfield opined that the power was definitely there, but he warned that the tax would be "a striking alteration to ignorant people," and suggested that Grenville have someone look into "the origin of the colonists' power to tax themselves and raise money at all."[25] The Stamp Act passed the House of Lords without debate and without a single vote against it.[26] The Act required that a stamp be purchased in order to validate all legal and many other types of documents, as well as newspapers.[27] Although this direct tax on the colonies was not expected to bring in a large amount of revenue, it aroused fury in America. The Virginia assembly condemned the Stamp Act on constitutional grounds, mobs in Boston attacked the collector of the tax, and riots spread throughout the colonies.[28] Local groups, calling themselves Sons of Liberty, forced merchants and judges to conduct their business without buying stamps and enforced an embargo on British goods.

In July 1765, the King and his uncle the Duke of Cumberland forced Grenville to resign as prime minister and persuaded Charles Watson-Wentworth, 2nd Marquess of Rockingham, to take the post. Rockingham was an enormously wealthy, universally respected nobleman who happened to have an aristocratic profile that went well with his station in life. He was a zealous Whig. At the age of fifteen he had slipped away from a family gathering to join the Duke of Cumberland's royal army in Carlisle near the Scottish border, and despite his youth, he served as a colonel in putting down the Jacobite Rebellion of 1745.[29] Something of a playboy and given to high-stakes gambling on horse races, he lived like a Continental prince and established a "distinct, separate social milieu, based on Brooks's Club" on St James's Street.[30] Rockingham was related to Lady Mansfield by marriage, and became Lord Mansfield's friend as well as one of his debtors.[31]

Rockingham was at first reluctant to take the helm of the government in the midst of the Stamp Act unrest, and even after he did, he could not decide how to handle the growing crisis. For several months he resisted efforts to repeal the Act, but after receiving letters from prominent English merchants describing their economic distress following the American embargo, he changed his mind.[32] In January 1766, the Rockingham ministry proposed to repeal the Stamp Act.[33]

Many Britons, including William Pitt, supported the Americans not only on the specific issue of the Stamp Act but also on the more general principle that Britain had no right to tax the colonies without their consent. Mansfield was of the opposite view and became a leading opponent of its repeal. This brought him once again into conflict with Pitt, as well as with Pitt's ally and Mansfield's judicial rival and political foe Charles Pratt, who had been raised to the peerage as Lord Camden.

On 14 January 1766, Pitt made a stirring speech in the House of Commons supporting repeal and condemning taxation without representation. He concluded: "The Americans have been wronged. They have been driven to madness by injustice. Will you punish them for the madness you have occasioned? Rather let prudence and temper come first from this side ... Let the sovereign authority over the colonies be ... made to extend to every point of legislation ... except that of taking money out of their pockets without their consent."[34] In the House of Lords, Camden made what Pitt later called a "divine" speech supporting Pitt's position that Britain had no right to tax the colonies,[35] and on 3 February 1766, Mansfield responded to Camden.

The issue of repeal of the Stamp Act created a dilemma for Mansfield. The violent reaction in America to the Act threatened the commercial interests that Mansfield normally supported; many London merchants who traded with North America sided with the Americans in their own self-interest.[36] On the other hand, repeal of the Act after it had been in effect for less than a year was a blow to the government's authority, of which Mansfield was always an ardent supporter. Ironically, this was the first time in his life he had ever opposed an important measure proposed by the government.[37]

He began his speech against repeal of the Stamp Act with the same kind of sanctimonious declaration of his own immunity from the lure of popularity that he was to make two years later in court in the *Wilkes* outlawry case and again in the *Somerset* slavery case: "I never was biased by any consideration of applause from without, in the discharge of my public duty." He then asserted that English law applied in colonial border disputes, in which he had represented various colonies many years earlier. These disputes, he said, show the necessity that there be "one superior decisive jurisdiction, to which all subordinate jurisdictions may recur." That jurisdiction, of course, was the British government.

Having made the point that the colonies were subject to English law, Mansfield turned to the question of taxation without representation. He made the ingenious argument that the colonists were represented in Parliament just as much as the English were. Eight million of England's population of nine million had no vote (women did not get the vote until the twentieth century[38]), but this was justified because, under a theory of "virtual representation," members of Parliament represented the disenfranchised of both sexes not just in their own constituencies but in the British nation at large, including the colonies.[39]

Mansfield then refuted the economic argument that the Stamp Tax was an internal tax, essentially different from external taxes, such as customs duties, which the colonists were accustomed to. He said that there was no difference between internal and external taxes. A tax was like a pebble thrown into a lake, causing ripples that agitate the entire lake. For example, a tax on tobacco at the ports in Virginia or London was in reality a duty upon the inland plantations of Virginia. Mansfield closed his speech on a personal note, saying that he bore no ill will toward Americans. He owed much to them, having been much concerned in many cases before the Privy Council involving the colonies, "and so I became a good deal acquainted with American affairs and people."[40]

According to David Hume, Mansfield spoke for two hours "in the most masterly manner: it is agreed on all hands that nobody ever remembers such a discourse for matter, for style, and for delivery."[41] But despite his eloquence, Parliament repealed the Stamp Act, to the great joy of the colonists. In order to gather the necessary votes for repeal, the Rockingham ministry was forced also to enact the face-saving American Declaratory Act, which asserted the continued right of Parliament to tax the colonies.[42]

A year later, Parliament used its authority under this law when, under the guidance of Chancellor of the Exchequer Charles Townshend, and with the support of Mansfield and Grenville,[43] it imposed customs duties on glass, paint, paper, and tea, when imported into America.[44] Predictably, the Townshend duties ensured that colonial unrest would continue. In a series of public letters entitled *Letters from a Farmer in Pennsylvania*, John Dickinson, who was actually a wealthy Philadelphia lawyer, pointed out the injustice of Britain claiming the right to prohibit the manufacture in America of certain articles and then imposing taxes on the import of these articles. "We are in the situation of a besieged city," he wrote, "surrounded in every part but one. If that is closed up no step can be taken but to surrender at discretion."[45] In effect, Dickinson was making the same point, albeit for opposite reasons, that Mansfield had made in his argument against repeal of the Stamp Act: namely, that there was no meaningful difference between internal and external taxes.

In the absence of any consistent policy toward the American colonists, the British government dithered. It was unfortunate for Britain that Mansfield's usual astuteness and pragmatism failed him in the dispute with the colonists. Despite his experience of American affairs, he did not use his influence with the King and the ministry to bring a political end to the crisis at a time when a more conciliatory approach might possibly have been successful.[46] Instead, he accused Pitt (who had been raised to the peerage as the Earl of Chatham in August 1766) and his followers of "giv[ing] up every point which the Crown has insisted upon from the Revolution [of 1688]." But Mansfield had less understanding of the colonists than either he or his colleagues believed. As a lawyer and politician, he had usually dealt with the British-appointed governors of the colonies, not with representatives of the colonists themselves. And during the Revolutionary War he was to get much of his information on American affairs from Thomas Hutchinson, the last royal governor of Massachusetts, who had been forced into exile because he attempted to enforce the measures taken by the British government.[47]

Again, the government, now headed by Lord North, backed down and repealed the Townshend duties, except for the duty on tea, which produced the most revenue.[48] By this time, however, the conflict between Britain and the colonies was no longer just about taxation; from the viewpoint of many Americans, it had turned into an attack on their rights and their liberties.[49] A mere colonial rebellion had been transformed into "a world-historical event that promised ... a new future not just for Americans but for all humanity."[50]

Furthermore, events in Britain that ostensibly had nothing to do with America had hardened the colonists' resolve to seek some form of autonomy. The colonists were fully aware that the House of Commons in 1768 had nullified the election of John Wilkes to represent Middlesex.[51] This action, according to historian George Guttridge, was "a principal cause of the American Revolution; for after such high-handed action ... Americans could no longer consider parliament as the representative of the people, but must regard its members as the packed adherents of a profligate ministry in whom it would be idle to invite American confidence."[52]

If the colonists' attitude had hardened, so had that of the British government. In December 1773 colonists protested the tax on tea by throwing three shiploads of tea into Boston harbour. The ministry, now headed by Lord North, responded to the Boston Tea Party with the punitive Boston Port Bill, which closed down the port of Boston until the tea was paid for. In addition, the bill contained several other provisions that moved the colonists toward war. It provided that the King would appoint the members of the upper house of the Massachusetts legislature, gave the British-appointed governor of Massachusetts discretion to transfer trials to England, and required inhabitants of Boston to billet British troops inside the city.[53]

North's harsh response to the Boston Tea Party was overwhelmingly supported by the King and Parliament.[54] In the House of Lords, Mansfield called the Boston Tea Party an act of high treason.[55] "The sword was drawn," he said, "and the scabbard thrown away." Like Julius Caesar, he said, Britain had "passed the Rubicon."[56] His words stuck – and provided ammunition with which his enemies taunted him. Sometime later, *The Public Advertiser* acidly juxtaposed Mansfield's brave words with his supposedly timid nature:

> The Rubicon is pass'd, great Julius cried;
> Mansfield, the Rubicon is pass'd, replied;
> Caesar press'd on, came, saw and won the day,
> What's become of Mansfield? – Run away![57]

For all that, Mansfield had become a leader of the militant opposition to the colonists that dictated British policy during the 1770s and led to armed conflict and the loss of the colonies. In the tug-of-war that ensued between a hawkish King and Tory ministry on one side and many members of the Whig elite on the other, Mansfield's advice was an important factor that led Britain to disaster.

While Mansfield was engaged in the political side of the dispute with America, a lawsuit came before his court dealing with the central issue of the conflict: Britain's right to tax its colonies. In 1774, a plantation owner in Grenada, a West Indies colony of Britain, challenged the right of the British-appointed governor to impose a 4.5 per cent tax on all exports from the island. In *Campbell v. Hall*,[58] Mansfield declared that there were two kinds of colonies, those acquired by conquest and those by settlement. For a conquered colony such as Grenada, the King (or a governor he appointed) could impose taxes (although in this case the tax was void because there was an error in the order imposing the tax). For a settled colony, such as the North American colonies, the elected colonial assembly must participate in the creation of taxes, but its legislative power was subordinate to the power of Parliament.

Mansfield's decision in *Campbell v. Hall* not only reasserted the power of Parliament over the American colonies but also aggravated the dispute with the colonies in another, quite different, way. The decision, as it applied to conquered colonies, encouraged Prime Minister North to push through Parliament the Quebec Act of 1774 to govern newly acquired Canada.[59]

The Quebec Act, which was sponsored (and probably drafted) by Mansfield,[60] called for a colonial government without an elected assembly and gave special rights to the Catholic Church, in which most French Canadians worshipped. The Quebec Act reflected Mansfield's support of religious toleration,[61] but it alarmed the North American colonists, who saw it as an ominous blueprint for London-controlled colonial governments throughout North America.[62]

By 1775, America had become the most pressing subject in British politics. King George III was a hawk throughout the conflict with the colonies, but his reputation in America as a tyrant was not shared by most of the British public, to whom he was a popular king who resolutely stood up for British power abroad. Although Mansfield had no specific responsibilities within the ministry, he had private audiences with the King and was a minister in all but name. The King needed little or no persuasion to take a strong line with the colonists, but Mansfield's support of his American policies was certainly a factor. Mansfield was also North's chief legal adviser and in frequent communication with him.[63]

In view of the King's bellicosity and North's lack of the qualifications as a war leader (he tried to resign several times during the American Revolution, but the King refused to accept his resignation), Mansfield's advice, both privately with the King and publicly in the House of Lords, was especially influential. In February 1775, Mansfield spoke in the House of Lords in favour of a motion "beseeching his Majesty to take the most effectual measures for enforcing due obedience to the laws and the authority" of Parliament. He conceded that the Townshend duties had been a mistake, but he said that making concessions to the Americans now would be an abdication of British sovereignty over the colonies.[64]

In August 1775, four months after the opening of hostilities at the Battle of Lexington and Concord, King George declared that the colonies were in open rebellion. Four months later Mansfield made his strongest (and best-remembered) speech in the House of Lords, recommending strong action against the colonists regardless of the impact it might have on commerce with North America. A bill to prohibit all trading with some of the colonies had been introduced in the House of Lords, and an argument was made that it would produce great distress. Mansfield responded: "Yet, my Lords, admitting all this to be true, what are we to do? Are we to rest inactive, with our arms folded, till they shall think proper to begin the attack, and gain strength to act against us with effect? We are in such a situation, that we must fight or be pursued. [As a Swedish general once said to his men,] 'if you do not kill them, they will kill you.'"[65]

Nevertheless, many politically active Englishmen opposed war with America. Several British army officers resigned their commissions rather than engage in what they regarded as a civil war.[66] The Scots, however, generally sided with the government because it provided them with an excellent opportunity to show their loyalty.[67] Many Englishmen who remembered the Jacobite Rebellion of 1745 continued to equate being a Scot with being a Jacobite. It should come as no surprise, therefore, that the American Revolution saw a resurgence in England of anti-Scottish feeling. By this time, Jacobitism was no longer seriously regarded as a threat to the government and the Hanoverian dynasty, but rather as a synonym for the authoritarian approach to government that George III favoured.[68]

Many patriotic Englishmen believed that the war with the colonies was a Scottish war.[69] Anti-government pamphleteers charged that the King was being secretly advised "behind the curtain" by two bloodthirsty Scots, Bute and Mansfield, to make war against the Americans.[70] Although Bute had resigned as prime minister a decade earlier and was no longer an influential political figure, Mansfield remained a confidant of the King and an adviser to the ministry. The notion advanced by their enemies that Bute and Mansfield had a system of secret influence over Britain's foreign policy was not just an exaggeration – it was nonsense.[71]

Pamphlets circulated in 1775 viciously attacked Mansfield and reminded readers of his background in dirt-poor Scotland, his Jacobite family connections, and the accusation made in 1753 that he had harboured Jacobite sympathies as a youth. The pamphlets republished the parts of his recent speeches in the House of Lords about crossing the Rubicon and killing Americans.[72] A vitriolic anonymous poem entitled "Casca's Epistle to Lord Mansfield" accused Mansfield of still being a Jacobite at heart; it even portrayed his prosecution of the Jacobite lords after the 1745 rebellion as an act of dissembling.[73]

It was not only pamphleteers who believed that Mansfield was a dominant and malignant influence in the government. The Earl of Shelburne inveighed against his secret influence immediately before and during the American Revolution and that "through his despotic counsels a Great Empire was being plunged in all the miseries and horrors of civil war while the domestic liberties of the country were equally endangered."[74] In debate in the House of

Lords, Mansfield urged strong measures against the colonists, adding that he never used his Cabinet position for his own personal profit. Shelburne responded by directly accusing Mansfield of interfering in Cabinet affairs when he no longer had any official responsibilities within the ministry.

Shelburne also said that influence in court had many allurements besides profit, and that even if Mansfield had nothing to ask for himself, he had many friends, relations, and dependents who had been amply provided for. This was a sensitive point for Mansfield, who was shameless in obtaining positions for his friends and relatives. "Rising in a great passion," Mansfield hotly accused Shelburne of failing to act like a gentleman and denied that he "had any hand in preparing *all* the bills of the last session" of Parliament (an implied admission that he may have prepared *some* of the legislation). Shelburne accused Mansfield of lying, but tempers cooled and a duel in Hyde Park was avoided.[75]

As chief justice, Mansfield used the laws against seditious libel to suppress opposition to the American war. In June 1775, several newspapers printed an advertisement by one John Horne (who was also known as John Horne Tooke) soliciting subscriptions to raise £100 "to be applied to the relief of the widows and orphans and aged parents of our beloved American fellow-subjects, who, faithful to the character of Englishmen, preferring death to slavery, were, for that reason only, inhumanly murdered by the King's troops at or near Lexington and Concord in the province of Massachusetts on the 19th of last April." The money raised was to be handed over to Benjamin Franklin to be applied for the stated purpose.[76]

The government brought seditious libel charges against the printers of four newspapers that had published the advertisement, and all were tried before Mansfield in December 1776. In each case, the jury found the printer guilty. On 4 July 1776 (ironically, the first American Independence Day), Horne was tried for libel in the Court of King's Bench. So confident was Mansfield of the anti-American feelings of the jury that he departed from his usual practice of telling the jury that the only question they had to decide was whether the defendant was the author or publisher of the alleged libel. In Horne's case he allowed the jury to decide whether the words in the advertisement were a criminal libel.[77] His confidence was justified: after a short deliberation, the jury brought in a guilty verdict. Horne was sentenced to a year's imprisonment and a £200 fine.[78]

The Royal Navy, the largest in the world, was the key to Britain's status as a world power. The navy safeguarded the nation's international commerce, provided a lifeline to its colonies, and protected its shores from foreign invasion. Britain's effort to suppress the American Revolution stretched the navy to the limit, with almost half its ships being engaged in defeating the colonists.[79] Since it was difficult to find enough volunteers for the hard life of a sailor on a man-of-war, the government resorted to the savage practice of "impressing" sailors – seizing men in taverns, on the street, or on merchant ships and forcing them to serve in the navy. In fact, during wartime, impressment was the navy's principal way of securing the manpower it needed.[80] Impressment provided a striking example of the conflict between the personal right to liberty and the public need for mutual security. It was a conflict that Mansfield was eventually called upon to resolve.

Impressment of sailors began well before the American Revolution. It was used in 1740, and again in 1755. Each time, when Britain was about to resume its intermittent warfare with France and needed to go on a war footing, the Admiralty issued warrants for press gangs to seize seamen and others who made their living on the water and conscript them into the navy.[81] By the next year, when war with France began, press gangs were in operation throughout England.[82] Twenty shillings was paid for each seaman they pressed. Non-seamen, however able-bodied, were not included in the authorization, because the navy wanted only those with seafaring experience. Impressment was extremely unpopular, not only with the common people, who sometimes attacked the press gangs, but also with many of the elite. George Grenville, who had recently served as treasurer of the navy, opposed the pressing of sailors, calling it a "tyrannical and unjust method."[83]

As attorney general, Mansfield had given a legal opinion to the Admiralty in a case where a press gang had detained three men who appeared to be able and fit for the navy but in fact were not seamen. The men were put in a cage and left in the charge of a constable. When the constable absented himself for a while, his assistant and several others used a poker to pry open the cage door, enabling the three men to flee. Mansfield was asked to opine whether the constable or the rescuers could be prosecuted. His opinion was careful and pragmatic. Since impressing non-seafarers was unauthorized, those who encouraged or assisted the wrongly impressed men to escape could not be prosecuted. Although the constable had acted illegally in detaining the men, he might have had the excuse that they looked like seamen.

In view of public outrage at impressment, Mansfield advised against prosecution: "I think a prosecution ... may be attended with too many difficulties to be advisable, because upon pressing it would be very imprudent to bring any matter to a judicial trial." The injustice of seizing men at random to serve in the navy touched a sensitive nerve in a public that jealously guarded its liberties, and Mansfield clearly thought it inadvisable for this issue to be discussed in an open forum.[84] In general, the government was reluctant to defend impressment, leaving it to the courts to clarify the law.[85]

Five days after he became chief justice, Mansfield issued a writ of habeas corpus on behalf of a man who claimed to have been illegally pressed.[86] However, in some cases he chose not to issue the writ but instead issued an order to the keeper of the Savoy prison (where persons seized by press gangs were held) to explain why they were holding the man.[87] Mansfield's avoidance of habeas corpus infuriated William Pitt, who believed giving judges discretion over so important a matter threatened the sacred liberty of the individual.[88] Pitt persuaded Attorney General Charles Pratt, who personally hated Mansfield,[89] to introduce a bill in the House of Commons requiring judges to issue a writ of habeas corpus in all cases where a person was "confined or restrained of his liberty, under any colour or pretence whatsoever."[90]

The Habeas Corpus Bill of 1758 had two purposes, one open and the other concealed. It was designed to protect men against illegal impressment, but it was also a move by Mansfield's political enemies to lower his prestige and credibility.[91] As an added insult, Pratt introduced the bill without consulting Mansfield or his political ally Lord Chancellor Hardwicke, then the only two lawyers who were members of the Cabinet. Pitt wanted "to throw a slur on Lord Mansfield, who had taken some liberties ... with [habeas corpus], which made him unpopular."[92] The bill passed the House of Commons, but it was defeated in the House of Lords, where Mansfield spoke for two and a half hours against it. Horace Walpole commented: "I never heard so much argument, so much sense, so much oratory, united;" but he added that he did not realize how much he loved liberty until he found that he was not staggered by Mansfield's eloquence.[93]

Two decades later, in the midst of the American Revolution, Mansfield was called upon to decide on the legality of impressment in the case of *Rex v. Tubbs*.[94] John Tubbs was one of thirty-two watermen retained by the mayor of the City of London to navigate his barge on the Thames.[95] When Tubbs was seized by a press gang pursuant to a warrant from the Admiralty, he claimed that he was exempt from impressment because he worked for the mayor. Mansfield had to decide two questions: whether impressment was legal and, if it was, whether Tubbs had a valid exemption.

Mansfield was unhappy that he could not avoid resolving what seemed an irreconcilable conflict between the private right of an individual to his freedom and the public need for an adequately manned navy. He was very sorry, he said, "that ... the City of London or ... the Admiralty ... have been prevailed upon to agitate this question." Given Mansfield's disinclination to undermine government authority, it was entirely predictable that he would find a way to uphold the legality of impressment, despite the absence of any statutory precedent. His fertile mind found a way: "The power of pressing," he said, "is founded upon immemorial usage, allowed for ages: if it be so founded and allowed for ages, it can have no ground to stand upon, nor can it be vindicated or justified by any reason but the safety of the State: and the practice is deduced from that trite maxim of the constitutional law of England, 'that private mischief had better be submitted to, than that public detriment and inconvenience should ensue.'"[96]

Mansfield went on to warn that pressing should "be exercised with the greatest moderation, and only upon the most cogent necessity." As to Tubbs's claim that he had an exemption, Mansfield conceded that there might be exemptions to the power to press sailors, which also were based on immemorial usage. However, poor Tubbs had not been able to point to any statute, law book, or other source showing that watermen working for the City of London were exempt from being pressed.[97] A year after the *Tubbs* case, a bill was introduced in Parliament to abolish the press gang. The bill was rejected by an overwhelming majority, and the manpower of the Royal Navy continued to be assured.[98]

Navy impressment applied only to "seamen, marines, sea-faring men or persons rowing or working on boats on rivers not under eighteen years of age or more than fifty-five,"[99] and did not reach foreigners, persons who were accidentally at sea or were boating for amusement, or those who had once been seamen but had changed their occupation. Mansfield, whose court heard most of the impressment cases brought on a writ of habeas corpus, ordered the release of many men who had a valid exemption from impressment. The rate of release in all habeas corpus cases during Mansfield's tenure was 80 per cent, and this included many impressment cases.[100] According to historian Paul Halliday, "nearly a thousand unfortunate seamen probably used habeas corpus to challenge their impressments during the final four decades of the eighteenth century."[101] Press gangs, which were paid according to the number of men they seized, did not always respect the limits of the impressment rules. A newspaper account, three weeks after Mansfield decided the *Tubbs* case, tells a story that unfortunately could have been common:

> Tuesday night as the son of Mr Yates, enameller, in Oxford Street, was shutting up his father's shop saw a prize-gang [*sic*] coming towards him, to avoid which he ran into a back parlor and locked the door. The gang followed and notwithstanding all the entreaties of the father who assured then he would produce his son and convince them he was not fit for their purpose, shattered the door to pieces where they found him, as the father had said, a poor, nerveless, feeble young fellow, not fit even for his father's business, which occasioned him setting him up in another way. The gang, therefore, contenting themselves with the mischief they had done and the alarm into which they had thrown the poor unhappy family left him on his father's hands with the door which he may or may not repair at his leisure. If there be no protection against outrages of this sort Englishmen are in a worse state than the inhabitants of Turkey.[102]

The war at sea also raised the question of the status of captured sailors on American warships. Were they to be treated as prisoners of war or as traitors, subject to trial and execution? In August 1776, a member of the Admiralty privately asked Mansfield for guidance. An American privateer, the *Yankee*, had captured two British merchant ships off the coast of New England and had taken their crew members aboard as prisoners. As the privateer continued its voyage, the prisoners turned the tables on their captors, took control of the ship, and brought it to London. The question asked of Mansfield was what to do with the four captured officers of the *Yankee*.

Mansfield's response, given as "the Confidential Conversation of a private friend," showed both his personal opinion of the status of the American belligerents and his usual pragmatic approach to solving a problem. It eerily reminds one of the present United States government's dilemma as to what to do with "enemy combatants" held at Guantanamo Bay. Mansfield stated that the four officers should not be set free or allowed to return to America, because they were guilty of the crime of piracy and high treason for levying war against Britain. On the other hand, if they were committed to prison, tried for treason, and perhaps executed, there would be calls in America for retaliation against imprisoned British officers. Mansfield's solution was for the King, as commander-in-chief, to hold them aboard a guardship as prisoners of war till further order. If they "are so wickedly advised as to claim to be considered as [British] Subjects and to apply for a writ of habeas corpus, that would be their own act, and the government would be forced to try them for their crime."[103]

When Mansfield was appointed to the bench in 1756, he had been made a baron, the lowest of the five ranks of the peerage, the others being, in ascending order: viscount, earl, marquess, and duke. His ambition was to attain the much more prestigious rank of earl and, since he was childless, to have his nephew Lord Stormont and Stormont's male heirs named as successors to the earldom. In September 1776, when the British army's victory against the Americans in the Battle of Long Island and its capture of New York seemed to justify Mansfield's belligerent advice to the King, Mansfield judged the time ripe to claim his earldom.[104] He mentioned his request privately to the King but asked that no step be taken until he had gone through proper channels by asking Lord North to petition the King to raise him to the rank of earl, with the title descending to the heirs of his father, the 5th Viscount Stormont.[105] As a practical matter, this meant that Mansfield's nephew, the 7th viscount, would inherit the title. Lord North supported Mansfield's promotion, but he reportedly objected to the Stormonts inheriting the title.[106] The King, however, immediately agreed to everything that Mansfield had asked. He wrote to North: "The request of Lord Mansfield after a zealous support of near sixteen years without ever asked any favour from the Crown seemed to entitle him very reasonably to ask the mark of favour he did yesterday."[107] The next day, Mansfield kissed the King's hand at a royal levee and became an earl. A newspaper commented: "It shows plainly how high the lawyer's interest is with the King."[108] Becoming an earl involved the payment of substantial tips: Mansfield's expenses totaled £652, including £175 for the King's household and various gratuities for trumpeters, the Garter King at Arms, etc.[109]

Mansfield's advice that King George treat the colonists as rebels and prosecute the American war vigorously turned sour in October 1777, when General John Burgoyne surrendered his army to the American forces at Saratoga. Saratoga was the turning point of the war. The defeat led France to recognize the independence of the United States of America in February 1778 and to sign a military alliance and commercial agreement with the new nation. A year later, Spain entered the war on the Americans' side.[110] For the first time in a century, Britain found itself in a major war without any allies.[111] For Britain, the war to suppress the rebellion had become secondary to the struggle against France and Spain for global supremacy.[112]

With the war turning against Britain, Mansfield tried to avoid the consequences of the American policy that he had advocated. In February 1778, he paid a visit to Lord Camden "with tears in his eyes confessing the probability of a French war," and asked Camden to do everything in his power to prevent it. Interestingly, Mansfield turned to his old political and legal adversary, not to his nephew Stormont, who was then serving as ambassador to France. Camden's reply was frosty, though hardly unjustified. He told Mansfield that "he had long foreseen the present situation, and endeavoured to prevent it without effect" and that "it was nothing more nor less than a concurrence with [Mansfield's] measures that had plunged us into the greatest distress."[113] In early 1778, when Lord North sent William Eden, a prominent member of Parliament, to America in an unsuccessful attempt to negotiate a settlement of the war, Mansfield made a point of meeting with him before he left.[114] It appears that Mansfield was heavily involved in the abortive peace mission.[115]

Edmund Burke and others attacked Mansfield as an architect of the failed American policy, a secret adviser to the King without ministerial responsibilities, "sitting in silence behind the curtain."[116] Mansfield was widely seen as the éminence grise of the Cabinet, and the true successor of Bute, the Scottish prime minister who had been a confidant of King George in the early 1760s.[117] Many held Mansfield personally responsible for Britain's loss of the colonies. On one occasion, while travelling on circuit, Mansfield was discussing the American war at a dinner and spoke angrily against the two brothers who commanded the British forces in America, Admiral Lord Richard Howe and General William Howe. The Howe brothers saw themselves as peacemakers; even while fighting the colonists, they were attempting to negotiate with General Washington and the Continental Congress.[118] Mansfield said that the two Howes "had no heads," to which his host pointedly – if tactlessly – replied: "Then what will become of the heads of those who sent them?"[119]

As usual, Mansfield's principal critic was William Pitt, Earl of Chatham.

In late 1777 and early 1778, Chatham constantly attacked the ministry in the House of Lords for its defence of the British government's policies and, in particular, its employment of Indians to scalp and torture Americans. According to Campbell, Mansfield, who continued to oppose all measures of conciliation,[120] "silently quailed under him, afraid of being blasted by the lightning of his wrath."[121] On 7 April 1778, Chatham, by then a sick man, delivered a passionate speech in the Lords, appealing to English patriotism and urging a negotiated peace with America and continued hostilities with France. "Shall this great kingdom that has survived whole and entire the Danish depredations, the Scottish inroads ... now fall prostrate before the House of Bourbon?" When Chatham referred to Scotland, he gave a meaningful glance at his old enemy Mansfield.[122] After concluding his speech, Chatham sat down, but then attempted to rise again to respond to another speaker. Camden, an eyewitness, described what happened next:

> He fell back upon his seat, and was to all appearance in the agonies of death. This threw the whole House into confusion; every person was upon his legs in a moment, hurrying from one place to another, some sending for assistance, others producing salts, and others reviving spirits. Many crowding about the Earl to observe his countenance – all affected – most part really concerned; and even those who might have felt a secret pleasure at the accident, yet put on the appearance of distress, except only the Earl of M., who sat still, almost as much unmoved as the senseless body itself.[123]

Some have doubted whether the "Earl of M.," who sat silently alone in the pandemonium that followed Chatham's collapse was Mansfield; there was at least one other earl present whose name began with *M*. Camden was a lifelong enemy of Mansfield, and his account of the event may not have been unbiased. It can also be questioned whether Camden had the time and the presence of mind, amid the bustle and chaos, to see what everyone on the floor of the House was doing, as well as observe the expression on Mansfield's face. Yet Camden's report on Mansfield's behaviour when Chatham collapsed has the ring of truth. For one thing, it was consistent with Mansfield's cold, proud nature. He had suffered humiliation from Chatham's unsparing attacks on him for over thirty years, and perhaps he believed it would be hypocritical to show a feigned concern for his old tormentor.

Camden's description of the scene, with Mansfield the only member of the House remaining seated in the hubbub, was memorably portrayed in

The Death of the Earl of Chatham by American painter John Singleton Copley, which 20,000 visitors paid 1 shilling each to see, and which now hangs in London's National Portrait Gallery.[124] Surprisingly, Mansfield was one of the subscribers for an engraved print of Copley's painting.[125] Two days after his collapse, Chatham was taken to his home in Kent, where he died on 11 May 1778.[126] Mansfield's name is not on the list of those who attended the funeral, and he did not support a bill for providing a pension to the great war leader's heirs.[127]

Chatham's death and the turning of the war against Britain marked the beginning of Mansfield's withdrawal from political life, although he remained a member of the Cabinet until the end of North's ministry in 1782. With the realization in Britain that the American war was lost, Mansfield's influence within the government declined.[128] In September 1779, he was present at a Cabinet meeting when the Earl of Sandwich, First Lord of the Admiralty, accused Lord Stormont, who had returned from Paris when France entered the war, of incompetence. He said that Stormont had failed to give the government timely intelligence about the French fleet, and this lack of intelligence had resulted in the inferiority of the British fleet and its inability to control the North American coast after France entered the war. Stormont not being present, Mansfield took up his nephew's defence and angrily retorted that the Admiralty was itself incompetent. This led to a general discussion of the American war, in which a majority of the Cabinet took a position of moderation toward the colonists, which Mansfield said was nothing less than a recognition of American independence. He accused them of timidity (a charge that, ironically, had often been made against him), and the meeting broke up in a mood of anger and resentment. Mansfield said that he would no longer provide advice to the government or attend Cabinet meetings.[129]

Although still greatly respected as a judge and an individual, he had become an unpopular political figure; the *London Courant* distinguished between his public and private life: "Lord Mansfield's political conduct must excite the indignity and abhorrence of every friend of his country; but considered in the character of a private gentleman no man has a claim to higher veneration. The poor in the neighbourhood of Highgate and Hampstead have been consistently relieved at this time by his Lordship's munificence and he is always a liberal benefactor to real objects of charity."[130]

While seemingly unforgiving toward Chatham, Mansfield displayed the puzzling ambivalence of his character by his willingness to let bygones be bygones when it came to representatives of the newly independent American republic. In 1783, John Adams, who had helped negotiate the treaty that ended the war, was in London. He asked John Singleton Copley, who had painted a magnificent portrait of Mansfield, which is reproduced in this book, (as well as his *Death of Chatham*), about gaining entrance to the House of Lords in order to hear the King's Speech at the opening of Parliament and to witness the formal introduction to the Lords of the Prince of Wales (later to be King George IV), who had reached the age of twenty-one. Copley asked Mansfield for a pass for Adams, and Mansfield willingly complied. Despite having been a leader in the Revolutionary War, Adams had a soft spot in his heart for the British monarchy and its ceremonies. This is how he described the scene:

> Standing in the lobby of the House of Lords, surrounded by a hundred of the first people of the kingdom, Sir Francis Molineux, the gentleman usher of the black rod, appeared suddenly in the room with his long staff, and roared out, with a very loud voice: "Where is Mr Adams, Lord Mansfield's friend?" I frankly avowed myself Lord Mansfield's friend, and was politely conducted, by Sir Francis, to my place. A gentleman said to me the next day: "How short a time has passed since I heard that same Lord Mansfield say, in that same House of Lords, My Lords, if you do not kill him, he will kill you."
>
> Pope had given me, when a boy, an affection for Murray. When in the study and practice of the law, my admiration of the learning, talents, and eloquence of Mansfield had been constantly increasing, though some of his opinions I could not approve. His politics in American affairs I had always detested. But now I found more politeness and good-humor in him than in Richmond, Camden, Burke, or Fox [all of whom had been supporters of the colonists].[131]

19

Protecting Authors and Inventors

Men of ability … may not be deprived of … the reward of their ingenuity and labour.

Lord Mansfield, in his opinion on a copyright case

Whether authors should be given an exclusive right to publish their works and, if so, how long the protection should last were controversial questions in eighteenth-century England. Copyright as we know it today did not exist before the eighteenth century.[1] Authors could obtain an exclusive right to publish their works only if they were able to obtain a licence directly from the King or indirectly from the Company of Stationers, which had a special charter from the King. Restrictions on the right to publish had a political purpose – to prevent the spread of subversive ideas.

The Licensing of the Press Act of 1662,[2] enacted soon after King Charles II's restoration to the throne, prohibited the printing or publication of books and pamphlets without a government licence. The largest London booksellers (who were also printers and publishers) used the statute to their commercial advantage in order to monopolize the book trade. Unlicensed books and pamphlets could be enjoined by the Court of Chancery.

In 1695, Parliament allowed the Press Act to expire. This legitimized piracy and led the booksellers to petition Parliament for protection against unauthorized copying of published works.[3] The result was the first English copyright statute, which came into effect on 10 April 1710.[4] Entitled "An Act for the Encouragement of Learning," it gave an author an exclusive right to publish a work for fourteen years, with renewal for another fourteen years if the author was alive at the expiration of the first period. The penalties for violating the statute were severe. All pirated copies of the work would be forfeited and destroyed, and the offender would be fined one penny for every sheet of the pirated edition found in his custody, with the fine being divided equally between the Crown and the owner of the copyright. This could amount to a sizable penalty.

As a practicing lawyer, Mansfield represented authors or publishers seeking protection against infringement of their works. In 1741 he represented his friend Alexander Pope, obtaining an injunction from the Chancery Court against Edmund Curll (the same publisher whom the Westminster boys had tossed in a blanket when Mansfield was a student there)[5] from publishing letters exchanged between Pope and Jonathan Swift.[6] Curll was not one of the leading booksellers but, rather, was a member of the "pirate realm," who challenged the alliance of the leading booksellers and criticized it as oligarchic and monopolistic.[7] When Curll moved in court to dissolve the injunction, Lord Chancellor Hardwicke ruled against him, saying that the Copyright Act of 1710 protected letters as well as books.

Hardwicke made another important legal point: while the recipient of a letter owned the paper on which the letter was written, the writer of the letter had the exclusive property right to publish the letter. Copyright was an "incorporeal" (i.e., intangible) right, separate from any physical property. This was a novel idea to eighteenth-century lawyers, who were trained to believe that there could be a common law property right only in land or physical goods. Thus, Pope was the owner of the copyright on the letters that he had written to Swift, but not on those that Swift had written to him.

In 1752 Mansfield asked the Chancery Court to enjoin the unauthorized publication of an edition of John Milton's *Paradise Lost*, with annotations by his old Westminster School friend Thomas Newton. Mansfield did not sue for money damages under the Copyright Act, probably because the twenty-eight-year statutory period of the Act on Milton's work had long since lapsed. His argument to the court foreshadowed the views he would later assert as a judge. He made three main points: first, before passage of the Copyright Act, authors had a perpetual property right in their works under the common law (this was a questionable assumption); second, the purpose of the Act was to *add to* authors' protection by imposing penalties on violators, not to *reduce* the protection by limiting the duration of the copyright; and, third, nothing in the Act altered an author's common law property right.

Mansfield also argued that preventing piracy was good public policy: the public was interested in having good, cheap editions, and in this case, the pirated edition of *Paradise Lost* was badly printed on bad paper. Finally, he argued that giving authors a property right in their books would encourage literary production. Chancellor Hardwicke agreed with Mansfield and granted the injunction.[8]

Despite Hardwicke's willingness to enjoin copyright infringers, wholesale piracy continued, particularly by Scottish publishers, who exported unauthorized editions of books to be sold in London. In 1759 about sixty London booksellers joined together in a well-financed campaign to eradicate piracy. Their aim was to control the publication of almost every book that had ever been published in London. Those who refused to join the cartel were threatened with blacklisting.[9]

One of the three trustees chosen to manage the booksellers' campaign was a publisher named Andrew Millar, an enterprising Scottish publisher who had moved to London and established a bookshop in the Strand.[10] Millar had bought the right to publish *The Seasons*, a poem by the Scot James Thomson, published in 1729, which had inspired Antonio Vivaldi to compose his famous violin concertos, *The Four Seasons*. In 1763, six years after the twenty-eight-year copyright on the poem expired, a printer named Robert Taylor published 1,000 unauthorized copies of the work, and Millar sued him.

It was on this dispute that Mansfield's authority as an interpreter of the law – hitherto unquestioned by his fellow judges – was challenged for the first time. *Millar v. Taylor*[11] was the first case to come before the Court of King's Bench under the Copyright Act. Two questions needed to be decided: Did a perpetual copyright under the common law exist before passage of the Copyright Act of 1710? If so, did the Act replace common law copyright or merely supplement it? The three associate justices stated their opinions in order of seniority, beginning with the most junior.

The first two judges opined that Millar owned a common law copyright in Thomson's poem, and that the copyright was not extinguished by the Copyright Act. The third judge, Joseph Yates, thought otherwise. Speaking for three hours, he argued that, while an author had an exclusive common law right to his works while they were in manuscript, this right ended upon publication, from which time his exclusive right was limited to the twenty-eight-year maximum period established by Parliament in the Copyright Act. While an author was entitled to the fruits of his labours, he said, the author had no right to expect that the fruits would be eternal.[12]

Finally, Mansfield delivered his opinion. He began by noting, with a mixture of pride and chagrin, that this was the first instance since he had become chief justice thirteen years earlier where there was a final difference of opinion in the court. He then repeated the point that Lord Chancellor Hardwicke had made when Mansfield was a lawyer representing Alexander Pope: the property right of an author in his work was an "incorporeal" right that "relates to Ideas detached from any Physical Existence."

Mansfield believed that the common law of England gave an author this right not only before publication but also forever afterwards. He conceded that, at first view, it seemed plausible that the Copyright Act, which limited the right to twenty-eight years, had abolished the common law copyright; but after consideration, he had come to the conclusion that abolition could not be *implied* from the Act. If Parliament had intended to take away the common law right, it would have done so *expressly*. Millar therefore was entitled to enforce his exclusive right to publish James Thomson's poem.

Today, Mansfield's support of a perpetual copyright seems misguided because it ignored the balance between the two competing interests that the Copyright Act attempted to achieve. Giving authors and artists an exclusive right to publish their works provided them with an incentive to engage in literary and artistic effort, while limiting the copyright period gave the public the benefit of eventual free access to their works.[13]

Even King George III, who like many of his subjects had great respect for Mansfield's legal wisdom, disagreed with his chief justice on this question. George was a diligent monarch who took an interest in almost everything pertaining to the government of his realm. After summarizing the opinions of the four judges in a letter, he wrote: "It may seem presumptuous ... to venture at deciding which opinion seems most agreeable to common sense; yet ... when an Author publishes to the World his works, he must rest satisfied with the sale of it as His reward, unless he obtains a patent which gives him an exclusive right for a certain number of Years."[14]

Ironically, Mansfield did recognize that the Copyright Act was designed to achieve such a balance in a later case, where the question before his court was not the length of time that an author was protected but, rather, the extent of the protection. He opined that the Act guards against the copying of words and sentiments, but that it does not prohibit a person from any writing on the same subject: "We must take care to guard against two extremes equally prejudicial; the one, that men of ability, who have employed their time for the service of the community, may not be deprived of their just merits, and the reward of their ingenuity and labour; the other, that the world may not be deprived of improvements, nor the progress of the arts be retarded."[15]

As we will see, Mansfield's refusal to place any time limit was later overruled by the House of Lords, but one aspect of his thinking has survived. As in so many other areas of the law, he seemed to have had an uncanny ability to see into the future. Modern legislation, often known by its French term "*droit moral*," gives authors and artists a "moral right" to protect the integrity of their works.[16] In the United Kingdom and Canada, the moral right extends to writers, composers, and visual artists;[17] in the United States, visual artists are protected by statute against the defacing or altering of a painting or sculpture, but writers and composers have no such protection for their works.[18] The moral right enables the creator of a work of art to retain some control over what happens to it, even after he or she sells it.

In *Millar v. Taylor*, Mansfield, without using the term "moral right," asserted that an author should be protected against degradation of his work and his reputation. This was an important part of his argument supporting an author's right to control his work, both before and after publication:

> It is just, that an author should reap the pecuniary profits of his own ingenuity and labour. It is just, that another should not use his name, without his consent. It is fit that he should judge when to publish, whether he ever will publish. It is fit he should not only choose the time, but the manner of publication; how many; what volume; what print. It is fit, he should choose to whose care he will trust the accuracy and correctness of the impression; in whose honesty he will confide, not to foist in additions ...
>
> But the same reasons hold, after the author has published. He can reap no pecuniary profit, if, the next moment after his work comes out, it may be pirated upon worse paper and in worse print, and in a cheaper volume ...
>
> The author may not only be deprived of any profit, but lose the expence he has been at. He is no more master of the use of his own name. He has no control over the correctness of his own work. He can not prevent additions. He can not retract errors. He can not amend; or cancel a faulty edition. Any one may print, pirate, and perpetuate the imperfections, to the disgrace and against the will of the author.[19]

Mansfield's view prevailed by a 3–1 vote of the court. *Millar v. Taylor* gave authors a perpetual copyright in their works, even though the Copyright Act limited copyright to twenty-eight years. But the dispute was not over. A few years later, Andrew Donaldson, a well-known Scottish bookseller who also sold his books in London, decided to challenge the London booksellers' group. He printed several thousand copies of Thomson's poem and displayed them in his London shop. Thomas Beckett, who had acquired the rights to *The Seasons* from Millar's heirs (Millar had died in 1768), obtained an injunction from Lord Chancellor Henry Bathurst. Donaldson then appealed the decision to the House of Lords.

The case came up before the House of Lords on 4 February 1774, and went on for eight sessions during that month. Huge crowds gathered to hear it, and only those who arrived early were able to find seats in the gallery of the House. Among those present were the politician Edmund Burke, the playwright Oliver Goldsmith, and the actor David Garrick.[20] Edward Thurlow, the attorney general (and future lord chancellor), started off, making a strong argument that Thomson's poem was in the public domain, saying that the Copyright Act "was not merely an accumulative act declaratory of the common law, and giving additional penalties, but that it was a new law that gave to learned men a property which they had not before, and that it was an incontrovertible proof that there previously existed no common law right."[21] Lord Camden, Mansfield's old political opponent, then proposed that each of the twelve "law lords" (the members of the House of Lords who were judges) state his opinion.[22] Five opined either that no copyright existed under the common law or, if such a right did exist, that the Copyright Act of 1710 had abolished it; five agreed with the majority decision in *Millar v. Taylor* that a perpetual copyright existed, independent of the statute.

Only Camden and Mansfield had not yet spoken. Camden rose and made an eloquent and persuasive speech, "with many dazzling metaphors and conceits."[23] He argued that copyright had never been recognized by the common law. Rather, it originated as a monopoly granted by the Stationers' Company and the royal prerogative (which had been abolished in the seventeenth century). The Copyright Act of 1710 was simply designed to give authors some limited protection.[24] While he spoke, he looked pointedly at Mansfield, who sat silently, seeming "to all appearance to be forming an oration with eyebrows and thumbs."[25] When Camden finished, everyone in the House looked at Mansfield, waiting for him to speak, but still he remained silent.[26] At that, Camden moved that the decision of the Chancery Court be reversed, and the House of Lords voted in favour of the motion. The Copyright Act protected authors' works for fourteen or twenty-eight years, but for no longer.

The House of Lords had overruled Mansfield's ruling in *Millar v. Taylor* that there was a perpetual copyright under the common law, and Mansfield said not a word in opposition. If he had spoken up in favour of his previous decree, the law lords would have divided evenly by a vote of 6–6, and the House of Lords might not have been willing to overrule him. Why didn't he speak, despite his strongly held views on this important issue? We do not know, but various explanations have been offered. His enemies believed that he "had not the courage to rise up in his place and defend his own judgment."[27] Others speculated that, having given his opinion on the issue, "he thought it becoming not then to repeat it."[28] This latter explanation seems unlikely, for he seldom hesitated to sit on cases in which his personal interest or connection might raise a question as to his ability to rule impartially. Another possible explanation is that Mansfield, who was not accustomed to having his rulings questioned, felt that it was presumptuous of lesser legal minds to challenge him and that it was beneath his dignity to argue with them. He had stated his views clearly and in detail five years earlier in *Millar v. Taylor*, and perhaps he felt no need to repeat them. But it is also possible that he was indeed cowed by Camden's persuasive argument, which swayed many members of the House.[29]

The public rebuke that Mansfield suffered in the *Donaldson* case was his first setback as a judge. James Boswell commented, likening Mansfield to a Scottish judge who had once been overruled: "Before that, whenever he opened his mouth, it was acquiesced in, but now they saw he could be in the wrong ... The charm was broke. [His defeat] destroyed his infallibility as the Literary Property Cause did Lord Mansfield's, who before that was a Pope in the House of Lords."[30]

In the mid-eighteenth-century, new inventions poured out, in spinning and weaving cloth, metalworking, and steam engines, among others. Patent law, however, remained undeveloped. Few cases involving patents came before the common law courts – only one case in the 1760s and four in the 1770s.[31] The first patents were royal grants of monopolies to inventors or entrepreneurs for the main purpose of improving the country's competitive position in an industry or trade. The first patent law, the Statute of Monopolies, enacted by Parliament in 1623, limited all future patents to fourteen years and required that patent disputes be resolved by the common law courts.[32] Yet, in practice, disputes continued to be decided by the King's Privy Council until early in the eighteenth century, when jurisdiction was finally transferred to the common law courts.[33]

As he had done in other areas of the law that affected commerce and industry, Mansfield studied the practices of merchants and industrialists and incorporated these practices into the common law. His patent-law decisions were characteristically pragmatic. For example, he ruled that, while there could not be two patents for the same machine, a patent could be granted for a new, differently constructed machine that would make the same goods as an existing machine.[34] In another case, he ruled that an invention did not have to be entirely new in order to be patented; a patent could be granted for an improvement on an existing machine (in this case a machine for making stockings).[35]

Mansfield's most important patent decision, *Liardet v. Johnson*,[36] involved the invention of a new kind of stucco, a kind of cement consisting of lime, sand, and water, used to coat the walls of buildings. During the eighteenth century, stucco was used on Palladian palaces in Italy, but when English builders tried to use it, they found that it was not durable in the damp, cool English climate.

John Liardet, a native of Switzerland who had settled in England, was granted a patent on an oil-based stucco that promised to overcome this problem. The patent grant was conditioned on Liardet filing, within four months, a "specification" that described his invention. The Earl of Northumberland, who apparently was providing the financing for Liardet's research, introduced him to the Adam brothers, two of whom, Robert and James, were noted Scottish architects and decorators. In exchange for a payment of £500, Liardet assigned his patent to the Adam brothers.[37] Robert Adam was the architect who made major alterations, which included the use of Liardet's stucco, on Kenwood, Mansfield's home on Hampstead Heath.[38]

In May 1777, the Adam brothers and Liardet sued John Johnson, a designer of country houses, claiming that he had inspected Liardet's specification, copied it, and used the patented stucco. There were two trials of the case, both before Lord Mansfield. The first trial produced a verdict for the plaintiffs, but there was criticism that Mansfield may have been biased because of his own relationship with Robert Adam; this may be why Mansfield granted the defendant a new trial.[39]

Nevertheless, Mansfield presided again at the second trial, which began at 9 a.m. on 18 July 1778 and lasted over fourteen hours. Several experienced and eminent architects, plasterers, and builders testified that Liardet's invention was not only new but also useful to the trade.[40] It was not until 10 p.m. that Mansfield delivered his instructions to the jury.[41] His instructions, based on common sense and his understanding of commercial practice, set the foundation of modern patent law.

Mansfield began by pointing out that, in deciding whether a patent should be granted, two extremes had to be avoided. Inventors should not be deprived of the benefit of their inventions, for it was in the interest of the public to give them an incentive to make new discoveries. On the other hand, monopolies should not be granted for inventions already in use by others. He told the jurors that they had to answer three questions in order to decide whether or not Johnson was liable for infringement of Liardet's patent: First, did the defendant use the plaintiff's invention? Second, was the invention new or old? And third, did the specification for the invention show others how to make it themselves?

The answer to Mansfield's first question was obvious; Johnson could not be liable unless he actually made use of Liardet's invention. The answers to the second and third questions also may seem clear today, at least to lawyers, because these principles are embedded in modern patent law, but they were not so obvious at the time. Without relying on any legal precedent, Mansfield was creating new law, or at least making the law conform to then-current commercial practices. What does it mean to say that an invention is new? Here, Mansfield referred to the expert testimony of the architects and plasterers. Newness was not an abstract concept, but one that related to commercial practice and experience: "The great point is, is it a new thing in the trade, or was it used and known by them?" An invention is new if it was not known to the trade at the time the patent was granted. In order to prevail, the defendant would have to show either that there was continuous and successful prior use of the invention, or that the invention was common knowledge *in the trade*.[42]

On his third question – did the specification enable others to make the invention? – Mansfield was making an important point that reflected the influence of the philosophy of John Locke on his thinking. Locke's theory of natural rights said that in the state of nature every individual possessed the right to life, liberty, and property.[43] According to Locke, when individuals join to live in a community, they give up some of their natural rights, in exchange for the civil rights that the community provides.[44] Mansfield applied Locke's theory to an inventor's patent rights: by disclosing his invention in a specification, an inventor made a bargain with society; he received "a temporary monopoly in return for revealing his invention."[45] Mansfield spelled it out: "For the condition of giving encouragement [to inventors] is this: that you must specify upon record your invention in such a way as shall teach an artist, when your term is out, to make it – and to make it as well as you by your directions; for then at the end of the term, the public shall have the benefit of it. The inventor has the benefit during the term, and the public have the benefit after that."[46] Justice Buller, Mansfield's colleague and disciple on the Court of King's Bench, put the matter succinctly a few years later: "The specification is the price which the patentee is to pay for the monopoly."[47]

The *Liardet* case was forward-looking in another way that had little to do specifically with patent law. It is well to remember that the eighteenth-century English courts had not yet developed rules of evidence. One of Mansfield's great contributions to the law was to provide some principles as to what evidence could or could not be admitted in a jury trial.[48] One of these principles involved the testimony of expert witnesses, i.e., persons possessing specialized knowledge, usually of a scientific kind, but not necessarily having any knowledge of the particular facts of the case being tried.

Consistent with his usual practice of looking to the customs and usages of trade and industry in formulating legal rules, Mansfield placed great emphasis in his instructions to the jury in the *Liardet* case on the testimony of expert witnesses. In fact, the decision rested largely on their testimony. The validity of Liardet's patent depended on whether his invention was new, and only those who worked in the construction industry – architects, plasterers, and builders – could say, as a practical matter, whether or not Liardet's stucco could be considered new.

A few years after the Liardet decision, Mansfield made explicit his support of the use of expert testimony. The question before the court in *Folkes v. Chadd*[49] was whether a sandbank that had been erected to prevent the sea from overflowing had caused the choking up of a harbour. An expert on the construction of harbours named Smeaton was called as a witness; his testimony was challenged because he was asked merely to give his opinion, not to testify about the facts of the case. Mansfield disagreed: "In matters of science, the reasonings of men of science can only be answered by men of science ... Mr Smeaton understands the construction of harbours, the causes of their destruction, and how remedied. In matters of science no other witnesses can be called ... I cannot believe that where the question is, whether a defect arises from a natural or an artificial cause, the opinions of men of science are not to be received."[50]

Today, expert testimony is commonly used and relied upon. In the United Kingdom, an expert's opinion "is admissible to furnish the court with ... information which is likely to be outside the experience and knowledge of a judge or jury."[51] In Canada, not more than five "professional or other experts entitled by the law or practice to give opinion evidence" may be called by each side in a criminal or civil trial.[52] The rules of the American federal courts echo Mansfield's language in the *Folkes* case: "If scientific, technical, or other specialized knowledge will assist the trier of fact to understand the evidence or to determine a fact in issue," an expert "may testify thereto."[53] As in so many other areas of the law, Mansfield was prescient in his willingness to rely on scientific experts to guide his court to a just decision.

In addition to copyright and patents, Mansfield heard several trademark cases, a third area of what is now collectively called intellectual property. Many of these cases involved a person's "passing off" his own product as someone else's. Mansfield was severe in punishing those guilty of this offence.[54] In the eighteenth century, London was famous all over Europe for the skill of its watchmakers and the beauty of the watches they made.[55] One watchmaker brought suit against another who had violated a seventeenth-century statute that penalized any watchmaker who put any name on a watch other than that of the person who had actually made it. Mansfield had no patience with an argument by defence counsel that his client was ignorant of this long-forgotten law, and that, anyway, it was a common practice of the trade to put names other than the maker's on watches. Mansfield told the jury: "There are two grounds for liability: First, the injury done a man of reputation [by] indifferent work; and, second, the injury it did the nation by bringing the trade into disrepute with foreigners. English watches were the best in Europe; when the buyer found himself disappointed in the quality, the maker's name fell into disrepute." The jury awarded the plaintiff £100 in damages. A newspaper that reported the case commented patriotically: "It is hoped this decision will put a stop to this mode of imposing … on all foreigners who give the preference to the English artist from the superior excellence of his work."[56]

In another case, Mansfield imposed a fine of £100 on a silversmith who put marks on silver-plated wares in imitation of the marks used in the industry to show that the silverware had been assayed and was made of pure silver. If the fine was not paid, the culprit was to serve a year in prison.[57]

Mansfield placed his imprint on patent law in a way that he was unable to do on copyright law. While he had argued unsuccessfully that an author's exclusive right to publish his works should be perpetual, he always acknowledged that a patent should give an inventor an exclusive right only for a limited period. It is unclear why Mansfield took a different approach to these two related areas of the law. One reason may have been that patents, unlike copyrights, had been regulated by statute since the early seventeenth century. Another possible reason was that Mansfield believed that the common law gave protection to authors but not to inventors. A third possibility is that the protection of literary works should be perpetual because it involved a conflict between an individual's right to publish at will and the government's right to create a monopoly, with Mansfield invariably coming down on the side of government authority. A patent, on the other hand, should be limited in duration because it created a monopoly that might inhibit commercial and industrial growth, which Mansfield wholeheartedly supported.

20

Women and Marriage

Forgetting he was a judge and remembering only that he was a man …
Morning Herald, reporting on Mansfield's actions in resolving a custody dispute

Mansfield treated the women in his life with affection and respect. His own long-lasting marriage was marked by mutual respect and untouched by scandal or by any apparent discord. He greatly enjoyed the company of women. He had several friends among well-educated, elite women, most notably the Duchess of Portland, with whom his friendship lasted from the 1740s until her death forty years later. As a widower he enjoyed the companionship of women at the fashionable spas of Bath and Tunbridge Wells. At Kenwood, he would go riding and visiting with his great-niece Lady Elizabeth Murray, who lived at Kenwood until she married and moved away in 1785. And in the last years of his life, he was looked after by two nieces and his illegitimate great-niece, Dido Elizabeth Belle, for whom he felt a warm affection and to whom he left sizable legacies.[1] In short, he "was surrounded by … vibrant and elegant young women."[2]

In his role as a judge, Mansfield was sensitive to the economic and social vulnerability of women, and there are numerous instances of his actively protecting them. A newspaper report of a custody dispute is eloquent proof of his humane approach to matters of this kind. The question before the court was whether a wife who had separated from her husband by mutual consent should have access to their only daughter. The husband claimed that, as a father, he should have sole authority over his child. Mansfield disagreed:

> We could not help observing ... that [Mansfield] showed a manifest inclination in favour of the fond and anxious affections of a tender mother. Forgetting he was a judge and remembering only that he was a man, he employed his eloquence, his address and even his influence in recommendation of a proposal made by himself; that the father should have the sole management of the child's education and that Mrs L. should have the privilege of enjoying her daughter's society at her own house during a visit for a week at certain stated periods.[3]

An example of how Mansfield's decency and sense of fairness influenced his judicial behaviour is *The King v. Wood*,[4] where a woman appeared in court to accuse her husband of "having attempted to take her away from a house where she had been, his pulling her out of bed before several people and some other indecencies and violences." Justice Buller, who usually agreed with Mansfield, said that the case should be dismissed, since it appeared that the woman had been away from her husband and that he had a right to reclaim her. But Mansfield was struck by the "indecency and cruelty of the proceeding as stated by the wife" (which had to be taken as true at this point in the proceeding), and stated that the court ought and would interpose its authority to protect the woman. Her husband denied all of his wife's allegations, but Mansfield said that he could apply to the court later to dismiss the case if he was willing to submit sworn affidavits.[5]

In another case, Mansfield refused to enforce a domestic agreement that he considered immoral. A man had promised in writing to support a woman and to give her an annuity of £60 a year if she lived with him in an unmarried state. But if she left him or went to another man, he would no longer be required to provide for her or leave her an annuity. After the man died, the woman sued the administrator of the man's estate for her annuity. In rejecting the woman's claim, Mansfield's judgment was severe, suggesting that he may have known more of the circumstances than the law report of the case discloses: "It [the annuity] is the price of prostitution ... for if she becomes virtuous, she is to lose the annuity ... The bond is illegal and void."[6]

Mansfield showed his concern for underprivileged women in other ways. He tried to get a bill through the House of Lords that would have relieved the misery of poor women with children in their arms who had to ride on the roof of stagecoaches enduring "storm and wind, rain, hail and the severity of frost, night after night, in long stages." When the bill was rejected, he had an experimental long carriage built, holding fourteen passengers inside and charging a reduced price. The carriage, which was called "The Lone Frigate," made a run from London to Portsmouth.[7] It is not known whether this ever became a commercial enterprise.

In the eighteenth century, a promise to marry, even if not made in writing, was enforceable.[8] As one newspaper put it, Mansfield "admired the spirit and resentment" shown by juries that punished "dangling lovers who obtain the affections of credulous young women, leave them in return the possession of broken hearts and ineffectual tears."[9] The jilted lover (usually, but not always, the woman) could recover damages from a person who breached a promise to marry, and Mansfield usually enforced these promises.[10] In summing up the evidence in one case, he said: "certainly each party has a right to retract at any time previous to the ceremony ... if they apprehend unhappiness to be the event but ... the retracting party if able, should make good the damages sustained to the other through the treaty."[11]

In *Morton v. Fenn*,[12] the defendant Fenn, a wealthy man of seventy, promised to marry Morton, a woman of fifty-three, if she went to bed with him that night. She agreed, and they evidently enjoyed it so much that they then lived together for a considerable time. Although Fenn several times repeated his promise to marry her, he eventually left her and married another woman. When Morton sued Fenn for £2,000 for breach of promise, his lawyer, the future Lord Chancellor Thomas Erskine, argued in defence that the contract was illegal because the "consideration" she gave for the promise (i.e., to go to bed with him) was immoral, and that she was equally at fault with him. Mansfield disagreed: the parties were not equally at fault; rather, it "was a cheat on the part of the man," and he was liable to her for breach of promise. Mansfield suggested, however, that they settle the case for £500, which they did.

In *Lowe v. Peers*,[13] Mansfield was unwilling to enforce a contract involving a marriage, but he, nevertheless, remained consistent in his support of the institution. After a long courtship, Newsham Peers had made an unusual promise in writing to Catherine Lowe: he did not agree to marry her, but he promised her that he would not marry anyone else, and that he would pay her £1,000 if he did. When he broke the promise and married another woman, Lowe sued for the promised £1,000. Mansfield pointed out that there was a great difference between promising to marry a particular person and promising not to marry anyone else. Because this was an agreement *in restraint of* marriage, it was against public policy, and the court refused to enforce it.

Mansfield expressed his support of the institution of marriage most clearly in a ruling that evidence given by a husband or a wife that a child was born out of wedlock was not admissible in court. As a modern writer has observed, until that time, "children born out of wedlock ... were left fatherless in the eyes of the law. Paternity actions could be brought, but in the absence of genetic testing capabilities, the outcome would depend solely on the man's access to the woman during the time of the child's conception. It was her word against his, and the burden of proof rested on the mother. This system typically left the child illegitimate and without access to financial support."[14]

The dispute in question was whether a boy had been born before or after his parents' marriage, and the narrow question raised in court was whether a written declaration by the now-deceased mother as to the date of the birth could be admitted in evidence. If the birth had occurred before the marriage, the boy was illegitimate and could not inherit his parents' estate. Mansfield allowed the declaration to be admitted, but, consistent with his practice of establishing a principle of law to guide future litigants, he added a proviso, which became known as the Mansfield Rule. He said: "As to the time of the birth, the father and mother are the most proper witnesses to prove it. But it is a rule, founded in decency, morality, and policy, that they shall not be permitted to say after marriage, that they have had no connection, and therefore that the offspring is spurious; more especially the mother, who is the offending party."[15]

Mansfield's views about marriage were, above all, humane and practical. In 1781, after deciding a case involving what is today referred to as common law marriage, he gave an informal, but revealing, discourse from the bench on the subject. A man and woman had lived together for several years without being married. On his death, the man left his estate to their children. He also left a certificate stating that he had married the woman before his death. More distant relatives sued to recover the estate from the children on the ground that they were illegitimate. Mansfield ruled that the couple's cohabitation as man and wife had the validity of a marriage.

Having ruled on the dispute before him, Mansfield then described an anonymous letter he had once received regarding the case of *Stapleton v. Stapleton*,[16] decided by Chancellor Hardwicke in 1736. Stapleton had lived for several years with a woman without marrying her, and the couple had several children. Fearing that the children would be bastardized, he married the woman. Upon his death, several relatives were able to wrest the estate from the children, successfully arguing that Stapleton's subsequent marriage was an acknowledgment that the couple's children born before the marriage were illegitimate.

Mansfield went on with his story: as a result of the *Stapleton* decision he had received a letter from a wealthy man who was living with a woman out of wedlock. He had fathered several children by her, and being a virtuous man, he wished to make her his wife; but now he wasn't sure that he should. He begged Mansfield, as a lawyer and a gentleman, to advise him how he should act. Mansfield replied "that in order to obtain peace of mind the proper person to apply to for advice and consolation was the rector of his parish ... but if he asked him [Mansfield] for advice as a lawyer and a gentleman he must advise him in that capacity not to marry the woman."[17]

In considering questions regarding marriage, Mansfield exercised his usual lawyerlike caution. Robert Trevor, the British minister to The Hague, met a Dutch woman whom he planned to marry, and he asked Mansfield whether a marriage in Holland would be recognized in England. Mansfield, then solicitor general, advised him that after his marriage under Dutch law, it would be prudent to have a second ceremony presided over by a priest of the Church of England. He wrote to Trevor: "Though the first kind of marriage would in my opinion answer all intents and purposes to the greatest degree of probability, yet I can't say with absolute certainty that no question can arise upon such a marriage ... Besides your public capacity seems an additional reason for your being married according to the laws of your country. There seems to me no possible objection to performing the ceremony twice, and I do by all means advise your so doing."[18]

A married woman had very few legal rights in eighteenth-century England. Basically, she could do nothing without her husband's consent. Under the law, a husband and wife were one person, and that person was the husband.[19] Lord Mansfield described a married woman's status this way: "The wife has no separate power of contracting. She has no property of her own; her personal estate absolutely, and her real estate during coverture [i.e., marriage] are her husband's; she, therefore cannot contract, but he is bound to support her."[20] A historian of social life in eighteenth-century England writes that "marriage turned the obsequious lover into the imperious husband ... Genteel wives took it absolutely for granted that their husbands enjoyed formal supremacy in marriage."[21] But, she continues, in practice the dynamics of any particular marriage "depended on the interplay of a variety of factors, including wealth, prior property agreements, relations with kindred, age, skills, personality and attractiveness. The extent of conjugal compatibility and affection [played] a determining rule in marital power relations."[22]

Mansfield decided several cases defining the contractual rights and obligations of women, a subject that was of significant concern to merchants who dealt with them.[23] Before Mansfield's time, the courts had created one very limited exception to the rule that a married woman lacked the legal capacity to make a contract or to sue or be sued: if a husband was exiled for life or if he was out of the country and swore never to return, and his wife remained in the country, she acquired the capacity to sue or be sued on her own behalf.

In a series of decisions, Mansfield progressively enlarged this exception. In *Ringsted v. Lady Lanesborough*,[24] a husband and wife had executed a separation agreement under which he paid her a large amount for her separate support. Afterwards they lived separately until his death, he in Ireland and she in England. During his lifetime, she ran up debts to a tradesman, who sued her for them. Her defence was that, as a married woman, she could not be sued.

Mansfield disagreed. He conceded that under the common law a wife had no power to make a contract, but he was unwilling to follow a precedent if it did not make sense: "General rules are ... varied by change of circumstances. Cases arise within the letter, yet not within the reason, of the rule; and exceptions are introduced, which, grafted upon the rule, form a system of law."[25] Turning to the case at hand, he pointed out that once the separation agreement was signed, the wife was no longer under her husband's control. "Credit was given to her as a single woman; and shall she now be permitted to say that she was not single?"[26]

Recognizing that there was no exact precedent for the case, Mansfield said that he therefore had to make a new precedent "from reason and analogy."[27] As in the cases involving exile, the husband was out of the country when the wife incurred the debt and so could not be sued. He had died before the lawsuit began, but even if he were alive, he would not be subject to the process of the court. Therefore, she could be sued alone and "cannot avail herself of this most iniquitous defence."[28]

At first glance, imposing liability on the wife does not seem to strike a blow for the emancipation of married women. But Mansfield, who always considered the practical consequences of his decisions, pointed out that holding a married woman liable under these circumstances not only gave justice to her creditor but also "mercy to the woman herself, for it enables her to obtain credit."[29]

In two cases decided soon after the *Ringsted* decision, Mansfield further loosened the exception to the rule that a married woman could not make a contract or be sued. In one of these cases, *Corbett v. Poelnitz*,[30] a husband and wife agreed to live separately, and he agreed to pay her £1,600 annually for her support. Unlike in *Ringsted*, where the husband could not be sued because he lived abroad, in this case the husband continued to live in England. Here, the wife had made a contract with a merchant, who sued her as a "feme sole" (i.e., a single woman).

The *Corbett* case provides an excellent example of how Mansfield shaped the law in order to do justice. After mentioning the exception to the rule, where a husband was out of the country, Mansfield asked rhetorically what was the reason for the exception, and then answered his own question:

> Because the wife acts as a single woman, gains credit as such, receives the benefit, and shall be liable to the loss: and where she had an estate to her separate use, in justice she ought to be liable to the extent of it ... The only question then is, whether a woman married, but living separate from her husband by agreement, having a large separate maintenance settled on her, continuing to live notoriously as a single woman, contracting and getting credit as such, and the husband not being liable, shall be sued as a feme sole? I think she should; it is just that it should be so.[31]

Following his undeviating view that a precedent must be based on a principle that future litigants can follow and rely on, Mansfield laid down the following principle: "where a woman has a separate estate, and acts and receives credit as a feme sole, she shall be liable as such."[32] Regardless of whether the husband was abroad or in England, this is what justice required.[33]

Mansfield did not allow the exceptions to swallow up the general rule that a married woman could not be sued. In one case, a woman ordered furniture and had work done on a house in St James's Street where she lived by herself in elegant style. Before all the furniture was delivered, the contractor learned that she was a married woman and that her husband lived in London. He went ahead with the work anyway, and when he later found out that the husband was insolvent, he sued the wife. Mansfield dismissed the suit: "If a married woman was to pass as a single woman, she would not be permitted afterwards to say she was married, for that would be a cheat. But here she never said she had no husband or was single and it was her debt.

And when [the contractor] knew she had a husband he continued to supply her with goods."[34]

Compared with the Victorian era that followed, the eighteenth century was an openly licentious period. The newspapers gleefully reported the details of any trial involving sex and marriage. Perhaps the most sensational case of the century was the bigamy trial of the Duchess of Kingston. Elizabeth Chudleigh, a maid of honour to the Princess of Wales, had married Augustus John Hervey, a lieutenant in the navy (who later rose to the rank of admiral), in 1744.[35] The marriage was kept secret, because celibacy was a condition of her job with the princess. They had a child in 1747, a boy who died in infancy.[36] The couple eventually separated, and for several years Elizabeth lived with the unmarried Duke of Kingston. In 1768, when she was forty-eight, she brought a suit against Hervey in an ecclesiastical court on the ground of "jactitation," i.e., that he was falsely claiming to be married to her. The suit was most likely collusive – she is reputed to have paid Hervey £16,000 to lose the case[37] – her reason for bringing the case being her desire to marry the duke. Although Hervey never remarried, he apparently was happy to be rid of her. In any case, he did not put up a credible defence to her fraudulent claim that she was a single woman. The ecclesiastical court co-operatively ruled that the couple was not married, and a few months later Elizabeth married the Duke of Kingston. The *Morning Post* stated that Hervey had sold his wife to the Duke of Kingston for £11,000, upon which Hervey brought a libel suit against the newspaper and was awarded damages of £300.[38]

After four years of married life, the duke died, leaving his wife all of his personal property and a life interest in his real estate. The duke's nephew and heir, Evelyn Meadows, who was disinherited by the duke's will, managed to get Elizabeth indicted for bigamy. She pleaded not guilty, on the ground that the ecclesiastical court's decision in the jactitation case that she was not married to Hervey was conclusive.

When she appeared in Mansfield's court to seek bail on 24 May 1775, she received astonishingly sympathetic treatment for a person accused of a felony. A newspaper reported the event:

> A stout lady of fifty or thereabouts, not without traces of former charm, was ushered into Lord Mansfield's presence. It was clear that she was a person of consideration, for she was attended by the Duke of

> Newcastle and Lord Northumberland as well as by the Sheriff of Middlesex. She had been waiting in an ante-chamber till Lord Mansfield and his brethren should announce that he was ready to receive her.
>
> Arrived in Court, the stout lady curtsied to the Judges, seated herself between Mr Justice Aston and her ducal companion, and calmly listened to the reading of a long and tedious document by the Clerk of the Court. This concluded, she entered into recognizances, undertook to appear in the House of Lords on a later date, and then … "in a very polite manner, took leave of the Court and retired."[39]

Mansfield granted her bail, although he later said that no person to be tried by the House of Lords for a felony had ever been let out on bail.[40] Elizabeth doubtless received deferential treatment from Mansfield because of her rank as a duchess. (Even if found to be married to Hervey, she would still be a peeress because in 1775 Hervey had succeeded to the title of Earl of Bristol; her correct title was either Duchess of Kingston or Countess of Bristol.) Another possible reason why Mansfield treated her with respect was her close connection with the Duke of Newcastle, who accompanied her to court. Newcastle had been a close friend of the deceased Duke of Kingston and was the nephew and heir of the 1st Duke of Newcastle, Mansfield's old patron, friend, and political associate, who had died in 1768.[41]

In any event, Mansfield seems to have befriended Elizabeth;[42] she later said that around this time, Mansfield met with her privately and reassured her that she was in no danger of punishment for bigamy, even if she were to be found guilty.[43] Bigamy was a "clergyable" offence, meaning that a first-time offender would not receive the death penalty; and as a peeress, she was unlikely to suffer the lesser (but cruel) penalty of being burned in the hand and jailed for a year.[44]

Throughout the proceeding, Mansfield did his utmost to help the duchess avoid being tried for bigamy. While Elizabeth was awaiting trial in November 1775, he argued in the House of Lords that the government had no interest in the case because her indictment had been instigated by a private individual, and that it was connected with disputes about property. Furthermore, even if she were convicted, no good would result to the public. Her conviction would not operate as an example because, as a peeress, she would not suffer any punishment.[45] Three weeks later, Mansfield again tried to persuade the Lords to drop the case, arguing, "I cannot perceive that any one consequence can possibly result from this trial, either in a private or public light."[46]

Despite Mansfield's arguments, the duchess was brought to trial before the House of Lords on 15 April 1776. The trial lasted five days and was the sensation of London. It was unprecedented for a peeress to be tried for a felony. A lady who was present described the scene:

> It was an event which caused more stir than the war with America, and a sight which, for beauty and magnificence, was exceeded only by a coronation. The social world rose at seven, and by eight was seated in full dress in Westminster Hall. The Duchess of Portland was there in the Queen's box on the opening day, and she "liked it very much." It was indeed as good as a play. When all were seated, "and the King-at-arms had commanded silence on pain of imprisonment (which, however, was very ill observed) the gentleman of the black rod was commanded to bring in his prisoner. Elizabeth, calling herself Duchess-dowager of Kingston, walked in ... [she] was dressed in deep mourning: a black hood on her head, her hair modestly dressed and powdered, a black silk sack, with crape trimmings; black gauze, deep ruffles, and black gloves." She was attended by "four virgins," dressed in white ... Peeresses came with their work bags full of good things to eat. Since the Duke of Newcastle's apartments were in Westminster, his party "had only to open a door to get at a very fine collation of all sorts of meats and wines with tea." Several of the elite stayed until seven; "then, after have been twelve hours fasting, they went to Mrs Delany's [a close friend of Lady Mansfield] [and] ate voraciously of mutton chops, lamb pye, lobster, and apple puffs."[47]

Elizabeth was convicted of bigamy, largely because of the testimony of Ann Cradock, a servant of Elizabeth's aunt who swore that she had been present at Elizabeth's wedding to Hervey in 1744.[48] The peers, having been advised by the twelve royal judges that the ecclesiastical court's ruling that Hervey and Elizabeth were not married was not binding on them, voted unanimously to find her guilty of bigamy. Even Mansfield concurred. Only Newcastle supported her in any manner, saying that she was "guilty erroneously, but not intentionally."[49]

As a peeress, Elizabeth was entitled to immediate discharge without suffering a burning of her hand or imprisonment.[50] (Her treatment may be contrasted with an earlier case of a soldier who was found guilty of bigamy; the judge (not Mansfield) ordered him to be burned in the hand, and the sheriff gave particular orders to the executioner to show no favour to the prisoner.[51])

So, although Elizabeth was convicted of bigamy, she suffered no punishment, just as Mansfield had predicted. She escaped in an open boat to France before Evelyn Meadows, the Duke of Kingston's nephew, could bring a legal proceeding against her to challenge his uncle's will. As a result, she kept the fortune that the duke had left to her and was able to live comfortably in St Petersburg and Paris, where she died in 1788.[52] She remained legally married to Hervey, with the title of Countess of Bristol, although they never lived together.

The case of the Duchess of Kingston gave Mansfield an opportunity to establish an important rule of evidence. During the trial, the solicitor general called Caesar Hawkins, a surgeon, as a witness for the prosecution. After establishing that Hawkins knew both Hervey and the duchess, he asked whether either of them had told him that they were married. Hawkins replied that he could not, consistent with his professional honour, disclose information that he had received in confidence. At this point, Mansfield intervened. He said that a surgeon's professional status alone did not give him a privilege to avoid giving evidence in court as to whether parties to a lawsuit were married or whether they had a child.[53] Hawkins was then allowed to answer the question. Mansfield did not, however, spell out exactly when a physician could assert a privilege on behalf of a patient.

Later in the trial, one of the duchess's lawyers called Hervey's attorney, William Berkley, as a witness. Berkley also demurred, saying that any knowledge he had of the case arose from his being Hervey's attorney, and that he could not testify, consistent with his honour and the duty he owed to Hervey. The defence lawyer replied that he had called Berkley merely to find out what had passed between him and the key witness Ann Cradock, "being sent to get her to attend and prove the marriage." Again, Mansfield spoke up, and this time he was more explicit on the question of privilege. He said that an attorney could refuse to testify only as to information revealed to him by his client in order to obtain the attorney's advice or instruction with regard to the client's defence. But an attorney was required to testify as to collateral facts, such as what a third party said to him.[54]

Mansfield's two rulings on the privilege of confidentiality that a physician or a lawyer may assert in court have had a lasting impact on the law. One modern writer states: "In this sensational case of private agendas and personal interests, is to be found the precedent that bound the whole of an evolving medical profession on this issue of medical confidentiality. The legacy of the bigamous Duchess is still with us today."[55]

Another *cause célèbre* where Mansfield showed a softness toward an aristocratic woman was the so-called Douglas Cause. The Duke of Douglas, the last survivor of the noblest family in Scotland, had no children, and his closest relative and heir was his beautiful headstrong sister, Lady Jane Douglas. She had secretly married a down-and-out Jacobite named Colonel John Stewart, and they had gone to live in Paris. In July 1748, at the age of about fifty, Lady Jane supposedly gave birth to twin boys. When Lady Jane told her brother about her marriage to a Jacobite, he cut off her allowance, leaving her and the colonel practically penniless.

The Duke of Douglas died in 1751, and some years later Archibald Douglas, one of Lady Jane's twins, claimed the inheritance to the Douglas lands (both Lady Jane and the other twin had died). Another branch of the large Douglas family, the Hamiltons, claimed that Archibald was an imposter and that they were the true heirs of the duke. They sent agents to Paris, who returned with evidence that Lady Jane had bought the infants from two impoverished Parisian families. The Hamiltons brought suit in the Scottish Court of Session, which upheld their claim by an eight-to-seven vote.[56]

Archibald appealed to the House of Lords, which heard the case on 27 February 1769. Mansfield was one of the law lords who argued in favour of Archibald's claim. He spoke for over an hour. Despite the season, at one point during his speech, the oppressive heat in the crowded chamber almost overcame him. He was about to faint and had to stop. The doors of the House were thrown open, and the lord chancellor rushed out with a servant and returned with a bottle of wine and glasses. After drinking two glasses of wine, Mansfield continued his speech. According to a spectator, "We, who had no wine, were nearly as much recruited by the fresh air which rushed in at the open doors as his lordship by the wine."[57]

Mansfield's speech was an unvarnished appeal to the peers' emotions – and to their aristocratic snobbery. Rather than discuss the detailed evidence that Hamilton's agents had unearthed in Paris and the contrary evidence presented by the Douglas supporters (Lord Camden, who also supported Archibald's claim, had already discussed the evidence), he dwelled instead on Lady Jane's ancestry. He told how she had come to see him in 1750 when she was destitute, and that he had used his influence to get her a pension of £300 a year from the King. His main argument was that a woman of Lady Jane's high birth could not possibly be guilty of fraud: "At that time I looked upon her to be a lady of the strictest honour and integrity, and to have the deepest sense of the grandeur of the family from whence she was sprung; a family conspicuously great in Scotland for a thousand years past … Is it possible, my lords, to imagine that a woman of such a family, of such high honour, and who had a real sense of her own dignity, could be so base as to impose false children upon the world?"[58] Mansfield's speech, supported by the authority that he commanded as chief justice, and by several other peers, had its desired effect. The House of Lords reversed the decision of the Scottish court in favour of the Douglas heir, with only five dissenters.[59]

Mansfield was severely criticized for the part he played in enabling Archibald to inherit the Douglas fortune. Four years after the case ended, Andrew Stuart, a lawyer who had represented the Hamilton faction, published four long letters addressed to Mansfield, setting forth the evidence of fraud in great detail and condemning him for ignoring it: "Your Lordship … knows, that in the Douglas cause there was not only a *suspicion*, but a *certainty* of forgery … proved by the clearest evidence, and even acknowledged at the bar by the counsel on that side of the question."[60] Campbell, Mansfield's nineteenth-century biographer, judged his speech as "very inferior to his usual judicial efforts," adding that he appealed to the lords' feelings and prejudices rather than making an exposition of the principles of law involved in the case and a masterly analysis of the evidence.[61]

Mansfield presided over several "criminal conversation" (the eighteenth-century term for adultery) cases, in which a cuckolded husband sued his wife's lover for damages.[62] *Cibber v. Sloper*, where Mansfield as a young lawyer represented the defendant, has been described earlier.[63] In that case, Mansfield was able to persuade the jury to award the plaintiff only nominal damages by showing that the supposedly injured husband had connived with his wife for her to commit adultery with the defendant.[64]

The most notorious criminal conversation case that Mansfield tried was that of Lord Grosvenor against the Duke of Cumberland, a brother of King George III.[65] Testimony taken at the trial showed that Lord Grosvenor's servants had, at his direction, bored two peepholes in the door of Lady Grosvenor's bedroom at an inn in the town of St Albans. Being satisfied that she was there with the Duke of Cumberland, they broke down the door and found them together in a state of undress. Other testimony elicited by

Cumberland's counsel indicated that Lord Grosvenor may himself have committed adultery some years earlier.[66]

At six-thirty in the evening, Mansfield began his summing up of the evidence, concisely explaining the law of criminal conversation to the jury. To make out a case, the plaintiff must prove that he was married to the woman involved (in another case, he said that "reputation will not do for that purpose")[67] and that the defendant "carnally knew" his wife: "no indecencies, no familiarities, no conjectures or probabilities, is sufficient to make out the ground of such an action. But there is no precise species of evidence that is defined, what shall or not be sufficient ... [In] my experience ... they generally have been able to prove what is almost equal to the very act, or to catching them in the act."[68]

After summing up the evidence, Mansfield turned to the question of damages, the most controversial issue in the case, given the fact that both parties were wealthy, high-ranking persons. He stated that the amount of damages should not depend on the circumstances of the parties but on the injury suffered by the plaintiff: "the injury is as great to a man of low as high rank, and therefore the situation of the parties is not the measure by which damages are to be governed."

If the plaintiff draws the defendant into a trap (as happened in the *Cibber* case), Mansfield continued, "though the crime before God is the same, he is not to recover damages." On the other hand, if the defendant takes advantage of his friendship with the plaintiff "and abuses that friendship, honour, and hospitality" in order to seduce the plaintiff's wife, "the measure of damages would certainly increase."[69] Finally, if the plaintiff himself is proved to have committed adultery, that would not be a bar to his recovering against the defendant; but "it goes a great way with regard to the injury he complains of, losing the comfort and society of his wife."[70]

After speaking for about half an hour, Mansfield handed the case to the jury and left for his home in Bloomsbury Square. The jury then retired to deliberate, and three hours later, having reached a verdict, hired four carriages to take them from Westminster Hall to Mansfield's house. They found in favour of the plaintiff and awarded damages of £10,000 against the royal duke. Although the award was only one-tenth of what Grosvenor had demanded, it was still a very substantial sum, and the jury seemed to have ignored Mansfield's instruction that the rank and situation of the defendant should not be a factor in measuring damages.[71] A newspaper correspondent suggested: "If [Mansfield's] doctrine is true in one instance, it will be applicable to every case of criminal conversation; and the consequence of it will be that a nobleman with ten thousand a year shall pay no greater damages than a peasant who labours for a shilling a day, or vice versa, that the seduction of a duchess and of a milliner stand upon the same footing in regard to the compensation due to the injured husband."[72] Mansfield's dictum that justice is blind puts one in mind of Anatole France's famous description of "the majestic equality of the law, which forbids the rich as well as the poor to sleep under bridges, to beg in the streets, and to steal bread."[73]

In another celebrated case, Sir Richard Worsley sued George Bissett for criminal conversation with Worsley's wife. At the trial several witnesses, including three noblemen, testified that Lady Worsley was sexually promiscuous. There also was sensational evidence about her in a public bathhouse; Sir Richard had encouraged Bissett to stand on his shoulders so that Bissett could see her through an upper-storey window.[74] Mansfield instructed the jury that the only question they had to decide was "Whether Sir Richard has not been privy to the prostitution of his Wife? Assenting to, encouraging and exciting even this Defendant?" After deliberating for less than an hour, the jury returned with a verdict for the plaintiff, giving him 1 shilling damages.[75]

One other criminal conversation case illustrates Mansfield's psychological acuity. A Mr Foley brought an action against Lord Peterborough for criminal conversation with his wife, Lady Ann Foley. (Peterborough was one of the witnesses who had testified about Lady Worsley's conduct three years earlier.) At the trial, it was proved that Foley knew that his wife was generally promiscuous, but may not have known about her dalliance with Peterborough. The jury awarded Foley a verdict of £2,500. On appeal, Peterborough's lawyer argued that a husband should not be allowed to take advantage of an injury he could have prevented. Mansfield rejected the argument. He said that it would be peculiarly unjust if a husband should be prevented from obtaining damages where, because of his fondness for his wife, he was blind to what all the rest of the world saw. In fact, Mansfield continued, the husband's very blindness made the injury more grievous to him, once he discovered it.[76]

Mansfield's most important contribution to the law of marriage was to expand the kinds of situation in which a married woman could be sued for the debts she incurred. While the direct effect of this was to help creditors, it was a step in freeing women from their subordinate status. In deciding other types of cases regarding women and marriage, Mansfield showed a basic humanity and concern for the helpless, qualities that were among the most salient elements of his conduct as a judge.

21

Religious Freedom

My desire to disturb no man for conscience' sake is pretty well known.

Lord Mansfield, after the 1780 Gordon Riots

All his life, Lord Mansfield was a member of the established Church of England and attended church services, but he kept his religious beliefs to himself. His last will and testament, executed at the age of seventy-seven, begins with the words, "When it shall please God, to call me to another State, to which, of all I now enjoy, I can only carry the Satisfaction of my own Conscience, & my firm Reliance upon his Goodness, through Jesus Christ." But this may have been less a declaration of a personal belief in God and the divinity of Christ than a conventionally religious way of referring to the end of his life.

Whatever his personal beliefs, Mansfield was a staunch supporter of religious freedom for others.[1] Throughout his judicial career, he sought to limit and soften the disabilities placed on Roman Catholics and Protestant dissenters. It is likely that, as a law officer of the Crown in 1753, he supported his government's abortive efforts to grant citizenship rights to Jews. As a judge who believed that law was based on reason and morality, he protected women accused of witchcraft.

Political and religious issues were inextricably intertwined in seventeenth- and early eighteenth-century Britain.[2] Rulers believed that religious toleration posed a threat to the existing political and social order – and, therefore, to their rule.[3] Protestant dissenters, the evangelical Puritans, had defeated the forces of King Charles I in the English Civil War, and had tried and executed him in 1649.[4] Forty years later, a Catholic king, James II, was forced to abdicate after he attempted to re-create Britain as a "modern, rational, centralized Catholic state."[5] Catholicism was associated with France, Britain's main enemy. The followers of King James and his son and grandson, the French-backed Jacobites, invaded England twice – in 1715 and 1745 – posing a constant threat to the established political and religious order. Many of the English regarded both Catholics and Protestant dissenters with suspicion and sometimes with hate and fear.

After the restoration of the monarchy in 1660, Parliament enacted the Corporations Act,[6] which, among other things, barred anyone from holding public office if he had not, within the previous year, taken the sacrament according to the rites of the Church of England. But religious toleration was a basic tenet of the architects of the Glorious Revolution of 1688. The leaders of the Church of England became more tolerant and were willing to allow religious practice outside the church.[7] Although religious toleration among the ruling elite increased during the eighteenth century, it barely overlay the violent prejudices held by many among the middle and lower classes.[8] Throughout the century there were sporadic outbreaks of religion-based mob violence, the worst of which occurred in 1715–16 (against dissenters), in 1753 (against Jews), and in 1780 (against Catholics).[9]

The Toleration Act of 1689[10] did not free Roman Catholics from the restrictive and punitive laws. They were prohibited from gathering together to practice their religion;[11] holding any form of government employment;[12] inheriting, purchasing, or owning land;[13] sending a child out of the country to be educated;[14] possessing a weapon, other than what was necessary for the defence of their house or person;[15] coming within ten miles of certain localities, including London;[16] and bringing a legal action or serving as an executor of an estate or legal guardian of a child.[17] Violators of these restrictions were subject to fines, and persons who discovered and reported the violations were rewarded with bounties.[18] A priest who held a Catholic mass could be imprisoned for life, and an informer who achieved a conviction was entitled to a £100 bounty.[19]

Protestant Nonconformists were subject to far fewer restrictions. The Toleration Act guaranteed them religious freedom but not political equality.[20] They could vote if they met the applicable property qualifications, worship in their own churches, bear arms, and be elected to Parliament; but they could not hold any public office unless they were willing to conform to Anglican rites of worship.[21] These political disabilities did not seriously affect the lives of most dissenters, but resentment remained that the Corporations Act infringed their rights as Englishmen.[22]

Mansfield's close friendship as a young man with the Catholic Alexander Pope may have contributed to his support of religious freedom. In 1753, when he successfully defended himself before the Cabinet against charges of Jacobitism, he emphasized both his loyalty to the state religion and his belief that everyone should be free to practise his or her own religion: "tyranny in the State and persecution in the Church are equally bad; and I would, upon principles of Christianity and sound policy, support the Toleration in its full extent, with the same warmth, and the same zeal, as I would the Established Church."[23]

In 1780, after his London home and all its contents had been destroyed by the anti-Catholic Gordon rioters, he pointed with pride to his long record of religious tolerance: "My desire to disturb no man for conscience' sake is pretty well known, and I hope, will be had in remembrance. I have no leaning to Roman Catholics ... I have shown equal favour to Dissenters from the established Church of all denominations; and ... I have always reprobated attempts to molest them in the celebration of their religious worship as unworthy of the apostolical protestantism which we profess."[24]

As a practicing lawyer, Mansfield represented clients in several matters involving religion, not always on behalf of Catholics or dissenters. As described earlier, he argued in the House of Commons on behalf of the Church of England against a bill that would have eased restrictions on Quakers;[25] on another occasion, he persuaded the Chancery Court that the deposition testimony of a Hindu who had taken a Hindu rather than a Christian oath should be admitted in evidence.[26] On yet another occasion, he wrote to a real estate conveyancer on behalf of a Roman Catholic family to whom a great estate had been bequeathed, asking him if he could "contrive a way by which an estate can be left to a papist."[27] However, these matters were part of a lawyer's daily work on behalf of clients and do not necessarily tell us much about Mansfield's personal views regarding the laws against Catholics and dissenters. We do learn a great deal more about his views after he became a judge.

On the bench, Mansfield consistently sought to lighten the legal burdens placed on Catholics, which he regarded as obsolete and unnecessarily punitive. When two justices of the peace faced criminal charges for refusing to compel two Catholics to take the prescribed oath of the Church of England, Mansfield set the justices free, expressing his disapproval "at this attempt to revive the severities of these very penal laws."[28] Given his duty as a judge to enforce the law, he invariably construed the anti-Catholic laws as narrowly as he could.

Perhaps the best example of this was the case of *Foone v. Blount*.[29] Warham, who owned real estate, left a sum of money to Foone, a Catholic, with instructions to his executor to sell the land and to pay the legacy out of the proceeds of the sale. After Warham died, Foone sued the executors for the money. The executors argued that Foone lacked the capacity to take the legacy because the law excluded a Catholic from any interest or profit arising out of land.

Mansfield disagreed. He interpreted the law narrowly and in accord with what he saw as the purpose of its enactment. The anti-Catholic laws were passed, he said, because they were thought to be necessary to the safety of the state, and they could be defended only on that ground: "From the nature of these laws, they are not to be carried by inference, beyond what the political reasons, which gave rise to them, require." The reason for the laws was to prevent Catholics from having the "weight and influence, which is necessarily connected with landed property," but here the creditor "can have nothing till the land is turned into money." Finally, Mansfield left no doubts about his aversion to laws that discriminated on the basis of a person's religious beliefs. Without a legal precedent that forced him to do so, he was unwilling to stretch these laws: "I should expect a precedent before I decided that a creditor should not be paid out of the assets, only because he happens to be of a different way of thinking from the established mode of religion."

Between 1766 and 1770, Mansfield heard six prosecutions of alleged Roman Catholic priests for saying a mass, none of which was successful.[30] The most celebrated of these cases was *Rex v. Webb*.[31] A carpenter named Payne accused James Webb of celebrating a Catholic mass. Payne was a professional informer who made a career out of bringing criminal proceedings against Catholics in order to earn bounties. When Payne testified, Mansfield asked him: "You are sure that this man is a Popish priest; and that he said Mass?" Payne answered: "Yes." Mansfield then asked: "You know then what a Mass is?" At this, Payne remained silent.[32] Mansfield's instructions to the jury provide a fine illustration of how he interpreted a law that he found repugnant:

> A Popish priest convicted of exercising his functions is subject to fine and perpetual imprisonment. But, first, he is to be proved a priest, for unless he is a priest, he cannot be touched for the enormity of saying mass; and then, unless he is proved to have said mass, the crime of being a priest will escape with impunity. Now the only witness to the

> mass is Payne – a very illiterate man, who knows nothing of Latin, the language in which it is said: and, moreover, he, as informer, is witness in his own cause; for, upon conviction, he is entitled to £100 reward.
>
> Several others were called, but not one of them would venture to swear that he saw the defendant say mass ...
>
> Then, as to the defendant being a priest, you are not to infer that because he preached; for laymen often perform this office with us, and a deacon may preach in the Church of Rome ... You must not infer that he is a priest because he said mass, and that he said mass because he is a priest.
>
> At the Reformation, they thought it in some measure necessary to pass these penal laws; for then the Pope had great power, and the Jesuits were then a very formidable body. Now the Pope has little power, and it seems to grow less every day ... These penal laws were not meant to be enforced except at proper seasons, when there is a necessity for it; or, more properly speaking, they were not meant to be enforced at all, but were merely made *in terrorem* ...
>
> Take notice, if you bring him in *guilty* the punishment is very severe; a dreadful punishment indeed! Nothing less than perpetual imprisonment![33]

The jury acquitted Webb. Mansfield had interpreted the anti-Catholic law so strictly that afterwards it was practically impossible to get a conviction against a priest for saying mass. The *Webb* case shows a great judge, informed by a spirit of religious freedom, using the tools of a lawyer to make public policy. According to Campbell, "many zealous Protestants were much scandalized, and rumours were spread that the chief justice was not only a Jacobite but a Papist, and some even asserted that he was a Jesuit in disguise."[34]

Unfazed by criticism, Mansfield continued to read the anti-Catholic laws narrowly, and in this he was able to obtain the concurrence of the eleven other royal judges, thus bringing a virtual halt to Payne's one-man campaign against the Catholics.[35] Before that, Payne had achieved some successes, most notably in 1767 when he was able to persuade a court to sentence an Irish priest, John Baptist Maloney, to life imprisonment.[36] Twenty years later, Mansfield appealed to King George III to pardon Maloney. The King replied: "God forbid, my Lord, that anyone should sanction persecution or attempt of one man within my realm to suffer unjustly. Therefore issue a pardon for Mr Maloney and see that he is set at liberty."[37]

In 1770, Payne brought an action against Mr Jones, "a reputable tradesman in Chancery Lane," alleging that he attended a Catholic service at the Sardinian ambassador's chapel in Lincoln's Inn Fields. The court acquitted him.[38] Despite his evident dislike of Payne, Mansfield stayed within the bounds of judicial even-handedness: when in a later case Payne's testimony was objected to on the ground that the promise of a reward made him an interested witness, Mansfield overruled the objection, saying "it was every day practice to admit the prosecutor of a highway robbery, burglary, etc. to be a witness."[39] Although Mansfield allowed Payne's testimony to be heard, he pointed out Payne's conflict of interest to the jury, as he had done in the *Webb* case. Nobody who was charged with saying mass was found guilty, and there were no more of these prosecutions after 1770.[40]

Mansfield invariably supported the rights of dissenters, i.e., members of Protestant denominations whose religious scruples prevented them from taking the oath and subscribing to the beliefs of the established Anglican Church. The dissenters were Presbyterians, Methodists, Quakers, and members of several smaller sects. In addition to middle-class tradesmen, shopkeepers, artisans, and professionals,[41] they also included many of the entrepreneurs, merchants, and inventors who were transforming England into the world's foremost commercial and industrial nation. Examples of prominent dissenters were James Watt, the inventor of the steam engine, and Josiah Wedgwood, who applied modern industrial methods to the production of pottery.[42]

By and large, the dissenters constituted a comfortable, urban, well-educated business class, who were influenced by the rational philosophy of the Enlightenment.[43] They owed their business success, at least in part, to the fact that they were a tight-knit group who did not indulge in the fashionable and often wasteful pursuits – principally gambling and drinking – of many upper-class Englishmen.[44] The dissenting community included a number of prominent families, including that of Sir Dudley Ryder, Mansfield's colleague when he was solicitor general and his predecessor as chief justice.[45]

The fact that support of commerce and industry was a central tenet of Mansfield's jurisprudence gave the dissenters a special claim to his favour. In one decision, Mansfield admitted the testimony in court of a Quaker who was willing to *affirm*, but refused to *swear* an oath, that he would tell the truth;[46] in another, he upheld the right of a congregation of Presbyterians to elect its own minister;[47] and in a third, he upheld the right of a dissenter to serve as a town clerk without taking the sacrament of the Church of England.[48] In one case, he went out of his way to state that "Methodists have a right to the protection of this Court, if interrupted in their decent and quiet devotion."[49]

It was in the House of Lords that Mansfield made his most famous effort to prevent the persecution of dissenters. Under the Corporations Act of 1661,[50] no person was allowed to serve in the government of any municipality unless he had received the sacrament of the Church of England within the previous year, but a dissenter could not in good conscience receive the sacrament. Although the purpose of the Act was to prevent dissenters from becoming public officials, the City of London used the Act as a convenient way to raise a very large amount of money, some of which was used to build Mansion House, which became the home of the mayor.[51]

In 1748, the City adopted a bylaw imposing a fine of £400 on any person who, having been nominated by the lord mayor for election as sheriff, declined to run for the office; and a fine of £100 on anyone who, being elected sheriff, refused to serve.[52] Several dissenters were elected sheriff and paid the fines because their religious beliefs prevented them from receiving the sacrament. Others refused to pay, and the City brought actions of debt against them in the Sheriff's Court. One of these was Allen Evans, who was elected in 1757 and ordered to pay the fine. Evans appealed, and for ten years his case wound its way through several courts, finally coming to the House of Lords on 4 February 1767.

Speaking as the most highly regarded of the law lords (the peers who were judges), Mansfield focused on the injustice that the City was attempting to visit on Evans, in a speech that has been described as "magnificent rhetoric and sound law."[53] He pointed out that the purpose of the Corporations Act was to bar dissenters from office, and that as a dissenter Evans was disabled from serving. Moreover, Evans could not be prosecuted for refusing to take the sacrament, because the Toleration Act freed all dissenters from that obligation.[54] He described the impossible dilemma in which the City's bylaw placed Evans and other dissenters: "If they accept, punish them; if they refuse, punish them; if they say, yes, punish them, if they say, no punish them."[55] He concluded:

> In the cause before your Lordships, the Defendant was by law incapable at the time of his pretended election: and it is my firm persuasion

> that he was chosen because he was incapable. If he had been capable, he had not been chosen; for they did not want him to serve the office. They chose him, because, without a breach of the law and a usurpation on the Crown, he could not serve the office. They chose him, that he might fall under the penalty of their By-law made to serve a particular purpose: in opposition to which, and to avoid the fine thereby imposed, he hath pleaded a legal disability grounded on two Acts of Parliament [the Corporations and Toleration acts].

Mansfield moved to acquit Evans, and the House of Lords immediately voted its agreement.[56] Although dissenters remained barred by the Corporations Act from serving in public office for another sixty years, they no longer could be fined for refusing to do what the law prohibited them from doing.[57]

Mansfield's vigorous and deeply felt toleration of Catholics and Protestant dissenters did not extend equally to Jews. He seems to have shared the mild anti-Semitic prejudice of the British upper classes, whose toleration of Jews was tempered by a patronizing attitude toward them. Their relatively enlightened attitude was not, however, shared by most of the public. The Jews had been expelled from England by King Edward I in 1290, but had been permitted to return by Oliver Cromwell in the 1650s. By the mid-eighteenth century, London had a small Jewish population, which included a few wealthy merchants and financiers.[58] Some Jews held local government office, and a few were members of the London Stock Exchange.[59] In 1758, a group of financiers, headed by an enormously rich Jewish stockbroker named Samson Gideon, a man who was "famed for his liberality, wit and common sense,"[60] had underwritten an £8 million loan to the government to finance the war against France.[61] The population of London also included middle-class Jewish merchants, as well as a number of poor Jews. A few Jews practised as attorneys (though not as barristers, who had the privilege of arguing cases in court).[62]

In 1753 the Pelham ministry introduced the Jewish Naturalization Bill, enabling some rich Jews to become British subjects. Pelham spoke at length in favour of the so-called "Jew Bill" in the House of Commons, arguing that its enactment would induce rich foreign Jews to live in England and "thus tend to increase, not only our manufactures and commerce, but our public revenue."[63] Pelham's emphasis on the economic benefits the country would gain by attracting Jews to its shores suggests at least the possibility that Mansfield, who consistently encouraged the growth of Britain's commerce, participated in drafting the speech in his official role as solicitor general. The passage of the bill in May 1753 was greeted by anti-Semitic riots. The fury of the public demonstrations, shortly before a national election, persuaded Pelham and Newcastle to have the Act repealed in the next session of Parliament.[64] Lord Chancellor Hardwicke, Newcastle's intimate adviser, had strongly supported the bill but accepted its repeal because of the public outcry.[65]

The enactment and subsequent repeal of the Jew Bill show the divide between the growing tolerance of the British ruling class and the savage religious prejudices of a large part of the population. A defamation suit between two Jewish butchers illustrates the popular anti-Semitism of the period. Two witnesses testified that, before a crowd of people, the defendant had called the plaintiff a thief, a highwayman, and a housebreaker. A newspaper account commented unfavourably on anti-Semitic prejudice: "But with all this wreck of character, good name and fame, so fully proved, a shameless Christian jury valued the difference between the reputation of two Jews at no more than a penny damages and one penny costs."[66]

Both as a practicing lawyer and later as a judge, Mansfield was condescending, but not hostile, toward Jews. On one occasion, when he was representing a client in court, his patronizing attitude backfired. General Sabine, the governor of Gibraltar, had tried without success to extort money from a North African Jew. As punishment, Sabine put the Jew on a ship sailing to Morocco, along with a sealed letter informing the country's Muslim ruler that he was being sent a pigeon to pluck. The Muslim, more tolerant than the Christian governor, freed the Jew and gave him Sabine's letter, which he took with him to England and then sued Sabine. Mansfield, acting as counsel for Sabine, argued that it had not been cruel to send the Jew back to Morocco, since that was his birthplace: "Where is the cruelty, the hardship, the injustice of banishing a man to his own country?" Knowing that Mansfield had never returned to Scotland since he left it at the age of thirteen, the Jew's lawyer answered: "Since my learned friend thinks so lightly of the matter I would ask him to suppose the case his own. Would *he* like to be banished to his native land?" (Loud laughter in the court.)[67]

A group of Jews, a number of them practically penniless, tried to make a living by writing bail bonds for defendants in the courts. Some Jewish bondsmen testified falsely that they had sufficient funds to be able to post the requested bail, and some were imprisoned for perjury.[68] This gave rise to the pejorative term "Jew bail." On one occasion, a Jewish bail bondsman came into court dressed in a tawdry suit of clothes, adorned with lace. William Davy, one of the barristers who often appeared before Mansfield, cross-examined him to find out whether he was worth the relatively small sum he had sworn to. The Jew answered affirmatively, but Davy persisted in his questioning. Mansfield interjected: "For shame, brother Davy, how can you tease the poor gentleman so? Don't you see, that he would *burn* for double the sum!"[69]

Mansfield's mixture of contempt and tolerance toward poor Jews is demonstrated by another incident, where a Jew named Mordecai Israel tried to justify writing a bail bond for £1,800. When asked if he was worth £1,800 after all his debts were paid, Israel admitted that he was not worth half that amount, but that the defendant's attorney had given him £20 to induce him to write the bail bond. Mansfield, who seemed struck by the answer, said: "You are an honest Jew and I would advise you by all means to keep it." As Mansfield was leaving the court, Israel bowed to him and said: "I humbly thank you, my lord; your lordship is the first that ever called me an *honest* man."[70]

Mansfield was a supremely rational man, opposed to all forms of superstition, including witchcraft. Belief in witchcraft and persecution of supposed witches persisted in England, particularly in rural areas, throughout the eighteenth century. The execution of witches was not forbidden until early in the next century,[71] although those who took it upon themselves to abuse or kill persons for alleged witchcraft were sometimes punished severely.[72] There were several newspaper reports of harmless women, and sometimes men, in their seventies or eighties, who were accused of being witches, then stripped of all their clothes and ducked into a pond or river. If they sank, they were innocent; if they didn't, they were deemed to be witches. Some drowned as a result of the mistreatment.[73] In one instance, a woman accused of being a witch was stripped and then weighed against the Bible; since she outweighed it, she was acquitted of the charge.[74]

There is only one known account of Mansfield dealing with an accusation of witchcraft. It was published shortly after his death, and if genuine, provides a wonderful example of his hatred of prejudice, his wisdom, and his sense of humour. While on circuit, he presided at a trial of a woman accused of witchcraft. Some witnesses testified that they had seen her walk upside down in the air. Mansfield calmly heard the evidence, and seeing that it would not be prudent to contradict the superstitions of the local jurors, he addressed them as follows:

> I do not doubt that this woman has walked in the air with her feet upwards, since you have all seen it; but she has the honour to be born in England as well as you and I, and consequently cannot be judged but by the laws of the country, nor punished but in proportion as she has violated them. Now I know not one law that forbids walking in the air with the feet upwards. We have all a right to do it with impunity. I see no reason therefore for this prosecution, and this woman may return home when she pleases.[75]

Mansfield's reputation for religious toleration was to cost him dearly in the anti-Catholic Gordon Riots of 1780.

22

The Gordon Riots

I have no books to consult.

Lord Mansfield, on his losses from the riots

It is likely that nowhere in the western world did so much wealth exist side by side with such abject poverty as in eighteenth-century London.[1] It was hard to imagine that the quiet oasis of Mansfield's Bloomsbury Square home was only a stone's throw from the scene of explosive violence and religious bigotry that erupted in 1780, eventually spilling out into the serenity of that square. Throughout the century, London had seen several outbreaks of mob violence based on political dissension, labour disputes, xenophobia, or religion intolerance, but the Gordon Riots were by far the most fierce and destructive. Many of those who participated in this unprecedented week-long disturbance were members of the "rabble," unskilled labourers, a class created by industrialization and urbanization. These people, as well as persons of the "middling sort" – apprentices, artisans, small shopkeepers – were motivated by anger at the inequities of the society, xenophobia against Irish immigrants, and intolerance of Catholics.[2]

The Gordon Riots were triggered by Parliament's enactment of the Catholic Relief Act of 1778,[3] a limited piece of legislation that did not give Catholics freedom of worship, but did repeal some of the onerous restrictions imposed on Catholics in the sixteenth and seventeenth centuries. In those years they were perceived in England as instruments of Catholic France and a threat to the state, in much the same way as during the Cold War many in the United States feared communists as agents of the Soviet Union.[4] But by the middle to latter part of the eighteenth century, as Mansfield himself had pointed out a few years earlier,[5] English Catholics were no longer a serious political force, and any valid political reason for the anti-Catholic laws had ceased to exist. The Catholic Relief Act repealed the provisions of the Popery Act of 1698 subjecting Catholic priests who said Mass to life imprisonment, and prohibiting Catholics from owning land and educating their children in their religion. The relief was conditioned on the swearing of an oath of allegiance to the King.

The Catholic Relief Act easily passed both Houses of Parliament and was supported by Britain's entire governing structure: the King, the ministry, the opposition, and the clergy of both the Anglican Church and the dissenting sects.[6] Nevertheless, there was a strong strain of intolerance among the Protestant working classes in both England and Scotland. Lord George Gordon, the hot-tempered younger son of the Duke of Gordon, mobilized the religious bigotry into a militant anti-Catholic movement, which soon got out of his control.[7]

Gordon was twenty-eight years of age in June 1780. According to a contemporary report: "He has the manners and air of a modern Puritan; his figure is tall and meager, his hair straight and his dress plain."[8] He had served as a naval officer in America but resigned his commission in 1772. He was elected to Parliament, where he denounced Britain's policy toward the American colonies. He neither spoke against the Catholic Relief Act when it was debated in the House of Commons nor voted against it.[9] However, soon after its passage, he began to agitate against it. He organized the Protestant Association, which gathered thousands of signatures on a petition to repeal the Act. On Friday, 2 June 1780, an extremely hot day, a crowd of about 60,000 of his supporters met at St George's Fields, on the south bank of the Thames. From there, they marched across the river to Westminster Palace, the home of Parliament, wearing blue cockades in their hats (signifying their anti-Catholicism) and carrying a huge roll of parchment listing the signers of the petition.[10] At 2:30 in the afternoon, they arrived in the Palace Yard, an open area facing Parliament with separate entrances for the House of Lords and the House of Commons.

Soon afterwards, members of Parliament began arriving in their carriages, only to find the Palace Yard filled with a large angry crowd. Up until then the crowd had been peaceful, but now it tried to force open the doors of Parliament. When the doorkeepers blocked their way, the marchers tried to obstruct the members from entering, although Lord Gordon pleaded with them to desist. The Westminster justices of the peace, with seventy-six constables under their command, were unable to control the increasingly violent crowd.[11] According to a newspaper report: "The multitude was so great that the carriages could not pass and those [members] who would not condescend to exclaim 'No Popery,' or whom they suspected to be unfriendly to their cause were treated with rough and wanton abuse."[12] Many noblemen and bishops were physically attacked and robbed of their possessions. The Archbishop of Canterbury had his wig pulled off and his canonical robes torn to pieces.[13] The Bishop of Lincoln was severely cut and was carried into the House in a fainting fit. The Duke of Northumberland escaped into the House with the loss of his watch,[14] while Lord Sandwich decided to turn his horses' heads and take refuge in flight.[15]

When Mansfield arrived, the mob broke the windows of his carriage, beat in the side panels, and threw mud in his face.[16] The still-athletic Archbishop of York dived through the mob and rescued him. With the help of the archbishop, Mansfield managed to enter the House of Lords, followed by several other peers, among them Lord Stormont, but not before having his coach broken to pieces and then being manhandled and pelted with mud by the mob for nearly half an hour.[17] Inside, it was a grotesque scene: "Some of their Lordships with their hair about their shoulders, others smutted with dirt; most of them as pale as the ghost of Hamlet."[18] Because Edward Thurlow, the lord chancellor, was ill, Mansfield presided over the House that day.[19] He showed considerable courage, though when he took his place on the chancellor's traditional woolsack seat, he was "quivering ... like an aspen."[20] Despite interruptions from the mob screaming and beating on the doors, the Duke of Richmond rose and spoke for half an hour on a motion he was about to make for annual parliamentary elections.[21] Then word trickled in that two of the peers, still outside, were in danger of losing their lives. They were brought in shortly after, "apparently much hurt." At this point, it was decided that no further business could be done, and the House adjourned.[22]

Many members of the House of Commons were able to shoulder their way through the rioters and enter the House, where they debated whether even to consider the petition to repeal the Act. From time to time, Lord Gordon left the chamber to report to the crowd on the progress of the debate.[23] The Commons voted to refuse to consider the petition by a vote of 192 to 6.[24]

Meanwhile, troops arrived and dispersed the crowd outside Parliament. The peers gradually departed, leaving Mansfield alone, except for the officers of the House and his own servants.[25] He made his escape by a back door facing the Thames and was rowed down the river, disguised in a green coat and bob-wig.[26]

The violence in the Palace Yard was bad enough, but far worse was to come. During the next few days, the rioters, their legislative mission abandoned, demolished the chapels of the Sardinian and Bavarian embassies (diplomats of friendly Catholic countries were permitted to exercise their religion[27]) and ransacked the home of Sir Charles Savile, the principal author of the Catholic Relief Act.[28] On Tuesday evening, the rioters stormed Newgate, the main prison for felons,[29] and released the prisoners, including some rioters who had been imprisoned during the previous days, many of whom now rejoined the mob.[30] The rioters then began to cry for vengeance against members of both the government and the opposition who were known to be sympathetic to the Act, including the Marquess of Rockingham, Edmund Burke, and Lord North.[31] It did not help that in eighteenth-century London the house of every notable or notorious citizen was well known.[32]

Later that evening, Mansfield was advised that the mob intended to destroy his house and those of several other judges. He sent for Sir John Hawkins, London's leading justice of the peace, who arrived at Bloomsbury Square, with several constables, to find Mansfield in a state of shock and at a loss as to what to do. Hawkins sent for military protection of the house, but when a contingent of soldiers arrived, Mansfield, against Hawkins's advice, insisted that they be stationed not in front of his house but around the corner in the vestry of nearby St George's Church.[33] Mansfield was afraid that the presence of the soldiers in front of his house would only enrage the rioters;[34] he might have saved his house if he had allowed the soldiers to show themselves and, if necessary, meet force with force.[35]

Mansfield's decision to keep his military protectors hidden turned out to be a mistake. At around the same time as the soldiers left Bloomsbury Square, Hawkins received a message from the Duke of Northumberland asking for protection for his home. Feeling that neither he nor the soldiers could be of any use at Lord Mansfield's, Hawkins took the soldiers over to Northumberland House. The homes of Northumberland and other notables who agreed to post guards around their houses were not attacked by the mob.[36] Prime Minister Lord North's house was saved by a troop of cavalry who rode over and wounded several of the rioters with their swords.[37]

The rioters plundered and destroyed several houses of judges and magistrates who lived in the neighbourhood of Bloomsbury Square. Shortly after midnight, one party, estimated by a witness at 2,000 strong,[38] arrived at Mansfield's house. They began by tearing up the iron railings around the house, and then they smashed the windows and forced the front door open with iron bars. Once inside the house, they proceeded to Mansfield's library and threw its contents out of the windows. "A fire was soon blazing at the corner of the Square, into which pictures, parchments, books, manuscripts, harpsichords, the choicest furniture ... were flung from the windows."[39] All of Lord and Lady Mansfield's clothing, including his judicial robes and wigs, was thrown into the street. An observer recalled seeing a chimney sweep dancing in front of the bonfire wearing one of Lady Mansfield's hoop skirts.[40] Among Mansfield's books that landed in the street was a volume of the letters of Alexander Pope, Mansfield's old friend from his days as a young lawyer. Picking up the book and seeing the name of the author, one of the rioters informed his companions that he had found definite proof that Mansfield was a Catholic. Discovering that Mansfield was (seemingly) a diabolical promoter of Popish plots so enraged the mob that they set to work burning every piece of paper they could find as well as the other contents of the house.[41]

Around four or five o'clock on Wednesday morning, 7 June, while the rioters were out on the street burning Mansfield's furniture, a detachment of soldiers belatedly arrived on the scene, accompanied by a justice of the peace, who ordered them to fire on the mob. They killed four men and a woman (another report says that six were killed) and wounded several others. The mob dispersed, and the officer commanding the soldiers, thinking that his job was done, marched his detachment away.[42] Fifteen minutes later, the rioters returned, this time with incendiary materials, and set the house on fire. Two fire engines arrived, but the mob would not allow the firemen to go to work until the house was burned to the ground.[43] An unverified report stated that some personal friends of Mansfield had earlier arrested three of the intruders and locked them in a room in the house, where they were forgotten and were burned to ashes.[44]

There were conflicting reports as to where Lord and Lady Mansfield were when their home was attacked. A month later, two newspapers reported that Sir Thomas Mills, reputed to be Mansfield's illegitimate son, was in the house when the mob began breaking the windows, and that he escorted Lady Mansfield to safety to a house in Lincoln's Inn Fields.[45] This story, however, may have been based on an account given to the newspapers by Mills, who was not always a reliable source. Another report stated that Mansfield had sent his wife and his great-niece, Lady Elizabeth Murray, to Kenwood before the house was attacked, but decided to remain there himself. According to this account, when the mob arrived, a servant persuaded Mansfield to make his escape through a back door, disguised in an old great coat. He was recognized by one of the rioters, who cried out: "There goes that old rogue, Mansfield," but he and his servant hurried on in silence and escaped.[46] Another report stated that Lord and Lady Mansfield escaped together through a back door,[47] while yet another account (perhaps the most likely one) stated that the mob did not arrive until half an hour after Mansfield had left for Kenwood.[48]

Whatever the time and manner of their escape, Lord and Lady Mansfield were not harmed, but his library of over 1,000 books and manuscripts, some of them autographed by Jonathan Swift, Alexander Pope, and other luminaries, was destroyed.[49] Perhaps the greatest loss was some two hundred notebooks containing Mansfield's handwritten notes on cases that he had decided, a loss that was instantly recognized at the time as "an irreparable loss to the gentlemen of the bar."[50] This sentiment likewise applied to future generations of lawyers and scholars, who were deprived of the benefit of Mansfield's thinking on numerous legal issues. Also destroyed was a manuscript, ready for press, containing eight speeches that he had made in Parliament on constitutional questions, which was to have been printed after his death; a picture painted by Pope (the only one he ever painted); and a manuscript of Lord Bolingbroke.[51] In financial terms, Mansfield's total losses were estimated at £30,000 (the equivalent of about US/CA$8 million in 2012), his library alone being valued at £10,000. The poet William Cowper wrote:

And Murray sighs o'er Pope and Swift
And many a treasure more,
The well-judged purchase and the gift
That graced his lettered store.

Their pages mangled, burnt and torn,
The loss was his alone;
But ages yet to come shall mourn
The burning of his own.[52]

It is not clear why Mansfield was a prime target of the rioters. Although he had always favoured religious toleration, he had not actively supported the Catholic Relief Bill, which was the immediate occasion for the riots.[53] On 19 June, twelve days after the destruction of his house, he told the House of Lords: "Although it so happened that I never once spoke in this House in support of the ... bill to mitigate Roman Catholic penalties, and, as far as I can recollect, was not present when it passed through any of its stages, I approved, and I approve, of its principles."[54]

In fact, the author of a letter to a newspaper shortly after the riots criticized Mansfield for not having been present in the House of Lords when the bill was debated. The writer stated that if Mansfield did not approve of the bill he should have attended the House and opposed it; and he contrasted Mansfield's inaction to the courage of Lord Temple, who in 1754 had made a special trip from his country home to the House of Lords to speak in opposition to the repeal of the Jewish Naturalization Act, a piece of legislation which, like the Catholic Relief Act, had provoked mob violence.[55]

Although the riots began as a protest against toleration of Catholics, there were other reasons for the disturbances. Until the later stages of the riots, the mob left untouched the thickly populated parishes of East London, where many of the poorer Catholics lived.[56] The attacks on the homes of Mansfield and several other judges, all of whom were Protestants, suggest that the mob was animated as much by a "levelling spirit" that enraged them against the upper classes as by anti-Catholic bigotry.[57] Mansfield was well known in London for his support of the prosecution of John Wilkes and other seditious-libel defendants, and for his severity in a broad range of criminal cases. The poorer classes hated Mansfield because they felt that his rulings unfairly persecuted them and, more generally, that he represented the law, which was stacked against those without title or wealth. One modern historian believes that Mansfield's house was targeted because he was part of "the whole cosmopolitan hierarchy, the powerful men whose tolerant or errant attitudes were undermining the 'true Protestantism.'"[58]

In the chaotic situation that existed on the day that Mansfield's house was destroyed, rumours circulated that the rioters had murdered him at his country home of Kenwood and burned down that house too.[59] The rumours were false, but on Wednesday morning, Stormont warned the military authorities that rioters were threatening to destroy Kenwood and asked that a cavalry detachment be sent there. This was done. About sixty rioters did indeed approach Kenwood with hostile intentions, but the soldiers dispersed them.[60]

The riots, which had begun with a legislative aim, quickly escalated into "senseless tumult, in the acts of a mad, unconnected rabble formed at once of the very lowest and worst part of the community, of robbers, thieves, pickpockets, unconnected and strangers to each other in every respect, further than they were collected for mere plunder or wanton unpremeditated mischief."[61] On Wednesday, 7 June, the King issued a proclamation giving discretionary powers to the military to suppress the riots,[62] and a £50 reward was offered for the discovery of anyone who aided and abetted the riots.[63] Nevertheless, the unrest continued, and for a week London was out of the control of the authorities. There was a report of three boys walking through the streets with iron bars taken from the railing in front of Mansfield's house, extorting money from shop owners.[64] After a distillery had been ransacked, liquor ran down the middle of the street, and many of the rioters drank themselves senseless. At Mansfield's house, "an ill-looking fellow, about nineteen, that was wounded, and had his hair clotted with blood, was too drunk, at one o'clock the next day, to be made sensible."[65]

Order was not restored until the evening of the 9th, a week after the riots began, after 17,000 troops had been marched into London.[66] The London magistrates and senior army officers had been reluctant to call in the military because they had not forgotten the slaughter at St George's Fields in Southwark in 1768, when soldiers had killed seven persons and wounded at least fifteen others who were protesting John Wilkes's imprisonment.[67] On 10 June, Lord Gordon was arrested on a charge of treason and committed to the Tower of London.

The riots caused property damage estimated at £100,000 – ten times that in Paris throughout the French Revolution[68] – but very few innocent citizens died.[69] Among them, according to one report, was a spectator at the burning of Mansfield's house, who was said to have become so hot that he went home and took a cold bath, which "produced a fever of which he died."[70] Thomas Hutchinson, the exiled Loyalist governor of Boston, witnessed the riots and died of fright, according to a report heard by Benjamin Franklin (who was living in Paris at the time) and passed on to a correspondent in America.[71] Hutchinson did indeed die during the week of the riots, but the statement that he died of fright probably stemmed from American patriotic contempt for a Tory.

Two hundred and ten of the rioters were killed outright by the troops, and seventy-five more died of their wounds. Out of sixty-two rioters who were sentenced to death, twenty-five were executed.[72] Among the latter were two crippled young men, John Gray and Charles Kent, who were convicted on 28 June of participating in the destruction of Mansfield's house and stealing his belongings. Gray, who had a broken leg and walked with a crutch, had carried a large iron bar and was seen breaking down a wall of a neighbouring house and coming out of Mansfield's house holding a bottle of his liquor; Kent, who had a wooden leg, also was seen carrying bottles out of the house.[73] Six weeks after the riots, Gray and Kent were taken by cart from Newgate Prison to Bloomsbury Square, where a gallows had been erected about twenty yards from the remains of Mansfield's house. The cart was placed under the gallows, but when it was noticed that the prisoners' backs were to the house, the cart was turned around so that when it was driven away they would see the ruins at the moment they were hanged.[74]

On Wednesday, 7 June, Mansfield told Stormont that he would not be able to preside over the House of Lords that day, but Stormont informed the King that Lord and Lady Mansfield were safe. King George, in a gesture that showed his personal affection and regard for Mansfield as well as respect for Mansfield's eminent status, ordered that Lord and Lady Mansfield be given apartments in the royal residence of St James's Palace until things calmed down.[75] One evening at the palace, Mansfield suggested that he read one of the sermons of Dr Blair, a Scottish clergyman, to the pious Queen Charlotte. The queen was so impressed with the sermon (and with Mansfield's delivery of it) that she persuaded the King to give Dr Blair an annual pension of £20.[76] In August, Mansfield moved to a rented house on Great Russell Street in Bloomsbury, not far from his previous residence.[77]

On 10 June, a day after the riots ended, the *Morning Post* reported that Mansfield had completely recovered from his ordeal,[78] but that he was unable to host a Cabinet dinner he had expected to give that evening. Prime Minister North filled in for him, "on account of his Lordship's indisposition and absence from town [presumably at Kenwood]."[79] On the 14th, however, Mansfield took his seat in court for the first time since the riots, clad in borrowed robes since all of his clothing had been destroyed.[80] According to an eyewitness: "The reverential silence ... which was observed when his Lordship resumed his place on the Bench, was expressive of sentiments of condolence and respect more affecting than the most eloquent address the occasion could have suggested."[81] In general, Mansfield was admired for his conduct during and after the riots. One noblewoman wrote to a friend: "Lord Mansfield's conduct has been great indeed; I thought I had long as high a respect for him as was possible, but my respect is heightened to almost adoration."[82]

Not everyone felt sympathy for Mansfield. Benjamin Franklin thought the Gordon Riots had administered a rough justice to him, in retribution for his support of British atrocities against the American colonists in the Revolutionary War, which had not yet ended. Franklin wrote: "It is not amiss that those who have approved the Burning our poor People's Houses and Towns should taste a little of the Effects of Fire themselves."[83] A year later, the *London Courant* took up the same theme. While observing that the loss of Mansfield's books was shocking, the newspaper report continued:

> Yet even this misfortune may be productive of some good by bringing home the feelings of every man in similar situations to rouse and by teaching men of influence and weight in a country from this horrid instance of literary destruction some little moderation before the cry: "Havoc and let slip the dogs of war." It is yet, however, in the memory of all Europe than no sooner had the British troops "passed the Rubicon" than their footsteps were marked with burnings and indiscriminate devastation. They devoted to the flames the college at Trenton with a most valuable library of books.[84]

Mansfield resumed his seat in the House of Lords on 19 June, where a debate ensued over the legality of the King ordering the military to suppress the rioting without the sanction of a civil magistrate.[85] The parochial constables and watchmen that comprised London's main police force were accustomed to guarding property but were ineffective in suppressing violent crime.[86] There was, therefore, no alternative to bringing in the troops. But a strong feeling persisted that the use of military forces to fight internal unrest was contrary to the unwritten British constitution and a threat to the civil liberties of citizens. A contemporary narrative of the riots expressed the view that, although the military had not in this instance abused its powers, "the possibility of abuse, the being but an hour under the control of a military force, was humiliating, derogatory, and alarming."[87]

In the House of Lords, Mansfield responded to these concerns, arguing rather implausibly that the soldiers had not acted in their military capacity but rather as citizens who, on seeing felonies being committed, were justified in putting the perpetrators to death.[88] In defending the legality of the measures ordered by the King, Mansfield mournfully declared: "I have not consulted books; indeed, I have no books to consult." There was a "deep sensation" in the House.[89] Mansfield also cited his long record of religious toleration: "I have no leaning to Roman Catholics. Many of those who are supposed to have directed the late mobs are not ignorant of my general tolerating principles when the toleration of sectaries [i.e., members of a sect] does not portend danger to the State."[90]

On 6 July, the House of Commons voted unanimously to authorize the government to compensate Mansfield for his losses. In a gracious letter to the Treasury, Mansfield turned down the offer:

> Besides what is irreparable, my pecuniary loss is great. I apprehended no danger and, therefore, took no precaution. But how great soever that loss may be I think it does not become me to claim or expect reparation from the State. I have made up my mind to bear my misfortune as I ought; with this consolation, that it came from those, whose objects manifestly were confusion [at home] and conflict and war abroad. If I should lay before you any account or computation of the pecuniary damage I have sustained it might seem a claim or expectation of being indemnified. Therefore, you shall have no further trouble, from your obedient, humble servant, Mansfield.[91]

In addition to his direct losses from the riots, Mansfield faced possible liability to his landlord. He did not own the ruined house in Bloomsbury Square, and a correspondent suggested in a letter to a newspaper that his decision to refuse the protection of the troops that had been sent to guard the house might make him liable to the landlord for the destruction of the house.[92] So far as is known, the landlord did not bring a lawsuit against Mansfield, but Mansfield may have paid him some compensation.

Mansfield presided over several lawsuits brought by property owners against insurance companies for the destruction of their property in the Gordon Riots. The most important of these suits was brought by Langdale, a wealthy distiller, who sued his insurer for fire damage to his house. Mansfield instructed a special jury that Langdale could not recover his losses because they came under an exception in the insurance policy for "civil commotion."[93] The case gave Mansfield an opportunity to sum up his view of the riots. He told the jury: "The insurrection that lately happened was certainly a species of civil commotion and its object was general, it aimed at the destruction of all law and government. It was [happening in] several different parts of the city at the time when the plaintiff's house was destroyed, it raged at the Bank [of England and other places and was] equally directed against public offices and private dwellings."[94]

Mansfield's observations in Langdale's case reflected his opinion, which he had first expressed in the House of Lords on 19 June, that the riots were the result of a systematic, planned scheme to destroy the government and the constitution.[95] The King seemed to agree, writing on the morning of 5 June (the day *before* Mansfield's house was destroyed): "we must get to the bottom of this; patching it up will only be preparing for further evils."[96] One contemporary account of the riots even suggested that French money had been used to incite the rioters.[97] There is no evidence to support these assertions. One newspaper pointed out that if the riots had been secretly directed, the Bank of England, the depository of the national wealth, would have been one of the first places attacked by the rioters. But no attempt was made on the bank until the very end of the riots, when it was adequately protected by the troops brought into London.[98]

No plan to bring down the government was ever unearthed, and none of the rioters who were tried even hinted that a ringleader had directed them. In fact, after Lord Gordon's initial attempt to petition the House of Commons to repeal the Catholic Relief Act, the riots seem to have been a totally unorganized affair. A witness at the trial of one of the rioters who helped destroy Mansfield's house testified that the defendant told him at the time: "I have done for that old fellow Lord Mansfield, I had fine fun; I made no less than six fires."[99] Fun in the form of mayhem, as well as class resentment, may have been the motivation for most of the rioters.

Historians generally agree with this assessment, pointing out that the riots did not spread beyond London and that the rioters had no political program, whether of revolutionary socialism or democracy.[100] In fact, many reformers were aghast at the riots; John Wilkes, who had been the idol of the London mob in the 1760s, courageously shouldered a musket as part of a citizens' effort to suppress the riots, only to be howled down by the mob.[101] For liberals as much as for political conservatives such as Mansfield, a lesson of the riots – which, it should be pointed out, occurred only nine years before the French Revolution – was that encouraging popular agitation against the established order could have unforeseen and terrible consequences.[102]

In March 1781, a criminal and civil action was brought against Brachley Kennett, the lord mayor of London, for neglect of duty during the riots. Mansfield again presided. One of the accusations against Kennett was that he did not read the Riot Act to the mob when it assembled. The Riot Act,[103] enacted in 1715, made it a felony for an assembly of more than twelve persons to fail to disperse after being ordered to do so and after being read certain portions of the Act by lawful authority. According to the evidence against Kennett, he not only failed to read the Riot Act to the mob but also, when it did not disperse, did not order the soldiers under his direction to arrest the rioters or, if all else failed, to fire at them.

Kennett was represented in court by Thomas Erskine, a brilliant lawyer who was later to become lord chancellor. Erskine argued that his client should not be harassed for errors of judgment, but only if he acted in bad faith or "heavily obstinately and perversely."[104] Mansfield disagreed. He told the jury that Kennett's fear of the rioters was no excuse for his inaction and that they must find him guilty of neglect of duty if he did not act as "a man of ordinary firmness."[105] After the jury had deliberated for about an hour, Mansfield left for his new home in Bloomsbury; an hour later, the jury took a coach there and told Mansfield that they found Kennett guilty of neglect of duty in the civil case but acquitted him in the criminal case. Mansfield told them that their verdict had to be either "guilty" or "not guilty"; the jury then found Kennett guilty.[106] He died before he could be sentenced, perhaps a suicide.[107]

The most noteworthy trial to come out of the Gordon Riots was the trial of Gordon himself, which took place in February 1781. After the riots, he had been brought before the Cabinet, where he disclaimed any intention of violating the public peace; he stated that he loved his country, that he had not foreseen the consequences of taking the anti-Catholic petition to Parliament, and that he was sorry the riots had occurred.[108]

Nevertheless, Gordon was indicted for high treason. Again, Mansfield presided and Erskine, joined by Lloyd Kenyon, who in 1788 was to succeed Mansfield as chief justice, represented the defendant. It did not go unnoticed that Mansfield, who had suffered such great losses in the Gordon Riots, had no compunction about sitting in judgment of the person accused of triggering the riots. The *Morning Herald* gently suggested that Mansfield "may ... from the point of delicacy absent himself ... lest the malevolent should, in case of ... conviction of the prisoner, attempt to slander his great name by insinuating that something more than a love of justice might have swayed his Lordship."[109]

But no such qualms deterred Mansfield from trying the Gordon case, despite his opinion, which he had expressed in the House of Lords two weeks after the riots, that the riots were part of a systematic plan to usurp the government and destroy the constitution. If that were the case, Mansfield must have believed that the organizer of the petition that led to the riots, Lord Gordon, had played a leading role in the scheme. Mansfield's private notes indicate that among the things he wanted to inquire into were: "What share Ld George Gordon had in procuring a number to attend the petition and calling the meeting in St George's Fields" and "What messages were sent into the country with his [illegible] to bring people up."[110] The notes are undated, but they probably were written about the time of Gordon's trial. Although these notes can be interpreted to mean that Mansfield was trying to ascertain the extent of Gordon's responsibility for the riots, his public statements before the trial strongly suggest that he had a preconceived notion of Gordon's complicity.

The treason trial of Lord Gordon riveted national attention to a degree comparable to the 1995 murder trial of O.J. Simpson in the United States. Mansfield put into place unusual security precautions, ordering that the main gate to Westminster Hall not be opened until he arrived and that guards be posted at all the entrances.[111] A large crowd of spectators attended the trial. One man climbed up one of the pillars in front of the Hall so that he could watch the trial through an open window. Mansfield ordered that the man be taken into custody, and what followed was a scene of farce incongruous to a treason trial. A bailiff politely asked the man to climb down, which he refused to do. The bailiff being too fat to climb up, Mansfield then repeated the request directly to the climber, adding that it was necessary for him to come down so that he could be taken into custody. When the man again refused, Mansfield gave up. The man remained on his perch taking notes all day and into the night.[112]

The trial began at eight o'clock on a Monday morning and continued until a quarter past five the next morning.[113] It was after midnight when Erskine rose to make his closing speech for the defendant. In a lengthy feat of advocacy that ensured his reputation as a great trial lawyer, Erskine emphasized that the crime of treason consisted of levying war against the King, but all that Gordon had done was present a petition to Parliament.

When Mansfield addressed the jury, he gave a rambling discourse, quite unlike his usual clear and concise jury instructions. He recounted at length the history of the restrictions on Catholics, going back to the time of Queen Elizabeth two hundred years earlier, which the Catholic Relief Act repealed. He gave an extraordinarily broad definition of levying war against the King, including an insurrection to raise the price of wages, to open all prisons, or even to destroy all brothels. Coming more to the point, he said that treason also encompassed presenting a petition to Parliament with the intent, by acts of force and violence, of compelling it to repeal a law. He told the jury that it had to decide two questions: first, whether Gordon's followers committed acts of violence to force Parliament to repeal the Act; and, second, if so, whether Gordon incited the insurrection.[114]

Finally, Mansfield summarized for the jury the evidence that had been presented at the trial. Erskine, and Gordon himself, interrupted Mansfield several times to say that he had misstated or omitted crucial facts. Coming to the testimony of Mr Pearson, the doorkeeper of the House of Commons, and what happened when Gordon and his followers tried to present their petition, Mansfield said he did not need to repeat this testimony since it did not contain any material fact. Gordon interrupted to say that Pearson's evidence was very material indeed: Pearson had testified that Gordon had not encouraged his supporters to block the entrance to the House of Commons, but on the contrary had begged them to keep back and leave room for the members of Parliament to go to their seats.

It may simply have been fatigue at the end of an exhausting trial, but Mansfield did not seem his usual self. He wearily asked the jury to use their own recollection of the testimony to make up for any deficiency in the notes he had made during the trial, or in his memory. When the jury finally left to deliberate, Mansfield was, according to a newspaper, "very much indisposed," whereas Gordon chatted cheerfully with his companions, seeming to have less interest in the outcome than anyone in the courtroom. In less than half an hour, the jury came back with a verdict of "not guilty."[115]

After the trial, Gordon became an outspoken promoter of liberal and radical causes, communicating with adherents in Britain, continental Europe, and America. In 1788, he was sentenced to five years in prison for publishing pamphlets criticizing Britain's justice system and libelling Queen Marie Antoinette of France. In the same year, he converted to Judaism, perhaps in the belief "current in certain dissenting circles, that the return of the Jews to Israel would herald the millennium." He grew a beard, underwent circumcision, and changed his name to Israel Abraham George Gordon. He died of gaol fever (i.e., typhus) in Newgate Prison in 1793.[116]

Mansfield was seventy-five at the time of the Gordon Riots, and it is hardly surprising that the violence and the loss of his papers and other possessions had a profound effect on him. Arthur Murphy, a writer and actor who sometimes attended trials in Mansfield's court, was saddened "to see that exalted genius sinking every day, till I saw him, who stood above all competition, dwindle into inferiority, and become no more than a common judge."[117] Murphy overstates Mansfield's decline: he remained chief justice for eight more years and handed down several important decisions during the first four of those years.[118] The riots, however, deepened his pessimism about the future of his country and hardened his innate political conservatism. A few weeks after the riots, he wrote to Philip Yorke, the son and successor to the title of Mansfield's former legal mentor, Lord Hardwicke, thanking him for a letter of sympathy:

> The kindness of your Lordship's letter touched me as it ought. It is a sore calamity which has befallen me and very unexpected. I do not feel more for myself at present than I do for the prospect of what hangs over this once happy but now [illegible] country from her own inhabitants in the midst of a foreign war [Britain was still at war with France and the American colonists]. The mischief is not over. The root is not got at ... They who wish riot and disturbance will agree to no doctrine which tends to quell it.[119]

23

Last Years

I go downhill with a gentle decay.

Lord Mansfield at the age of eighty, in a letter to the Duke of Rutland

As early as 1766, when Lord Mansfield was sixty-one and had been chief justice for ten years, London newspapers were publishing rumours that he was planning to retire.[1] Five years later, it was rumoured that he was about to retire or accept the post of lord chancellor, in either case with Sir Fletcher Norton, a prominent barrister and the speaker of the House of Commons, succeeding him as chief justice.[2] Norton was said to be "greatly disgusted" when it turned out that Mansfield had no plans to either retire or accept the chancellorship.[3] There were more reports of Mansfield's impending resignation in 1776, after he was raised to the rank of earl, with the line of succession passing to his nephew, Lord Stormont. The rumour mongers thought that once the childless chief justice had received an earldom and perpetuated his name, he would be content to devote the evening of his life to leisure pursuits. Reportedly, only negotiation over the size of his pension prevented Mansfield from retiring.[4] A year later, the King expressed his opinion that Edward Thurlow, the attorney general, was "by far the fittest person in [Westminster] Hall to succeed Lord Mansfield."[5] Thurlow did not get the job, but in 1778 he became lord chancellor.

Anticipation that Mansfield would retire at the age of seventy – or even sixty – was not unreasonable. He was of retirement age, and only one of the six chief justices who immediately preceded him had served for longer than ten years.[6] No one could possibly imagine that he would remain chief justice for an unprecedented thirty-two years. But the people who believed the rumours of Mansfield's resignation did not understand him. To be sure, both perpetuating his name and accumulating wealth were important to him, but his work was his only passion. He loved the law and he loved being chief justice. At the age of seventy, he participated in a House of Lords debate "with all the fire and eloquence as if he had been in the prime of life."[7] He was in good health; when staying at Kenwood, he tried to ride every day.[8] When he was seventy-six, a friend said he looked no older than fifty-five and that he walked three-and-a-half miles with no sign of fatigue;[9] another friend observed that he had "all the fire of 30 with his Senses in the Fullest Perfection."[10]

Despite mistaken (and in certain cases wishful) comments by some that he had outlived his abilities and was no longer capable of performing his duties as a judge,[11] Mansfield was able to recover from the shock and the personal losses caused by the Gordon Riots. He continued to entertain members of the nobility and the legal profession at Kenwood and at his newly leased home on Great Russell Street in London.[12] Although he suffered a painful injury to his right shoulder when he fell from his horse in March 1781,[13] within a month he had recovered sufficiently to engage in a debate in the House of Lords, speaking for over an hour "with his usual eloquence and accuracy."[14] For the next three years, he followed his usual routine, trying cases and hearing appeals in court, meeting with his fellow judges, participating in debates in the House of Lords and sitting as speaker of the House when the chancellor was unavailable or when the post was vacant, attending royal levees, and acting as a confidential adviser to the King.[15] In January 1784, a newspaper reported that in court "he appears so much in health and spirits that the coolness of the season seems to brace up his nerves and thereby vigour to his constitution."[16]

Mansfield divided his time between London and Kenwood. A July 1781 letter written by Mary Delany, a close friend of Lady Mansfield, to Mrs Delany's sister provides a glimpse of the Mansfields' social life at Kenwood:

> Last Friday morning Lady Mansfield and Miss Murray [Mansfield's niece] came here from Kenwood and invited Mrs.Boscawen and all her guests to dine there yesterday, which we did; and a most agreeable day it proved. Lord Mansfield in charming spirits; and after dinner, when the sun was declining, he invited me to walk around his garden and thro' the wood, and by the time we came back to tea it was 8 o'clock; we had walked two miles at least, and tho' I felt a little tired, the pleasure of the place and his conversation [made] me not sensible of it till I came home.[17]

This happy pattern of work and leisure ended with the sudden death of Lady Mansfield, after a marriage of forty-six years. She had been dangerously ill in 1778, when she was seventy-four, and again in 1782, though we do not know the nature of the illness or illnesses. Each time she apparently made a complete recovery, perhaps because she had a competent doctor and sensibly refused to use the most common remedies of the day, which included swallowing bark and ass's milk.[18]

Two years later she again fell ill. A friend wrote: "I have just had a most melancholy account of dear Lady Mansfield's health; she was seized yesterday morning. I fear there is little or no hope."[19] During her last illness, Mansfield sat up with her at night, administering the medicines that her doctors prescribed.[20] She died on 10 April 1784. Mansfield was shattered by her death. Shortly afterwards, he wrote to the Duke of Rutland: "I cannot speak upon the subject. The shock has overset me, and though I hope I am able to bear up my mind, with God's assistance, to any calamity, a nervous disorder has seized my whole body and every part. I get no sleep."[21] Two years later, he wrote to Rutland that he had suffered a return of the nervous disorder he had felt from the shock of his wife's passing.[22]

For six months after Lady Mansfield's death, Mansfield seemed to have totally lost interest in his work on the bench. Instead of travelling on circuit as usual in the summer, in June 1784 he left for the spa resort of Tunbridge Wells, in the county of Kent about twenty-five miles from London.[23] This was on the advice of his physician, though it is not clear what malady he was suffering from, other than his persistent rheumatism, which had afflicted him for at least thirty years.[24] Soon after arriving at Tunbridge, he left for the seaside resort of Brighthelmstone (it was not called by its modern name of Brighton until the early nineteenth century), again on the advice of his physician, but returned to Tunbridge a few days later.[25] One correspondent wrote on 11 June: "Lord Mansfield is just returned from the sea side & quite a new man ... I trembled for his life when he went away but has brought an additional supply of health & spirits back with him."[26] Nevertheless, Mansfield did not resume his place on the bench until the court's Michaelmas term in early November.[27] His absence from the court and apparent ill health gave rise to new rumours that he was about to retire. As usual, the rumours were false.[28]

From the late seventeenth century on, Tunbridge Wells had been popular among the elite for its easy accessibility from London by private carriage or stagecoach, commodious accommodations, pleasant walks, shops, and plentiful supply of good food from the surrounding countryside as well as fish from the nearby ports of Rye and Deal. Although many people went to Tunbridge Wells in the hope that its medicinal springs would restore their health, the social scene was at least an equal attraction. Defoe wrote of Tunbridge that it "wants nothing ... that can make a man or woman completely happy, always provided they have money."[29]

A big attraction of Tunbridge, like that of other eighteenth-century spas, was its assembly, which was described as "a stated and general meeting of the polite persons of both sexes, for the sake of conversation, gallantry, news and play."[30] A newspaper reported in a letter from Tunbridge Wells in October 1784: "Earl Mansfield, who seems by the help of the waters, to have taken a new term for terms [a weak pun conflating a term at court with the thermal waters at Tunbridge], rallies the women, young and old, every morning at eight o'clock, on the walks, with a voice as clear as a bell."[31] The same month, another newspaper commented: "Lord Mansfield leaves us today in perfect health. He has been the life of the place for the last three months; mixes in all companies and never failed to create sympathy and good humour wherever he went, still preserving his companionable qualities superior to any man living."[32]

The ladies at Tunbridge Wells idolized Mansfield, and he thoroughly enjoyed the adulation. When Sir Thomas Parker, a fellow judge some ten years older than Mansfield, bemoaned their increasing years, Mansfield is said to have replied: "Poh! Sir Thomas, let you and I talk about the young ladies, and not dwell on old age."[33] According to one observer: "He would take his share in the small talk of the ladies with all imaginable affability: he was, in fact, like most men, not in the least degree displeased at being incensed by their flattery."[34] And the ladies at Tunbridge Wells (not all of them young) did flatter Mansfield. One wrote a poem about her sadness when he returned to London in October 1784:

The Muse, quite desponding, and almost in tears,
Like a tragedy queen, on the pantiles [i.e., the promenade] appears;
For Mansfield she mourns, on those comfortless walks,
Of Mansfield she thinks, and of Mansfield she talks.[35]

Other ladies (and even gentlemen) at Tunbridge Wells wrote flowery poems praising Mansfield, which were published in the London newspapers. A stanza from one written by a lady, about his falling from a bench in the Tunbridge Wells ballroom and losing his wig, is worth quoting:

Mourn not, ye judges, when we tell
How from the bench Earl Mansfield fell,

For Justice thus replies:
"Without a Wig, without a Gown,
He still must equally be known
Pre-eminently wise."[36]

There were also cultural activities at Tunbridge Wells. On one occasion Thomas Sheridan, an actor and theatre manager and the father of playwright Richard Brinsley Sheridan, read passages from the poets Milton, Dryden, and Gray to the company after breakfast. A lady who sat next to Mansfield at this event wrote to a friend that she had the honour of making his tea, "which I delighted in, because I had the opportunity of hearing his conversation, which was as lively and as pleasant as possible."[37]

On his return to London, Mansfield resumed his usual activities. He had recovered from his unspecified illness of the summer, and he handled the workload of the court with ease, deciding as many cases each day as he had twenty years earlier.[38] William Smith, a former chief justice of colonial New York, described vividly in his diary a visit to Mansfield's court one afternoon in December 1784, when Mansfield, alone on the bench, wearing a black silk gown, a small wig, and a cocked hat, disposed of several minor cases, at least three of them involving assaults:

> I think my Lord M is crusty as well as quick, very peremptory & the Bar seem all to stand in Awe of him ... And tho' all seem to dread him yet the Room is noisy and he not very anxious for preserving Decorum upon the whole. His Language is: I shant [*sic*] suffer that; That shall not be; What do you say to this; The Witness has answered you over & over again; you shan't draw him ...
>
> He affects Sagacity riseing up: I see your Defence by the first Question, &c &c ... A Battery had been proved by one Witness who swore there was no other Person as a Witness present. Bearcroft [lawyer for the defendant] opened that he should prove the Deft. beaten and that the Plf. gave his Client a black Eye. When his Witness came in they failed him, but the Judge had his Case and took the Examination off his Hands with Rigor towards the Witness & adding as he went on, And that's all you can say You know nothing else, I am glad of it. To the 2d he said, now be careful to speak Truth, & to every Answer said, that's all is it not ... In short the whole Barr seem afraid of the Judge. The Jurors appeared to be

> as insignificant as Dogs. My Lord in the Course of Trials makes short Observations to them, but with no manner of Formality in his Address to them.[39]

On 2 March 1785, Mansfield celebrated his eightieth birthday by trying cases at Guildhall in the City of London. As soon as he entered the courtroom, Thomas Gorman, a merchant who often sat as a juror, presented him with a bouquet, "which the Chief Justice received with his usual politeness and affability."[40] A visitor to the court on that day commented: "There is the appearance of Years in his Body, none in the Exertion of the Faculties of his Mind."[41] In April he moved from Great Russell Street to a house in Lincoln's Inn Fields, which placed him closer to the courts in Westminster Hall and Guildhall; perhaps he also felt nostalgic for the neighbourhood where he had lived during the first years of his marriage.

In the summer of 1785, Mansfield went on circuit in the Home Counties (near London), taking the opportunity to make a two-day visit to Tunbridge Wells, where Lord Sheffield was staying. Sheffield wrote to a friend: "That fine old man, Lord Mansfield, having dispatched eighteen causes in one day at Maidstone, came here on Wednesday and stays till Thursday, when he goes to Lewes to open the Sussex assizes. He is wonderfully well; I am mostly with him, and he entertains me well with past and present history ... I crammed with turtle with him, and shall do the same with venison this day."[42]

Beginning in 1785, Mansfield began spending most of his time at Kenwood, where he was cared for by a number of his female relatives. These included his two unmarried nieces, Anne and Marjory Murray, the daughters of his deceased eldest brother, David; his great-niece, Lady Elizabeth Murray, the daughter of his nephew Lord Stormont; and Dido Elizabeth Belle, the illegitimate daughter of his nephew Captain John Lindsay and a black slave.[43] He would often go by his coach into London in the morning to visit friends, and return to Kenwood in time for dinner with his relatives and guests.[44]

He had a particular affection for Lady Elizabeth, with whom he would go riding to visit neighbours.[45] In late 1785, when she married George Finch-Hatton, a member of an ancient and illustrious family and a nephew of Lady Mansfield, Mansfield made the enormous gift of £10,000 to the bride. At the same time he gave £7,000 to her father, Lord Stormont, to help him get out of debt.[46]

As Mansfield entered his eighties, he continued to work with much of his old energy, although his health was beginning to decline. An incident at this time involving Lord George Sackville provides a rare glimpse of Mansfield's inner feelings about his own mortality, which he would normally have kept hidden beneath an urbane facade. In the summer of 1785, Sackville, then sixty-nine and suffering from a terminal illness, was at Tunbridge Wells. Learning that Mansfield was there too, he wanted to say his last goodbye to an old friend. A mutual friend who was present described what happened:

> Lord Sackville, just dismounted from his horse, came into the room, where he had waited a very few minutes, and staggered as he advanced to reach his hand to his respectable visitor; he drew his breath with palpitating quickness, and if I remember never rode again: there was a death-like character in his countenance, that visibly affected and disturbed Lord Mansfield in a manner, that I did not quite expect, for it had more of horror in it, than a form man [i.e., an old schoolmate] ought to have shown, and less perhaps of other feelings than a friend, invited to a meeting of that nature, must have discovered, had he not been *frightened from his propriety*.
>
> As soon as Lord Sackville had recovered his breath, his visitor remaining silent, he began by apologizing for the trouble he had given him, and for the unpleasant spectacle he was conscious of exhibiting to him in the condition he was now reduced to; "but, my good lord," he said, "though I ought not to have imposed upon you the painful ceremony of paying a last visit to a dying man, yet so great was my anxiety to return you my unfeigned thanks for all your good to me, all the kind protection you have shown me through the course of my unprosperous life, that I could not know you was so near me, and not wish to assure you of the invariable respect I have entertained for your character, and now in the most serious manner to solicit your forgiveness, if ever in the fluctuations of politics or the heats of party, I have appeared in your eyes at any moment of my life unjust to your great merits, or forgetful of your many favours."

The report goes on to say that Mansfield, quickly recovering from his shock, made a "perfectly becoming and highly satisfactory" reply.[47] Sackville died later that summer.

Mansfield's insight and humour did not desert him in his old age. His biographer, Campbell, relates a telling anecdote. Mansfield went to visit his friend Bishop Trevor, who was seriously ill. While Mansfield was with Trevor's secretary waiting to go upstairs to see the bishop, Dr Addington, Trevor's physician, himself pale and wan, arrived in a chair carried by two men, who started to take him upstairs. At this point, the secretary, fearing that the bishop would be depressed by seeing the debilitated doctor, urged Mansfield to go upstairs first. Mansfield replied: "By no means; let him go: you know nothing of human nature: the bishop will be put in good spirits by seeing any one in a worse condition than himself."[48]

As 1785 ended, Mansfield, still following his usual work routine, wrote to the Duke of Rutland: "I go downhill with a gentle decay, and, I thank God, without gout or stone. The load of business grows too great; since the last term I have 107 causes in Middlesex and 118 in London, and they must all be dispatched before Christmas Day."[49] About this time, the Duke of Rutland commissioned Sir Joshua Reynolds to paint Mansfield's portrait. Reynolds, who had been trying to persuade Mansfield to sit for him for years, jumped at the chance. He wrote, somewhat whimsically, to the duke:

> It is thought one of my best portraits, but he should have sat eight or ten years before; his countenance is much changed since he lost his teeth. I have made him exactly what he is now, as if I was upon my oath to give the truth, the whole truth, and nothing but the truth. I think it necessary to treat great men with this reverence, though I really think his Lordship would not have been displeased if this strict adherence to truth had been dispensed with, and drawn a few years younger.[50]

While painting the portrait, Reynolds asked Mansfield whether he thought it was a good likeness. Mansfield replied that he had no way of telling: he had not looked at himself in a mirror for thirty years, since his servant always dressed him and put on his wig.[51] Despite Reynolds's honesty in depicting Mansfield's aged face, Mansfield liked the portrait so much that he had an engraving made of it so that he could send copies to his friends.[52] The correspondent for a newspaper gushed that Reynolds not only paints "the lucid eye, the dimpled smile," but he also catches "the mind's interior grace and all the beauties of the soul. Even the sentenced criminal adores his placid smile."[53]

In May 1786, Mansfield complained of rheumatism in his right hand, which gave him sleepless nights and was so bad that he could not take off his hat when ceremony required it.[54] From then until Mansfield retired two years later, he seldom presided over the court, and Francis Buller, the associate judge with whom he was closest, usually acted as chief justice in his absence.[55] Inevitably, rumours of his imminent retirement resurfaced, but he returned to court in June 1786 for Trinity Term. On the first day of the new term, the judges of the three central courts, the lawyers, and court officials went in procession from Mansfield's house in Lincoln's Inn Fields to Westminster Hall, before separating to go to their respective courts.[56] A newspaper reported: "On entering the [court]room a great number of his friends flocked around him and inquired after his health with the utmost eagerness and solicitude. His lordship addressed them with his usual cheerfulness: 'I have not (said he) altered my resolution of going a very long journey but I am happy to have it once more in my power of publicly taking leave of you all before I set out.'"[57] James Boswell, who was present in court a few days later, wrote: "Lord Mansfield's taking his seat again upon the bench was a striking sight. Yet one could not help perceiving that all was vanity."[58]

Mansfield, now suffering from rheumatic pain in both arms, continued to hold the office of chief justice but he no longer sat as a judge. In July he returned to Tunbridge Wells and stayed there until October. In August, referring to himself in the third person, he wrote to a friend that he "is so ill, and suffers so extremely at present from rheumatic and nervous irritations, he is incapable of enjoying the company of those he loves the most."[59] He joined the usual procession of judges at the opening of the Michaelmas Term, but did not attend court. The London newspapers kept their readers posted on the state of Mansfield's health. In January 1787, one paper reported that although his condition weakened every day, he was taken with the idea of going to Westminster the second day of the term but the idea had to be dropped.[60]

Seeking to improve his health, Mansfield, accompanied by one of his nieces, set out in March 1787 for the watering place of Bath, going there by easy stages. Bath, a hundred miles from London in England's West Country, had become "the cynosure of elegance" by the late eighteenth century. As with Tunbridge Wells, many people went there ostensibly to "take the waters," but more likely to enjoy themselves. Bath was replete with "punch-drinkers, port-drinkers, and claret-clubs [as well as] rakes and dowagers." It was a place for watching the beautiful people, attending elaborate balls, and gambling. Parents went there to find matches for their daughters, widows to find husbands, and the sick and elderly to find health.[61] A man convalescing at Bath wrote in 1780 that it was "the pleasantest town to inhabit that ever I was in. I mean merely on account of its beautiful streets and public buildings; for as to society or public places, the little I have seen of either does not tempt me." Nevertheless, the writer may have been at least slightly tempted, for he continued: "There are a number of beautiful women offered for show on the ball nights ... with the most splendid shapes ... One glance at the rearguards had more effect upon my increasing health than all the hot water I daily swallow."[62]

Back in October 1754, when he was attorney general, Mansfield had visited Bath on the advice of his physician, who thought that bathing in the waters might cure his rheumatism.[63] Perhaps he too ogled the beautiful women. Now, more than thirty years later, whether or not he benefited from Bath's waters, he enjoyed the social life. A newspaper reported: "he rises early, cracks his jokes on the parade and is very much in the fashion of the place."[64] His conversation was chiefly about the past, on topics unrelated to politics or law.[65] One paper recounted whimsically that, although transcripts of the debates in the House of Lords were constantly sent to him, he still could not sleep without opiates.[66] According to a visitor to Bath, he "sleeps everywhere but in bed."[67]

In May Mansfield returned to London, his health not much improved.[68] He began to be criticized for continuing to draw his salary while not performing his duties as a judge.[69] It was even suggested that Parliament would be forced to intervene to get him to resign.[70] *The World*, a daily newspaper that began publishing in 1787, continually criticized his clinging to office.[71] In early November, it remarked that he had outlived everything but his salary;[72] three weeks later it opined: "Making the judges independent was justly one of the most applauded measures of his Majesty's reign, but it certainly was not in the intention of the legislature to render them independent of their employment."[73] A week later, the same newspaper expressed regret "that no kind person might be found ... to set him agoing."[74]

There were rumours that Lord Stormont had urged Mansfield not to resign in hopes that, in order to get him to step down, the government would agree to Stormont's direct succession to the earldom.[75] When Mansfield had been created an earl in 1776, the heirs of his father, the 5th Viscount Stormont, were designated his successors, which made his nephew, the 7th Viscount, his presumptive heir. Nevertheless, there was some doubt about Stormont's right to inherit the earldom because a resolution passed by the House of Lords in 1711 prohibited any Scottish peer from sitting in Parliament, even if he inherited a British peerage. The year before Mansfield died, any doubt about the succession was removed by the creation of a new earldom of Mansfield (of Kenwood in Middlesex County), specifying that Stormont would succeed to the title directly.[76]

Mansfield had a more substantive reason for remaining in office. During his long tenure on the bench, he had introduced many changes in the law to conform it to the economic and social conditions of modern England, and he did not want to see his changes reversed by an unsympathetic successor. In 1782, when the most often mentioned candidates were Sir Fletcher Norton and John Dunning, Mansfield declared his determination to stay on because he was resolved not to see his adjudications overturned or treated with contempt, which he thought would happen if either of the two were to succeed him.[77] Both Norton and Dunning were highly competent lawyers and had long-standing personal relationships with Mansfield, but Norton was known as "Sir Bullface Doublefee" for his corruption and indiscretion,[78] and Dunning's politics were opposed to Mansfield's on important issues, including Mansfield's virtually unquestioning support of the prerogatives of the King.[79]

Mansfield's choice as successor was Sir Francis Buller. He had served with Mansfield on the Court of King's Bench since 1778, when at the age of thirty-two, upon Mansfield's recommendation, he became the youngest judge ever appointed to that court.[80] Buller, in his own words, "respected and revered [Mansfield] as a second father."[81] Like Mansfield, Buller had a reputation for severity in criminal cases; he was best known for having allegedly stated that a husband could punish his wife with impunity if he used a "stick no thicker than his thumb." There is no actual evidence that Buller ever made the statement, but cartoonist James Gillray indelibly characterized him by drawing a merciless caricature of Buller as "Judge Thumb."[82]

Although Buller was no carbon copy of Mansfield, they shared a common judicial philosophy and had a close working relationship.[83] Like Mansfield, Buller was willing to bring the more flexible principles of equity into English common law, an approach that did not appeal to judges and lawyers with more traditional views. From 1784 on, Mansfield made it clear that he would not resign unless Buller was named as his successor.[84] In 1786, Mansfield wrote to Lord Chancellor Edward Thurlow, offering to resign if Buller was named, and he was "much vexed" when he learned that the government, then under the leadership of William Pitt the Younger, the son of his old political enemy Chatham, planned to appoint Sir Lloyd Kenyon instead.[85] Kenyon, who since 1784 had served as master of the rolls, the kingdom's third highest-ranking judge, was inclined to preserve the traditional formality and rigour of the common law, a position directly opposed to Mansfield's tendency to introduce equitable principles into the common law.

The impasse continued into 1788. *The World* asserted that Mansfield was well enough to go out riding every day, "yet too bad to be in Westminster Hall."[86] In March, he celebrated his eighty-third birthday with a number of his relatives in a convivial party at Kenwood.[87] Sir John Macpherson visited Kenwood that autumn and found Mansfield sitting in front of the door of the house, obviously in some physical pain. Their conversation sheds some interesting light on Mansfield's views on law and politics:

> He received me with the utmost politeness, and conducted me to his library, where we walked up and down; conversed with me on the leading events of the day, and at last asked me what was my opinion of Mr Pitt. I replied that I considered him a great Minister. "A Great Minister!" Answered Lord Mansfield, "a great young Minister you mean, Sir John. [Pitt was twenty-nine at the time and had been prime minister since he was twenty-four, the youngest person ever to serve in that office.] What did he intend by impeaching [Warren] Hastings or suffering him to be impeached?" "He meant," said I, "as I apprehend, to let justice take her course." "Justice, sir," rejoined Lord Mansfield, "pray where did he find her? Where is she?" "If you, my Lord," returned I, "do not know where to find justice, who have been dispensing her favours these fifty years, how can any man attempt it?" "Yes, sir," answered he, "that is justice between man and man. All which is thus done is well done. It is terminated. Criminal justice I can understand. But political justice, where is she? What is her colour? Sometimes she is black. Sometimes she is red too. No, Sir John, Mr Pitt is not a great Minister. He is a great young Minister. He will live to repent allowing Mr Hastings to be impeached. He has made a precedent which will

some future day be used against himself. Mr Pitt is only a great young Minister."[88]

When Macpherson related the conversation to Thurlow at dinner, Thurlow, who, like Mansfield, was a supporter of Hastings, said that only Mansfield could have said this. "He was a surprising man. Ninety-nine times out of a hundred he was right in his opinions or decisions; and when once in a hundred times he was wrong, ninety-nine men out of a hundred could not discover it. He was a wonderful man."[89]

Eventually, circumstances forced Mansfield to retire. In February, Buller had suffered a stroke, which for a while prevented him from sitting in court, and the other two King's Bench judges were unwilling to make important decisions by themselves.[90] When a third member of the court became indisposed, King's Bench was left with only one active judge.[91] On 14 April, Mansfield informed Kenyon that he planned to resign, despite his continued preference for Buller: "Except Mr Justice Buller, to whom Lord Mansfield is bound by many ties," Kenyon wrote, referring to himself in the third person, "there is no man in Westminster Hall by whom Lord Mansfield had rather be succeeded than by the Master of the Rolls."[92] On the same day, Mansfield wrote to King George III, citing "bodily infirmities" that prevented him from executing his office as his reason for resigning. On 17 April, the King cordially accepted his resignation, replying that he "has ever been conscious of the ability and zeal with which ... Mansfield has presided in [court], as well as of the attachment he has shown to his person and government."[93]

It was not until June, however, that Mansfield summoned an official of the Chancery Court to Kenwood and handed him his formal resignation.[94] After the King appointed Kenyon chief justice, Kenyon called on Mansfield, who received him "most kindly and cordially."[95] Mansfield received a letter from Thomas Erskine (who had successfully represented Lord George Gordon in his treason trial), on behalf of the gentlemen of the bar, praising his "enlightened and regular administrations of justice." Without detaining the servant who brought the letter more than five minutes, Mansfield wrote a gracious reply.[96]

As was customary, the incoming chief justice bought the gold chain of office from his predecessor (for 100 guineas), and he also paid Mansfield an additional £147, 3 shillings, and threepence for the unexpired portion of Mansfield's rent of his chambers at Serjeant's Inn.[97] Like Mansfield, Kenyon was made a peer on his appointment; Buller also received a peerage as a compensation prize.

Mansfield's fear that Kenyon would try to reverse the changes in the law that he had set in motion was justified. While Mansfield had introduced some principles of equity into the English common law, Kenyon insisted that the traditional boundary between law and equity must be maintained. "Our courts of law only consider legal rights," he wrote a few years later; "our courts of equity have other rules, by which they sometimes supersede those legal rules, and in so doing they act most beneficially for the subject. We all know, that if the courts of law were to take into their consideration all the jurisdiction belonging to courts of equity, many bad consequences would follow."[98]

Kenyon's attempts to reverse Mansfield's reforms were generally popular with the bar. One evening a year and a half after Mansfield's resignation, James Boswell was dining with Sir Joshua Reynolds, Thomas Erskine, and others, when Erskine said that Kenyon was a better chief justice than Mansfield. Boswell asked Erskine how, at the time of Mansfield's retirement, he and his fellow lawyers could have made "a complimentary address to that old fellow who you know did all he could to destroy the law of England?" According to Boswell, "Erskine was abashed, for what he did was from ostentation, contrary to his opinion; but he answered quickly: '... It was pious to give a cordial to an old man.'"[99]

At least one London newspaper praised Kenyon and, by implication, criticized his predecessor. In January 1789, *The Public Advertiser* stated that Kenyon had introduced into King's Bench "the more immediate and important use of a principle of justice than we recollect to have been impressed upon the mind so forcibly of late years: that is *sound morals*; to establish this principle and to make it the criterion of judicial determinations is the true merit of the English laws."[100] This comment, however applicable it may have been to Kenyon, was unfair to Mansfield, who had always recognized and promoted the central place of morality in his legal judgments. But *The Public Advertiser* was a long-time foe of Mansfield. In the 1770s it had published the letters of the anonymous Junius, one of which was a personal attack on the chief justice. An earlier Junius letter criticizing the King and the ministry had led to the editor of *The Public Advertiser* being charged with seditious libel; he was tried before Mansfield, but the jury acquitted him.[101]

Immediately after his retirement, Mansfield was back at Tunbridge Wells. *The World* reported: "Now that poor Lord Mansfield has been so properly relieved of all care as to public business nothing can exceed him for colloquial turn and convivial pleasantry." Nonetheless, he was taking opiates at night and purges in the morning to gain some relief from pain and sleeplessness.[102] He soon returned to Kenwood, where he spent his remaining years, looked after by his two nieces and his great-niece, Dido Elizabeth Belle. Although he sometimes visited London,[103] soon this was no longer possible because he had difficulty moving his hands and arms, presumably as a result of his rheumatism.[104] By September 1788, he was no longer able to write without great difficulty and pain. The several codicils to his will that he made from then until his death were dictated to his nieces (and in one instance to Stormont), who then read them back to him; after approving them, he made his "mark" on the codicil. In response to a letter from a friend in July 1792, he replied: "I am forced to Borrow another hand to return my thanks ... Dictated by the 1st Earl of Mansfield in his 88th year."[105]

His routine at Kenwood was to rise early and have several of the morning papers read to him at breakfast, presumably by one of his nieces. He would dine early by himself, then drink a glass or two of wine and go to bed at nine or ten in the evening.[106] He had occasional visitors, including Erskine, who would go to Kenwood on behalf of the members of the bar to inquire about his health, which continued to decline. In September 1791, he was suffering from severe stomach pains and fainting fits.[107]

Mansfield remained in full possession of his intellectual powers, although he was too weak to exert himself mentally for any long period.[108] Not long before Mansfield's death, a visitor to Kenwood recalled seeing him "sitting with a cloth under his chin, as he was then dribbling, but that he was reading some causes heard before a chief justice of the United States and remarked that out of the whole number in the volume there were not above one or two that he should have decided otherwise ... Though he had lost all muscular control and could scarcely swallow his saliva, his intellectual powers were still sufficiently unimpaired to render that kind of reading the most agreeable to him."[109]

For many years, Mansfield had been pessimistic about England's future. Early in George III's reign, when an unstable government was dithering over how it should respond to the demands of the rebellious American colonists, he wrote to the Duke of Newcastle: "I see no hope of salvation for this undone country from any human means. All quarters in different ways & degrees contribute to her ruin. Confusion comes apace & will soon be general. France does foment and will soon avail herself of it."[110] The onset of the French Revolution a year after his retirement increased his pessimism. When the French National Assembly agreed on a constitution in 1791, Mansfield's apothecary ventured the opinion that the troubles in France were now over. Mansfield presciently replied: "*Over*, sir, do you say? My dear sir, they are not yet begun."[111] On another occasion, when his physician asked him what he thought of the French Revolution, Mansfield exploded in fury, at the same time making clear his own view that developments to meet new circumstances should come about not by sweeping constitutional or statutory changes but by incremental changes in the law, only in response to a proven need:[112]

> *A nation* which, for more than twelve centuries, has made a conspicuous figure in the annals of Europe: a nation where the polite arts first flourished in the Northern Hemisphere: ... *a nation* whose philosophers and men of science cherished and improved civilization: ... to think that *a nation* like this should not, in the course of so many centuries, have learned *something* worth preserving, should not have hit upon some little code of laws, or a few principles sufficient to form one! Idiots! who, instead of retaining what was valuable, sound, and energetic in their constitution, has at once sunk into barbarity, lost sight of first principles, and brought forward a farrago of laws fit for Botany Bay! It is enough to fill the mind with astonishment and abhorrence![113]

In fact, during his final years, the French Revolution was his favourite topic of conversation.[114] He was very inquisitive and anxious about the momentous events taking place in France, and he was especially shocked by the execution of Louis XVI in January 1793, only two months before his own death.[115]

By early 1793, it was clear that Mansfield was failing. Although he said he was not afraid of death (the incident with George Sackville at Tunbridge Wells, described earlier, casts some doubt on this), he was afraid of suffering and asked his doctor to let him die quietly.[116] He repeatedly commanded that no poultices (which were designed to raise blisters) or other methods should be tried to bring him out of any delirium or stupor.[117] On 16 March, he was reported to be dangerously ill at Kenwood.[118] He retained his mental faculties until three or four days before he died, when he refused to be taken from his bed as usual; soon afterwards he lost the ability to speak. He died on 17 March 1793, two weeks after his eighty-eighth birthday.[119]

His will, kept with no fewer than nineteen codicils in a tin box at Kenwood, had been executed in 1782, two year's before his wife's death. Written in his own hand in plain non-technical language on little more than half a sheet of paper, the will shines an interesting light on his character and personal relationships.[120]

Aside from many specific bequests, the original will provided that Lady Mansfield would enjoy all his personal property during her life, and that "after the death of my dear Wife I leave my whole real & personal Estate ... to my Nephew David Viscount Stormont" and his heirs. He appointed his wife and Stormont as his executors.

He made generous bequests to several relatives. His nieces, Anne and Marjory Murray, were to receive £6,000 each, and an additional £300 a year after the death of his wife, with the survivor of them receiving £600 a year for her life. His great-niece, Elizabeth Murray, was to get £10,000, a bequest he had satisfied in 1785 by giving her this amount upon her marriage. Smaller bequests were made to his nephew, Sir John Lindsay, and to the children of another nephew, Sir David Lindsay. The will stated that Lady Stormont was to get "my best Diamond Ring, to Lady David Lindsay my second, and to Lady John Lindsay my third Diamond Ring which I hope they will wear for my Sake." Mansfield confirmed the freedom of his great-niece, Dido Elizabeth Belle, who, after his wife's death, was to receive £100 a year for life.[121]

Mansfield also made bequests to a large number of his servants, the most important of whom was John Way, who had served him as an accountant and investment manager, and in many other capacities. Way was to receive £1,000, and several servants were to receive amounts ranging from £100 to £300. Other servants who had lived with him for more than five years were to receive three years' wages if they were still in his service at the time of his death.

In the eleven years that passed between the execution of his will and his death, Mansfield made nineteen codicils, all but one of them after Lady Mansfield's death in 1784. Several of the codicils added to the bequests to his nieces, Anne and Marjory. In May 1786, in two separate codicils, he left an additional £500 to Dido Elizabeth Belle. Clearly, he wished to show his gratitude to the women who looked after him in his old age. Other codicils increased the amount of the bequests to his servants and made new bequests to servants who had more recently entered his service.

In two separate codicils executed in November 1786, Mansfield increased the bequest to Way by £1,000 and left him an annuity of £500. Mansfield also asked Stormont, his successor to the earldom, to use Way "as he has done for me in the Management of my Rents Securitys & Effects, but I leave this to his Honour, of which I have no doubt, & do not make it a Condition." Way did provide Stormont with information and advice about Mansfield's investments immediately after his death, but it is not known whether the 2nd Earl kept Way in his employ during the three years until his own death in 1796.[122] Mansfield also had used his patronage as chief justice to compensate Way, by giving him the sinecure of a life appointment as "filazer" of the Court of King's Bench, i.e., the court official who filed writs and issued processes.[123]

The timing of several of the codicils to Mansfield's will is curious. He executed three codicils within less than two weeks of each other in May 1786, and two of them increased the amounts bequeathed to Anne and Marjory Murray and Dido Elizabeth Belle. Similarly, he executed two codicils within two weeks in November 1786, both of which increased the amounts bequeathed to John Way. One can only speculate, but it is possible that Mansfield was being pressured by the people upon whom he depended to increase their compensation for the time and effort they were spending on his behalf. Five years later, in October 1791, Mansfield executed four codicils within four *days* of each other. These codicils contained diverse bequests, mostly to his servants, and the fact that they were bunched within a short period suggests that Mansfield, anticipating his death, was anxious to make sure that his affairs were in order.

Two other codicils raise an interesting question. The first one, executed in May 1786, revokes any bequest to William Lindsay, the eldest son of Mansfield's nephew Sir David Lindsay; but a codicil executed three years later states that Mansfield did not mean to revoke the bequest to William. It would be interesting to know why Mansfield decided to cut William out of his will and then changed his mind.

The entire legal profession of London, including the score of judges and the three hundred lawyers who practised before them, had planned to pay their respects to the great man by accompanying his corpse in a five-mile procession from Kenwood to Westminster Abbey. That idea was dropped when Stormont informed the judges that Mansfield's will stated that he desired to be buried privately, and "from the love I bear to the place of my early Education, I wish it to be in Westminster Abbey."[124] He was buried at nine o'clock on the morning of 28 March in the North Transept of the Abbey, about twenty paces from a little gate that led into the churchyard, in the same vault as Lady Mansfield, and next to the grave of his old enemy William Pitt, Earl of Chatham.[125] Honouring his wishes, only a few relatives and personal friends attended the funeral in the Abbey.

A former client from the time Mansfield was a practicing lawyer, for whom he had successfully recovered a very large share of disputed property, had left £1,500 in his will to build a monument to Mansfield and to award a prize for the best inscription to be carved on the monument.[126] The monument, one of the largest in the Abbey, shows a seated figure of Mansfield, flanked by two allegorical figures representing justice and learning. It was designed by John Flaxman, a well-known sculptor, who had also been a designer of relief figures for the Wedgwood pottery factory.[127] The inscription on the monument states:

> Here Murray, long enough his country's pride,
> Is now no more than Tully or than Hyde.
> Foretold by Pope and fulfilled in the year 1793.[128]

An epitaph written by a Mr David Rees paid tribute not only to Mansfield's pre-eminence as a judge but also to his emulation of his classical forbears:

> Sacred to the immortal memory
> of WILLIAM MURRAY, Earl of Mansfield
> late Lord Chief Justice of England
> who
> during the course of thirty years
> and upwards
> not only discharged the duties
> of that High Office
> with unexampled assiduity
> and
> unquestionable reputation,
> but happily united
> the wisdom of Socrates

the eloquence of Cicero
the harmony of Virgil
and
the wit and pleasantries of Horace
with the beauties of his own unbounded genius
became and was confessedly
the brightest ornament of human nature
that any age or country has hitherto
been able to boast of.
The Venerable Peer
having passed the age fourscore
and finding his corporeal powers too feeble
much longer to display his
wonderful talents
with the wonted energy
withdrew himself from the Bench
and, willing to appear with those talents
undimmed at the throne of his
Divine Creator
by whom he had been so peculiarly and
abundantly endued
shook off the cloak of mortality
in his eighty-ninth year.

Epilogue

Lord Mansfield's Legacy

More than two hundred and fifty years after he became a judge, Lord Mansfield remains a dominant presence, not just to legal scholars but also to judges and lawyers in Britain, the United States, Canada, and other nations that follow the Anglo-American legal tradition. Every year, his decisions and pronouncements are cited as relevant to present-day conditions (or in some cases explicitly rejected because they are no longer relevant). Courts and governments around the globe continue to learn from Mansfield's wisdom.

Initially, there was resistance in the United States to Mansfield's influence. In view of his opposition to the colonists before and during the Revolutionary War, and his generally conservative political views, it is not surprising that some of the founders of the infant republic showed considerable hostility toward him. After independence, the English common law formed the basis for the American legal system, but Thomas Jefferson, the drafter of the Declaration of Independence and the leader, later, of the Democratic-Republican Party, wanted to exclude any trace of Mansfield's jurisprudence from the United States. Jefferson believed that the wide discretion exercised by Mansfield and other English common law judges was a threat to liberty.[1] He wrote from Paris in 1788: "I hold it essential, in America, to forbid that any English decision which has happened since the accession of Lord Mansfield to the bench [in 1756], should ever be cited in a court; though there have come many good ones from him, yet there is so much sly poison instilled into a great part of them, that it is better to proscribe the whole."[2]

Several years later, Jefferson repeated this advice, although he revised it slightly by saying that American law should exclude English cases from the beginning of George III's reign in 1760. Regarding Mansfield as the evil genius of English law, Jefferson observed that his proposal "would add the advantage of getting us rid of all Mansfield's innovations."[3] He was particularly concerned that Mansfield had imported, through a process that Jefferson called the "civilization" of the common law, portions of the civil law of continental Europe into English law. "It is well known," wrote Jefferson, "that a man of one system of law can never become pure and sound in any other. Lord Mansfield was a splendid proof of this."[4] More fundamentally, Jefferson's democratic tenets were at odds with Mansfield's invariable respect for the authority of the state.

Chief Justice John Marshall of the United States Supreme Court, a Federalist in party politics, disagreed with Jefferson, calling Mansfield "one of the greatest Judges who ever sat on any bench, & who has done more than any other to remove those technical impediments which grow out of a different state of society, & too long continued to obstruct the course of substantial justice."[5] John Adams, the second United States president and also a Federalist, referred to him in 1783 as "the great Lord Mansfield."[6] Marshall's and Adams's view has prevailed over Jefferson's. After the Revolution, the American states, either by statute or by judicial decisions, adopted the English common law as precedents without excluding Mansfield's decisions.[7] His commercial-law decisions, in which he assimilated mercantile custom into the common law, were especially influential in New York, the hub of American commerce.[8]

Thus, Mansfield's decisions influenced American law from the very beginning of the republic. In 1804, only eleven years after Mansfield died, the New York attorney general, prosecuting a criminal case, cited with approval Mansfield's instructions to the jury in the John Horne seditious-libel case. Alexander Hamilton, representing the defendant in the New York case, was wary of adopting Mansfield's doctrines into American law, presumably because of Mansfield's harsh rulings in seditious-libel cases,[9] but he, nonetheless, joined the prosecutor in praise of the great judge:

> The attorney-general has taken vast pains to celebrate Lord Mansfield's character. Never, till now, did I hear that his reputation was high in republican estimation; never, till now, did I consider him as a model for republican imitation. I do not mean, however, to detract from the fame of that truly great man, but only conceived his sentiments were not

> those fit for a republic. No man more truly reveres his exalted fame than myself; if he had his faults, he had his virtues; and I would not only tread lightly on his ashes, but drop a tear as I passed by. He indeed, seems to have been the parent of the doctrines of the other [i.e., the prosecutor's] side. Such, however, we trust, will not be proved to be the doctrines of the common law nor of this country.[10]

Mansfield's reputation in the United States continued to grow. According to Campbell, writing in the mid-nineteenth century, "Beyond the Atlantic the reputation of Mansfield is as high as in his own country, and his decisions are regarded of as great authority in the courts of New York and Washington as in Westminster Hall."[11] Joseph Story, after John Marshall the most eminent American judge of the early nineteenth century, paid tribute to Mansfield's contributions to American law, citing particularly his influence on maritime law and his borrowing what was most useful from the commercial law of continental Europe.[12] One writer coupled Mansfield's name to those of John Marshall and Daniel Webster as legal philosophers and reformers with an "intrepid love of right."[13]

Although Oliver Wendell Holmes Jr, whose long career as a judge and legal philosopher spanned the late nineteenth and early twentieth centuries, did not share Mansfield's judicial philosophy, he did share Mansfield's impatience with blind adherence to precedent. On this question, he flattered Mansfield, perhaps unconsciously, by imitation. In *The Path of the Law*, he wrote: "It is revolting to have no better reason for a rule of law than so it was laid down in the time of Henry IV. It is still more revolting if the grounds upon which it was laid down have vanished long since, and the rule simply persists from blind imitation of the past,"[14] echoing Mansfield over a century earlier in his opinion in *Jones v. Randall*: "The law would be a strange science ... if ... we must go to the time of Richard I ... to see what is the law."[15]

Today, Mansfield's legacy in the United States is secure. The Supreme Court has cited Mansfield's decisions over three hundred and thirty times, in cases that bear on almost every area of the law. Just a few are mentioned here as illustrations of Mansfield's continuing influence and relevance.

- On corporate law, the Court, citing Mansfield, ruled in the famous *Dartmouth College* case[16] that the government cannot deprive a corporation of rights that were given to it in its original charter.[17]

- On commercial law, the Court cited Mansfield in ruling that a bona fide purchaser of a negotiable instrument acquires title to it. Thus, a person who buys a stolen banknote, reasonably believing that the seller has acquired it honestly, becomes the owner of the note.[18]
- On defamation, the Court cited Mansfield in ruling that a libellous publication is not protected by the First Amendment. Freedom of speech does not include the right to tell harmful lies about people.[19]
- On unjust enrichment, the Court cited Mansfield in deciding that a person can recover assets that are rightfully his, even if the person holding the assets never agreed to return them. In such cases, a promise will be implied. For example, money obtained from someone by mistake must be returned to the rightful owner.[20]
- On parental rights, the Court cited Mansfield in deciding that a court had discretion to resolve custody disputes in a manner best suited to serve the welfare of the child.[21]
- On contracts, the Court cited Mansfield in holding that a promise made for an immoral purpose is not binding.[22]
- On criminal law, the Court cited Mansfield in holding that a confession must be voluntary to be admissible in evidence.[23]
- On searches and seizures, the Court cited Mansfield in holding that electronic surveillance in domestic security matters requires an appropriate warrant procedure.[24]
- On the writ of habeas corpus, the Court cited Mansfield in ruling that the writ is available to a prisoner at Guantanamo Bay, a location that is under the control of the government although outside its sovereignty. Thus, a prisoner cannot be deprived of his right to challenge his detention simply because he is being held outside the geographical limits of the United States.[25]

The lower federal and state courts in the United States have cited Mansfield countless times, as have legal scholars and even government officials. For example, in 1976 New York's highest court cited Mansfield when it ruled that an attempt to commit a crime, even if ultimately unsuccessful, can be a criminal act.[26] Another example is a 2012 opinion of the Nebraska Supreme Court that discussed the longstanding rule known as "Lord Mansfield's Rule," which established a presumption that a child born during wedlock was legitimate, and prohibited a husband and wife from testifying against each other to overcome the presumption. The court decided that, in view of the advent of genetic testing, the rule should no longer be followed.[27]

On a completely different kind of matter, the authors of a 2008 working paper of the Federal Reserve Bank of Cleveland made a detailed analysis of Mansfield's 1758 decision that a bona fide purchaser of a banknote held the note free and clear of any claims that conflicted with his ownership of the note. The authors concluded that the application of Mansfield's "holder in due course" rule to home mortgage notes should be reconsidered.[28]

Although both the Nebraska court and the authors of the Federal Reserve Bank working paper questioned the modern-day applicability of a Mansfield decision, both felt it necessary to explain carefully why a rule that he established more than two centuries ago should no longer be followed. It is undeniable that the mind of Lord Mansfield is with us as a living presence today.

Mansfield's jurisprudence remains equally relevant in Canada and Britain. In the late twentieth and early twenty-first centuries, Canadian courts have continued to cite his rulings numerous times to support their own decisions. To cite only a few, the Canadian courts have referred to Mansfield when holding that a court has the inherent power to prevent injustice, even in the absence of a statute;[29] that different statutes on the same subject, though made at different times, should be taken together as explanatory of each other;[30] that an insured must disclose all material facts to the insurer, except for facts that the insurer may be presumed to already know;[31] that a court will not lend its aid to a person whose claim is based upon an immoral or illegal act;[32] that a person who is unjustly enriched must return the money or property to the rightful owner;[33] that a person holding an office of trust and confidence may be punished for acting with a corrupt motive, as opposed to an error of judgment;[34] that a court may not violate the privacy of jury deliberations;[35] and that a balance must be struck between rewarding the efforts of artists and inventors and not depriving the public of improvements or retarding the progress of the arts.[36]

Meanwhile, Canadian legal writers continue to discuss Mansfield's decisions and legal philosophy, and their impact on Canadian law. A survey of recent literature encompasses articles on unjust enrichment,[37] copyright,[38] contracts,[39] slavery,[40] jury deliberations,[41] the influence of conscience on the law,[42] Mansfield's use of special juries in commercial cases,[43] and the role of the courts in effecting legal change.[44]

In Britain, Mansfield's jurisprudence remains equally relevant today. For example, in a 2012 case, a husband sued his wife for breach of confidence for breaking into his computer and stealing valuable and confidential files. The question before the court was whether there was a duty of confidence between husband and wife that could be enforced in a court of equity. In ruling that such a duty existed, the court reached back over two hundred years to Mansfield:

> The notion that a husband cannot enjoy rights of confidence as against his wife in respect of information which would otherwise be confidential as against her if they were not married, seems to us to be simply unsustainable. The idea that a husband and a wife should be regarded as a single unit in law was a fiction which has been abandon[ed] for a long time. Thus more than two centuries ago ... Lord Mansfield ... said that: "The fashion of the times has introduced an alteration, and now husband and wife may, for many purposes, be separated, and possess separate property, a practice unknown to the old law."[45]

Other recent British cases citing Mansfield include decisions that a public officer may be held criminally liable for misbehaviour in office;[46] that the law prohibits prior restraint of the freedom of the press;[47] that in a judicial proceeding, a party, witness, counsel, juror, and judge all enjoy immunity from liability for words spoken in the course of the proceeding;[48] that a court may not invade the privacy of jury deliberations;[49] and that a court will not lend its aid to a person who bases his case on an immoral or illegal act.[50] In the year 2011 alone, at least ten reported cases in the United Kingdom cited Mansfield's decisions to support their rulings. Mansfield continues to be a source of legal wisdom for courts in countries or jurisdictions that have adopted, to a greater or lesser extent, the English common law, including Australia, Hong Kong, India, Israel, New Zealand, and South Africa.[51]

The question naturally arises: Why are Mansfield's decisions in virtually every important area of the law still being cited by judges and legal scholars today? No judge of the eighteenth – or perhaps even the twentieth – century is so often referred to when seeking an answer to a question of law.

One reason may be the broad jurisdiction of Mansfield's court. He both conducted trials and heard appeals on an enormous range of issues that came before him, from questions of fundamental human rights, such as the legality of slavery or the scope of the writ of habeas corpus, to critical questions of procedure and evidence, such as whether an expert witness could give testimony in court or the scope of the attorney-client privilege.

But this is only a small part of the answer. Other prominent eighteenth-century judges exercised similarly broad jurisdiction, but they are largely or completely forgotten today. To understand Mansfield's enduring influence, we have to look at his method of deciding cases as well as the fundamental values on which he based his decisions. He believed that, while it was important that the common law provide precedents that lawyers and clients could use to guide themselves in their conduct, a precedent is valuable only if it is based on a principle. Thus, when he followed, modified, or established a precedent, he distilled from it a principle that clarified the law and could be applied to a variety of basically similar, although perhaps superficially different, situations. These principles, clearly expressed and standing like guideposts, have stood the test of time. Even as social and economic conditions have changed over more than two centuries, many of the principles that Mansfield articulated are sufficiently general to be relevant in many different circumstances *and* sufficiently specific to be of practical value to lawyers and judges.

But the usefulness of a principle, however well expressed, depends on its substance, and here we must turn to Mansfield's personal qualities and the values he espoused. He was, first and foremost, a learned lawyer. His diligence, knowledge, and judgment were extraordinary. As a young man, he took the initiative to become familiar with the laws of ancient Rome and modern Europe, some of which he incorporated into the then overly formalistic common law of England. His study of the great philosophers of law instilled in him a belief that all law was based on morality, reason, and human nature, which were the same everywhere, even though customs, mores, and traditions differ from country to country. He was familiar with mercantile customs, which to a large extent were common to all trading countries, and he brought these too into the common law. As a result of his deep and broad understanding of the law and of practical affairs, the lasting principles he established were realistic and full of common sense.

One final characteristic completed Mansfield's genius, causing its brilliance to shine all the way to the twenty-first century. He combined his astute understanding of human nature with a vigorous aspiration to achieve justice. To him, morals were an essential element of law, and he made his court the custodian of the morals of the people. To him, morality was an essential part of the English common law. The principles of law he established were always aimed at a result that was fair. And his humanist focus on the intent of the individual, whether in making a contract, writing a will, committing a crime, or some other action, is consistent with modern sensibility.

Mansfield was criticized in his own time, and has been criticized since, for softening the rigid common law by infusing it with the more flexible procedures of equity. Many of his contemporaries believed that he wanted simply to decide cases according to his own unfettered discretion. But posterity has refuted this view. With few exceptions, Mansfield's rulings were solidly grounded on his encyclopedic knowledge of the law, his understanding of human nature, his diligence in ascertaining the facts of a dispute, his sound common sense, and his overriding instinct for justice. Ironically, innovations denounced by some as nothing but products of his personal preference have become part of the bedrock of Anglo-American law.

There is perhaps no better way to end this book than to quote a nineteenth-century English lawyer's summary of Lord Mansfield's contribution to Anglo-American law and society:

> England and America, and the civilized world, lie under the deepest obligations to him: – Wherever commerce shall extend its social influences; wherever justice shall be administered by enlightened and liberal rules; wherever contracts shall be expounded upon the eternal principles of right and wrong; wherever moral delicacy and juridical refinement shall be infused into the municipal code, at once to persuade men to be honest, and to keep them so; wherever the intercourse of mankind shall aim at something more elevated than that groveling spirit of barter, in which meanness, and avarice, and fraud strive for the mastery over ignorance and folly – the name of Lord Mansfield will be held in reverence by the good and the wise, by the honest merchant, the enlightened lawyer, the just statesman and conscientious Judge.[52]

Acknowledgments

Brooklyn Law School provided me access to its library facilities and databases, and provided financing for the thirteen law students who acted as my research assistants over a period of six years. These individuals performed a variety of tasks with great spirit and efficiency, including some highly creative detective work, tracking down elusive facts and delving into the lives of Mansfield and his contemporaries. They are Kerry Fox, Shannon Hahn, Edward Heppt, James Spencer Hoffman, Won-Hyung (Warren) Lee, Courtney Maccarone, Kenneth Marx, Sonal Mehta, Anthony Mongone, Mitul Patel, Ross Shikowitz, David Sienko, and Sylvia Simson.

Several librarians helped me with my research. Librarians, in my experience, are the most admirable professionals on Earth, combining literary expertise, technological proficiency, a keenly felt service mentality, and unbounded cheerfulness and enthusiasm. My special thanks go to Jean Davis of the Brooklyn Law School Library for the many obscure books, articles, and dissertations that she found for me, in print or online, at the Brooklyn library and from other locales. I also extend my gratitude to the late Sara Robbins, and Rosemary Campagna and Victoria Szymczak of the Brooklyn Law School Library; Suzy Taraba and Valerie Gillispie of the Special Collections and Archives at the Olin Library, Wesleyan University, who for over eighteen months greatly facilitated my research into the Arthur T. Vanderbilt Collection of Mansfield papers; Mary Robertson, chief curator of manuscripts at the Huntington Library; Tessa Spencer of the National Register of Archives for Scotland; Jennifer Johnstone and Keren Guthrie of the Archive Services, University of Dundee. I also thank the many librarians who helped me at the British Library; New York Public Library; J.P. Morgan Library in New York; New York Historical Society; Columbia

University Library; and Rare Book, Manuscript, and Special Collections Library at Duke University.

My deep appreciation goes to the people at Scone Palace, home of the present Lord and Lady Mansfield, who helped me with the research that went into this book: Sarah Adams, Elspeth Bruce, Gwen Haxton, and Thomas MacFarlane. Others who assisted me in many different, but always valuable, ways are Jacqueline Aronson, Carol Haralson, Bailey Kuklin, James Oldham, Elizabeth Varon, and the late Melvin P. Antell.

Arthur T. Vanderbilt II, grandson of Judge Vanderbilt, read the entire manuscript in draft and gave me many helpful suggestions. Equally important, he was a continual source of encouragement and wise advice throughout the process of researching and writing this book. The members of the Brooklyn Law School faculty who participated in a faculty workshop on Lord Mansfield in January 2009 asked searching questions that set me on new paths of thinking and research on Mansfield's jurisprudence. Over numerous lunches, my friend and law school classmate, Michael Finkelstein, gave me the benefit of his always prudent and creative thoughts on how the book should be organized.

I want to express my gratitude to all the individuals with whom I had contact at McGill-Queen's University Press, and special thanks go to Jacqueline Mason, who guided me through every step of the publishing process with efficiency and friendliness, and to Eleanor Gasparik, whose thorough and sensitive editing improved the book enormously. I am greatly beholden to the two anonymous readers of the manuscript whose reports contained many helpful suggestions.

My daughter, Susan Poser, read several chapters of the manuscript and discussed every aspect of the project with me. Her astute comments and suggestions have immeasurably improved the book.

Finally, it is difficult for me to express adequately my gratitude to my wife and soulmate, Judy Cohn, who was with me throughout the process of researching and writing this book, beginning with our first visit to Scone Palace in the summer of 2006, when seeing a portrait of Lord Mansfield by Sir Joshua Reynolds started me thinking about this biography. Judy read the entire manuscript, most of it more than once, and her perspective as a non-lawyer was particularly valuable to me. If a sentence or a paragraph was not clear to her, then it had to be rewritten. On a personal note, her admirable patience with my Mansfield obsession, which often dominated our dinner-table conversations of the past six years, is deeply appreciated.

Notes

ABBREVIATIONS

BL	British Library, London
JPML	J.P. Morgan Library, New York City
NAS	National Archives of Scotland, Edinburgh
NYHS	New York Historical Society, New York City
ODNB	*Oxford Dictionary of National Biography*
SP	Mansfield papers at Scone Palace, Scotland (examined at Dundee University Library, Dundee, Scotland)
VC	Arthur T. Vanderbilt (1888–1957) Political, Professional, and Judicial Papers in the Collection on Legal Change at the Olin Library, Wesleyan University, Middletown, Connecticut (A detailed register of the Vanderbilt Collection was compiled by Clement E. Vose in 1972 and is available at the Olin Library. The material concerning Lord Mansfield is in Boxes 315–331.)

Note: When quotations are not indicated with an endnote number, it is because the same source will be quoted again shortly following the first quotation. The last quotation from the same source will be marked with a note number.

PREFACE

1 C.H.S. Fifoot, *Lord Mansfield* (Oxford: Clarendon Press, 1936. Reprinted by Darmstadt: Scientia Verlag Aalen, 1977).
2 Edmund Heward, *Lord Mansfield* (Chichester and London: Barry Rose Publishers Ltd, 1979).
3 James Oldham, *The Mansfield Manuscripts and the Growth of English Law in the Eighteenth Century*, 2 vols. (Chapel Hill and London: University of North Carolina Press, 1992).

4 James Oldham, *English Common Law in the Age of Mansfield* (Chapel Hill and London: University of North Carolina Press, 2004).
5 John Holliday, *The Life of William, Late Earl of Mansfield* (London: Printed for P. Elmsly and D. Brenner, etc., 1797).
6 Baron John Campbell, *The Lives of the Chief Justices of England: From the Norman Conquest till the Death of Lord Mansfield*. 2 vols. (London: John Murray, 1849).
7 John Buchan, *Memory Hold-the-Door* (London: Hodder and Stoughton Ltd, 1940), 90.
8 Hamilton to Vanderbilt, 11 Jul. 1938; Vanderbilt to Hamilton (telegram), 19 Jul. 1938 (VC).
9 Those interested in other decisions of Mansfield should consult Oldham, *The Mansfield Manuscripts*.

INTRODUCTION

1 Steve Pincus, *1688: The First Modern Revolution* (New Haven and London: Yale University Press, 2009), 8.
2 Bertrand Russell, *A History of Western Philosophy* (New York: Simon and Schuster, 1945), 543.
3 Roy Porter, *The Creation of the Modern World: The Untold Story of the British Enlightenment* (New York and London: W.W. Norton & Company, 2000), 136–7.
4 See, for example, *Doe v. Exxon Mobil*, 654 F.3d 11 (D.C. Cir. 2011), holding that residents of Indonesia could sue in a United States court for wrongs allegedly done to them in Indonesia by a United States corporation. The court cited *Mostyn v. Fabrigas*, 1 Cowp. 160 (1774), where Mansfield said: "A subject born in Minorca has as good a right to appeal to the King's Courts of Justice, as one who is born within the sound of Bow Bell." Mansfield was referring to the London church of Mary-le-bow; only a person born within the sound of its bell could claim to be a Cockney.
5 See, for example, *Teelucksingh v. R.*, 2011 CarswellNat 25, 2011 TCC 22 (2011), where the Canadian Tax Court ruled that, where a party or its witness in a trial decides not to give evidence that was within its power to give, the court is justified in drawing the inference that the evidence would have been unfavourable to that party. The court cited Mansfield's ruling in *Blatch v. Archer*, 1 Cowp. 63, 65, 98 Eng. Rep. 968, 970 (1774): "It is certainly a maxim that all evidence is to be weighed according to the proof which was in the power of one side to have produced, and in the power of the other to have contradicted."
6 See, for example, *Jones v. Kaney*, 2011 UKSC 13 (2011), where the Supreme Court of the United Kingdom held that expert witnesses retained in litigation enjoyed immunity from liability. The court quoted Mansfield in *R. v. Skinner*, Lofft. 55, 56, 98 Eng. Rep. 529, 530 (1772): "Neither party, witness, counsel, jury, or Judge, can be put to answer, civilly or criminally, for words spoken in office."

7 *Rasul v. Bush*, 542 U.S. 466, 482 (2004); *Boumediene v. Bush*, 533 U.S. 723 (2008), both citing *King v. Cowle*, 2 Burr. 834, 97 Eng. Rep. 587 (1759).

8 The scope of parliamentary legislation during the eighteenth century is summarized by Joanna Innes, "Governing diverse societies" in Paul Langford, ed., *The Eighteenth Century: 1688–1815* (Oxford: Oxford University Press, 2002), 123.

9 Bernard I. Shientag, "Lord Mansfield Revisited: A Modern Assessment," *Fordham Law Review* x (1941): 345.

10 John Buchan, *Some Eighteenth Century Byways* (Edinburgh and London: William Blackwood & Sons, 1908), 70–1.

CHAPTER ONE

1 John Campbell, Lord Mansfield's nineteenth-century biographer, states that King James, "caught by the good looks, pleasing manners, and skill in all sorts of games which he discovered in David Murray … made him his companion, knighted him, and promoted him to be Master of the Horse, Comptroller of the Household, and Captain of the Body-Guard." John Campbell, *The Lives of the Chief Justices of England: From the Norman Conquest till the Death of Lord Mansfield* (London: John Murray, 1849), ii, 305. Campbell does not, however, cite any source for this information.

2 SP, Bundle 1852.

3 *Scots Magazine* (March 1793), 154–5 (VC, Box 322).

4 The abbey and palace had been destroyed in the religious wars of the sixteenth century, but a new abbey and palace were built in the seventeenth century. J.J. Bell, *The Glory of Scotland* (London: G.G. Harrap and Co., 1932), 284. Nothing except the gateway remains of the seventeenth-century palace; the present palace was built in the early nineteenth century. Scone is pronounced "Skoon."

5 Alan R. MacDonald, "Murray, David, first Viscount Stormont," in H.C.G. Matthew and Brian Harrison, eds., *Oxford Dictionary of National Biography*, rev. ed. (hereinafter *ODNB*) (Oxford and New York: Oxford University Press, 2004).

6 Charles Sanford Terry, *The Chevalier de St. George and the Jacobite Movements in his Favour 1701–1720* (London: David Nutt, 1901), 99.

7 Sir Robert Grierson of Lag was not a direct ancestor of William Murray. Sir Robert's father was the younger brother of Sir John Grierson of Lag, Murray's great-grandfather on his mother's side. http://www.thepeerage.com/p22823.htm#i228229 (accessed 22 Dec. 2011).

8 The fate of the Wigtown martyrs is described in Blackwood's *Edinburgh Magazine*, American Edition, 57 (1863): 742–8: Charlotte M. Yonge, ed., *The Monthly Packet of Readings for Members of the English Church* 15: 555. A fictional account of the atrocities during the war on the Covenanters appeared in "The Laird of Redgauntlet," *Macmillan's Magazine* 54 (1886): 116–24.

9 Before the reform of the English calendar in 1752, the year officially began on 25 March, so that Mansfield's birth date is sometimes given as 1704 or 1704/5.

10 James based his claim to the English throne as the great-grandson of Henry VIII's sister, Margaret Tudor, who had married James IV of Scotland.
11 James II's mother, Queen Henrietta Maria of Britain, was an aunt of Louis XIV.
12 The word "Pretender" had nothing to do with pretense; it meant a claimant to the throne.
13 The term "Jacobite" came from "Jacobus," the Latin for James.
14 Terry, *The Chevalier de St George*, 104–9; Edmund Heward, *Lord Mansfield* (Chichester and London: Barry Rose, 1979), 2.
15 George Penny, *Traditions of Perth, Containing Sketches of the Manners and Customs of the Inhabitants, and Notices of Public Occurrences, During the Last Century; Interesting Extracts from Old Records; Notices of the Neighbouring Localities of Historical Interest* (Perth, 1836).
16 Martin Daunton, "The wealth of the nation," in Paul Langford, ed., *The Eighteenth Century, 1688–1815* (Oxford: Oxford University Press, 2002), 161.
17 Geoffrey Holmes and Daniel Szechi, *The Age of Oligarchy: Pre-industrial Britain 1722–1783* (London and New York: Longman, 1993), 189.
18 *Perth Academy, Historical Notes* (VC, Box 322).
19 Undated letter from Murray to his brother Charles. SP, Bundle 933.
20 Penny, *Traditions of Perth* (VC, Box 322).
21 Campbell, *The Lives of the Chief Justices of England,* ii, 310. The only contemporaneous evidence known to this author that Viscount Stormont was in straitened financial condition is that upon his release from prison in 1708, he complained about his lack of money. Stormont to Alexander Barclay, 12 June 1708. SP, Bundle 1258.
22 Campbell, *The Lives of the Chief Justices*, ii, 310. Camlongan is near Annandale, where Stormont had family connections. Stormont's mother (William's paternal grandmother) had been married to John Murray, Earl of Annandale, who was also the 3rd Viscount Stormont. After his death in 1658, she married his cousin David Murray, William's grandfather, who succeeded to the title as the 4th Viscount Stormont. Thus, Stormont's father and stepfather both preceded him as Viscount Stormont. George E. Cokayne, *The Complete Peerage of England, Scotland, Ireland, Great Britain and the United Kingdom, Extant, Extinct, or Dormant* (London: G. Bell and Sons, 1898).
23 Henry G. Graham, *The Social Life of Scotland in the Eighteenth Century*, 4th ed. (London: Adam and Charles Black, 1937). (VC); Edgar, *The Boyhood of Great Men: Intended as an Example to Youth* (London: R. Bentley, 1861–2), 88–100; Campbell, *The Lives of the Chief Justices*, ii, 310.
24 Ibid.
25 David Hayton, "Contested Kingdoms, 1688–1756," in Langford, ed., *The Eighteenth Century*, 38. King George's claim to the throne was through his grandmother, Elizabeth Stuart, the daughter of King James I of England and Scotland. Although the Catholic descendants of King James had a better hereditary claim, they were disqualified under the Act of 1701.

26 William Matthews, ed., *The Diary of Dudley Ryder, 1715–1716* (London: Methuen and Co., 1939), 61–2.
27 James Browne, *A History of the Highlands and of the Highland Clans* (London, Edinburgh, and Dublin: A. Fullarton and Co., 1851) ii, 266.
28 SP, Bundle 1253.
29 Daniel Szechi, *1715: The Great Jacobite Rebellion* (New Haven and London: Yale University Press, 2006), 206.
30 Murray G.H. Pittock, *Jacobitism* (New York: St Martin's Press, Inc.), 1998), 54.
31 Eveline Cruickshanks and Howard Erskine-Hill, *The Atterbury Plot* (New York: Palgrave Macmillan, 2004), 109.
32 Horace Walpole, *Memoirs of the Reign of George II*, edited by John Brooke. (New Haven and London: Yale University Press, 1985), i, 286–7; Campbell, *The Lives of the Chief Justices*, ii, 311–12.
33 Mrs Thomson, *Memoirs of the Jacobites of 1715 and 1745* (London: Richard Bentley, 1846), i, 93.
34 See Chapter 3.
35 Browne, *History of the Highlands*, 363.
36 Bruce Lenman, *The Jacobite Uprisings in Britain, 1689–1746* (London: Eyre Methuen, 1980), 203–4.
37 Mrs Thomson, *Memoirs of the Jacobites*, i, 214–15.
38 *Gazetteer*, 8 Nov. 1788 (VC).
39 Edgar, *Boyhood of Great Men*, 88–100.
40 Campbell, *The Lives of the Chief Justices*, ii, 312.
41 Cruickshanks and Erskine-Hill, *The Atterbury Plot*, 223.
42 Edgar, *Boyhood of Great Men*, 88–100.
43 Ibid.
44 Linda Colley, *Britons: Forging the Nation 1707–1837*, 2nd ed. (New Haven and London: Yale University Press, 2005), 16–17.
45 H.J. Dyos and D.H. Aldcroft, *British Transport: An Economic Survey from the Seventeenth Century to the Twentieth* (Leicester: Leicester University Press, 1969), 29–34; Joan Parkes, *Travel in England in the Seventeenth Century* (London: Oxford University Press, H. Milford, 1925), 152–3, 158–60.
46 Campbell, *The Lives of the Chief Justices*, ii, 244.

CHAPTER TWO

1 Jerry White, *London in the Eighteenth Century: A Great and Monstrous Thing* (London: The Bodley Head, 2012), 2.
2 Although historians have not been able to determine the size of the population with any degree of certainty, "a kind of consensus around 575,000 for 1700 and 750,000 for 1750 has emerged." Ibid., 3, 108.
3 Langford, *A Polite & Commercial People: England 1727–1783* (New York: Oxford University Press), 161.

4 White, *London in the Eighteenth Century*, 7, 186–7.
5 Ibid., 106.
6 Ibid., 8.
7 Ibid., 198–202.
8 Ibid., 224. The noise and sights of the London streets are also described in Walter Besant, *London in the Eighteenth Century* (London: Adam and Charles Black, 1903), 88–105.
9 Ibid., 323.
10 White, *London in the Eighteenth Century*, 390.
11 Dorothy George, *London Life in the Eighteenth Century* (London: Penguin Books Ltd, 1966), 24.
12 White, *London in the Eighteenth Century*, 5.
13 William Baskerville Hamilton, "The Education of Solicitor-General William Murray: A Preliminary Chronological Sketch, 1705–1742" (1936), 1.
14 Hamilton, "The Education of Solicitor-General William Murray," 4.
15 Safalra, "Historical UK Inflation and Price Conversion," http://safalra.com/other/historical-uk-inflation-price-conversion (accessed 18 Jan. 2013).
16 Langford, *A Polite and Commercial People*, 83.
17 Frederic H. Forshall, *Westminster School, Past and Present* (London: Wyman and Sons, 1884).
18 Hamilton, "The Education of Solicitor-General William Murray," 14.
19 Sir John Mowbray, *Seventy Years at Westminster* (Edinburgh and London: W. Blackwood and Sons, 1898), 164.
20 Ibid., 164.
21 Paul Baines and Pat Rogers, *Edmund Curll, Bookseller* (Oxford: Clarendon Press, 2007), 1.
22 Maynard Mack, *Alexander Pope: A Life* (New York and London: W.W. Norton & Company, 1985), 48, 653–4, 656.
23 Baines and Rogers, *Edmund Curll, Bookseller*, 94; Reginald Airy, *Westminster … With Fifty-One Illustrations. Handbooks to the Great Public Schools* (London: G. Bell and Sons, 1902) (VC).
24 Reed Browning, *The Duke of Newcastle* (New Haven and London: Yale University Press), 102–03.
25 Hamilton, "The Education of Solicitor-General William Murray," 4.
26 Cruickshanks and Erskine-Hill, *The Atterbury Plot*, 223; Geoffrey Treasure, *Early Hanoverian Britain 1714–1789* (Mechanicsburg, PA: Stackpole Books, 1992), 16–18.
27 Heward, *Lord Mansfield*, 5.
28 John Sargeaunt, *Annals of Westminster School* (London: Methuen and Co., 1898), 168.
29 Campbell, *The Lives of the Chief Justices,* ii, 308.
30 Forshall, *Westminster School*.

31 *The World*, 26 Mar. 1787.
32 *Scots Magazine*, June 1790.
33 John Holliday, *The Life of William, Late Earl of Mansfield* (London: P. Elmsly and D. Brenner, 1797), 3.
34 "Westminster School," *Old and New London*, vol. 3 (1878), 462–83. http://www.british-history.ac.uk/report.aspx?compid=45168 (accessed 22 Dec. 2011).
35 Airy, *Westminster*; Campbell, *The Lives of the Chief Justices*, ii, 318.
36 Rudolph Ackermann, *History of the Public Schools*; Rev. H.L. Thompson, *History of Christ Church* (London: F.E. Robinson and Co., 1900).
37 Hamilton, "The Education of Solicitor-General William Murray," 12.
38 Henrietta Tayler, "The First Lord Mansfield," *Scottish Notes & Queries*, 3rd Series, 13 (April 1935), 51–2.
39 Forshall, *Westminster School.*
40 Ibid.
41 F.W. Forshall, *Westminster School*. The story reminds one of the famous "Who's on first?" vaudeville dialogue of Abbott and Costello.
42 Hamilton, "The Education of Solicitor-General William Murray," 10–12.
43 Ibid., 10–11.
44 For example, Lord George Sackville's Westminster connection secured his constant access to the Duke of Newcastle, then the prime minister. Sargeaunt, *Annals of Westminster School*, 157.
45 Hamilton, "The Education of Solicitor-General William Murray," 11.
46 It should be noted that Hamilton wrote this in the 1930s, when very few women were able to participate in public life.
47 Hamilton, "The Education of Solicitor-General William Murray," 11–12.
48 Ibid., 9.
49 Minutes of the Deposition of the Solicitor-General, 23 Feb. 1753. Egerton Ms. 3440, f.61 (VC).
50 Hamilton, "The Education of Solicitor-General William Murray," 9.
51 Holliday, *Life of Lord Mansfield*, 51–2. In 1786 John Way, Mansfield's steward and financial manager, stated that Mansfield owned landed property in Cheshire. This may have been Vernon's bequest. SP, Bundle 58; Heward, *Lord Mansfield*, 35.
52 See Chapter 7.
53 Hamilton, "The Education of Solicitor-General William Murray," 7. Murray's entry into politics and relationship with Newcastle are described in Chapter 5.
54 Hamilton, "The Education of Solicitor-General William Murray," 8.
55 Bath to Newcastle, 4 Oct. 1742. Add. MSS 32,699, f. 432v (VC).
56 Murray to Johnson, 9 May 1752, Add. MSS 32,727 (VC).
57 *Whitehall Evening Post*, 20 Apr. 1758 (VC). Hamilton, "The Education of Solicitor-General William Murray," 16.
58 *Scots Magazine*, June 1790 (VC). Although Christ Church was one of the Oxford colleges, it has always been referred to simply as "Christ Church."

59 *Public Advertiser*, 22 Jul. 1789.

60 Wilfrid Prest, *William Blackstone: Law and Letters in the Eighteenth Century* (Oxford: Oxford University Press, 2008), 53.

61 Graham Midgely, *University Life in Eighteenth-Century Oxford* (New Haven: Yale University Press, 1996), 21.

62 Ibid., 26–7.

63 Walter S. Sichel, *Bolingbroke and his Times* (London: James Nisbet and Co., 1901–2), 236; Matthews, ed., *Diary of Dudley Ryder*. 74. Oxford's close connection with the Stuart kings goes back to the 1640s, when King Charles I made the town his headquarters during the English Civil War. Blair Worden, *The English Civil Wars 1640–1660* (London: Weidenfeld and Nicolson, 2009), 46.

64 James, Earl of Waldegrave, *Memoirs and Speeches of James, 2nd Earl of Waldegrave, 1742–1763*, edited by J.C.D. Clark (Cambridge: Cambridge University Press, 1988), 11–12.

65 Matthews, ed., *Diary of Dudley Ryder*, 74.

66 Ibid., 143.

67 Campbell, *The Lives of the Chief Justices*, ii, 321.

68 Midgely, *University Life in Eighteenth-Century England*, 112.

69 Ibid., 143.

70 E.G.W. Bill, *Education at Christ Church Oxford 1660–1800* (Oxford: Clarendon Press, 1988), 164n1.

71 Henrietta Tayler, ed., *The Jacobite Court at Rome in 1719, from Original Documents at Fettercairn House and at Windsor Castle* (Edinburgh: T. and A. Constable), 132.

72 Murray's Speech before the Cabinet Council, 23 Feb. 1753. Add. MSS. 33050, ff. 331 et seq. (reproduced in Hamilton, "The Education of Solicitor-General William Murray," 18–19).

73 Sir Charles Mallet, "Education, Schools and Universities," in A.S. Turberville, ed., *Johnson's England: An Account of the Life and Manners of His Age* (Oxford: Oxford University Press, 1933), ii, 226.

74 Matthews, ed., *Diary of Dudley Ryder*, 133.

75 Bill, *Education at Christ Church*, 227, 327.

76 In 1725, rebellious students at Christ Church circulated a couplet: "Would you have all as dull as he that does preside, / Keep Sherman in, and Wigan [a popular lecturer] lay aside." Ibid., 49.

77 Ibid., 327.

78 Ibid., 303.

79 Ibid., 245.

80 W.H. Davenport Adams, *Learned in the Law; or, Examples and Encouragements from the Lives of Eminent Lawyers* (London: S.W. Partridge and Co., 1882).

81 Holliday, *Life of Lord Mansfield*, 5–8.

82 *Bill, Education at Christ Church*, 198.

83 Ibid., 196–7.

84 Ibid., 311–12.

85 Holmes and Szechi, *The Age of Oligarchy*, 192.

86 Norman Sykes, *Edmund Gibson, Bishop of London, 1669–1748: A Study in Politics and Religion in the Eighteenth Century* (London: Oxford University Press, H. Milford, 1926), 82–9; Hamilton, "The Education of Solicitor-General William Murray," 19–21.

87 Firth, "Modern History in Oxford," *English Historical Review*, 125, 1; Sykes, *Edmund Gibson, Bishop of London,* 81.

88 Murray's Speech before the Cabinet Council (reproduced in Hamilton, "The Education of Solicitor-General William Murray," 21).

89 Campbell, *The Lives of the Chief Justices*, ii, 324.

90 Under the Treaty of Utrecht, which was signed in 1713, France agreed to ban the Pretender from French soil. France did not immediately comply, but by 1717 it no longer supported the Jacobite cause, at least for the time being. After sojourns in the Duchy of Lorraine, the Papal enclave of Avignon, and Urbino, the Jacobite court settled in Rome. Lenman, *The Jacobite Risings in Britain*, 109, 182; Sir Charles A. Petrie, *The Jacobite Movement: The Last Phase 1716–1807* (London: Eyre and Spottiswoode, 1950), 15–17.

91 Murray (from Paris) to Lord Inverness, 6 Aug. 1725. Henrietta Tayler, *The Jacobite Court at Rome*, 230.

92 Ibid.

93 Hamilton, "The Education of Solicitor-General William Murray," 18.

CHAPTER THREE

1 Campbell, *The Lives of the Chief Justices*, ii, 311.

2 "*Provided their political allegiance was not suspect* [Scots] could expect no obstruction to be placed in the way of their preferment." (Italics added.) James Hayes, "Scottish Officers in the British Army 1714–63," *The Scottish Historical Review* 37, no. 123, part 1 (Apr. 1958): 25–6.

3 Campbell, *The Lives of the Chief Justices*, ii, 319.

4 Ibid.

5 Stuart Handley, "Foley, Thomas, First Baron Foley," *ODNB*.

6 Hamilton, "The Education of Solicitor-General William Murray," 25–6.

7 Edgar, *Boyhood of Great Men*, 88–100.

8 Holliday, *Life of Lord Mansfield*, 131.

9 *Morning Post*, 17 Mar. 1778, 16 May 1778.

10 Matthews, ed., *Diary of Dudley Ryder*, 44.

11 Sir Frank D. Mackinnon, "The Law and the Lawyers," in Turberville, ed., *Johnson's England*, ii, 289.

12 David Lemmings, *Professors of the Law: Barristers and English Legal Culture in the Eighteenth Century* (Oxford: Oxford University Press, 2000), 124–6.

13 Ibid, 118–19.
14 *A Treatise on the Study of the Law, written by Lords Mansfield, Ashburton and Thurlow* (London: Harrison, Cluss and Co., 1797) (VC). This "treatise" consists of six letters, four of which were written by Mansfield.
15 Lemmings, *Professors of the Law*, 63. Gray's Inn, which had once been the most important of the Inns of Court, faded into insignificance during the eighteenth century. Ibid, 144–5.
16 Ibid., 64.
17 Matthews, ed., *Diary of Dudley Ryder*, 7–8.
18 Ibid, 49.
19 Roy Porter, *English Society in the Eighteenth Century*, rev. ed. (London and New York: Penguin Books, 1991), 264.
20 Hamilton, "The Education of Solicitor-General William Murray," 28.
21 Richard Tuck, *The Rights of War and Peace: Political Thought and the International Order From Grotius to Kant* (Oxford and New York: Oxford University Press, 1999), 78–98.
22 Samuel Pufendorf, *On the Duty of Man and Citizen According to Natural Law*. Cambridge Texts in the History of Political Thought, edited by James Tully, translated by Michael Silverthorne (Cambridge: Cambridge University Press, 1991), 34–6.
23 Ibid. xviii.
24 See Chapter 21.
25 *A Treatise on the Study of the Law*, 48–56. The letter quoted from was written by Mansfield. It was undated but was probably written in the 1770s.
26 John H. Baker, *An Introduction to English Legal History*, 2nd ed. (London: Butterworths, 1979), 164–5.
27 The first volume of the *Commentaries* was published in 1765.
28 *Diary of Dudley Ryder*, 1715–1716 (VC). The excerpts from Ryder's diary relating to education are not included in the printed volume edited by William Matthews.
29 *Journal of the Board of Trade*, 1735–41, 292 (VC).
30 Adams, *Learned in the Law*, 144; Campbell, *The Lives of the Chief Justices*, ii, 328.
31 Yorke, *Hardwicke*, ii, 488n1.
32 Arnold D. McNair, "Dr. Johnson and the Law," *The Law Quarterly Review* 68 (July 1847): 305.
33 Sir William Holdsworth, *A History of English Law* (London: Methuen and Co. Ltd and Sweet and Maxwell, 1938), xii, 555–6.
34 Adams, *Learned in the Law*.
35 Ryder's unpublished diaries, 109 (VC).
36 William Seward, *Anecdotes of Some Distinguished Persons, Chiefly of the Present and Two Preceding Centuries: Adorned with Sculptures*, 4 vols. (London: T. Cadell and W. Davies, 1795–96), iv, 491ff.

CHAPTER FOUR

1 *Phineas Finn*, 1869 (Oxford University Press edition, 1973), ii, 226.
2 Langford, *A Polite and Commercial People*, 73.
3 Matthews, *Diary of Dudley Ryder*, 6.
4 Ibid., 88.
5 Paul Langford, *Public Life and the Propertied Englishman, 1689–1798* (Oxford: Clarendon Press; New York: Oxford University Press, 1991), 37; Browning, *Newcastle*, 201.
6 John Ashton Cannon, *Aristocratic Century: The Peerage of Eighteenth-Century England* (Cambridge: Cambridge University Press, 1984), 128.
7 Hamilton, "The Education of Solicitor-General William Murray," 97 (quoting Edward & Anne Porritt, *The Unreformed House of Commons, Parliamentary Representation Before 1832*, i, 517).
8 Hamilton, "The Education of Solicitor-General William Murray," 9.
9 Campbell, *The Lives of the Chief Justices*, ii, 331.
10 John Buchan wrote that "he had no money to make the grand tour with which certain biographers have credited him." *Some Eighteenth Century Byways, and Other Essays* (Edinburgh and London: W. Blackwood and Sons, 1908), 79.
11 Hamilton, "The Education of Solicitor-General William Murray, 29n72.
12 In 1736, he was in arrears with his rent at Lincoln's Inn. Heward, *Lord Mansfield*, 13.
13 Besant, *London in the Eighteenth Century*, 311.
14 Campbell, *The Lives of the Chief Justices*, ii, 333.
15 Ibid., 335–6.
16 McNair, "Dr Johnson and the Law," *The Law Quarterly Review* 68 (Jul. 1947): 305.
17 Campbell, *The Lives of the Chief Justices*, ii, 336–7.
18 Ibid.
19 8 Brown 281, 3 Eng. Rep. 584 (1734).
20 William S. Holdsworth, *A History of English Law*, 12 vols. (London: Methuen and Co., Ltd, 1938), xii, 465.
21 William S. Holdsworth, *Some Makers of English Law: The Tagore Lectures, 1937–38* (Cambridge: Cambridge University Press, 1966), 179; George T. Kenyon, *The Life of Lloyd, First Lord Kenyon, Chief Justice of* England (London: Longmans, Green, 1873), 1.
22 Seward, *Anecdotes*, ii, 360–1.
23 N.W. Barber, "The Separation of Powers and the British Constitution," Legal Research Paper No. 03/2012, University of Oxford (Jan. 2012), 7 (citing S.A. de Smith, "The Separation of Powers in New Dress," *McGill Law Journal* xii, 491 (1966).
24 R.L. Schuyler, "The Life of Lord Hardwicke," *Political Science Quarterly*, xxix, 310 (1914).

25 *Waldegrave Memoirs*, 154.

26 Baron John Campbell, *The Lives of the Lord Chancellors and Keepers of the Great Seal of England: From the Earliest Times till the Reign of King George IV* (Philadelphia: Blanchard and Lea, 1851), v, 65.

27 Peter D.G. Thomas, "Yorke, Philip," *ODNB*.

28 Yorke, *Hardwicke*, ii, 539.

29 Peter D.G. Thomas, "Yorke, Philip," *ODNB*.

30 Ibid.

31 Although the United Kingdom, Canada, and the United States (with the important exception of Delaware) have merged their common-law and equity courts, important vestiges of this bifurcated system still exist in all three countries. In general, common law principles and procedures govern a lawsuit brought for damages, whereas equitable principles and procedures govern a lawsuit brought for an injunction. In the United States, the parties are entitled to a jury in a suit in "law" but not in one in "equity." J.H. Baker, *An Introduction to English Legal History*, 2nd ed. (London: Butterworths, 1979), 98–9; Leonard I. Rotman, "The Fusion of Law and Equity: A Canadian Perspective" (2011), available at SSRN http://ssrn.com/abstract=1846694; Morton J. Horwitz, *The Transformation of American Law: 1780–1860* (Cambridge, MA, and London: Harvard University Press, 1977), 265.

32 David Lieberman, *The Province of Legislation Determined: Legal Theory in Eighteenth-Century Britain* (Cambridge: Cambridge University Press, 1989), 75.

33 *Lloyd's Evening Post*, 6 Mar. 1776.

34 Kenyon, *Life of Lord Kenyon*. A century later, Charles Dickens famously described the endless intricate procedures of Chancery in his novel *Bleak House*.

35 Yorke, *Hardwicke*, ii, 511–12.

36 *The King v. Gratwicke*, Gundry MSS (KB) B.1 vol. 10, fo. 38 (VC).

37 The Riot Act was a statute enacted in 1714 allowing the authorities to order any unlawful group of more than twelve persons to disperse. Any person who did not leave the scene within an hour after the reading of the Riot Act was guilty of a felony, which was punishable by death.

38 Andrew C. Thompson, *George II: King and Elector* (New Haven and London: Yale University Press, 2011), 90.

39 Heward, *Lord Mansfield*, 18–20.

40 Apparently no relation to the smuggler Andrew Wilson.

41 Browning, *Newcastle*, 75.

42 Campbell, *The Lives of the Chief Justices*, ii, 338–9; Matthews, *Diary of Dudley Ryder*, 23; Hamilton, "The Education of Solicitor-General William Murray," 52–5.

43 Ibid., 55–6.

44 Seward, *Anecdotes*, iv, 491ff.

45 *Ex parte Thomas Lamprey*, 25 Eng. Rep. 899 (1737).

46 Campbell, *The Lives of the Chief Justices*, ii, 349–51.
47 David Hayton, "Contested Kingdoms, 1688–1756," in Langford, ed., *The Eighteenth Century*, 53.
48 Hamilton, "The Education of Solicitor-General William Murray," 57–9.
49 Susannah Cibber was also a sister of Thomas Arne, the composer of the patriotic song "Rule Britannia." She was the victim of her husband's persecution but escaped from him and, protected from him by Sloper, became an important figure on the London stage. George Winchester Stone Jr and George M. Kahrl, *David Garrick: A Critical Biography* (Carbondale and Edwardsville: Southern Illinois University Press, 1979), 58. She was a theatrical colleague of the great David Garrick, once writing to him, "I desire you always to be my lover upon the stage, and my friend off of it." James Boaden, ed., *The Private Correspondence of David Garrick*, 2 vols. (London: H. Colburn and R. Bentley, 1831–32), i, 38.
50 Campbell, *The Lives of the Chief Justices*, ii, 341, 343; *The Tryal of a Cause for Criminal Conversation, Between Theophilus Cibber, Gent. Plaintiff, and William Sloper, Esq; Defendant* (London: Printed for T. Trott, 1739), Harvard Law School Library.
51 Robert Pye Donkin, *The Trial Between The Rt. Hon. Sir Richard Worsley, Bt. Plaintiff and George Maurice Bisset, Esq. Defendant* (London, 1782), Harvard Law School Library.
52 William Cowper to William Hayley, Weston, 27 Aug. 1793. Wright, *Correspondence of Cowper*, iv, 441–2 (VC).
53 The portrait is in the National Portrait Gallery in London.
54 Heward, *Lord Mansfield*, 29.
55 William Cooke, *Memoirs of Samuel Foote* (New York: Peter A. Mesier, 1806), ii, 111.
56 *Commons Journal*, 23, 127–8 (1739) (VC).
57 Hamilton, "The Education of Solicitor-General William Murray," 71–2.
58 Frances Harris, *A Passion for Government: The Life of Sarah, Duchess of Marlborough* (Oxford: Clarendon Press, 1991), 1.
59 Campbell, *The Lives of the Chief Justices*, ii, 343.
60 Harris, *A Passion for Government: The Life of Sarah, Duchess of Marlborough*, 340.
61 Olivia Spencer-Churchill Colville, *Duchess Sarah* (London, New York, and Bombay: Longmans, Green, and Co., 1904), 293.
62 Pope to Spence, 1735. Samuel Weller Singer, *Anecdotes, Observations, and Characters … Collected by the Rev. Joseph Spence*, 239 (VC). Campbell, writing in mid-nineteenth century, states that Lord Marchmont introduced Murray to Pope while Murray was a student at Westminster School. Campbell, *The Lives of the Chief Justices*, ii, 329–30.
63 Maynard Mack, *Alexander Pope: A Life* (New York and London: W.W. Norton and Co., 1985), 97, 153–5, 185; Hamilton, "The Education of Solicitor-General William Murray," 30.

64 See, for example, Pope's letter to William Warburton in January 1742, referring to Murray's house as "home." George Wiley Sherburn, *Alexander Pope, Correspondence* (Clarendon Press, 1956), iv, 380. Pope's home at Twickenham is described in Mack, *Alexander Pope,* 358–65.
65 Hamilton, "The Education of Solicitor-General William Murray," 33.
66 J.J. Sexby, *The Municipal Parks, Gardens, and Open Spaces of London: Their History and Associations* (London: E. Stock, 1898).
67 The principal anti-Catholic statutes were the Conventicles Act, 16 Car. II, c.4 (1664); the Test Act, 25 Car. II, c.2 (1673); and the Popery Act, 11 Gui. III, c.4 (1698).
68 Mack, *Alexander Pope,* 39–40, 77, 660.
69 Pope to William Fortescue, 26 Aug. 1736; Sherburn, *Alexander Pope, Correspondence*, iv, 29.
70 Pope to Fortescue, 31 Jul. 1738; Pope to Swift, 17 May 1739. Elwin and Courthope, eds. *The Works of Alexander Pope*, ix, 142 (quoted in Hamilton, "The Education of Solicitor-General William Murray," 32).
71 Pope to Swift, 17 May 1739. Elwin and Courthope, vii, 374.
72 Pope to Lyttelton, 3 Nov. 1741. Phillimore, *Memoirs of G. Lyttelton*, i, 180 (VC).
73 Ibid., *Scots Magazine*, June 1793, 264–5.
74 Mack, *Alexander Pope,* 761.
75 Ibid., 686.
76 Campbell, *The Lives of the Chief Justices*, ii, 330.
77 For example, Murray assisted his friend William Warburton in a dispute that Warburton had with his publisher. Pope to Ralph Allen, 19 Jan. 1742. Sherburn, *Alexander Pope, Correspondence*, iv, 383.
78 Mack, *Alexander Pope*, 808; White, *London in the Eighteenth Century*, 265.
79 Add. MSS. 65161, ff. 5–32v.37, 41, 55 (BL). For more on Murray's involvement in copyright cases, both as a lawyer and judge, see Chapter 19.
80 The Ode, which cost one shilling, was advertised in several newspapers in 1756 (VC).
81 Campbell, *The Lives of the Chief Justices*, ii, 339–41.
82 Mack, *Alexander Pope,* 673.
83 Cecil Headlam, *The Inns of Court: Painted by Gordon Home, Described by C. Headlam* (London: Adam & Charles Black), 103–4.
84 William Kent to an unknown correspondent, 28 Nov. 1737. George Paston, *Mr Pope: His Life and Times* (London: Hutchinson and Co., 1909), ii, 576.
85 Heward, *Lord Mansfield*, 24.
86 Elwin and Courthope, eds., *Pope's Works*, ii, 267.
87 Warburton to Birch, 3 Jul. 1738, and 13 Jul. 1738. John Nichols, *Illustrations of Literary History of the Eighteenth Century,* 8 vols. (London: Nichols, Son and Bentley, 1817–58), ii, 90–1; Murray to Warburton, 28 Dec. 1754, Egerton 1959, f.18, 18v, 20 (VC); Hamilton, "The Education of Solicitor-General William Murray," 33.

88 Warburton to Charles Yorke, 5 Oct. 1754 (VC).
89 See Chapter 9.
90 Geoffrey R.R. Treasure, *Who's Who in British History: Early Hanoverian Britain 1714–1789* (Mechanicsburg, PA: Stackpole Books, 1992), 112–13.
91 John Nichols, *Literary Anecdotes of the Eighteenth Century*, 9 vols. (London: Nichols, Son and Bentley, 1812–16), v, 629.
92 Simon Varey, *Henry St. John, Viscount Bolingbroke* (Boston: Twayne Publishers, 1984).
93 Brean S. Hammond, *Pope and Bolingbroke: A Study of Friendship and Influence* (Columbia, MO: University of Missouri Press, 1984), 159.
94 Giles S. H. Ilchester, *Henry Fox, First Lord Holland: His Family and Relations*, 2 vols. (London: John Murray, 1920), i, 153.
95 George Lyttelton to William Warburton, 2 Sep. 1745. Kelvert, *Unpublished Papers of Warburton* (VC): ("You will consider how many friends you have that are also friends of Lord Bolingbroke, particularly Lord Chesterfield and Mr Murray. . . .")
96 Hamilton, "The Education of Solicitor-General William Murray," 79–81.
97 An eighteenth-century biographer of Pope states that the dinner took place at Murray's home in London and that Bolingbroke also was present at the dinner. Owen Ruffhead, *The Life of Alexander Pope, Esq. Compiled from Original Manuscripts, with a Critical Essay on His Writings and Genius* (London: 1769), 219–20. There is no contemporary evidence, however, supporting this account. Moreover, King George II had issued a proclamation in mid-February 1744 that, in view of the threat of a Jacobite invasion, an existing law (1 Gui. and Mar., c.9 (1688)) that banned Catholics from coming with ten miles of London, which had fallen into disuse, would henceforth be enforced. In view of this restriction and the fact that by early 1744 Pope's deteriorating health would have made a trip into London difficult, it is unlikely that the dinner took place in Murray's home.
98 Hammond, *Pope and Bolingbroke*, 107–8.
99 Campbell, *The Lives of the Chief Justices*, ii, 352.
100 Anonymous letter written in 1756 by Murray to Warburton, caused by Warburton's attack on Bolingbroke. The letter is endorsed "N.B. From Lord Mansfield, 1756." Egerton MSS, 1959, f.31, 31v-32, 33v-34, 34v (VC).
101 Ibid.
102 Ibid.
103 Frances E. Anderson, *Christopher Smart* (New York: Twayne Publishers, 1974), 23–4.
104 Chris Mounsey, *Christopher Smart: Clown of God* (Lewisburg, PA: Bucknell University Press, 2001), 40–1.
105 Ibid., 49.
106 *The Annotated Letters of Christopher Smart, Edited by Betty Rizzo and Robert Mahony* (Carbondale: Southern Illinois University Press, 1991), 2–3.

107 Ibid., 8–9.

108 Ibid., 6.

109 Mounsey, *Christopher Smart: Clown of God*, 7.

110 Hamilton, "The Education of Solicitor-General William Murray," 36–7.

111 *Journal of the Board of Trade, 1735–41*, 312–13 (VC).

112 Ibid., 185–8 (VC). The dispute, which had begun in the early seventeenth century, continued until 1750, when Chancellor Hardwicke ordered specific performance of a 1732 agreement between the Penn brothers and Lord Baltimore that divided up between them the land between the Delaware River and Chesapeake Bay. Mansfield continued to represent the Penn brothers until the time of Hardwicke's decision. Hamilton, "The Education of Solicitor-General William Murray," 41–5.

113 Ibid., 48–50.

114 John Telford, ed., *Journal of Charles Wesley* (London: Hodder and Stoughton, 1886), 118–19; Hamilton, "The Education of Solicitor-General William Murray," 51.

115 *Journal of the Board of Trade, 1735–41*, 292 (VC).

116 Theodore F.T. Plucknett, *A Concise History of the Common Law* (Boston: Little, Brown and Company, 1956), 62–3.

117 John Locke, "Some Considerations of the Consequences of the Lowering of Interest, and Raising the Value of Money," in *Several Papers Relating to Money, Interest and Trade &c.*, London 1696, 2–3 (reprinted by Augustus M. Kelley, New York, 1968).

118 *Journal of the Board of Trade, 1735–41*, 343–4; E.B. Russell, *The Review of the American Colonial Legislation by the King in Council*, 171 (VC).

119 Hamilton, "The Education of Solicitor-General William Murray," 51–2.

120 *Marriage settlement of William Murray and Elizabeth Finch*. SP, Bundle 1407.

121 Holdsworth, *Some Makers of English Law*, 145–50.

122 D.E.C. Yale, "Finch, Heneage, First Earl of Nottingham," *ODNB*.

123 Baker, *An Introduction to English Legal History*, 289.

124 An example is Section 2-201 of the Uniform Commercial Code.

125 Henry Horowitz, "Finch, Daniel, Second Earl of Nottingham and Seventh Earl of Winchilsea," *ODNB*.

126 Cokayne, *Complete Peerage*.

127 The picture hangs in Mansfield's former home, Kenwood House, now an English Heritage museum.

128 Holliday, *Life of Lord Mansfield*, 40.

129 Russell Kirk, *Edmund Burke: A Genius Reconsidered* (Wilmington, DE: Intercollegiate Studies Institute, 1997), 16.

130 Vickery, *The Gentleman's Daughter*, 307–8.

131 Ibid., 376.

132 *British Journal*, 16 Jul. 1726.

133 *Daily Post*, May 21, 1732.
134 Vickery, *The Gentleman's Daughter*, 86.
135 Mansfield to W. Eden, 28 Aug. 1776. Add. MSS. 34413, f. 75 (BL).
136 Lady Mary Montagu to Lady Pomfret, 1738. *The Letters and Works of Lady Mary Montagu, edited by Lord Wharncliffe and William Moy Thomas*, 2 vols. (Cambridge and New York: Cambridge University Press, 2011), ii, 208 (VC).
137 Hon. Grace Granville to Mrs Ann Granville, 1 Nov. 1738. Mary Delany, *The Autobiography and Correspondence of Mary Granville, Mrs Delany*, 3 vols. (London: R. Bentley, 1861), ii, 8.
138 John Almon, *Biographical, Literary, and Political Anecdotes*, 3 vols. (London: T.N. Longman, and L.B. Seeley, 1797). i, 218, 220–1.
139 For an instance of the nobility's contempt for lawyers, see Vickery, *The Gentleman's Daughter*, 292.
140 Basil Williams, *The Life of William Pitt, Earl of Chatham*, 4th impression, 2 vols. (London: Frank Cass and Co., 1966), i, 104n2.
141 Thompson, *George II: King and Elector*, 180.
142 Elaine Chalus, *Elite Women in English Political Life c.1754–1790* (Oxford: Clarendon Press, 2005), 119.
143 Ibid., 120.
144 Ibid.
145 See Chapter 6.
146 *Chesterfield v. Janssen*, 1 Atk. 299, 334 (1750).
147 See Chapter 5.
148 James Oswald to Henry Home (later Lord Kames), 24 Dec. 1741. *Memorials of James Oswald*, 10 (VC).
149 Campbell, *The Lives of the Chief Justices*, ii, 348, 348n*.
150 Besant, *London in the Eighteenth Century*, 77.
151 George Walter Thornbury and E. Walford, *Old and New London*, 6 vols. (London: Cassell, Petter, and Galpin, 1872–78?), iii.
152 Arthur Houlton Marks, *Historical Notes on Lincoln's Inn Fields* (London: Hertford Record Co., 1922), 27.
153 George Besant, *London in the Eighteenth Century*, 79.
154 White, *London in the Eighteenth Century*, 303, 377.
155 Besant, *London in the Eighteenth Century*, 194, 247, 429, 446.
156 Heward, *Lord Mansfield*, 25.

CHAPTER FIVE

1 Langford, *A Polite and Commercial People*, 334.
2 Romney Sedgwick, ed., *Letters from George III to Lord Bute 1756–1766* (London: Macmillan and Co. Ltd, 1939), xivn.
3 David Hayton, "Contested Kingdoms, 1688–1756," in Langford, ed., *The Eigh-*

teenth Century, 55–64; Basil Williams, *The Whig Supremacy 1714–1760*, 2nd ed., revised by C.H. Stuart (Oxford: Clarendon Press, 1960), 211–12.

4 D. Nichol Smith, "The Newspaper," in Turberville, ed., *Johnson's England*, ii, 335.

5 Geoffrey Holmes and Daniel Szechi, *The Age of Oligarchy: Pre-industrial Britain 1722–1783* (London and New York: Longman, 1993), 12–26; David Hayton, "Contested Kingdoms, 1688–1756," in Langford, ed., *The Eighteenth Century*, 56–7.

6 Williams, *The Whig Supremacy*, 211–12.

7 Steve Pincus, *1688: The First Modern Revolution* (New Haven and London: Yale University Press, 2009), 16–17, 21.

8 Thompson, *George II*, 103.

9 John Carswell, *The South Sea Bubble* (Dover, NH: Alan Sutton, 1993), 132.

10 Edward Pearce, *Pitt the Elder: Man of War* (London: The Bodley Head, 2010), 24.

11 A daughter of an earlier Viscount Cornbury was the first wife of King James II and the mother of Queens Mary II (of William and Mary) and Anne.

12 Harris, *A Passion for Government: the Life of Sarah, Duchess of Marlborough*, 1.

13 Treasure, *Early Hanoverian Britain 1714–1789*, 43.

14 Langford, *A Polite and Commercial People*, 188.

15 Walpole to Lady Ailesbury, 10 Oct. 1761. W.S. Lewis, ed., *The Yale Editions of Horace Walpole's Correspondence* (New Haven: Yale University Press, 1974), xxxviii, 131.

16 Diary of Earl Marchmont, 1 Oct. 1744. G.H. Rose, ed., *A Selection from the Papers of the Earls of Marchmont*, 3 vols. (hereinafter "Marchmont Papers"), (London: J. Murray, 1831), i, 51–2.

17 Cornbury to George Grenville, 3 Aug. 1742. Richard Grenville, Earl Temple, *The Grenville Papers*, edited with notes by William James Smith, 4 vols. (London, John Murray, 1852–53), i, 6–7.

18 Cornbury to G. Grenville, 14 Oct. 1742. *Grenville Papers*, i, 11–12.

19 Murray to George Grenville, 3 Nov. 1742. *Grenville Papers*, i, 16–17.

20 Mack, *Alexander Pope*, 612.

21 Ibid., 83.

22 John M. Aden, *Something Like Horace: Studies in the Art and Allusion of Pope's Horatian Satires* (Nashville: Vanderbilt University Press, 1969), 75.

23 Williams, *Chatham*, i, 54.

24 Hamilton, "The Education of Solicitor-General William Murray," 96–8.

25 Langford, *A Polite and Commercial People*, 43.

26 Williams, *The Whig Supremacy*, 69.

27 Hamilton, "The Education of Solicitor-General William Murray," 46–8.

28 Eighteen years later, when defending himself against a charge of having been a secret Jacobite, Murray emphasized his ties to the established Church: "It was imagined that, by my appearance ... upon the occasion of the Quakers Bill, I had

gained some credit with the clergy." Murray's speech before the Cabinet Council, 23 Feb. 1753. Add. MSS. 33050, f. 331 (BL).

29 Holmes and Szechi, 65–6; Williams, *The Whig Supremacy*, 208.

30 Stephen Conway, *War, State and Society in Mid-Eighteenth Century Britain and Ireland* (Oxford: Oxford University Press, 2006), 147.

31 Pincus, *1688*, 19.

32 Hamilton, "The Education of Solicitor-General William Murray," 61–2.

33 Ibid., 61–4.

34 Campbell, *The Lives of the Chief Justices*, ii, 344; Williams, *The Whig Supremacy*, 208.

35 Hamilton, "The Education of Solicitor-General William Murray," 64; Williams, *Chatham*, i, 75.

36 Williams, *The Whig Supremacy*, 210.

37 Hamilton, "The Education of Solicitor-General William Murray," 76–8.

38 Walpole to Horace Mann, 22 Dec. 1741. W.S. Lewis, ed., *The Yale Editions of Horace Walpole's Correspondence* (New Haven: Yale University Press, 1952), xvii, 252.

39 Langford, *A Polite and Commercial People*, 190.

40 Jonathan Swift, "A Vindication of his Excellence John Lord Carteret," in *The Works of Jonathan Swift* (Dublin: G. Faulkner, 1751), 174.

41 Walpole to Horace Mann, 18 June 1744. W.S. Lewis, ed., *The Yale Editions of Horace Walpole's Correspondence* (New Haven: Yale University Press, 1954), xviii, 464.

42 Bob Harris, *Politics and the Nation: Britain in the Mid-Eighteenth Century* (Oxford and New York: Oxford University Press, 2002), 22.

43 Ray A. Kelch, *Newcastle: A Duke Without Money: Thomas Pelham-Holles 1693–1768* (London: Routledge and Kegan Paul, 1974), 17.

44 Newcastle was secretary of state for the southern department from 1724 to 1748 and for the northern department from 1748 to 1754. Geoffrey Treasure, *Who's Who in Early Hanoverian Britain 1714–1789* (Mechanicsburg, PA: Stackpole Books, 1992), 96.

45 Williams, *Chatham*, i, 325.

46 J.C.D. Clark, *Dynamics of Change: The Crisis of the 1750s and English Party Systems* (Cambridge: Cambridge University Press, 1982), 66; Browning, *Newcastle*, 44.

47 Conway, *War, State and Society*, 40.

48 Browning, *Newcastle*, 77.

49 Kelch, *Newcastle: A Duke Without Money*, 9.

50 Yorke, *Hardwicke*, i, 286–87.

51 Kelch, *Newcastle: A Duke Without Money*, 38–50.

52 Browning, *Newcastle*, 126.

53 Kelch, *Newcastle: A Duke Without Money*, 115.

54 Harris, *Politics and the Nation*, 27.

55 Langford, *A Polite and Commercial People*, 226.

56 Browning, *Newcastle*, 87.

57 Hamilton, "The Education of Solicitor-General William Murray," 87.

58 George Harris, *The Life of Lord Chancellor Hardwicke: With Selections from His Correspondence, Diaries, Speeches, and Judgements*, 3 vols. (London: E. Moxon, 1847), iii, 10.

59 Browning, *Newcastle*, 18.

60 Ibid., 63.

61 A.F. Pollard and Rev. M.J. Mercer, "Stone, Andrew," *ODNB*.

62 Sedgwick, *Letters from George III to Lord Bute*, xxvii.

63 Browning, *Newcastle*, 63.

64 Horace Walpole, *Memoirs of the Reign of King George II* , edited by John Brooke (New Haven and London: Yale University Press, 1985), i, 283–4.

65 Murray to Newcastle, 29 May 1756. Add. MSS. 34523, f.85 (BL).

66 Newcastle to Murray, 30 May 1756. Add. MSS. 34523, f.143 (VC).

67 Sedgwick, *Letters from George III to Lord Bute*, xxvii.

68 Newcastle to Mansfield, 20 Aug. 1758. Add. MSS. 32882, f. 472 (VC).

69 Kelch, *Newcastle: A Duke Without Money*, 90.

70 The Vanes were also distantly related by marriage to Lady Mansfield. Henry Vane, Earl of Darlington, was a brother-in-law of Lady Mansfield's sister, Henrietta, Duchess of Cleveland.

71 Browning, *Newcastle*, 126–7.

72 Kelch, Newcastle: *A Duke Without Money*, 96.

73 Undated letter from Murray to Stone. Add. 33065, f.436 (BL); Murray to Stone, 16 Aug. 1741. Add 33065, ff. 438–40 (VC).

74 Harris, *Hardwicke*, i, 522–3.

75 Heward, *Lord Mansfield*, 94.

76 Alexander Pulling, *Order of the Coif* (W. Clowes and Sons, Ltd, 1897), 201n2 (Google ebook); see also http://www.stanford.edu/group/auden/cgi-bin/auden/individual.php?pid=I22476&ged=auden-bicknell.ged

77 Hamilton, "The Education of Solicitor-General William Murray," 91.

78 Edward Porritt, assisted by Annie G. Porritt, *The Unreformed House of Commons: Parliamentary Representation Before 1832*, 2 vols. (Cambridge: Cambridge University Press, 1903), i, 4.

79 Hamilton, "The Education of Solicitor-General William Murray," 95.

80 Newcastle to Hardwicke, 9 Sep. 1742 (quoted in Yorke, *Hardwicke*, i, 307).

81 Hamilton, "The Education of Solicitor-General William Murray," 95.

82 Browning, *Newcastle*, 142, 205.

83 Williams, *Chatham*, i, 104n2.

84 Richmond to Newcastle, 3 Dec. 1742 (quoted in Yorke, *Hardwicke*, i, 307)

85 Diary entry of 24 Apr. 1772. Scott and Pottle, *Boswell Papers*, ix, 257 (VC). Dr Johnson was not overly impressed by Mansfield. When somebody in Scotland observed that he had heard that Mansfield was not a great English lawyer, Johnson replied: "Why, sir, supposing Lord Mansfield not to have the splendid talents

which he possesses, he must be a great English lawyer from having been so long at the bar and having passed through so many of the great offices of the law. Sir, you may as well maintain that a carrier who has driven a pack-horse between Edinburgh and Berwick for thirty years does not know the road, as that Lord Mansfield does not know the law of England." Boswell's *Journal of a Tour to the Hebrides* (New York: The Literary Guild, Inc., 1936), 386.

86 Hamilton, "The Education of Solicitor-General William Murray," 93.

87 *Minutes of the Deposition of the Solicitor General,* 23 Feb. 1753. Egerton MS. 3440, f.61 (BL).

88 William Hamilton (from London) to Arthur Vanderbilt, 19 Jul. 1938 (VC).

89 Hamilton, "The Education of Solicitor-General William Murray," 92.

90 Browning, *Newcastle*, 116.

91 Wilbur L. Cross, *The History of Henry Fielding*, 3 vols. (New Haven: Yale University Press, 1918), ii, 4–5.

92 Bolingbroke to Marchmont, 2 Aug. 1742. *Marchmont Papers*, ii, 288–9.

93 Williams, *Chatham*, i, 96.

94 Hamilton, "The Education of Solicitor-General William Murray," 96.

95 Mansfield to Newcastle, 4 Dec. 1776. Add. MSS. 32987, ff. 165–6 (VC).

CHAPTER SIX

1 Clark, *Dynamics of Change*, 96.

2 Edmund G.P. Fitzmaurice, *Life of William, Earl of Shelburne, afterwards First Marquess of Lansdowne: With Extracts from His Papers and Correspondence*, 2 vols. (London: Macmillan and Co., 1875. Reprinted by Elibron Classics, 2006), i, 108–9.

3 *Public Advertiser*, 28 Jul. 1789 (VC).

4 Edward Raymond Turner, *The Cabinet Council of England in the Seventeenth and Eighteenth Centuries, 1622–1784* (New York: Russell and Russell, 1930), i, 19–20.

5 Prest, *Blackstone*, 200.

6 David Lemmings, "Ryder, Sir Dudley," *ODNB*; Matthews, *Diary of Dudley Ryder*, 2.

7 James Oldham, "The Work of Ryder and Murray as Law Officers of the Crown," in Thomas G. Watkin, ed., *Proceedings of the Eighth British Legal History Conference* (Cardiff, 1987), 159.

8 James Oldham, *English Common Law in the Age of Mansfield* (Chapel Hill, NC, and London: University of North Carolina Press, 2004), 7.

9 Norton-Kyshe, *The Law and Privileges Relating to the Attorney-General and Solicitor-General of England* (London: Steven and Haynes, 1897), 4–5, 116–17.

10 *Black Books*, iii, 331–4 (VC).

11 Holliday, *Life of Lord Mansfield*, 52.

12 *Lord Chesterfield's letters to his son*. Letter CCXL III, 11 Feb. 1751 (O.S.) (VC).

13 Adams, *Learned in the Law*, 156.

14 *Edinburgh Review*, 57 (Jan. 1834): 526–7.
15 Sir Egerton Brydges, *A Biographical Peerage of the Empire of Great Britain*, 4 vols. (London: J. Johnson, 1808–17), i, 3.
16 John Forster, *Biographical Essays*, 3rd ed. (London: John Murray, 1860), 388.
17 Abraham Hayward, *Lord Chesterfield and George Selwyn* (Longman, 1854), 37 (VC).
18 *Samuel Martin's Parliamentary Journal*, Nov.–Dec. 1754. Add. MSS. 41355, ff.14–28v. (Martin Papers, vol. 10) (VC).
19 Williams, *Chatham*, i, 104.
20 George II visited Hanover over ten times during his thirty-three-year reign. Thompson, *George II*, 86. Thompson mentions visits in 1732, 1735, 1736, 1740, 1741, 1743, 1745, 1748, 1752, and 1755, but it is clear from letters between Murray and Newcastle (who was in Hanover with the King) that the King also visited Hanover in 1750.
21 The King's title of "elector" derived from the fact that he was one of the German princes and bishops who, at least in theory, elected the Holy Roman Emperor.
22 Langford, *A Polite and Commercial People*, 190–1.
23 Holliday, *Life of Lord Mansfield*, 56–65.
24 Walpole, *Memoirs of the Reign of King George II*, i, 48–9, 283–4.
25 Adams, *Learned in the Law*, 255.
26 Harris, *Politics and the Nation*, 26.
27 Williams, *Chatham*, i, 105–6.
28 Ibid., i, 105.
29 Heward, *Lord Mansfield*, 31.
30 Williams, *Chatham*, i, 104–5.
31 Walpole, *Memoirs of the Reign of King George II*, i, 408,
32 Ilchester, *Henry Fox*, i, 294.
33 Walpole, *Memoirs of the Reign of King George II*, i, 114.
34 Ilchester, *Henry Fox*, i, 191–2.
35 Holliday, *Life of Lord Mansfield*, 90–7.
36 Heward, *Lord Mansfield*, 97.
37 TNA [The National Archives], SP [State Papers] 36/152, f.66, 9 Mar. 1748 (VC).
38 Ibid., 27 Jun., 1754 (VC).
39 Leman Thomas Rede and Edward, Wynne, *Strictures on the Lives and Characters of the Most Eminent Lawyers of the Present Day* (London: G. Kearsley, 1790), 32.
40 Harris, *Politics and the Nation*, 28.
41 Williams, *The Whig Supremacy*, 264–5; Langford, *A Polite and Commercial People*, 210.
42 Harris, *Politics and the Nation*, 28.
43 Holliday, *Life of Lord Mansfield*, 82–7.
44 Murray to Newcastle, 25 May 1750. Add. MSS. 32720, f. 411 (VC).
45 Newcastle to Murray, 31 May 1752. Add. MSS. 32927 (VC).
46 Murray to Newcastle, 31 May 1752. Add. MSS. 32729, f.204 (VC).
47 Stone to Newcastle, 17 Jul. 1752, Add. MSS. 32728, f.292 (VC).

48 Murray to Newcastle, 24 Jul. 1752. Add. MSS. 32728, ff. 378–379 (VC).
49 Stone to Newcastle, 18 Aug. 1755. Add. MSS. 32858, f. 197 et seq. (VC).
50 Murray to Newcastle, 2 Nov. 1750. Add. 32723, f. 219 (VC).
51 Kelch, *Newcastle: A Duke Without Money*, 126.
52 Ibid., 140.
53 Ibid., 143.
54 Ibid.
55 *Paper on the private affairs of the Duke of Newcastle*, 13 Jan. 1753. Add. MSS. 32731, ff.39–44 (BL).
56 Lord Chesterfield to his son, 12 Feb. 1754. *Lord Chesterfield's Letters* (Oxford and New York: Oxford University Press, 1992), 297.
57 George O. Trevelyan, *The Early History of Charles James Fox*, 3rd ed. (London: Longmans and Co., 1881), 100.
58 Baker, *An Introduction to English Legal History*, 142. Charles Yorke, who was solicitor general in 1758, received fees from private clients of about £5,000 a year. Theobald Mathew, *For Lawyers and Others* (London: William Hodge and Co., 1937). It should be remembered that Murray was already a hugely successful practitioner at the time he was appointed solicitor general. In addition to his salary and his fees from private practice, Murray received fees for attending meetings of the Board of Trade.
59 In *Chesterfield v. Janssen*, 28 Eng. Rep. 82 (1750), discussed in Chapter 16, Ryder and Murray both argued for the defendant.
60 In *Roach v. Beardley,* Hill MS. Rep. vol. 5. Fol. 116 MS Room. S. 4. (1744), a dispute over a will, Attorney General Ryder represented the defendants, while Solicitor General Murray represented the plaintiff.
61 Mrs Delany to Mrs Dewes, 28 Oct. 1752. *Correspondence of Mrs Delany*, series 1, iii, 167–8.
62 Holdsworth, *History of English Law*, vi, 475.
63 *The King v. Burgess*, 96 Eng. Rep. 942 (1754).
64 26 Eng. Rep. 14 (1744).
65 The emphasis is in the report of the case.

CHAPTER SEVEN

1 *The Later Diaries of Sir Dudley Ryder*, 11 Sep. 1741 (VC).
2 Harris, *Politics and the Nation*, 23–4.
3 Pittock, *Jacobitism*, 98.
4 Conway, *War, State and Society*, 18–19, 1t98.
5 Thomson, *Memoirs of the Jacobites*, iii, 250.
6 Pittock, *Jacobitism*, 100–2; Petrie, *The Jacobite Movement: The Last Phase,* 93.
7 Harris, *Politics and the Nation*, 28–9.
8 Conway, *War, State and Society*, 18–19.

9 Colley, *Britons*, 74–6.
10 Pittock, *Jacobitism*, 102–11.
11 Ibid., 113.
12 Petrie, *The Jacobite Movement: The Last Phase*, 118–19.
13 Colley, *Britons*, 79, 83.
14 *Report on the Mayor of Carlisle's Case*. Add. MSS. 35408, f.214 (BL).
15 MS Opinion Book of the Law Officers in Library of Congress, ff. 14–16. 1746–47 (VC).
16 *The King v. Townley*, Rep. of Cases, 15 Jul. 1746. 10–24 Geo. II. MSS. Room G.3. Vol. 3. Fo. 1355 (VC).
17 Langford, *A Polite and Commercial People*, 210–11.
18 Walpole to Horace Mann, 1 Aug. 1746. W.S. Lewis, ed., *The Yale Editions of Horace Walpole's Correspondence* (New Haven: Yale University Press, 1954), xix, 283.
19 Langford, *A Polite and Commercial People*, 210–11.
20 Amanda Vickery, *The Gentleman's Daughter: Women's Lives in Georgian England* (New Haven and London: Yale University Press, 1999), 238.
21 Pittock, *Jacobitism*, 31; Edward M. Furgol, "Fraser, Simon, Eleventh Lord Lovat," *ODNB*.
22 Ibid., 113; Petrie, *The Jacobite Movement: The Last Phase*, 122–4.
23 The ODNB gives Lovat's birthdate as 1667 or 1668, which would have made him about eighty at the time of his trial. Furgol, "Fraser, Simon, Eleventh Lord Lovat," ODNB. One of his biographers, however, concludes, implausibly, that he was nine years younger. W.C. Mackenzie, *Simon Fraser, Lord Lovat: His Life and Times* (London: Chapman and Hall, Ltd, 1908), 3. If so, he would have married at the age of ten. See n25 below.
24 A report of Lovat's trial, published in 1747, is available at the New York City Bar Association, Document No. Q4201379069.
25 Lovat was related to Murray by marriage. In 1697, when he was about twenty, he had, probably forcibly, married the thirty-three-year-old daughter of John Murray, a distant relative of William Murray, in order to gain an inheritance. He was accused of raping her, but she, having become attached to him, refused to prosecute him. Mackenzie, *Simon Fraser, Lord Lovat: His Life and Times*, 24–6.
26 A report of Lovat's trial, published in 1747, is available at the New York City Bar Association, Document No. Q4201379069.
27 Conway, *War, State and Society*, 204.
28 Harris, *Politics and the Nation*, 28–9.
29 Oldham, "The Work of Ryder and Murray," 167–73.
30 Harris, *Politics and the Nation*, 27.
31 Walpole, *Memoirs of the Reign of King George II*, i, 74–5.
32 William Coxe, *Memoirs of the Administration of the Right Honourable Henry Pelham, Collected from the Family Papers, and Other Authentic Documents*, 2 vols. (London: Longman, Rees, Orme, Brown and Green, 1829), ii, 236.

33 Horace Walpole, *Memoirs of the Reign of King George II*, i, 283–4.

34 Coxe, *Memoirs of the Administration of Henry Pelham*, ii, 236; Walpole, *Memoirs of the Reign of King George II*, i, 289–90.

35 James Waldegrave, *The Memoirs and Speeches of James, 2nd Earl of Waldegrave, 1742–1763* (hereinafter "*Waldegrave Memoirs*"), edited with an introduction by J.C.D. Clark (Cambridge: Cambridge University Press, 1988), 53–4.

36 Murray to Newcastle, 11 Aug. 1752. Add. MSS 32729, f.73 (VC).

37 Coxe, *Memoirs of the Administration of Henry Pelham*, ii, 237; Walpole, *Memoirs of the Reign of King George II*, i, 289–90; Heward, Lord *Mansfield*, 35.

38 William Coxe, *Memoirs of the Administration of Henry Pelham*, ii, 238; Horace Walpole, *Memoirs of the Reign of King George II*, i, 289–90.

39 Ilchester, *Fox*, i, 181–3.

40 Sedgwick, *Letters of George III to Lord Bute*, xxvii.

41 Walpole, *Memoirs of the Reign of King George II*, i, 298n1.

42 Sedgwick, *Letters from George III to Lord Bute*, xxx.

43 Walpole, *Memoirs of the Reign of King George II*, i, 304. Another version of the story was that the newspaper Fawcett was reading reported that Dr Johnson had been appointed an instructor to the Prince of Wales. Ibid., i, 314.

44 Ibid., i, 305.

45 See Chapter 2.

46 Horace Walpole's account of the episode states that Fawcett accused Murray and Stone of drinking toasts to the Pretender when Fawcett first accused Dr Johnson. Walpole, *Memoirs of the Reign of King George II*, i, 304.

47 Trench, *George II*, 269.

48 Campbell, *The Lives of the Chief Justices*, ii, 371.

49 George Bubb Dodington, *The Diary of the Late George Bubb, Baron of Melcombe Regis; from March 4, 1749, to February 6, 1761* (hereinafter "*Dodington Diary*"); entry of 8 May 1753 (London: J. Murray, 1823), 241–2.

50 Walpole accused Murray of having tampered with Fawcett. According to Walpole, Murray went to Fawcett's home and advised him to contradict what he had said. Walpole, *Memoirs of the Reign of King George II*, i, 309, 318n1. It is impossible to know whether this is true, and Walpole clearly had a bias against Murray.

51 *Minutes of the Deposition of the Solicitor General,* 23 Feb. 1753. Egerton MS. 3440, f.61 (BL).

52 Investigation of charges of Jacobitism, 26 Feb. 1753. Add. 43428, f.318–320v. (BL).

53 Newcastle to the King, 23 Feb. 1753. Add. 32731, p. 27365 (VC). Fawcett's accusation and its aftermath are described in Coxe, *Memoirs of the Administration of Henry Pelham*, ii, 254–63.

54 Walpole, *Memoirs of the Reign of King George II*, i, 315.

55 Coxe, *Memoirs of the Administration of Henry Pelham*, ii, 261.

56 *Waldegrave Memoirs*, 254, 257–8.

57 Pitt to Temple, 19 Mar. 1753, *Grenville Papers*, i, 101.
58 William Coxe, *Memoirs of the Administration of Henry Pelham*, ii, 263.
59 E.G.W. Bill, *Education at Christ Church Oxford 1660–1800* (Oxford: Clarendon Press, 1988), 164n1.
60 Nicholas Rogers, *Crowds, Culture, and Politics in Georgian Britain* (Oxford: Clarendon Press; New York: Oxford University Press, 1998), 22–3.
61 Ibid., 46–7.
62 Ibid., 40–1.
63 Petrie, *The Jacobite Movement: The Last Phase*, i, 106–7.
64 Ilchester, *Fox*, i, 183n1.
65 Browning, *Newcastle*, 189.
66 Almon, *Anecdotes*, 227–8.
67 Chesterfield to unknown person, 4 Apr. 1753. Bonamy Dobree, ed., *Letters of Chesterfield*, v. 2014.
68 Oldham, *The Mansfield Manuscripts*, i, 196–7.
69 Williams, *Chatham*, i, 258.
70 *Waldegrave Memoirs*, 62, 62n197.
71 "Casca's Epistle to Lord Mansfield," *The Crisis*, No. XVII. (New York: Anderson, 1775), 137–48. AAS copy. NYHS. 13983.

CHAPTER EIGHT

1 *Diary of the Earl of Egmont* (Historical Manuscripts Commission, 1922–23) iii, 314 (VC).
2 Campbell, *The Lives of the Chief Justices*, ii, 379–81.
3 Harris, *Hardwicke*, iii, 11–12. The master of the rolls was originally a clerk who kept the records of the Chancery Court. In the Middle Ages, the position evolved into a judicial one. The master of the rolls was deputy to the lord chancellor; he was the third highest English judge, inferior only to the lord chancellor and the chief justice of King's Bench. Baker, *An Introduction to English Legal History*, 85, 95.
4 Hardwicke to Newcastle, 17 May 1754. Add. MSS. 32735, f.283–284 (VC).
5 *Whitehall Evening Post*, 22–25 May 1756.
6 Ibid.
7 Ibid.
8 *Waldegrave Memoirs*, 174–5.
9 Browning, *Newcastle*, 242.
10 Newcastle to Murray, 30 May 1756. Add. MSS. 32865, f.143 (VC).
11 Walpole, *Memoirs of the Reign of King George II*, i, 380.
12 Newcastle to Murray, 30 May 1756. Add. MSS. 32865, f.143 (VC).
13 Potter to Pitt, 4 Jun. 1756 (quoted in Rosebery, *Chatham*, 455).
14 Harris, *Politics and the Nation*, 34.

15 Walpole, *Memoirs of the Reign of King George II*, ii, 162.
16 Harris, *Politics and the Nation*, 34; Conway, *War, State and Society*, 130–1.
17 Browning, *Newcastle*, 238.
18 Newcastle to Murray, 30 May 1756. Add. MSS. 32865, f.143 (VC).
19 Ibid.
20 Walpole, *Memoirs of the Reign of King George II*, ii, 227–8.
21 Clark, *Dynamics of Change*, 47, 83–4.
22 Newcastle to Murray, 4 Jun. 1756. Add. MSS. 32865, f.203 (VC).
23 Newcastle to Stone, 25 Jun. 1756. Add. MSS. 32865, f.430 (VC).
24 Newcastle to Hardwicke, 12 Jun. 1756. Add. MSS. 32865, f. 277 (VC).
25 Campbell, *The Lives of the Chief Justices*, ii, 389.
26 Newcastle to Hardwicke, 25 Jun. 1756. Add. MSS. 32865, f. 432 (VC).
27 Hardwicke to Newcastle, 26 Jun. 1756. Add. MSS. 32865, f. 440 (VC).
28 Murray to Hardwicke, 26 Jun. 1756. Add. MSS. 35954, f.85 (VC).
29 Hardwicke to Newcastle, 28 Jun. 1756. Yorke, *Hardwicke*, ii, 301–3.
30 Amanda Vickery, *Behind Closed Doors* (New Haven and London: Yale University Press, 2009), 130.
31 Ilchester, *Henry Fox*, i, 69.
32 Thompson, *George II*, 250.
33 Ibid., 106.
34 Hardwicke to Newcastle, 30 Jun. 1756. Add. MSS. 32865, f.470 (VC).
35 Newcastle to Murray, 2 Jul. 1756. Add. MSS. 32866, f.8 (VC).
36 Murray to Newcastle, 2 Jul. 1756. Add. MSS. 32866, f. 10 (VC).
37 Rosebery, *Chatham*, 453–54.
38 *Waldegrave Memoirs*, 174–5.
39 Thompson, *George II*, 252.
40 Social historians have pointed to Lady Bell's considerable influence at George II's court. Hannah Barker and Elaine Chalus, eds., *Women's History: Britain, 1700–1850, An Introduction* (London; New York: Routledge, 2005), 223.
41 Newcastle to Murray, 20 Oct. 1756. Add. MSS. 32868, f.376 (VC).
42 Murray to Hardwicke, 24 Oct. 1756 (Yorke, *Hardwicke*, ii, 329).
43 Coxe MSS. P. 3–4 E.E., p. 226 (VC).
44 Campbell, *The Lives of the Chief Justices*, ii, 389.
45 Lady Mansfield to Stormont, 7 Dec. 1756. SP, Bundle 1390.
46 Holliday, *Life of Lord Mansfield*, 109.
47 *Whitehall Evening Post*, 6–9 Nov. 1756.
48 The legal historian William Holdsworth asserted that Hardwicke was the only lawyer of the eighteenth century whose fame rivals that of Mansfield. Holdsworth, *Some Makers of English Law*, 180.
49 Campbell, *The Lives of the Chief Justices*, ii, 391.
50 *Ryder Diary*.
51 Campbell, *The Lives of the Chief Justices*, ii, 393.

52 H.W.V. Temperley, "Inner and Outer Cabinet and Privy Council, 1679–1783," *English Historical Review*, 27, no. 108 (Oct. 1912): 684–7.
53 *London Evening Post*, 2 Dec. 1756.
54 Campbell, *The Lives of the Chief Justices*, ii, 398.

CHAPTER NINE

1 Yorke, *Hardwicke*, i, 143.
2 Journal entry of 11 Apr. 1773. James Boswell, *Boswell for the Defence 1769–1774*, William K. Wimsatt Jr and Frederick Poddle, eds. (New York: McGraw-Hill, 1959), 173–9.
3 See Chapter 14.
4 See Chapter 23.
5 Mansfield to Newcastle, 27 Jul. 1767. Add. MSS. 32984, f.67 (VC).
6 *London Chronicle*, 27 May 1773 (VC).
7 Correspondence between Mansfield and Granville, 3–8 Apr. 1767, Add. MSS. 42085, ff. 14–17 (BL).
8 Holliday, *Life of Lord Mansfield*, 489.
9 Campbell, *The Lives of the Chief Justices*, ii, 447–8.
10 Holdsworth, *Some Makers of English Law*, 162–3.
11 Browning, *Newcastle*, 235–6, 241.
12 Harris, *Politics and the Nation*, 34.
13 Conway, *War, State and Society*, 131.
14 Browning, *Newcastle*, 236.
15 Mansfield to Miss Ann Pitt, 7 Dec. 1756. Hist. MSS. Comm. 13th Rep., Appx., pt. 3, Fortescue MSS, vol. 1, 139 (VC).
16 Mansfield to Holdernesse, 14 Feb. 1757. Eg. 3438, f.20 (BL).
17 Horace Walpole, *Memoirs of the Reign of King George the Second*, ii, 318.
18 Clark, *The Dynamics of Change*, 334–5.
19 Walpole, *Memoirs of the Reign of King George II*, ii, 351–2.
20 John H. Langbein, "The Criminal Trial before the Lawyers," *University of Chicago Law Review*, xlv (1978): 263, 297.
21 Horace Walpole, *Horace Walpole: Memoirs and Portraits*, edited by Matthew Hodgart (London: B.T. Batsford, 1963), 248.
22 Walpole, *Memoirs of the Reign of King George II*, ii, 353. This was not the only time that Walpole accused Mansfield of having unpleasant traits that Walpole regarded as feminine: "As he had all the mischievous qualities of a woman, even to the alacrity of uttering the grossest untruths, he hated juries with a feminine animosity." Walpole, *Memoirs and Portraits*, 249.
23 Thompson, *George II*, 259.
24 Voltaire, *Candide*, ch. 23 (quoted in Shapiro, ed., *The Yale Book of Quotations*, 792).
25 Browning, *Newcastle*, 261.

26 Ilchester, *Fox*, i, 189n1.
27 Ibid., i, 157; Peter Luff, "Fox, Henry, first Baron Holland of Foxley," *ODNB*.
28 See Chapter 8.
29 Clark, *The Dynamics of Change*, 340.
30 Ibid, 347.
31 Newcastle to Hardwicke, 5 Mar. 1757. Add. MSS, 35416, ff.178–79 (VC).
32 Clark, *The Dynamics of Change*, 340.
33 Newcastle to Mansfield, 5 Mar. 1757. Add. MSS. 32870, f.239 (BL).
34 Newcastle to Hardwicke, 26 Mar. 1757. Add. MSS. 32870, f.340 (VC).
35 Stone to Newcastle, 26 Mar. 1757. Add. 32870, MSS. f. 342 (VC).
36 Turner, *The Cabinet Council of England in the Seventeenth and Eighteenth Centuries, 1622–1784*, i, 19–20; Thompson, *George II*, 215–18.
37 Turner, *The Cabinet Council of England in the Seventeenth and Eighteenth Centuries, 1622–1784*, ii, 10–11.
38 Ibid., ii, 51.
39 Ibid., ii, 110.
40 Ibid., ii, 38.
41 Ibid., ii, 33.
42 Temperley, "Inner and Outer Cabinet and Privy Council, 1679–1783," *The English Historical Review* xxvii, No. 108 (Oct. 1912): 696n60.
43 Turner, *The Cabinet Council of England in the Seventeenth and Eighteenth Centuries, 1622–1784*, ii, 34.
44 Accounts by leading politicians of their private meetings with the King were not always an accurate record of what did happen, as opposed to what they wished, or wanted others to believe, had happened. Thompson, *George II*, 71.
45 Newcastle to Hardwicke, 15 Apr. 1757. Add. MSS. 32870, f.421 (VC).
46 Newcastle to Mansfield, 13 Apr. 1757. Add. MSS. 32870, f.411 (BL).
47 Mansfield to Newcastle, 15 Apr. 1757. Add. MSS. 32870, f.427 (BL).
48 Clark, *The Dynamics of Change*, 387–9.
49 Mansfield to Hardwicke, 11 Jun. 1757 (Sat. 4 o'clock). Add. MSS.35595, f.39 (BL).
50 Dupplin to "Madam," 13 Jun. 1757. Add. MSS. 32871, ff.298–99 (VC).
51 Ilchester, *Henry Fox*, ii, 58–60. Waldegrave, *Memoirs*, 128–9 (VC).
52 Newcastle to Mansfield, 10 Dec. 1767. Add. MSS.32985, ff.57–61v (VC).
53 Clark, *The Dynamics of Change*, 423–4.
54 Mansfield to Hardwicke, 11 Jul. 1757 (Sat. 4 o'clock). Add. MSS. 35595, f.39 (BL).
55 Devonshire to Hardwicke, 14 Jun. 1757 (quoted in Yorke, *Hardwicke*, ii, 400).
56 Clark, *The Dynamics of Change*, 429.
57 Harris, *Politics and the Nation*, 26.
58 Richard Middleton, *The Bells of Victory: The Pitt-Newcastle Ministry and the Conduct of the Seven Years War, 1757–1762* (Cambridge: Cambridge University Press, 1985), 19, 49.
59 Luff, "Fox, Henry, first Baron Holland of Foxley," *ODNB*; John Heneage Jesse,

Memoirs of Celebrated Etonians, 2 vols. (London: Richard Bentley and Sons, 1875), i, 51.

60 Newcastle to Hardwicke, 23 Aug. 1757. Yorke, Hardwicke, iii, 312.

61 Holdernesse to Newcastle, 9 Sep. 1757. Add. MSS. 32874 (VC).

62 Holdernesse to Mansfield, 14 Sep. 1757. Eg. 3438, f.158 (BL).

63 Mansfield to Holderness, 14 Sep. 1757. Eg. 3438, f.160 (BL).

64 Newcastle to Hardwicke, 5 Nov. 1757. Add. MSS. 35417, f.152 (VC); Browning, *Newcastle*, 269.

65 Newcastle to Mansfield, 8 Jun. 1759 (VC).

66 Mansfield to Newcastle, 15 Apr. 1757, Add. MSS. 32870, f.427 (BL); Mansfield to Newcastle, 21 Apr. 1760 (VC). Add. 35429, MSS. f.13 (BL); Mansfield to Newcastle, 18 Jul. 1760. Add. 32902, MSS. ff.355–56 (VC); Newcastle to Mansfield, 9 Sep. 1760. Add. MSS. 32911, f.202 (VC).

67 Newcastle to Mansfield, 9 Sep. 1760, and memo. Add. MSS. 32911, ff. 202–205 (VC).

68 Newcastle to Mansfield, 16 Sep. 1760. S. MSS. 32911 (VC).

69 Mansfield to Newcastle, 20 Aug. 1758. Add MSS. 32822, f.470 (VC).

70 Newcastle's Memo for the King. Add. MSS. 32891, f.358 (VC); Newcastle to Mansfield, 15 Jun. 1759. Add. 32892, MSS. ff.92–93v (VC); Newcastle to Hardwicke, 20 Nov. 1759. Add. MSS. 35419, ff.101–02v (VC).

71 Mansfield to Newcastle, 27 Jul. 1758. Add. MSS. 32882, f.77 (VC).

72 Williams, *Chatham*, ii, 71.

73 Memo of Newcastle, 16 Mar. 1759. Add. MSS. 32889, f.100 et seq. (VC).

74 Newcastle to Hardwicke, 31 Aug. 1759 (quoted in Yorke, *Hardwicke*, iii, 56–57).

75 Mansfield to Newcastle, 1 Nov. 1759 (quoted in Yorke, *Hardwicke*, iii, 80).

76 Newcastle's Memo for the King, 6 Jun. 1759. Add. 32892, f.312 (VC).

77 John B. Owen, *The Eighteenth Century 1714–1815* (New York and London: W.W. Norton and Company, 1974), 100.

78 Williams, *The Whig Supremacy*, 28.

79 Owen, *The Eighteenth Century*, 103.

80 Porter, *English Society in the Eighteenth Century*, 110.

81 Ibid., 76.

82 Browning, *Newcastle*, 183.

83 Rosebery, *Chatham*, 138.

84 Hamilton, "The Education of Solicitor-General William Murray," 85.

85 Browning, *Newcastle*, 44; Donald G. Barnes, "The Duke of Newcastle, Ecclesiastical Minister, 1724–54," *The Pacific Historical Review* 3, no. 2 (June 1934): 164–91.

86 Porter, *English Society in the Eighteenth Century*, 114.

87 Harris, *Politics and the Nation*, 27.

88 Porter, *English Society in the Eighteenth Century*, 113.

89 See Chapter 10.

90 Nichols, *Illustrations of the Literary History of the Eighteenth Century*, v, 199.

91 Katherine Harriet Porter, "Margaret, Duchess of Portland," Ph.D. thesis, Cornell University (June 1930): 94–8.

92 Murray to Newcastle, 3 Nov. 1752. Add. MSS. 32730, ff. 201–202 (VC).

93 Newcastle to Murray, 18 Oct. 1752. Add. MSS. 32730, f.140 (VC).

94 Mansfield to Lyttelton, 12 Oct. 1759. Maud Mary Lyttelton Wyndham, *Chronicles of the Eighteenth Century, Founded on the Correspondence of Sir Thomas Lyttelton and His Family*, 2 vols. (London: Hodder and Stoughton, 1924), ii, 295 (VC).

95 Boaden, *Private Correspondence of David Garrick*, i, 294–5.

96 He died of a heart attack while having a bowel movement. "Death came to George ... wearing the cap and bells of low comedy; for this, like other crises in the King's life, was coloured by farce." Trench, *George II*, 298–9.

97 Jeremy Black, *George III: America's Last King*, (New Haven: Yale University Press, 2006), 109–10.

98 Thomas Macnight, *Life of Henry St John, Viscount Bolingbroke* (London: Chapman and Hall, 1863), 630–1, 635.

99 Black, *George III: America's Last King*, 121, 123, 142. "His preference for frugal meals and his sober habits became a source of fun for the graphic satirists." John Cannon, "George III," *ODNB*.

100 Black, *George III: America's Last King*, 122, 137, 162–84.

101 May, *The Constitutional History of England since the Accession of George the Third, 1760–1860*, ii, 87; Fitzmaurice, *Shelburne*, i, 98–100.

102 J.A. Lovat-Fraser, *John Stuart Earl of Bute* (Cambridge, UK: Cambridge University Press, 1912), 96–7.

103 Karl Wolfgang Schweizer, "Stuart, John, Third Earl of Bute," *ODNB*.

104 Newcastle to an unknown person, 14 Dec. 1760, Add. MSS. 32916, f.53v (VC).

105 Arthur T. Bolton, *The Architecture of Robert and James Adam (1758–1794)*, 2 vols. (London: Country Life and George Newnes; New York: C. Scribner's Sons, 1922), ii, 32.

106 Newcastle to Hardwicke, 14 Nov. 1760. Add. MSS. 35420, f.114 (VC).

107 Ilchester, *Henry Fox*, i, 216.

108 Roscoe, *Lives of Eminent British Lawyers*, 215.

109 Elaine Chalus, *Elite Women in English Political Life c.1754–1790* (Oxford: Clarendon Press, 2005), 120.

110 Mansfield to Newcastle, 24 Dec. 1760. Add. MSS. 32916, f.296 (VC).

111 Newcastle to Mansfield, 18 Mar. 1761. Add. MSS. 32920 ff.295–96 (VC).

112 Mansfield to Newcastle, 23 Aug. 1761. Add. MSS. 32927, f.179–83 (VC).

113 Browning, *Newcastle*, 282.

114 Ilchester, *Henry Fox*, ii, 213; Browning, *Newcastle*, 282.

115 Ibid., 285.

116 Newcastle to Joseph Yorke, 14 May 1762 (quoted in Yorke, *Hardwicke*, iii, 355–7).

117 Horace Walpole, *Memoirs of the Reign of King George III*, 4 vols. (London: Lawrence and Bullen, 1894), i, 132.

118 Sargeaunt, *Annals of Westminster School* (VC).
119 Mansfield to Newcastle, 3 May 1762. Add. MSS. 32938, ff.28–29v (VC).
120 "Essay on Chatham," *Edinburgh Review*, 80 (Oct. 1844): 547–8.
121 Newcastle to Kinnoull, 3 Jun. 1763. Add. MSS. 32949, ff. 21–22 (VC).
122 Newcastle to the Attorney General, 25 Oct. 1762 (quoted in Yorke, *Hardwicke*, iii, 426).
123 *Waldegrave Memoirs*, 308–9 (quoting Horace Walpole).
124 Holmes and Szechi, *The Age of Oligarchy*, 283–4.
125 *Waldegrave Memoirs*, 239–40.
126 Schweizer, "Stuart, John, Third Earl of Bute," *ODNB*.
127 "Essay on Chatham," *Edinburgh Review* 80, 558.
128 Sedgwick, ed., *Letters from George III to Lord Bute*, 116–17.
129 Ibid., 131–2.
130 Ibid.,157.
131 Ibid., 184. Dr Johnson too thought Mansfield vain. He told Boswell that flattery was like a bellows and that Lord Mansfield received flattery "till cheeks like to burst." James Boswell, *The Life of Samuel Johnson*, edited by David Womersley (London: Penguin Group, 2008), 380–1.
132 Sedgwick, ed., *Letters from George III to Lord Bute*, 193, 226.
133 Fitzmaurice, *Shelburne*, i, 284.
134 Heward, *Lord Mansfield*, 81.
135 See Chapter 18.
136 John L. Bullion, *A Great and Necessary Measure: George Grenville and the Genesis of the Stamp Act: 1763–1765* (Columbia, MO: University of Missouri Press, 1982), 43.
137 Thomas Erskine May, *The Constitutional History of England since the Accession of King George the Third, 1760–1860*, 2 vols. (New York: A.C. Armstrong and Son, 1899), i, 34.
138 See Chapter 14.
139 Newcastle to Devonshire, 11 Aug. 1763. Add. MSS. 32950, ff. 71v-72v (VC).
140 Walpole, *Memoirs of the Reign of King George III*, i, 231–2.
141 Newcastle to Hardwicke, 11 Aug. 1763. Add. MSS. 32950, ff. 71v-72v (VC).
142 Mansfield and the marriage contract, 22–23 Aug. 1763. Add. MSS. 35353, ff. 266, 338, 346 (VC).
143 Newcastle to Devonshire, 24 Sep. 1763. Add. MSS. 32951, f. 151 (VC).
144 Ibid.
145 Sandwich to Fox, 26 Sep. 1763. Earl of Ilchester, ed., *Letters to Fox* (London, Privately printed for presentation to the members of the Roxburghe Club, 1915), 179–84 (VC).
146 Newcastle to Devonshire, 3 Dec. 1763. Add. MSS. 32954, f. 64v (VC).
147 Heward states that "Murray ceased to have much influence in public affairs after Newcastle resigned in 1762." Heward, *Lord Mansfield*, 88. But contemporaneous

evidence shows that he continued to exercise great political influence with the King and the ministry well into the 1770s, particularly in American affairs. He remained a Cabinet member until 1782. See Chapter 18.

148 Williams, *Chatham*, ii, 221.

149 Lord March to George Selwyn, Nov. 1766. Hayward, *Lord Chesterfield and George Selwyn*, 91 (VC).

150 Portland to Newcastle, 17 Dec. 1766. Add. MSS 32978, f.378 to 379v (VC). By Whiggism, Portland was presumably referring to the independence of Parliament from the Crown, implementing the political theories of John Locke and embodied in the Glorious Revolution of 1688. George H. Guttridge, *English Whiggism and the American Revolution* (Berkeley and Los Angeles: University of California Press), 1–16.

151 Newcastle to Rockingham, 11 Jun. 1767. Add. MSS. 32982, ff.303–303v (VC).

152 The six were the Duke of Newcastle (1757–62), Earl of Bute (1762–63), George Grenville (1763–65), Marquess of Rockingham (1765–66), Earl of Chatham (1766–68), and Duke of Grafton (1768–70).

153 Newcastle's minute, 4 Apr. 1767. Add. MSS.32981, ff.31–32 (VC).

154 Richard Rigby to the Duke of Bedford, 12 Sep. 1767. *Bedford Correspondence*, iii, 389–90 (VC).

155 Lyttelton to Lord Temple, 25 Nov. 1767. Phillimore, *Memoirs of G. Lyttelton*, ii, 734–41 (VC).

156 Peter D.G. Thomas, *Lord North* (Edinburgh: Allen Lane, 1976), 39.

157 Ibid., 42–3.

158 Ibid., 69. See Chapter 18.

159 Holliday, *Life of Lord Mansfield*, 322–3.

160 Prest, *Blackstone*, 256n74.

161 Langford, *A Polite and Commercial People*, 522.

162 North to Mansfield, 3 Sep. 1781. SP, Bundle 641.

163 *Public Ledger*, 8 Aug. 1775.

164 SP, Box 117/Bundle 4.

165 *Morning Post*, 11 Nov. 1776 (VC).

166 Fitzmaurice, *Shelburne*, ii, 315–16.

167 Kirk, *Burke*, 71.

168 *Public Advertiser*, 4 Dec. 1777 (VC).

169 Comte de Vergennes to Marquis de Noailles, 30 Aug. 1777 (VC).

170 Richard Butterwick, *Poland's Last King and English Culture: Stanislaw August Poniatowski, 1732–1798* (Oxford: Clarendon Press; New York: Oxford University Press), 113–14, 124.

171 Ibid., 126. Mansfield to the Duchess of Portland, 30 Nov. 1757. Hist. MSS. Comm. Bath, vol. 1, 364–5 (VC).

172 Davies, *God's Playground*, ii, 390.

173 H.M. Scott, "Murray, David, Seventh Viscount Stormont and Second Earl of Mansfield," *ODNB*.

174 See, for example, Lord Suffolk to the King, 5 Feb. 1774. Fortescue, *Correspondence of George III*, iii, 60 (forwarding to the King an extract from a letter from the King of Poland to John Lind, Poland's envoy to Britain, which Lind had passed on to Mansfield. As to Lind's role, see Butterwick, *Poland's Last King*, 132.).

175 NAS, Ex NRAS 776 second series bundle 578. RH4/151/10.

176 H.M. Scott, *The Emergence of the Eastern Powers, 1756–1775*, (Cambridge, UK; New York: Cambridge University Press), 221–2.

CHAPTER TEN

1 Knight, *Gallery of Portraits with Memoirs*, vi, 62–8.

2 A copy of the will is in VC, Box 319.

3 Lewis Saul Benjamin, *Lady Suffolk and Her Circle, by Lewis Melville [pseudo.]* (London: Hutchinson, 1924), 269.

4 *Aurora*, 22 Feb. 1781 (VC).

5 Langford, *A Polite and Commercial People*, 111.

6 Newcastle to the Bishop of Worcester, 22 Jun. 1768. Add. MSS. 33072, f.50, 50v. (VC)

7 SP, Bundle 1400.

8 Lady Mansfield to Stormont, 8 Jan. 1757. SP, Bundle 1390.

9 Ibid., 13 May 1757. SP, Bundle 1390.

10 Chalus, Elite Women in English Political Life, 55–60.

11 Lady Mansfield to Stormont, 8 Jan. 1757. SP, Bundle 1390.

12 Ibid., 7 Dec. 1756. SP, Bundle 1390.

13 Ibid., 13 May 1757. SP, Bundle 1390

14 Lady Hervey to Rev. Edmund Morris, 30 Nov. 1765 (VC).

15 Journal entry of 26 Dec. 1765. James Boswell, *Boswell on the Grand Tour: Italy, Corsica and France, 1765–1766*, edited by Frank Brady and Frederick A. Pottle (New York: McGraw-Hill, 1955), 250–2.

16 Heward, *Lord Mansfield*, 91.

17 The accounts that John Way kept for Mansfield show that Mansfield banked at C. Hoare & Co. over the course of many years. SP, Bundle 1400. The bank continued to handle the accounts of Mansfield's heirs after his death. John Way to the 3rd Earl of Mansfield, 24 Dec. 1798. SP, Box 117/Bundle 4.

18 Way's employment by Mansfield had begun at the latest by December 1757, and it continued until Mansfield's death in 1793. SP, Box 75/Bundle 1.

19 Way to the 2nd Earl of Mansfield, May 1793. SP, Box83/Bundle 4.

20 In a letter to the 3rd of Mansfield in 1798, Way stated that the profits of the office of chief clerk for that year amounted to £3,386, and that he and Mansfield had

agreed twenty years earlier that after Mansfield's death, these profits, "after deducting what is due to myself," should be paid to the 2nd earl and his heirs. Way wished to know to whom the money should be paid or deposited. Way to the 3rd Earl of Mansfield, 24 Dec. 1798. SP, Box 117/Bundle 4.

21 Account by John Way of interest paid to Mansfield (1791). SP, Bundle 2347.
22 Way to Mansfield, 24 Dec. 1787. SP, Box 93, Bundle 3.
23 See Chapter 23.
24 Memorandum written by Lord Stormont describing conversation with Way, 19 Sep. 1786. SP, Bundle 58. The land in Cheshire presumably had been bequeathed to him by Vernon, who had befriended him while he was at Westminster School. See Chapter 2.
25 *London Chronicle*, 7–9 Oct. 1788 (VC).
26 Langford, *Public Life and the Propertied Englishman*, 63–4.
27 *Morning Herald*, 16 Aug. 1782 (VC).
28 Account by John Way of interest paid to Lord Mansfield (1791). SP, Bundle 2347.
29 *The Royal Kalender; or Complete and Correct Annual Register for England, Scotland, Ireland and America for the Year 1772, etc.* London 1772 (VC).
30 Yorke, *Hardwicke*, i, 87.
31 Mansfield to Stormont, 28 Jun. 1784. Ex NRAS 776 second series bundle 2347.
32 Matthews, *Ryder Diary*, 5 May 1754.
33 *Parker's General Advertiser*, 11 Nov. 1784 (VC).
34 *London Courant*, 5 Feb. 1780 (VC). "Going snacks" means to divide profits. *Oxford English Dictionary*, ii (New York: Oxford University Press, 1971), 2886.
35 NAS, RH/151/10.
36 *London Courant*, 5 Feb. 5 1780 (VC).
37 White, *London in the Eighteenth Century*, 52–4.
38 Bolton, *The Architecture of Robert & James Adam*, i, 113.
39 Gore-Browne, *Chancellor Thurlow*, 130–1.
40 Roscoe, *Lives of Eminent British Lawyers*, 190.
41 Conway, *War, State and Society*, 153–4.
42 Newcastle to the Duke of Cumberland, 4 Sep. 1745. Add. MSS. 32705, f.136 (VC). Lindsay was a son of Mansfield's sister Emilia, who had married Sir Alexander Lindsay of Evalie, Perth. Hamilton, "The Education of Solicitor-General William Murray," 2.
43 Newcastle to the Duke of Devonshire, 2 Jan. 1756. Add. MSS. 32862, f.10 (VC).
44 Mansfield to Newcastle, 11 Oct. 1758. Add. MSS. 32884, f.329 (VC). It is not clear whether this is the same Mr Lindsay that Mansfield was pushing for earlier.
45 Edward Trelawney to Andrew Stone, 12 Nov. 1747. Add. MSS. 32713, f.432 (VC).
46 *The World*, 1 Jan. 1787 (VC).
47 Journal entry of 2 Apr. 1783. James Boswell, *Boswell, the English Experiment, 1785–1789*, edited by Irma S. Lustig (New York: McGraw-Hill, c1986), 92–3.
48 Mansfield to Newcastle, 21 Apr. 1761. Add. MSS. 32922, f.112 (VC).

49 Newcastle to Mansfield, 22 Apr. 1761. Add. MSS. 32922, f.133 (VC).
50 Mansfield to Newcastle, 23 May 23 1761. Dd. MSS. 32923, ff. 235–236v (VC).
51 Mansfield to Stormont, 24 Apr. 1761. SP, Box 18/Folder 8.
52 Sedgwick, *Letters of George III*, 7 Apr. 1763, 211–12.
53 Mansfield to Newcastle, 1761. Add. MSS. 35429, f.15 (BL).
54 Campbell, *The Lives of the Chief Justices*, ii, 494, 494n.
55 Mme. Necker to Stormont, 9 Nov. 1779 and 20 Jun. 1780. SP, Box 14.
56 *Morning Chronicle*, 15 Apr. 1776 (VC).
57 *Gazetteer*, 28 Dec. 1776 (VC).
58 Under the terms of the earldom created in 1776, the title would pass to the heirs of Mansfield's father, which meant that Stormont would inherit the title when Mansfield died. Because it was believed that a Scottish nobleman could not inherit an English title of nobility, a new earldom of Mansfield was created shortly before Mansfield's death, which provided that Stormont would inherit the title directly from his uncle.
59 H.M. Scott, *British Foreign Policy in the Age of the American Revolution* (Oxford: Clarendon Press; New York: Oxford University Press, 1990), 240.
60 Sir Nathaniel William Wraxall, *The Historical and the Posthumous Memoirs of Sir Nathaniel William Wraxall, 1772–1784*, edited by Henry B. Wheatley, 5 vols. (New York: Scribner and Welford, 1884).
61 *Adams's Weekly Courant*, 21 Sep. 1779 (VC).
62 *Morning Herald*, 31 Jul. 1782 (VC).
63 H.M. Scott, "Murray, David, Seventh Viscount Stormont and Second Earl of Mansfield," *ODNB*.
64 Mansfield to an unidentified correspondent, 15 Aug. 1776 (JPML). Since Mansfield addressed the letter to "My dearest," it is possible that the addressee was his close (and influential) friend, the Duchess of Portland. In the letter, Mansfield asked the addressee to suggest Stormont's name for the position, emphasizing that Stormont had heavy expenses as ambassador to Paris.
65 Stormont to the Earl of Suffolk, 20 Oct. 1778. SP, Bundle 641. Various newspapers, 24 Oct. 1778.
66 *Morning Post*, 29 Oct. 1778 (VC).
67 *London Evening Post*, 21–23 Oct. 1779 (VC).
68 Scott, "Murray, David, Seventh Viscount Stormont and Second Earl of Mansfield," *ODNB*.
69 *London Courant*, 31 Oct. 1780 (VC).
70 *Morning Post*, 6 Nov. 1779 (VC). The actor, playwright, and wit Samuel Foote was another who commented on Stormont's parsimony. When Foote dined with Stormont at the British embassy in Paris, Stormont brought out his wine in a small decanter and poured it into tiny glasses, pontificating about its exquisite growth and enormous age. "It is very little of its age," said Foote, holding up his glass. Forster, *Biographical Essays*, 336.

71 *Morning Post*, 9 Nov. 1779.

72 Scott, "Murray, David, Seventh Viscount Stormont and Second Earl of Mansfield," ODNB.

73 Mansfield to Stormont, 17 Sep. 1756. SP, Box 18/Folder 8.

74 Ibid., 25 Jan. 1757. SP, Box 18/Folder 8.

75 Ibid., 17 Sep. 1756. SP, Box 18/Folder 8.

76 Ibid., 30 Nov. 1756. SP, Box 18/Folder 8.

77 In November 1756, Mansfield found it necessary to inform Stormont that "the King desires you wou'd go to Warsaw." Mansfield to Stormont, 30 Nov. 1756. SP, Box 18/Folder 8. Lady Mansfield wrote: "I'm very much vex'd to find they intend sending you to Poland." Lady Mansfield to Stormont, 7 Dec. 1756. SP, Bundle 1390.

78 Mansfield to Stormont, 8 Nov. 1757. SP, Box 18/Folder 8.

79 Lady Mansfield to Stormont, 23 Dec. 1757. SP, Bundle 1390.

80 Ibid., 23 Dec. 1757. SP, Bundle 1390.

81 Mansfield to Stormont, 2 Jan. 1758. SP, Box 18/Folder 8.

82 Ibid., 6 Jan. 1758. SP, Box 18/Folder 8.

83 Ibid., 7 Mar. 1758. SP, Box 18/Folder 8.

84 *Journal of Capt. E. Thompson, R.N.*, 2 Jan. 1785. *Cornhill Magazine* xvii, 638.

85 The rumours that Marjory Hay was the Pretender's mistress are plausible, in view of the "endless quarrels" between the Pretender and his wife, Clementina Sobieski, and the animosity that Clementina displayed to Marjory. Lenman, *The Jacobite Risings in Britain*, 203. Tayler, ed., *The Jacobite Court at Rome*, 28. Of course, even if Marjory was the Pretender's mistress, that does not mean that Mills was their son.

86 *Morning Chronicle*, 31 Mar. 1774, 15 Apr. 1776 (VC); *Public Advertiser*, 14 Jul. 1785 (VC).

87 Sylvester Douglas, Baron Glenbervie. *The Diaries of Sylvester Douglas, Lord Glenbervie*, edited by Francis Bickley, 2 vols. (London: Constable and Co.; Boston and New York: Houghton Mifflin Co., 1928): Entry of 3 Jan. 1810, ii, 77.

88 Ibid.

89 *Morning Chronicle*, 31 Jul. 1766 (VC).

90 Garrick to Samuel Martin, 29 Apr. 1776. David M. Little and George M. Kahrl, eds., *The Letters of David Garrick* (London: Oxford University Press, 1963), iii, 1096.

91 *London Evening Post*, 11–13 Feb. 1777 (VC).

92 *Public Advertiser*, 28 Nov. 1774 (VC).

93 Sylvester Douglas referred to him as "a sort of pseudo-Mæcenas." *Diaries of Sylvester Douglas*, ii 2, 77 (Entry of 3 Jan. 1810). Mæcenas was a generous patron of the arts in Ancient Rome.

94 *Memoirs of Richard Cumberland*, 173.

95 *London Evening Post*, 8 Aug. 1772 (VC).

96 C. Hoare and Co., *Untitled Paper on the Adelphi Terrace Financial Scandal of 1772*, July 2010.
97 Mills to Stormont, 7 Nov. 1777. SP, Bundle 664.
98 *General Evening Post*, 1–4 Jul. 1780 (VC).
99 *Public Advertiser*, 16 Feb. 1782 (VC).
100 Garrick to James Boswell, 17 Nov. 1772. Little and Kahrl, eds., *The Letters of David Garrick*, ii, 828.
101 A diarist wrote in 1785 that she had gone off to France with her footman. *Journal of Capt E. Thompson*, R.N., 2 Jan. 1785. *Cornhill Magazine* xvii, 638.
102 It was not the first time Mansfield had approached Hastings for employment for his relatives. In 1775, he recommended to Hastings a Mr Hay, presumably a relative of Mansfield's sister Marjory and her husband, John Hay. Mansfield to Hastings, 3 Mar. 1775. Add. MSS. 39871, f.1 (BL).
103 Mansfield to Hastings, 23 Jan. 1782. Add. MSS. 39871, ff. 29, 29v. (VC).
104 *Gazetteer*, 20 Apr. 1782 (VC).
105 *Morning Post*, 21 Sep. 1784 (VC).
106 *Gazetteer*, 7 Mar. 1787 (VC).
107 Greenwood, F. Murray. "Sir Thomas Mills." *Dictionary of Canadian Biography Online*, iv, 200. University of Toronto/Universite Laval.
108 *Memoirs of Richard Cumberland*, 173.
109 L.F.S. Upton, ed. *The Diary and Selected Papers of Chief Justice William Smith, 1784–1793*, 3 vols. (Toronto: Champlain Society, 1963–65), i, 110–11 (Entry of 12 Aug. 1784).
110 Sir William Grant to Sir Thomas Mills, 3 Oct. 1777. SP, Bundle 664.
111 Another letter among the Scone Papers, also about the Revolutionary War, was written by Mills to Lord Stormont. 7 Nov. 1777. SP, Bundle 664.

CHAPTER ELEVEN

1 Heward, *Lord Mansfield*, 39.
2 Arthur T. Vanderbilt II, *Changing Law: A Biography of Arthur T. Vanderbilt* (New Brunswick, NJ: Rutgers University Press, 1976), 25.
3 SP, vol. 270.
4 *Southampton Observer*, 13 Jun. 1874 (VC).
5 C. Yorke to Warburton, 10 Aug. 1754. Add. MSS. 35404 (VC).
6 Sexby, *The Municipal Parks, Gardens, and Open Spaces of London*, 417–19.
7 Caroline A. White, *Sweet Hampstead and Its Associations* (London: Elliot Stock, 1900), 6–7.
8 Sexby, *The Municipal Parks, Gardens, and Open Spaces of London*, 419.
9 F.E. Baines, ed., *Records of the Manor, Parish, and Borough of Hampstead, in the County of London* (London: Whittaker and Co., 1890), 161–2, 224.
10 White, *Sweet Hampstead and Its Associations*, 42.

11 *Public Advertiser*, 24 Aug. 1786 (VC).
12 *General Advertiser*, 16 Dec. 1786 (VC).
13 Proceedings of the Old Bailey. Reference Numbers t17860718 (19 Jul. 1786) & t17870711-36 (11 Jul. 1787).
14 Lady Mansfield to Lord Stormont, 13 May 1757. SP, Bundle 1390.
15 *Lloyd's Evening Post*, 1 Jan. 1773 (VC).
16 *Morning Chronicle*, 6 Feb. 1776 (VC).
17 He appears to have purchased land there in 1757 and 1763. SP, Box No. 3.
18 The accounts of John Way, Mansfield's steward, of money paid to Mansfield in 1791 show that he received £731 in rents from the Kenwood estate. SP, Bundle 2347.
19 Eileen Harris, *The Country Houses of Robert Adam* (London: Aurum Press Limited, 2007), 99. James Adam, Robert's brother and architectural partner, also contributed to the work, with designs for the interiors of the library and its anteroom. Ibid.
20 Vickery, *Behind Closed Doors*, 12.
21 Holmes and Szechi, *The Age of Oligarchy*, 205.
22 Harris, *The Country Houses of Robert Adam*, 101.
23 Ibid.
24 Newcastle to Mansfield, 15 Jul. 1768. Add. MSS. 32990, f.305 (VC).
25 Harris, *The Country Houses of Robert Adam*, 101–2. The glass cost Mansfield £170. SP, Bundle 1400. Chippendale worked with Adam on "a number of grand projects in the 1760s." White, *London in the Eighteenth Century*, 216.
26 Harris, *The Country Houses of Robert Adam*, 101.
27 Samuel Curwen, *The Journal and Letters of Samuel Curwen: an American in England from 1775 to 1783*, edited by George Atkinson Ward, 4th ed. (Boston: Little, Brown and Co., 1864).
28 Mary Hamilton Dickenson, *Letters and Diaries from 1756 to 1816*, edited by Elizabeth and Florence Anson (London: J. Murray, 1925), 245.
29 *Morning Chronicle*, 1 Apr. 1793 (VC).
30 *Kenwood: The Iveagh Bequest*, published by English Heritage, 2007.
31 *Evening Standard*, 31 Dec. 1938 (VC).
32 Although the exact date that Mansfield moved to Bloomsbury Square is difficult to determine, it appears that it was about fifteen or sixteen years after he moved to Lincoln's Inn Fields in 1759. Edwin Beresford Chancellor, *The Romance of Lincoln's Inn Fields and Its Neighbourhood* (1932). The British Museum had been established in 1753.
33 Lawrence Hutton, *Literary Landmarks of London* (New York: Harper and Brothers, 1892), 128.
34 Mrs E.T. Cook, *Highways and Byways in London*, 244 (1903).
35 Edwin Beresford Chancellor, *The Squares of London*, 184 (1907).
36 Thomas Pennant, *Some Account of London*, 247 (5th ed., 1813).

37 Cook, *Highways and Byways in London*, 233n1 (1903).
38 Chalus, *Elite Women in English Political Life*, 50.
39 Campbell, *The Lives of the Chief Justices*, ii, 575–6.
40 *Morning Post*, 21 Oct. 1777 (VC).
41 Journal entry of 29 Mar. 1772. Boswell, *The Heart of Boswell*, 323.
42 Journal entry of 26 Mar. 1775. Boswell, *Boswell: The Ominous Years*, 96–8.
43 *Morning Post*, 29 Oct. 1778 (VC).
44 *Morning Chronicle*, 14 Oct. 1784 (VC).
45 Upton, ed., *The Diary and Selected Papers of Chief Justice William Smith*, i, 234.
46 Kenyon, *Lord Kenyon*, 25.
47 *Public Advertiser*, 2 May 1757 (VC).
48 Trevelyan, *English Social History*, 408.
49 Wroughton to Edward Weston, 27 Apr. 1762. Hist. MSSD. Comm., Report on the MSS. of C.F. Underwood, 331 (VC).
50 Newcastle to Mansfield, 26 Jun. 1767. Add. MSS. 32982, f.431, 431v. (VC).
51 Browning, *Newcastle*, 6.
52 Vickery, *Behind Closed Doors*, 274.
53 Jeaffreson, *A Book about Lawyers*, ii, 232.
54 Mansfield to Stormont, 25 Jan. 1757. SP, Box 18/Folder 8.
55 Mansfield to Stormont, 6 Jan. 1758. SP, Box 18/Folder 8.
56 Thompson, *George II*, 193.
57 Newcastle to Rockingham, 17 Sep. 1766. Add. MSS. 32977, f.94v (VC).
58 *Morning Chronicle*, 2 Sep. 1776 (VC).
59 Stella Tillyard, *A Royal Affair: George III and his Scandalous Siblings* (New York: Random House, 2006), 74.
60 Mansfield to Newcastle, 6 Sep. 1768. Add. MSS. 32991A, f.69 (VC).
61 Mansfield to Newcastle, 3 Aug. 1767. Add. MSS. 32984, ff.159, 159v. (VC); Newcastle to Mansfield, 7 Aug. 1767. Add. MSS. 32984, f.204 (VC).
62 *Public Advertiser*, 18 Sep. 1767 (VC).
63 Chalus, *Elite Women in English Political Life*, 84, 94.
64 Ibid., 91.
65 Vickery, *Behind Closed Doors*, 274.
66 Abbott, *Sugar*, 57; Vickery, *Behind Closed Doors*, 293.
67 Richard Cumberland, *Memoirs of Richard Cumberland*, 2 vols. (London: Lackington, Allen and Co., 1807), ii, 344–6 (quoted in Roscoe, *Lives of Eminent British Lawyers*, 225).
68 Boswell showed his admiration for Mansfield in a conversation with Johnson that he recorded in his *Life of Johnson*, iii, 268:

"We talked of war.

Johnson: 'Every man thinks meanly of himself for not having been a soldier, or not having been at sea.'

Boswell: 'Lord Mansfield does not.'

Johnson [his temper obviously rising]: 'Sir, if Lord Mansfield were in a company of General Officers and Admirals who have been in service, he would shrink; he'd wish to creep under the table.'

Boswell: 'No; he'd think he could *try* them all.'"

McNair, "Dr Johnson and the Law," *The Law Quarterly Review* 68 (Jul. 1947): 302, 308–9.

69 Journal entry of 11 Apr. 1773. Boswell, *The Heart of Boswell*, 333–4.

70 Journal entry of 9 Apr. 1775. Boswell, *Boswell: The Ominous Years*, 136–7.

71 Journal entry of 11 Apr. 1773, Wimsatt and Pottle, eds., *Boswell for the Defence 1769–1774*, 333–4.

72 Mansfield to Duchess of Portland, 30 Nov. 1757. Hist. MSS. Comm. Bath, i, 364–5 (VC).

73 Alexander Murray to the Duchess of Portland, 13 Jun. 1770. Hist. MSS. Comm. Bath, i, 368–9 (VC).

74 A.S. Turberville, *A History of Welbeck Abbey and Its Owners*, 2 vols. (London: Faber and Faber, 1938–39), ii, 154.

75 Edward Young to the Duchess of Portland, 20 Jan. 1756. H.M.C. Bath, i, 322 (VC).

76 Lord Sheffield to William Eden, 15 Jul. 1785. *Correspondence of Auckland*, i, 346 (VC).

77 Hamilton, "The Education of Solicitor-General William Murray," 9.

78 Valentine, *Lord George Germain*, 3–13, 49, 55–6. Fitzmaurice, *Shelburne*, i, 351, 355.

79 Mansfield to Newcastle, 16 Jun. 1759. Add. MSS. 32872, f.108–108v (VC).

80 *Morning Herald*, 30 Aug. 1781 (VC).

81 Evans, *Warburton and the Warburtonians: A Study in Some Eighteenth-Century Controversies* (London: Oxford University Press, 1932), 188.

82 Kilvert, *Memoirs of the Life and Writings of the Right Rev. Richard Hurd* (London: Richard Bentley, 1860), 38.

83 Ibid., 325.

84 Percy H. Fitzgerald, *Samuel Foote: A Biography* (London: Chatto and Windus, 1910), 223.

85 John Forster, *Biographical Essays*, 3rd ed. (London: John Murray, 1860), 373–4.

86 Shapiro, ed., *The Yale Book of Quotations*, 281.

87 Hastings was five years younger than Stormont, so it is unlikely they were schoolboy friends, but they seem to have known each other. Moreover, as an old Westminster, Hastings had a natural claim to Mansfield's friendship.

88 John Scott to Hastings, 3 Jan. 1782. Add. MSS. 29152, ff. 291v-292v (VC).

89 Mansfield to Hastings, in response to a letter from Hastings to Mansfield of 21 Mar. 1774. Add. MSS. 39871, ff. 2–3 (VC).

90 Their correspondence on this subject is described in Chapter 12.

91 P.J. Marshall, "Hastings, Warren," *ODNB*.
92 Scott to Hastings, 25 Dec. 1781. Add. MSS. 29152, ff. 221v, 227–228v (VC).
93 Scott to Hastings, 3 Jan. 1782. Add. MSS. 39152, ff. 291v-292v (VC).
94 Scott to Hastings, 3 Jan. 1782. Add. MSS. 39152, ff. 291v-292v (VC); Scott to Hastings, 26 Jun. 1782, Add. MSS. 29154, f.416 et seq. (VC).
95 Scott to Hastings, 21 Oct. 1783. Add. MSS. 29161, f.31 (VC).
96 Scott to Hastings, 28 Sep. 1782. Add. MSS. 29156, ff. 124–125 (VC).
97 Much earlier, Mansfield had recommended a Mr Hay for employment in Bengal. Mansfield to Hastings, 3 Mar. 1775. Add. MSS. 39871, f.1 (VC, Box 322). Hay may have been a relative of Mansfield's sister Marjory, who had married John Hay.
98 Scott to Hastings, 11 Jul. 1782. Add. MSS. 29155, ff.67–68v (VC).
99 Mansfield to Hastings, 27 Sep. 1783. Add. 29160, f.397 (VC).
100 Scott to Hastings, 1 Jul. 1782. Add. MSS. 29155, ff. 8–8v (VC).
101 Scott to Mrs Hastings, 25 Jul. 1783. Add. MSS 29160, ff. 145–147 (VC).
102 Scott to Hastings, 16 Jun. 1782. Add. MSS. 29154, f.339 (VC).
103 Marshall, "Hastings, Warren." *ODNB*.
104 Scott to Mrs Hastings, 25 Jul. 1783. Add. MSS. 29160, ff. 145v-147 (VC).
105 Scott to Hastings, 3 Aug. 1782. Add. MSS. 29155, ff. 320–321v (VC).
106 Jeremy Bernstein, *Dawning of the Raj: The Life and Trials of Warren Hastings* (Chicago: Iva R. Dee, 2000), 172.
107 Scott to Hastings, 27 Mar. 1784. Add. MSS. 29163, f.f.51v-52v (VC).
108 Major Scott to Hastings, 15 Oct. 1784. Add. MSS. 29166, f.297 (VC). *London Chronicle*, 9–12 Oct. 1784 (VC).
109 Colley, *Britons*, 131.
110 Heward, *Lord Mansfield*, 91–2.
111 Heward, *Lord Mansfield*, 96.
112 Mansfield to Rutland, 14 Oct. 1784. Hist. MSS. Comm. 14th Rep. Appx. Part 1, Rutland MSS, iii, 142–3 (VC).
113 Lord Sydney to Cornwallis, 4 Nov. 1787. Charles Cornwallis, *Correspondence of Charles, First Marquis Cornwallis*, edited by Charles Ross (London: John Murray, 1859), i, 336.
114 John Murray, the 2nd Earl of Annandale, was also the 3rd Viscount Stormont. When he died in 1658, his widow, Lady Elizabeth Carnegy, married William Murray's grandfather, the 4th Viscount Stormont. In 1661, William Johnstone, also a Scot, was created Marquess of Annandale. The 3rd Marquess, whose meeting with Murray is described in the letter quoted from in the text, was his descendant. Duncan Adamson, "Johnstone, William, first Marquess of Annandale," *ODNB*.
115 Mansfield to Marchioness of Annandale, 17 Oct. 1743 (JPML).
116 *Debrett's Illustrated Peerage and Baronetage* (London: Debrett's Peerage Ltd. and MacMillan).

117 Mansfield to Marchioness of Annandale, 2 Jun. 1744 (JPML).
118 David Hume, *The Letters of David Hume*, edited by J.Y.T. Greig, 2 vols. (Oxford: Clarendon Press, 1932), i, xxiii, 61n2.
119 Ibid., i, 62.
120 *Evening Advertiser*, 5 Apr. 1757 (VC).
121 *Scots Magazine,* xv (1753): 629.
122 Arthur Collins, *Collins's Peerage of England: … Greatly Augmented, and Continued to the Present Time, by Sir Egerton Brydges*, 9 vols. (London: F.C. and J. Rivington, 1812.), v, 146.
123 Newcastle memorandum, 15 Dec. 1758. Add. MSS. 32886, f.326 (VC).
124 Rockingham to Newcastle, 6 Sep. 1763. Add. MSS. 32950, f.339 (VC).
125 Hardwicke to Newcastle, 15 Oct. 1763. Yorke, *Hardwicke*, iii, 536.
126 Newcastle to the Duke of Cumberland, 31 Oct. 1763. Add. MSS. 32952, f. 151 (VC).
127 Tracy Borman, *King's Mistress, Queen's Servant: the Life and Times of Henrietta Howard* (London: Pimlico, 2008), 270.
128 Mansfield to Lady Suffolk, 16 Sep. 1761. Add. MSS. 22628, f.63 (VC). Morton was elected; whether Mansfield voted for him is not known.
129 Archbishop of Canterbury to Newcastle, 25 Oct. 1766 and 27 Oct. 1766. Add. MSS. 32977, f.281 (VC).
130 Porter, *The Creation of the Modern World*, 22.

CHAPTER TWELVE

1 Sylvester Douglas, *The Diaries of Sylvester Douglas, Lord Glenbervie,* edited by Francis Bickley, 2 vols. (London: Constable and Co.; Boston and New York: Houghton Mifflin Co., 1928), ii, 77.
2 Mansfield's successor, Lord Kenyon, also was offered the post of lord chancellor and also thought that being chief justice was preferable. Kenyon, *Life of Lord Kenyon*, 257n.
3 Ernest Brown Rowlands, *Seventy-Two Years at the Bar: A Memoir [of Sir Harry Bodkin Poland]* (London: Macmillan and Co., 1924), 225.
4 Lemmings, *Professors of the Law*, 271. Saikrishna Prakash and Steven Smith, "How to Remove a Federal Judge," *Yale Law Journal* cxvi (2006): 92–102.
5 G.M. Trevelyan, *English Social History: A Survey of Six Centuries Chaucer to Queen Victoria* (London: Longmans, Green and Co., 1942), 350.
6 The King's Speech to both Houses of Parliament, 3 Mar. 1761 (VC).
7 *Read's Weekly Journal*, 1 May 1761 (VC). The poem was entitled "Truth in Rhyme."
8 Trevelyan, *English Social History*, 350.
9 Campbell, *The Lives of the Chief Justices*, ii, 446–7.

10 Baker, *Introduction to English Legal History*, 18.

11 Oldham, *The Mansfield Manuscripts*, i, 44.

12 In the Middle Ages, King's Bench was concerned with crimes and other wrongs, like trespass or assault, that threatened a breach of the king's peace; Common Pleas was concerned with litigation between subjects; and Exchequer dealt with the revenues of the Crown. Long before Mansfield's time, the use of fictional pleading (for example, that a breach of contract constituted a trespass) made these jurisdictional distinctions virtually meaningless. Sir Frank MacKinnon, "The Law and the Lawyers," in Turberville, ed., *Johnson's England*, ii, 291–2. While the history of common law pleading is beyond the scope of this biography, a brief summary of it can be found in Baker, *Introduction to English Legal History*, 49–61.

13 Baker, *Introduction to English Legal History*, 46–7; MacKinnon, "The Law and the Lawyers," in Turberville, ed., *Johnson's England*, ii, 291–2.

14 Ibid., ii, 292. Mansfield's finances are discussed in more detail in Chapter 10.

15 MacKinnon, "The Law and the Lawyers," in Turberville, ed., *Johnson's England*, ii, 292; Oldham, *The Mansfield Manuscripts*, i, 124; John Stoughton, *Shades and Echoes of Old London* (London: Leisure House Office, 1864[?]); David A. Lockmiller, *Sir William Blackstone* (Chapel Hill, NC: University of North Carolina Press), 107; MacKinnon "The Law and the Lawyers," in Turberville, ed., *Johnson's England*, ii, 292.

16 Oldham, *English Common Law in the Age of Mansfield*, 48.

17 MacKinnon, "The Law and the Lawyers," in Turberville, ed., *Johnson's England*, ii, 292.

18 White, *London in the Eighteenth Century*, 270.

19 Lemmings, *Professors of the Law*, 73.

20 Oldham, *The Mansfield Manuscripts*, i, 68, 79.

21 Samuel Johnson [not the famous Dr Samuel Johnson] to his sister Elizabeth, 27 Jan. 1775. Samuel Johnson, *Sir Joshua's Nephew*, edited by Susan M. Radcliffe (London: J. Murray, 1930), 32–4.

22 Stoughton, *Shades and Echoes of Old London*.

23 Oldham, *The Mansfield Manuscripts*, i, 119–20.

24 Lemmings, *Professors of the Law*, 46.

25 *The World*, 20 Nov. 1787.

26 Lemmings, *Professors of the Law*, 141; Oldham, *The Mansfield Manuscripts*, i, 77–8.

27 William N. Welsby, Lives of *Eminent Judges of the Seventeenth and Eighteenth Centuries* (London: Sweet, 1846), 443.

28 Baker, *Introduction to English Legal History*, 53.

29 He did not go on circuit in 1760–61 or 1776–79, perhaps because he was too busy, or in 1784, the year Lady Mansfield died. Heward, *Lord Mansfield*, 65–70.

30 Oldham, *English Common Law in the Age of Mansfield*, 36–7.

31 Oldham, *The Mansfield Manuscripts*, i, 130.

32 Ibid., i, 128–9.

33 Lemmings, *Professors of the Law*, 51, 51n103.

34 Joseph Cradock, *Literary and Miscellaneous Memoirs* (London: J.B. Nichols, 1826). 99.

35 Mansfield to the Duke of Newcastle, 27 July 1758. Add. MSS. 32882, f.77 (VC).

36 Mansfield to Justice Wilmot, 14 Aug. 1758. Add. MSS. 9828, f.35 (VC).

37 Heward, *Lord Mansfield*, 71.

38 Oldham, *The Mansfield Manuscripts*, i, 134.

39 John H. Langbein, "Shaping the Eighteenth-Century Criminal Trial: A View from the Ryder Sources," *University of Chicago Law Review* 50 (1983) 117–20.

40 *Public Advertiser*, 12 Oct. 1778.

41 Mansfield to the Duke of Newcastle, 27 Jul. 1758. Add. MSS. 32882, f.77 (VC).

42 *Public Ledger*, 25 Mar. 1761 (VC).

43 Vickery, *The Gentleman's Daughter*, 237–8.

44 *Morning Herald*, 22 Sep. 1784. This incident was reported many years after Mansfield had ceased going on the Northern Circuit.

45 Oldham, *The Mansfield Manuscripts*, i, 119.

46 *Somerset v. Stewart*, Lofft, 1, 98 Eng. Rep. 499 (1772).

47 *Rex v. Wilkes*, 4 Burr. 2527, 98 Eng. Rep. 327 (1770).

48 A newspaper commented: "After a hearing of several hours the plaintiff was non-suited which it is hoped will be a warning not to proceed in such frivolous cases." *Public Ledger*, 23 May 1760 (VC).

49 This conclusion is based on the author's review of numerous summaries of cases on index cards prepared by Judge Arthur Vanderbilt's research assistants.

50 Oldham, *The Mansfield Manuscripts*, i, 51.

51 4 Burr. 2303 (1769); *Scots Magazine*, June 1793, 261–5. The case is described in Chapter 19.

52 4 Burr. 2577, 98 Eng. Rep. 355 (1770). The case involved the Rule in Shelley's Case, a rule of law dating back to the fourteenth century, which said that where a testator devises property to a man and his heirs, the man gets complete ownership and may sell or give away the property, leaving nothing to the heirs. In *Perrin*, the testator left his estate to his son and then to the heirs of his daughter but made clear his intention that his son should have the property only during his lifetime. Mansfield and two of his three associate justices were willing to disregard established precedent in order to fulfill the testator's clear intention to give his son only a life interest in the property. Justice Yates dissented, and on appeal, the Court of Exchequer Chamber reversed the court's decision. Oldham, *The Mansfield Manuscripts*, ii, 1354.

53 Heward, *Lord Mansfield*, 57–8. Oldham notes that there were additional dissents in unreported cases, but that "the degree of unanimity in the decisions was high." Oldham, *The Mansfield Manuscripts*, i, 47.

54 Jane Dianne Samson, "Ex Aequo et Bono: Mansfield and Commercial Law," dissertation, University of Victoria (1983), 160.

55 Charles Francis Adams, *The Works of John Adams, Second President of the United States: With a Life of the Author,* 10 vols. (Boston: Little, Brown and Co., 1850–56), ii, 257 (quoting Robert Morris, a barrister at law).

56 Oldham, *The Mansfield Manuscripts*, i, 47–60.

57 *Diary of Woodfall's Journal*, 30 Mar. 1793 (VC).

58 John C. Jeaffreson, *A Book about Lawyers*, 2 vols. (London: Hurst and Blackett, 1867) ii, 164.

59 Rev. Samuel Denne to Rev. John Denne, 17 Feb. 1757, in *Illustrations of the Literary History of the Eighteenth Century,* 8 vols. John Nichols, (London: Nichols, Son and Bentley, 1817–58), vi, 806.

60 Lewis C. Warden, *The Life of Blackstone* (Charlottesville, VA: Michie Co., 1938), 40, 58, 76, 81–2.

61 Ibid., 237.

62 Prest, *Blackstone*, 176.

63 Holliday, *Life of Lord Mansfield*, 89; Browning, *Newcastle*, 184. A recent biographer of Blackstone casts doubt on the story, pointing out that nobody else was present at the interview and that Newcastle did not fill the vacancy until nine months later. Prest, *Blackstone*, 108–9. Nonetheless, Newcastle's control of the patronage system and his frequent use of patronage for political purposes make the story plausible.

64 Campbell, *The Lives of the Chief Justices*, ii, 378–9.

65 Lieberman, *The Province of Legislation Determined*, 31–2.

66 Prest, *Blackstone*, 222.

67 Oldham, *The Mansfield Manuscripts*, i, 48. Prest, *Blackstone*, 259–60.

68 Ibid.

69 Ibid., 271.

70 MacKinnon, "The Law and the Lawyers," in Turberville, ed., *Johnson's England*, ii, 300.

71 Oldham, *The Mansfield Manuscripts*, i, 195.

72 Fitzmaurice, *Life of Shelburne*, i, 89.

73 See Chapter 20.

74 The axiom (but not the thought) postdated Mansfield. It was stated by William E. Gladstone in the House of Commons in 1868. Fred E. Shapiro, ed., *The Yale Book of Quotations* (New Haven and London: Yale University Press, 2006), 312. In his "To be, or not to be" soliloquy, Hamlet included "the law's delay" as one of several reasons for ending one's life. *Hamlet*, Act III, Scene 1.

75 1 Burr. 6 (1756).

76 Welsby, *Eminent Judges*, 400–1.

77 Lewis Bernstein Namier and John Brooke, *The House of Commons: 1754–1790* (New York: Published for the History of Parliament Trust by Oxford University Press, 1964), ii, 367.

78 *Morning Chronicle*, 19 May 1777 (VC).

79 *Star*, 30 Mar. 1793 (VC).
80 *Gazetteer*, 20 Jul. 1778 (VC).
81 *Public Advertiser*, 21 Dec. 1778 (VC).
82 Mansfield to William Eden, 5 Mar. 1778. *Journal and Correspondence of Auckland*, vol. 1, xv (VC); *Morning Chronicle*, 13 May 1777 (VC).
83 *Morning Herald*, 29 Jun. 1781 (VC).
84 Paterson, *Curiosities of Law and Lawyers*, 67.
85 Jeaffreson, John C., *A Book about Lawyers*, ii, 164.
86 Mansfield to Justice Wilmot, 29 Dec. 1757. Add. MSS. 9828, f.33 (VC).
87 *Rex v. Wilkes*, 4 Burr. 2527, 2549, 98 Eng. Rep. 327, 339 (1770).
88 Charlotte Moore, book review of Mark Bostridge, *Florence Nightingale*, in *The Spectator*, 25 Oct. 2007, 41.
89 Heward, *Lord Mansfield*, 46.
90 Seward, *Anecdotes*, iv, 491 ff.
91 Johnson to his sister Elizabeth, 27 Jan. 1775. Samuel Johnson, *Sir Joshua's Nephew*, 34.
92 Journal entry of 30 Mar. 1772. James Boswell, *Boswell for the Defence, 1769–1774*, edited by William K Wimsatt Jr and Frederick A. Pottle (New York: McGraw-Hill, 1959), 80–1.
93 Roscoe, *Lives of Eminent British Lawyers*, 218.
94 The Butler Memoir of Mansfield prior to Holliday. Seward, *Anecdotes*, 1795–6 ed., IV (VC).
95 *Scots Magazine*, June 1793 (quoting from a letter published in two London newspapers on 23 Jul. 1776).
96 Holliday, *Life of Lord Mansfield*, 120–1.
97 Campbell, *The Lives of the Chief Justices*, ii, 580.
98 Diary of William Samuel Johnson, 25 Nov. 1767. Conn. Hist. Soc., vol. 3 (VC, Box 328).
99 *Morning Post*, 21 Nov. 1780 (VC).
100 Journal entry of 10 Apr. 1772. James Boswell, *The Heart of Boswell: Six Journals in One Volume,* edited by Mark Harris (New York: McGraw-Hill, 1981), 326.
101 *General Advertiser*, 24 Oct. 1785.
102 Kenyon, *Life of Lord Kenyon*, 106.
103 Paterson, *Curiosities of Law and Lawyers* (VC).
104 Duke of Newcastle to Duke of Devonshire, 11 Aug. 1763 (quoted in Yorke, *Hardwicke*, iii, 517).
105 Campbell, *The Lives of the Chief Justices*, ii, 564.
106 Laetitia Matilda Hawkins, *Memoirs, Anecdotes, Facts, and Opinions*, 2 vols. (London: Longman, Hurst, Rees, Orme, Brown, and Green, 1824), i, 255–6.
107 Oldham, *The Mansfield Manuscripts*, i, 81.
108 Hawkins, *Memoirs*, i, 255–6.
109 Heward, *Lord Mansfield*, 62.

110 Paterson, James, *Curiosities of Law and Lawyers*, 22.

111 Ibid., 35; Lord Henry Brougham, *Sketches of Statesmen of the Time of George III* (London: Richard Griffin and Co., 1836), iv, 327. This anecdote has been attributed to both Dunning and Serjeant William Davy, another barrister who was known for his humour and who likewise was not intimidated by Mansfield. J.H. Baker, "Davy, Sir William," ODNB. Humphry William Woolrych, *Lives of Eminent Serjeants-at-Law of the English Bar* (London: W.H. Allen, 1869), 625.

112 John Cannon, "Dunning, John, First Baron Ashburton," ODNB.

113 Folarin O. Shyllon, *Black Slaves in Britain* (London: Oxford University Press, 1974), 90.

114 Kenyon, *Life of Kenyon*, 35.

115 *Gazetteer*, 24 Jan. 1776.

116 William Samuel Johnson to William Pittkin, 11 Apr. 1767 ("Sir Fletcher Norton ... is generally esteemed one of the first counsel at the bar, and has peculiar influence with Lord Mansfield.") Collections of Mass. Hist. Soc., 5th Series, ix. (Part 1 of Jonathan Trumbull Papers, 223.

117 Charles Kendall Adams, *Representative British Orations*, i, 143–9 (VC).

118 Paterson, *Curiosities of Law and Lawyers*, 135.

119 *Morning Post*, 12 Jun. 1777 (VC).

120 Campbell, *The Lives of the Chief Justices*, ii, 570.

121 Harold Wentworth and Stuart Berg Flexner, eds. *Dictionary of American Slang* (Second Supplemented Edition) (New York: Thomas Y. Crowell Company, 1975), 543.

122 Jeaffreson, *A Book About Lawyers*, ii, 169.

123 Catley became a successful singer and actress. She was "without beauty, vulgar in speech, amoral, and mercenary, but undeniably witty, with a graceful carriage and an exquisite voice." William Appleton, *Charles Macklin: An Actor's Life* (Cambridge, MA: Harvard University Press, 1960), 134.

124 Delaval was a friend of the King's brother, the Duke of York, and of members of the nobility, as well as being a patron of the stage. John Forster, *Biographical Essays*, 351.

125 *Rex v. Delaval*, 3 Burr. 1434, 97 Eng. Rep. 913 (1763).

126 Not all judges agreed with Mansfield that it was the job of the common law courts to regulate morality. Only four years after the *Delaval* decision, a judge stated that morals were the concern of the ecclesiastical courts, not the common law courts. "From the Restoration to the Regency: Kept Mistresses and Legal Contracts," text at n111. Legal Studies Research Paper No. 2009-03, University of Warwick School of Law (the author is not named).

127 *Rex v. Delaval*, 3 Burr. 1434, 97 Eng. Rep. 913 (1763).

128 *General Evening Post*, 22 Apr. 1777 (VC).

129 *Gazetteer*, 26 Apr. 1777 (VC).

130 *Morning Post*, 25 Apr. 1777 (VC).
131 *Rex v. Felix MacDonald*, 3 Burr. 1645, 97 Eng. Rep. 1026 (1765).
132 White, *London in the Eighteenth Century*, 153.
133 Ibid., 309–10. Allardyce Nicoll, *A History of English Drama 1660–1900: Late Eighteenth Century Drama 1750–1800* (Cambridge: Cambridge University Press, 1969), 5–10.
134 The riot was created by adherents of the actor David Garrick, who objected to Macklin playing the role of Macbeth, a role that they considered to be exclusively owned by Garrick. Edward Abbott Parry, "Charles Macklin," in William Archer, ed., *Eminent Actors* (London: Kegan Paul, Trench, Trübner and Co., Ltd, 1891), 162–5.
135 *Morning Chronicle*, 24 Feb. 1784 (VC).
136 Paterson, *Curiosities of Law and Lawyers*, 372.
137 Mansfield expressed a similar view in dealing with labour disputes, stating that, while an employee may request higher wages, it was an illegal conspiracy for employees to combine in order to force an employer to raise wages. See Chapter 13.
138 Parry, "Charles Macklin," in William Archer, ed., *Eminent Actors*, 172–7.
139 *London Chronicle*, 4 Aug. 1775) (VC).
140 Elizabeth N. Chatten, *Samuel Foote* (Boston: Twayne Publishers, 1980), 92.
141 Campbell, *The Lives of the Chief Justices*, ii, 570.
142 Paterson, *Curiosities of Law and Lawyers*, 42–3.
143 Horace Twiss, The Public and Private *Life of Lord Chancellor Eldon*, 3 vols. (London: John Murray, 1844), iii, 116–17 (quoted in Hamilton, "Education of Solicitor-General William Murray," 15).
144 See Chapter 20.
145 Theobald Mathew, *For Lawyers and Others* (London: William Hodge and Co., 1937), 89.
146 Conversation of Boswell with Foote, 19 Apr. 1776. James Boswell, *Boswell: The Ominous Years 1774–1776*, edited by Charles Ryskamp and Frederick Poddle (London: William Heinemann, 1963), 342–3.
147 Holliday, *Life of Lord Mansfield*, 184–5.
148 Mansfield to Hastings, 3 Mar. 1775. Add. MSS. 39871, f.1 to f.2 (BL). Eleven years earlier, Mansfield had expressed dismay to Prime Minister George Grenville on learning that British laws were to be imposed on newly conquered, largely Catholic, French-speaking Canada: "Is it possible that we have abolished their laws, and customs, and forms of judicature all at once? – a thing never to be attempted or wished. The history of the world don't furnish an instance of so rash and unjust an act by any conqueror whatsoever: much less by the Crown of England, which has always left to the conquered their own laws and usages, with a change only so far as the sovereignty was concerned." Mansfield to Grenville, 24 Dec. 1764. Grenville Papers, ii.

149 Mansfield to Hastings, 3 Mar. 1775. Add. MSS. 39871, f.2 (BL).

150 Roscoe Pound, *An Introduction to the Philosophy of Law* (New Haven: Yale University Press, rev. ed. 1959), 62. Natural law is often contrasted to legal positivism, a legal theory that states that law has nothing to do with morals, unless the legislature has enacted a moral principle. Oliver Wendell Holmes, perhaps the leading exponent of positivism, wrote: "The primary rights and duties with which jurisprudence busies itself ... are nothing but prophesies ... [A] legal duty ... is nothing but a prediction that if a man does or omits certain things he will be made to suffer in this or that way by judgment of the court." Oliver Wendell Holmes, "The Path of the Law" in *Collected Legal Papers* (New York: Peter Smith, 1952), 168–9.

151 Pound, *An Introduction to the Philosophy of Law,* 12.

152 S. Todd Lowry, "Lord Mansfield and the Law Merchant: Law and Economics in the Eighteenth Century," *Journal of Economic Issues* vii, no. 4 (Dec. 1973), 605, 610–11.

153 Sir Henry *Maine, Ancient Law* (New York: Everyman's Library, E.P. Dutton and Co Inc, 1954. First published 1861), 56.

154 Bertrand Russell, *The History of Western Philosophy* (New York: Simon and Schuster, 1945), 623.

155 See Chapter 3.

156 John Locke, *Two Treatises of Government* (New York: E.P. Dutton and Co. Inc. Everyman's Library, 1943), 118–20, 181; Roy Porter, *The Creation of the Modern World*, 185–6.

157 See, for example, *Perrin v. Blake*, 4 Burr. 2577, 98 Eng. Rep. 355 (1770).

158 In *Rex v. Scofield*, Cald. 397 (1784), Mansfield ruled that a person who attempted to burn down a house was guilty of a crime, even though his attempt failed. The decision is transcribed in Oldham, *The Mansfield Manuscripts*, ii, 1421–4. Like many of Mansfield's decisions, this case has been influential; it was cited by New York's highest court for the proposition that there can be criminal liability for an attempt, even if ultimately unsuccessful, to commit a crime. *People v. Dlugash*, 41 N.Y.2d 725, 732 (1977).

159 Charles Phineas Sherman, *Roman Law in the Modern World*, 3 vols. (Boston: Boston Book Co., 1917), i, 240.

160 Campbell, *The Lives of the Chief Justices*, ii, 404.

161 *Ringsted v. Lady Lanesborough*, 3 Doug. 197, 99 Eng. Rep. 610 (1783).

162 *Omychund v. Barker*, 26 Eng. Rep. 14 (1744).

163 Charles Knight, *Gallery of Portraits with Memoirs* (London: C. Knight, 1833–37), (1836), vi, 62–8.

164 Paterson, *Curiosities of Law and Lawyers*, 73.

165 Holdsworth, *Some Makers of English Law*, 170–1.

166 *Jones v. Randall*, 3 Cowp. 37, 39 (1774).

167 *Omychund v. Barker*, 26 Eng. Rep. 14 (1744). He argued this case as a lawyer, but he adopted the same method of decision-making as a judge.

168 Oldham, *The Mansfield Manuscripts*, i, 203.

169 *Scottish Notes and Queries*, ix, 106 (VC).

170 *Barwell v. Brooks*, 3 Doug. 372, 373, 99 Eng. Rep. 702, 703 (1784).

171 "Law and Social Sciences Today," Gaston Lecture, Georgetown University, 25 Nov. 1957.

172 Sir William Holdsworth, *A History of English Law* (London: Methuen and Co. Ltd and Sweet and Maxwell, 1938), xii, 555.

173 Samson, "Lord Mansfield and Commercial Law," 132.

174 *Hodgson v. Ambrose*, 1 Doug. 337, 341, 99 Eng. Rep. 216, 219 (1780).

175 Holdsworth, *A History of English Law*, xii, 557.

176 Duncan M. Kerly, *An Historical Sketch of the Equitable Jurisdiction of the Court of Chancery* (Cambridge: Cambridge University Press, 1890), 180.

177 Susan A. Bandes, "Moral Imagination in Judging," *Washburn Law Journal* (2011): li, 1, 12.

178 Heward, *Lord Mansfield*, 173.

179 Roscoe, *Lives of Eminent British Lawyers*, 216.

180 In the sensational 1776 trial of the Duchess of Kingston in the House of Lords for bigamy, Mansfield advised the House that these privileges were limited to matters arising within the professional relationship with the client or patient. See Chapter 20.

181 Alfred Dalzel to Lord Stormont, June 1793. NAS, RH4/151/10. Ex NRAS 776 second series bundle 578.

182 As to the common sense Mansfield brought to the law, Holliday tells of a case early in his tenure on the bench, where a lawyer had taken up a considerable time of the court citing several cases to prove the construction of an old woman's will. Finally, Mansfield stopped him and asked whether he thought the old woman had ever heard of these cases and, if not, what common sense and justice must say to the matter. He immediately gave judgment in favour of common sense against the precedents, to the satisfaction of the whole court. Holliday, *Life of Lord Mansfield*, 127.

183 Heward, *Lord Mansfield*, 177.

184 Emma Rothschild, *The Inner Life of Empires: An Eighteenth-Century History* (Princeton and Oxford: Princeton University Press, 2011), 252.

CHAPTER THIRTEEN

1 Pincus, *1688*, 8, 20, 37.

2 *Whitehall Evening Post*, 25–27 Sep. 1759 (VC). This was not the only ship to be named after him; in the 1790s, a 128-foot-long spar to be used as a mast for the

navy was shipped from Canada on board another *Lord Mansfield*. Patrick Campbell and William F. Ganong, *Travels in the Interior Inhabited Parts of North America in the Years 1791 and 1792* (Toronto: Champlain Society, 1937), 28.

3 Campbell, *The Lives of the Chief Justices*, ii, 403.

4 Holmes and Szechi, *The Age of Oligarchy*, 133.

5 Quoted in C.H.S. Fifoot, *Lord Mansfield* (Oxford: Oxford University Press, 1936; reprinted Darmstadt: Scienta Verlag Aalen, 1977), 4.

6 White, *London in the Eighteenth Century*, 168.

7 Langford, *Public Life and the Propertied Englishman*, 61.

8 Ibid., 4.

9 Holmes and Szechi, *The Age of Oligarchy*, 144; Daunton, "The Wealth of the Nation," in Langford, ed., *The Eighteenth Century*, 168.

10 Trevelyan, *English Social History*, 371.

11 *Diary of Dudley Ryder*, 52. Ryder's dinner companion also suggested that all holidays "but the necessary ones, be entirely cut off [because] every holiday costs England £100,000 by the loss of so much labour." Ibid. The practice of subdividing manufacturing functions among specialists was already common in London's coachmaking and watchmaking industries. According to one historian: "No man was expected to make a complete watch." White, *London in the Eighteenth Century*, 215.

12 Fitzmaurice, *Shelburne*, i, 402–3 (quoting from Lady Shelburne's diary).

13 Holmes and Szechi, The Age of Oligarchy, 162; R.M. Healey, Review of Shena Mason, ed., *Matthew Boulton*, *Times Literary Supplement,* 11 Sep. 2009, 27.

14 Holmes and Szechi, *The Age of Oligarchy*, 335–6. A Nobel Prize winner of the twenty-first century has observed: "There is no such thing as useless fundamental knowledge. The silicon revolution would have been impossible without quantum physics. Abstract maths allows internet security and computers not to crash every second. Albert Einstein's theory of relativity might seem irrelevant but your satellite navigation system would not work without it." Andre Geim, "Be afraid, be very afraid, of the world's tech crisis," *Fin. Times*, 6 Feb. 2013, 9.

15 Michio Kaku, "A Second Big Bang In Geneva?" *Wall St J*, 1 Apr. 2010: A19.

16 Trevelyan, *English Social History*, 390.

17 Daunton, "The Wealth of the Nation," in Langford, ed., *The Eighteenth Century*, 171–3; Langford, *A Polite and Commercial People*, 655, 661; H. Heaton, "Industry and Trade," in Turberville, ed., *Johnson's England*, i, 237–38.

18 Trevelyan, *English Social History*, 350–1.

19 Daunton, "The Wealth of the Nation," in Langford, ed., *The Eighteenth Century*, 158.

20 Heaton, "Industry and Trade," in Turberville, ed., *Johnson's England*, i, 233–4.

21 Trevelyan, *English Social History*, 386.

22 Holmes and Szechi, *The Age of Oligarchy*, 159.

23 White, *London in the Eighteenth Century*, 175.

24 Pincus, *1688*, 44.

25 White, *London in the Eighteenth Century*, 175, 252–5; Smith, "The Newspaper," in Turberville, ed., *Johnson's England*, ii, 340–5.

26 Holmes and Szechi, *The Age of Oligarchy*, 160.

27 Helen Saberi, *Tea: A Global History* (London: Reaktion, 2010), 93–4.

28 Elizabeth Abbott, *Sugar: A Bittersweet History* (London and New York: Duckworth Overlook, 2008), 50–1; Matthew Parker, *The Sugar Barons: Family, Corruption, Empire, and War in the West Indies* (New York: Walker and Company, 2011), 127.

29 Saberi, *Tea: A Global History*, 148–55.

30 Conway, *War, State, and Society*, 288; Holmes and Szechi, *The Age of Oligarchy*, 149.

31 Ibid., 149–50; Heaton, "Industry and Trade," in Turberville, ed., *Johnson's England*, i, 231.

32 See Chapter 17.

33 Daunton, "The Wealth of the Nation," in Langford, ed., *The Eighteenth Century*, 163.

34 Holmes and Szechi, *The Age of Oligarchy*, 152; White, *England in the Eighteenth Century*, 177.

35 There had been earlier trading in securities in coffee houses, but in 1773 a group of brokers acquired a building of their own on Threadneedle Street, which for the first time was called the Stock Exchange; admission was open to everyone for sixpence a day. Trading on an exchange with limited membership began in 1802 in a newly erected building. E. Victor Morgan and W.A. Thomas, *The Stock Exchange: Its History and Functions* (London: Elek Books, 1962), 68–71; White, *London in the Eighteenth Century,* 184.

36 Oldham, *The Mansfield Manuscripts*, i, 687–90.

37 See Chapter 6.

38 Mansfield's reasoning was reminiscent of Portia's ruling in *The Merchant of Venice* that the contract Shylock had made with Antonio allowed him to get his pound of Antonio's flesh but not a drop of his blood. Act IV, Scene 1.

39 *Dyson v. Villiers*, Hill MS. Rep. Vol. 10. Fo. 330. MS. Room S.4 (VC); *London Chronicle*, 20–23 Feb. 1773 (VC).

40 White, *London in the Eighteenth Century*, 222–3.

41 *Aldis v, Finmore*, Yorke Mss., vol. 4, Fo. 162, 11 Dec. 1773 (VC).

42 *Morning Post*, 19 Aug. 1775 (VC).

43 Colley, *Britons*, 56.

44 Fifoot, *Lord Mansfield*, 8.

45 Ibid., 14.

46 Lieberman, *The Province of Legislation Determined*, 102.

47 Ibid., 102–3.

48 Holdsworth, *A History of English Law*, xii, 524.

49 *Metcalfe v. Hall*, Hill Mss. Rep. Vol. 18. Fol. 16. MS. Room. S. 1. (1782). B.R. Durnf. 168, 408 (VC).
50 Samson, "Ex Aequo et Bono: Lord Mansfield and Commercial Law," 58–9.
51 Scott Cooper, Colin Rule, and Louis Del Duca, "From Lex Mercatoria to Online Dispute Resolution: Lessons from History in Building Cross-Border Redress Systems," Legal Studies Research Paper No. 9-2011. Penn State, The Dickinson School of Law, 2011.
52 Oldham, *The Mansfield Manuscripts*, i, 600–2.
53 Lawrence M. Friedman, *A History of American Law*, 2nd ed. (New York: Simon and Schuster, Inc., 1985), 28; *Goodwin v. Robarts*, L.R. 10 Ex. (1875); Oldham, *The Mansfield Manuscripts*, i, 605–9.
54 Bernard I. Shientag, "Lord Mansfield Revisited – A Modern Assessment," *Fordham Law Review* x (1941): 345, 351.
55 *Pillans v. Van Mierop*, 3 Burr. 1664, 1669 (1765).
56 Holdsworth, *A History of English Law*, xii, 524–5.
57 Oldham, *The Mansfield Manuscripts*, i, 206.
58 *Lewis v. Rucker*, 2 Burr. 1167, 1168, 97 Eng. Rep. 769, 770 (1761).
59 Sir Frank MacKinnon, "The Law and the Lawyers," in Turberville, ed., *Johnson's England*, ii, 296.
60 *Wigglesworth v. Dallison*, 1 Doug. 201, 207, 99 Eng. Rep. 132, 135 (1779).
61 Campbell, *The Lives of the Chief Justices*, ii, 404.
62 *Luke v. Lyde*, 97 Eng. Rep. 614, 617 (1759).
63 *Anthon v. Fisher*, 3 Dougl. 166, 99 Eng. Rep. 594 (1782).
64 *Luke v. Lyde*, 2 Burr. 882, 889, 97 Eng. Rep. 614, 619 (1759). Mansfield's willingness to consider foreign law when deciding cases resonates today in the United States, where the Supreme Court has considered the question of whether foreign law can be appropriately considered in interpreting the Constitution. In *Roper v. Simmons*, 543 U.S. 551 (2005), Justice Anthony Kennedy used foreign law to buttress the Supreme Court's decision that it was unconstitutional to sentence to death a person who was under the age of eighteen when he committed a capital crime. Justice Scalia and two other Justices disagreed. The issue is discussed in Ganesh Sitaraman, "The Use and Abuse of Foreign Law in Constitutional Interpretation," *Harvard Journal of Law and Public Policy* xxxii (2005): 653–93.
65 Jane Dianne Samson, "Lord Mansfield and Negotiable Instruments," *Dalhousie Law Journal* xi, no. 3 (1987–88): 935–6.
66 *Goss v. Withers*, 2 Burr. 683, 97 Eng. Rep. 511 (1758);
67 *Lewis v. Rucker*, 2 Burr. 1167, 1172, 97 Eng. Rep. 769, 772 (1761).
68 *Bexwell v. Christie*, 1 Cowp. 396, 98 Eng. Rep. 1150 (1776).
69 Shientag, "Lord Mansfield Revisited," 351.
70 Langford, *A Polite and Commercial People*, 300.
71 *Trueman v. Fenton*, 2 Cowp. 544, 547, 98 Eng. Rep. 1232, 1233 (1777).

72 Oldham, *The Mansfield Manuscripts,* i, 231.
73 3 Burr. 1664, 1669 (1765).
74 Lieberman, *The Province of Legislation Determined,* 109–10; according to Holdsworth, Mansfield's decision in *Pillans* was based on Scots law, in which he found "a theory of contract which he considered more reasonable than the English theory based on consideration." *A History of English Law*, xii, 556.
75 *Rann v. Hughes*, 7 T.R. 750, 2 Eng. Rep. 18 (1778).
76 1 Cowp. 289, 98 Eng. Rep. 1091 (1782).
77 *Morning Chronicle*, 8 May 1777 (VC).
78 *Lloyd's Evening Post*, 7 Jun. 1776 (VC).
79 *Morning Post*, 23 Dec. 1777 (VC). Other Mansfield decisions involving the sale of defective goods are described in Oldham, *The Mansfield Manuscripts*, i, 232–40.
80 White, *London in the Eighteenth Century*, 275.
81 *Morning Post*, 7 Feb. 1777 (VC).
82 *Gazetteer*, 15 Jul. 1778 (VC).
83 See Chapter 4.
84 Oldham, *The Mansfield Manuscripts*, i, 185.
85 *Moses v. MacFerlan*, 2 Burr. 1010, 97 Eng. Rep. 679 (1760).
86 Oldham, *The Mansfield Manuscripts*, i, 226–31.
87 1 Doug. 138, 99 Eng. Rep. 91 (1779).
88 Vickery, *The Gentleman's Daughter*, 244. For more on Cornelys's career, see White, *London in the Eighteenth Century*, 293–302.
89 *Hawkes v. Saunders*, 1 Cowp. 289, 98 Eng. Rep. 1091 (1782).
90 Oldham, *The Mansfield Manuscripts*, i, 231.
91 Colley, *Britons*, 66–7; Heaton, "Industry and Trade," in Turberville, ed., *Johnson's England*, i, 257–8.
92 MacKinnon, "The Law and the Lawyers," in Turberville, ed., *Johnson's England*, ii, 296.
93 The history of the bill of exchange and the promissory note is described in *Goodwin v. Robarts*, L.R. 10 Ex., 346–7 (1875).
94 John Downes and Jordan Elliot Goodman, *Dictionary of Finance and Investment Terms*, 6th ed. (Hauppauge, NY: Barron's Educational Series, Incl., 2003), 62. The drawee of a bank cheque is the bank and the cheque is payable on demand; whereas the drawee of a bill of exchange might be a merchant or other person, and the bill might not be payable until a period of time had passed.
95 Quoted in Oldham, *The Mansfield Manuscripts*, i, 596–7.
96 Holdsworth, *A History of English Law*, xii, 529.
97 Oldham, *The Mansfield Manuscripts*, i, 596; Samson, "Lord Mansfield and Negotiable Instruments," 932.
98 1 Burr. 452, 97 Eng. Rep. 398 (1758).
99 1 Burr. 452, 457, 97 Eng. Rep. 398, 401.

100 Ibid., 402.
101 T.J. Stiles, *The First Tycoon, The Epic Life of Cornelius Vanderbilt* (New York: Alfred A. Knopf, 2009), 97.
102 Oldham, *The Mansfield Manuscripts*, i, 204–6.
103 *Edie v. East India Company*, 2 Burr. 1217, 97 Eng. Rep. 797 (1761).
104 2 Burr. 1217, 1222, 97 Eng. Rep. 797, 800.
105 Samson, "Lord Mansfield and Negotiable Instruments," 938.
106 Seward, *Anecdotes*, ii, 360–1 (1795).
107 2 Doug. 634, 99 Eng. Rep. 402 (1781).
108 2 Doug. 634, 635, 99 Eng. Rep. 402, 403.
109 2 Cowp. 753, 98 Eng. Rep. 1344 (1778).
110 Under the harsh criminal law of the time, the letter-sorter was executed for the theft.
111 2 Cowp. 753, 766, 98 Eng. Rep. 1344, 1350.
112 Mansfield's trial notes included over thirty nuisance cases, most of which were brought as public (i.e., criminal) actions, as opposed to private lawsuits. Oldham, *English Common Law in the Age of Mansfield*, 252–3. The predominance of criminal cases is understandable because nuisances typically created discomfort for an entire locality, not just a single individual. Ibid., 250–1.
113 Heward, *Lord Mansfield*, 56.
114 Oldham, *English Common Law in the Age of Mansfield*, 256.
115 Ibid., 248.
116 *British Mercury*, 7 Dec. 1780 (VC).
117 *Gazetteer*, 6 Jul. 1776 (VC).
118 *Rex v. Minish*, Yorke MSS. Vol. 4, Fo. 107 (1776) (VC).
119 *Rex v. White*, 1 Burr. 333, 97 Eng. Rep. 338 (1757).
120 This business developed in the early eighteenth century among underwriters who met in Edward Lloyd's coffee house. Ibid., 181.
121 1 Doug. 231, 99 Eng. Rep. 151 (1779).
122 1 Doug, 231, 233, 99 Eng. Rep. 151, 152.
123 Oldham, *The Mansfield Manuscripts*, i, 450.
124 *Morning Chronicle*, 23 Apr. 1777 (VC).
125 *London Chronicle*, 17 Nov. 1781 (VC).
126 *Lewis v. Rucker*, 2 Burr. 1166, 1172, 97 Eng. Rep. 769, 772 (1761).
127 3 Burr. 1237, 1240, 97 Eng. Rep. 808, 810 (1761).
128 3 Burr. 1909, 97 Eng. Rep. 1162 (1766).
129 1 Burr. 341, 97 Eng. Rep. 342 (1757).
130 Oldham, *The Mansfield Manuscripts*, i, 476.
131 1 Black. W. 313, 96 Eng. Rep. 175 (1761).
132 *Gazetteer*, 29 May 1780 (VC).
133 Holmes and Szechi, *The Age of Oligarchy*, 168.
134 Ibid., 165.

135 Ibid,. 164, 166.
136 Williams, *The Whig Supremacy*, 143.
137 1 Leach 275, 168 Eng. Rep. 240 (1783).
138 *Daily Universal Register*, 26 May 1785 (VC).
139 *London Evening Post*, 4 Dec. 1762 (VC).
140 *Lloyd's Evening Post*, 1 Jun. 1776 (VC).
141 Oldham, *The Mansfield Manuscripts*, ii, 1322–3.
142 *Aurora*, 20 Feb. 1781 (VC).
143 Paterson, *Curiosities of Law and Lawyers*, 42.

CHAPTER FOURTEEN

1 Oldham, *The Mansfield Manuscripts*, ii, 782.
2 *The Scourge*, 23 Jan. 1771 (BL)
3 *Public Advertiser*, 14 Jul. 1790; Shapiro, ed., *Yale Book of Quotations*, 489.
4 *Whitehall Evening Post*, 19 Jun. 29–1 Jul. 1776 (VC).
5 *Morning Post*, 12 Dec. 1776 (VC).
6 Yorke, *Hardwicke*, i, 84–6.
7 Trial of William Owen for publishing a libel entitled "The Case of Alexander Murray, Esq.," 6 Jul. 1752. 18 State Trials 1203 (VC)
8 29 Nov. 1755. Boswell's *Johnson*. Hill, ed.: Oxford 1887, i, 294n9 (VC).
9 Ernest Rhys, ed., *Boswell's Life of Johnson* (New York: Everyman's Library, E.P. Dutton and Co., 1906), i, 180n2.
10 Walpole to Horace Mann, 3 May 1749. W.S. Lewis, ed., *The Yale Editions of Horace Walpole's Correspondence* (New Haven: Yale University Press, 1960), xx, 46.
11 Murray to Hardwicke, 31 Dec. 1755. Add. MSS. 35593, f. 356v (VC).
12 *Whitehall Evening Post*, 19–22 Jun. 1756; White, *London in the Eighteenth Century*, 451.
13 Mrs Boscawen to Mrs Delany, 20 Nov. 1776. *Correspondence of Mrs Delany*, series 2, ii, 278.
14 Colley, *Britons*, 100.
15 Pincus, *1688*, 18.
16 Arthur H. Cash, *John Wilkes: The Scandalous Father of Civil Liberty* (New Haven: Yale University Press, 2006) 7, 46–7.
17 *Wilkes v. Wilkes*, Dickens 789, 21 Eng. Rep. 478 (1757).
18 Cash, *John Wilkes*, 32–3, 46–7, 56, 300–2.
19 Heward, *Lord Mansfield*, 112.
20 Wilkes, *The North Briton, from No. I to No. XLVI inclusive, with Several Useful and Explanatory Notes*, 1763. Reprinted by Kessinger Publishing's Rare Reprints.
21 West to Newcastle, 23 Apr. 1763. Add. MSS. 32989, f. 375v (BL); Fitzmaurice, *Shelburne*, i, 274.
22 Holmes and Szechi, *The Age of Oligarchy*, 318; Cash, *John Wilkes*, 101, 106–8.
23 Newcastle to Devonshire, 2 May 1763. Add. MSS. 32948, ff. 203–204 (VC).

24 Henry Eeles, *Lord Chancellor Camden and His Family* (London: P.Allan), 1934, 149.
25 Campbell, *The Lives of the Lord Chancellors*, vi, 301–2, 350–1.
26 Eeles, *Lord Chancellor Camden and His Family*, London, 103.
27 Peter D. G. Thomas, "Glynn, John," ODNB.
28 William Pitt, *Correspondence of William Pitt, Earl of Chatham*, edited by William Stanhope Taylor and Captain John Henry Pringle, 4 vols. (London: John Murray, 1839), iii, 483.
29 Walpole, *Memoirs of the Reign of George III*, ii, 11; Cash, *John Wilkes*, 380.
30 Cash, *John Wilkes*, 106–13.
31 Newcastle to Devonshire, 2 May 1763. Add. MSS. 32948, ff. 203–204 (VC).
32 Cash, *John Wilkes*, 31
33 Ibid., 31–5, 130–1.
34 Ibid, 121–2.
35 For Canada, see *R. v. Coté*, 2011 SCC 46, [2011] 3 S.C.R. 215; for the United States, see *Mapp v. Ohio*, 367 U.S. 643 (1961).
36 Warburton to Allen Kilvert, 17 Nov. 1763. *Unpublished Papers of Warburton*, 1841, 227–31 (VC).
37 Cash, *John Wilkes*, 150.
38 Ibid., 143.
39 White, *London in the Eighteenth Century*, 519.
40 Walpole, *Memoirs of the Reign of King George III*, i, 262–4.
41 Letter from Wilkes, 20 Jan. 1764. Percy Hetherington Fitzgerald, *The Life and Times of John Wilkes, M.P., Lord Mayor of London, and Chamberlain*, 2 vols. (London: Ward and Downey, 1888), i, 252.
42 Oldham, *English Common Law in the Age of Mansfield*, 224.
43 *Money v. Leach*, 3 Burr. 1741, 97 Eng. Rep. 1075 (1765).
44 J. Almon to Wilkes, 12 May 1767. Add. MSS. 30869, f. 123 (VC).
45 The several proceedings against Wilkes are described in *Rex v. Wilkes*, 4 Burr. 2527, 98 Eng. Rep. 328 (1770).
46 Diary of William Samuel Johnson, 20 Apr. 1768. Conn. Hist. Soc., vol. 4 (VC).
47 West to Newcastle, 20 Apr. 1768. Add. MSS. 32989, ff. 363–365v. (VC).
48 West to Newcastle, 24 Apr. 1768. Add. MSS 32989, ff. 377–377v (VC).
49 Newcastle to Mansfield, 13 May 1768. Add. MSS. 32990, f. 55–55v. (VC).
50 Diary of William Samuel Johnson, 27 Apr. 1768. Conn. Hist. Soc., vol. 4 (VC).
51 Cash, *John Wilkes*, 217.
52 White, *London in the Eighteenth Century*, 517.
53 Rockingham to Newcastle, 10 May 1768. Add. MSS. 32990, ff. 35–36v. (VC).
54 Newcastle to Mansfield, 13 May 1768. Add. MSS. 32990, ff. 55–55v. (VC).
55 West to Newcastle, 16 May 1768. Add. MSS. 32990, ff. 77–77v. (VC).
56 Newcastle to Rockingham, 3 Jun. 1768. Add. MSS. 32990, f. 153 (VC).
57 Extract of Mansfield's judgment against J. Wilkes. Add. MSS. 57818, f.134 (BL). Mansfield asserted several times in his life that popularity should not be sought

after. Later in his life, he wrote to the Duke of Rutland, who was then lord lieutenant of Ireland: "By not running after, or otherwise courting popularity than by deserving it, I hear it now follows you ... Be assured the true popularity is that which follows." Mansfield to Rutland, 19 Jun. 1786. Hist. MSS. 14th Rep. Appendix, part 1, Rutland MSS., vol. 3, 311 (VC). For another example of Mansfield's expressed disdain for popularity, see Roscoe, *Eminent British Lawyers*, 196.

58 *Rex v. Wilkes*, 4 Burr. 2527, 2566 (1770).

59 Walpole, *Memoirs of the Reign of King George III*, iii, 151–2.

60 Knight, *Gallery of Portraits with Memoirs*, vi, 62–8.

61 Heward, *Lord Mansfield*, 117.

62 Rockingham to Newcastle, 9 Jun. 1768. Add. MSS. 32990, f. 186 (VC); Walpole, *Memoirs of the Reign of King George III*, iii, 151–2.

63 He could not be freed from prison while the outlawry was in force. *Rex. v. Wilkes*, 4 Burr. 2527, 2532.

64 4 Burr. 2527, 2575–6.

65 Walpole, *Memoirs of the Reign of King George III*, iii, 154n2; Almon, *Anecdotes*, i, 373–6.

66 Cash, *John Wilkes*, 227.

67 White, *London in the Eighteenth Century*, 526.

68 Cash, *John Wilkes*, 254.

69 Holliday, *Life of Lord Mansfield*, 27–72.

70 Mansfield's view that a legislature could overrule the voters on the question of the qualification of its members was rejected 200 years later by the United States Supreme Court. Adam Clayton Powell was the first African-American ever elected to Congress from New York. In 1967, a committee of the House of Representatives accused Powell of misusing public funds. A hearing was held, at which Powell refused to answer questions. The House of Representatives then voted to exclude Powell and declared his seat vacant. Powell brought suit, claiming that his exclusion violated the U.S. Constitution. The Supreme Court held that the House of Representatives was without power to exclude Powell from membership. Chief Justice Earl Warren, after describing the events surrounding the Wilkes elections in some detail, concluded that the Court's decision was supported by English precedent, in particular by the vote of the House of Commons in 1782 to expunge from its records its resolutions expelling Wilkes. *Powell v. McCormack*, 395 U.S. 486, 490–93, 527–29 (1969).

71 Cash, *John Wilkes*, 308–9, 380.

72 1793. Hist. MSS. Comm. Fourth Report, App. Macauley MSS, 401 (VC).

73 *The World*, 18 Aug. 1787 (VC).

74 Mansfield to Wilkes, 1 Aug. 1788. Add. MSS. 30873, f. 114 (*John Wilkes Correspondence*, vii) (VC).

75 Barré was an Irish Member of Parliament who coined the name "Sons of Liberty" for the American patriots.

76 Several persons have been suspected of being Junius, among them Sir Philip Francis, an opponent of Warren Hastings, the British Indian politician and friend of Mansfield; and Sir Edward Newenham, who was passionately devoted to the American cause. P.W. Wilson, *William Pitt, the Younger*, 156; Smyth, *Writings of Benjamin Franklin*, i, xvi (VC).

77 D. Nichol Smith, "The Newspaper," in A.S. Turberville, ed., *Johnson's England*, ii, 344.

78 Ibid., ii, 332.

79 Heward, *Lord Mansfield*, 128–9.

80 *Rex v. Woodfall,* 5 Burr. 2661, 98 Eng. Rep. 398 (1770); Campbell, vol. 2, 479–80.

81 Campbell, *The Lives of the Chief Justices*, ii, 480.

82 See Chapter 9.

83 Letter XLI, addressed to Mansfield, 14 Nov. 1770. *The Letters of Junius* (London: J. Mundell and Co., 1798).

84 Campbell, *The Lives of the Chief Justices*, ii, 483–4.

85 *Rex v. Woodfall*, Lofft. 776, 98 Eng. Rep. 914 (1774). A mark was two-thirds of a pound, or about thirteen shillings.

86 *Rex v. Almon*, 5 Burr. 2686, 98 Eng. Rep. 411 (1770).

87 Professor Oldham has expressed a similar opinion. *The Mansfield Manuscripts*, ii, 808.

88 Fitzmaurice, *Life of William, Earl of Shelburne*, ii, 218.

89 *The Poetical Works of Thomas Chatterton* (Cambridge: W.P. Grant, 1842), ii, 452–3. Chatterton probably wrote the poem in 1770 shortly before he committed suicide at the age of eighteen.

CHAPTER FIFTEEN

1 Criminal cases of all kinds were heard at Westminster Hall and on circuit. Felonies were heard at Old Bailey and misdemeanors at Guildhall. Oldham, *The Mansfield Manuscripts*, i, 108.

2 *St James's Chronicle*, 1 Apr. 1770 (VC).

3 Oldham, *The Mansfield Manuscripts*, ii, 926.

4 Holliday, *Life of Lord Mansfield*, 134–5.

5 *Rex v. Delaval*, 3 Burr. 1434, 97 Eng. Rep. 913 (1763). The case is described in Chapter 12.

6 4 Burr. 2495, 98 Eng. Rep. 308 (1769). See Francis Bowes Sayre, "Criminal Attempts," *Harvard Law Review*, xli (1928), 821, 833–4.

7 Cald. 397 (1784). The case is transcribed in Oldham, *The Mansfield Manuscripts*, ii, 1421–4.

8 Like so many of Mansfield's decisions, this case has been influential; for example, it was cited by New York's highest court for the proposition that there can be criminal liability for an attempt, even if ultimately unsuccessful, to commit a crime. *People v. Dlugash*, 41 N.Y.2d 725, 732 (1977).

9 These are described in Chapters 14 and 22.
10 *London Chronicl.e*, 24–26 Jan. 1758 (VC).
11 Langford, *A Polite and Commercial People*, 455.
12 Besant, *History of London*, 209–10.
13 *London Chronicle*, 28–30 Nov. 1758 (VC).
14 White, *London in the Eighteenth Century*, 391–3.
15 *Public Advertiser*, 6 Nov. 1788 (VC).
16 White, *London in the Eighteenth Century*, 356–61.
17 Pierre Jean Grosley, *A Tour to London*, iii, 59–60 (1772) (VC).
18 *London Chronicle*, 22–24 Apr. 1760 (VC).
19 *London Evening Post*, 10–12 May 1759 (VC).
20 The price of Rotterdam gin was 10 shillings (or half a pound) a gallon. *Morning Herald*, 5 Dec. 1783 (VC).
21 *London Chronicle*, 15 Feb. 1757 (VC).
22 White, *London in the Eighteenth Century*, 327–8.
23 Yorke, *Hardwicke*, i, 133; White, *London in the Eighteenth Century*, 330–1.
24 Besant, *History of London*, 214–16.
25 *Public Advertiser*, 23 Aug. 1787 (VC).
26 Porter, *English Society in the Eighteenth Century*, 119.
27 Mansfield to Newcastle, 27 Sep. 1757. Add. MSS. 32874, ff. 318–320v. (VC).
28 Langbein, "Shaping the Eighteenth-Century Criminal Trial: A View From the Ryder Sources," 56–7 (1983); Porter, *English Society in the Eighteenth Century*, 123.
29 *Whitehall Evening Post*, 26–28 Nov. 1761 (VC).
30 *Gazetteer*, 26 May 1780 (VC).
31 J.M. Beattie, "Sir John Fielding and Public Justice: The Bow Street Magistrates' Court, 1754–1780," *Law and History Review*, xxv (Spring 2007), 61, 69.
32 Ibid., 69; White, *London in the Eighteenth Century*, 436; Porter, *English Society in the Eighteenth Century*, 140; Langbein, "Shaping the Eighteenth-Century Criminal Trial: A View From the Ryder Sources," 67–8.
33 Beattie, "Sir John Fielding and Public Justice," passim.
34 *British Mercury*, 11 Dec. 1780 (VC).
35 Ibid.
36 Beattie, "Sir John Fielding and Public Justice," 98. Another modern historian presents a less flattering picture of the Fielding brothers: "Both were arrogant, proud and willful in office" and they "despised and feared any collective expression of the London poor and waged war on their pleasures." White, *London in the Eighteenth Century*, 425.
37 Until 1790, the law permitted a judge to impose the sentence of burning at the stake for a woman guilty of murder or making counterfeit coins, but there were few such sentences and the executioner usually strangled the woman before she suffered the agony of burning. White, *London in the Eighteenth Century*, 462. The

Eighth Amendment to the United States Constitution forbids cruel or unusual punishment.

38 Andrea McKenzie, "'This Death some Strong and Stout Hearted Man Doth Choose': The Practice of Peine et Dure in Seventeenth- and Eighteenth-Century England," *Law and History Review*, xxiii (Summer 2005), 279–313.

39 Ibid., 280.

40 A prisoner might be willing to undergo the torture and death of pressing for a number of possible reasons, including defiant rejection of the court's authority, an attempt to plea bargain with the court, or to avoid a public execution. Ibid., 289–90. Death might come in a few minutes or the agony could last as long as two days. McKenzie cites a brutal example from 1735: "When [the prisoner] continued obstinate, weights were laid on him in hundred-pound increments; and after three hundred, in increments of fifty. At four hundred pounds, he was just dead, having all the Agonies of Death upon him: Then the Executioner, who weighs about 16 or 17 Stone [about 235 pounds/105 kilograms] laid down upon the Board which was over him, and, adding to the Weight, kill'd him in an Instant." Ibid., 286–7.

41 *London Chronicle*, 1 Aug. 1757.

42 McKenzie, "'This Death some Strong and Stout Hearted Man Doth Choose,'" 282.

43 Lieberman, *The Province of Legislation Determined*, 26.

44 Yorke, *Hardwicke*, i, 131.

45 Langbein, "Shaping the Eighteenth-Century Criminal Trial: A View From the Ryder Sources," 37–40.

46 McKinnon, "The Law and the Lawyers," in Turberville, ed., *Johnson's England*, ii, 304.

47 White, *London in the Eighteenth Century*, 393, 395–6.

48 In January 1776, for example, Mansfield attended a Cabinet meeting to consider the merits of several petitions of condemned criminals for remission of their death sentences. *Morning Chronicle*, 15 Jan. 1776 (VC).

49 Langbein, "The Criminal Trial before the Lawyers," 263, 297.

50 J.M. Beattie, *Crime and the Courts in England, 1660–1800* (Oxford: Clarendon Press, 1986), 431–2.

51 According to Langbein, "Very few people of those accused of non-clergyable property crimes were executed." Langbein, "Shaping the Eighteenth-Century Criminal Trial: A View From the Ryder Sources," 47. On the other hand, Porter writes that two-thirds of those convicted of forgery were executed. Porter, *English Society in the Eighteenth Century*, 135.

52 Proceedings of the Old Bailey for 5 Oct. 1757 and 23 Nov. 1757. Reference Numbers OA17571005 and OA17571123. On a single day in 1740 there were six hangings at Tyburn. *Daily Post*, 8 May 1740.

53 Simon Devereaux, "Recasting the Theatre of Execution: The Abolition of the Tyburn Ritual," *Past & Present* 202 (Feb. 2009), 127, 148–9. During a longer period than is being considered here (1660–1800), 38 per cent of those convicted of crimes against property (principally robbery and burglary) and 76 per cent of those convicted of murder were executed. Beattie, *Crime and the Courts in England*, 1660–1800, 434–5.
54 Holliday, *Life of Lord Mansfield*, 213.
55 *London Evening Post*, 5 Aug. 1775 (VC).
56 Porter, *English Society in the Eighteenth Century*, 18; White, *London in the Eighteenth Century*, 461.
57 *Owen's Weekly Chronicle*, 10 Jun. 1758 (VC).
58 *London Evening Post*, 13–15 Jun. 1758 (VC).
59 *Owen's Weekly Chronicle*, 8 Jul. 1758 (VC).
60 *London Chronicle*, 11–13 Jul. 1758 (VC).
61 The procession is described in the *Norwich Gazette*, 12 Sep. 1741 (VC).
62 White, *London in the Eighteenth Century*, 418.
63 Around this time, in order to eliminate the unpleasant connotations of "Tyburn," the names of the two main thoroughfares that intersected at the place of execution were changed. Tyburn Road became Oxford Street, and Tyburn Lane became Park Lane. Devereaux, "Recasting the Theatre of Execution: The Abolition of the Tyburn Ritual," 136.
64 Porter, *English Society in the Eighteenth Century*, 287.
65 Conway, *War, State and Society*, 69, 76–7, 90, 271–2.
66 *London Chronicle*, 15 Jul. 1757 (VC).
67 *London Evening Post*, 6 Mar. 1775 (VC).
68 *Whitehall Evening Post*, 18–20 May 1758 (VC).
69 *Pamphleteer*, xiv (1814).
70 *Whitehall Evening Post*, 19–22 Jun. 1756 (VC).
71 *Royal Westminster Journal*, 6 Nov. 1762 (VC); *Town and Country Journal*, 5 Jun. 1739 (VC).
72 *British Chronicle*, 10–13 Mar. 1758 (VC).
73 Ibid., 19–21 Apr. 1758 (VC).
74 *London Evening Post*, 25–27 Oct. 1761 (VC).
75 *Public Advertiser*, 11 Aug. 1758 (VC).
76 *St James's Chronicle*, 11 Apr. 1780 (VC).
77 *Say's Gazetteer*, 9 Mar. 1756 (VC).
78 *Town and Country Journal*, 5 Jun. 1739 (VC).
79 Porter, *English Society in the Eighteenth Century*, 138.
80 Ibid., *Daily Advertiser*, 26 Jun. 1776 (VC).
81 *London Evening Post*, 25–27 Oct. 1761 (VC).
82 See Chapter 14.
83 Walpole, *Memoirs of the Reign of George II*, iii, 39–40.

84 *British Chronicle*, 19–21 Apr. 1758 (VC).
85 Almon, *Anecdotes*, i, 373–6.
86 White, *London in the Eighteenth Century*, 449.
87 *Lloyd's Evening Post*,.12–14 Aug. 1761 (VC).
88 Porter, *English Society in the Eighteenth Century*, 139.
89 *The Times*, 25 Apr. 1793 (VC).
90 *Morning Chronicle*, 14 Jul. 1781 (VC).
91 Act for the Relief of certain Insolvent Debtors, 21 Geo. III, c. 63.
92 16 Geo. III, c.43. Simon Devereaux, "The Making of the Penitentiary Act, 1775–1779," *The Historical Journal* 42. No. 2 (Jun. 1999), 405, 415.
93 *McKinnon*, "The Law and the Lawyers," in Turberville, ed., *Johnson's England*, ii, 307–8.
94 *London Evening Post*, 26 Apr. 1777 (VC).
95 *Lloyd's Evening Post*, 11 Dec. 1776 (VC).
96 Williams, The *Whig Supremacy*, 135.
97 White, *London in the Eighteenth Century*, 450.
98 Robert Gore-Browne, *Chancellor Thurlow: The Life and Times of an XVIIIth Century Lawyer* (London: Hamish Hamilton, 1953), 233.
99 *Morning Chronicle*, 14 Nov. 1780 (VC); *Gazetteer*, 15 Nov. 1780 (VC).
100 *The World*, 7 Dec. 1787 (VC); White, *London In the Eighteenth Century*, 484–5.
101 Ibid., 452; Williams, *The Whig Supremacy*, 135.
102 Murray to Stone, 18 May 1751. Add. MSS. 32720, f. 359 (BL).
103 *London Evening Post*, 23 Nov. 1780 (VC).
104 White, *London in the Eighteenth Century*, 446.
105 *Morning Chronicle*, 28 Apr. 1781 (VC).
106 *Public Advertiser*, 10 Nov. 1758 (VC).
107 *Morning Post*, 28 Jun. 1776 (VC).
108 *St James's Chronicle*, 7 Jul. 1781 (VC).
109 Porter, *English Society in the Eighteenth Century*, 119–20.
110 James F. Stephen, *A History of the Criminal Law of England*, 3 vols. (London: Macmillan, 1883), i, 495.
111 *St James's Chronicle*, 7 Nov. 1780 (VC).
112 See Chapter 21.
113 *Morning Post*, 27 Jan. 1778 (VC).
114 *Morning Herald*, 7 Dec. 1782 (VC).
115 Langbein, "Shaping the Eighteenth-Century Criminal Trial: A View From the Ryder Sources," 91.
116 *The King v. Rudd*, 1 Leach 115, 119, 168 Eng. Rep. 160, 162 (1775).
117 *Morning Post*, 22 Nov. 1776 (VC).
118 *Gazetteer*, 8 May 1777 (VC).
119 Beattie, *Crime and the Courts in England, 1660–1800*, 415.
120 Langbein, "The Criminal Trial before the Lawyers," 263, 308, 315–16.

121 Ibid., 263, 279–86.
122 *London Chronicle*, 5 Aug. 1775 (VC).
123 Proceedings of the Old Bailey, 9 Jan. 1776. Reference Number t17760109-24.
124 Beattie, *Crime and the Courts in England, 1660–1800*, 432.
125 *Gazetteer*, 17 Jul. 1780 (VC).
126 Campbell, *The Lives of the Chief Justices*, ii, 443–4.
127 Colley, *Britons*, 66.
128 Between 1757 and 1759, Mansfield tried four forgery cases at Old Bailey of three men and one woman. He was accompanied on the bench by the lord mayor of London, a justice of the Court of Common Pleas, and a baron of the Court of Exchequer. All four defendants were convicted, and all except one of the men were executed. Proceedings of Old Bailey, Reference Numbers OA17571005, OA17580405-26, t17591024-27.
129 Campbell, *The Lives of the Chief Justices*, ii, 443–4.
130 Oldham, *The Mansfield Manuscripts*, i, 118.
131 White, *London in the Eighteenth Century*, 500.
132 *Account of the Trial of the Rev. Doctor Dodd* (London: Richardson and Urquart, 1777). Harvard Law School Library. Gale Document No. Q4200463747.
133 Mathew, *For Lawyers and Others*, 155–6.
134 Howson, *The Macaroni Parson*, 200.
135 Ibid. Howson does not provide a source for his statement that there had been several recent cases of forgery; the same statement is also made in Earl of Birkenhead, *Famous Trials of History*, 2 vols. (New York: Clark Boardman, Ltd, 1929), i, 159. Sitting at Old Bailey, Mansfield presided over nine forgery trials, eight of which resulted in convictions. Oldham, *The Mansfield Manuscripts*, i, 118. Furthermore, several commercial cases decided by Mansfield involved forged or stolen negotiable instruments.
136 For a report of the *Perreau* case, see *The King v. Rudd*, 1 Leach 115, 168 Eng. Rep. 160 (1775); Mathew, *For Lawyers and Others*, 156.
137 Howson, *The Macaroni Parson*, 200.
138 Birkenhead, *Famous Trials of History*, i, 152–9; Fitzgerald, *A Famous Forgery*, 148.
139 *Morning Post*, 6 Jul. 1766 (VC).
140 Oldham, *The Mansfield Manuscripts*, ii, 107.
141 See, for example, *Morning Post*, 8 Mar. 1775 (VC); *Morning Chronicle*, 23 Apr. 1778 (VC); *Morning Post*, 6 Jul. 1778 (VC).
142 See Chapter 21.
143 Oldham, *The Mansfield Manuscripts*, ii, 1066, citing the *London Chronicle* of 23 Nov. 1786. Another account states that it was a meeting of lawyers, held in Mansfield's chambers in 1766. Paterson, *Curiosities of Law and Lawyers*, 14, citing *Lady's Magazine*, vol. 17, 667. It is possible that there were two meetings, one in 1766 and the other in 1786.
144 *Morning Chronicle*, 22 Nov. and 29 Nov. 1784 (VC).

145 Oldham, *The Mansfield Manuscripts*, i, 113–14.
146 *Calendar of Home Office Papers, 1760–1765*, 273, 13–14 Apr. 1763 (VC, Box 324).
147 *London Evening Post*, 15–17 Jan. 1779 (VC).
148 *Morning Chronicle*, 22 Dec. 1779 (VC); *General Evening Post*, 10 Feb. 1780 (VC).
149 *London Evening Post*, 8–10 Feb. 1780 (VC).
150 *London Courant*, 30 Mar. 1780 (VC).

CHAPTER SIXTEEN

1 Clark, *Waldegrave Memoirs*, 43.
2 White, *London in the Eighteenth Century*, 341–3.
3 Porter, *English Society in the Eighteenth Century*, 238.
4 Gore-Browne, *Chancellor Thurlow*, 224. For more on Beckford, see White, *London in the Eighteenth Century*, 165–7.
5 *Morning Herald*, 7 Aug. 1783 (VC).
6 Porter, *English Society in the Eighteenth Century*, 238.
7 *Payne's Universal Chronicle*, 22 May 1758 (VC).
8 *St James's Chronicle*, 5 Sep. 1780 (VC).
9 Murray to Newcastle, 1 Jun. 1750. Add. MSS. 32,721, f.13 (VC).
10 *Morning Post*, 10 Jul. 1775 (VC).
11 9 Anne, c. 19.
12 A.S. Cuming, "Sports and Games," in Turberville, ed., *Johnson's England*, i, 379.
13 18 Geo. II, c. 34.
14 18 Geo. II, c. 34, §VI.
15 *Universal Chronicle*, 9 Jan. 1760 (VC).
16 *London Chronicle*, 19–21 Feb. 1760 (VC).
17 Holdsworth, *History of English Law*, xii, 520.
18 1 Cowp. 37, 98 Eng. Rep. 954 (1774).
19 *Daily Universal Register*, 25 Nov. 1785 (VC).
20 130 S.Ct. 876 (2010).
21 Ibid., 961.
22 *Rex v. Le Chevalier D'Eon*, 3 Burr. 1513 (1764). This was a criminal case brought against D'Eon for libelling Count de Guerchy, the new French ambassador to England. It did not involve a wager.
23 *Gazetteer*, 2 Feb. 1778 (VC).
24 Kimberly Chrisman-Campbell, "Dressing d'Eon," in Simon Burrows et al., eds., *The Chevalier d'Eon and his Worlds* (London; Continuum, 2010), 99.
25 There is no court report of the case, but it was reported in several newspapers.
26 *Gazetteer*, 2 Jul. 1777 (VC).
27 Neville Williams. *Knaves and Fools* (New York: The Macmillan Company, 1960), 134–6.
28 *Morning Chronicle*, 2 Jul. 1777 (VC).

29 Williams, *Knaves and Fools*, 138.
30 2 Cowp. 729, 98 Eng. Rep. 1331 (1778).
31 2 Cowp. 729, 735, 98 Eng. Rep. 1331, 1334.
32 2 Cowp. 729, 736, 98 Eng. Rep. 1331, 1335.
33 See, for example, *Jones v. Tsige*, 2012 ONCA 32, 2012-01-18 Ct. App. Ont.).
34 381 U.S. 479 (1965).
35 93 S.Ct.705 (1973).
36 Ibid., 726–7.
37 *Gazetteer*, 2 Feb. 1778 (VC).
38 d'Eon may have claimed to be a woman because, while he presumably derived sexual pleasure from wearing women's clothes, if he were to be identified as a man he would have been subject to a strong social taboo against cross-dressing. Chrisman-Campbell, "Dressing d'Eon," in Burrows et al., eds., *The Chevalier d'Eon and his Worlds*, 98.
39 Ibid., 109.
40 Mrs Boscawen to Mrs Delany, 27 May 1786. *Correspondence of Mrs Delany*, iii, 355–6.
41 12 Anne, st. 2, c.16 (1713). Sybil Campbell, "The Economic and Social Effect of the Usury Laws in the Eighteenth Century," *Transactions of the Royal Historical Society*, 4th Series, xvi (1933): 197–8.
42 Campbell, "Usury Laws," 200.
43 See the discussion of Locke's theory of money in Chapter 4.
44 *Stanhope v. Executors of Spinks*, Chancery 1741 (VC).
45 1 Atk. 301, 26 Eng. Rep. 191 (1750).
46 1 Atk. 301, 326–331, 26 Eng. Rep. 191, 208–11.
47 1 Atk. 301, 331, 26 Eng. Rep. 191, 211.
48 Oldham, *The Mansfield Manuscripts*, i, 645.
49 *Morning Herald*, 9 Dec. 1782 (VC).
50 *Morning Chronicle*, 17 Dec. 1777 (VC).
51 *Richards v. Brown*, 2 Cowp. 769, 98 Eng. Rep. 1352 (1778).

CHAPTER SEVENTEEN

1 C.R. Boxer, *The Portuguese Seaborne Empire 1415–1825* (London: Hutchinson and Co., 1969), 24–7; Seymour Drescher, *Abolition: A History of Slavery and Antislavery* (New York: Cambridge University Press, 2009), 37.
2 Drescher, *Abolition*, 80.
3 About two-thirds of the ten million Africans who survived the Atlantic crossing were taken to the sugar colonies. Ibid., 46.
4 Ibid., 58.
5 Ibid., 30.
6 Holmes and Szechi, *The Age of Oligarchy*, 255.

7 Drescher, *Abolition*, 61.
8 Ibid., 36.
9 Liverpool also became the principal market for cotton. Porter, *English Society in the Eighteenth Century*, 200.
10 Conway, *War, State and Society*, 89; Parker, *The Sugar Barons*, 298.
11 Trevelyan, *English Social History*, 391.
12 Cash, *John Wilkes*, 269.
13 White, *London in the Eighteenth Century*, 165–6.
14 David Brion Davis, *The Problem of Slavery in the Age of Revolution 1770–1823* (New York: Oxford University Press, 1999), 470.
15 Drescher, *Capitalism and Antislavery: British Mobilization in Comparative Perspective* (New York and Oxford: Oxford University Press, 1987), 25.
16 Estimates of the black population in Britain in the 1770s vary. Compare Drescher, *Capitalism and Antislavery*, 28 (10,000 blacks) with Porter, *English Society in the Eighteenth Century*, 157 (14,000 blacks), and with White, *London in the Eighteenth Century*, 127 (5,000 to 10,000 blacks in London). In his opinion in the *Somerset* case, Mansfield referred to there being 14,000 or 15,000 black men in Britain whom abolition would set free.
17 Davis, *The Problem of Slavery in the Age of Revolution*, 495; Porter, *English Society in the Eighteenth Century*, 136.
18 Archbishop of Canterbury to Earl of Hardwicke, 19 Jul. 1760. Add. MSS. 35596, ff. 155, 155v. (VC).
19 Signed Opinion by P. Yorke (AG) and C. Talbot (SG), 14 Jan. 1729, BM. Egerton Mss., 1074, f.70 (VC).
20 Davis, *The Problem of Slavery in the Age of Revolution*, 479.
21 *Public Advertiser*, 24 Jun. 1772 (VC).
22 *Gazetteer*, 4 Nov. 1760 (VC).
23 Drescher, *Capitalism and Antislavery*, 32.
24 John Locke, *Two Treatises of Government*, Everyman's Library, edited by Ernest Rhys (London: J.M. Dent and Sons Ltd; New York: E.P. Dutton and Co. Inc., 1943), 3. Locke, nevertheless, believed that a West Indian planter had power over slaves that he had bought. Drescher, *Abolition*, 77.
25 Shyllon, *Black Slaves in Britain*, 157.
26 Davis, *The Problem of Slavery in the Age of Revolution*, 495.
27 Porter, *English Society in the Eighteenth Century*, 180; Davis, *The Problem of Slavery in the Age of Revolution*, 82.
28 White, *London in the Eighteenth Century*, 128.
29 Shyllon, *Black Slaves in Britain*, 28–9.
30 White, *London in the Eighteenth Century*, 321.
31 Davis, *The Problem of Slavery in the Age of Revolution*, 375–6.
32 *Butts v. Penny*, 2 Lev. 201, 83 Eng. Rep. 518 (1677).
33 *Chamberlain v. Harvey*, Carthew 397, 90 Eng. Rep. 830 (1697).

34 *Smith v. Gould*, 2 Salkeld 667, 3 Ld. Raym. 1275, 91 Eng. Rep. 567 (1705); Oldham, *The Mansfield Manuscripts*, ii, 1223–4.
35 Signed Opinion by P. Yorke (AG) and C. Talbot (SG), 14 Jan. 1729, BM. Egerton Mss., 1074, f.70 (VC).
36 Drescher, *Capitalism and Antislavery*, 32.
37 Blackstone, *Commentaries*, bk. 1, ch. 1, 123.
38 Ibid., bk. 1, ch. 1, 127. The two passages are quoted in Shyllon, *Black Slaves in Britain*, 59.
39 Fifoot, *Mansfield*, 71.
40 Shyllon, *Black Slaves in Britain*, 60–1.
41 Archbishop of Canterbury to Earl of Hardwicke, 19 Jul. 1760. Add. 35596, ff. 155, 155v. (VC).
42 Oldham, *The Mansfield Manuscripts*, ii, 1221.
43 Drescher, *Capitalism and Antislavery*, 36.
44 Adam Smith, *The Theory of Moral Sentiments*, edited by Knud Haakonssen (Cambridge, UK: Cambridge University Press, 2002), 242.
45 Treasure, *Who's Who in Early Hanoverian Britain, 1714–1789*, 113.
46 Davis, *The Problem of Slavery in the Age of Revolution,* 84.
47 James Beattie, *An Essay on the Nature and Immutability of Truth* (London: Edward and Charles Dilly; Edinburgh: William Creech, 1778), 426.
48 Ibid., 428.
49 Margaret Forbes, *Beattie and His Friends* (Westminster: Archibald Constable and Co., 1904), 101n.
50 Beattie to Dr. John Gregory, 28 Aug. 1771. Forbes, *Beattie and His Friends*, 60.
51 Ibid., 94.
52 *Owen's Weekly Chronicle*, 24 Jun. 1758 (VC).
53 Oldham, *The Mansfield Manuscripts*, ii, 1226.
54 Paul D. Halliday, *Habeas Corpus: From England to Empire* (Cambridge, MA; London: Harvard University Press, 2010), 1–2, 14.
55 Ibid., 1–2.
56 Ibid., 32, 48. Impressment of seamen into the navy is discussed in Chapter 18.
57 Oldham, *The Mansfield Manuscripts*, ii, 1226.
58 Shyllon, *Black Slaves in Britain*, 43–54.
59 Davis, *The Problem of Slavery in the Age of Revolution,* 488.
60 His name was spelled Steuart or Stuart in some accounts of the case. Somerset's name was sometimes spelled Somersett.
61 Alfred W. and Ruth G. Blumrosen, *Slave Nation: How Slavery United the Colonies and Sparked the American Revolution* (Naperville, IL: Sourcebooks, Inc., 2005), 4–5.
62 The factual background of the *Somerset* case is described in Davis, *The Problem of Slavery in Age of Revolution*, 480–1; Shyllon, *Black Slaves in Britain*, 77–9; Oldham, *The Mansfield Manuscripts*, ii, 1228; and Blumrosen, *Slave Nation*, 1–14.
63 Ibid., 7.

64 Shyllon, *Black Slaves in Britain*, 113; Blumrosen, *Slave Nation*, 9.
65 Ibid., 115–17.
66 Charles Stewart to Mr Murray, 15 Jun. 1772 (VC).
67 James Oldham, "New Light on Mansfield and Slavery," *The Journal of British Studies* xxvii, no. 1 (Jan. 1988): 61.
68 Drescher, *Capitalism and Antislavery*, 40.
69 Drescher, *Abolition*, 100.
70 *London Evening Post*, 20–23 Jun. 1772; Drescher, *Abolition*, 102.
71 Shyllon, *Black Slaves in Britain*, 128.
72 Peter D. G. Thomas, "John Glynn," ODNB. See Chapter 14.
73 Shyllon, *Black Slaves in Britain*, 130.
74 Ibid., 92–106.
75 This opinion is discussed in Chapter 18.
76 *Somerset v. Stewart*, Lofft 1, 17, 98 Eng. Rep. 499, 509 (1772).
77 Although Mansfield first used the words in the *Wilkes* case, which is described in 14, they are best remembered for his use of them in the *Somerset* case.
78 Shyllon, *Black Slaves in Britain*, 106–8.
79 *Somerset v. Stewart*, Lofft 1, 19, 98 Eng. Rep. 499, 510 (1772).
80 The report of the case that I have quoted from is that of Capel Lofft, 1, 98 Eng. Rep. 499 (1772). There were four other reports of the case, none of which is inconsistent with Lofft, though, according to a detailed analysis by Professor Oldham, they expand and clarify it. Oldham, "New Light on Mansfield and Slavery." The decision was also reported in several London newspapers. *Public Advertiser*, 24 Jun. 1772 (VC); *London Evening Post*, 23–25 Jun. 1772 (VC).
81 Langford, *A Polite and Commercial People*, 517–18.
82 Drescher, *Abolition*, 102.
83 Ibid., 105.
84 Shyllon, *Black Slaves in Britain*, 157.
85 Drescher, *Capitalism and Antislavery*, 37, 41, 49.
86 Ibid., 41.
87 *Gazette and New Daily Advertiser*, 28 May 1772 (VC).
88 Davis, *The Problem of Slavery in the Age of Revolution*, 501.
89 *Daily Universal Register*, 29 Apr. 1785 (VC); Shyllon, *Black Slaves in Britain*, 165.
90 Oldham, *The Mansfield Manuscripts*, ii, 1237.
91 *The King v. The Inhabitants of Thames Ditton*, 4 Dougl. 299, 99 Eng. Rep. 891 (1785)
92 Halliday, *Habeas Corpus: From England to Empire*, 175.
93 Shyllon, *Black Slaves in Britain*, 176.
94 *Gregson v. Gilbert*, 3 Dougl. 233, 99 Eng. Rep. 629 (1783).
95 According to one account, the captain decided to throw the slaves overboard in the belief that if he did, the loss of the slaves would fall on the insurer, while if they died of natural causes, the loss would fall on the owners. Shyllon, *Black Slaves in Britain*, 184.

96 A spectator at the trial wrote: "The narrative seemed to make every person present shudder and I waited with some impatience expecting that the jury by their foreman would have applied to the Court for information how to bring the perpetrator of such a horrid deed to justice." *Morning Chronicle*, 17 Mar. 1783 (VC).
97 Oldham, *The Mansfield Manuscripts*, ii, 1222.
98 Rothschild, *The Inner Life of Empires*, 229, 292–3.
99 Drescher, *Capitalism and Antislavery*, 40.
100 Ibid., 43.
101 Davis, *The Problem of Slavery in the Age of Revolution*, 377.
102 Stephen Usherwood, "The Abolitionists' Debt to Lord Mansfield," *History Today* xxxi, issue 3 (Mar. 1981): 40.
103 Rothschild, *The Inner Life of Empires*, 162.
104 Sarah Minney, "The Search for Dido," *History Today* lv, issue 10, (Oct. 2005): 2–3. Carolyn Steedman, "Lord Mansfield's Women," *Past and Present*, issue 176 (Aug. 2002): 105, 107–8.
105 A photocopy of Mansfield's will and codicils is in VC, Box 319.
106 Sarah Minney, "The Search for Dido."
107 Drescher, *Abolition*, 104–5.
108 Samuel Johnson, *Taxation No Tyranny* (1775) (quoted in Shapiro, ed., *The Yale Book of Quotations*, 401).
109 Drescher, *Abolition*, 105.
110 This argument is the basic thesis of Blumrosen, *Slave Nation*.
111 See Chapter 18.

CHAPTER EIGHTEEN

1 See Chapter 4.
2 See Chapter 6.
3 Acts of the Privy Council, Col. Ser. IV, 4, 23 Jul. 1746 (VC).
4 See Chapter 17.
5 Yorke, *Hardwicke*, i, 89.
6 George Chalmers, *Opinions of Eminent Lawyers* (Burlington, VT: C. Goodrich and Co., 1858), 333–6.
7 The Kennebeck Land Patent Case, 5 Sep. 1755. Add. MSS. 15488 L.C. Transcripts, 127–45 (VC).
8 Murray to Newcastle, 6 Oct. 1754. Add. MSS 32737, f. 45. L.C. Transcripts (VC).
9 See, for example, Mansfield to Newcastle, 30 Aug. 1760. Add, MSS. 32910, f. 427–431 (VC).
10 Newcastle's minutes of a conversation with Mansfield, 13 May 1767. Add. MSS. 32981, f. 382 (BL).
11 Mansfield to George Grenville, 24 Dec. 1764. *Grenville Papers*, ii, 476–8.

12 H.T. Dickinson, *Britain and the American Revolution* (London; New York: Longman, 1998), 73–4.

13 Gordon S. Wood, *Empire of Liberty: A History of the Early Republic, 1789–1815* (New York: Oxford University Press, 2009), 40.

14 Conway, War, *State and Society*, 247.

15 Colley, *Britons*, 135.

16 Letter from Mansfield praising William Robertson's *History of Scotland*. Dugal Stewart, *Account of the Life and Writings of William Robertson*, 1802 (VC).

17 Gordon S. Wood, *The American Revolution: A History* (London: Phoenix, 2002), 4, 55.

18 Don Cook, *The Long Fuse: How England Lost the American Colonies, 1760–1785* (New York: The Atlantic Monthly Press, 2006), 3.

19 Holmes and Szechi, *The Age of Oligarchy*, 380.

20 Cook, *The Long Fuse*, 52.

21 Ian R. Christie, *Crisis of Empire, Britain and the American Colonies, 1754–1783* (London: Edward Arnold, 1966), 39.

22 Bullion, *A Great and Necessary Measure: George Grenville and the Genesis of the Stamp Act: 1763–1765*, 43–4.

23 Ibid.

24 Wood, *The American Revolution*, 6, 10, 17.

25 P.D.G. Thomas, *British Politics and the Stamp Act Crisis: The First Phase of the American Revolution 1763–1767* (Oxford: Clarendon Press, 1975), 87.

26 Ibid., 98.

27 Wood, *The American Revolution*, 24; Watson, *The Reign of George III*, 106.

28 Holmes and Szechi, *The Age of Oligarchy*, 285–6.

29 George H. Guttridge, *The Early Career of Lord Rockingham: 1730–1765* (Berkeley: University of California Press, 1952), 4.

30 S.M.Farrell, "Wentworth, Charles Watson-, second Marquess of Annandale,"ODNB; Holmes and Szechi, *The Age of Oligarchy*, 144, 293.

31 Lady Mansfield's sister Mary was Rockingham's mother. Rockingham's political and social friendship with Mansfield is referred to in many letters. See, for example, Rockingham to Newcastle, 6 Sep. 1766. Add. MSS. 32950, f.339. (BL)

32 Paul Langford, *The First Rockingham Administration: 1765–1766* (London: Oxford University Press, 1973), 111.

33 Holmes and Szechi, *The Age of Oligarchy*, 286.

34 Williams, *Chatham*, ii, 194–5.

35 Ibid., ii, 210.

36 Porter, *English Society in the Eighteenth Century*, 345.

37 *Scots Magazine* (June 1793), 264–5 (VC).

38 In the late eighteenth century, a few elite women did vote, but they were generally barred by custom from doing so. Chalus, *Elite Women in English Political Life*, 25, 35–6.

39 Wood, *The American Revolution*, 38–9; Chalus, *Elite Women in English Political Life*, 33.
40 Holliday, *Life of Lord Mansfield*, 242–8.
41 Hume to Earl of Hertford, 27 Feb. 1766. Hume, *Letters of David Hume*, ii, 19.
42 Conway, *War, State and Society*, 248.
43 Fitzmaurice, *Shelburne*, i, 259.
44 Wood, *The American Revolution*, 29.
45 Fitzmaurice, *Shelburne*, ii, 125–6.
46 Conway, *War, State and Society*, 251.
47 London Evening Post, 6 Jun. 1775, VC, Box 325.
48 Conway, *War, State and Society*, 251.
49 Wood, *The American Revolution*, 35; Conway, War, *State and Society*, 252.
50 Wood, *Empire of Liberty*, 37.
51 See Chapter 14.
52 Guttridge, *English Whiggism and the American Revolution*, 29.
53 Watson, *The Reign of George III*, 197.
54 Holmes and Szechi, *The Age of Oligarchy*, 295.
55 Fitzmaurice, *Shelburne*, ii, 303.
56 Almon, *Anecdotes*, 357–8.
57 *The Public Advertiser*, 6 Nov. 1775 (VC).
58 Lofft. 653, 98 Eng. Rep. 848; 1 Cowp. 204, 98 Eng. Rep. 1045 (1774)
59 Conway, *War, State and Society*, 239.
60 Langford, *A Polite and Commercial People*, 709.
61 See Chapter 21.
62 Conway, *War, State and Society*, 239.
63 Langford, *A Polite and Commercial People*, 708–9; Campbell, *The Lives of the Chief Justices*, ii, 499.
64 Ibid., ii, 495–6.
65 Ibid., ii, 499–500.
66 Wood, *The American Revolution*, 76.
67 Colley, *Britons*, 141.
68 Conway, *War, State and Society*, 182.
69 George Otto Trevelyan, *The American Revolution*, ed. Richard B. Morris (New York: D. McKay Co., 1964).
70 Holmes and Szechi, *The Age of Oligarchy*, 292.
71 H.T. Dickinson, *Britain and the American Revolution* (London; New York: Longman, 1998), 114.
72 *Plea of the Colonies, on the Charges Brought against Them by Lord Mansfield and Others* (London: J. Almon, 1775) (JPML).
73 *The Crisis*, No. XVII. New York, Anderson, [1775], 137–48. AAS copy (NYHS). A portion of the poem is quoted in Chapter 7.
74 Fitzmaurice, *Shelburne*, ii, 315–16.

75 Campbell, *The Lives of the Chief Justices*, ii, 498–9.
76 *Gazetteer*, 18 Dec. 1776 (VC).
77 Oldham, *The Mansfield Manuscripts*, ii, 803, 803n104.
78 Campbell, *The Lives of the Chief Justices*, ii, 504.
79 Wood, *The American Revolution*, 74.
80 Colley, *Britons*, 65.
81 Nicholas Rogers, *The Press Gang: Naval Impressment and Its Opponents in Georgian Britain* (London; New York: Continuum, 2007), 21.
82 Ilchester, *Henry Fox*, ii, 325.
83 Conway, *War, State and Society*, 130, 154.
84 Opinion of Murray, Attorney General, on impressment, 6 Mar. 1755. P.R.O. Ad. 7/298, No. 99 (VC).
85 Rogers, *The Press Gang*, 19.
86 Halliday, *Habeas Corpus: From England to Empire*, 71.
87 Ibid., 115.
88 Newcastle to Hardwicke, 14 Apr. 1758. Add. MSS. 32879, ff. 157–158 (VC).
89 Walpole, *Memoirs of the Reign of King George II*, iii, 11.
90 SP, Bundle 1352; Williams, *Chatham*, ii, 38.
91 Newcastle memo, 19 Dec. 1758. Add. MSS. 32886 (VC).
92 Yorke, *Hardwicke*, iii, 4–6.
93 Walpole, *Memoirs of the Reign of King George II*, iii, 21.
94 2 Cowp. 512 (1776).
95 *Morning Post*, 29 Nov. 1776 (VC).
96 2 Cowp. 512, 517–18. Mansfield's invoking of "immemorial usage" to legitimize impressment was not original. Thirty years earlier, a local court in Bristol had used the same justification. *The Case of Alexander Broadbent*, Fost. 154, 168 Eng. Rep. 76 (1743). The *Broadbent* case is discussed in Rogers, *The Press Gang*, 19–20.
97 2 Cowp. 512, 517–19.
98 Gore-Browne, *Thurlow*, 94–5.
99 *Gazetteer*, 2 Dec. 1776 (VC).
100 Halliday, *Habeas Corpus: From England to Empire*, 55.
101 Ibid., 32–3.
102 *Public Advertiser*, 21 Dec. 1776 (VC).
103 P.R.O. Colonial Office 5, Bundle 43. Draft of a letter to Mansfield dated Marble Hill, 6 Aug. 1776 and the original of Mansfield's answer, dated 8 Aug. 1776, from Guilford (VC). In addition to the four officers, the captives included nineteen crew members and two slaves. The Admiralty apparently intended to impress them as sailors on a British ship bound for the East Indies.
104 *Morning Post*, 22 Oct. 1776 (VC).
105 Lord North to the King, 17 Sep. 1776; the King to Lord North, 17 Sep. 1776. Sir John W. Fortescue, *Correspondence of George III from 1760 to 1783*, 6 vols. (London:

Macmillan and Co., 1927–28), iii, 392–3. Campbell says that the earldom would descend to the heirs of Louisa Cathcart Murray, the wife of Mansfield's nephew, because it was believed at the time that a Scottish peer could not inherit a British peerage through his mother. Campbell, *The Lives of the Chief Justices*, ii, 501–2. This, however, is contradicted by the correspondence between the King and Lord North.

106 *Morning Post*, 8 Nov. 1776 (VC).
107 The King to Lord North, 17 Sep. 1776. Fortescue, *Correspondence of George III*, iii, 392–3.
108 *Morning Post*, 8 Nov. 1776 (VC).
109 NAS, RH4/151/10.
110 Wood, *The American Revolution*, 80.
111 Holmes and Szechi, *The Age of Oligarchy*, 305.
112 Wood, *The American Revolution*, 80.
113 John Adams to M. Derimple in care of Mr Lee in Paris, 24 Feb. 1778. MS in Franklin Papers, Library of Congress (VC).
114 Mansfield to William Eden, 10 Apr. 1778. Add. MSS. 34461, f.48 (VC).
115 William Hamilton to Arthur Vanderbilt, 9 Aug. 1942 (discussing letters between the French in London and Paris after the outbreak of the American Revolution) (VC).
116 Guttridge, *English Whiggism*, 104; Campbell, *The Lives of the Chief Justices*, ii, 504.
117 Langford, *A Polite and Commercial People*, 522.
118 Wood, *The American Revolution*, 76–7.
119 Almon, *Anecdotes*, 359.
120 Roscoe, *Lives of Eminent British Lawyers*, 191.
121 Campbell, *The Lives of the Chief Justices*, ii, 505.
122 Williams, *Chatham*, ii, 330.
123 Camden to the Duke of Grafton, Apr. 1778. *Law Review and Quarterly Journal* ii, 315 (VC).
124 White, *London in the Eighteenth Century*, 286.
125 *Public Advertiser*, 5 May 1780 (VC).
126 Williams, *Chatham*, ii, 331.
127 Campbell, *The Lives of the Chief Justices*, ii, 508.
128 Ibid., ii, p. 510.
129 *Adams's Weekly Courant*, 21 Sep. 1779 (VC).
130 *London Courant*, 22 Mar. 1780 (VC).
131 Adams, *The Works of John Adams*, i, 406.

CHAPTER NINETEEN

1 Adrian Johns, *Piracy: The Intellectual Property Wars from Gutenberg to Gates* (Chicago and London: University of Chicago Press, 2009), 109.

2 14 Car. II c. 33.

3 H. Tomas Gomez-Arostegui, "The Untold Story of the First Copyright Suit under the Statute of Queen Anne in 1710," *Lewis and Clark Law School, Legal Research Paper No. 2010–11*, (2010): 4–9.

4 8 Anne c. 19.

5 See Chapter 2.

6 *Pope v. Curll*, 2 Atk. 342, 26 Eng. Rep. 608 (1741).

7 Johns, *Piracy*, 111.

8 *Tonson v. Walker*, 3 Swans. 671, 36 Eng. Rep. 1017 (1752); Harris, *Hardwicke*, ii, 524–6.

9 Johns, *Piracy*, 119–20.

10 Ibid., 120; White, *London in the Eighteenth Century*, 265.

11 4 Burr. 2302, 98 Eng. Rep. 201 (1769). The facts of the case are described in *Donaldson v. Beckett*, 1 Eng. Rep. 837 (1774)

12 4 Burr. 2302, 2355–7, 98 Eng. Rep. 201, 229–31.

13 This balance is reflected in the United States Constitution, which states: "The Congress shall have Power ... to promote the Progress of Science and useful Arts, by securing *for limited Times* to Authors and Inventors the exclusive Right to their respective Writings and Discoveries." Art. 1, sec. 8, clause 8 (emphasis added).

14 Fortescue, *Correspondence of George III*, ii, 93.

15 *Sayre v. Moore*, sittings after Hil. 1785. The facts of the case and Mansfield's opinion are set forth in *Cary v. Longman*, 102 Eng. Rep., 138, 139 n(b).

16 Thomas F. Cotter, "Pragmatism, Economics, and the Droit Moral," *North Carolina Law Review* lxxvi (1997): 1.

17 Copyright, Designs and Patents Act 1988, §§77–89 (UK); Copyright Act of Canada, §14.1, R.S.C. 1985, c.10 (4th Supp.).

18 Visual Artists Rights Act of 1990, 17 U.S.C. §106A. In the United Kingdom, Canada, and the United States, an artist may waive the moral right. The Berne Convention for the Protection of Literary and Artistic Works (Berne Convention), which has 166 member countries, provides a broad moral right. Even after an author has transferred his work, the Berne Convention perpetually protects all literary and artistic works from "distortion, mutilation or other modification of ... the ... work, which would be prejudicial to his honor or reputation." Articles 2, 6*bis*. Although the United States is a member of the Berne Convention, its laws do not give authors all of its protections. See Graeme W. Austin, "The Berne Convention as a Canon of Construction: Moral Rights After Dastar," *Victoria University of Wellington Legal Research Papers*. 3 VUWLRP 4/2013.

19 4 Burr. 2398, 98 Eng. Rep. 252. The point that Mansfield's opinion in *Millar v. Taylor* was a statement of the moral right has also been made by Professor Oldham, *The Mansfield Manuscripts*, i, 726; and by Professor Gerald Dworkin, "The Moral Right of the Author: Moral Rights and the Common Law Countries," *Colum.-VLA J.L. and Arts* 19 (1994–95): 229.

20 Johns, *Piracy*, 136.

21 Proceedings in the House of Lords on the Question of Literary Property. 4 Feb. 1774. *Parliamentary History of England*, xvii, 953 (1771–74).

22 Ibid., xvii, 971.

23 Lord Townshend to John A. Hutchinson, 25 Feb. 1774. Hist. MSS. Comm., 12th Report, Appendix, Part IX, MS of the Earl of Donomoughmore, 278. (VC).

24 Proceedings in the House of Lords on the Question of Literary Property. 15 Feb. 1774. *Parliamentary History of England*, xvii, 992–1001 (1771–74).

25 Lord Townshend to John A. Hutchinson, 25 Feb. 1774. Hist. MSS. Comm., 12th Report, Appendix, Part IX, MS of the Earl of Donomoughmore, 278. (VC).

26 Ibid.

27 Almon, *Biographical Anecdotes*, 354.

28 John Forster, *The Life and Times of Oliver Goldsmith* (London: Chapman and Hall, 1871), ch. 21.

29 Lord Townshend to John A. Hutchinson, 25 Feb. 1774. Hist. MSS. Comm. 12th Report. Appendix, Part IX. MS. of the Earl of Donomoughmore, 278 (VC).

30 *Boswell Papers*, Isham Collection, Scott and Pottle, xv, 279. Conversation with Lord Kames, 20 Dec. 1778). The Scottish judge was Lord Arniston.

31 Edward C. Walterscheid, "The Early Evolution of the United States Patent Law: Antecedents (Part 3)," *Journal of the Patent and Trademark Society* (1995): 775.

32 Adam Mossoff, "Rethinking the Development of Patents: An Intellectual History, 1550–1800," *Hastings Law Journal* 52 (2001): 1271–2.

33 Oldham, *The Mansfield Manuscripts*, i, 731.

34 *Morning Chronicle*, 8 Dec. 1775 (VC).

35 Ibid., 1 Jun. 1776 (VC).

36 The case was not reported, but it was widely discussed in the press at the time. Mossoff, "Rethinking the Development of Patents: An Intellectual History, 1550–1800," 1293; Oldham, *The Mansfield Manuscripts*, i, 723.

37 John N. Adams and Gwen Averley, "The Patent Specification: The Role of *Liardet v. Johnson*," *Journal of Legal History* 7 (1986): 162–3.

38 Liardet's composition proved to be defective and had to be removed from all the stucco ornaments at Kenwood in 1793. Harris, *The Country Houses of Robert Adam*, 99.

39 Adams and Averley, "The Patent Specification: The Role of *Liardet v. Johnson*," 164.

40 E.W. Hulme, "On the History of Patent Law in the Seventeenth and Eighteenth Centuries," *Law Quarterly Review* 18 (1902): 284, 286.

41 *Gazetteer*, 20 Jul. 1778.

42 Hulme, "On the History of Patent Law in the Seventeenth and Eighteenth Centuries," 284–7.

43 The axiom in the American Declaration of Independence that every individual has a right to life, liberty, and the pursuit of happiness reflects Locke's theory with only a slight reformulation.

44 John Locke, *Two Treatises of Government* (New York: E.P. Dutton and Co. Inc. Everyman's Library, 1943), 164–6.
45 Johns, *Piracy*, 258. Mossoff, "Rethinking the Development of Patents: An Intellectual History," 1298.
46 Hulme, "On the History of Patent Law in the Seventeenth and Eighteenth Centuries," 285.
47 Boulton and Watt v. Bull, 1 Carp. P.C. 105, 99 Eng. Rep. 1274 (1787).
48 John H. Langbein, "The Criminal Trial Before the Lawyers," 315–16.
49 3 Doug. 157, 99 Eng. Rep. 589 (1782).
50 3 Doug. 157, 159, 99 Eng. Rep. 589, 590 (1782).
51 R. Turner [1975] QB 834, 841 (UK). See Civil Procedure Rules Part 35 Section 1 and Criminal Procedure Rules Part 22.
52 Canada Evidence Act, R.S. 1985, c. E-10, s. 7.
53 Rule 702 of the Federal Rules of Evidence. See *Daubert v. Merrell Dow Pharmaceuticals, Inc.*, 509 U.S. 579, 589 (1993).
54 Oldham, *The Mansfield Manuscripts*, i, 728.
55 White, *London in the Eighteenth Century*, 215.
56 *Westminster Journal*, 21 Feb. 1778 (VC).
57 *London Evening Post*, 9 Dec. 1757 (VC).

CHAPTER TWENTY

1 See Chapter 23.
2 Carolyn Steedman, "Lord Mansfield's Women," *Past and Present*, Oxford: Oxford University Press, Issue 176 (1952): 105, 108.
3 *Morning Herald*, 16 Feb. 1781 (VC).
4 There is no court report of the case, but it was described in a newspaper report. *Daily Universal Register*, 1 Jun. 1785 (VC).
5 It appears that in a later trial before Mansfield of a criminal case against the husband, Mansfield told the jury that no cruelty or beating had been proved, and that a man had a right to take the person of his wife. The jury acquitted him. Yorke MSS, vol. 4, f.217. Sittings after Westminster, 26 Geo. III, 3 B.R. (VC).
6 *Walker v. Perkins*, 3 Burr. 1568, 97 Eng. Rep. 985 (1764).
7 *St. James's Chronicle*, 1 Aug. 1781 (VC).
8 Oldham, *The Mansfield Manuscripts*, ii, 1251–2.
9 *Morning Post*, 18 Dec. 1776 (VC).
10 Oldham, *The Mansfield Manuscripts*, ii, 1257.
11 *Morning Post*, 6 Jul. 1780 (VC).
12 3 Doug. 212, 99 Eng. Rep. 618 (1783).
13 4 Burr. 2225, 98 Eng. Rep. 160 (1768).
14 Janyna Morse Caccioppo, "Voluntary Acknowledgements of Paternity: Should

Biology Play a Role in Determining Who Can Be a Legal Father?" *Indiana Law Review* xxxviii (2005): 479, 484.

15 *Goodright v. Moss*, 2 Cowp. 591, 593, 98 Eng. Rep. 1257, 1258 (1777). Although the Mansfield Rule has endured, several American courts have rejected it, in view of the advent of DNA testing and the lessening of the social stigma of illegitimacy. See the discussion in *Serafin v. Serafin*, 258 N.W.2d 461 (Mich. 1977).

16 Cas. T. Hard. 277, 95 Eng. Rep. 178 (1736). This report of the case states facts that are somewhat different from the version that Mansfield recounted.

17 *Whitehall Evening Post*, 15 Feb. 1781 (VC).

18 Murray to Robert Trevor, 8 Jan. 1743. (NS). Hist. MSS. Comm. 14th Rep., App. 9 Trevor MSS, 84–5 (VC).

19 Chalus, *Elite Women in English Political Life*, 33.

20 *Ringsted v. Lady Lanesborough*, 3 Doug. 196, 202, 99 Eng. Rep. 610, 613 (1783). A wife could be protected, however, by a marriage settlement that placed her property in a trust that sheltered the property from any claims of her husband's creditors. In one case, a marriage settlement placed the wife's thirty-four cows in a trust. *Haslington v. Gill*, 3 Doug. 415, 99 Eng. Rep. 725 (1784).

21 Vickery, *The Gentleman's Daughter*, 59.

22 Ibid., 59–60.

23 Oldham, *The Mansfield Manuscripts*, ii, 1245.

24 3 Doug. 196, 99 Eng. Rep. 610 (1783).

25 3 Doug. 196, 203.

26 Ibid.

27 3 Doug. 196, 204.

28 Ibid.

29 3 Doug. 196, 200.

30 1 T.R. 4, 99 Eng. Rep. 940 (1785). The other case was *Barwell v. Brooks*, 3 Doug. 372, 99 Eng. Rep. 702 (1784).

31 1 T.R. 4, 9.

32 Ibid.

33 After Mansfield's retirement, the courts pulled back from his expansion of the exception, ruling that a married woman could be sued only if her husband was outside the jurisdiction of the English courts. Oldham, *The Mansfield Manuscripts*, ii, 1247–9.

34 *Crompton v. Mackrill*, Yorke MSS, vol. 4, fo. 133 (1777) (VC).

35 *The Trial of Elizabeth Duchess Dowager of Kingston for Bigamy* (London: Charles Bathurst, 1776), 104.

36 Ibid., 105.

37 T.A.B. Corley, "Chudleigh, Elizabeth," ODNB.

38 *Public Advertiser*, 2 Jun. 1775 (VC).

39 Mathew, *For Lawyers and Others*, 89.

40 *Public Advertiser*, 2 Apr. 1776 (VC).

41 Kingston had entrusted Newcastle with his will. *Trial of the Duchess of Kingston*, 142.

42 Arthur Vincent, ed., *Twelve Bad Women: Illustrations and Reviews of Feminine Turpitude Set Forth by Impartial Hands* (London: T. Fisher Unwin, 1897), 247.

43 *London Chronicle*, 13 Sep. 1788 (VC).

44 *The Duchess of Kingston's Case*, 1 Leach 146, 148 (1776).

45 *London Chronicle*, 21 Nov. 1775.

46 *Gazetteer*, 14 Dec. 1775.

47 Katherine Harriet Porter, "Margaret, Duchess of Portland," *A Thesis Presented to the Faculty of the Graduate School of Cornell University for the degree of Doctor of Philosophy*, June 1930.

48 *Trial of the Duchess of Kingston*, 109.

49 Ibid., 154–5.

50 *The Duchess of Kingston's Case*, 1 Leach 146, 147–8 (1776).

51 *Daily Post*, 26 May 1740 (VC).

52 T.A.B. Corley, "Chudleigh, Elizabeth," *ODNB*.

53 *Trial of the Duchess of Kingston*, 119–20.

54 Ibid., 146.

55 Angus H. Ferguson, "The Lasting Legacy of a Bigamous Duchess: The Benchmark Precedent for Medical Confidentiality," *Social History of Medicine* 19 (2006): 51.

56 John Maxcy Zane, *The Story of Law* (Garden City, NY: Doubleday, Doran and Company, Inc., 1927), 329–36.

57 Alexander Carlyle, Burton, *Autobiography of the Rev. Dr Alexander Carlyle*, edited by John H. Burton (Edinburgh: W. Blackwood and Sons, 1860), 537–8.

58 *Second Letter to a Noble Lord: On the Speeches of the Lord Chancellor and of Lord Mansfield on February the 27th, 1769, on the Douglas Cause* (London: A. Henderson), 12–14.

59 Zane, *The Story of Law*, 329–36.

60 Andrew Stuart, *Letters to The Right Honourable Lord Mansfield from Andrew Stuart, Esq.* (London: Wakefield, 1773). 9.

61 Campbell, *The Lives of the Chief Justices*, ii, 445.

62 In 1770 Mansfield said that in his experience "a great number" of criminal conversation cases had been tried. *Proceedings at Large, in a Cause on an Action Brought by Lord Grosvenor v. Duke of Cumberland; for Criminal Conversation with Lady Grosvenor* (London: J. Wheble, 1770), 74. It is not clear whether he was referring to trials where he presided or to all those he was aware of. Oldham states that Mansfield tried twenty such cases that reached a verdict. Oldham, *The Mansfield Manuscripts*, ii, 1259.

63 See Chapter 4.

64 *The Tryal of a Cause for Criminal Conversation, Between Theophilus Cibber, Gent.*

Plaintiff, and William Sloper, Esq., Defendant (London: Printed for T. Trott. 1739). Harvard Law School Library.

65 *Proceedings in Grosvenor v. Cumberland.*

66 Ibid., 38–42.

67 *Hemmings v. Smith.* Dampier MSS (VC).

68 *Proceedings in Grosvenor v. Cumberland*, 74.

69 Ibid., 77–8.

70 Ibid., 78.

71 Stella Tillyard, *A Royal Affair: George III and His Scandalous Siblings*, 134–74.

72 *Public Advertiser*, 11 Jan. 1771.

73 *Le Lys Rouge*, ch. 7 (quoted in Shapiro, ed., *The Yale Book of Quotations*), 285.

74 *The Trial with the Whole of the Evidence between Sir Richard Worsley and George Maurice Bissett, for Criminal Conversation with the Plaintiff's Wife* (London: G. Kearsley, 1782), 12–18. A book about the case, Hallie Rubenhold, *Lady Worsley's Whim: An Eighteenth-Century Tale of Sex, Scandal and Divorce* (London: Chatto and Windus, 2008), was published in 2008.

75 *The Trial with the Whole of the Evidence between Sir Richard Worsley and George Maurice Bissett, for Criminal Conversation with the Plaintiff's Wife*, 19.

76 *Daily Universal Register*, 27 Apr. 1785 (VC).

CHAPTER TWENTY-ONE

1 Robert Aubrey Noakes, "Lord Mansfield and Toleration," *The Month* (Aug. 1940): 87.

2 White, *London in the Eighteenth Century*, 502.

3 Thompson, *George II*, 34.

4 Blair Worden, *The English Civil Wars: 1640–1660* (London: Weidenfeld and Nicolson, 2009), 9–10, 50, 53–4.

5 Pincus, *1688*, 143.

6 13 Car. II, st. ii, C.1.

7 Pincus, *1688*, 12.

8 Colley, *Britons*, 22–3; Langford, *A Polite and Commercial People*, 291–2.

9 Holmes and Szechi, *The Age of Oligarchy*, 171–2. The Gordon Riots of 1780, in which Mansfield was a prime target of the rioters, are described in Chapter 22.

10 1 Gui. and Mar., c. 18 (1689).

11 The Conventicles Act, 16 Car. II, c.4 (1664).

12 The Test Act, 25 Car. II, c.2 (1673).

13 The Popery Act, 11 Gui. III, c.4 (1698).

14 The Popery Act, 11 Gui. III, c.4 (1698).

15 The Papists Disarming Act, 1 Gui. and Mar., c.15 (1688).

16 1 Gui. and MR., C.9 (1688).

17 The Papists Disabling Act, 30 Car. II, St.2, c.1 (1678).

18 For example, any Catholic who sent a child out of the country to be educated would forfeit £50 to the Crown and £50 to the person who discovered and reported the offence. The Popery Act, 11 Gui. III, c.4 (1698). See Colley, *Britons*, 19; Mack, *Alexander Pope*, 40.
19 The Popery Act, 11 Gui. III, c.4 (1698).
20 Charles F. Mullett, "The Corporations Act and Election of English Protestant Dissenters to Corporation Offices," *Virginia Law Review* xxi, no. 6 (Apr. 1935): 642.
21 Colley, *Britons*, 19; Oldham, *The Mansfield Manuscripts*, ii, 864.
22 Mullett, "The Corporations Act and the Election of English Protestant Dissenters to Corporation Offices," 641–2.
23 William Murray's speech on 23 Feb. 1753. The Council Examination of the Jacobite Charges. Add. MSS. 33050, ff.200–368 (VC).
24 Campbell, *The Lives of the Chief Justices*, ii, 529–30.
25 See Chapter 4.
26 The case was *Omychund v. Barker*, which is discussed in Chapter 6.
27 William Murray to Mr Booth, 1735. Roscoe, *Lives of Eminent British Lawyers*, 173–4.
28 *London Chronicle*, 18 Nov. 1776 (VC).
29 2 Cowp. 463, 98 Eng. Rep. 1188 (1776).
30 Oldham, *The Mansfield Manuscripts*, ii, 872.
31 Although there is no report of the case, it is described in detail in Oldham, *The Mansfield Manuscripts*, ii, 877–9; in Holliday, *Life of Lord Mansfield*, 176–9; and in Campbell, *The Lives of the Chief Justices*, ii, 514–16.
32 John Adams, *Elegant Anecdotes and Bon Mots* (London: C. and G. Kearsley, 1794), 19–20.
33 Campbell, *The Lives of the Chief Justices*, ii, 514–16.
34 Ibid., ii, 516.
35 Oldham, *The Mansfield Manuscripts*, ii, 870–1.
36 Ibid., ii, p. 870.
37 *Public Advertiser*, 28 Nov. 1788 (VC).
38 *Gazetteer*, 6 Dec. 1770 (VC).
39 *Rex v. Dylone*, Yorke MSS, vol. 4, f. 85. Westminster Sittings after Trin. 7 G.3. (VC).
40 Heward, *Lord Mansfield*, 57.
41 White, *London in the Eighteenth Century*, 489.
42 Andrew Scull, book review of Mike Jay, *The Atmosphere of Heaven*, Times Literary Supplement, 30 Oct. 2009, 3.
43 Holmes and Szechi, *The Age of Oligarchy*, 114–15.
44 Porter, *English Society in the Eighteenth Century*, 321.
45 Oldham, *The Mansfield Manuscripts*, ii, 866.

46 *Atcheson v. Everitt*, 1 Cowp. 382, 98 Eng. Rep. 1142 (1775).
47 *Rex v. Barker*, 3 Burr. 1264, 97 Eng. Rep. 823 (1762).
48 *Crawford v. Powell*, 2 Burr. 1013, 97 Eng. Rep. 681 (1760).
49 *Rex v. Wroughton*, 3 Burr. 1682, 97 Eng. Rep. 1045 (1765).
50 13 Car. II, St.2, c.1 (1661).
51 Mullett, "The Corporations Act and Election of English Protestant Dissenters to Corporation Offices," 650.
52 *Speech of Mansfield in the House of Lords in the Cause between the City of London and Dissenters*. 4 Feb. 1767 (BL, Rare Books Room).
53 Mullett, "The Corporations Act and Election of English Protestant Dissenters to Corporation Offices," *Virginia Law Review* 21, No. 6 (Apr. 1935): 663.
54 Ibid., 660.
55 Ibid., 663.
56 *Speech of Mansfield in the House of Lords in the Cause between the City of London and Dissenters*. 4 Feb. 1767 (BL, Rare Books Room).
57 Mullett, "The Corporations Act and Election of English Protestant Dissenters to Corporation Offices," 664.
58 In 1800, there were about 15,000 Jews in London, most of whom had immigrated during the previous fifty years. White, *London in the Eighteenth Century*, 145.
59 Porter, *English Society in the Eighteenth Century*, 172.
60 White, *London in the Eighteenth Century*, 146.
61 Holmes and Szechi, *The Age of Oligarchy*, 152.
62 *Morning Chronicle*, 12 Jun. 1773 (VC).
63 Coxe, *Memoirs of the Administration of Henry Pelham*, ii, 249; White, *London in the Eighteenth Century*, 150–1.
64 Holmes and Szechi, *The Age of Oligarchy*, 268; Browning, *Newcastle*, 190–1.
65 Thomas, "Yorke, Philip, First Earl of Hardwicke," *ODNB*.
66 *General Evening Post*, 29 May 1777 (VC).
67 Paterson, *Curiosities of Law and Lawyers*, 474–5.
68 *Morning Post*, 6 Jul. 1766 (VC).
69 Holliday, *Life of Lord Mansfield*, 213.
70 *London Evening Post*, 2–4 Feb. 1779. The newspaper account has Israel speaking with a foreign accent, but I have eliminated this in the quoted language.
71 Henry Joseph Haskell, *This Was Cicero: Modern Politics in a Roman Toga* (New York: A.A. Knopf, 1942), 55.
72 A rioter who helped cause the death of an elderly couple accused of witchcraft in 1760 was executed and afterwards hanged in chains. *London Evening Post*, 21–24 Jun. 1760 (VC).
73 *London Evening Post*, 21–24 Jun. 1760 (VC); *Public Advertiser*, 10 Jul. 1776 (VC).
74 *Payne's Universal Chronicle*, 24 Feb.–3 Mar. 1759 (VC).
75 John Adams, *Elegant Anecdotes and Bon Mots*, 19–20.

CHAPTER TWENTY-TWO

1 Paul Langford, *A Polite and Commercial People*, 161; White, *London in the Eighteenth Century*, 106.
2 Ibid., 158, 160, 536.
3 18 Geo. III, c.60 (1778).
4 The legal disabilities imposed on Catholics are described in Chapter 21.
5 *Rex v. Webb*, discussed in Chapter 21.
6 *Gazetteer*, 21 Dec. 1780 (VC).
7 Colley, *Britons*, 23.
8 *Narrative of the Late Riots and Disturbances in the Cities of London and Westminster* (hereinafter *Narrative of the Late Riots*) (London: Fielding and Walker, 1780), 11; *Whitehall Evening Post*, 8 Feb. 1781 (VC).
9 Colin Haydon, "Gordon, Lord George," *ODNB*.
10 *Narrative of the Late Riots*, 15–16, 55; White, *London in the Eighteenth Century*, 534–5.
11 Rogers, *Crowds, Culture and Politics in Georgian Britain*, 159.
12 *London Courant*, 3 Jun. 1780 (VC).
13 Rogers, *Crowds, Culture and Politics in Georgian Britain*, 159.
14 *London Courant*, 3 Jun. 1780 (VC).
15 Ibid.
16 William Connor Sydney, *England and the English in the Eighteenth Century: Chapters in the Social History of the Times*, 2 vols. (New York: Macmillan, 1891), ii, 203.
17 *Narrative of the Late Riots*, 17–19.
18 21 Parliamentary History, 665 (quoted in Heward, *Lord Mansfield*, 155).
19 Campbell, *The Lives of the Chief Justices*, ii, 518–20.
20 Walpole to Lady Ossory, 3 Jun. 1780. W.S. Lewis, ed., *The Yale Editions of Horace Walpole's Correspondence* (New Haven: Yale University Press, 1965), xxxiii, 175. Walpole apparently heard this from the Duke of Devonshire, who was present. John Paul De Castro, *The Gordon Riots* (London: H. Milford, Oxford University Press, 1926), 37. A few years later, when another peer said that he hoped Mansfield was not the worse for having sat on the woolsack all day in the absence of the lord chancellor, Mansfield replied: "My Lord, nobody is worse for doing his duty." *Public Advertiser*, 4 May 1786 (VC).
21 Rogers, *Crowds, Culture and Politics in Georgian Britain*, 159.
22 De Castro, *The Gordon Riots*, 37–8.
23 Haydon, "Gordon, Lord George," *ODNB*.
24 *Narrative of the Late Riots*, 22.
25 Campbell, *The Lives of the Chief Justices*, ii, 518–21.
26 Mrs Lloyd Kenyon to Mrs Kenyon, 6 Jun. 1780. Hist. MSS. Comm., 14th Rep., Appendix, Part IV, Kenyon MSS, 510 (VC).
27 White, *London in the Eighteenth Century*, 506.

28 Ibid., 22–3; Rogers, *Crowds, Culture and Politics in Georgian Britain*, 159–60; Benjamin Franklin to William Carmichael, 17 Jun. 1780; Benjamin Franklin, *The Writings of Benjamin Franklin*, edited by Albert Henry Smyth, 10 vols. (New York and London: Macmillan and Co., 1905–07), viii, 99.
29 White, *London in the Eighteenth Century*, 453.
30 *Narrative of the Late Riots*, 27; White, *London in the Eighteenth Century*, 539.
31 Rogers, *Crowds, Culture and Politics in Georgian Britain*, 161.
32 Peter Ackroyd, *London: The Biography* (London: Chatto and Windus, 2000), 489.
33 Hawkins, *Memoirs*, ii, 108–9. The author was Sir John Hawkins's daughter.
34 Campbell, *The Lives of the Chief Justices*, ii, 523.
35 *Public Advertiser*, 12 Jun. 1780 (VC).
36 De Castro, *The Gordon Riots*, 95–6; Holliday, *Life of Lord Mansfield*, 410–11.
37 *Narrative of the Late Riots*, 26.
38 Testimony of Constable Thomas Learing in the trial of John Gray for breaking the peace and rioting, 28 Jun. 1780. Proceedings of the Old Bailey. Reference Number t17800628-69.
39 De Castro, *The Gordon Riots*, 98.
40 Mrs Boscawen to Mrs Delany, *Life and Correspondence of Mrs Delany*, v.
41 *Morning Post*, 6 Oct. 1780 (VC).
42 De Castro, *The Gordon Riots*, 99. The officer, Colonel John Woodford, happened to be a brother-in-law of Lord George Gordon. Ibid.
43 *Morning Chronicle*, 8 Jun. 1780 (VC).
44 *London Courant*, 4 Jul. 1780 (VC).
45 *General Evening Post*, 1–4 Jul. 1780 (VC); *Morning Chronicle*, 4 Jul. 1780 (VC). Mills testified to this in a trial of a person accused of inciting the rioting. Thomas Jones Howell and William Cobbett, *Collection of State Trials*, xxi, 664–88.
46 *Public Advertiser*, 12 Dec. 1780.
47 *Narrative of the Late Riots*, 29; *Public Advertiser*, 9 Jun. 1780.
48 *Gazetteer*, 4 Jun. 1780.
49 Adams, *Learned in the Law*, 207.
50 *Gazetteer*, 4 Jun. 1780.
51 Edward Malone (a Shakespeare scholar) to Charlemont, 5 Jul. 1780. Hist. MSS. Comm. 12th Rep., Appendix, Part 10, Charlemont Memoirs, L. 374 (VC).
52 Adams, *Learned in the Law*, 207.
53 *Scots Magazine* (June 1793): 261–3 (VC).
54 De Castro, *The Gordon Riots*, 204–6.
55 *London Courant*, 30 Jun. 1780 (VC).
56 Holmes and Szechi, *The Age of Oligarchy*, 178–9. Although the rioters targeted working-class Irish Catholics, that was more for economic than for religious reasons. The rioters believed that Irishmen were taking away their jobs. White, *London in the Eighteenth Century*, 158.
57 *Morning Post*, 9 Jun. 1780 (VC).

58 Rogers, *Crowds, Culture and Politics in Georgian Britain*, 161.
59 *Public Advertiser*, 9 Jun. 1780 (VC).
60 De Castro, *The Gordon Riots*, 112–13. A newspaper reported that 1,500 armed persons had assembled at Highgate to attack Kenwood, but they were deterred by a large party of militia. *Public Advertiser*, 9 Jun. 1780 (VC). The number was probably an exaggeration, stimulated by public hysteria.
61 *Whitehall Evening Post*, 13 Jul. 1780 (VC). The Gordon Riots were famously depicted in Charles Dickens's novel *Barnaby Rudge*.
62 *Narrative of the Late Riots*, 31.
63 *London Courant*, 28 Jun. 1780 (VC); *Narrative of the Late Riots*, 40–1.
64 *Narrative of the Late Riots*, 30.
65 Ibid., 36.
66 *London Courant*, 28 Jun. 1780 (VC).
67 Holmes and Szechi, *The Age of Oligarchy*, 186, 320.
68 Porter, *English Society in the Eighteenth Century*, 101.
69 *Narrative of the Late Riots*, 34.
70 *Morning Chronicle*, 20 Mar. 1786 (VC).
71 Franklin to William Carmichael, 17 Jun. 1780. Franklin, *The Writings of Benjamin Franklin*, viii, 99.
72 Holmes and Szechi, *The Age of Oligarchy*, 178–9.
73 Proceedings of the Old Bailey. Reference Numbers t17800628-69 and t17800628-81.
74 *Public Advertiser*, 24 Jul. 1780 (VC).
75 Ibid., 13 Jun. 1780.
76 Ibid., 11 Aug. 1780.
77 *Morning Post*, 5 Aug. 1780 (VC).
78 Ibid., 10 Jun. 1780 (VC).
79 *Morning Chronicle*, 12 Jun. 1780 (VC).
80 *Morning Post*, 10 Jun. 1780 (VC).
81 *Scots Magazine* (June 1793): 264–5 (VC).
82 Elizabeth Montagu to the Duchess of Portland, 29 Jun. 1780. Hist. MSS. Comm. Bath, i, 348 (VC).
83 Franklin to Samuel Wharton, 17 Jun. 1780. Franklin, *The Writings of Benj. Franklin*, viii, 94–5.
84 *London Courant*, 23 Jun. 1781 (VC).
85 *Gazetteer*, 21 Jun. 1780 (VC).
86 There was also a small police force known as the Bow Street Runners, but it was not strong enough to be effective against large-scale violence. See Chapter 15.
87 *Narrative of the Late Riots*, 41.
88 *London Courant*, 21 Jun. 1780 (VC).
89 Campbell, *The Lives of the Chief Justices*, ii, 527–30. Mansfield's first biographer

gives a slightly different version of what Mansfield said: "I speak not from books, for books I have none." Holliday, *Life of Mansfield*, 413. One newspaper was unimpressed with the pathos, quoting Caliban's speech in Act III of *The Tempest*: "Remember first to possess his books; for without them he's but a sot." *Morning Chronicle*, 18 Jan. 1781 (VC).

90 Noakes, "Mansfield and Toleration," 91.

91 *Morning Chronicle*, 9 Jun. 1781, quoting Mansfield's letter of 21 Aug. 1780 to Whitfield Keene of the Treasury (VC). A slightly different version of the letter is printed in Charles Knight, *Gallery of Portraits with Memoirs*, vi, 62–8 (1836). I have used the Knight version and have made a minor change in the letter in order to make it more comprehensible.

92 *London Courant*, 1 Aug. 1780 (VC); *Whitehall Evening Post*, 31 Oct. 1780 (VC).

93 *Langdale v. Mason*, 486 nb 163 (London, 14 Dec. 1780), cited in Oldham, *The Mansfield Manuscripts*, i, 478. See *London Chronicle*, 16 Dec. 1780 (VC).

94 *Morning Chronicle*, 16 Dec. 1780 (VC).

95 De Castro, *The Gordon Riots*, 204–6; *London Courant*, 28 Jun. 1780 (VC).

96 SP, Box 14.

97 *Narrative of the Late Riots*, 45.

98 *London Courant*, 28 Jun. 1780 (VC).

99 Trial of Thomas Crankshaw, 28 Jun. 1780. Proceedings of the Old Bailey. Reference Number t17800628-78.

100 Porter, *English Society in the Eighteenth Century*, 104.

101 Langford, *A Polite and Commercial People*, 551.

102 Porter, *English Society in the Eighteenth Century*, 347.

103 1 Geo. I.

104 *Morning Chronicle*, 12 Mar. 1781 (VC).

105 Oldham, *The Mansfield Manuscripts*, ii, 1113–14. The case is *Rex v. Kennett*, 5 Car. and P. 282 (1781).

106 *Morning Chronicle*, 12 Mar. 1781 (VC). The jury's proposed verdict would make perfect sense today. A person cannot be convicted of a crime unless a jury finds him or her guilty "beyond a reasonable doubt," whereas civil liability requires only the less rigorous standard of "by a preponderance of the evidence."

107 White, *London in the Eighteenth Century*, 543.

108 *Narrative of the Late Riots*, 48–9.

109 *Morning Herald*, 29 Jan. 1781 (VC).

110 SP, Bundle 641.

111 *Lloyd's Evening Post*, 5 Feb. 1781 (VC).

112 *Whitehall Evening Post*, 8 Feb. 1781 (VC).

113 *The Trial of Lord George Gordon for High Treason at the Bar of the Court of King's Bench*. London: Kearsly and Gurney, 1781, ii, 65.

114 Ibid., ii, 63–4.

115 *Whitehall Evening Post*, 8 Feb. 1781 (VC).
116 Haydon, "Gordon, Lord George," *ODNB*; Geoffrey Treasure, *Who's Who in British History: Early Hanoverian Britain 1714–1789*, 314–15.
117 Jesse Foot, *Life of Arthur Murphy, Esq*., (London: J. Faulder, 1811), 16–17.
118 These included cases on commercial law, contracts, conspiracy, trade unions, and the rights of married women.
119 Mansfield to the 2nd Earl of Hardwicke, 21 Jul. 1780. Add. MSS. 35616 (BL).

CHAPTER TWENTY-THREE

1 The *Morning Post* of 9 Jul. 1766 reported that his resignation and retirement were talked of more than ever (VC).
2 William Stratton to Lord Stormont, 27 Jan. 1771. NAS. Ex NRAS 776 second series bundle 578.
3 *Public Advertiser*, 22 Feb. 1771 (VC); *Gazetteer*, 4 Mar. 1771 (VC).
4 *Morning Post*, 11 Nov. 1776 (VC).
5 The King to Lord North, 28 Oct. 1777. Fortescue, *Correspondence of George III*, iii, 486.
6 The exception was Sir William Lee, who held the office from 1737 to 1754.
7 *Public Advertiser*, 9 Mar. 1775 (VC); *Morning Chronicle*, 12 Oct. 1775 (VC).
8 Mansfield to Stormont, 10 Apr. 1777. SP, Bundle 641.
9 Forbes, *Beattie and His Friends*, 173.
10 Scott to Hastings, 25 Dec. 1781. Add. 29152, f.221v. (VC).
11 Lord Sydney to Earl Cornwallis, 6 Jan. 1783. Cornwallis, *Correspondence of Charles, First Marquis Cornwallis*, i, 267 (VC).
12 *Morning Chronicle*, 22 Mar. 1784 (VC).
13 Ibid., 26 Mar. 1781.
14 *London Chronicle*, 3 May 1781 (VC).
15 *Morning Chronicle*, 3 Jan. 1784, 26 Feb. 1784, 4 Mar. 1784 (VC).
16 *Morning Herald*, 29 Jan. 1784 (VC).
17 Mrs Boscawen to Mrs Delany, 28 Oct. 1778, 10 Nov. 1778. *Correspondence of Mrs Delany*, series 2, ii, 393, 487; Mrs Delany to Mrs Port, 23 Jul. 1781. Ibid., series 2, iii, 40.
18 Mansfield to Bishop Newton, Jan. 1782; Holliday, *Life of Lord Mansfield*, 132.
19 Duchess of Portland to Mrs Delany, undated and unsigned letter, *Correspondence of Mrs Delany*, series 2, iii, 212.
20 *Gazetteer*, 29 Apr. 1784 (VC).
21 Mansfield to Rutland, 29 May 1784. Hist. MSS. Comm. 14th Rep., Appendix, Part I, Rutland MSS. iii, 99 (VC).
22 Mansfield to Rutland, 19 Jun. 1786. Hist. MSS. Comm. 14th Rep., Appendix, Part I, Rutland MSS. iii, 311 (VC).
23 *Parker's General Advertiser*, 4 Jun. 1784 (VC).

24 In 1754 he had gone to the spa of Bath to cure his rheumatism. C. Yorke to Warburton, 10 Aug. 1754. Add. MSS. 35404, f.95 (VC). Five years later, he wrote to Lord Stormont: "Yesterday morning I was very well but before dinner seized with a violent rheumatick pain in the small of my back so at present I am unable to stir. I hope it won't continue." Mansfield to Stormont, 30 Oct. 1759. SP, Box 18/Folder 8.

25 *Morning Herald*, 7 Jun. 1784 (VC); Scott to Hastings, 11 Jun. 1784. Add. MSS. 29164, f.220–221 (VC).

26 Scott to Hastings, 11 Jun. 1784. Add. MSS. 29164, ff. 220–221 (VC).

27 *Morning Chronicle*, 6 Nov. 1784, 3 Dec. 1784 (VC).

28 *Morning Herald*, 2 Aug. 1784 (VC).

29 Holmes and Szechi, *The Age of Oligarchy*, 211.

30 Amanda Vickery, *The Gentleman's Daughter*, 240.

31 *Morning Herald*, 9 Oct. 1784 (VC).

32 *London Chronicle*, 9–12 Oct. 1784 (VC).

33 Holliday, *Life of Lord Mansfield*, 463.

34 *Memoirs of Richard Cumberland*, ii, 344–6.

35 *Correspondence of Mrs Delany*, series 2, iii, 298.

36 *Morning Chronicle*, 5 Nov. 1784 (VC).

37 Mrs Boscawen to Mrs Delany, 7 Sep. 1784. *Correspondence of Mrs Delany*, series 2, ii, 229.

38 *Morning Chronicle*, 3 Dec. 1784, 7 Dec. 1784 (VC); *Morning Herald*, 22 Jun. 1785 (VC).

39 William Smith, *The Diary and Selected Papers of Chief Justice William Smith, 1784–1793*, edited by L.F.S. Upton, 2 vols. (Toronto: The Champlain Society, 1963) i, 168–70.

40 *General Advertiser*, 7 Mar. 1785 (VC).

41 *Diary of Chief Justice William Smith*, i, 204.

42 Lord Sheffield to William Eden, 15 Jul. 1785. *Correspondence of Auckland*, i, 346. (VC).

43 Carolyn Steedman, "Lord Mansfield's Women," 107–8.

44 Mrs Boscawen to Mrs Delany, 13 Jan. 1786, 19 May 1786. *Correspondence of Mrs Delany*, series 2, iii, 335, 352.

45 Mrs Boscawen to Mrs Delany, 28 Oct. 1778. *Correspondence of Mrs Delany*, series 2, ii, 393.

46 Mansfield to Rutland, 11 Dec. 1785. Hist. MSS. Comm. 14th Rep., Appendix, Part I, Rutland MSS. Vol. III, 268 (VC).

47 Cumberland, *Memoirs of Richard Cumberland*, ii, 492–3.

48 Campbell, *The Lives of the Chief Justices*, ii, 549n.

49 Mansfield to Rutland, 11 Dec. 1785. Hist. MSS. Comm. 14th Rep., Appendix, Part I, Rutland MSS. Vol. III, 268 (VC). Mansfield's reference to stone probably meant a kidney or bladder stone.

50 Reynolds to Rutland, 4 Jan. 1786. Hist. MSS. Comm. 14th Rep., Appendix, Part I, Rutland MSS., iii (VC). The painting now hangs in Scone Palace, the home of the current Earl of Mansfield. A copy of the print, by the engraver Bartolozzi, is in the British Museum. Many years earlier, when Mansfield was thirty-seven, he was painted by Reynolds's teacher, Thomas Hudson, who was a renowned painter in his own right. White, *London in the Eighteenth Century*, 268, 278.

51 James Northcote, *The Life of Sir Joshua Reynolds*, 2 vols. (London: Henry Colburn, 1818), ii, 98.

52 Mansfield to Rutland, 11 Dec. 1785. Hist. MSS. Comm. 14th Rep., Appendix, Part I, Rutland MSS., iii (VC).

53 *Morning Chronicle*, 20 Apr. 1786 (VC).

54 Thomas Orde to Rutland, 31 May 1786. Hist. MSS. Comm., 14th Rep., Appendix, Part I, Rutland MSS., iii, 305 (VC).

55 *Morning Chronicle*, 10 May 1786 (VC).

56 *Morning Herald*, 17 Jun. 1786 (VC).

57 *Public Advertiser*, 8 Jun. 1786 (VC).

58 Journal entry of 16 Jun. 1786. Boswell, *Boswell, the English Experiment*, 72.

59 Mansfield to Charles Jenkinson, Earl of Liverpool, 21 Aug. 1786. Add. MSS. 38223, f.147 (VC).

60 *The World*, 31 Jan. 1787 (VC).

61 Porter, *English Society in the Eighteenth Century*, 227; John Timbs, *Anecdote Lives of Wits and Humourists* (London: Richard Bentley and Sons, 1872), i, 220.

62 Gore-Browne, *Thurlow*, 155–6.

63 Charles Yorke to Warburton, 10 Aug. 1754. Add. 35404, f. 95. (VC). Apparently, visitors to Bath both bathed in the restorative mineral waters and drank them. Today, immersion in the waters is not permitted.

64 *London Chronicle*, 27–29 Mar. 1787 (VC).

65 *The World*, 31 Mar. 1787 (VC).

66 Ibid., 6 Apr.1787.

67 Lt-Gen. Grant to Earl Cornwallis, 16 Apr. 1787. Cornwallis, *Correspondence of Charles, First Marquis Cornwallis*, i, 287.

68 *The World*, 17 May 1787 (VC).

69 Lt-Gen. Grant to Earl Cornwallis, 16 Apr. 1787. Cornwallis, *Correspondence of Charles, First Marquis Cornwallis*, i, 287.

70 *The World*, 9 May 1787 (VC).

71 Smith, "The Newspaper," in Turberville, ed., *Johnson's England*, ii, 358.

72 *The World*, 22 Nov. 1787 (VC).

73 Ibid., 29 Nov. 1787 (VC).

74 Ibid., 6 Dec. 1787 (VC).

75 Lt-Gen. Grant to Earl Cornwallis, 16 Apr. 1787. Cornwallis, *Correspondence of Charles, First Marquis Cornwallis*, i, 287.

76 G.E. Cokayne, *Complete Peerage* (VC).

77 *Morning Post*, 4 Nov. 1782 (VC).

78 Oldham, *The Mansfield Manuscripts*, i, 72.

79 Lewis Bernstein Namier and John Brooke, *The House of Commons: 1754–1790*, 3 vols. (New York: Published for the History of Parliament Trust by Oxford University Press, 1964), ii, 368.

80 Rede and Wynne, *Strictures on the Lives and Characters of the Most Eminent Lawyers of the Present Day*, 108–9.

81 Buller to Stormont, 1793. NAS, Ex NRAS 776 second series bundle 584.

82 Townsend, *The Lives of Twelve Eminent Judges of the Last and of the Present Century*, 2 vols. (London: Longman, Brown, Green, and Longmans, 1846), i, 19–21; Edward Foss, *The Judges of England*, 9 vols. (London: John Murray, 1848–64), viii, 251–2.

83 Oldham, *The Mansfield Manuscripts*, i, 192–4.

84 *Morning Herald*, 21 Jun. 1784 (VC).

85 Kenyon, *Lord Kenyon*, 164–6.

86 *The World*, 8 Feb. 1788 (VC).

87 *Public Advertiser*, 4 Mar. 1788 (VC).

88 Nathaniel William Wraxall, *The Historical and Posthumous Memoirs of Sir Nathaniel William Wraxall 1772–84*, vol. v (New York: Scribner and Welford, 1884), 12–13.

89 Ibid.

90 Lt-Gen. Grant to Earl Cornwallis, 6 Apr. 1788. Cornwallis, *Correspondence of Charles, 1st Marquess Cornwallis*, i, 322.

91 *Public Advertiser*, 8 Apr. 1788 (VC).

92 Mansfield to Kenyon, 14 Apr. 1788. Hist. MSS. Comm. 14th Rep., Appendix, Part IV, Kenyon MSS., 526 (VC).

93 Mansfield to the King, 14 Apr. 1788; the King to Mansfield, 17 Apr. 1788. Fortescue, *Correspondence of George III.*

94 *London Chronicle*, 7 Jun. 1788 (VC).

95 Kenyon, *Lord Kenyon*, 164–6.

96 *London Chronicle*, 24 Jun. 1788 (VC).

97 Hist. MSS. Comm. 14th Rep. Appendix, Part IV, Kenyon MSS., 526 (VC). When Mansfield was appointed chief justice in 1756, he had bought the gold chain and the chambers in Serjeant's Inn from Sir Dudley Ryder's widow and executrix for similar amounts. NAS, RH4/151/10.

98 Holdsworth, *Some Makers of English Law*, 204–5 (quoting *Bauerman v. Radenius*, 7 T.R. 663 (1798). See Chapter 4.

99 Journal entry of 1 Jan. 1790. James Boswell, *Boswell, the Great Biographer, 1789–1795*, edited by Marlies K. Danziger and Frank Brady (New York: McGraw-Hill, *c.* 1989), 27.

100 *Public Advertiser*, 3 Feb. 1789 (VC).

101 See Chapter 14.

102 *The World*, 14 Jun. 1788 (VC).

103 *London Chronicle*, 14–16 Apr. 1789 (VC).
104 Ibid., 21 Dec. 1789.
105 Mansfield to Lord Fitzwilliam, 27 Jul. 1792. SP, Bundle 584.
106 *Public Advertiser*, 25 Apr. 1791 (VC).
107 *London Chronicle*, 15–17 Sep. 1791 (VC).
108 *Public Advertiser*, 20 Aug. 1791 (VC).
109 Viscount Sandon to Arthur Vanderbilt, 8 Feb. 1955 (quoting from the diaries of Lord Hatherton) (VC).
110 Mansfield to Newcastle, June 1768. Add. MSS. 32990, f.202 (VC).
111 Campbell, *The Lives of the Chief Justices*, ii, 558.
112 Holdsworth, *Some Makers of English Law*, 165.
113 Campbell, *The Lives of the Chief Justices*, ii, 558–9. Botany Bay was the early settlement by convicts in Australia.
114 *Public Advertiser*, 30 Aug. 1791 (VC).
115 *Scots Magazine*, June 1793 (VC).
116 Holliday, *Life of Lord Mansfield*, 479.
117 Obituary in *Gentleman's Magazine* (VC).
118 *London Chronicle*, 16 Mar. 1793 (VC).
119 *The Star*, 18 Mar. 1793 (VC).
120 Campbell, *The Lives of the Chief Justices*, ii, 562. A photocopy of Mansfield's will and codicils is in VC, Box 319.
121 See Chapter 17.
122 Way to the 2nd Earl of Mansfield, May 1793. SP, Box 83/Bundle 4. In some documents, Way refers to himself as chief clerk. See Chapter 10.
123 Kenyon, *Life of Lord Kenyon*, 330–1.
124 *St James's Chronicle*, 28–30 Mar. 1793 (VC).
125 *Morning Herald*, 29 Mar. 1793 (VC); Scots Magazine, June 1793, 264–5 (VC).
126 *Gentleman's Magazine* lxiii (Apr. 1793): 370 (VC).
127 2nd Earl of Mansfield to John Flaxman, 24 Jun. 1793. Add. MSS. 36652, f. 123 (VC). White, *London in the Eighteenth Century*, 284.
128 Tully was the name sometimes applied to Marcus Tullius Cicero, the great Roman philosopher and orator of the first century BC. Hyde refers to Edward Hyde, 1st Earl of Clarendon, a leading English statesman of the seventeenth century who was known for his eloquence.

EPILOGUE

1 Gordon S. Wood, *Empire of Liberty*, 449.
2 Jefferson to Mr Cutting, 2 Oct. 1788. *Writings of Jefferson,* memorial edition, edited by Andrew A. Lipscomb and Albert Ellery Bergh, 20 vols. (Washington, DC: 1904), vii, 155.
3 Jefferson to Judge John Tyler, 17 Jun. 1812. Ibid., xiii, 166–7.

4 Jefferson to Albert Gallatin, 27 Sep. 1810. Ibid., xii.
5 Wood. *Empire of Liberty*, 449.
6 Adams, *The Works of John Adams*, i, 406.
7 Louis F. Del Duca and Alain A. Levasseur, "Impact of Legal Culture and Legal Transplants on the Evolution of the U.S. Legal System," *Legal Studies Research Paper No. 23-2010* (2010): 4–5.
8 John Theodore Horton, *James Kent: A Study in Conservatism 1763–1847* (New York and London: D. Appleton-Century Company, Inc., 1939), 104.
9 See Chapter 14.
10 Speech for the defendant in *People v. Croswell*, N.Y. Sup. Ct. (1804). Alexander Hamilton, *The Works of Alexander Hamilton*, edited by Henry Cabot Lodge, 9 vols. (New York and London: G.P. Putnam's Sons, 1904), viii, 425.
11 Campbell, *The Lives of the Chief Justices*, ii, 582.
12 Ibid., 582–3.
13 Henry T. Tuckerman, *The Collector: Essays on Books, Newspapers, Pictures, Inns, Authors, Doctors, Holidays, Actors, Preachers* (London: J.C. Hotten, 1868), 196–7.
14 Oliver Wendell Holmes, "The Path of the Law," in *Collected Legal Papers* (New York: Peter Smith, 1952), 187. This was an address given by Holmes at the Boston University School of Law on 8 Jan. 1897. Holmes presumably was referring to King Henry IV of France, who reigned from 1589 to 1610.
15 98 Eng. Rep. 706 (1774). Richard I was King of England from 1189 to 1199. The similarity between the two quotations was noted by Albert W. Alschuler, *Law without Values: The Life, Work, and Legacy of Justice Holmes* (Chicago and London: University of Chicago Press, 2000), 249.
16 *Trustees of Dartmouth College v. Woodward*, 17 U.S. 518 (1819).
17 *Rex v. Vice-Chancellor of Cambridge*, 3 Burr. 1648, 97 Eng. Rep. 1027 (1765).
18 *Holly v. Domestic & Foreign Missionary Society of Protestant Episcopal Church*, 180 U.S. 284 (1901), citing Mansfield in *Miller v. Race*, 4 Burr. 452 (1758).
19 *Herbert v. Lando*, 441 U.S. 153 (1979), quoting Mansfield in *King v. Woodfall*, 5 Burr. 2661 (1770).
20 *Stone v. White*, 301 U.S. 532, 534–5 (1937), quoting Mansfield in *Moses v. Macferlan*, 2 Burr. 1005 (1770).
21 *Lehman v. Lycoming Country Children's Services Agency*, 458 U.S. 502 (1982), citing Mansfield in *King v. Delaval*, 97 Eng. Rep. 913 (1763).
22 *Trist v. Child*, 88 U.S. 441 (1874), citing Mansfield in *Jones v. Randall*, 1 Cowp. 37, 98 Eng. Rep. 954 (1774).
23 *Dickerson v. United States*, 530 U.S. 428 (2000), citing Mansfield in *King v. Rudd*, 168 Eng. Rep. 160 (1783).
24 *United States v. U.S. District Court for E.D. of Mich.*, 407 U.S. 297 (1972), citing Mansfield in *Leach v. Three of the King's Messengers*, 19 How. St. Tr. 1001 (1765).
25 *Resul v. Bush*, 542 U.S. 466 (2004), citing Mansfield in *King v. Cowle*, 2 Burr. 834, 97 Eng. Rep. 587 (1759).

26 *People v. Dlugash*, 41 NY.2d 725, 732 (1977), citing Mansfield in *Rex v. Scofield*, Cald. 397. (1784). See Chapter 15. I thank April Newbauer for bringing the *Dlugash* case to my attention.

27 *Alisha C. v. Jeremy C.*, 808 N.W.2d 875 (Neb. 2012), citing Mansfield in *Goodright v. Moss*, 2 Cowp. 591, 593, 98 Eng. Rep. 1257, 1258 (1777). See Chapter 20. I thank Susan Poser for bringing the Nebraska case to my attention.

28 Mark B. Greenlee and Thomas J. Fitzpatrick IV, "Reconsidering the Application of the Holder in Due Course Rule to Home Mortgage Notes." Federal Reserve Bank of Cleveland Working Paper 08-08 (Nov. 2008). The Mansfield case was *Miller v. Race*, 1 Burr. 452, 97 Eng. Rep. 398 (1758). See Chapter 13. I thank Kelly Skalicky for bringing the working paper to my attention.

29 *Blencoe v. British Columbia (Human Rights Commission)*, [2000] 2 S.C.R. 307, citing Mansfield in *Rex v. Barker*, 3 Burr. 1265, 97 Eng. Rep. 823 (1762).

30 *Sharbern Holding Inc. v. Vancouver Airport Centre Ltd*, [2011] 2 S.C.R. 175, citing Manfield in *Rex v. Loxdale*, 1 Burr. 445, 97 Eng. Rep. 394 (1758).

31 *Canadian Indemnity Co. v. Canadian Johns-Manville Co.*, [1990] 2 S.C.R. 549, citing Mansfield in *Carter v. Boehm*, 3 Burr. 1905, 97 Eng. Rep. 1162 (1766).

32 *Still v. Minister of National Revenue*, 1997 Fed. Ct. Appeal LEXIS 283, citing Mansfield in *Holman v. Johnson*, 1 Cowp. 341, 98 Eng. Rep. 1120 (1775).

33 *Soulos v. Korkontzilas*, 1997 Can. Sup. Ct. LEXIS 31, citing Mansfield in *Moses v. Macferlan*, 2 Burr. 1005, 97 Eng. Rep. 676 (1760).

34 *Regina v. Boulanger*, [2006] 2 S.C.R. 49, citing Mansfield in *Rex v. Bembridge*, 3 Doug. 327, 99 Eng. Rep. 679 (1783).

35 *Regina v. Pan*, 2001 SCC 42, citing Mansfield in *Vaise v. Delaval*, 1 T.R. 11, 99 Eng. Rep. 944 (1785).

36 *CCH Canadian Limited v. The Law Society of Upper Canada*, 2002 FCA 187, citing Mansfield in *Sayer v. Moore*, 501 nb 79 (1785).

37 Dennis R. Klimchuk, "Restitution and Realism," *Canadian Journal of Law and Jurisprudence* 20 (Jan. 2007): 225; Abraham Drassinower, "Unrequested Benefits in the Law of Unjust Enrichment," *University of Toronto Law Journal* 48 (Fall 1998): 459.

38 Katie Sykes, "Towards a Public Justification of Copyright," *University of Toronto Faculty of Law Review* 61 (Winter 2003): 1.

39 John F. Dolan, "What Is the Matter with the UCP?" *Banking and Finance Law Review* 15 (1999–2000): 501.

40 Barry Cahill, "Slavery and the Judges of Loyalist Nova Scotia," *University of New Brunswick Law Journal* 43 (1994): 73.

41 Travis Hreno, "Necessity and Jury Nullification," *Canadian Journal of Law and Jurisprudence* 20 (July 2007): 351.

42 Dennis R. Klimchuk, "The Nebulous Equitable Duty of Conscience," *Queen's Law Journal* 31 (Fall 2005): 206.

43 George Walker, "Bank Recovery: The Development of Judicial and Arbitral Redress under English Law," *Banking and Finance Law Review* 15 (1999–2000): 369.

44 Jason Weinrib, "What Can Kant Teach Us about Legal Classification?" *Canadian Journal of Law and Jurisprudence* 23 (Jan. 2010): 203.

45 *Tchenguiz v. Imerman*, [2010] EWCA Civ 908; (2011) 2 W.L.R. 592, citing Mansfield in *Barwell v. Brooks*, 3 Doug. 371, 373 (1784).

46 *R. v. Belton (Alicia Taria)* [2010] EWCA Crim 2857; (2011) 1 Cr. App. R. 20., citing Mansfield in *Rex. V. Bembridge*, 3 Doug. 327, 99 Eng. Rep. 679 (1783).

47 *Webster (A Child)*, Re, [2006] EWHC 2898 (Fam), citing Mansfield in *Rex. v. Dean of St. Asaph*, 3 term Rep 428n (1784).

48 *Meadow v. General Medical Council*, [2006] EWHC 146 (Admin), citing Mansfield in *Rex v. Skinner*, Lofft 54, 98 Eng. Rep. 529 (1772).

49 *R. v. Mirza (Shabbir Ali)*, [2004] UKHL 2; [2004] H.R.L.R. 11, citing Mansfield in *Vaise v. Delaval*, 1 T.R. 11, 99 Eng. Rep. 944.

50 *Zarkasi v. Anindita*, (UKEAT 18 Jan. 2012), citing Mansfield in *Holman v. Johnson*, 1 Cowp. 341, 343 (1775).

51 For Australia, see *Legal Services Commissioner v. Rushford* [2012] (Victoria Supreme Court), VSC 632, citing Mansfield in Ex parte Brounsall, 2 Cowp. 830, 98 Eng. Rep. 1385 (1778) for the proposition that the court's power to disbar an attorney is for protective, not punitive, reasons. For Hong Kong, see *Fu Kor Kuen Patrick v. HKSAR (Court of Final Appeal)*, HKEC 705, citing Mansfield in *Folkes v. Chadd*, 99 Eng. Rep. (1782), for the proposition that the testimony of expert witnesses is admissible in court. For India, see *K.A. Mohammed Ibrahim v. District Revenue Officer*, M.M No. 39893/2008/C4 Madras High Court (2010), on Mansfield's views on freedom of the press. For Israel, see *CA 337/62 Riezenfeld v. Jacobson* 17(2) PD 1009, 1014 [1963] (Isr.), citing Mansfield in *Holman v. Johnson*, 1 Cowp. 341 (1775), for the proposition that the court will not lend its aid to a man who bases his claim on an immoral or illegal act. For New Zealand, see *The Healy Holmberg Trading Partnership v. Grant* [2012] NZCA 451, citing Mansfield in *Blatch v. Archer*, 98 Eng. Rep. 969 (1774) for the proposition that in a trial all evidence must be weighed according to the proof which it was in the power of one side to have produced, and in the power of the other to have contradicted. For South Africa, see Stuart Woolman, Theunis Roux, and Michael Bishop in Constitutional Law of South Africa (2nd ed. 2012), ch. 64, citing Mansfield's decision on slavery in *Somerset v. Stewart*, 99 Eng. Rep. 499 (1972).

52 J. Anderson Rose, *The Necessity for Additional Common Law Judges: A Paper Read Before the Metropolitan and Provincial Law Association* (London: Butterworths, 1867), 29.

Bibliography

UNPUBLISHED PAPERS

Hamilton, William Baskerville. "The Education of Solicitor-General William Murray: A Preliminary Chronological Sketch, 1705–1742 (1936)." Unpublished paper in the Vanderbilt Collection, Olin Library, Wesleyan University.

Porter, Katherine Harriet. "Margaret, Duchess of Portland," Ph.D. thesis, Cornell University (June 1930).

Samson, Jane Dianne. "Ex Aequo et Bono: Lord Mansfield and Commercial Law," dissertation, University of Victoria (1983).

PUBLISHED ARTICLES AND PAPERS

Adams, John N. and Gwen Averley. "The Patent Specification: The Role of *Liardet v. Johnson*." *The Journal of Legal History* 7 (1986): 156–77.

Barnes, Donald G. "The Duke of Newcastle, Ecclesiastical Minister, 1724–54," *The Pacific Historical Review* 3, no. 2 (Jun. 1934): 164–91.

Beattie, J.M. "Sir John Fielding and Public Justice: The Bow Street Magistrates' Court, 1754–1780," *Law and History Review* 25 (Spring 2007): 61–100.

Campbell, Sybil. "The Economic and Social Effect of the Usury Laws in the Eighteenth Century." *Transactions of the Royal Historical Society*, 4th Series, 16 (1933): 197–210.

Devereaux, Simon. "The Making of the Penitentiary Act, 1775–1779," *The Historical Journal* 42, no. 2 (Jun. 1999): 405–33.

– "Recasting the Theatre of Execution: The Abolition of the Tyburn Ritual," *Past & Present*. Oxford: Oxford University Press. Issue 202 (2009): 127–74.

Ferguson, Angus H. "The Lasting Legacy of a Bigamous Duchess: The Benchmark Precedent for Medical Confidentiality," *Social History of Medicine* 19, no. 1 (2006): 37–53.

Hayes, James. "Scottish Officers in the British Army 1714–63," *The Scottish Historical Review* 37, no. 123, part 1 (Apr. 1958): 23–33.

Hulme, E.W. "On the History of Patent Law in the Seventeenth and Eighteenth Centuries," *Law Quarterly Review* 18 (1902): 284.

Langbein, John H. "The Criminal Trial before the Lawyers," *University of Chicago Law Review* 45 (1978): 263.

– "Shaping the Eighteenth-Century Criminal Trial: A View from the Ryder Sources," *University of Chicago Law Review* 50 (1983): 1.

Longley, John. "Observations on the Trial by Jury: Particularly on the Unanimity Required in the Verdict (1812)." *Pamphleteer* X, 5 (Feb. 1812): 331–52.

Lowry, S. Todd. "Lord Mansfield and the Law Merchant: Law and Economics in the Eighteenth Century," *Journal of Economic Issues* 7, no. 4 (Dec. 1973): 605.

McKenzie, Andrea. "'This Death Some Strong and Stout Hearted Man Doth Choose': The Practice of Peine Forte et Dure in Seventeenth- and Eighteenth-Century England," *Law and History Review* 23 (Summer 2005): 279–313.

McNair, Arnold D. "Dr Johnson and the Law," *Law Quarterly Review* 68 (Jul. 1947): 302–22.

Mossoff, Adam. "Rethinking the Development of Patents: An Intellectual History, 1550–1800," *Hastings Law Journal* 52 (2001): 1255.

Mullett, Charles F. "The Corporations Act and Election of English Protestant Dissenters to Corporation Offices," *Virginia Law Review* 21, no. 6 (Apr. 1935): 641–64.

Noakes, Robert Aubrey. "Lord Mansfield and Toleration," *The Month* (Aug. 1940): 85–92.

Oldham, James. "Law-making at *Nisi Prius* in the Early 1800s," *Journal of Legal History* 25, no. 3 (Dec. 2004): 221–47.

– "New Light on Mansfield and Slavery," *Journal of British Studies* 27, no. 1 (Jan. 1988): 45–68.

– "The Work of Ryder and Murray as Law Officers of the Crown," Thomas G. Watkin, ed., *Proceedings of the Eighth British Legal History Conference*, Cardiff (1987): 157.

Rose, J. Anderson. "The Necessity for Additional Common Law Judges," *Paper Read before the Metropolitan and Provincial Law Association*. London: Butterworths, 1867.

Samson, Jane Dianne. "Lord Mansfield and Negotiable Instruments," *Dalhousie Law Journal* 11, no. 3 (1987–88): 931.

Sayre, Francis Bowes. "Criminal Attempts," *Harvard Law Review* 41(1928): 821.

Shientag, Bernard L. "Lord Mansfield Revisited: A Modern Assessment," *Fordham Law Review* 10 (1941): 345.

Steedman, Carolyn. "Lord Mansfield's Women," *Past & Present*. Oxford: Oxford University Press. Issue 176 (1952): 105.

Temperley, H.W.V. "Inner and Outer Cabinet and Privy Council, 1679–1783," *English Historical Review* 27, no. 108 (Oct. 1912): 682–99.

BOOKS

Abbott, Elizabeth. *Sugar: A Bittersweet History*. London and New York: Duckworth Overlook, 2008.

Ackermann, Rudolph. *The History of Westminster School: Dedicated to the Very Rev. the Dean and the Rev. the Prebendaries of the Collegiate Church of St Peter's, Westminster*. London: R. Ackermann, 1816.

Ackroyd, Peter. *London: The Biography*. London: Chatto and Windus, 2000.

Adams, Charles F. *The Works of John Adams, Second President of the United States: With a Life of the Author, Notes, and Illustrations, by His Grandson Charles Francis Adams*. 10 vols. Boston: Little, Brown and Co., 1850–56.

Adams, Charles K., ed. *Representative British Orations, with Introductions and Explanatory Notes by Charles Kendall Adams*. 3 vols. New York and London: G.P. Putnam's Sons, 1884.

Adams, John. *Elegant Anecdotes, and Bon-mots, of the Greatest Princes, Politicians, Philosophers, Orators, and Wits of Modern Times; ... Calculated to Inspire the Minds of Youth with Noble, Virtuous, Generous, and Liberal Sentiments*. 3rd ed. London: C. and G. Kearsley, 1794.

Adams, W.H. Davenport. *Learned in the Law; or, Examples and Encouragements from the Lives of Eminent Lawyers*. London: S.W. Partridge and Co., 1882.

Aden, John M. *Something like Horace: Studies in the Art and Allusion of Pope's Horatian Satires*. Nashville: Vanderbilt University Press, 1969.

Airy, Reginald. *Westminster ... With Fifty-One Illustrations*. Handbooks to the Great Public Schools. London: G. Bell and Sons, 1902.

Almon, John. *Biographical, Literary, and Political Anecdotes, of Several of the Most Eminent Persons of the Present Age*. 3 vols. London: T.N. Longman, and L.B. Seeley, 1797.

Alschuler, Albert W. *Law without Values: The Life, Work, and Legacy of Justice Holmes*. Chicago and London: University of Chicago Press, 2000.

Anderson, Frances E. *Christopher Smart*. New York: Twayne Publishers, 1974.

Anson, Elizabeth and Florence, eds. *Mary Hamilton, afterwards Mrs John Dickenson, at Court and at Home. From Letters and Diaries, 1756 to 1816*. London: J. Murray, 1925.

Appleton, William. *Charles Macklin: An Actor's Life*. Cambridge, MA: Harvard University Press, 1960.

Archer, William, ed. *Eminent Actors*. London: Kegan Paul, Trench, Trubner and Co., Ltd, 1891.

Austin, John. *Lectures on Jurisprudence or the Philosophy of Positive Law*. Revised and edited by Robert Campbell. 5th ed. 2 vols. London: John Murray, 1885.

Baines, F.E., ed. *Records of the Manor, Parish, and Borough of Hampstead, in the County of London*. London: Whittaker and Co., 1890.

Baines, Paul. *Edmund Curll, Bookseller*. Oxford: Clarendon Press, 2007.

Baker, John H. *An Introduction to English Legal History*. 2nd ed. London: Butterworths, 1979.

Barker, G.F. Russell, and Alan H. Stenning. *The Record of Old Westminsters: A Biographical List of All Those Who Are Known to Have Been Educated at Westminster School from the Earliest Times to 1927*. 2 vols. London: Chiswick Press, 1928.

Barker, Hannah and Elaine Chalus, eds. *Women's History: Britain, 1700–1850, an Introduction*. London and New York: Routledge, 2005.

Beattie, James. *An Essay on the Nature and Immutability of Truth*. London: Edward and Charles Dilly; Edinburgh: William Creech, 1778.

Beattie, J.M. *Crime and the Courts in England, 1660–1800*. Oxford: Clarendon Press, 1986.

Beavan, Arthur H. James and Horace Smith. *A Family Narrative Based upon Hitherto Unpublished Private Diaries, Letters, and Other Documents ... With Five Portraits*. London: Hurst and Blackett, 1899.

Bell, J.J. *The Glory of Scotland*. London: G. G. Harrap and Co., [1932].

Bellamy, George Anne. *An Apology for the Life of George Anne Bellamy, Late of Covent Garden Theatre, Written by Herself*. 6 vols. London, 1785.

Bellot, Hugh H.L. *The Inner and Middle Temple: Legal, Literary, and Historic Associations ... With Ninety Illustrations*. London: Methuen and Co., 1902.

Bernstein, Jeremy. *Dawning of the Raj; The Life and Trials of Warren Hastings*. Chicago: Iva R. Dee, 2000.

Besant, Sir Walter. *The History of London*. London: Longmans, Green, and Co., 1893.

– *London in the Eighteenth Century*. London: Adam and Charles Black, 1903.

Bill, E.G.W. *Education at Christ Church Oxford 1660–1800*. Oxford: Clarendon Press, 1988.

Birkenhead, Earl of. *Famous Trials of History*. 2 vols. New York: Clark Boardman, Ltd, 1929.

Bishop, Joel Prentiss. *New Criminal Procedure or New Commentaries on the Law of Pleading and Evidence and the Practice in Criminal Cases*. Edited by R.H. Underhill. 2nd ed. 3 vols. Chicago: T.H. Flood and Company, 1913.

Black, Jeremy. *George III: America's Last King*. New Haven: Yale University Press, 2006.

Black's Guide to Scotland. 15th ed. London: Adam and Charles Black, 1920.

Blackstone, William. *The Commentaries on the Laws and Constitution of England*. London, 1796.

Blumrosen, Alfred W. and Ruth G. Blumrosen. *Slave Nation: How Slavery United the Colonies and Sparked the American Revolution*. Naperville, Illinois: Sourcebooks, Inc., 2005.

Boaden, James, ed. *The Private Correspondence of David Garrick*. 2 vols. London: H. Colburn and R. Bentley, 1831–32.

Bolton, Arthur T. *The Architecture of Robert and James Adam, 1758–1794*. 2 vols. London: Country Life and George Newnes; New York: C. Scribner's Sons, 1922.

Borman, Tracy. *King's Mistress, Queen's Servant: The Life and Times of Henrietta Howard*. London: Pimlico, 2008.

Boswell, James. *Boswell, the English Experiment 1785–1789*. Edited by Irma S. Lustig and Frederick A. Pottle. New York: McGraw-Hill, *c.*1986.

– *Boswell for the Defence, 1769–1774*. Edited by William K. Wimsatt Jr and Frederick A. Pottle. New York: McGraw-Hill, 1959.

– *Boswell: The Great Biographer, 1789–1795*. Edited by Marlies K. Danziger and Frank Brady. New York: McGraw-Hill, *c.*1989.

– *Boswell on the Grand Tour: Italy, Corsica and France, 1765–1766*. Edited by Frank Brady and Frederick A. Pottle. New York: McGraw-Hill, 1955.

– *Boswell's Life of Johnson, Including Boswell's Journal of a Tour to the Hebrides, and Johnson's Diary of a Journey into North Wales*. Edited by George Birkbeck Hill. 6 vols. Oxford: Clarendon Press, 1887.

– *The Heart of Boswell: Six Journals in One Volume*. Edited by Mark Harris. New York: McGraw-Hill, *c.*1981.

– *Journal of a Tour to the Hebrides with Samuel Johnson, LL.D.* New York: The Literary Guild, 1936.

– *Letters of James Boswell*. Collected and edited by Chauncey Brewster Tinker. 2 vols. Oxford: Clarendon Press, 1924.

– *The Life of Samuel Johnson, LL.D.* Oxford, 1887.

– *Private Papers of James Boswell from Malahide Castle: In the Collection of Lt Colonel Ralph Heyward Isham*. Prepared for the press by Geoffrey Scott and Frederick A. Pottle. New York: W.E. Rudge, [1928]–34.

Boxer, C.R. *The Portuguese Seaborne Empire 1415–1825*. London: Hutchinson and Co., 1969.

Brougham, Lord Henry. *Sketches of Statesmen of the Time of George III*. London: Richard Griffin and Co., 1856.

Browne, James. *A History of the Highlands and of the Highland* Clans. 4 vols. London, Edinburgh, and Dublin: A. Fullarton and Co., 1851

Browning, Oscar, ed. *The Political Memoranda of Francis Fifth Duke of Leeds*. Westminster: Printed for the Camden Society, 1884.

Browning, Reed, *The Duke of Newcastle*. New Haven and London: Yale University Press, 1975.

Bryce, James, Viscount. *Studies in History and Jurisprudence*. 2 vols. Oxford: Clarendon Press, 1901.

Brydges, Sir Egerton S. *A Biographical Peerage of the Empire of Great Britain: In Which Are Memoirs and Characters of the Most Celebrated Persons of Each Family*. 4 vols. London: J. Johnson, 1808–17.

Buchan, John. *Some Eighteenth Century Byways, and Other Essays*. Edinburgh and London: W. Blackwood and Sons, 1908.

Bullion, John L. *A Great and Necessary Measure: George Grenville and the Genesis of the Stamp Act: 1763–1765*. Columbia, MO: University of Missouri Press, 1982.

Burney, Fanny. *The Early Diary of Frances Burney, 1768–1778, with a Selection from Her Correspondence, and from the Journals of Her Sisters Susan and Charlotte Burney*. Edited by Annie Raine Ellis. 2 vols. London: George Bell and Sons, 1889.

Butterwick, Richard. *Poland's Last King and English Culture: Stanislaw August Ponia-*

towski, 1732–1798. Oxford: Clarendon Press; New York: Oxford University Press, 1998.

Campbell, John, Baron. *The Lives of the Chief Justices of England: From the Norman Conquest till the Death of Lord Mansfield*. 2 vols. London: John Murray, 1849.

– *The Lives of the Lord Chancellors and Keepers of the Great Seal of England, from the Earliest Times till the Reign of King George IV*. 7 vols. Philadelphia: Blanchard and Lea, 1851.

Cannon, John Ashton. *Aristocratic Century: The Peerage of Eighteenth-Century England*. Cambridge: Cambridge University Press, 1984.

Carlyle, Alexander. *Autobiography of the Rev. Dr Alexander Carlyle, Minister of Inveresk, Containing Memorials of the Men and Events of His Time*. Edited by John H. Burton. Edinburgh: W. Blackwood and Sons, 1860.

Carswell, John. *The South Sea Bubble*. Dover, NH: Alan Sutton, 1993.

Cash, Arthur H. *John Wilkes: The Scandalous Father of Civil Liberty*. New Haven, CT: Yale University Press, 2006.

Chalmers, George. *Opinions of Eminent Lawyers on Various Points of English Jurisprudence, Chiefly Concerning the Colonies, Fisheries and Commerce of Great Britain: Collected and Digested, from the Originals in the Board of Trade and Other Depositories*. Burlington, VT: C. Goodrich and Co., 1858.

Chatten, Elizabeth N. *Samuel Foote*. Boston: Twayne Publishers, 1980.

Christie, Ian R. *Crisis of Empire, Britain and the American Colonies, 1754–1783*. London: Edward Arnold, 1966.

Clark, J.C.D. *The Dynamics of Change: The Crisis of the 1750s and English Party Systems*. Cambridge: Cambridge University Press, 1982.

Cokayne, George E. *The Complete Peerage of England, Scotland, Ireland, Great Britain and the United Kingdom, Extant, Extinct, or Dormant*. London: G. Bell and Sons, 1898.

Colley, Linda. *Britons: Forging the Nation 1707–1837*. 2nd ed. New Haven and London: Yale University Press, 2005.

Collins, Arthur. *Collins's Peerage of England ... Greatly Augmented, and Continued to the Present Time, by Sir Egerton Brydges*. 9 vols. London: F.C. and J. Rivington, 1812.

Colville, Olivia Spencer-Churchill. *Duchess Sarah*. London, New York, and Bombay: Longmans, Green, and Co., 1904.

Conway, Stephen. *War, State, and Society in Mid-Eighteenth-Century Britain and Ireland*. Oxford: Oxford University Press, 2006.

Cook, Don. *The Long Fuse: How England Lost the American Colonies, 1760–1785*. New York: The Atlantic Monthly Press, 1995.

Cooke, William. *Memoirs of Samuel Foote*. 2 vols. New York: Peter A. Mesier, 1806.

Cornwallis, Charles. *Correspondence of Charles, First Marquis Cornwallis*. Edited, with notes, by Charles Ross. 3 vols. London: John Murray, 1859.

Cowper, William. *The Correspondence of William Cowper*. Arranged in chronological order, with annotations, by Thomas Wright. 4 vols. London: Hodder and Stoughton, 1904.

– *Westminster School and the Nonsense Club*.

Coxe, William, Archdeacon of Wiltshire. *Memoirs of the Administration of the Right Honourable Henry Pelham, Collected from the Family Papers, and Other Authentic Documents*. 2 vols. London: Longman, Rees, Orme, Brown and Green, 1829.

Cradock, Joseph. *Literary and Miscellaneous Memoirs*. London: J.B. Nichols, 1826.

Cruickshanks, Eveline. *The Atterbury Plot*. New York: Palgrave Macmillan, 2004.

Cumberland, Richard. *Memoirs of Richard Cumberland. Written by Himself. Containing an Account of His Life and Writings, Interspersed with Anecdotes and Characters of Several of the Most Distinguished Persons of His Time, with Whom He Has Had Intercourse and Connexion*. 2 vols. London: Lackington, Allen and Co., 1807.

Cunningham, Peter, ed. *The Letters of Horace Walpole*. London: R. Bentley, 1857–59.

Cunningham, Timothy. *The Law of Simony: Containing, All the Statutes, Cases at Large, Arguments, Resolutions, and Judgments Concerning It, etc*. London: Printed by His Majesty's Law-Printers; sold by G. Robinson, 1784.

Curwen, Samuel. *Journal and Letters of the Late Samuel Curwen, Judge of Admiralty, etc., an American Refugee in England, from 1775 to 1784, Comprising Remarks on the Prominent Men and Measures of that Period: To which Are Added, Biographical Notices of Many American Loyalists and Other Eminent Persons*. Edited by George Atkinson Ward. 4th ed. Boston: Little, Brown and Co., 1864.

Darlington, Richard. *Diary and Notes*, 1860.

Davies, Norman. *God's Playground: A History of Poland*. 2 vols. New York: Columbia University Press, 2005.

Davis, David Brion. *The Problem of Slavery in the Age of Revolution 1770–1823*. New York: Oxford University Press, 1999.

Debrett's Illustrated Peerage and Baronetage. London: Debrett's Peerage Ltd and MacMillan) [Published every 5 years.]

De Castro, John Paul. *The Gordon Riots*. London: H. Milford, Oxford University Press, 1926.

Delany, Mary. *The Autobiography and Correspondence of Mary Granville, Mrs Delany: With Interesting Reminiscences of King George the Third and Queen Charlotte*. Edited by the Right Honourable Lady Llanover. 3 vols. London: R. Bentley, 1861.

Dicey, Albert V. *Lectures on the Relation Between Law and Public Opinion in England During the Nineteenth Century*. London: Macmillan and Co., 1914.

Dickenson, Mary Hamilton. *Mary Hamilton, afterwards Mrs John Dickenson, at Court and at Home. From Letters and Diaries, 1756 to 1816, Edited by her Great-Granddaughters, Elizabeth and Florence Anson*. London: John Murray, 1925.

Dickinson, H.T., ed. *Britain and the American Revolution*. London and New York: Longman, 1998.

Dodington, George Bubb, Baron of Melcombe Regis. *The Diary of the Late George Bubb Dodington, Baron of Melcombe Regis: From March 8, 1749, to February 6, 1761. With an Appendix, Containing Some Curious and Interesting Papers, Which Are Either Referred to, or Alluded to, in the Diary*. Published From His Lordship's Original Manuscripts, by Henry Penruddocke Wyndham. Salisbury: E. Easton, 1783.

Douglas, Sylvester, Baron Glenbervie. *The Diaries of Sylvester Douglas, Lord Glenbervie*. Edited by Francis Bickley. 2 vols. London: Constable and Co.; Boston and New York: Houghton Mifflin Co., 1928.

Drescher, Seymour. *Abolition: A History of Slavery and Antislavery*. New York: Cambridge University Press, 2009.

– *Capitalism and Antislavery: British Mobilization in Comparative Perspective*. New York and Oxford: Oxford University Press, 1987.

Duff, James, Second Earl of Fife. *Lord Fife and His Factor: Being the Correspondence of James, Second Lord Fife, 1729–1809*. Edited by Alistair and Henrietta Tayler. London: William Heinemann, 1925.

Dyos, H.J. and D.H. Aldcroft. *British Transport: An Economic Survey from the Seventeenth Century to the Twentieth*. Leicester: Leicester University Press, 1969.

Eden, William, Baron Auckland. *The Journal and Correspondence of William, Lord Auckland*. With a preface and introduction by the Bishop of Bath and Wells. Edited by George Hogge. 4 vols. London: R. Bentley, 1861–62.

Edgar, John G. *The Boyhood of Great Men: Intended as an Example to Youth*. 4th ed. London: David Bogue, 1857.

Evans, Arthur W. *Warburton and the Warburtonians: A Study in Some Eighteenth-Century Controversies*. London: Oxford University Press, 1932.

Fifoot, Cecil H.S. *Lord Mansfield*. Oxford: Clarendon Press, 1936. Reprint, Darmstadt: Scientia Verlag Aalen, 1977.

Fitzgerald, Percy H. *A Famous Forgery*. London: Chapman and Hall, 1865.

– *The Life and Times of John Wilkes, M.P., Lord Mayor of London, and Chamberlain*. 2 vols. London: Ward and Downey, 1888.

– *Samuel Foote: A Biography*. London: Chatto and Windus, 1910.

Fitzmaurice, Edmund G.P. *Life of William, Earl of Shelburne, afterwards first Marquess of Lansdowne: With Extracts from His Papers and Correspondence*. 2 vols. London: Macmillan and Co., 1875. Reprint, Elibron Classics, Adamant Media Corp., 2006.

Foot, Jesse. *The Life of Arthur Murphy, Esq*. London: J. Faulder, 1811.

Forbes, Esther. *Paul Revere and the World He Lived in*. Boston: Houghton Mifflin Co., 1942.

Forbes, Margaret. *Beattie and His Friends*. Westminster: Archibald Constable and Co., 1904.

Forshall, Frederic H. *Westminster School: Past and Present*. London: Wyman and Sons, 1884.

Forster, John. *Biographical Essays*. London: John Murray, 3rd ed. 1860.

Forsyth, William. *History of Trial by Jury*. Prepared by James Appleton Morgan. 2nd ed., 1875.

Fortescue, Sir John W. *The Correspondence of King George the Third from 1760 to December 1783: Printed From the Original Papers in the Royal Archives at Windsor Castle*. 6 vols. London: Macmillan and Co., 1927–28.

Foss, Edward. *The Judges of England; With Sketches of Their Lives, and Miscellaneous No-*

tices Connected with the Courts at Westminster, from the Time of the Conquest. 9 vols. London: Longman, Brown, Green, and Longmans, 1848–64.

Foster, Sir Michael. *A Report of Some Proceedings on the Commission of Oyer and Terminer and Goal Delivery for the Trial of the Rebels in the Year 1746 in the County of Surry, and of Other Crown Cases: To Which Are Added Discourses upon a Few Branches of the Crown Law.* With Additional Notes and References by His Nephew, Michael Dodson. 3rd ed. London: E. and R. Brooke, 1792.

Fox, Henry. *Letters to Henry Fox, Lord Holland, with a Few Addressed to His Brother Stephen, Earl of Ilchester.* Edited by the Earl of Ilchester. London: Privately printed for presentation to the members of the Roxburghe Club, 1915.

Franklin, Benjamin. *The Writings of Benjamin Franklin.* Collected and edited, with a life and introduction, by Albert Henry Smyth. 10 vols. New York and London: Macmillan and Co., 1905–07.

Friedman, Lawrence M. *A History of American Law.* 2nd ed. New York: Simon and Schuster, Inc., 1985.

Furber, Holden. *Henry Dundas, First Viscount Melville, 1742–1811: Political Manager of Scotland, Statesman, Administrator of British India.* London: Oxford University Press, 1931.

Gell, Edith M. *Under Three Reigns, 1860–1920.* London: Kegan Paul, Trench, Trubner and Co., 1927.

George, M. Dorothy. *England in Transition: Life and Work in the Eighteenth Century.* London: G. Routledge and Sons, 1931.

George III, King of Great Britain. *Letters from George III to Lord Bute, 1756–1766.* Edited with an introduction by Romney Sedgwick. London: Macmillan and Co., 1939.

Gibbon, Edward. *The Miscellaneous Works of Edward Gibbon, Esq., with Memoirs of His Life and Writings, Composed by Himself: Illustrated from His Letters, with Occasional Notes and Narrative, by the John Lord Sheffield.* 2 vols. London, 1796.

Giftis, Steven H. *Law Dictionary.* 5th ed. New York: Barron's, 2003.

Gleig, George R. *Memoirs of the Life of the Right Hon. Warren Hastings, First Governor-General of Bengal.* 3 vols. London: Richard Bentley, 1841.

Goodeve. *Lord Mansfield, C.J.: A Founder's Day Speech at Christ Church, Oxford, June 17, 1865.*

Gore-Browne, Robert. *Chancellor Thurlow: The Life and Times of an XVIIIth Century Lawyer.* London: Hamish Hamilton, 1953.

Graham, Henry G. *The Social Life of Scotland in the Eighteenth Century.* 4th ed. London: Adam and Charles Black, 1937.

Gray, Thomas. *Correspondence of Thomas Gray.* Edited by the late Paget Toynbee and Leonard Whibley. 3 vols. Oxford: Clarendon Press, 1935.

Great Britain, Home Office. *Calendar of Home Office Papers of the Reign of George III: 1760 (25 Oct.)–1765 [etc.] Preserved in Her Majesty's Public Record Office.* [vols. 1, 2] Edited by J. Redington. [vols. 3, etc.] Edited by R.A. Roberts. London: Longman and Co., 1878.

Great Britain, Privy Council. *Acts of the Privy Council of England: Colonial Series*. Edited through the direction of the Lord President of the Council by W.L. Grant and James Munro, under the general supervision of Almeric W. Fitzroy. 6 vols. Hereford, 1908–66.

Grenville, Richard, Earl Temple. *The Grenville Papers: Being the Correspondence of Richard Grenville, Earl Temple, K.G., and the Right Hon. George Grenville, Their Friends and Contemporaries*. Edited, with notes, by William James Smith. 4 vols. London: John Murray, 1852–53.

Guttridge, George H. *The Early Career of Lord Rockingham: 1730–1765*. Berkeley: University of California Press, 1952.

– *English Whiggism and the American Revolution*. Berkeley and Los Angeles: University of California Press, 1966.

Halliday, Paul D. *Habeas Corpus: From England to Empire*. Cambridge, MA, and London: Harvard University Press, 2010.

Hammond, Brean S. *Pope and Bolingbroke: A Study of Friendship and Influence*. Columbia: University of Missouri Press, 1984.

Harris, Bob. *Politics and the Nation: Britain in the Mid-Eighteenth Century*. Oxford and New York: Oxford University Press, 2002.

Harris, Eileen. *The Country Houses of Robert Adam*. London: Aurum Press Limited, 2007.

Harris, Frances. *A Passion for Government: The Life of Sarah, Duchess of Marlborough*. Oxford: Clarendon Press, 1991.

Harris, George. *The Life of Lord Chancellor Hardwicke: With Selections from His Correspondence, Diaries, Speeches, and Judgements*. 3 vols. London: E. Moxon, 1847.

Harrison, Frederic. *Chatham: Series on Twelve English Statesmen*. London: Macmillan and Co., 1905.

Haslip, Joan. *Lady Hester Stanhope: A Biography*. London: Cobden-Sanderson, 1934.

Hawkins, Laetitia Matilda. *Memoirs, Anecdotes, Facts, and Opinions*. 2 vols. London: Longman, Hurst, Rees, Orme, Brown, and Green, 1824.

Hayward, Abraham. *Lord Chesterfield and George Selwyn*. N.p., Longman, 1854.

Headlam, Cecil. *The Inns of Court: Painted by Gordon Home, described by C. Headlam*. London: Adam and Charles Black, 1909.

Henley, Robert, First Earl of Northington, Lord Chancellor of England. *Reports of Cases Argued and Determined in the High Court of Chancery, from 1757 to 1766: From the Original Manuscripts of Lord Chancellor Northington. Collected and arranged, with notes and references to former and subsequent determinations, and to the Register's books, by the Honourable Robert Henley Eden*. 2nd ed. 2 vols. London: 1827.

Hervey, Mary Lepell, Baroness. *Letters of Mary Lepel, Lady Hervey: With a Memoir and Illustrative Notes*. Edited by Edmund Morris. London: John Murray, 1821.

Heward, Edmund. *Lord Mansfield*. Chichester and London: Barry Rose, 1979

Hirst, Francis W. *Adam Smith. English Men of Letters*. London: Macmillan and Co., 1904.

Holdsworth, Sir William S. *A History of English Law*. 16 vols. London: Methuen and Co. Ltd; Sweet and Maxwell, 1938.

– *Some Makers of English Law: The Tagore Lectures, 1937–38*. Cambridge: Cambridge University Press, 1966.

Holmes, Geoffrey and Daniel Szechi. *The Age of Oligarchy: Pre-Industrial Britain 1722–1783*. London and New York: Longman, 1993.

Horton, John Theodore. *James Kent: A Study in Conservatism 1763–1847*. New York and London: D. Appleton-Century Company, Inc., 1939.

Horwitz, Morton J. *The Transformation of American Law: 1780–1860*. Cambridge, MA, and London: Harvard University Press, 1977.

Hostettler, John. *A History of Criminal Justice in England and Wales*. Winchester, Waterside Press, 2009.

Howson, Gerald. *The Macaroni Parson: The Life of the Unfortunate Doctor Dodd*. London: Hutchinson and Co., 1973.

Hume, David. *The Letters of David Hume*. Edited by J.Y.T. Greig. 2 vols. Oxford: Clarendon Press, 1932.

Hunt, Leigh. *The Town: Its Memorable Characters and Events*. London: Smith, Elder and Co., 1848.

Hutton, James. *A Hundred Years Ago: An Historical Sketch, 1755 to 1756*. London: Longman, 1857.

Ilchester, Giles S.H., Earl. *Henry Fox, First Lord Holland: His Family and Relations*. 2 vols. London: John Murray, 1920.

Jeaffreson, John C. *A Book About Lawyers*. 2 vols. London: Hurst and Blackett, 1867.

Jefferson, Thomas. *The Writings of Thomas Jefferson*. Memorial Edition. Edited by Andrew A. Lipscomb and Albert Ellery Bergh. 20 vols. Issued under the auspices of the Thomas Jefferson Memorial Association of the United States, Washington, DC, 1904–05.

Jesse, John Heneage. *Memoirs of Celebrated Etonians*. 2 vols. London: Richard Bentley and Son, 1875.

Johns, Adrian. *Piracy: The Intellectual Property Wars from Gutenberg to Gates*. Chicago and London: University of Chicago Press, 2009.

Johnson, Samuel. *Sir Joshua's Nephew, being Letters Written, 1769–1778, by a Young Man to His Sisters*. Edited by his great-great-great-niece, Susan M. Radcliffe. London: J. Murray, 1930.

Johnson, William S. *The Superior Court Diary of William Samuel Johnson, 1772–1773, with Appropriate Records and File Papers of the Superior Court of the Colony of Connecticut for the Terms, December 1772, through March 1773*. Edited by John T. Farrell, etc. Washington, DC: American Historical Association, 1942.

Jones, Benjamin M. *Henry Fielding, Novelist and Magistrate*. London: G. Allen and Unwin, 1933.

Kelch, Ray A. *Newcastle: A Duke without Money: Thomas Pelham-Holles 1693–1768*. London: Routledge and Kegan Paul, 1974.

Kenyon, George T. *The Life of Lloyd, First Lord Kenyon, Lord Chief Justice of England*. London: Longmans, Green, 1873.

Kerly, Duncan M. *An Historical Sketch of the Equitable Jurisdiction of the Court of Chancery*. Cambridge: Cambridge University Press, 1890.

Kilvert, Francis. *Memoirs of the Life and Writings of the Right Rev. Richard Hurd. With a selection from his correspondence and other unpublished papers*. London: Richard Bentley, 1860.

Knight, Charles. *Gallery of Portraits with Memoirs*. 7 vols. London: C. Knight, 1833–37.

Landau, Norma, ed. *Law, Crime and English Society, 1660–1830*. Cambridge, UK; New York: Cambridge University Press, 2002.

Langford, Paul, ed. *The Eighteenth Century, 1688–1815*. Oxford: Oxford University Press, 2002.

– *The First Rockingham Administration: 1765–1766*. London: Oxford University Press, 1973.

– *A Polite and Commercial People: England, 1727–1783*. The New Oxford History of England. New York: Oxford University Press, 1989.

– *Public Life and the Propertied Englishman, 1689–1798*. Oxford: Clarendon Press; New York: Oxford University Press, 1991.

Lecky, William E.H. *A History of England in the Eighteenth Century*. 8 vols. New York: D. Appleton and Company, 1892.

Ledward, K.H., ed. *Journals of the Board of Trade and Plantations: January 1735–1741*. vol. 7. London, n.d.

Lemmings, David. *Professors of the Law: Barristers and English Legal Culture in the Eighteenth Century*. Oxford: Oxford University Press, 2000.

Lenman, Bruce. *The Jacobite Uprisings in Britain, 1689–1746*. London: Eyre Methuen, 1980.

Lieberman, David. *The Province of Legislation Determined: Legal Theory in Eighteenth-Century Britain*. Cambridge: Cambridge University Press, 1989.

Little, David M. and George M. Kahrl, eds. *The Letters of David Garrick*. 3 vols. London: Oxford University Press, 1963.

Locke, John. *Two Treatises of Government*. Everyman's Library. Edited by Ernest Rhys. London: J.M. Dent and Sons Ltd; New York: E.P. Dutton and Co. Inc., 1943.

Lockmiller, David A. *Sir William Blackstone*. Chapel Hill, NC: University of North Carolina Press, 1938.

Lovat-Fraser, James A. *Erskine*. Cambridge: Cambridge University Press, 1932.

– *John Stuart Earl of Bute*. Cambridge: Cambridge University Press, 1912.

Lyon, Hastings. *The Constitution and the Men Who Made It: The Story of the Constitutional Convention, 1787*. Boston and New York: Houghton Mifflin Co., 1936.

Mack, Maynard. *Alexander Pope: A Life*. New York and London: W.W. Norton and Company, 1985.

Macnight, Thomas. *Life of Henry St John, Viscount Bolingbroke*. London: Chapman and Hall, 1863.

Magnus, Sir Philip. *Edmund Burke: A Life*. London: John Murray, 1939.

Marsden, Reginald G. *Documents Relating to Law and Custom of the Sea*. 2 vols. Greenwich: Navy Records Society, 1915–16.

Marshall, William. *Historic Scenes in Perthshire*. Edinburgh: W. Oliphant, 1880.

Martin, Sir Theodore. *A Life of Lord Lyndhurst from Letters and Papers in Possession of His Family*. London: John Murray, 1883.

Mathew, Theobald. *For Lawyers and Others*. London: William Hodge and Co., 1937.

Matthew, H.C.G. and Brian Harrison, eds. *Oxford Dictionary of National Biography: in association with the British Academy: from the earliest times to the year 2000*. 61 vols. Oxford: Oxford University Press, 2004.

May, Thomas Erskine. *The Constitutional History of England since the Accession of George the Third, 1760–1860*. 2 vols. New York: A.C. Armstrong and Son, 1899.

Melville, Lewis [Lewis S. Benjamin]. *Lady Suffolk and Her Circle*. London: Hutchinson and Co., 1924.

Middleton, Richard. *The Bells of Victory: The Pitt-Newcastle Ministry and the Conduct of the Seven Years War, 1757–1762*. Cambridge: Cambridge University Press, 1985.

Midgely, Graham. *University Life in Eighteenth-Century Oxford*. New Haven: Yale University Press, 1996.

Montagu, Elizabeth R. *Elizabeth Montagu, the Queen of the Blue-Stockings, Her Correspondence from 1720 to 1761*. Edited by her great-great-niece, Emily J. Climenson. 2 vols. London: John Murray; New York: E.P. Dutton, 1906.

– *Mrs Montagu, "Queen of the Blues," Her Letters and Friendships from 1762 to 1800*. Edited by Reginald Blunt from material left to him by [and in continuation of the collection edited by] her great-great-niece Emily J. Climenson. 2 vols. London: Constable and Co., *c.* 1923.

Montagu, Lady Mary Wortley. *The Letters and Works of Lady Mary Wortley Montagu*. Edited by her great-grandson, Lord Wharncliffe. London: R. Bentley, 1837.

Moore, Frank F. *The Life of Oliver Goldsmith … With Nine Illustrations*. London: Constable and Co., 1910.

Morgan, E. Victor and W.A. Thomas. *The Stock Exchange: Its History and Functions*. London: Elek Books, 1962.

Mounsey, Chris. *Christopher Smart: Clown of God*. Lewisburg, PA: Bucknell University Press, 2001.

Mowbray, Sir John. *Seventy Years at Westminster*. Edinburgh and London: W. Blackwood and Sons, 1898.

Namier, Sir Lewis B. *England in the Age of the American Revolution*. London: Macmillan and Co., 1930.

– *The Structure of Politics at the Accession of George III*. London: Macmillan and Co., 1929.

Namier, Sir Lewis B. and John Brooke. *The House of Commons: 1754–1790*. 3 vols. New York: Published for the History of Parliament Trust by Oxford University Press, 1964.

The New Statistical Account of Scotland: By the Ministers of the Respective Parishes, Under the Superintendence of a Committee of the Society for the Benefit of the Sons and Daughters of the Clergy. 15 vols. Edinburgh and London: W. Blackwood and Sons, 1845.

Nichols, John. *Illustrations of the Literary History of the Eighteenth Century: Consisting of*

Authentic Memoirs and Original Letters of Eminent Persons, and Intended as a Sequel to the "Literary Anecdotes." 8 vols. London: Nichols, Son and Bentley, 1817–58.

– *Literary Anecdotes of the Eighteenth Century: Comprising Biographical Memoirs of W. Bowyer, and Many of His Learned Friends; An Incidental View of the Progress and Advancement of Literature in This Kingdom during the Last Century, and Biographical Anecdotes of a Considerable Number of Eminent Writers and Ingenious Artists; With a Very Copious Index.* 9 vols. London: Nichols, Son and Bentley, 1812–16.

Nicoll, Allardyce. *A History of English Drama 1660–1900: Late Eighteenth Century Drama 1750–1800*. Cambridge: Cambridge University Press, 1969.

Northcote, James. *The Life of Sir Joshua Reynolds*. 2 vols. London: Henry Colburn, 1818.

Northey, Sir Edward. *Legal Opinion on Cases re. America and the West Indies, 1716–1750.*

Norton-Kyshe, James William. *The Law and Privileges Relating to the Attorney-General and Solicitor-General of England*. London: Steven and Haynes, 1897.

Oldfield, Thomas H.B. *An Entire and Complete History, Political and Personal, of the Boroughs of Great Britain (Together with the Cinque Ports): To Which is Prefixed, An Original Sketch of Constitutional Rights, etc.* London, 1792.

Oldham, James. *English Common Law in the Age of Mansfield*. Studies in Legal History. Chapel Hill, NC, and London: University of North Carolina Press, 2004.

– *The Mansfield Manuscripts and the Growth of English Law in the Eighteenth Century*. 2 vols. Chapel Hill, NC, and London: University of North Carolina Press, 1992.

Osborn, Edward B. *Literature and Life: Things Seen, Heard and Read*. London: Methuen and Co., 1921.

Osborne, Francis Godolphin, Duke of Leeds. *The Political Memoranda of Francis, Fifth Duke of Leeds*. Edited, together with other papers, and with notes, introduction, and appendix, by Oscar Browning. London: Camden Society, 1884.

Oswald, James. *Memorials of the Public Life and Character of the Right Hon. James Oswald of Dunnikier: Contained in a Correspondence with Some of the Most Distinguished Men of the Last Century*. Edinburgh: Archibald Constable and Co., 1825.

Owen, John B. *The Eighteenth Century 1714–1815*. New York and London: W.W. Norton and Company, 1974.

Parker, Matthew. *The Sugar Barons: Family, Corruption, Empire, and War in the West Indies*. New York: Walker and Company, 2011.

Parkes, Joan. *Travel in England in the Seventeenth Century*. London: Oxford University Press, 1925.

Paston, George. *B.R. Haydon and His Friends*. London: James Nisbet and Co., 1905.

– *Mr Pope: His Life and Times*. 2 vols. London: Hutchinson and Co., 1909.

Paterson, James. *Curiosities of Law and Lawyers, by Croake James [pseudo]*. Albany and New York: Banks and Brothers, 1883.

Pearce, Edward. *Pitt the Elder: Man of War*. London: The Bodley Head, 2010.

Penny, George. *Traditions of Perth, Containing Sketches of the Manners and Customs of the Inhabitants, and Notices of Public Occurrences, during the Last Century; Interesting Extracts from Old Records; Notices of the Neighbouring Localities of Historical Interest*. Perth, 1836.

Perceval, John, First Earl of Egmont. *Manuscripts of the Earl of Egmont: Diary of Viscount Percival, Afterwards First Earl of Egmont*. 3 vols. London, H.M. Stationery Off., 1920–23.

Petrie, Sir Charles A. *The Jacobite Movement: The First Phase, 1688–1716*. London: Eyre and Spottiswoode, 1948.

– *The Jacobite Movement: The Last Phase, 1716–1807*. London: Eyre and Spottiswoode, 1950.

Phillimore, Robert J. *Memoirs and Correspondence of George, Lord Lyttelton, from 1734 to 1773*. 2 vols. London: J. Ridgway, 1845.

Pincus, Steve. *1688: The First Modern Revolution*. New Haven and London: Yale University Press, 2009.

Pitt, William. *Correspondence of William Pitt, Earl of Chatham*. Edited by William Stanhope Taylor and Captain John Henry Pringle. 4 vols. London: John Murray, 1838–40.

Pittock, Murray. *Jacobitism*. New York: St Martin's Press, 1998.

Pope, Alexander. *The Works of Alexander Pope*. Edited by Whitwell Elwin and William J. Courthope. 10 vols. London: John Murray, 1871–89.

Porritt, Edward, assisted by Annie G. Porritt. *The Unreformed House of Commons: Parliamentary Representation before 1832*. 2 vols. Cambridge: Cambridge University Press, 1903.

Porter, Roy. *The Creation of the Modern World: The Untold Story of the British Enlightenment*. New York and London: W.W. Norton and Company, 2000.

– *English Society in the Eighteenth Century*. Revised ed. London and New York: Penguin Books, 1991.

Potter, Harold, assisted by O. Hood Phillips. *A Short Outline of English Legal History*. 3rd ed. London: Sweet and Maxwell, 1933.

Prest, Wilfrid. *William Blackstone: Law and Letters in the Eighteenth Century*. Oxford: Oxford University Press, 2008.

Prior, James. *Memoir of the Life and Character of the Right Hon. Edmund Burke: With Specimens of His Poetry and Letters, etc.* London: Baldwin, Cradock and Joy, 1826.

Radclyffe, Charles W. *Memorials of Westminster School*. London, 1845.

Rede, Leman Thomas and Edward Wynne. *Strictures on the Lives and Characters of the Most Eminent Lawyers of the Present Day*. London: G. Kearsley, 1790.

Riker, Thad W. *Henry Fox, First Lord Holland: A Study of the Career of an Eighteenth Century Politician*. 2 vols. Oxford: Clarendon Press, 1911.

Rogers, Nicholas. *Crowds, Culture, and Politics in Georgian Britain*. Oxford: Clarendon Press; New York: Oxford University Press, 1998.

Roscoe, Henry. *Lives of Eminent British Lawyers*. London: Longman, Rees, Orme, Brown and Green, 1830.

Rose, George H., ed. *A Selection from the Papers of the Earls of Marchmont, in the Possession of the Right Hon. Sir George Henry Rose: Illustrative of Events from 1685 to 1750*. 3 vols. London: John Murray, 1831.

Rosebery, Archibald Philip Primrose, Earl. *Lord Chatham, His Early Life and Connections*. New York and London: Harper and Brothers, 1910.

Rothschild, Emma. *The Inner Life of Empires: An Eighteenth-Century History*. Princeton and Oxford: Princeton University Press, 2011.

Rowlands, Ernest Bowen. *Seventy-two Years at the Bar: A Memoir [of Sir Harry Bodkin Poland]*. London: Macmillan and Co., 1924.

Ruffhead, Owen. *The Life of Alexander Pope, Esq.: Compiled from Original Manuscripts, with a Critical Essay on His Writings and Genius*. London, 1769.

Russell, Bertrand. *A History of Western Philosophy*. New York: Simon and Schuster, 1945.

Russell, John, Fourth Duke of Bedford. *Correspondence of John, Fourth Duke of Bedford, Selected from the Originals at Woburn Abbey*. 3 vols. London: Longman, Brown, Green, and Longmans, 1842–46.

Ryder, Sir Dudley. *The Diary of Dudley Ryder, 1715–1716*. Transcribed from shorthand and edited by William Matthews. London: Methuen and Co., 1939.

Ryley, Robert M. *William Warburton*. Boston: Twayne Publishers, 1984.

Saberi, Helen. *Tea: A Global History*. London: Reaktion, 2010.

Sackville, Caroline Harriet Stopford. *The Manuscripts of Mrs Stopford Sackville of Drayton House, Northamptonshire*. [Calendared by Richard B. Knowles and William O. Hewlett.] Royal Commission on Historical Manuscripts, Report 9, vol. 3. N.p.: 1884.

Sargeaunt, John. *Annals of Westminster School*. London: Methuen and Co., 1898.

Scott, H.M. *British Foreign Policy in the Age of the American Revolution*. Oxford, UK: Clarendon Press; New York: Oxford University Press, 1990.

– *The Emergence of the Eastern Powers, 1756–1775*. Cambridge, UK; New York: Cambridge University Press, 2001.

Scott, Sir Walter, ed. *The Works of Jonathan Swift, D.D., Dean of St Patrick's, Dublin; Containing Additional Letters, Tracts, and Poems, Not Hitherto Published; with Notes and Life of the Author*. 2nd ed. Edinburgh: Archibald Constable and Co.; London: Hurst, Robinson, and Co., 1824.

Seward, William. *Anecdotes of Some Distinguished Persons, Chiefly of the Present and Two Preceding Centuries: Adorned with Sculptures*. 4 vols. London: T. Cadell and W. Davies, 1795–96.

– *Biographiana: By the Compiler of Anecdotes of Distinguished Persons*. 2 vols. London: Printed for J. Johnson, 1799.

Sexby, J.J. *The Municipal Parks, Gardens, and Open Spaces of London: Their History and Associations*. London: E. Stock, 1898.

Shapiro, Fred E., ed. *The Yale Book of Quotations*. New Haven and London: Yale University Press, 2006.

Shenstone, William. *The Letters of William Shenstone*. Arranged and edited with introduction, notes, and index by Marjorie Williams. Oxford: Basil Blackwell, 1939.

Sherburn, George Wiley, ed. *Alexander Pope, Correspondence*. 5 vols. Oxford: Clarendon Press, 1956.

Sherman, Charles P. *Roman Law in the Modern World*. 3 vols. Boston: Boston Book Co., 1917.

Shyllon, Folarin O. *Black Slaves in Britain*. London: Oxford University Press, 1974.

Sichel, Walter S. *Bolingbroke and His Times*. 2 vols. London: James Nisbet and Co., 1901–02.

Smart, Christopher. *The Annotated Letters of Christopher Smart*. Edited by Betty Rizzon and Robert Mahony. Carbondale: Southern Illinois University Press, 1991.

Smith, John T. *Antiquities of Westminster: The Old Palace; St Stephen's Chapel (Now the House of Commons). Containing Two Hundred and Forty-six Engravings of Topographical Objects, of which One Hundred and Twenty-two No Longer Remain*. London: Printed by T. Bensley for J.T. Smith, 1807–[09].

Smith, John W. *A Compendium of Mercantile Law*. Edited by J. Macdonell, assisted by G. Humphreys. 10th ed. 2 vols. London: Stevens and Sons, 1890.

Smith, William. *The Diary and Selected Papers of Chief Justice William Smith, 1784–1793*. Edited by L.F.S. Upton. 2 vols. Toronto: The Champlain Society, 1963.

Society for the Diffusion of Useful Knowledge. *The Gallery of Portraits: With Memoirs*. Under the Superintendence of the Society for the Diffusion of Useful Knowledge. Biographical sketches by Arthur T. Malkin. 7 vols. London: Charles Knight, 1833–37.

Stanhope, Philip Dormer, Fourth Earl of Chesterfield. *The Letters of Philip Dormer Stanhope, Fourth Earl of Chesterfield*. Edited by Bonamy Dobrée. 6 vols. London: Eyre and Spottiswoode; New York: Viking Press, 1932.

Stephen, James F. *A History of the Criminal Law of England*. 3 vols. London: Macmillan, 1883.

Stern, Seth and Stephen Wermiel. *Justice Brennan: Liberal Champion*. Boston and New York: Houghton Mifflin Harcourt, 2010.

Stewart, Dugald. *Account of the Life and Writings of William Robertson ... Read Before the Society of Edinburgh*. London: T. Cadell and W. Davies; Edinburgh: E. Balfour, 1801.

Stone, George Winchester, Jr and George M. Kahrl. *David Garrick: A Critical Biography*. Carbondale and Edwardsville: Southern Illinois University Press, 1979.

Stoughton, John. *Shades and Echoes of Old London*. London: Leisure House Office, 1864[?].

Surtees, William E. *A Sketch of the Lives of Lords Stowell and Eldon: Comprising, with Additional Matter, Some Corrections of Mr Twiss's Work on the Chancellor*. London: Chapman and Hall, 1846.

Sydney, William Connor. *England and the English in the Eighteenth Century: Chapters in the Social History of the Times*. 2 vols. New York: Macmillan, 1891.

Symons, Jelinger C. *William Burke the Author of Junius: An Essay on His Era*. London, 1859.

Szechi, Daniel. *1715: The Great Jacobite Rebellion*. New Haven: Yale University Press, 2006.

Tanner, Lawrence E. *Westminster School: A History*. London: Country Life, 1934.

Tayler, Henrietta, ed. *The Jacobite Court at Rome in 1719, From Original Documents at Fettercairn House and at Windsor Castle*. Edinburgh: Printed at the University Press by T. and A. Constable, for the Scottish History Society, 1938.

Temple, Richard Grenville. *The Grenville Papers*. 4 vols. New York: AMS Press, 1970.

Terry, Charles Sanford. *The Chevalier de St George and the Jacobite Movements in His Favour 1701–1720*. London: David Nutt, 1901.

Thomas, P.D.G. *British Politics and the Stamp Act Crisis: The First Phase of the American Revolution 1763–1767*. Oxford: Clarendon Press, 1975.

Thompson, Andrew C. *George II: King and Elector*. New Haven and London: Yale University Press, 2011.

Thompson, Rev. H.L. *History of Christ Church*. N.p.: n.d.

Thomson, Mrs *Memoirs of the Jacobites of 1715 and 1745*. 3 vols. London: Richard Bentley, 1846.

Tillyard, Stella. *A Royal Affair: George III and His Scandalous Siblings*. New York: Random House, 2006.

Timbs, John. *Anecdote Lives of Wits and Humourists*. 2 vols. London: Richard Bentley and Sons, 1872.

Townsend, William. *The Lives of Twelve Eminent Judges of the Last and of the Present Century*. 2 vols. London: Longman, Brown, Green, and Longmans, 1846.

Treasure, Geoffrey R.R. *Who's Who in Early Hanoverian Britain: 1714–1789*. Who's Who in British History Series, 6. Mechanicsburg, PA: Stackpole Books, 1992.

Trench, Charles Chenevix. *George II*. London: The History Book Club, 1973.

Trevelyan, G.M. *English Social History: A Survey of Six Centuries Chaucer to Queen Victoria*. London: Longmans, Green and Co., 1942.

Trevelyan, Sir George O. *The American Revolution*. Edited by Richard B. Morris. New York: D. McKay Co., 1964.

– *The Early History of Charles James Fox*. 3rd ed. London: Longmans and Co., 1881.

Tuckerman, Henry T. *The Collector: Essays on Books, Newspapers, Pictures, Inns, Authors, Doctors, Holidays, Actors, Preachers*. With an introduction by Dr [John] Doran. London: John Camden Hotten, 1868.

Turberville, Arthur S. *A History of Welbeck Abbey and Its Owners*. 2 vols. London: Faber and Faber, 1938–39.

– ed. *Johnson's England: An Account of the Life and Manners of His Age*. 2 vols. Oxford: Oxford University Press, 1933.

Turner, Edward Raymond. *The Cabinet Council of England in the Seventeenth and Eighteenth Centuries, 1622–1784*. 2 vols. New York: Russell and Russell, 1930.

Twiss, Horace. *The Public and Private Life of Lord Chancellor Eldon, with Selections from His Correspondence*. 3 vols. London: John Murray, 1844.

University of Oxford. *Alumni Oxonienses: The Members of the University of Oxford, 1715–1886: Their Parentage, Birthplace, and Year of Birth, with a Record of Their Degrees. Being the Matriculation Register of the University*. Alphabetically arranged, revised, and annotated by Joseph Foster. 4 vols. Oxford and London: Parker and Co., 1888.

Valentine, Alan. *Lord George Germain*. Oxford, UK: Clarendon Press, 1962.

Vanderbilt, Arthur T., II. *Changing Law: A Biography of Arthur T. Vanderbilt*. New Brunswick, NJ: Rutgers University Press, 1976.

Varey, Simon. *Henry St John, Viscount Bolingbroke*. Boston: Twayne Publishers, c.1984.

Vickery, Amanda. *Behind Closed Doors: At Home in Georgian England*. New Haven and London: Yale University Press, 2009.

– *The Gentleman's Daughter: Women's Lives in Georgian England*. New Haven and London: Yale University Press, 1999.

Vincent, Arthur, ed. *Lives of Twelve Bad Women: Illustrations and Reviews of Feminine Turpitude Set Forth by Impartial Hands*. London: T. Fisher Unwin, 1897.

Wakeman, Henry O. *An Introduction to the History of the Church of England from the Earliest Times to the Present Day*. London: Rivington, Percival and Co., 1896.

Waldegrave, James, Earl. *The Memoirs and Speeches of James, 2nd Earl of Waldegrave, 1742–1963*. Edited with an introduction by J.C.D. Clark. Cambridge: Cambridge University Press, 1988.

Walpole, Horace. *Horace Walpole: Memoirs and Portraits. Edited by Matthew Hodgart*. London: B.T. Batsford, 1963.

– *The Letters of Horace Walpole, Edited with Notes and Indices by Mrs Paget Toynbee*. 16 vols. Oxford: Clarendon Press, 1903–05.

– *Letters of Horace Walpole, Selected by W.S. Lewis, with an introd. by R.W. Ketton-Cremer*. London: Folio Society, 1951.

– *Memoirs of the Reign of King George II, Edited by John Brooke*. 3 vols. The Yale Edition of Horace Walpole's Memoirs. New Haven, CT, and London: Yale University Press, 1985.

– *Memoirs of the Reign of King George III*. 4 vols. London: Lawrence and Bullen, 1894.

– *Reminiscences Written by Mr Horace Walpole in 1788 for the Amusement of Miss Mary and Miss Agnes Berry. With notes and index by Paget Toynbee*. Oxford: Clarendon Press, 1924.

Warden, Lewis C. *The Life of Blackstone*. Charlottesville, VA: Michie Co., 1938.

Watson, J. Steven. *The Reign of George III, 1760–1815*. London: Oxford University Press, 1960.

Watson, John S. *Biographies of John Wilkes and William Cobbett*. Edinburgh and London: W. Blackwood and Sons, 1870.

Weitman, Sophia. *Warren Hastings and Philip Francis*. Publications of the University of Manchester: Historical Series no. 56. Manchester: Manchester University Press, 1929.

Welch, Joseph, comp. *Alumni Westmonasterienses*. London, 1852.

Wellman, Francis L. *The Art of Cross-Examination: With the Cross-Examinations of Im-*

portant Witnesses in Some Celebrated Cases. 4th ed. Garden City, NY: Garden City Books, 1948.

– *Day in Court: Or, the Subtle Arts of Great Advocates*. New York: Macmillan Co., 1910.

Welsby, William N., ed. *Lives of Eminent English Judges of the Seventeenth and Eighteenth Centuries*. London: Sweet, 1846.

White, Caroline A. *Sweet Hampstead and Its Associations*. London: Elliot Stock, 1900.

White, Jerry. *London in the Eighteenth Century: A Great and Monstrous Thing*. London: The Bodley Head, 2012.

Wilkes, John. *The Correspondence of the Late John Wilkes: With His Friends, Printed from the Original Manuscripts, in which Are Introduced Memoirs of His Life*. Edited by John Almon. London: Printed for R. Phillips, by T. Gillet, 1805.

– *The North Briton: From No. 1 to No. 46 Inclusive, with Several Useful and Explanatory Notes*. London, 1763 [Reprinted by Kessinger Publishing's Rare Reprints].

Williams, Basil. *The Life of William Pitt, Earl of Chatham*. 4th impression. 2 vols. London: Frank Cass and Co., 1966.

– *The Whig Supremacy, 1714–1760*. Revised by C.H. Stuart. 2nd ed. Oxford: Clarendon Press, 1960.

Williams, Neville. *Knaves and Fools*. New York: The Macmillan Company, 1960.

Wilson, Philip W. *William Pitt, The Younger*. Garden City, NY: Doubleday, Doran and Co., 1930.

Wood, Gordon S. *The American Revolution: A History*. London: Phoenix, 2002.

– *Empire of Liberty: A History of the Early Republic, 1789–1815*. New York: Oxford University Press, 2009.

Woolrych, Humphry William. *Lives of Eminent Serjeants-at-Law of the English Bar*. London: W.H. Allen, 1869

Worden, Blair. *The English Civil Wars 1640–1660*. London: Weidenfeld and Nicolson, 2009.

Wraxall, Sir Nathaniel W. *Historical Memoirs of My Own Time … from 1772 … to 1784*. 2 vols. London, 1815.

– *The Historical and Posthumous Memoirs of Sir Nathaniel William Wraxall 1772–84*. 5 vols. New York: Scribner and Welford, 1884.

Wyndham, Maud Mary Lyttelton. *Chronicles of the Eighteenth Century, Founded on the Correspondence of Sir Thomas Lyttelton and His Family*. 2 vols. London: Hodder and Stoughton, 1924.

Yorke, Philip C. *The Life and Correspondence of Philip Yorke, Earl of Hardwicke, Lord High Chancellor of Great Britain*. 3 vols. New York: Farrar, Strauss and Giraux, 1977.

Zane, John Maxcy. *The Story of Law*. Garden City, NY: Doubleday, Doran and Company, Inc., 1927.

Index